A
POET'S
GUIDE
TO
POETRY

Chicago Guides
to *Writing*, Editing,
and Publishing

On Writing, Editing, and Publishing
Jacques Barzun

Getting into Print
Walter W. Powell

Writing for Social Scientists
Howard S. Becker

Chicago Guide for Preparing Electronic Manuscripts
Prepared by the Staff of the University of Chicago Press

Tales of the Field
John Van Maanen

A Handbook of Biological Illustration
Frances W. Zweifel

The Craft of Translation
John Biguenet and Rainer Schulte, editors

Style
Joseph M. Williams

Mapping It Out
Mark Monmonier

Indexing Books
Nancy C. Mulvany

Writing Ethnographic Fieldnotes
Robert M. Emerson, Rachel I. Fretz, and Linda L. Shaw

Glossary of Typesetting Terms
Richard Eckersley, Richard Angstadt, Charles M. Ellerston,
Richard Hendel, Naomi B. Pascal, and Anita Walker Scott

The Craft of Research
Wayne C. Booth, Gregory G. Colomb, and Joseph M. Williams

A Manual for Writers of Term Papers, Theses, and Dissertations
Kate L. Turabian

Tricks of the Trade
Howard S. Becker

A
POET'S
GUIDE
TO
POETRY

〰〰

MARY KINZIE

THE UNIVERSITY OF CHICAGO PRESS

CHICAGO

Mary Kinzie is a poet, editor, and critic who founded the creative writing program at Northwestern University, where she teaches. She is the author of five books of poems, including *Summers of Vietnam* (Sheep Meadow), *Autumn Eros,* and *Ghost Ship* (Knopf), and two earlier critical books, *The Judge Is Fury* (Michigan) and *The Cure of Poetry in an Age of Prose* (University of Chicago Press).

The University of Chicago Press, Chicago 60637
© 1999 by The University of Chicago
All rights reserved. Published 1999
Printed in the United States of America

08 07 06 05 04 03 02 01 00 99 1 2 3 4 5
ISBN 0-226-43738-8 (cloth)
      0-226-43739-6 (paper)

Library of Congress Cataloging-in-Publication Data

Kinzie, Mary.
A poet's guide to poetry / Mary Kinzie.
    p. cm.—(Chicago guides to writing, editing, and publishing)
    Includes bibliographical references and indexes.
    ISBN 0-226-43738-8 (cloth : alk. paper). —ISBN 0-226-43739-6
    (paper : alk. paper)
    I. Title. II. Series.
    PN1059.A9K56 1999
    808.1—dc21   98-10248
                                                         CIP

for my fellow students of poetry

CONTENTS

A Note on Sources ix

Introduction: The Enchantment of the Work 1

1   Writing the Poem You Read: A View of Artistic Process 13

Part I   **The Elements of Relation and Resemblance** 45

2   Line and Half-Meaning 51

3   Syntax and Whole Meaning 75

4   Diction and Layers in Meaning 111

5   Trope and Thought 142

6   Rhetoric and Speech 187

7   Rhythm as Combination 212

Part II   **The Elements, Controlled in Time** 215

8   Accentual-Syllabic Meter: The Role of Stress
and Interval 217

9   Stanza and Rhyme: The Role of Echo 262

10   Further Rhythms in English—Counted Forms:
Accentual Verse and Syllabic Verse (including Haiku) 290

11   Further Rhythms in English—Non-Counted Forms:
The Four Freedoms of Free Verse 330

Part III   Writing in Form   **345**

   12   Exercises for Beginning and Advanced Writers   347

   13   Poetic Terms   380

   14   Annotated Bibliography of Further Reading   483

            List of Poems by Form   503

            Author and Title Index   508

            Subject Index   517

            Credits   558

A NOTE ON SOURCES

The editions used for poets of this century appear in the Credits section at the end of the book. For poems in the public domain, except where noted below and in the text, I have relied on the five-volume anthology edited by W. H. Auden and Norman Holmes Pearson, *Poets of the English Language* (New York: Viking/Penguin, 1950; 1978): *I. Medieval and Renaissance Poets, Langland to Spenser; II. Elizabethan and Jacobean Poets, Marlowe to Marvell; III. Restoration and Augustan Poets, Milton to Goldsmith; IV. Romantic Poets, Blake to Poe; V. Victorian and Edwardian Poets, Tennyson to Yeats*. The Bible used is the King James Version. The Shakespeare edition is Alfred Harbage's (Penguin, 1969), with various editors for the individual works. For the sonnets not in Auden's anthology, I return as he does to the 1609 printing by Thorpe. For Milton I have used Merritt Y. Hughes's edition, *The Complete Poems and Major Prose of John Milton* (Indianapolis: Bobbs-Merrill/Odyssey, 1957). Other texts for frequently cited poets are: *The Poems of Alexander Pope,* edited by John Butt (New Haven: Yale University Press, 1963); *The Oxford Authors: William Wordsworth,* edited by Stephen Gill (Oxford & New York: Oxford University Press, 1984) (note that Gill's line numberings are somewhat different from those in previous editions of Wordsworth); *The Complete Poems of Emily Dickinson,* edited by Thomas H. Johnson (Boston: Little, Brown, 1955); and *The Complete Poems of Thomas Hardy,* edited by James Gibson (New York: Macmillan, 1976). The issue of modernizing old spellings will be taken up with regard to Wyatt in chapter 3.

~This symbol is used to indicate a break between sections or stanzas of a poem wherever such breaks are lost due to pagination.

Introduction:
The Enchantment of the Work

Poetry as an Art

I believe poets read poetry differently than non-poets do. When some readers talk, I am amazed by the appetite for paraphrase. When critics talk, I am just as amazed by how completely they hear poetry as a function of culture (another sort of paraphrase). But when I hear poets, I hear the enchantment of the work. Their ideas about a poem are always borne by some conception of intimacy or distance of voice, rigor or looseness of attitude, delicacy or directness of treatment. Above all, poets always seem to listen, even as they compose, to the voice of that something that decides the rightness of their designs.

In this guide, I attempt to reintroduce into the discourse about poetry some awareness of these promptings that motivate the writing of poems. I would like to counter the claims of culture and paraphrase by pointing to the call of a more impersonal task—that of overhearing music that is not yet made. All poetry comes into being in respect to its sounds, tormented into perfection or near-perfection by the logical and prosaic resistance of language in response to the disturbance of occasion.

A Poet's Guide to Poetry began as a practical response to the need for a handbook and writing guide that would reassert the claims of poetry as an art. But it is an art with a past and it is an art whose linguistic and imaginative components can be known and discussed. Thus the guide should approach the major traditions of lyric and meditative poetry in English since the medieval period in two ways. First, the book should present the sounds and rhythms of poetry alongside consideration of the ideas and thought-units within the poems. It sounds simple enough, yet few introductions to formal poetry now treat sense and sound as parallels that continuously co-operate even when one seems dominant. And few of my recent predecessors give essential space to the chief mechanism of thought: the sentence, along with the other elements of grammatical construction.

Second, because poetry is an art that reading, at its best, can imitate, the book should present argument and example from the perspective of the writing of the poems we read. Note that I did not say "from the perspective of the writer," for the issue of intention can best be discovered from within an art rather than within a biographical subject. Of course, historical perspective must be invoked whenever the work of any period is studied, but by historical I mean primarily the conventions of various kinds of poems within their various climates of viewpoint and desire. A poem is neither the clone of a convention nor a mere wildcat product of will, but rather a rescue, within the horizon suggested by a convention, of a sequence of new turnings.

In order to fathom poems from within, I make one assumption some may find hard to accept: Any poem is best imagined as provisional. Even if it does leap already formed and completed from the poet's imagination, that leap rises from something precarious. Most of the poetry that interests me is not closed-off, polished down, or predictable from its very first word. Even after a poem has hardened into print, it may continue to represent a risk, a chance, a surmise, or a hypothesis about itself. This quality of hypothesis and provisionality takes shape against the background of all the other poems that make a new one possible—poems by others perceived by those writers who commit themselves to reading and by readers who strive to learn what it means to write as forming a tradition or literary inheritance. In other words, I assume that most poetry is the product of experiments on the past, acts of recombining already invented substances in such a way that they are transformed. I therefore concentrate on the frequency with which many poems confront conventions: how they stand back from themselves, turn off onto new paths, question their purpose in relation to both theme and shape, even begin again. In short, my aim is to uncover the poem that is uncovering itself.

How to Use This Guide

Several audiences will gain by once again linking form with content through taking on the perspective of the poem-in-progress with its many turns. Writers and would-be writers are my primary concern; but I also address the interests of those who wish to get closer to reading the very words—and the very order of the words—in literary works. New writers and readers are encouraged to move through the Introduction to the discussion of elements in Parts I and II, and those who are ready to experiment will delve more thoroughly into Part III's chapters on "Writing in Form," particularly the exercises in chapter 12. Those who have a wide acquaintance with poetry or who would like to pursue questions of creation will, I hope, find the view of the artistic process in chapter 1, "Writing the Poem You Read," properly challenging; it is a kind of *ars poetica,* in which I suggest writing as a model not only for making art but also for making sense of art. At the core of both enterprises is a series of thresholds into the unwritten and the unknown.

What follows this look at artistic process is a thorough consideration of the elements of verse, first in their role as basic threads that weave among each other (Part I), then from the perspective of how poems move through time (Part II). (Three working concepts central to both Parts I and II are presented in the introduction to Part I.) Part III presents practicum chapters on writing, poetic terms, and reading on critical topics. For quick reference to the poems used as examples, the indexes (a List of Poems by Form and an Author-Title index) should prove beneficial.

Very little I say here is being said for the first time. Even so, I hope the focus on the horizon of tradition from the perspective of risk will help new readers to learn to think about the relations between technique and meaning and expert readers to refresh their hold on the forces and subtleties of the poem. I have found it helpful, both in composing and comprehending a poet's work, to undertake the imaginative consciousness of the artist. So I recommend that the readers of this book also look through the artists' eyes. In all literary exercises, critical as well as creative, the critical should merge with the creative. The hope is that the blending of viewpoints in this way will make those who wish to write more daring and accomplished poets and those who read more discerning thinkers in their comprehension of poetry as the art of resemblance, precariously controlled in time.

Sounding Like Others

Imagine yourself as a student in a poetry course facing the writing of your first poem. It will, perhaps, be an assignment putting you in touch with a metrical line used by many writers before you, starting with Chaucer and continuing to the present day. This heritage is important because, in fact, your job is to create and construct a poem that sounds like other poems. In this first exercise, and perhaps for some time thereafter, your goal should be to sound like others rather than to create a completely original composition. Let's say the pattern you will follow in the first poem is that of blank verse—unrhymed lines of five stresses interspersed with five unstressed syllables:

> I DARE not MOVE my DIMME[1] eyes ANy WAY.

> This SHAKing KEEPS me STEADy. I should KNOW.

> In CUBES like BUILDing BLOCKS of DUSTy GOLD

The line is called iambic pentameter—it is five (*penta-*) measures long—and each measure is an iambic foot (two syllables, the first of which is weakly stressed, the second strongly). The first step toward writing your own poem is to read other blank-verse poems, noting the fluctuations in two main features of style:

1. Phrases and sentences in blank-verse poems do not regularly stop with the end of the line; many run on (or **enjamb**[2]) from one line to the next.

2. But their speed is not constant: Sentences in blank verse enjamb from one line to the next in various ways, sometimes slowly, at other times energetically.

Sentence and Line

So now you will begin to think about sentences as they work against line. You will also begin to understand how the different kinds of sentences, from simple to complex, change depending on whether the sentence stops where the line stops or moves on beyond the line. The first example above was one sentence long, and it took exactly one line to say. The second was two sentences long and neatly filled one line; there was a sense of ample room to go at the idea twice. But the third line was only a part of a sentence. More than one line was needed to complete the

---

1. The adjective *dimme* (an older spelling of dim) is one syllable long, not two.

2. Throughout the book, **boldface type** is used to indicate defined terms. The defined terms, frequently with examples, are discussed in chapter 13, "Poetic Terms," which is set up as an annotated dictionary.

thought (as you can see in the complete poem, quoted on p. 127), so the excerpt we have suggests a higher pressure to move off of one line.

One result of such pressure is that some blank verse is not just a sequence of finished sentences, each on its own closed line, but an enjambing network of sentences *across* many lines, weaving entire paragraphs of verse. You will start noticing the length of these verse paragraphs and what kinds of sentences make them up. Before you have moved very far into the poem, however, you can already begin to sense an implied relation of theme to the brevity or the expansion of the linear style. Some themes that find support in a style that is end-stopped would not work as well if the lines were to run on; the reverse is also true.

Theme, Order, Voice, and Form

Meantime, there comes explicit subject matter and the poet's treatment of theme at the level of plot and organization. How does the poem before you, which you are writing your way through as a reader and fellow writer—how does this poem unfold? Temporally (moving from then to now)? causally (because *x* therefore *y*)? Does it take the form of an explanation? description? confession? history? (and of what sort, personal or universal?) You will now also be starting to wonder: Who is speaking? Is this person truthful? dull? vicious? seductive? Are you being directly addressed (you, the person reading, on this day of your own life)? Or is someone nearer to the poet, in time and place and shared feeling, being directly or generally addressed? If nobody is being addressed, what other purpose do the words put upon the page serve? Are you being sung to? told a story? presented with a description? involved in reading an argument or logical proposition?

Before going further, consider four points you can apply to all verse:

1. *Context:* You are approaching this one poem in light of all the other poems like it that you are coming to know.

2. *Unfolding:* You are reading and writing *from within* and questioning what unfolds next while imagining that the poem is being composed alongside all the others in its field.

3. *Words:* You are not just reading messages or extracting meanings or drafting editorials to put into lines: You are thinking *in words*. You are thinking so hard in the atmosphere created by words that they enter you like your breathing. This means, first, looking at words by themselves,

with all their weight and subtlety; it helps to think about their length, complexity, and language of origin, too.

4. *Sentence versus Line:* Along with the form and sound of words by themselves, you are concerned with their connection into sentences, in whole or in part; some of these parts fall neatly into lines, others work against the lines.

In other words, like the poet, you are doing everything at once. Moreover, you are moving through uncertainties. You are thinking not only about field and form and characters and speeches and the voice and its reason for speaking/writing: You are thinking about the right word to use and also about the best phrase and sentence to put that word in, as you might when you look for a frame for a picture. But you are also peering into something that is, on every dimension—picture and frame—*not finished yet,* still growing.

Growing Words

One of the ways a poem grows, which the act of reading imitates, is to send out tendrils from the word toward the sentence of which it becomes a part, and from the sentence to the surrounding trellis of the lines. Think ahead and complete sentences up to the words that strike you as original or odd. Composition lives by word choice and word choice is possible only when you care enough about language to have an informed preference: You care about the word's form as the vehicle of your meaning. Composition then proceeds from word to word and choice to choice. But at the same time, it is also moving from one sentence frame to the next. Choice of sentence frame affects the choice of word (and conversely, words suggest the sentences that lead to them).

Or try to imagine how it feels to cast your thought in one kind of sentence, as if it were a mold; ask how alternative sentence forms make one kind of line sound—and even *look*—different from the next. This awareness will help you decide why, in one poem, there might be examples of several kinds of sentence. You might also want to think of casting your thought (in the sentence that gives it shape) out beyond the boundaries of the lines, as if you were fishing in unseen waters.

Note that you will need the vantage of the writer because you are soon—if you are not already—exploring a poem actually of your making that is coming into existence beneath your hand. (In fact, I also offer my literature students the option of creating poems in certain forms as ambitious alternatives to essays and papers.) Imitation helps you read; reading prepares you to imitate.

Among the poems you should consider at this stage (preparing to write in blank verse) are five meditations about places and attachments, three of them readily available in poetry anthologies, William Wordsworth's (1770–1850) "Tintern Abbey" ("Lines Written a Few Miles Above Tintern Abbey on Revisiting the Banks of the Wye During a Tour, July 13, 1798"); Samuel Taylor Coleridge's (1772–1834) "Frost at Midnight"; and Philip Larkin's (1922–1985) "Whitsun Weddings." The other two are in this book: Thom Gunn's (b. 1929) "His Rooms in College" and Howard Nemerov's (1920–1991) "Landscape with Self-Portrait." Each of the five differs from the others in theme and treatment of line and sentence; but all enjamb periodically, using sentences larger/longer than the line. In addition, these five poems share a similar movement of mind, from a landscape or view through a window, to a meditation of a personal nature, to a glance again at the now changed external scene. This out/in/out movement is one you will imitate in the following writing exercise.

The First Exercise

So now you are getting or giving a poem assignment that might run something like this. (Newcomers shouldn't fret about the terms: those not yet explained will soon become familiar while reading Part I; terms are also defined and exemplified in the annotated dictionary-style chapter 13 in Part III.)

Form: Minimum twenty lines of **blank verse** (unrhymed iambic pentameter with occasional—and necessary—enjambment).

Argument: Use the three-part organization of the poems by Coleridge, Wordsworth, Larkin, Nemerov, and Gunn: that is, first the description of a scene, which then triggers a meditation on something in the speaker's experience, which enables the speaker to return to the initial scene with a sense of resolution or understanding.[3] The poem should close with a reference to the

---

3. Some readers may recognize the insight about three-part form from M. H. Abrams's description in "Structure and Style in the Greater Romantic Lyric," in *From Sensibility to Romanticism: Essays Presented to Frederick A. Pottle,* edited by Frederick W. Hilles and Harold Bloom, pp. 527–60 (New York: Oxford University Press, 1965).

place where the poem began, which has been implicitly altered by the meditation that intervenes.

Subject: Someone in your family looks at the season.

The task of writing your own poem may become easier when you voice the ideas and longings of another person whom you know fairly well. Further help can come from drafting a preliminary 250- to 300-word creative meditation in prose on the same subject as the poem. This prose should probably reach at least the third-draft stage. Don't be content with a first sketch, whether in verse or prose. The better the trial run in creative prose, the better the poem that takes off from it.

Getting to the End of the First Line

There is no getting around it: The first poem is a large task. This is especially true if you are reading your first poems and making your initial attempts at thinking like a writer. Thinking like a writer means using language—words and sentences. To be sure, ideas are important; plots essential; illustrations and comparisons and descriptive features—these, too, are excellent and often necessary. But neither plots nor ideas can be separated from the words and sentence frames that convey them: In poetry, plots and ideas are produced by and constantly dependent on language. One thing the poem must discover is a language to speak in.

Words are your medium—both individual words and the sentences formed by individual words. Without some attention to them, there is no way to get to the end of the first line. (This is true of reading also.) On the other hand, when you begin to question the poem's form of expression in light of alternatives, you have, in effect, begun to read, and write, *in language* and to train your verbal skills so as to do both.

For both activities, reading and writing, you will find yourself responding on many levels of expression at the same time. Part I presents some categories for this experience of multiple levels or strands crisscrossing in the poem and discusses the six elements that work together in the poem's web of language: the line, the sentence, diction (word-choice), trope (comparison), rhetoric (argument and voice), and rhythm. The fashion of their working-together is far from linear, but the chapters in Part I will help you teach yourself how each element contributes to (and is changed by) each of the others in turn and in combinations. (You may want to revisit the first chapter's discussion of beginnings after you have worked through the six elements in Part I.)

The learning process you will experience is subtle and ultimately takes more than a few weeks of thinking-by-writing-your-way-through the shifting combinations of a handful of poems. So you must be patient as you teach yourself (or others) and not look for automatic routines or shortcuts to accomplishment. If you can live with a certain amount of uncertainty at the start (as you might expect to do when taking up any new skill), you will find that you understand more about blank verse and the other forms with each day of reading and each attempt at imitation. Even a few weeks will find you more ready to tackle the blank verse poem, for example, than you were before you began studying in this way. You may write surprisingly good apprentice poems as a result of your efforts. (More will be said about possible exercises and themes in the practicum exercises in chapter 12.)

Context and Tradition

Now a word about the environment in which poems grow. Although individual poets differ, all poems emerge from a literary culture. The better you come to understand the poetic background, the more sense you can make of the immediate, unfolding foreground.

Let us say you are reading **sonnets,** a closed form of fourteen lines popular in the fourteenth to seventeenth centuries in Europe and involving certain intentionally extreme assumptions about love—including the threshold assumption that love is the central arena of human experience. (Our own culture has absorbed this assumption about the centrality of love, although earlier poetic formulas of response may strike us first as odd.) The student who wants to learn to read by writing must approach sonnets by putting the elements together so as to think about the following:

1. The poem's plots (and even logical arguments have plots, complete with projections of motive).

2. You have to think about ideas (and even visual images like leaves clinging to a tree limb and rocky beaches abound in ideas; so do actions like laughing, gazing, and departing, and more complex acts such as approval or recoil).

3. As readers/writers you will try to incorporate into your understanding your knowledge of what other poets have written (because no poem comes into being without carrying on its back—or trying to get out from under—its particular ancestry within a tradition).

4. And finally, you will also have to think about sentences and vo-cabulary—because poetry is an art of words, and an art of wrestling with the forms we are given, and of remaking their frames.

With respect to sonnets, the theme of love was given. By knowing how love themes were elaborated in the early Renaissance, you can pre-pare for the surprise created in the late Renaissance, when sonnet writers switched from the pursuit of the beloved as a governing theme to the worship of God. Once you can grasp in a general way this religious in-flection given to a verse form identified with secular love, you can begin to appreciate the great political and philosophical sonnets in which later writers enlarged the sonnet's scope. We will come back to these ideas throughout the chapters in Part I and in chapter 9's discussion of the stanza.

How is understanding reached? By reading within centuries and within forms and then by reading across centuries and across forms. One needs good instruction and a good grasp of the essential processes of po-etic thought. This book aims to help in the provision of these essentials.

The Order of Part I

I would be surprised if I did not surprise some of you in the particular choices I make in discussing the six elements in Part I of this guide. One of the most devilling things about the unities of poems is that they cannot be treated as if one clear thing could be laid, like a transparent crystal, on a second clear thing until the perfect visionary temple was complete. Po-etry does not declare the best angle from which to be, initially, learned about. In my approach to the six elements and their overlap, I have tried to begin with what are, to me, the most important and interdependent of all the features of poetry:

1. This art form in English has for the better part of six centuries been spoken or written in *lines*.
2. Scored across the pattern of lines is the subversive pattern of com-position in *sentences*.

From sentence and line follow all the other features of the plain-style lyric and meditative poems that are my chief concern here—the features of diction, trope, rhetoric, and rhythmic sound. Sometimes, however, the order of their arrival is not well-behaved; all too often, when we talk about one element, others nudge their way into the discussion. This is a book one may want to reread, but I hope the movement from one thought and example to the next will help you begin to explore poetry like writers—patiently, repeatedly, ever more deeply imbedded in the work, yet poised on a new threshold each time you enter the poem.

1

Writing the Poem You Read: A View of Artistic Process

The Limbo of Beginning

The first rule of thumb is simply put: To become better acquainted with poetry you must read poems as if you were writing them. Then you must accept the even stranger idea that the process of reading is instructive because it retraces the intricate paths of composition. Reading is like writing in beginning in uncertainty and driving toward speculation and experiment. The reader follows, via the poem as a ghostly map, the many paths that were not taken by the author, but whose possibility leaves a shadow like crosshatching on the paths that remain. To read this way keeps a poem always provisional and still in the making, which is how the process of reading absorbs the act of writing to their mutual improvement in terms of skills and understanding. Eventually writer and reader see their present way more clearly than the paths not taken.

Furthermore, reading in the present detects what writing in the present also suffers: a list toward something precarious. Reading, like writing, hangs over the abyss: The ways poetry *can* be written in a given period trail off into nothingness. The solid conventions hover, break up, and eerily recombine when subjected to experiments that distort them (and even obedience, at the extremes—such as William Shakespeare's or Gerard Manley Hopkins's obedience to the sonnet tradition—can produce difference and distortion). Reading becomes the process of recognizing how poets stand upon the given in order to peer over into the unshaped but unfolding present. What aids both writer and reader to fill out this partial presence are the forms of verse.

Pursuit of the poem, by reader or writer, involves trial and error against the backdrop of form. I would call error a form of blessedness: The best poems satisfy by surprise, either because they reject something more familiar, or because they teeter on the edge of confusion in know-ing something else. Reading, like writing, requires us to uncover a poem that is in the process of uncovering itself.

Understanding the poem we are reading is a process that moves from ignorance through partial insights to higher levels of understanding. Sim-ilarly, to *write* the poem is to move from ignorance to higher levels of understanding (understanding being seen, in part, as achievement). But first it is necessary to explore one's ignorance, to feel about in the dark-ness ignorance makes. The aim even in rereading a poem we already know is to climb back down into the limbo of the half-shaped.

Perceiving how shape emerges from the half-shaped background provides the reader with a lens, or vantage, similar to the writer's. But this does not require us to say much about the lives of the poets or how they went about making their works; I am more interested in how the poems themselves wrestle with their tasks and occasions. For task and occasion arise only from a clear sense of poetic mission, a mission that articulates itself most strongly when responding (among other spurs) to a poetic tradition. Therefore, reading cannot be limited to the poem on the page—or to data about its author—at the expense of relevant context about the poem's medium and its imaginative scope.

"Context" implicates the language of poetry with its movement in verbal time (prosody) and its movement in intellectual time (poetic mode—the analogue of plot in fiction). Definitions of relevance may be debated, but I am drawn to a definition by familiarity: You know that you have begun to master the poem's relevant context when you can take on the perspective of the artist and follow the clues planted in the work to the curious rightness of its shape. Background turns into foreground and apparent digression turns into primary signal if you move through the poem from within. (New Criticism, by contrast, typically insists on a distanced role for the reader.) I believe the effect of the craft of writing is actually to entice readers into the same domain as the creative imagina-tion. The most dependable map for the re-creation of a work of literature (and I would include fiction here, too) comes with the creative work itself through its address to the unknown as an ethical idea realized aes-thetically. "Realization" as a metaphor for literary art thus asks us to dis-cern what needed realizing, what was once less than perfectly formed—intuitions and resemblances. Over time one becomes better at reading and interpreting from within and participates more subtly in the unpre-dictable unfolding of intuitions and their embodied forms as they weave through each other, like bands of mist above a landscape only partly visible.

Of course, the landscape we reconstruct is not the writer's—the work viewed in hindsight by the writer is always the perfectly visible unfolding of a success story in which certainty and completion overcame doubt. The *poet's* poem is, in a sense, dead. This may be why the poet and critic Howard Nemerov once said to me, responding to a query about one of his works, "You never *ask* a poet what he means, you *tell* him!" The poem *we* work through is more instructive because it will not let us cancel out, with anecdotal information, the primal question about beginnings: *Why now?* Why does the poem start where it does? What unfulfilled intentional set or pose is still partially glimpsed between the gathering lines of development? Why does the poem hover over this particular occasion? What threshold of uncertainty is preserved by the beginning?

I would like to put these questions to the following beginnings without (for the moment) worrying about their endings:

(1) Sometimes a lantern moves along the night,
    That interests our eyes.

    〰〰[1]

(2) Who
    are these two women, walking
    through the great forum of the plain . . .

    〰〰

(3) The sea is calm tonight.
    The tide is full, the moon lies fair
    Upon the straits; on the French coast the light
    Gleams and is gone . . .

    〰〰

(4) Four-fifty. The palings of Trinity Church
    Burying Ground, a few inches above the earth,
    are sunk in green light. The low stones
    like pale books knocked sideways.

    〰〰

(5) Those bowers that with gentle work did frame
    The lovely gaze where every eye doth dwell . . .

    〰〰

1. A colophon 〰〰 will separate quotations from different texts.

(6) Across the floor flits the mechanical toy,
    fit for a king of several centuries back.
    A little circus horse with real white hair . . .

                                    ~~~~~
(7) A bird half wakened in the lunar noon
    Sang halfway through its little inborn tune.[2]

All the excerpts but (5) invite us into the present moment. The most vigorous in insisting on the immediacy of real time is (4), which impales us on the exact numerals of the time of day, as the bus pauses to take on more working girls from the stores and businesses that are letting out; the pale blocks of episcopal stone, which resemble books (and which, like books, are ignored by the young, exhausted women), increase the poignancy of the lives beautiful and lofty images cannot rescue from labor, for the stones remind us, too, that their bodies will lie beneath them. (See III in the "Poetry Sampler.")

Competing to be next in immediacy are (2), whose question (*who are they?*) produces an urgency laid over the indefinite plane of time across which the two woman are walking, and the beginning lines of the poem about the little circus horse (6), in which we catch the lightsome flitting of the mechanical toy against a darker background of a far-away, aristocratic past. The depths of the past dwarf the autonomy of the little circus horse while paradoxically increasing the vividness of his traits (the "real white hair").

Poems (1), (3), and (7) all posit actions less pressing and more generalized, within time frames more extended. Poem (5), of course, asks nothing of the immediate moment in its setting (although the complete sonnet implies the speaker's enormous admiration—in an unavoidable present—for the other person's beauty). Its threshold is more reticent about local appearances—although presence and confrontation and immediacy are nevertheless built into the poem. In general, therefore, because poems can embody intense and immediate feeling *without* scenic props, localization in setting or situation cannot be the only index of immediacy in feeling-time, or time as lived.

---

2. All poems above except (3), "Dover Beach," which is readily available, and (7), discussed later in the chapter, are given in full in the Poetry Sampler at the end of this chapter because they are either recent or rarely anthologized.

Looking at these seven opening passages will nevertheless remind us that, no matter what ideas feed the works, mental and emotional content must depend on objective counters and local embodiments to some degree. Without material embodiment, no spirit can come through the pattern. The sonnets by Hopkins (1) and Shakespeare (5) explore the need of spiritual and intellectual content for embodied or physically inhabited forms, Shakespeare's poem by imagining the beloved's growth through self-cultivation into a graceful and coherent mind, Hopkins's by dramatizing in the figure of the lantern all of visual perception as the test of Christ's presence.

The need for projection into thing and shape may, indeed, force from poets settings, characters, and dramas primarily tonal or atmospheric and perhaps in part accidental. Much of the natural setting of (3) is tangential to the poet's purpose, which is to present the historical inevitability of struggle, in a world that overrides individuals, as an analogue to the erosion of religious belief. Emphasis falls on inevitability and coercion even in so private a matter as one's disposition toward God. But the tender look of the French coast is irrelevant to thoughts of faith and war. In the realm of belief, France is not notably more stalwart than the speaker's own country. As for struggle and the hint of war especially late in the poem where "ignorant armies clash by night"—these tracks feel cold. History does not seem specifically invoked. Even if we look for coded reference to the time, it has been fifty years since the Napoleonic wars engaged the two countries against each other (the Crimean War, with France as an ally, would end in 1856; the Franco-Prussian War, another conflict that touched both France and England though not as enemies, would begin three years after the 1867 publication of "Dover Beach"). The "ignorant armies" of the poem's final line might continue to work their carnage throughout history even if the poet had seen the Channel (across which so many armies have passed) in a drizzle. The lyrical moment does not derive directly from a historical crux or a particular national occasion:

> on the French coast the light
> Gleams and is gone; the cliffs of England stand,
> Glimmering and vast . . .

But there is a secondary impulse in seeing the moonlight on the French coast glisten then extinguish, and that is piquancy of association with the two women nearest him, his fiancée, with whom he visited

Dover in 1848, and the woman known only as "Marguerite," a "Daughter of France" who inspired a brilliant series of lyrics.[3] Add to this the poet's Francophilia and the fabric of attachment thickens, making more poignant the undeniable details of the scene.[4] The white chalk cliffs at Dover, up the coast from where he stands, thus tremble with brilliant reflected moonlight and suggest that his own country is huge, extensive and solid, whereas clouds cover the moon on the other shore until France, with its variegation of personal associations from his university years onward, is visible only in shadows; that country comes to hint, however indirectly, through the pain of distance, at the pain of God's invisibility in the modern world.

In being English, Matthew Arnold's speaker is protected and affirmed—and he acknowledges this citizenship; but he is made into a feeling person as far as the poem is concerned only through the fitful nearness to France. It is, furthermore, the feeling person who is in touch with his deepest anxieties and who is vulnerable to the ideas in the poem about war, personal loyalties, and the haunting failure of faith in general and in his own outlook.[5] Thus the beginning of "Dover Beach" makes us reexperience the never fully explored association through which fond feeling, and a dramatized self-pity close to remorse, are fathomed for the release of religious dismay. By looking through the first lines as if they were all we had, we thus appreciate more completely how their mingled

3. A stanza from one of these presages the oceanic turmoil and imagery of an island fastness in "Dover Beach":

Yes! in the sea of life enisled,
With echoing straits between us thrown,
Dotting the shoreless watery wild,
We mortal millions live *alone*.
The islands feel the enclasping flow,
And then their endless bounds they know.

4. By the time of completing "Dover Beach" (which he worked on intermittently from 1848 to 1861), Matthew Arnold had distinguished himself as a cultural ambassador to France, among writers and thinkers whose acceptance he found flattering. A hint of melancholy pride at successes of self-presentation in another language filters through the English situation, touching him from the perspective on the shore with its tall, luminous cliffs.

5. I cannot entirely accept the idea of Nicholas Murray in his new biography that Arnold is concerned not with his own loss of faith but with the stiff-necked and resistant nature of the *Zeitgeist* (although I am willing to be persuaded that many critics have taken "Dover Beach" too literally). See Murray, *A Life of Matthew Arnold* (New York: St. Martin's Press, 1997), pp. 117 and 234.

layers of imminence and uncertainty both remain on the page and dissolve themselves in the fullness of the poem.

Indirection at the start typifies all seven poems quoted. Poem (2) is about the Gulf War in 1990–91; its historical moment is part of its stated theme. But the two women shuffling through the dreck of the battlefield are premonitions of Antigone and Ismene, talking about their loss of their brother (Polyneices); the shadow of Creon lowers over them. All this we discover in time. The beginning, however, commemorates neither the war nor the last two plays of Sophocles' Oedipus cycle, but images with no names under a featureless sky abandoned by civilization. We see these women whose talk we cannot yet overhear trudging through the plain's huge "forum"; later, "broken tablets / of illegible laws cobble the ground." Echoes of social discourse and covenant racket in the air and disappear. In the dry pool, no images of enchanted water rise up as we might find in T. S. Eliot's "Burnt Norton," which the following passage echoes,—no lotus of communion, no mystic emanation—only the suggestion of a hollow vessel filled with ash:

> It is as if time itself
> were a dry fountain, where the urn fills only
> with pale ashes . . .
> where church and court alike are built of bones . . .

20

The title preceding these lines of Eleanor Wilner's irradiates the beginning of the poem with antimystical and anticommunal system. She names the poem "Operations: Desert Shield, Desert Storm" (see the "Poetry Sampler"). These were the two code names under which the successive military operations against Saddam Hussein were conducted by the American military. We must also remember that the war was, for us, largely a matter of the deployment of war machines, not foot soldiers. The poem's preliminary movements thus contradict the specific horror of the missiles and earth-movers and their victims by focusing on two people who have little to do with war—they are women, and they are walking and talking. The ground may have been littered with metal and strafed with fire, and men buried despite their screams, but the women walk (as so often women have done) frustratingly far from the event.

That distance between the title, with its general spread of aggression, and human figures, with their implied specialization of affect, is what Wilner embodies by indirection, or displacement of focus. We wait in limbo with the poet until we have wandered so far beyond the present

imposed by the title that we are in a second and earlier time that embraces
the eras of the Hebrew Bible, Greek tragedy, and, later, Roman law.

Displacement occurs in this substituted time as well. The great
schemes become archeologies "built of bones," gods and governments
reducing to the same furious idea—that brothers must be killed and
beautiful things ruined. Anonymity ("boys," "two women") protects us
from detail but requires us to repeat and compare. The few bits of evi-
dence before us need to be placed against other partial portraits from the
past—Creon in his trappings; Henry at Agincourt ("Once more into the
breach, dear friends, once more; / Or close the wall up with our English
dead!" *King Henry V,* III.i); the fields of struggle in many periods strewn
with bodies broken open like rotting fruit, spilling the many seeds:

> the air itself a deadly trench
> to these benighted boys, condemned
> to fall again into the ranks
> of what repeats: into the breach
> once more, another city broken open like   35
> a rotting fruit, the flies rising,
> the delicate seeds exposed
> to the sun, a book with a broken
> spine . . .

From her controlled aimlessness of occasion come the revisionary
fragments and copious metaphors that digress into Wilner's theme. These
many-layered meditations connect backwards from the moment of writ-
ing to generations of victim and tyrant and many forebears in the reading
of experience. This lineage includes those who read the body, as above,
like a usurped town, and those who agree that human history stretches
like a page the beings on earth can walk upon but never turn because

> it extends and extends, the smoking cities
> scattered like open lesions
> to the periphery of sight, these wounds
> that memory worries so they
> cannot close, this sand   50
> littered with the bodies of brothers.

The mediating limbo of this poem-in-the-making also forces a connec-
tion between all who realize—as poets and soldiers must—that we live

the world over again (we "fall again into the ranks / of what repeats"). Hence experiences such as picking our way over the anonymous sand— or hurling our bodies across it—mount up with an effect of living a mir- rored life, a life refracted by the belief that we are repeating ourselves— indeed, that we are being repeated, projected upon these copies.

Such copyings and rehearsals reach back not just through individual time but beyond the individual life-span until there can be no beginning to the thought we think. To start a train of thought is to encounter a rich, particular perturbation of copies and patterns from before, very like the turmoil from which the poet selects her images. In Wilner's "Opera- tions," the sprung dimension of uncertainty and repetition out of which poetry grows in general thus becomes her particular poem's theme. She is exploring the threshold where known responses cease, amid a clamor of competing recognitions.

Thresholds of Choice

Imagine that period in the life of a poem when the words left behind on the page start to record an intellectual and imaginative game, a kind of hide-and-seek with the always elusive picture of the poem's whole. This picture of the poem's whole increasingly draws us, as it drew the poet, across its many thresholds of choice, always going one way rather than any of the others that crowded up at the time. My discussion of the long poems of Arnold and Wilner touched on this idea but could not treat their unfoldings in full. So I will quote a few short poems to illustrate what I mean about choices, starting with poem (7).

Robert Frost's sonnet on hearing a bird who begins to sing, then stops, changes direction as a poem once the speaker realizes that his real subject is neither his own waking in the middle of the night, nor the sleepy automatic quality of the little bird's song, but some alternative sys- tem of meaning that only indifferently suffers an analogy with human experience. The theme of the work has to do with our exclusion from the world about which the speaker puzzles:

On a Bird Singing in Its Sleep

A bird half wakened in the lunar noon
Sang halfway through its little inborn tune.
Partly because it sang but once all night
And that from no especial bush's height,

Partly because it sang ventriloquist   5
And had the inspiration to desist
Almost before the prick of hostile ears,
It ventured less in peril than appears.
It could not have come down to us so far,
Through the interstices of things ajar   10
On the long bead chain of repeated birth,
To be a bird while we are men on earth,
If singing out of sleep and dream that way
Had made it much more easily a prey.

Frost toys with the desire we all have to be sought out by the creatures in the unspeaking animal realm. (He is drawn to the idea of signals from that realm; in his poem "The Most of It," the natural world sends him a powerful buck whose indifference is both magisterial and annoying.) Frost drops hints here and there in "On a Bird Singing in Its Sleep" that there is some warm link between the sleepy bird and ourselves—almost as if that link made us, too, drowsily vulnerable to some predator, whether real or internal to our souls. But all the hints of fellowship and shared frailty are canceled by the long argument of the last six lines: The bird can survive into our period only because it has persisted *despite* us and all its other enemies. Nearness and friendship between such realms is a dream.

I said that the image of the poem's whole was elusive. Even for fairly brief poems, such as Frost's sonnet, wholeness can be experienced but never pointed to or turned into a sum. The way a poem comes to a dramatic peak and then subsides can feel like the poem's whole point, but the climax is never the entire production. In addition, the further back in the composition of the poem we start, the more unpredictable its twists and turns will be. We must wonder what it is like to be writing a poem that, like Frost's, seems to stop right at its start, lurching to a halt after the second line ("Sang halfway through its little inborn tune"). It is a halt that mimics the little blurt of melody from the bird.

But the poem desires to penetrate further than the blurts of its first closed couplet. So at line 3, Frost skips across to a more cerebral and complex mode of speaking, less focused on sense impressions and more on arguments (*Partly because X, . . . Partly because Y . . .*). Once the speaker begins to argue so reasonably, he must reach beyond the appearance of accident to some more logical origin. This is the idea that, just as the bird is primed to sing as soon as it wakes, the creature is programmed to *stop* singing when it is the wrong time, too. It would have to be so, Frost says, otherwise the species would have perished. Note, however, that the last couplet teeters over the remnant hint of danger (the last word of the poem, *prey*, connects the bird [it] with what threatens it) rather than resolving on the bird's present safety ("If singing out of sleep and dream that way / Had made it much more easily a prey").

Frost's choice moves us owing to its stress on precariousness. The logical plot—the argument—has a happy ending; sense says that the bird stopped singing in time and was safe from predators. But the illogical plot of implications deriving from language and word-order balances *for all time* on the bird's vulnerability; the poem closes on the resonant word *prey*, thereby resisting neatness, and weakening the logical rescue that began in line 3. One conclusion (the assertion compressed in the final word *prey*) contradicts the other (the gist of the long contrary-to-fact sentence from which we derive the rational comfort that the bird was not made easily into prey). Even in its ending the poem mirrors the jaggedness of its start; the poem shuts up prematurely just as the little bird does.

Indeed there are many poems which come anything but directly to their conclusions. Some poems appear to settle only at the last minute upon an ending, as in the last line of this brief lyric by Thomas Hardy:

The Self-Unseeing

Here is the ancient floor,
Footworn and hallowed and thin,
Here was the former door
Where the dead feet walked in.

She sat here in her chair,   5
Smiling into the fire;
He who played stood there,
Bowing it higher and higher.

Childlike, I danced in a dream;
Blessings emblazoned that day;   10
Everything glowed with a gleam;
Yet we were looking away!

For the most part, one assumes that the order of the poem's lines reflects (even if it does not exactly match) the order of composition in time. This ordinal assumption is true to the logic of increasing complexity, even if the poet did not hit on the right opening words or stanza until completing the rest. In "The Self-Unseeing," Hardy is picking his way with a sad stringency through the visual details so as to record—at last—what escaped his speaker's notice at the time. And his particular naming of the ordinary things without overstating the pathos they acquired in time is a slowly intensifying process (see especially lines 6 and 9–11, where the wife and the child are enraptured by the father's fiddle playing). Rather than a snapshot of a scene that is uniform in its radiance, the scene and its verbal rendering in the beginning lines must be noncommittal to suggest the speaker's boyhood security within a household he took for granted on ordinary and somewhat empty days. Hardy's stark utterances suggest the paralysis of nostalgia about a past in which he was half-asleep.

From this perspective of the initiating themes, the fact that the image of the whole is not yet articulated limits the possible images the poet can adopt for the first glimpses of that whole. Hindsight can polish the beginning but must also retrace the work's evolution and so can neither erase nor replace the essential testing by which a beginning is made. In poems, the beginning will often remain uncertain of its end.

A poem underway is provisional; its making is what we want to call to mind in order to gain a sympathetic sense of the unknown that always confronts writers. By imagining the opportunities they had to make certain choices rather than others, we can estimate the values of the choices the poets actually made. The first two stanzas of a poem by Emily Dickinson suggest, as the first line has it, "'Tis good—the looking back on Grief—" (#660). But it turns out that the looking back on something is a staying action against an event we never directly see:

> 'Tis good—the looking back on Grief—
> To re-endure a Day—
> We thought the Mighty Funeral—
> Of All Conceived Joy—
>
> To recollect how Busy Grass
> Did meddle—one by one—
> Till all the Grief with Summer—waved
> And none could see the stone.
> ~

5

And though the Woe you have Today
Be larger—As the Sea   10
Exceeds its Unremembered Drop—
They're Water—equally—[6]

The speaker hopes by looking back to feel kindly, even indulgent and a little patronizing, toward her own past experience, which is minor compared with the nearly unmentionable, major grief in the present moment. (The present is described and shaped *only* in the contrast, in stanza three, between the ocean of itself and the water drop it used to be.)

The poem is hardly the best that Dickinson wrote, but what beguiles me is the ambiguous second stanza. We come to it with the hint pertaining from stanza one that plants us at a grave site (see line 3). When we meet the "Busy Grass" of line 5, we might at first imagine that the burial scene returns during the same long-ago summer as the death. But Dickinson is viewing the action of time—she is looking back first to an earlier funeral day and then to days of the ensuing summer during which "Busy Grass" grew up and hid the tomb marker; in the process, that first grief, originally sharp and engrossing, became blended in with the softness of the mild and fertile season.

The passage of time purports to take away the strength of that past grief (which was not as great as her present bereavement). But like Robert Frost's poem, which closes on "prey" while insisting that we imagine escape from predation, and Thomas Hardy's, which ends "looking away" from the scene the speaker is so desperate to recover and scrutinize, Dickinson's poem still *says* "stone" at the end of a sentence designed to negate the stone's existence ("Till all the Grief with Summer—waved / And none could see the stone"). Although we are supposed to be unable to see it now, the stone memorial asserts its place in the mental record by putting itself down so irrevocably in the verbal one. Further, the stanza also rhymes on that word "stone," and thus makes it more audible and (so to speak) visible. Thus the present grief of the speaker, however it

6. Poem #660, composed during the banner year, 1862, when poems #326 through #664 were written. Emily Dickinson used the dash as her primary mode of punctuation. Sometimes the dash stands for a comma, sometimes for a semicolon, at other times for a period, and in some rare cases, as at the end of the third line of #660, for a mere line break ("the Mighty Funeral— / Of All Conceived Joy"). One task for the reader of Dickinson is deciding where her sentences begin and end.

may outstrip that earlier one, still implicitly competes with it, taking on some of the features (such as stubbornness and refusal to be comforted) of the loss from long ago.

Conventions and Time

Of course, Dickinson, like Hardy and Frost, was not entirely free to take up her themes. In part, a poet's choices are determined by conventions that change in time; the poetic horizon is not the same during all literary periods. Subjects change. Some become more available. The bird has a more deterministic significance for Robert Frost than for Shakespeare or for the writer of the ballad of the silver swan, "who living had no note," or for John Keats, who wrote of a nightingale "pouring forth [its] soul abroad." Other subjects recede. Deaths were more commonplace and domestic in the time of Dickinson than in ours, and Dickinson herself attended scores of deathbeds, particularly those of children and young women; graveyard visits to the long departed were also part of the domestic round. Still other subjects rise and fall in unpredictable cycles. Poets like Hardy and Frost are never far from the outdoors in their poems, whereas nature is considerably muted as a subject in many poems by their Edwardian and early twentieth-century contemporaries—not to mention what we view as the alienation of landscape from medieval, Renaissance, and eighteenth-century poems, owing to the conventions of literary representation. One of our tasks in reading amounts to developing a sense of the horizon of thematic and stylistic possibility that beckons the practicing poet, just as one of the tasks in writing is to push out beyond the verge traced by what has once been expressed.

Without tradition, there can be no sense of the outer limit; without disdain for the bounds worn by practice, there can be no new poems. The horizon of possibility both attracts and defines a sense of threshold. The poet's scope is both broadened by tradition and limited by those assumptions about what needs to be explored. But whenever tradition undergoes a jolt, owing to the experiments of certain poets, subjects change; so do postures. For example, the array of choices awaiting the poet was different in the eighteenth century when convention favored poetic wit and a rhetorical stance much like the political journalist's today. The tone of the two poems last quoted above diverges fundamentally from that of verse like the following:

from "Retaliation"

Here lies David Garrick, describe me who can,
An abridgment of all that was pleasant in man;
. . . .
On the stage he was a natural, simple, affecting;
'Twas only that, when he was off, he was acting:
With no reason on earth to go out of his way,
He turn'd and he varied full ten times a day;
Tho' secure of our hearts, yet confoundedly sick,
If they were not his own by finessing and trick,
He cast off his friends, as a huntsman his pack;
For he knew when he pleased he could whistle them back.[7]

(Oliver Goldsmith)

Goldsmith's satiric portrait of the famous actor, his friend David Garrick
(who had earlier written a humorous and premature epitaph for *him*),
works by a system of polarities and reversals of style. These extremes in
style reflect a view of psychology as itself based on reversal or at least
conflict of attitude: Garrick repels his friends in order to stage their return
to him; he is only himself when on stage, for it is when he is off-stage
that he is the most disposed to play-act; Garrick requires the devotion of
others but does not value such devotion unless he is aware of having con-
nived to get it (hence the devotion is marred by his own artifices). He is
the sort of person who must always *work* on others, even when there is
not much to be gained by doing so. The curious angularity of Oliver
Goldsmith's galloping couplets is well suited to the portrayal of this canny
and perverse theatrical artist, David Garrick. His style provokes Gold-
smith's to paradox and undercutting until invention and insult are hard
to tell apart: Garrick is not a splendid final sum but rather a stunted and
wilful "abridgement," which is to say a diminished contraction, of pleas-
ant human features.

Conventions can be overturned even within a convention's frame.
For example, at a time when the **Petrarchan** conventions of sonnet
writing gave the writer certain stereotypes of devotion to a beloved out
of reach and often cruel to the lover, some writers elect to retreat from

7. Arthur Friedman, ed., *Collected Works,* by Oliver Goldsmith (Oxford: Oxford
University Press, 1966), vol. 4, p. 357.

these stereotypes of extreme self-sacrifice into feelings less noble. In many of the sonnets of William Shakespeare, we detect a sensibility that instead of being lovelorn and long-suffering (let alone ennobled by his yearning) is fretful and dissatisfied—above all, dissatisfied with looking at an idea all from one perspective (even if it was this extreme perspective which initially seemed to gratify his hunger for confession):

Sonnet 110

Alas 'tis true, I have gone here and there
And made my selfe a motley to the view,*   *a fool in public
Gor'd mine own thoughts, sold cheap what is most deare,
Made old offences of affections new.
Most true it is that I have lookt on truth   5
Askonce* and strangely: But by all above,   *askance; skewed
These blenches* gave my heart another youth,   *turnings aside
And worse essais* prov'd thee my best of love,   *worse indulgences
Now all is done, have what shall have no end,
Mine appetite I never more will grin'de*   *whet 10
On newer proofe, to trie an older friend,
A God in love, to whom I am confin'd.
    Then give me welcome, next my heaven the best,
    Even to thy pure and most most loving brest.

This sonnet supposes a speaker who is already vexed and tormented when we meet him. No remoteness is permitted to intrude, nor gradual approach, and no accretion of details. Instead, the poem bursts upon us in full swing—so abruptly, in fact, that the good intentions the speaker lays down in the final six lines keep being swamped by the unwieldiness of his recent (and apparently chronic) misbehavior: Despite the claim, "Mine appetite I never more will grin'de / On newer proofe," what draws him onward across even these lines is the continuing avid whetting and sharpening and teasing out of his pleasures. Under "pleasures," we should include the craving to show off, play the fool, and amuse others by exorbitance (including the exaggerated self-accusations during the poem— for example, "*Gor'd* mine own thoughts," piercing them painfully and publicly), instead of guarding his privacy and his closest personal bonds.

This exorbitance in theme, which veers off from the conventional orbit of sonnets, is matched by exorbitance in stance: Note Shakespeare's speaker's irritable rehearsal of his faults. Something like irritability also goads the speaker of a later poem on less personal themes:

Great Men have been among us; hands that penned
And tongues that uttered wisdom—better none:
The later Sidney, Marvel, Harrington,
Young Vane, and others who called Milton friend.
These moralists could act and comprehend: 5
They knew how genuine glory was put on;
Taught us how rightfully a nation shone
In splendour: what strength was, that would not bend
But in magnanimous meekness. France, 'tis strange,
Hath brought forth no such souls as we had then.   10
Perpetual emptiness! unceasing change!
No single volume paramount, no code,
No master spirit, no determined road;
But equally a want of books and men!

(William Wordsworth, "Great Men have been among us")

I said this poem was less personal than Shakespeare's. But it is also an attempt to fit political content to the highly personal frame of the sonnet. Wordsworth turns the sonnet's strict limitation of fourteen lines, which might have disabled him, into a strength. Since one cannot, convincingly, contrast two nations such as England and France in respect to both moral and literary thought in the space of so few lines, Wordsworth turns brevity to his advantage by summing up the brooding on the topic that has taken place outside the poem. This poet-speaker comes before us in the attitude not of emotional upheaval but of pensive citizenship.

Today, on the other hand, the range of possible poetic attitudes often excludes such opportunities for satire, argument, and moral opinion as we have seen in the three poems above, favoring instead detailed particulars of person and setting, confessionalism, and the anti-intellectual role of seeming sincere. These preferences leave out formality and the play of rhetoric, especially any rhetoric with heroic content, as in Wordsworth's poem. But also in Shakespeare's 110th sonnet we witnessed a willingness to explore extremes not of experience only but even of culpability; it is this possibility of guilt that is even further antipathetic to most late-twentieth-century poets' threshold of self-esteem.

I said earlier that one of our tasks in reading is to acquire a sense of the horizon of stylistic possibility that lies before the poet. This horizon draws the writer on in part because it defines the poem's scope. Depending on these defining and limiting features of style and stance—

some of them necessarily different from those in our own time—the style
of a particular poem that is still new to us will trace a unique path and
perhaps exhibit unusual handling *as the writer moves through the poem.* Not
all the elements and movements can be familiar ones; while some of
course are predictable (within the norms of the period, at least), their
coordination in a given poem may yet be tentative and daring. Consider
the risk Louise Bogan takes in addressing not just a person or even a col-
lection of individuals but an entire tradition of writing:

> Single Sonnet
>
> Now, you great stanza, you heroic mould,
> Bend to my will, for I must give you love:
> The weight in the heart that breathes, but cannot move,
> Which to endure flesh only makes so bold.
>
> Take up, take up, as it were lead or gold   5
> The burden, test the dreadful mass thereof.
> No stone, slate, metal under or above
> Earth, is so ponderous, so dull, so cold.
>
> Too long as ocean bed bears up the ocean,
> As earth's core bears the earth, have I borne this;   10
> Too long have lovers, bending for their kiss,
> Felt bitter force cohering without motion.
>
> Staunch meter, great song, it is yours, at length,
> To prove how stronger you are than my strength.

Bogan addresses the final, valedictory couplet to a poetic form. But by
this late point we are no longer beguiled by our early inkling as to her
intent. Her theme was greater than a mere poetic form. By lines 13–14,
we can feel how passion itself has been analyzed and driven into catego-
ries—the passion of erotic surrender to which the young woman suc-
cumbs *and* the drive of a young writer's self-devotion as person and poet
to an unconditional feeling she perceives as crushing.

The demands of a poetic form used both by Shakespeare and by Sir
Philip Sidney, the last a poet with whom she was much in sympathy, may
be extraordinary, even (in their way) "heroic" (see Bogan's first line), but
these are slight as compared with the accompanying task of reconstituting
the feelings she judges essential, as theme and process, to any proper son-
net. For such sensual yielding produces a paralyzed intensity. Her analo-

gies for this suggest both heat and coercion: earth's core blazing beneath the heavy mantle of the earth's many layers—a picture she juxtaposes to the "bitter force" compelling one to bend again to taste pleasure despite the fact that its enjoyment is weirdly deadening and foreknown.

When we read Bogan's poem we are learning something about how it felt to *write that poem* and not others in which she also addresses the contest between flesh and spirit with the ideas common to Renaissance poets—poems such as "The Alchemist," in which the substance left over after the fierce burning to which Bogan's speaker subjects her entire being is only base metal, "unmysterious flesh," not gold, "the mind's avid substance." In "Single Sonnet," we follow the oppression and constriction of a particular and even eccentric conflict: The poet's conflict in writing about love becomes a contest between a woman's living flesh and a rigid mold (the latter a play on both the sonnet form and the weight of earth—"mould" as humus, earth, or soil, with its sluggish morbidity). Further, in lines 4 through 8 we see a heated confrontation between imposed fleshly being and imposed (and enormously demanding) poetic convention.

From both directions, the types of heaviness and pressure cohere, so that the form of the sonnet—that heavy burden of tradition she tries to lift again in the words we read—becomes almost light relative to the leaden horror of sexual feeling. The body is tugged at by the same monster that gnaws at the speaker's limbs—the distasteful urge to repeat. When, in the second stanza, Bogan's projected voice urges the heroic mould of the sonnet form to take up the dreadful leaden mass of unsatisfied desire and lighten it through fulfillment, she is also enacting the consequence of such pressures on her own slight frame. She becomes the sonnet and is beaten by its truth as if that were the measure of its strength.

What happens in the last six lines is her doubly triumphant surrender to the sonnet because not only has Bogan said her piece, she has composed a splendid sonnet about being crushed by the sonnet. However, she is not saying that she cannot write in sonnet form. Instead, she is saying that as a human being she is sapped by the struggle to make psychological torment and disorder (the domain of the sonnet as she views it) the subject of a perversely perfect poem. The latter is achieved, but the cost in human terms is prohibitive.

The perspective we can undertake—moving through the poem from the inside—can bring home to us how that poem's themes and techniques might have begun to strike out at a tangent from the expected direction and perhaps at an unexpected speed. Bogan's personal address to the sonnet releases all the energy and anarchy of seduction, which must be excluded from view, or seen only through the contradiction of control ("which to endure flesh only makes so bold"). Elizabeth Bishop's description of the little circus horse in "Cirque d'Hiver" opens in the fifth line to include the little dancer, and indeed lines 6 through 10 describe her graceful turns seemingly without derision (except for the judgmental spell cast by the spray of artificial roses). But by line 11 another plot has unfolded and the circus horse is ennobled by the comparison with the painter Chirico, while the dancer diminishes into a state that is limp and physical (her "pink toes dangle . . . along the little pole" that easily, glibly, and with no apparent resistance "pierces both her body and her soul").

Bishop's speaker identifies with the animal and not the dancer; the latter has only a minimal soul, the horse by contrast a complete sensibility. These personalities emerge incrementally, but erratically and by implication, up to the point at which the dancer is entirely frivolous and one-dimensional and the little circus horse the figure bearing all the complexity of full being. This fullness is constrained by circumstance as (by virtue of her discovery of it) Bishop's speaker's also is. Lorrie Goldensohn reminds us of the genital appearance of the big tin key planted under the horse's haunch.[8] But let us not forget that the horse cannot turn that key himself and that he is a mechanized toy. Then, too, the dance begun by the torque applied to the clockwork key has run down: He "clicks and stops, and looks at me." The last stanza of "Cirque d'Hiver" staggers to an eerie stasis until at last the two figures constrained by life and halted in their movements—the circus horse and the speaker who watches him—penetrate each other's reserve: "'Well, we have come this far.'" It is an eccentric finale. The words *this far* coincide with and represent the poem's end, suggesting the blank space that follows, full of unspoken understanding yet melancholy now that the machine has run out of energy—and out of words. To read Bishop's poem is to experience the tug of absent meanings, among them the sudden involvement of the speaker as the little circus horse breaks the proscenium, standing out from the frame that contains him, and makes it possible for them to address each other. Yet the plot of the poem does not aim at this breach from the start—even

8. But Goldensohn is not quite focused on the implications, claiming that the big tin key "may blur or decentralize" questions of sexuality. See her *Elizabeth Bishop: The Biography of a Poetry* (New York: Columbia University Press, 1992), pp. 57–58.

at line 13 Bishop is preparing only the first mild overtures of sympathy as the speaker imagines horse and dancer ("He *feels* her pink toes dangle"), while direct acknowledgment doesn't emerge until six lines from the end (the horse "canters, then clicks and stops, and looks at me"). So precarious is their link that it was nearly not formed at all.

This method of understanding poems as both imbedded in progression and indebted to surprise is essential if we are to read in order to write: It allows us to skirt the barrier of the poem as a completed "object" and to appreciate some of the lessons of the past while they were still fresh and chancy. Above all, it is a method that allows us to chart our experience of any poem, over years, according to where the work continues to digress from the course within that poem which *we* might have taken. In "course," we must include "point of origin," too. Thus in Bishop's poem we detect a swerve from dancer to horse almost from the start—a striking avoidance for a woman writer whose speaker is presumably also female. In Shakespeare's Sonnet 5, too, there is a start that is instantly countered; it may be that many of us would have resisted such a quick turn as Shakespeare's from temporality as the fair seed time of the beloved's soul (ll. 1–2) to time as his running-down biological clock (ll. 3–8). But a further detour redoubles this turn, in reverse, when in the last six lines the past perfection of the other's summerlike being returns, still ravishing and aromatic, in a prison of glass (a perfume bottle). And in the Hopkins sonnet, the lantern is first a hint (as isolated objects in space, by virtue of what I call the **law of simplified focus,** often are) of the speaker's self-projection when he sees that wistful mark of human journeying. The lantern's meaning alters, however, in the fourth through the eighth lines, to summon up a picture of those other human beings one meets in life who bravely shine out, perfect either "In mould [form] or mind." Hopkins's composition then fills with affection and awe, two emotions that lift the poem across the surprising threshold of death into eternal grace.

In the other poems also, the digressions are continuous and surprising. Wilner and Winters and Arnold repeatedly shift from present to a multifarious past in which historical time also operates. More locally still, we continue to be deflected from expectation by the last line of Hardy's poem ("Yet we were looking away!"), by line 7 of Sonnet 110 by Shakespeare ("These blenches gave my heart another youth"), by the third line in Bogan ("The weight in the heart that breathes, but cannot move"), by the third line in Frost ("Partly because it sang but once all night"), and by the ambiguous catchphrase in line 5 of the excerpt from Goldsmith

("With no reason on earth to go out of his way"): all are points of pivot and imbalance that keep surprising us as we reread. Caroming off of expectation, these lines in their contexts remind their emerging subjects that it is often in their resistance to us that poets teach us the most.

Poetry and Intention

If we imagine from now on that we are writing whatever we read, we will be participating in one of the most important tasks of the contemporary reader and writer, which is to rejoin meaning to its fashion of saying. When we appreciate style as the subtle medium of sense, we can see how the *way* works are written also discloses the meanings these works of art intend. Meaning in poetry is imbedded in the saying.

Such meaning in poetry does not just happen: It is the product of a trained writer's strength, all of which in one way or another is formed and fueled by intention. In art, it is only by intending a saying, with all its effects of meaning, that a work in words can become a coherent piece of literature. Similarly, it is only by imagining *how artistic intention grows* through the work that a reader can get inside it.

This approach asks the reader to depart from processes of reading that may have become habitual. We reach the threshold of this change when we accept that we can no longer read as if the poem were reaching out to us and manipulating us; instead, we can think of how *we* are moving inside the growing poem. But we are not imposing our meaning on the poem—we are actively remaking the work's own meaning, tracking the path of the poem from among the tangle of possible routes it might have taken but did not. In effect, we accompany the poet through the ambiguous emergence of the eventual artistic pattern.

It takes time for us to read carefully; we must look words up, think about the meter and stanza form, decide who is being addressed and in what situation, decide what is the literal surface of the poem and how that is symbolic, then adjust to the subtler insights about stance, nuance, and rhythm that come with repeated readings. Just as it takes time to read and read again, so the poem took time to come into being. As time makes us more confident of our tact in reading, so too any one poem must have taken a while to grow in a writer's mind and under the writer's hand. Elizabeth Bishop used to keep a poem she was working on scotch-taped to her refrigerator for many months, making minute changes, giving those changes time to grow strange again, before she felt she had come through to the exact degree of casual rightness that she craved. All the more reason for the reader not to hasten to any conclusion without support from the poet's often tedious discipline, which so often paves the way for such rapid movements of mind.

~~~~~

Poetry Sampler

I

The Lantern Out of Doors

Sometimes a lantern moves along the night,
    That interests our eyes. And who goes there?
    I think; where from and bound, I wonder, where,
With, all down darkness wide, his wading light?

Men go by me whom either beauty bright   5
    In mould or mind or what not else makes rare:
    They rain against our much-thick and marsh air
Rich beams, till death or distance buys them quite.

Death or distance soon consumes them: wind
    What most I may eye after, be in at the end   10
I cannot, and out of sight is out of mind.

Christ minds; Christ's interest, what to avow or amend
    There, eyes them, heart wants, care haunts, foot follows kind,
Their ransom, their rescue, and first, fast, last friend.

                 (Gerard Manley Hopkins; composed 1877)

II

Operations: Desert Shield, Desert Storm

1.
Who
are these two women, walking
through the great forum of the plain, walking
under the sun's blinded white eye,
under a hard, featureless sky, bright steel   5
without a trace of blue. Two women,
their shadows trailing them
like assassins.
~

What
are they speaking of,   10
so rapt in conversation they scarcely
seem to see the vacancy through which
they walk. One kicks reflexively at bits
of junk that litter the dry ground, raising
white spurts of dust that hover   15
at their feet like slavish hounds
of cloud, assiduous on the trail of
all lost things.
        It is as if time itself
were a dry fountain, where the urn fills only
with pale ashes; where broken tablets   20
of illegible laws cobble the ground;
where church and court alike are built of bones,
a filigreed white latticework of chalk
through which the white sun casts
a black lace of shadows, widows' weeds;   25
where a small wind picks through debris,
an indigent in search of scraps; where
in the desert of our god-drenched origins
the armies grow again, human beetles in
their masks, vague hatred with its poison   30
gas, the air itself a deadly trench
to these benighted boys, condemned
to fall again into the ranks
of what repeats: into the breach
once more, another city broken open like   35
a rotting fruit, the flies rising,
the delicate seeds exposed
to the sun, a book with a broken
spine, anything where enough
is left to name.   40

Antigone and Ismene,
or so we might call them,
these two women walking across this page
of history, this page that is not
a page, because no one can turn it, because   45

it extends and extends, the smoking cities
scattered like open lesions
to the periphery of sight, these wounds
that memory worries so they
cannot close, this sand   50
littered with the bodies of brothers.
These two women, whoever they might be,
have the look of those daughters
caught in the line of a self-blinded king
(a father who is also a brother)   55
debating again the choice
of terms—imprisoned in life, or death.
One is full of argument and heat,
an intellect who can face down a tyrant
with her tongue. The other has a downcast   60
face and sorrow even in the way her garments
hang, folds that hold the shadows deep
inside; though young, her soul
weighs like an ancient thing; Ismene
takes her sister's arm, to whom her life   65
is bound, for whose futility she feels
such a ravaged pity, and such
affection she agrees to lose
their argument, pretend to a weakness
she could never own, because she knows   70
the anger of Antigone must speak
although it end as an echo in a chamber
sealed in the granite hills, a tomb
whose stone is always rolled away
too late. Ismene, grieving,   75
lives, and walks the olive groves
alone, a lively shade for company.

Again, the dictator
in his empty boots
stalks the narrowing tunnels   80
of the streets, his little voice
widened by the megaphones of war,
death's echo amplified.

And then it is Ismene
recalls her sister to her side,   85
steels herself to animate
that shade, and lose her yet again,
if lose she must.

2.
What vicious agency of farce
recalled that ancient sister's act   90
of love, that wish for a brother's
burial? The stage darkens, the shadows
of the sisters merge, and deepen
to a common night:
                        the end of light
those young men, living, saw   95
(to think that horror stops the mind)
as the earthmovers pushed the tons of sand
up over them, and then rolled on.

And after the cheering crowds have gone
home, after the last yellow ribbon of sun   100
has faded in the west, where shall Ismene hide
when they open the cave where defiance
hangs, when those swaying sandals
brush her face, after they cut
the body down, where shall she turn   105
from all that is buried in the desert plot
made for headlines and parades,
a place too dry for even grief.
Yesterday's news.
Too topical for poems.   110
Welcome home, this is
America, welcome home.

                                          (Eleanor Wilner)

III

The Mill-Race

Four-fifty. The palings of Trinity Church
Burying Ground, a few inches above the earth,
are sunk in green light. The low stones
like pale books knocked sideways. The bus so close to the curb
that brush-drops of ebony paint stand out wetly, the sunlight   5
seethes with vibrations, the sidewalks
on Whitehall shudder with subterranean tremors. Overhead, faint
                                                                flickers

crackle down the window-paths, limpid telegraphy of the
late afternoon July thunderstorm unfurling over Manhattan.
Its set and luminous velocity, the long stalks of stormlight, and then
                                                    the first drops   10
strike their light civic stripes on the pavement.
Between the palings, oat-panicles sift a few bright
grains to the stonecourse. Above it, at shoulder height,
a side door is flung open, a fire-exit; streaming from lobbies

come girls and women, black girls with ripples of cornrows and
                                                          plaits,   15
ear-hoops, striped shadowy cotton-topped skirts, white girls in
                                              gauzy-toned nylons,
one girl with shocked-back ash hair, lightened eyebrows;
one face from Easter Island, mauve and granitic;
thigh on thigh, waist by waist; the elbow's curlicue and the finger's;
                                          elbow-work, heel-work,
are suddenly absorbed in the corduroyed black-rubber stairs of the
                                                      bus. Humid   20
sighs, settlings, each face tilts up to the windows'
shadowless yards of mercuric green plateglass. In close-up

you can see it in the set and grain of each face,
despite the roped rainlight pouring in the bus-windows—
it's the strain of gravity itself, life-hours cut off and offered   25
to the voice that says, "Give me this day your
life, that is LABOR, and I'll give you back

one day, then another. For mine are the terms."
It's gravity, spilling in capillaries, cheek-tissue trembling
despite the makeup, the monograms, the mass-market designer
scarves,   30
the army of private signs disowning the workplace and longing for
night. . . .

But this, at least, is the interspace. Like the slowing of some ritual
water mill, a creaking and dipping pause
of black-splintered paddles, the irregularly
dappled off-lighting—bottle-green—the lucid slim sluice   35
falling back in a spittle-stream from the plank-edge. It won't take us
altogether, we say, the mill-race—it won't churn us up, altogether.
We'll keep
this glib stretch of leisure-water, like our self's self—to reflect the
sky.
But we won't (says the bus-rider, slumped, to herself). Nothing's
left over, really, from labor. They've taken it all for the mill-race.
Even now,   40

as the driver flicks off the huge felt-edged wipers,
the rain slackening, lifting, labor
lengthens itself along Broadway. Fresh puddles
mirror in amber and crimson the night signs
that wit has set up to draw money: O'Donnell's,   45
Beirut Cafe, Yonah's Knish . . . People dart out from awnings.
The old man at the kiosk starts his late shift, whipping off rain-
streaked
Lucite sheets from his new stacks of newsprint.

If there is leisure, bus-riders, it's not for you,
not between here and uptown or here and the Bronx. . . .   50
Outside Marine Midland, the black sea of unmarked corporate
hire-cars
waits for the belated office-lights, the long rainy run to the exurbs.
Somewhere it may be, on a converted barn-roof in Connecticut,
leisure silvers the shingles, somewhere the densely packed
labor-mines running a half-mile down from the sky   55

to the Battery's bedrock rise, metamorphic, in water-gardens,
lichened windows where the lamp lights Thucydides or Gibbon.

It's not a water-mill really, work. It's like the nocturnal
paper-mill pulverizing, crushing each fiber of rag into atoms,
or the smooth-lipped workhouse   60
treadmill, that wore down a London of doxies and sharps,
or the paper-mill, faerique, that raised the cathedrals and wore out
                                        hosts of dust-demons,
but it's mostly the miller's curse-gift, forgotten of God yet still
                                        grinding, the salt-
mill, that makes the sea, salt.

                                                    (Anne Winters)

IV

    Sonnet 5

Those howers that with gentle worke did frame,
The lovely gaze where every eye doth dwell
Will play the tirants to the very same,
And that unfaire★ which fairely doth excell: ★*make ugly*
For never resting time leads Summer on,   5
To hidious winter and confounds him there,
Sap checkt with frost and lustie leav's quite gon.
Beauty ore-snow'd and barenes every where,
Then were not summers distillation left
A liquid prisoner pent in walls of glasse,   10
Beauties effect with beauty were bereft,
Nor it nor noe remembrance what it was.
    But flowers distil'd though they with winter meete,
    Leese★ but their show, their substance still lives sweet.   ★*lose*

                                                (William Shakespeare)

V

    Cirque d'Hiver[9]

Across the floor flits the mechanical toy,
fit for a king of several centuries back.
A little circus horse with real white hair.
His eyes are glossy black.
He bears a little dancer on his back.   5

She stands upon her toes and turns and turns.
A slanting spray of artificial roses
is stitched across her skirt and tinsel bodice.
Above her head she poses
another spray of artificial roses.   10

His mane and tail are straight from Chirico.[10]
He has a formal, melancholy soul.
He feels her pink toes dangle toward his back
along the little pole
that pierces both her body and her soul   15

and goes through his, and reappears below,
under his belly, as a big tin key.
He canters three steps, then he makes a bow,
canters again, bows on one knee,
canters, then clicks and stops, and looks at me.   20
~

9. *Cirque d'hiver* (French: literally, winter circus): a covered circus building at 110
Rue Amelot (in the quarter of Paris called "Boulevards," originally laid out by Louis
XIV—in the 1930s it was still the most affluent district). The Cirque d'hiver itself was
built, in the shape of a tent, for Napoleon III in 1857.

10. *Chirico, Giorgio de* (1888–1978). Originator of metaphysical painting; also con-
sidered the founder of futurism. Born in Greece of Sicilian parents, Chirico studied in
Athens, Munich, Italy, and Paris. His pictures convey an inexplicable atmosphere of
strangeness and uneasiness, in the immobility of the empty perspectives and his illusory
perspectives. During the 1920s, Chirico painted his most powerful and disturbing
works—obsessive compositions of naked figures that are half-human, half-dummies, and
the famous series of riotous horses on unreal shores with broken Greek columns. See
Harold Osborn, ed., *The Oxford Companion to Art* (Oxford: Clarendon Press, 1970), pp.
237–38.

The dancer, by this time, has turned her back.
He is the more intelligent by far.
Facing each other rather desperately—
his eye is like a star—
we stare and say, "Well, we have come this far."

25

(Elizabeth Bishop)

PART I

The Six Elements of Relation and Resemblance

Three Working Concepts

As writers move through their poems, they discipline themselves to respond to language on many fronts at once. But active experiment is usually limited to one or two of these elements. We can distinguish six that play major roles. The elements are: **line, syntax, diction, trope, rhetoric** or argument, and **rhythm.** The elements, or avenues of approach, are by turns fostered and suppressed, followed and ignored. Out of the coordination of their contours and directions—the rising and falling of certain elements in turn—a poem is moved forward from its starting point. The reaching of an endpoint coincides not only with the completion of the poem but also with the comprehension of its terrain by writer and reader. However, "comprehension" means, in some measure, recollection of uncertainty. Poems remain mysterious territory at the start—even long after they've been written and reread.

To shift from the idea of a journey to the act of composition, we could say the poem is drawn together out of its parts like a tapestry or even a piece of music. As in those other kinds of making, the treatment of one thread affects the entire design, just as the prominence of a few notes requires the quiet cooperation of the multitude of others in the piece. Even when they do not come into the foreground, all of the stylistic elements are being deliberately managed by the maker, and their management requires the conscious acknowledgment of the attentive audience. Along these lines, we will experiment—as readers and as writers—with Donald Davie's notion that all good poetry fends something off. What a poet keeps out of a poem is as necessary to its success as what the poet lets into it. In a complementary way, what the poet lets into the poem is a choice from among a number of poetic ideas that are (if not exactly banished) displaced into a background. Here they not only serve to throw the chosen elements into higher relief but also form the support against which the active elements can lean.

The Continuum

To discuss the elements and their links, three working concepts will be used. The first is the continuum, which helps us to read within centuries and within forms and also across centuries and across forms. The continuum is a constant line expressing some feature or relation, on which we can display the range from one extreme to the other. For example, at its extremes, the voice of the poem will either be singing or logically arguing, with other stages in between:

SONG	STORY	DESCRIPTION	ARGUMENT

All poems can be placed on the line close to one of these stylistic options or midway between two of them. (You might imagine for yourself where a form like the conversational poem might fall.)

For each of the elements of a poem, a continuum can help us visualize the range of possibilities and the gradual stages of difference. The more finely these stages are discriminated, the more points there will be along the continuum. The more points named on the continuum, the more comprehensive the account of stylistic mode. A continuum of syntax, or sentence frame, would begin with three basic defining points:

SIMPLE DECLARATIVE	COMPOUND SENTENCE	COMPLEX SUBORDINATING

Such a continuum assumes that all poems are written in complete sentences. Because some poems are not, greater scope may be required for this particular continuum. You might want to allow for fragments and incomplete phrases at one end of the continuum of sentences; at the complex end, you could discriminate between two forms of subordination of the parts of the whole sentence—descriptive subordination and more argumentative use of subordinating clauses:

PHRASES & SENTENCE FRAGMENTS	SIMPLE DECLARATIVE	COMPOUND	COMPLEX (A) [DESCRIPTIVE]	COMPLEX (B) [ARGUMENTATIVE]

The continuum of syntax can also be applied to examples from one poet, to indicate range, as well as to poems by various hands from the same time period—not to mention poems from different periods.

Note that a minimum of three points must be described for a continuum to begin to acquire the shape of a useful working concept. Thus the continuum will also help guard against both vagueness and absolute claims. Let me give an example. Instead of saying that Poet X is a simple writer, one should first suggest the area of style in which the simplicity is most visible: for example, "Poet X uses simple sentences, or simple, one-syllable words, or short, simple lines." Then you need at least two other writers for comparison and contrast along the chosen continuum. If you say, "Poet X uses simple declarative sentences," situate him or her on the continuum shown above by designating at one extreme Poet A as a user of fragments, and Poet B, at the other extreme, as a user of complex argumentative sentences. Poet X would then either move closer to A or B or pivot halfway between the practices of both. If a writer strikes you as representing an extreme usage, provide that poet with his or her opposite, with a moderating poet in between them. These relationships are the first step toward using the continuum to reach clearer judgments about individual writers.

What can work for poets can also be useful for clusters of poems. Lines of relation, or continua, can be imagined for the voices and themes within the complete works of single individuals, too, with groups of more songlike poems during one period, more argumentative poems at another. In addition, some eras are more given than others to usages such as punning; a continuum from flat or un-nuanced vocabulary to the other extreme of diction with multiple layers (as in a pun) would help analyze these trends.

Coincidence, Tension, and Recession of Technique

Each of the elements of poetic relation and resemblance involve balance between competing urges. As the examples above show, each element (or type of continuum) provides for simplicity at one end and complexity at the other, with all the conceivable points between. Some writers choose to coordinate simplicity of language (or diction) with simplicity of sentence frame with simplicity of rhythm with simplicity of idea with end-stopping in the lines. Such coordination occurs in the early Scottish ballads. We say of such poetry that the elements coincide with each other.

But not all poems are content with simplicity on all fronts and decide to vary one of the elements—say, sentence frame (or syntax)—while maintaining all the other elements toward the pole of the plain and simple. In this case, style of sentence works in tension with the style of word-choice or diction and the style of line and rhythm. The subtle music of poetry is often produced by the tension between a few elements of style against a background of coincidence among the rest. Some techniques must recede in order that others stand out. The only provisos about using the coincidence/tension and recession idea are these:

1. Thorough coincidence at the complex pole is not as pleasing as coincidence at the simple. A little complexity goes a long way in a poem, and if every element is being stretched to its utmost complication, the poem may grow too dense, and even hard to follow.

2. Coincidence at the simple end of the various continua can lead to monotony, as for example when line and sentence unit always coincide. Some variation is preferred by the ear.

3. In order for one or more of the elements to stand out, all the others must still be deliberately controlled so as to recede or remain in the background. For example, the comparisons in a poem may be brilliant, but if the lines and their rhythms are not also carefully managed to buffer that brilliance and make it expressive, the poem's lines will unravel into prose.

Thresholds of Choice

Thresholds and Standards

Some writers, like some literary cultures, maintain different standards for tension and coincidence than we do. We may need to redefine the thresholds for stylistic tension and coincidence not only for each stylistic element but for each tradition, each era, and each individual body of work we encounter. With regard to the rhythms of the poetic line, for example, poets in the eighteenth century had a fairly narrow set of ideas about acceptable variations. Slight liberties were felt as more significant than they are in our own time. Their notion of experimental threshold was highly circumscribed; ours is more open.

Threshold and Half-Meaning

There is a second sense of threshold that is helpful to keep in mind, and that is the limber margin belonging to the first two elements of relation—the line and the sentence. Each of these stylistic features has a limit. In addition, the line often ends before the sentence does. (The reverse case is less common, as there are only so many sentences you can bring to completion in the space of a line.) When the line ends before the sentence does, we can say that the threshold of the line is in tension with that of the sentence. In cases of such tension, the line can provide a partial or temporary meaning or suggestion that is at odds with the meaning of the completed sentence. I call these provisional meanings before moving off the line **half-meanings.** The half-meanings of lines that run on would be in tension with the whole meaning that emerges when the sentence has come to its end. Of course, the meanings that derive from any isolated part of a poem are also partial (although I do not call them half-meanings)—a partiality that reminds us of the need to keep moving through the poem.

The Threshold of the Known

By rereading poems in their context, we encounter the last of the three senses of threshold that pertain to poetic creation. This is the poem's comprehensive and repeating encounter with the unknown. Every poem tries to cross *some* kind of boundary so as to push off from what poems have already been and start laying claim to something different. Sometimes difference is achieved by returning to older forms now fallen into disuse (this has already happened with bardic Welsh rhyme and Anglo-Saxon verse). At other points, experiment results in something genuinely new. The dramatic poets of the sixteenth century made one such daring move, away from rhymed dramatic verse, by colonizing the then somewhat awkward terrain of blank verse; the first poets to make the shift teeter a bit. Even early Shakespeare wavers on the threshold, but his later work is electric with the discovery of the new mode of enjambing. In the seventeenth century, Milton extended the transgression by pushing iambic pentameter—the heroic line of the drama—into the complex toils of narrative meditation. Wordsworth then softened blank verse by his thematic stress on personal memory and a protected rural boyhood, thus opening blank verse as a medium of consciousness in time.

A new poem in the making (which is also to say, in the making of the reader's imagination, too) is always stepping across the threshold of the past where content and forms already exist, into a future where, so far, the maps are incomplete.

2

Line and Half-Meaning

The Logic of the Line

The first threshold we cross in a poem is the one that distinguishes it from prose. Indeed, the most obvious thing about a poem is that it is arranged in **lines,**[1] not paragraphs. The right-hand margins of poems are not even and symmetrical as are paragraphs of printed prose. In poems, by contrast, the lines stop for reasons of their own. One reason—and the primary one in literary history—will be numerical; many of the poems you will be encouraged to read (and to think about writing) are those that obey some numerical rule. We will come back to these in a while.

But another reason to end a line may be logical and prosaic. Hebrew poetry consists of lines that close at the ends of phrases; the lengths of these lines vary. Either they have identical opening or closing phrases, called **tags** (these repeated tags are found in much devotional and oral poetry in the form of litanies and refrains), or the lines of **Hebrew verse** have parallel or antithetical units of phrasing. New lines begin with capital letters.

> *Let them be* ashamed and confounded that seek after my soul: *let them be* turned backward, and put to confusion, that desire my hurt.
> *Let them be* turned back for a reward of their shame that say, Aha, aha.

---

1. As in the Introduction, defined terms, indicated by **boldface type,** are discussed in chapter 13, "Poetic Terms," which is set up as an annotated dictionary.

Let all those that seek thee rejoice and be glad in thee: *and let such* as
    love thy salvation say continually, *Let God be* magnified. . . .

(Psalms 70:2–4)

～～～

As he that bindeth a stone in a sling, *so is he that giveth* honour to a
    fool.
As a thorn goeth up into the hand of a drunkard, *so is a parable*
    in the mouth of fools.
. . . .
As a dog returneth to his vomit, *so a fool returneth* to his folly.
. . . .
As the door turneth upon his hinges, *so doth the slothful* upon his bed.

(Proverbs 26:8–9, 11, 14)

In these passages, the sameness of the initial tag reinforces the larger
balance of repeating sentence pattern and analogous illustration.[2] In the
second type of Hebrew verse, parallelism and complement tighten the
mesh of the pattern in a somewhat subtler way:

Sing, O heavens; and be joyful, O earth; and break forth into
    singing, O mountains.

(Isaiah 49:13)

～～～

And he hath made my mouth like a sharp sword, in the shadow of
    his hand hath he hid me; and made me a polished shaft; in his
    quiver he hid me away.

(Isaiah 49:2)

Here, the parallels of the sentences support parallels in theme; and when
syntax so closely parallels the comparisons, we have an interwoven net of
resemblances that controls our expectations.

What I have described is not as tight a form of control as meter and
rhyme in other kinds of verse like the sonnet or even the ballad (song).
But the method (which is characteristic of Hebrew poetry) of writing in

---

2. This use of tags resembles **isocolon** or sameness of sentence-frame in a speech.
Both are examples of **anaphora** (see the dictionary entry in chapter 13 for further discus-
sion and examples).

phrases that fall into parallel rankings with conspicuous likeness or con-
spicuous contrast between the themes nevertheless does create patterns
of anticipation *at intervals* in the English translations, much as meter does.[3]
And when it uses **antithesis** (close contrast in neighboring phrases), He-
brew poetry achieves closure still more succinctly:

> The sun shall not smite thee by day,
> nor the moon by night.

(Psalms 121:6)

All verses in Hebrew poetry contain phrases or sentences that are
wholes. In English verse of the twentieth century, on the other hand,
the tradition of **free verse** has permitted two kinds of **lineation:** lines
composed of broken phrases (one might describe this practice as anti-
grammatical) as well as free-verse lines organized in syntactically com-
plete units, all the phrases set off and complete:[4]

> To my right,
> In a field of sunlight between two pines,
> The droppings of last year's horses
> Blaze up into golden stones.
> I lean back, as the evening darkens and comes on.   5
> A chicken hawk flies over, looking for home.
> I have wasted my life.

(James Wright, "Lying in a Hammock at William Duffy's Farm
in Pine Island, Minnesota")

The lines above could be said to lineate by phrase, breaking where the
clusters of words also divide. His free verse is syntactically complete, even
if, unlike what occurs in Hebrew verse, the modern poet's phrases are
not rhetorically balanced in parallel. Wright has deliberately avoided or
"fended off" that sort of symmetry.

---

3. The original Hebrew has a free variation of stresses between two and four and a
limit to the number of intervening unstressed syllables, much as Anglo-Saxon verse does.
See Robert Alter, "Ancient Hebrew Poetry," in *The Literary Guide to the Bible,* edited by
Robert Alter and Frank Kermode, pp. 611–24 (Cambridge, MA: Harvard University
Press, 1987).

4. Because the decision to break the unit of grammar is such a central distinguishing
feature within the practice of free verse, I divide the **imagist free-verse** readings into
two categories, end-stopped (or grammatical) and enjambed (or antigrammatical). See
the "List of Poems by Form."

But lines of free verse may also enjamb (run over) across continuing phrases and clauses, thus creating an effect of "tugging." There are many degrees of tugging between line and grammatical phrase. In the passages from free-verse poems below, there is greater spring or suspension than in Wright as the line boundary is approached. The *substance* of the poem runs on, even if there is a mild breaking, or hesitation, at line ends:

But how does one feel?
One grows used to the weather,
The landscape and that;
And the sublime comes down
To the spirit itself,   15

The spirit and space,
The empty spirit
In vacant space.
What wine does one drink?
What bread does one eat?   20
                        (Wallace Stevens, "The American Sublime")

⌇⌇⌇⌇

     Dark flows up from his feet
To his shoulders and throat, then has his face in its mask,
Then lifts.   85
                              (Louise Bogan, "Summer Wish")

Still other kinds of free verse use prominent breaks at the ends of the lines, between the individual words or phrases—but without necessarily creating a sensation of violence in the expression:

     Why couldn't
We have been more considerate? These figures leaving   30

The platform or waiting to board the train are my brothers
In a way that really wants to tell me why there is so little
Panic and disorder in the world, and so much unhappiness.
                              (John Ashbery, "Melodic Trains")

One has the sense in reading an excerpt like the one above, however, that although form supports theme in the direction of a sudden insight, there is little conviction about the revelation. The acts of "leaving / The plat-form" and of discovering that there is surprisingly "little / Panic and dis-order" are not nearly as sudden and decisive as either the theme of parting or the literal parting in the line breaks would seem to suggest. The reason is that the local breaks within these threshold phrases are moderated by the lengths of John Ashbery's lines and the ample reach of his sentences; these act to buffer the breaks and create a norm against which even the cutting apart of words in the same phrase is not noticeable. Variety of sentence and length of line make any sort of break less surprising.

John Ashbery, like his contemporary James Schuyler, has created a number of long poetic works in long lines—works in which the line boundaries are effortlessly but not metrically bridged.[5] Even brief lines such as these, from Schuyler's "A Few Days," need not be dramatic:

> I'd like to   330
> find a new place, somewhere where there are friends and
>   not too many
> houses. This summer has passed like a dream. On the last
>   day of August
> I feel much better than I felt in June, heaven be praised.   335
>   Who said, "Only
> health is beautiful"? There's truth in the old saw. I
>   have always been
> more interested in truth than in imagination: I
>   wonder if that's   340
> true?

Schuyler's great gift as a poet is to mask the artistry with which his seem-ingly unhindered free-verse lines are bridged. This formal ease reflects his themes, musing about the ordinary jumble of life—friends, books, visiting, the stretch of the seasons. The anchor of Schuyler's practice is his evenness of temper.

But in the work of other poets, particularly those who tend to use the brief line for shocking effects, the violence of the line breaks that interrupt the units of syntax can mirror authentic unease in the feeling of

---

5. This is an idea I borrow from Charles Hartman and apply to Ashbery in a long study of his work that appears in my volume *The Cure of Poetry in an Age of Prose: Moral Essays on the Poet's Calling* (Chicago: University of Chicago Press, 1993).

the whole, which soon dominates the atmosphere. However, when they become the norm, even those line breaks that dramatize certain exaggerations of meaning and feeling become unmarked (that is, they recede into the background).

The free-verse examples given thus far, to the extent that they suggest adherence to a norm, are also unmarked. This want of distinctive shape occurs because they contain line breaks in which the pausing signifies little more than the introduction of a new phrase and topic or (in the case of Ashbery and Schuyler) they announce a deliberate erasure of the borders between lines. Whatever becomes a habit of style cannot be used to surprise:

> Not only underground are the brains of men
> Eaten by maggots.
> Life in itself
> Is nothing,
> An empty cup, a flight of uncarpeted stairs.   15
>
> > (Edna St. Vincent Millay, "Spring")

~~~~~~

> Her bare
>
> Feet seem to be saying:
> We have come so far, it is over.
>
> Each dead child coiled, a white serpent,
> One at each little   10
>
> Pitcher of milk, now empty.
> She has folded
>
> Them back into her body as petals
> Of a rose close when the garden
>
> Stiffens and odors bleed   15
> From the sweet, deep throats of the night flower.
>
> > (Sylvia Plath, "Edge")

In the two excerpts above we observe the relative brevity of the lines that break hardest and the eventual subsidence of the first sharp effect.

Lines in Place

The free-verse excerpts above illustrate another point about all **verse.** Not only is verse *in lines,* also the substance on any one line is made to seem equivalent to that on any other line. This equivalence (which I call **isomorphism**) is an almost automatic result of the mere fact of the line as a unit, and it holds true for the old ballads as well as for the work of contemporary poets.[6] The pairs of lines in James Wright's poem bear out the idea that the hawk and the speaker of the poem are actors performing a similar drama. In the same way, Wright insists that the sun between the pine trees and the casual gesture of the speaker's body (we assume he is nodding or pointing when he says, "To my right") are equal in importance. Furthermore, the horse droppings and their unexpectedly glorious appearance (they "Blaze up") are one: The differences between the low and the high fade before the sudden new resemblances.

A more self-conscious half-meaning occurs in the middle line below, from Eleanor Wilner's "Operations: Desert Shield, Desert Storm" (quoted in full in the "Poetry Sampler" in chapter 1):

> the armies grow again, human beetles in
> their masks, vague hatred with its poison   30
> gas, the air itself a deadly trench . . .

While reading line 30 and being guided by it, we will try to connect hatred both with a mask (as though it were a grimace rather than protective gear) and with the poison hate secretes. Although neither is the strictly accurate reading, both links inevitably release operative meanings into the poem, adding to the turmoil of feeling.

Eleanor Wilner's poem works relatively quickly; the lines are short and their tempo insistent, and thus the life-span of the half-meanings brief when compared with the following more somber free verse by Louise Bogan. The instinctive granting of equivalent weight to equivalent forms (in this case, lines) requires of us here a more speculative imaginative weighting of each syntactically complete line with all the others.

---

6. Although he does not use the term isomorphism for the instinctive granting of equivalent weight to equivalent forms (in this case, lines), the phenomenon itself is discussed with some care by Charles O. Hartman throughout his *Free Verse: An Essay on Prosody* (Princeton, NJ: Princeton University Press, 1980).

Anaphora, or the repetition of an initial tag, highlights the linear paral-
lels. The poem is essentially a carefully crafted catalogue:

> Baroque Comment
>
> From loud sound and still chance;
> From mindless earth, wet with a dead million leaves;
> From the forest, the empty desert, the tearing beasts,
> The kelp-disordered beaches;
> Coincident with the lie, anger, lust, oppression and death in many
>   forms: 5
>
> Ornamental structures, continents apart, separated by seas;
> Fitted marble, swung bells; fruit in garlands as well as on the
>   branch;
> The flower at last in bronze, stretched backward, or curled within;
> Stone in various shapes: beyond the pyramid, the contrived arch
>   and the buttress;
> The named constellations;   10
> Crown and vesture; palm and laurel chosen as noble and enduring;
> Speech proud in sound; death considered sacrifice;
> Mask, weapon, urn; the ordered strings;
> Fountains; foreheads under weather-bleached hair;
> The wreath, the oar, the tool,   15
> The prow;
> The turned eyes and the opened mouth of love.

Note how the brief lines ("The named constellations," "The prow") rise
out of and define themselves against the elegant and impassioned cata-
logue of civilized achievements to steer toward new thresholds of signi-
fying power.

Bogan coordinates the shifts to briefer lines with a thoughtful mode
of emphasis. By contrast, in Plath's poem, the bareness of the dead wom-
an's feet is given such a strong—even rough—emphasis by the radically
broken line, "Her bare," that this quality competes in importance with
the words the feet are given to say ("We have come so far, it is over"). In
the excerpt from Schuyler's poem, the break after "many" isolates the
prior referent ("friends") in a limbo of not-being ("friends and / not too
many"); this is an isolation that thematically complements the in-and-out
between solitude and sociability, soul and matter, elsewhere in the poem,

although the line is quickly drawn down to a milder development of feeling characteristic of Schuyler's temperament ("not too many / houses. This summer has passed like a dream").

In the excerpts from Millay and Plath, with their violent breaks, and even in the gentler Schuyler, another principle has come into play. The radical splitting apart of phrases creates provisional meanings in the orphaned lines. These momentary meanings may counteract or clash with the meaning of the sentence—once the sentence has been pieced back together. When a metrical verse enjambs, it, too, can hover between "half" and "whole" meanings in this way. Whatever the mode in which the poet controls the lines, metrical or free, the same rule applies: *An enjambed line always creates a **half-meaning** in addition to the "whole" meaning of the sentence.* Shakespeare uses one such line when Ulysses encourages perseverance because it "keeps honour bright: To have done is to hang," thus suggesting that being idle is like dying in disrepute (as in hanging for a crime). But a more comprehensive meaning overrides that melodramatic hint with a comparison that is strategically material:

> . . . perseverance, dear my lord,
> Keeps honour bright: To have done is to hang
> Quite out of fashion, like a rusty mail
> In monumental mockery.
>
> (Troilus and Cressida III.iii)

Inaction is as embarrassing as owning a suit of mail for use in combat but never taking it down from its peg.

Consider the following sampler of metrical lines whose meaning is so dependent on completed context that they make little sense in isolation:

> And flash of his authority? It's well . . .
>
> is character. The Universe induces . . .
>
> Companionable streams or climb the air . . .
>
> Eve separate; he wished, but not with hope
>
> As every day, yet outcast, safe and outcast . . .

Of anyone to please, it withers so . . .
~~~~~~
With three still pools by passage work[7]

Now, some of these lines occur in passages whose meaning is not substantively altered by out-of-context use. But even when the disturbance created by half-meaning is slight, it is still a disturbance and must be accommodated by both poet and reader.

Note, on the other hand, that as we found in Ulysses's speech from *Troilus and Cressida,* some of the half-meanings created in the lines above are not merely ambiguous but also misleading. And even if the fairly bland final line just quoted announces no pitfalls, eventually we realize that the line has put into intimate connection two prepositional phrases that are only nominally geographical (introduced by "with" and "by"): What the completed syntactic context of Howard Nemerov's "Landscape with Self-Portrait" shows instead is the logic of instrumental causation as the creek is joined to pools by means of hydraulic "passage work":

> And further down, through trees, the streaming creek   5
> With three still pools by passage work
> Of rapids and rills in fretted rhythms linked . . .

On the whole, however, the Nemerov poem (quoted in its entirety in chapter 4) exhibits only a mildly distorting half-meaning.

A more disorienting music of misunderstanding obtains in the excerpt that heads the list; this line from "Mr. Edwards and the Spider" by Robert Lowell suggests that the "flash of the authority" of some presence is "well," that is, doing what is expected, salutary, and right. Whereas in fact, as Lowell wrote it, the new sentence beginning "It's well" asks us to believe that it is better that God destroy us than that we imagine in death that we have any defense against his raging will:

> A very little thing, a little worm,
> Or hourglass-blazoned spider, it is said,   20
>   Can kill a tiger. Will the dead
>   Hold up his mirror and affirm
>   To the four winds the smell

7. These lines appear in poems excerpted at greater length elsewhere in the text: the poets are Robert Lowell, Howard Nemerov, W. B. Yeats, John Milton, Edwin Muir, Philip Larkin, and (again) Howard Nemerov.

And flash of his authority? It's well
If God who holds you to the pit of hell,   25
Much as one holds a spider, will destroy,
Baffle, and dissipate your soul . . .

One index of the limited interpretability of the twenty-fourth line when
it is read alone is that the agent of the sentence, the force upholding to
the general view His wishes, is not God at all, as we at first assumed, but
rather the collective dead (line 21).

Observe, however, that the hovering between half-meanings and
whole meanings is true of only a few of the lines in Lowell's stanza and
that the line I quoted first is the most serious offender in his stanza. In
fact, half-meaning, which introduces such an interesting threshold of un-
certainty at which we waver, depends on a solid background of lines that
assert more or less whole meanings. Constant use of tension leads in time
to no tension. Some techniques must be quieter and recede so that others
can be more forceful. Without some recession of the syntax resulting in
coincidence between sense and linear form, tension in meaning at the
apt moment will have no springboard. Unless the poem lays a basis in
lines that balance sound and sense—lines that are whole—the effect of
half-meanings simply can't be obtained.

Before leaving Lowell's stanza, it's well (as he might have said) to feel
with the poet how that plateau of confusion owing to half-meaning at
line 24 supplies an indispensable thrill of a thwart and contrary emotion.
Whether or not the dead affirm God's power in slavish fashion, God's
power is, simply by virtue of being itself, always affirmed—in place,
"well," potent, in control. I will risk mentioning the joke that seems to
circulate among repeated generations of children: God is like the five-
hundred-pound gorilla, who sleeps—where? Wherever he wants. The
style of the poem may sound more sophisticated, yet there's an element
of the peevish child about the rhetorical twists in Lowell's poem imper-
sonating Jonathan Edwards in Calvinist eighteenth-century New En-
gland. And at many points the rhetorical twisting is framed by just such
perverse and aggressive turns of half-meaning as the one at line 24 we
have just examined.

Now throughout Lowell's stanza, the sentence takes priority over the
line. In his work, we are usually moving beyond the line-ends onto the
next line—even when we hear echoes of a metric and stanzaic pattern.
But in much metrical verse—verse that measures and repeats—the psy-

chological equivalence called isomorphism, which urges the lines upon
us with equal weight, is further strengthened by numerical conformity.
A recurring pattern brackets together what is said on or within the lines
in ways the ear as well as the eye can compare. This linear huddling in-
creases the dramatic effect of parallel placement:

> The Daemon
>
> Must I tell again
> In the words I know
> For the ears of men
> The flesh, the blow?
>
> Must I show outright   5
> The bruise in the side,
> The halt in the night,
> And how death cried?
>
> Must I speak to the lot
> Who little bore?   10
> It said, *Why not?*
> It said, *Once more.*
>
> (Louise Bogan)

Bogan exploits contradictions growing from the parallels in otherwise
evenly matched, neighboring lines. The technique is called **juxtaposi-
tion.** Indifference and compulsion are joined in the demon's answers to
the speaker of this poem by the writer; inevitable pain is made to seem
casual. The equivalence between two modes of feeling is supported not
just by the metrical symmetry of the last two lines but also by rhyme and
by the repeating sentence form ("It said"). What's more, these forced
symmetries occur at the moment when all the earlier questions (ten lines
of them) are going to be answered but not by being made more sensible,
let alone more bearable. When we think of "writing our way" through
Bogan's "The Daemon," we register as far more shocking the "answer"
spoken by the demon's question, with its hint of the random and blurred
origins of our worst fate, which is, to repeat ourselves dully and relent-
lessly "Once more." It's the carelessness of "*Why not?*" that makes us
squirm.

A second example of the juxtaposition of isomorphic lines with
differing meanings, this one a more conversational poem, is "At a Low

Bar" by David Ferry, where we find two lines juxtaposed in order to compromise the speaker's self-esteem: "Dumb, ignorant creatures, / My fellow, my self, my fool":

from "At a Low Bar"

I looked along the bar
And saw my fellow creature
Bravely standing there.
By word, sign, or touch,   20
I cried in my mute heart,
Tell me, be my teacher,
Be learnèd in that art,[8]
What is my name and nature?

My pulse ticked in my wrist;   25
The noon hung around unawares;
Outside the traffic passed.
Like quiet cattle or such,
Standing about a pool,
Dumb, ignorant creatures,   30
My fellow, my self, my fool,
Ignorant of our natures.

Unlike most of the other lines in Ferry's poem (see, for example, 17, 25, and 27), lines 30–31 do not match up very well metrically—an effect by displacement that emphasizes the difficult task of humility (his theme) by making the rhythms of its expression as awkward and weak as (by implication) the speaker's moral resolve.

Juxtaposition is intensified by imbalances lurking beneath the surface of a poem by Theodore Roethke. On the surface, cause and effect neatly divide the line-pairs:

We romped until the pans   5
Slid from the kitchen shelf;
My mother's countenance
Could not unfrown itself.

(from "My Papa's Waltz")

---

8. For the accent over *learnèd* in David Ferry's line, *Be learnèd in that art,* see note 11 below.

The line divisions are so neat that we do not at first recognize how disparate the content of the two couplets is. Lines 5 and 7 counteract each other in sentence (**syntax**) and **diction** (level and type of vocabulary)[9]— one line active, narrative, and lively ("We romped until the pans"), the other line unfinished in syntax and somber in tone ("My mother's countenance . . ."). In the end, however, the somber, unfinished seventh line takes command of the father and son, who are frozen by the mother's deepening and more potent displeasure (even if it is grammatically inactive: her face "Could not unfrown itself").

The main logic of the line-pairings in "A Drinking Song," by William Butler Yeats, derives from juxtaposition; the lines (and what he says in them) must be perceived as in some way equivalent before we can register the equally clear hint of qualification (wine does one thing, love another). Rather than contradicting on one hand or working exactly parallel on the other, the lines and their themes are equally contrasted:

A Drinking Song

Wine comes in at the mouth
And love comes in at the eye;
That's all we shall know for truth
Before we grow old and die.
I lift the glass to my mouth,   5
I look at you and I sigh.

What is grossly physical (drinking wine) is equated with, or rendered in terms of, what is lastingly spiritual ("drinking in" the radiant aura of the loved one). As physical acts issue in spiritual effects, so the spiritual ennobles the physical ("I lift the glass to my mouth, / I look at you and I sigh").

Now juxtaposition can also achieve its effects in free verse. Recall the end of James Wright's poem:

A chicken hawk flies over, looking for home.   6
I have wasted my life.

The demeanor of the speaker in this last line is, I believe, only nominally miserable. For the two mismatched statements here feed off each other, and the elevation of ordinary detail earlier in the poem raises the temper-

---

9. **Syntax** is discussed more thoroughly in the next chapter; **diction** is the focus of chapter 4.

ature of the speaker's apparent depression until it seems that to have wasted his life is very nearly an announcement of a new resolve. The speaker seems to have been transformed by opening his eyes to the details his description has discovered, making the mood of a depressing insight euphoric.

Similarly, in Bogan's "Baroque Comment," juxtaposition of lines of uneven lengths draws our attention to divergences in their meaning—or to the pointedness of their having been selected by the poet. As a result, one of these in particular, "The prow," becomes a beacon for the lines before (about ornament and daily craft) and after (in which Bogan is responding to the religio-erotic transport imaged in the sculptor Bernini's rendering of St. Theresa):

> The wreath, the oar, the tool,   15
> The prow;
> The turned eyes and the opened mouth of love.

Juxtaposition as a device can thus *imply* opposition while providing a chance for drawing the juxtaposed assertions closer, as if in **apposition.** The central location of "The prow" connects the baroque items in line 15 with the voyages of exploration and acquisition that in the sixteenth century financed high art and encouraged the pervasive use of skilled ornament. The prow of the explorers' ship generates crafts ("Wreath"), shipbuilding ("the oar, the tool"), as well as the art of Bernini ("The turned eyes" of St. Theresa in the sculpture group).

This drawing-near by means of juxtaposition is more irregular in its approaches in free verse than in metered verse. The formal neutrality of each free-verse line to the others around it is in tension with the idea of likeness. Poems supported by rhyme and that other technique of parallels, meter, on the other hand, often echo their thematic contrasts by means of auditory symmetry. In "The Oxen," by Thomas Hardy, for example, rhyme symmetry highlights an ironic juxtaposition that is never resolved. Lines 2 and 4 contrast the awe of the elders with their long-established "ease":

> Christmas Eve, and twelve of the clock.
>   "Now they are all on their knees,"
> An elder said as we sat in a flock
>   By the embers in hearthside ease.   4

Belief (the idea that the oxen worship the Christ-child by going down on their knees) is at odds with action in the poem (the ease of the elders keeps them from going out to the barn to see if they are right). Note that Hardy's two lines rhyme in a way that diffuses the pointed rhyming effect, since the rhyming words *knees/ease* are embedded in phrases that have a colloquial ring, particularly line 2: "'Now they are all *on their knees.*'"

The verses of A. E. Housman, too, often rhyme on the phrase: "And if my ways are not as theirs, / Let them *mind their own affairs.*" Robert Herrick and Alexander Pope are other notorious exploiters of the overlap between rhyme and catchphrase:

> A Conjuration, to Electra
>
> By these soft Tods★ of wooll   ★*tufts*
> With which the aire is full:
> By all those tinctures there,
> That paint the Hemisphere:
> By Dewes and drisling Raine,   5
> That swell the Golden Graine:
> By all those sweets that be
> I' th' flowrie Nunnerie:
> By silent Nights, and the
> Three Formes of Heccate★;   ★*pronounced* heck-a-tee 10
> By all Aspects that blesse
> The sober Sorceresse,
> While juice she strained, and pith
> To make her Philters★ with: ★*love potions*
> By Time, that hastens on   15
> Things to perfection:
> And by your self, the best
> Conjurement of the rest:
> O my Electra! be
> In love with none but me.   20
>   (Robert Herrick)

from "Delight in Disorder"

A sweet disorder in the dresse
Kindles in cloathes a wantonnesse:
A Lawne* about the shoulders thrown   *length of fine lace
Into a fine distraction: 4

. . . .

A winning wave (deserving Note)
In the tempestuous petticote: 10
A carelesse shooe-string, in whose tye
I see a wilde civility:
Doe more bewitch me, then when Art
Is too precise in every part.[10]

(Robert Herrick)

In each couplet, Herrick walks lightly over the first occurrence of the rhymed sound, more heavily over the second rhymes (in the even-numbered lines), which embed the more vivid if not the more serious meanings. For example, in the first poem the name of the witch *Heccate* (surely more ponderable than the article *the,* with which it rhymes) and *Hemisphere* (versus the tame *there*); in the second poem, *perfection* (which clearly takes precedence over the preposition *on,* even when the latter is an adverbial part of the verb *hastens*), and the most striking of them all, *wilde civility*—a rhyme phrase—to rhyme with the *tye,* or tying-up, of the little shoe string. First or "pre-rhymes" (words that carry the initial syllable to be rhymed upon) can be brief and bland if the second rhymes are vivid and command more of their lines.

Alexander Pope will also often save catchphrase for last: "Had Cole-pepper's whole wealth been hops and hogs," he asks in the "Epistle to Bathurst," "Could he himself have *sent it to the dogs?*" But in other couplets, Pope achieves the *effect* of catchphrase by "seeding" a more familiar expression in the first line of the couplet, then bringing up a phrase so lucid and almost proverbially tuned at the end of the second line of the couplet that this newly coined expression seems the inevitable one: "Willing to wound, and yet *afraid to strike,* / Just hint a fault and *hesitate dislike*" ("Epistle to Dr. Arbuthnot"). W. H. Auden is another poet alert

10. Robert Herrick, "Delight in Disorder," in *Major Poets of the Earlier Seventeenth Century,* edited by Barbara K. Lewalski and Andrew J. Sabol (Indianapolis: Bobbs-Merrill/Odyssey, 1973), p. 946.

to the effect of **rhyming on the phrase:** "Caesar's double-bed is warm /
As an unimportant clerk / Writes I DO NOT LIKE MY WORK /
On a pink official form." Here, in the practice of couplets dependent on
preexisting phrases, we meet another of those situations that persuade us
that we can learn to read a poem by remaining open to how the poet
might be composing it. To understand the composition of good couplet
rhyme is to register as also *prior* the aptness of this final rhyme-phrase
toward which the rest of the couplet aims itself. Further discussion of the
technique of finding the second rhyme first will be found in chapter 9
and intermittently throughout Part I.

Lines in Tension

Rhyme affects enjambment by curbing it. But enjambment also tugs
against rhyme, because **sentence** tugs against **line.** The more **enjamb-
ment,** or run-on, there is from one line to the next, the less the lines
function as individual entities. Pausing at the line-end is needed, both to
make rhyme audible and to make the line evident as such. Bear in mind
that the most natural way to pause is to come to the end of a phrase,
clause, or sentence. That is, pauses depend on the syntax of the sentence.
Note that a pause is produced only by syntax, *not* by punctuation. Marks
of punctuation are merely the symptoms of the syntax, not the cause of
sentence form. (When such a syntactic pause occurs in the middle of a
metrical line, it is called a **caesura,** which means a *cut* caused by the
sentence-form within the line.)

Whenever phrases end at the ends of the lines, thus creating pauses,
the *lines themselves* are emphasized as rhythmical units and as units of
meaning. For rhyme to be audible, and the line closed off or capped by
rhyme to be audible as a line, then some pausing will be mandatory, and
phrase will close with the close of the line. We noted earlier that this
does not happen often in Lowell because his forward momentum is so
headlong. So he rhymes *in passing.* More stanzaically oriented is the work
of poets like Edwin Muir, Hardy, Thomas Gray, and Auden. Something
of a highly developed line consciousness accompanies their exercise of
syntax within the linear, stanzaic grid. What this means during the writ-
ing of a poem is that the rhythmical breaths with their rhyming keynotes,
now in the background, now in foreground, regulate the passage of the
mind through the assertions that take the form of sentences.

As one becomes more sure of the available technical context in the working through of ideas in a poem, one naturally becomes more attentive to **grammar.** One grows more aware of the shape of the sentence—aware of where one has tacked up the first pieces of the frame, and then of where one might thicken it for some texture, say in the form of apposition, and even where to turn the entire frame upside down (in a mode called **syntactic inversion**). In a poem of normal sentence order of subject-verb-object (s-v-o), inverted syntax is "marked," or significant. It will worry and make obsessive the idea expressed, as in Edwin Muir's "The Enchanted Knight": "Long since the rust its gardens here has planned":

> The Enchanted Knight
>
> Lulled by La Belle Dame Sans Merci he lies
>   In the bare wood below the blackening hill.
> The plough drives nearer now, the shadow flies
>   Past him across the plain, but he lies still.
>
> Long since the rust its gardens here has planned,   5
>   Flowering his armour like an autumn field.
> From his sharp breast-plate to his iron hand
>   A spider's web is stretched, a phantom shield.
>
> When footsteps pound the turf beside his ear
>   Armies pass through his dream in endless line,   10
> And one by one his ancient friends appear;
>   They pass all day, but he can make no sign.
>
> When a bird cries within the silent grove
>   The long-lost voice goes by, he makes to rise
> And follow, but his cold limbs never move,   15
>   And on the turf unstirred his shadow lies.
>
> But if a withered leaf should drift
>   Across his face and rest, the dread drops start
> Chill on his forehead. Now he tries to lift
>   The insulting weight that stays and breaks his heart.   20

One might speculate that this inversion in line 5 is provoked by Muir's need to suggest that time has a different "schedule" here in the second stanza than it did in the first, where cause followed effect in the present time. The contortion of sentence order in 5 also provides an alternative to static description, which might have chosen the shield as the sentence's subject, but which chooses instead a mimicry of the slow, extruded drama of oxidation eating its patterns into the outer surface of the helpless knight's shield. *Rust* is now the sentence's mysterious agent.

By contrast in the work of a poet like John Milton, where inversion is so frequent, one must learn to distinguish the passages that have thematic formal significance where inverted sentences are concerned from those inversions that are mere fretwork. Examples of the latter occur in the tags introducing speeches, for example, "To whom thus *Adam* fervently repli'd," an inversion of the form o-s-v that we encounter at almost every shift in the dialogue. But the inversion in *Paradise Lost* IX.397–98 is a different matter (Eve in a desire for independence has persuaded Adam to let her work apart from him; she gazes back at Adam as she walks away and he follows her gaze with his own): "Her long and ardent look his Eye pursu'd / Delighted, but desiring more her stay."[11] The Latinate syntax is not simply a tic but a means of promoting the importance of Eve's gaze in Adam's eyes and keeping her in the forefront of the field of attention for as long as possible.

In Thomas Hardy's work, often the climactic stanzas are multifariously staggered and inverted in their syntax. Consider the stanza from the poem in which a man recalls how as a youth he and a girl had stepped down from the coach to make it lighter for the pony to pull uphill:

> And to me, though Time's unflinching rigour,   30
> > In mindless rote, has ruled from sight
> The substance now, one phantom figure
> > Remains on the slope, as when that night
> > Saw us alight.

The loops of inversion and qualification almost bury the kernel sentence ("to me . . . one . . . figure [that of the girl] . . . Remains"). But perhaps these postponements, in a stanza about the past, conceal something energetically moving *in the present,* long after the events to which the poem tries to return. It may be that the tortuous syntactic indirections accurately reflect the unmediated but evolving experience of the speaker

---

11. The elision of the letter *e* in past participles indicates that there is no extra syllable pronounced; David Ferry imitates earlier orthography when he uses a grave accent to indicate when the past suffix *-ed* in *learnèd* is voiced—that is, made into a separate syllable. See also entries in the indexes and chapter 13 under **pronunciation.**

finding his way through the thought of the present, so baffled by waves of memory and yearning. The speaker has to move back through time, age, and loss, before even so much as reaching a phantom of the figure of that girl who once, even further back, in flesh and blood, alighted on solid ground. To have placed her as the subject of the sentence would have solved the mystery before it could be posed.

Occasionally, a gnarled syntactic inversion, easily shown in an excerpt—

Yet ev'n these bones from insult to protect
Some frail memorial still erected nigh,
With uncouth rhimes and shapeless sculpture deck'd,
Implores the passing tribute of a sigh.   80

—will show a more genial relation to ordinary sentence-form when the surrounding syntax is grasped. The one-stanza sentence above from Thomas Gray's "Elegy Written in a Country Church-Yard" shows with its ungainly and confusing inversion a discomfort with neat and orderly expression that is more understandable when we feel how close to having to end the poem Gray had just come:

Far from the madding crowd's ignoble strife,
Their sober wishes never learn'd to stray;
Along the cool sequester'd vale of life   75
They kept the noiseless tenor of their way.

The stanza that follows this one would of necessity have the enormous unstated task of keeping the poem afloat and making it seem to continue—and to *need* to continue—after such stirring end-stopping. Just as Robert Lowell has a bent toward the excessively enjambed (see the excerpt earlier in this chapter), Gray has a bent toward the excessively regular that threatens to keep shutting the poem down. Although his rhymes are more audible thereby, the tempo lags. In fact the lag leads too quickly into something finished. Lines 77 to 80 drive the poet into an uncompleted present time again where he can toy with uncertainty of sentence-frame and event (*does* someone pass? *does* anyone sigh? *does* some memorial structure have a true shape of feeling beneath its artistic shapelessness?) Clearly, Gray needs to struggle against closure (even the closure of perfection of expression), which leads to sobriety and anonymity of another kind than he examines in his theme.

There is, however, some leeway in exploring the principle of coincidence with respect to rhyme (the rule that, to be heard, rhyme words must coincide with the end of a unit of meaning, that is, with a phrase or a sentence). Gray's two stanzas suggest something like two extremes in a stanza, the elaborately well-behaved and the aggressively disobedient. Along the continuum of stanza-frame and rhyme-use, there are more options between these two. It can happen that even in counteracting the principle we might gain strength from the psychological rhythms of our native language-use. Exceptions can be measured only by reference to the norms they seem to ignore. Tension needs coincidence to play against. The following exceptions to coincidence, by masters of line/syntax play, suggest the power of the rule, for we hear in them how odd the breaking of the convention sounds and how habitually the poems have built up and supported the technique they would violate. Above all, we can follow these poems only by trying to follow the path of the lines as they are being thought through into sentences:

> Altogether elsewhere, vast   25
> Herds of reindeer move across
> Miles and miles of golden moss,
> Silently and very fast.
>
> (W. H. Auden, "The Fall of Rome")

By making the last three lines of the stanza progressively more well-behaved as they perch upon their metric frames, Auden reduces the drain on rhythm caused by the first harsh enjambment ("vast / Herds").

> . . . while I wait, ‖ a cry
> As from beneath the glass,   30
> Pierces me with ‖ "Alas
> That the beloved must die."
>
> (Janet Lewis, "In the Egyptian Museum")[12]

Janet Lewis provides a two-stage detonation of abrupt emotion in the first and third lines of her poem's final stanza (the complete text is given in chapter 4). The most interesting effect is the metrical parallelism; the caesuras fall at the same points in both lines. And any parallels, even if they involve disjunctions, act to bind the lines *as lines*. Lewis's control is

---

12. Note: Two parallel vertical lines ‖ are used to indicate **caesuras** or syntactic junctures within lines of verse.

further shown by the semantic parallel, since the "cry" *is* (it has the phonetic form) "'Alas.'"

Louise Bogan in the second stanza of "Single Sonnet" (see the full text on p. 30) masks one enjambment with devices of balance (the repeated "Take up," the choice of heavy "lead *or* gold"), while she suspends the second and much stronger enjambment between two series comprising three items each ("stone, slate metal," then "so ponderous, so dull, so cold"). The milder enjambment is marked with a single curved arrow, the stronger with a double arrow:

> Take up, take up as it were lead or gold ⤵   5
> The burden; test the dreadful mass thereof.
> No stone, slate, metal under or above ⤵⤵
> Earth is so ponderous, so dull, so cold.

Bogan's two "splits" hint that the weight and dullness of unexpressed and paralyzing feeling make the poet-speaker on edge, not merely plodding. Although the semantic meaning of the words points to something dully crushing and recurrent in the pressure to speak, the meter, enjambment, and syntax (of the first sentence in particular) suggest that shouldering this burden of feeling is also precarious.

When enjambment—that is, when syntax—overruns the line, a pleasant "counterpoint" can be created if the balance is carefully managed.

> For the present stalks abroad
> Like the past and its wronged again
> Whimper and are ignored,
> And the truth cannot be hid;
> Somebody chose their pain,   35
> What needn't have happened did.
>
> (W. H. Auden, "A Walk After Dark")

By the close of Auden's sentence and the stanza, rhyme rings in the closure of the line. Resolution of line with sentence is achieved, but it is not morally comfortable. With irony and disparagement Auden implies that the present is as mean and inchoate as the past. Still, fatalism and its self-important bossiness are buffered by a colloquial shrug; the agent is the long-awaited and casually embedded verb "did," which stands for "did happen."

When rhyme is extremely vivid and witty, as in Auden, Herrick, and

Pope, the poem as a whole slows down; the forward narration is balked. In many rhyming poems, however, rhyme is a background technique, unremarkable, "behaved," quiescent, as in Edwin Muir's poems and the old ballads. What the **recession of technique** permits is the emergence of other kinds of emphasis. In the purest story poems, rhymes are at once audible (falling at heavy pauses) and almost drab, as, in fact, are many of the other mechanisms of verbal "thickening," like puns, heavier diction, and metaphor. The goal in the great Scottish ballads is not so much to create pleasure in language; rather, the ballads aim to create a sense of life and death that has been "intensified to one point." There is, wrote Edwin Muir, nothing in these early Scottish poems except "passion, terror, instinct, action"; the ballads "achieve great poetry by an unconditionality which rejects, where other literatures use, the image."[13] We will return to the ballads, image, and trope later on.

13. "A Note on the Scottish Ballads," *Latitudes* (essays), by Edwin Muir (New York: Huebsch, 1924), pp. 17, 18, 19.

3

Syntax and Whole Meaning

Syntax and Line

It is impossible to speak adequately about one of the "threads" in a poem without crossing one or more of the others. Just as the subject of a poem cannot be considered apart from the use of voices, things, and images, so the line of verse cannot be discussed, let alone produced, without attention to the form of speech it contains. In fact, **syntax**—or the way the sentence is organized—is one necessary defining principle of the poetic **line.** All lines of verse either coincide with the phrase, clause, or sentence, or diverge from the phrase, clause, or sentence, thus splitting the phrasal units and causing tension between line and syntax.

A **clause** is a syntactically dependent unit in which a subject and verb occur. Examples (first, clauses that coincide with the poetic line): "a still pond / That opened upon no sight a quiet eye" (Edwin Muir, "The Gate"); "That doe not do the thing, they most do showe" (Shakespeare, Sonnet 94). Clauses that diverge from the line: "if thou think, trial unsought may find / Us both securer" (Milton, *Paradise Lost* IX.370–71); "from boughs sets free / Summer" (Bogan, "Song for a Lyre"); "the open water, which long / remembers nothing" (Nemerov, "Writing").

A **phrase** is a coherent group of words (not containing both subject and verb) that act together. Examples (first, of **coincidence** of phrase with line) include: "Beautiful, my delight / " (Bogan, "To Be Sung on the Water"); "Two shadows racing on the grass, / Silent and so near" (Muir, "Ballad of Hector in Hades"—both lines are complete phrases and each phrase takes up a complete line); "Now and again / One fish slides" (Nemerov, "The Sanctuary"; the phrase need not appear on the same line with the noun or verb it modifies). Examples of phrases that diverge from the line include: "Bred to a harder thing / Than triumph"

(Yeats, "To a Friend Whose Work Has Come to Nothing"—the comparative "harder" is divided from its paired term "than"); the scholar is "surprised / Less by the loss" (Thom Gunn, "His Rooms in College"); "stressed, / Slightly" (Raymond Oliver, "Structures"). Both of the last two examples create significant half-meanings that are at odds with the whole.

Enjambment is minimal or maximal depending on how line and syntax merge, or diverge. Viewed as competitors for the rhythmic control of the poem, the line is the conservative force and the sentence the anarchist as it pulls attention away from meter and line, which seek to contain it. Consider Bogan's framing sentence in the second stanza of her melodious lyric quoted in passing in the paragraph above:

> To Be Sung on the Water
> Beautiful, my delight,
> Pass, as we pass the wave.
> Pass, as the mottled night
> Leaves what it cannot save,
> Scattering dark and bright.   5
>
> Beautiful, pass and be
> Less than the guiltless shade
> To which our vows were said;
> Less than the sound of the oar
> To which our vows were made,—   10
> Less than the sound of its blade
> Dipping the stream once more.

Line 6 is strongly enjambed. Lines 7 and 8 close line with phrase or sentence, and the eighth line (a dependent clause) is complete on its line, but we are still trying to recover from the ragged break between the verb of command at the end of line 6 ("be") and the completed predicate that spills far forward into 7: "be / Less than the guiltless shade." It's important to note that some variations are long-lasting; their effects influence the feeling of the poem long after the line has passed. Worth noting, too, is that line 7 produces at its end a bond between line and syntax, which is clear—but *not* between line and the meanings it cannot possibly contain, for "guiltless" applied to "shade" immediately suggests the possibility that shade can partake of an ethical dimension where such judgments as guilt and innocence are vitally relevant. Thus the line winds down to closure in one sense—the phrase is complete on its line—while being thrown off-balance in another—the wider lexical uneasiness of the word "guilt-less" jars against the more contained materiality of "shade."

Another rule of thumb is that the strongest enjambments are those in which a new phrase, new clause, or new sentence is begun close to the end of the line (Auden is fond of these, as we see, for example, in the line already quoted from "The Fall of Rome," "Altogether elsewhere, vast," and the line from "Lady, Weeping at the Crossroads," "Push on to the world's end, pay the," which continues, ". . . pay the / Dread guard with a kiss"). Equal in strength are the enjambments in which a split phrase is abruptly concluded at the very start of the next line, as in the last line below from *Paradise Lost:*

But, if thou think, trial unsought may find
Us both securer than thus warn'd thou seem'st,
Go; for thy stay, not free, absents thee more;

(IX.370–72)

The leftover "Go" satisfies on one level because it concludes a long inverted sentence in which there are no **caesuras** (or midline grammatical pauses). But "Go" also teeters off balance by turning to an abrupt stoppage after the very first syllable of the line: [*Go;*‖].[1] The stress on "Go" seems more awkward than the reversal of iambic stress for the strong initial monosyllables in "To Be Sung on the Water" (for example, in "Less than the sound of its blade," line 11), owing to the finality of the pause that falls right away. Supported by a semicolon, this stoppage in the Milton line in turn seems to attract further dramatic stops: [*Go;* ‖ *for thy stay,* ‖ *not free,* ‖ *absents thee more*].

Few poets attempt both kinds of caesural pausing, end-line and beginning-line, at once. But see the lines in which form follows theme in Raymond Oliver's "Structures," where there are three caesuras in a row:

1. Note: Two parallel vertical lines [‖] are used to indicate caesuras or syntactic junctures within lines of verse. However, when poems are quoted in prose texts, one diagonal slash [/] is the signal for a line break, while two diagonals signal a passage that carries across two stanzas [//]. See also chapter 8 on accentual-syllabic meter.

Structures

This is the structure of the early dawn:
Before its colors are defined like tone
In a becoming poem, there's a rest,
As when a line ends with a comma—stressed,
Slightly, but showing that the sense runs on,   5
That more is coming than one could have known.

The middle of the three grammatical breaks is further emphasized by fall-
ing at the line boundary: [*comma*— ‖ *stressed,* ‖ / *Slightly,* ‖]. The question
is, how often does the writer wish to bring together so much disjunction
at once? And how much can any poem afford? Raymond Oliver's poem
is, in tone and method, cautionary and didactic; with such ends in view,
and such determined brevity with which to effect these ends, Oliver must
not only slow down but then, immediately, begin to quicken his speed
and his ideas. (These effects of tempo, in this poem and in general, will
be discussed further in Part II.)

Consider, though, how it must have been for Raymond Oliver as the
author of "Structures" to move toward the comparison of the dawn with
a moment in a poem—a moment very like the one in *this* poem—before
either his hypothetical poem or his own emerging poem could be fin-
ished. Say that the poet has the idea that rhythm in the sentence might
reflect the start of definition in the sky. The example (he might have
thought) could occur just where a line boundary appeared to close and
then failed to do so entirely. Consider, that is, how the analogy might
grow from rough to exact as the slight roughening of the rhythm and of
the sentence-with-line-coincidence also began to unfold as a possibil-
ity—say at the beginning of line 4 ("As when a line . . ."). Oliver is now
also alert to the idea of the colors in the morning sky drawing them-
selves—ever so tentatively—out of the grainy indistinction of the gray
half-light and into a hue of greater definition, the sky still a smudge of
charcoal, but suggesting something unnameably chromatic. . . . It is in
this kind of intuition (ours of the poet's; the poet's of a thought and image
closely bound up with the starting of saying) that writers and readers can
make the most sense of the links between content and form. Only as we
try to follow the braillelike code of the growing poem do we properly
register the way in which small shifts in stress and pause register huge
gains in resolution of theme. (This is how form opens to theme.) We see

those tentative dawn pastels more acutely because the poem's auditory logic (its **prosody**) is their lens.

Extremes of Syntax

Because syntax, or sentence-frame, is such a critical tool for meaning in writing and for considering the unfolding of the line of verse, it will help to have the kinds of syntax in mind when we read. In a general way, it will be clear to most readers that Gascoigne's title-line, "Give money me, take friendship whoso list," uses a more complicated style than Yeats's "I look at you and I sigh" (from "A Drinking Song"), just as we find a stylistic disparity between the following two passages:

> So set its Sun in Thee
> What Day be dark to me—
> What Distance—far—
> So I the ships may see
> That touch—how seldomly—   5
> Thy shore?
>
> (Dickinson, #808)

> The moon sets; after a little   5
> The reeds sigh from the shore.
> Then silence. There is a whisper,
> "Thou art here once more."
>
> (Randall Jarrell, "A Soul")

Jarrell's lines are so simple their series of assertions seem halting, whereas Dickinson bursts in on us with a thought at once passionate and knotted-up—even strangled. But it may need some review before we can classify these differences in syntactic terms.

The most obvious way in which sentences may be formed is by adding a verb to a subject in simple **declaration:** *Helen fell,* or, adding an adverb, *Helen fell down.* This is the syntax of "His Rooms in College," by Thom Gunn: "He reads, / He reads," and of J. V. Cunningham's comment in "For My Contemporaries," "Verse is not easy." With an object, this simple declarative form might read: *Helen loves Jack;* adding a prepositional phrase, we might have *Helen fights with Jack.* Compare Hardy's title-line, "I look into my glass." Such declarative thrift is also the essential force in that great line of John Donne, "I dare not move my dimme eyes any way," from the first of the "Divine Meditations."

Sentences may also be formed by joining one simple **declarative sentence** to another in parallel series (**parataxis**), usually with a coordinating conjunction (*and, or, nor, but, yet, for*): *Helen loves Jack and Jack loves her. Helen loves Jack but Jack loves Moira.* These are called **compound sentences.** Auden writes a compound without conjunction in one of his sonnets: "The peaks came into focus; it had rained." This is the form of Jarrell's lines from "A Soul": "The moon sets; after a little / The reeds sigh" (see further Jarrell excerpts in chapter 5 on trope). Robert Frost writes a compound sentence with conjunction at the end of "The Strong Are Saying Nothing": "There may be little or much beyond the grave, / But the strong are saying nothing until they see." So does William Blake in his lines from "And Did Those Feet": "I will not cease from Mental Fight, / Nor shall my sword sleep in my hand." Obviously, the shorter the compound sentence the sooner it will end and the greater will be the coincidence of sentence with line-end.

Yet a third variety of sentence subordinates one part of the sentence or clause to another clause in descriptive fashion: *Helen loves Jack, who has a nasty cold.* Roethke describes his heron with a cleverly extruded descriptive clause built on adverbial and prepositional phrases: "The heron stands in water *where the swamp / Has deepened to the blackness of a pool.*" Notice how David Ferry spins his descriptive sentence down from the relative pronoun "that" in the tenth line:

> The man is all his own hunched strength, the body's
> Self and strength, *that* bears, like weariness,   10
> Itself upon itself, as a stone's weight
> Bears heavily on itself to be itself.

("Seen Through a Window")

More subtle still is the logical dependence of one clause upon another in complex rather than descriptive subordination (**hypotaxis**): *Although Helen loves Jack, she cannot give him much of her time.* Or: *Even if Jack loved her, Helen would still be unhappy.* The relational bent of hypotactic sentences is used to good effect by many couplet writers, with their disposition to elaborate checks and balances: "*As* Crusoe made his clothes, *so* he [Friday] no less / Must labour to invent his nakedness" ("Man Friday," by A. D. Hope). Notice, however, Hope's unexpected disparity between clause and line; "As" introduces a clause of three feet, "so" a clause of seven feet. This disparity runs counter to the symmetry of the thematic contrast between Friday and Crusoe without undermining it.

There is more anxiety embodied in the relation of subordinate to main clause in Muir's cause-and-effect sentence (with its *if* . . . *then* frame) as the clauses reproduce the dead knight's Christ-like spiritual struggle to rise again:

> But if a withered leaf should drift
> Across his face and rest, the dread drops start
> Chill on his forehead.　　　　　　　　　　　　　　　　20
> ("The Enchanted Knight")

We can hear how Muir coordinates the logical struggle with a rhythmical one, the sluggish tempo an echo of the mental effort made by the enchanted knight. There is considerably less struggling and a much livelier tread in the witty use by George Gordon, Lord Byron of his **adversative** (or oppositional) clause starting with "although": "Oh Pleasure! you're indeed a pleasant thing, / Although one must be damned for you, no doubt." Auden's adversative ("no matter") and contrary-to-fact syntax is considerably more withering: "Far off, no matter what good they intended, / The armies waited for a verbal error. . . ."

Some hypotactic structures like Muir's ("if a withered leaf *should drift*") involve a form of hypothesis called the **subjunctive mood** (it is distinguished from the **indicative mood,** which belongs to statements about things as they are rather than as they might be).[2] Subjunctive patterns include (1) the optative (hopeful) construction (introduced by *if only* or *would that* or *[if] that*)—as in the line from "The Flower," by George Herbert, "Oh that I once past changing were!" and in Thomas Hardy's poem about the disparity between his shrunken body and his still vigorous desire:

> I look into my glass,
> And view my wasting skin,
> And say, 'Would God it came to pass
> My heart had shrunk as thin!'　　　　　　　　　　　　4
> ("I Look into My Glass")

---

2. The sense of struggle I mention in the paragraph above is borne out by Muir's mismatch of hypothesis with conclusion, the former subjunctive, the latter indicative (the dread drops of blood *start,* not *would start*).

A sentence that uses the hopeful subjunctive begins in line 3 and contin-
ues to the end of line 4. (2) The hypothetical subjunctive (whose verbal
counters are clauses beginning *if* followed by those beginning or implying
then; so (or *such*) followed by *that; when* leading to *then*. A good example
occurs in a poetic fragment attributed to John Keats:

> Lines Supposed to Have Been Addressed to Fanny Brawne
>
> *This living hand,* now warm and capable
> Of earnest grasping, *would if it were* cold
> And in the icy silence of the tomb,
> *So haunt* thy days and chill thy dreaming nights
> *That thou wouldst* wish thine own heart dry of blood   5
> *So* in my veins red *life might* stream again,
> *And thou be* conscience-calm'd—see, here it is—
> I hold it towards you.[3]

The elaborate conditional syntax is highlighted in italics. Note how all
the lines down to the seventh twist and turn the boundaries between
dying and renewed life. (3) The third form of subjunctive argues like
Sherlock Holmes from the impossibility of a negative. The argument is
called "contrary to fact":

> The twain are blest
> Do eastern stars slope never west   5
> Nor pallid ashes [ever] follow fire:
> If hours be years the twain are blest.
>
> (Thomas Hardy, "At a Hasty Wedding")

If stars never move from east to west, writes Hardy, and if ashes never
remain after a fire, then this couple marrying so hastily is blest. But since
these hypotheses are all false, especially line 7's—hours can never be
years—then the union is doomed.

The Renaissance poets, who so often argue metaphysics in songlike
stanza forms, are drawn to the syntax of the contrary-to-fact subjunctive
mood because it opens the door on exaggerated conjecture. The speaker
of the following quatrains says he is sure love continues as long as the soul

---

3. Carlos Baker, ed., *Keats: Poems and Selected Letters* (New York: Charles Scribner's
Sons, 1962), p. 367.

does because the sins we commit never die and always remain in the soul as a stain:

Much more that true and reàl joy
    Which in a virtuous love is found
    Must be more solid in its ground
Than fate or death can e'er destroy;   100

Else should our souls in vain elect,
    And vainer yet were heaven's laws,
    When to the everlasting cause
They give a perishing effect.

Nor here on earth then, nor above,   105
    Our good affection can impair,
    For where God doth admit the fair,
Think you that he excludeth love?[4]

The poet argues in *two* contrary-to-fact stanzas, the second and third above. To paraphrase: If love didn't continue forever, then it would be fruitless for our souls to find their mates; love's origins being everlasting, the search for a noneternal mate would lead to that impossibility, "a perishing effect [or result]." Our affection for one another must be eternal because, in the second place, argues Herbert of Cherbury, God promotes what is beautiful and he could not exclude love from these realms. The penultimate stanza above illustrates that age's habit of knotting the thought within a brief but complex stanza, while the last four lines quoted exhibit the breaking-through of simplicity and sweetness; the last-minute leap to a question (another syntactic choice) speeds this result. Less songlike but no less extreme is Shakespeare's assertion in the final couplet of Sonnet 116: "If this be error and upon me proved, / I never writ, nor no man ever loved."

Extremes attract extremes. Hypotaxis (complex subordination) and subjunctives (hypothetical and wishful argument) in the poems by Shakespeare and Hardy and Herbert of Cherbury above draw in another device affecting the sentence—**inversion,** or the disturbance, by reversing or

4. Edward, 1st Baron Herbert of Cherbury, "An Ode upon the Question Moved, Whether Love Should Continue Forever?" in *Poetry of the English Renaissance 1509–1660,* edited by J. William Hebel and Hoyt H. Hudson (New York: Appleton-Century-Crofts, 1957), p. 557.

interrupting (which I have just illustrated in my own sentence), of normal sentence order (s-v-o). Not *proved upon me* but *upon me proved*. In "At a Hasty Wedding," Hardy writes *Do eastern stars slope never west* instead of *Do* (or *if*) *eastern stars never slope west*. Herbert of Cherbury likewise inverts: *Else should our souls in vain elect;* and *When to the everlasting cause / They give*. And we might smooth out the sentence order in the last stanza quoted from "An Ode upon . . . Whether Love Should Continue Forever" to read: *Neither here nor there **can** our good affection **weaken** or die out*.

"Deep though it may be and bitter," writes Auden of the everlasting ocean, "You must drink it dry," employing an inversion emphatic and elegant in preference to a lackluster alternative such as *Though it may be deep and bitter* (see the full text of "Lady, Weeping at the Crossroads" in chapter 5 on trope). Emily Dickinson's #808 quoted above in this chapter employs both condensation (*So* rather than *So long as* or *If I can only*) as well as inversion in the first line, *So set its Sun in Thee*.[5]

Adding to her inversions and interruptions are Dickinson's complexity of clause and hopeful conditionals, which we can paraphrase: *So long as the sun goes down in a condition of unity with you (God), what day would be dark or distance far?* Then Emily Dickinson repeats (with one hitch) the idea of that conditional setting of the day and of life (again in paraphrase): *I can bear anything in life so long as I can see the ships that touch your shore (even if they do so infrequently)*. The ships may represent luckier spirits, as well as natural emanations that travel to and from the far-off hemisphere of God. In an effort to make Dickinson's meaning clear, this wordy paraphrase neglects the chief trait of the poem—economy. However, the six trimeter lines are also syntactically overwrought, in the fashion of a riddle. Subjunctives can, in fact, become too complicated with their overlapping uncertainties. Eliot seems to be mocking this tendency when he can't pin the blame on either Mungojerrie or Rumpelteazer, "or could you have sworn that it mightn't be both?" The sprinkle of negatives snarls up this comically fussy sentence even more.

Sometimes we can see the advantage of juxtaposing a complex subjunctive with parataxis in the same poem. See the final pair of stanzas in Hardy's "The Darkling Thrush," the first of which states a hypothesis bluntly, the second taking a more indirect approach:

5. Dickinson exemplifies interrupted syntax here too, writing of the ships "That touch—how seldomly— / Thy shore."

At once a voice arose among
    The bleak twigs overhead
In a full-throated evensong
    Of joy illimited;   20
An aged thrush, frail, gaunt, and small,
    In blast-beruffled plume,
Had chosen thus to fling his soul
    Upon the growing gloom.

So little cause for carolings   25
    Of such ecstatic sound
Was written on terrestrial things
    Afar or nigh around,
That I could think there trembled through
    His happy good-night air   30
Some blessed Hope, whereof he knew
    And I was unaware.

Lines 17 through 24 employ a relatively straight declarative directness, contrary to the extended and complex subjunctive of the kernel assertion in lines 25 through 32, "So little cause . . . Was written . . . That I could think there trembled. . . ." Hardy's style of indirection imitates the tentativeness of hope. Note that the subjunctive mood changes the form of the verb (for example, *If this be* error instead of *If this is error; If hours be years* rather than *If hours are years; if it were* cold and not *if it was cold; That I could* think instead of *That I can* think; *This living hand would* instead of *This living hand will*). All are verbs in the subjunctive mood.

The Keats lines illustrate another cluster of technical features related to complex patterns of thought. Long sentences promote tension with line boundary. Furthermore, long sentences with subordinating syntax (hypotaxis) promote a tension with line boundary that is decidedly more dramatic and cerebral than the tension born merely of splitting compound phrases or clauses. Coleridge illustrates the difference in quoting as his epigraph ("I fear, I fear, my master dear! / We shall have a deadly storm") a passage from the ballad "Sir Patrick Spens," in which there is close coincidence of syntax with line,[6] and then launching out upon a stanza in which the unit is no longer line but verse paragraph:

6. See chapter 10 for the text of the poem.

Well! If the bard was weather-wise who made
The grand old ballad of Sir Patrick Spens,
This night . . . will not go hence
Unroused by winds . . .   4
("Dejection: An Ode")

At the break between lines 1 and 2, there is strenuous pressure to con-
tinue: not only does *made* need its object (*who made / the ballad*), the *if-*
clause needs its resolving main clause (*If the author of the old ballad was correct
about the early signs of storm [the rim around the moon], then tonight the wind
will rage*). Clearly, it is more disruptive to split the provisions of an argu-
ment than to divide (for a brief moment) phrases and clauses that have
been added on to each other in supportive compound and coordinating
forms. Despite the length of the contrary-to-fact sentence in the sestet of
Frost's "On a Bird Singing in Its Sleep," the coincidence between line
and clause creates a balance, as the logic spills carefully down from one
provision to the next ("It could not have come down to us so far . . . If
singing out of sleep and dream that way / Had made it much more easily
a prey"). This is the balance necessarily broken by Sir Thomas Wyatt in
the last three lines of "Stand Whoso List":

Stand whoso list* upon the slipper* top   *whoever likes / slippery
   Of court's estates, and let me here rejoice,
And use me quiet without let or stop,
      Unknown in court that hath such brackish joys.
         In hidden place, so let my days forth pass,   5
     That when my years be done, withouten noise,
       I may die aged after the common trace:
For him death gripeth right hard by the crope*   *throat
     That is much known of other; and of himself, alas,
      Doth die unknown, dazed with dreadful face.[7]   10

7. This smoothed-out version of Wyatt's "Stand Whoso List" appears in the fourth
Norton (1996), the Stallworthy, Ferguson revision of the Allison, Barrows, et al., edition
of the *Norton Anthology of Poetry,* third edition (New York: W. W. Norton, 1983). There
is disagreement about the value of modernization. Auden reasons as follows for keeping
to the original spelling and punctuation: "to present the poetry of earlier ages in modern
spelling, punctuation, and capitalization," he says, "does violence to both the meaning
and the poetic effect of the lines." Retaining the original versions means to retain "impor-
tant evidence . . . as to pronunciation, syllabic values, emphasis, and breath pauses, as well
as to the unit of phrasing" (W. H. Auden and Norman Holmes Pearson, eds., *Poets of the
English Language* [New York: Viking/Penguin, 1950; 1978], vol. 1, p. vii). These are

Wyatt promotes a tension between the sentence that whips forward these images of a bad death, to which a wasted life might bind him, and the linear frame to which they are unevenly lashed. But clearly it is a tension that makes palpable the danger of wasting his inward self—a self still unfinished, like his verse—on slavish outward opportunities.

Not that such tension and complexity as Wyatt's are in any way absolutes toward which the writer should always strive—any more than coincidence or simplicity are. These thresholds of invention in poetry are closely bound up with thematic suggestion. It makes as little sense to work toward complexity and tension in a poem that aims to express contentment as to compose the lines simply and uniformly in a poem of fretful brooding. Form should follow theme. For the beginning reader and writer, at any rate, it is helpful to try to coordinate theme with the form of expression, and to experiment with formal complexity when *mental* complexity is at issue, and then, when singleness of mind guides the speaking of the poem, to strive for simplicity and transparency.

"Singleness of mind" is a slippery concept, but no more slippery than the syntax that is supposed to convey it. Often it seems that a poem powerfully addresses and makes coherent a state of mind that has more than

---

values which, as a poet as well as a scholar, Auden may have felt more strongly than most. Here is the version of "Stond Who So List" from Kenneth Muir's edition of Wyatt (1949), which Auden and Holmes use; they change only the *"v"* and *"i"* of words like *vpon* and *ioyes* back to *"u"* and *"j"*:

> Stond who so list upon the Slipper *toppe*
>> Of courtes estates, and *lett* me *heare* rejoyce;
> And use me *quyet* without lett or stoppe,
>> *Unknowen* in courte, that hath suche *brackishe joyes:*
>> In hidden place, so lett my *dayes forthe passe,*   5
> That when my yeares be done, withouten noyse,
>> I may dye aged after the common trace.
> For hym death *greep'the* right hard by the croppe
>> That is *moche knowen* of other; and of him self alas,
>> Doth dye unknowen, dazed with dreadfull face.   10

The words and phrases I have italicized (and their rhymes) are decidedly different in rhythm and feeling when quoted as they were originally printed.

In the hope that some readers may interest themselves in the subtle rhythmic differences that emerge in original spellings and punctuation of texts from the fourteenth through the seventeenth centuries, I have sprinkled many original versions throughout this book. In particular, all of Shakespeare's sonnets appear in the versions of 1609. (To quote from the plays, however, began to require so many textual explanations that modernization was preferred.)

one quality, and for which the poet adopts more than one kind of syntax—more, perhaps, than one *attitude* toward syntax as a method of transmission. One poet whose attitude is complex but never uniform in approach is Louise Bogan. And one measure of her range of style is the variety of nondeclarative syntaxes she employs—exclamation, entreaty, command, exhortation, curse, derision, and interrogative. Almost any sample of her lyrics shows the tonal fluidity of her imperatives: "Let the crystal clasp them / When you drink your wine, in autumn," she writes in "After the Persian." In "Last Hill in a Vista," we hear the encouraging "Come, let us tell the weeds in ditches / How we are poor, who once had riches." And in "Single Sonnet," as we have heard, she wants that great stanza-form to "Bend to my will." **Imperatives** all three—yet what freshness of approach as we move from the elegiac wineglass to the happy conspiratorial whisper and then to the steely command that the sonnet *Bend*.

Nor is Bogan ever far from the cry, whether of loss ("O not departure, but a voyage done!" [Song for the Last Act"]) or of achievement ("O, as with arm and hammer, / Still it is good to strive" ["Roman Fountain"] . As for questions, she asks the demon whether she must repeat the painful mission of the poet; of the lover, she accusingly inquires, "How could I judge you gentle or unkind / When all bright flying space was in your care?" ["Fifteenth Farewell"]). And throughout her work there is a sensibility pressing harder than usual on the commonest poetic means; even declarative syntax becomes vivid and aggressive: "Too long as ocean bed bears up the ocean, / As earth's core bears the earth, have I borne this" ("Single Sonnet"); "When the bare eyes were before me / And the hissing hair" ("Medusa"); "The bales stand on the stone; the anchor weeps / Its red rust downward" ("Song for the Last Act"); "Softly awake, its sound / Poured on the chilly ground" ("Song for a Lyre").

In these declarative clauses and sentences, Bogan posits or "declares" events and states as far removed as we can imagine from one another. Further, as in "Song for a Lyre," where the unexpected verb *Poured* makes an active metaphor for *sound* (as if the sound did its own pouring of itself onto the chilly ground), Bogan everywhere enlivens her syntax with active verbs: "the serpents on the forehead / *Formed* in the air" ("Medusa"); "the fireflies *wink and snap* / Close to the cool ground" ("After the Persian"); "the anchor *weeps* / Its red rust *downward*"; "The staves [of music] *are shuttled over* with a stark / Unprinted silence" ("Song for the Last

Act"). For all its brevity, Bogan's poetic oeuvre is prodigious in its syntactic breadth, which so often leads her to metaphor.

> Song for a Lyre
>
> The landscape where I lie
> Again from boughs sets free
> Summer; all night must fly
> In wind's obscurity
> The thick, green leaves that made   5
> Heavy the August shade.
>
> Soon, in the pictured night,
> Returns—as in a dream,
> Left after sleep's delight—
> The shallow autumn stream: 10
> Softly awake, its sound
> Poured on the chilly ground.
>
> Soon fly the leaves in throngs;
> O love, though once I lay
> Far from its sound, to weep,   15
> When night divides my sleep,
> When stars, the autumn stream,
> Stillness, divide my dream,
> Night to your voice belongs.
>
>   (Louise Bogan)

The sentences in lines 2–3, 3–4, 5–6, and 7–8 invert normal syntax as a response to the unnatural change through which the autumn night has compelled the speaker to pass (and of which the autumnal wind and ever shallower stream are the emblems). She does not give up her mature passions with ease but seems confused about the terms this experience is setting for her. She is shaken by it even as she struggles to see why it should be confusing. Inversions mirror that strain. By contrast, the absence of inversion in the last stanza (until the final line) corresponds to the achievement of distance from earlier painful passages. The final line is thus a statement less of torment than of dignified triumph and its inversion a token of the eloquence granted by clarity of insight—insight possible only after a serious effort at relinquishment has been made.

Minimal Syntax: The Fragment

A final possibility in sentence-frame is the syntactic fragment (a broken-off and incomplete sentence), the most common form of which is the noun fragment, made up of a noun and modifying phrases or clauses. Philip Larkin ends "Home Is So Sad" with two noun fragments, with no clauses: "Look at the pictures and the cutlery. / *The music in the piano stool. That vase.*" Here the clipped style of Larkin's fragments emphasizes the diminished hardness and wistful visibility of the things referred to. They represent the taste of the formerly young parents when first married. The light that shines on all of these things is as harsh as the attempt at reticence in the rough fragments is curiously heartbreaking—for all the irony that comes so easily to Larkin's sensibility.

> Home Is So Sad
>
> Home is so sad. It stays as it was left,
> Shaped to the comfort of the last to go
> As if to win them back. Instead, bereft
> Of anyone to please, it withers so,
> Having no heart to put aside the theft   5
>
> And turn again to what it started as,
> A joyous shot at how things ought to be,
> Long fallen wide. You can see how it was:
> Look at the pictures and the cutlery.
> The music in the piano stool. That vase.   10

Larkin implies that we are looking at a very different style of decor from the style favored by the "the last to go," who are the (now-grown) children whose school things remain behind in neatly kept nostalgia by the bereft middle-aged parents. The fragments suggest that the things speak for themselves, but that, in the accusatory glare of a new generation that has rejected home, the parents no longer have much heart to argue or excuse.

The fact that a fragment is a broken-off sentence is the trait that augments negative judgment in the last four lines of the sonnet by William Wordsworth in which he is condemning the French for failing to solidify in culture and government the gains of the Revolution. Instead, there is only the fragmentary debris of pointless movement, with no syntax to hold it together: "Perpetual emptiness! unceasing change!" (see full text above in chapter 1, p. 29). The fragmentary nature of Wordsworth's phrases coheres with his speaker's explosive impatience with postrevolutionary France. So too in "Moly" the speaker is too hard-pressed to fill his question in: "What beasthood skin she made me take?" (see the entire poem later in this chapter).

But **sentence fragments** can also be highly formalized. Samuel Johnson employs a classical suspension in the two phrases that open this stanza, prior to the appearance of the main subject and verb:

> No summons mocked by chill delay,   21
> No petty gain disdained by pride,
> The modest wants of every day
> The toil of every day supplied.

("On the Death of Dr. Robert Levet")

These **absolute** phrases, not quite affiliated with Dr. Levet and yet the result of his behavior, prepare us for the impersonal frame of the main sentence (lines 23–24). Less processional and balanced is the sentence fragment in the last **quatrain** (four-line rhyming stanza) of Louise Bogan's poem "Memory." As ever, her syntax is complex, weaving intricate modifying clauses in and about the subject terms, even if there are no main subject and verb. This fragment pivots on the latecomer pronoun "it" in the eleventh line, which is synonymous with idle remembering:

> Rather, like shards and straw upon coarse ground,
> Of little worth when found,—   10
> Rubble in gardens, it and stones alike,
> That any spade may strike.

The technical incompleteness of Bogan's sentence confirms the temper of the speaker's mental movement as vacant and fruitless. The mood is also one of retreat and cancellation, perhaps too emphatic for an occasion whose contours are suppressed; we do not know the content of the memory—in fact, the poem keeps content at a distance in order to master its emotional pull. Thus, despite the absence of a main verb in the stanza, the implications and interrelations between the phrases and clauses that define the term "it" (that is, memory) are pretty complicated. It's true that we are off on the broken outskirts of syntax, yet we are being asked to respond more aggressively in our allegiances (and our enmities) than in either Johnson's laudatory quatrain about Dr. Levet or Larkin's guardedly pessimistic "Home Is So Sad."

Trope also comes in here, by exclusion as well as by different forms of inclusion: in Johnson's work, there are abstractions to which we must supply imagined human gestures and routines; whatever emerges as visualizable is guided by the assertions (about modesty, hard labor, and the alacrity of Dr. Levet's sympathy with his patients)—there is no indication of setting, personal idiosyncrasy, or real "mood." With Larkin, there are recognizable *things* in the poem's setting whose meaning we are asked to decode, while in the stanza from Bogan's "Memory," there are remembered *passions* whose resemblance to literal rubble we must actively imagine and ponder. Her poem is thus more sophisticated than Larkin's in its use of trope but more reliant than Johnson's on the aura of illustrative detail. Recall, however, that we have been speaking of lines of verse that appear to be deprived of one of the main carriers of meaning, namely the full sentence. Given the exceptional variety these poets derive from fragments, we might suspect that no technique, even one of truncation or fragmentation, can be limited in its effect, let alone discounted or proscribed.

Descriptive Syntax

A corollary to this lesson is that full syntax won't ensure interesting syntax. Sentences in some works seem filled to overflowing with action—strong verbs and violent agency—while giving an impression of sameness. This apparent contradiction holds in Byron's eighty-line phantasmagoria about the end of the human race:

> . . . some lay down
> And hid their eyes and wept; and some did rest   25
> Their chins upon their clenchèd hands, and smiled;
> And others hurried to and fro, and fed
> Their funeral piles with fuel, and look'd up
> With mad disquietude on the dull sky,
> The pall of a past world; and then again   30
> With curses cast them down upon the dust,
> And gnash'd their teeth and howl'd: the wild birds shriek'd
> And, terrified, did flutter on the ground,
> And flap their useless wings; the wildest brutes
> Came tame and tremulous; and vipers crawl'd   35
> And twined themselves among the multitude,
> Hissing, but stingless—they were slain for food.

Too incessant a rehearsal of action, as in Byron's "Darkness," can be as tiring as too great a reliance on adjectival embellishment, as in the work of Byron's contemporary, John Keats. The syntax in some of Keats's poems may be nominally complete and yet serve as excuse for a catalogue of noun phrases—sometimes heavily guarded by adjectives. In Keats's narrative poem "The Eve of St. Agnes," each stanza presents a little cameo of descriptive texture, as in XXX, in which the young lover Porphyro brings dainties to Madeline's bed chamber; the operative verbs are the fairly passive *slept* and the bare hinge for the catalogue, *brought forth:*

And still she slept an azure-lidded sleep,	
In blanchèd linen, smooth and lavender'd,	
While he from forth the closet brought a heap	
Of candied apple, quince, and plum, and gourd;	265
With jellies soother* than the creamy curd,	*softer
And lucent syrops, tinct with cinnamon;	
Manna and dates, in argosy transferr'd	
From Fez; and spicèd dainties, every one,	
From silken Samarcand to cedar'd Lebanon.	270

In his defense, Keats's lines, however profuse, do vary the length and "breath" taken by the units of thought and expression. On occasion, the catalogue contracts into a line (265), at other times one item on the list requires a lengthier derivation (268–69; 269–70). This variety keeps Keats's stanzas from becoming entirely line-bound (or **stichic**), and yet they lack the flexibility provided by the larger rhetorical frame in Milton's description of Satan prone on the flood of the burning lake after being hurled into hell; here also the main verb is a plain counter, *Lay:*[8]

> [He] Lay floating many a rood, in bulk as huge
> As whom the Fables name of monstrous size,
> *Titanian,* or *Earth-born,* that warr'd on *Jove,*

---

8. Milton's verb *Lay,* the past tense of the **intransitive verb** *lie,* belongs with a category I call **non-verbs**—those that do the work of an equals sign between nouns and qualities. This verb is one of the many that tends to perform little or no actual work in sentences. Copulas are clearly the worst offenders where real work is concerned, promoting equations between nouns and other nouns and adjectives. See a list of non-verbs in chapter 12.

Briareos* or *Typhon,*** whom the Den   **hundred-armed Titan in Hesiod epic*
                                                    **monster who dared to scale Olympus
                                                    and was hurled to earth

By ancient *Tarsus* held, or that Sea-beast   200
Leviathan, which God of all his works
Created hugest that swum th' Ocean stream:
Him haply slumb'ring on the *Norway* foam
The Pilot of some small night-founder'd Skiff,
Deeming some Island, oft, as Seamen tell,   205
With fixèd Anchor in his scaly rind
Moors by his side under the Lee . . .

(*Paradise Lost* I)

Typography in Milton's poem gives readers the means to track visually the placement of the items in his lists, since according to the usage of the time, the important nouns are capitalized and the proper nouns and exotic terms are also italicized. These visual cues alert us to the location of items along the line (note how position shifts so as to place *Jove* and *Leviathan* at opposite ends of their lines, and how in lines 204 and 205 the capitalized nouns take up complementary positions). If topical and proper nouns appear at different places, among different concentrations of terms with similar type-display (sometimes in a cluster, sometimes all alone), and if some lines want any topic-nouns at all (196), we discover a rhythm that is not just visual but syntactic as well. Milton thus far exceeds Keats in the variety of his noun-oriented syntax. As Paul Fussell suggests, the poet who writes stichic poetry that is primarily end-stopped creates poems that are like mosaics, thereby giving us the "sense of a whole constructed out of tiny parts of roughly the same size and weight," whereas with sentences that reach beyond the line boundaries, we get "a symphonic sense of flow and flux, a sort of tidal variation."[9] The tidal movement is stronger in Milton than in Byron or Keats.

Similarly, Daryl Hine's rhymed **pentameter** (or five-measure lines) in "Bluebeard's Wife" suggests profusion without clogging the syntax with repetitive fragments. Enjambment is the key, and for enjambment (by definition) one needs the pressure against the line boundary, which

9. Paul Fussell, *Poetic Meter and Poetic Form* (New York: Random House, 1965), p. 116. Fussell makes a primary distinction between poetry that is stichic, or proceeding by lines (whether end-stopped *or* enjambed), and poetry that is strophic (or **stanzaic**), in which a greater degree of end-stopping, hence line integrity, will obtain.

only syntax can provide. The sentence in stanza two of the Hine excerpt "hovers" over the enjambment on the ambiguous word "understood," which at first seems to be a verb but soon proves to be an adjective derived from a verb; it modifies "secret" (l. 13):

from "Bluebeard's Wife"

Impatiently she tampered with the locks,
One by one she opened all the doors;
The music boxes and the cuckoo clocks
Stopped in alarm; dust settled on the floors
Like apprehensive footsteps. Then the stores   5
Of silence were exposed to her soft touch:
Mute diamonds and still exquisite ores.
She had not thought the squalid world had such
Treasure to proffer, nor so easy, nor so much.

She did not listen to the hinges' groans,   10
Complaints in metal, warnings in the wood,
But room by room progressed from precious stones
To tears, and at each secret understood,
Exclaimed, amused, "How simple!" or "How good!"
As she took up some fragile, painted jar.   15
Throughout the palace doors and windows stood
Whether in dread or sympathy ajar
Upon a pale horizon seeming very far.[10]

Daryl Hine's syntax has to be reconstructed to register the appositions: "and at each secret [which had been] understood, / [She] Exclaimed, amused, 'How simple!' or 'How good!' / As she took up some fragile, painted jar." The half meaning with the possibility we must reject ("at each secret [she] understood") creates a moment of excess in the field of syntactic possibility that makes a nice eddy in the smooth current of narrative sentences all about it.[11]

It's interesting to note that, for enjambment to function as a limbering and expressive technique, it must avoid repetition and not fall into

---

10. The final line in each of Daryl Hine's nine-line stanzas in "Bluebeard's Wife" is not pentameter but **hexameter,** or six-measure. See **Spenserean Stanza** in chapter 13, "Poetic Terms."

11. Note that we can also hover between two *rhythms* when a line is heard in isolation. See chapter 10.

the same "turn" at the same place in every line. Such patterning would be just that—an exchange of one kind of fixed pattern for the uniformity of the line. Consider the variety provided by Howard Nemerov's **blank** (unrhymed) **iambic pentameter**[12] sonnet "Again," which carries its descriptive phrases along a swiftly moving syntax. In fact, the poem is a single fourteen-line sentence. It proceeds through a sequence of nouns modified by clauses. But the method of forward propulsion differs from line to line. All the nouns are objects of the kernel sentence, with its command to "sing the slow change / That makes" the various autumnal phenomena occur.

> Again
>
> Again, great season, sing it through again
> Before we fall asleep, sing the slow change
> That makes October burn out red and gold
> And color bleed into the world and die,
> And butterflies among the fluttering leaves   5
> Disguise themselves until the few last leaves
> Spin to the ground or to the skimming streams
> That carry them along until they sink,
> And through the muted land, the nevergreen
> Needles and mull and duff of the forest floor,   10
> The wind go ashen, till one afternoon
> The cold snow cloud comes down the intervale
> Above the river on whose slow black flood
> The few first flakes come hurrying in to drown.

The compositional goal, which keeps the Nemerov poem sinuous and pleasantly on-edge, dictates that we must entertain different phrasal "bondings" (as for lines 9 through 12). We have in view streams that carry along the leaves that have broken loose from the last, weak summer butterflies, which have disguised themselves among those leaves. Thus when we come to the verbs *Spin* and *sink* in the subordinate clauses, we still have the butterflies in mind, too. Both leaves and the ghost-shapes of butterflies "Spin to the ground or to the skimming streams / That carry them along until they sink." The syntax of line 9 coheres with that of line

---

12. Terms describing accentual-syllabic poetry will be found in chapter 8 on meter as well as in chapter 13, "Poetic Terms."

8, and indeed the thought *could* proceed in some other way, for example: "And through the muted land . . . [8] / The leaves slip down and crumble" [9]; but in fact there is a serious parting or lurch in meaning just where we expect a turn in a sonnet, between lines 8 and 9—a turn of whose seriousness we may not be fully aware until we stumble over line 11, "The wind go ashen."

To make sense of this seemingly ungrammatical statement, we have to pore back through the poem to the kernel syntax from lines 2 and 3: "sing the slow change / That makes . . . The wind go ashen." The local structure of line 9 may permit us to follow the leaves (with their hidden butterflies) along the stream and to carry that stream "Through the muted . . . forest," but the local structure of line 11 ("The wind go"), with a syntactic link postponed from line 3 ("makes . . . The wind go"), insists that we shift slightly from the streams to the land in order for the wind of the coming winter—one could call winter the result of a greater "shift"—to blow through everything. The poem "Again" thus illustrates further possibilities of dramatic difference within a syntax that is basically additive (**paratactic**).

The Sentence and the Pentameter Passage

When Milton describes Eve's flowers in a long parallel series, he animates the parallels by disparities—shifts in phrasing and breaks in line—by means of which the sentence strikes out ahead of the lines' control, then falls back into order.

> He sought them both, but wish'd his hap might find
> *Eve* separate, he wish'd, but not with hope
> Of what so seldom chanc'd, when to his wish,
> Beyond his hope, *Eve* separate he spies,
> Veil'd in a Cloud of Fragrance, where she stood,   425
> Half spi'd, so thick the Roses bushing round
> About her glow'd, oft stopping to support
> Each Flow'r of slender stalk, whose head though gay
> Carnation, Purple, Azure, or speckt with Gold,
> Hung drooping unsustain'd, them she upstays   430
> Gently with Myrtle band, mindless the while,
> Herself, though fairest unsupported Flow'r,
> From her best prop so far, and storm so nigh.

> (*Paradise Lost* IX)

Milton believed this ability of syntax to overreach the line differently each time to be the true source of the musical delight essential to poetry, following his rejection of "the troublesome and modern bondage of Riming" in favor of the liberated movement of **blank verse**—namely its "sense variously drawn out from one Verse into another."[13] Milton animates even his catalogues, like the flowers above, or the list of rivers in *Paradise Lost* IX.76–82, of diseases in XI.479–95, and of monsters resembling Satan in the passage quoted earlier (I.196–204), by placing the parallel terms (in the following case, the river names) at different points along the successive lines; he also varies by length of phrase and complexity of clause. Satan is searching for a hiding place:

> Sea he had searcht and Land
> From *Eden* over *Pontus,* and the Pool
> *Maeotis,* up beyond the River *Ob;*
> Downward as far Antarctic; and in length
> West from Orontes to the Ocean barr'd   80
> At *Darien,* thence to the land where flows
> *Ganges* and *Indus:* thus the Orb he roam'd
> With narrow search . . .

> *(Paradise Lost* IX)

Still another feature of their complexity is the sentences' relation to line and run-on. A brief passage from *Paradise Lost* VI.867–70 shows the shifting of sentence within line as the parallels in each strikingly alter with respect to each other:

> Hell heard th' insufferable noise, Hell saw
> Heav'n ruining from Heav'n, and would have fled
> Affrighted; but strict Fate had cast too deep
> Her dark foundations, and too fast had bound.   870

Note how the lines tug the phrasal units back in, by devices like repetition, balancing, and rhyme (for example, *Hell heard/Hell saw; strict/deep; too deep/too fast; dark/fast; cast/fast*). A thoroughly embedded **alliteration** (use of the same sounds) on the letter *f* also binds and balances. Allitera-

---

13. See Milton's introduction to the second edition (1674) of *Paradise Lost* in Merritt Hughes's edition (Bobbs-Merrill/Odyssey, 1957), p. 210.

tion on vowels (sometimes called **assonance**) is also an important bind-
ing device in Milton, audible here in the short *a* of *cast/fast* and in other
passages in which the primary movement involves vowels, as in the play
on *u* and *o* in the passage below describing the shield of Satan:

> . . . the broad circumference
> Hung on his shoulders like the Moon, whose Orb
> Through Optic Glass the *Tuscan* Artist views
> At ev'ning from the top of *Fesole* . . .

> > *(Paradise Lost* I.287–89)

So, although it's true that syntax works *against* line here, and in tension
with it, nevertheless sound and diction work to surround the lines with
a ghostly pattern of integrity and balance. When the syntax tends to break
away from the line, the pattern just described acts to rein the line in. (We
will see similar binding effects when we discuss prosody in chapter 8.)

Milton extends the alliteration we have just examined in at least two
ways: by verbatim repetition of linked terms and by a repetitive device
called **adnomination,** where the poet rings changes on a root word.
These two devices can be illustrated by three passages spoken by Adam
in Book IX. In the first, we notice how Adam (who tends to be more
interested in this kind of word play than Eve) elaborates a mild intercon-
nected free-association on the key terms *labor (toil), food, love, life,* and *de-
light:*

> Yet not so strictly hath our Lord impos'd   235
> Labor, as to debar us when we need
> Refreshment, whether food, or talk between,
> Food of the mind, or this sweet intercourse
> Of looks and smiles, for smiles from Reason flow,
> To brute deni'd, and are of Love the food,   240
> Love not the lowest end of human life.
> For not to irksome toil, but to delight
> He made us, and delight to Reason join'd.

> > *(Paradise Lost* IX)

Somewhat less windily, in the second speech (although still more
elaborately punning than might be strictly consonant with natural pas-

sion), Adam illustrates adnomination by ringing changes on the root-
term *tempt*.[14] He is trying to persuade Eve that it is dangerous for her to
work the garden alone:

> Not diffident* of thee do I dissuade   **mistrustful*
> Thy absence from my sight, but to avoid
> Th' attempt itself, intended by our Foe.   295
> For hee who tempts, though in vain, at least asperses*   **maligns*
> The tempted with dishonor foul, suppos'd
> Not incorruptible of Faith, not proof
> Against temptation . . .
>
>   (IX.293–99)

It's clear how the pertinent words coast about within the line, now
middle, now early, now late, thus adding a visual dimension to the many
auditory designs: the *-dent* of *diffident* creates an interior vowel-rhyme
with all the *tempt*s and with the *-tend-* in *intended,* increasing the verbal
overlay on the syntactic frame. Adam is still exercised in the identical vein
when, seventy lines later, he mingles in *attempt* with another flurry of
alliterations, *approve, attempt, attest:*

> Trial will come unsought.
> Wouldst thou approve thy constancy, approve
> First thy obedience; th' other who can know,
> Not seeing thee attempted, who attest?
> But if thou think, trial unsought may find   370
> Us both securer than thus warn'd thou seem'st,
> Go; for thy stay, not free, absents thee more.

More pompous still is what might seem to us the fairly dry diction of
the pulpit speech Adam had just made (in IX.343ff.) about reason and
will. But its play between poetic line, muscular syntax, and verbal echo
(including *will/well, right/erect/Reason,* and even *fair/false/free/forbid*), is
undeniably vivid and passionate, while showing presence of mind in
acute language-use:

---

14. In this example of adnomination, note how *tempt* appears at the root of words
that over time have accumulated different meanings as they assumed prefixes and suffixes
(*attempt, tempted, temptation*).

To whom thus *Adam* fervently repli'd.
O Woman, best are all things as the will
Of God ordain'd them, his creating hand
Nothing imperfect or deficient left   345
Of all that he Created, much less Man,

. . . .
. . . within himself
The danger lies, yet lies within his power:
Against his will he can receive no harm.   350
But God left free the Will, for what obeys
Reason, is free, and Reason he made right,
But bid her★ well beware, and still erect,   ★*Reason*
Lest by some fair appearing good surpris'd
She dictate false, and misinform the Will   355
To do what God expressly hath forbid.

This is a situation in which the joy the poet and his mouthpiece Adam take in figuring out and breaking through the style burnishes the theme to a more than customary depth.

The Implications of End-Stopping

Because it is unrhymed, blank verse *requires* **enjambment** in order to move itself forward. The reverse situation, end-stopped blank verse, raises the longing for rhyme and a disappointment at its lack. See "The Idea of Order at Key West," by Wallace Stevens, for a good example of the way **end-stopping** seems to *attract* rhyme. Also consider these two versions of a du Bellay sonnet made by Edmund Spenser, particularly the unrhymed version, which seems to yearn after rhymes as the lines huddle over their pauses at each line boundary.

I Saw the Bird That Dares Behold the Sun

I saw the bird that dares behold the sun,
With feeble flight venture to mount to heaven.
By more and more she gan to trust her wings,
Still following th' example of her dame.
I saw her rise, and with a larger flight   5
Surmount the tops even of the highest hills,
And pierce the clouds, and with her wings to reach

The place where is the Temple of the Gods.
There she was lost, and suddenly I saw
Where tumbling through the air in lompe* of fire,   *mass 10
All flaming down she fell upon the plain.
I saw her body turnèd all to dust,
And saw the fowl that shuns the cheerful light
Out of her ashes as a worm arise.

                              (Joachim du Bellay, trans. by Edmund Spenser)[15]

Even at lines 5, 7, 9, and 13, where there is nominal run-on, the syntax
is so amply parallel and orderly that no serious **half-meaning** can occur.
It is probable that Spenser's decision to turn his translation from an un-
rhymed to a rhymed form is owing to his habit of end-line pausing:

I Saw the Bird That Can the Sun Endure

I saw the bird that can the sun endure,
With feeble wings essay to mount on hight;
By more and more she gan her wings t'assure,
Following th'ensample of her mother's sight:
I saw her rise, and with a larger flight   5
To pierce the clouds, and with wide pinions
To measure the most haughty mountain's height,
Until she raught* the gods' own mansions: *reached
There she was lost, when sudden I beheld,
Where, tumbling through the air in fiery fold,   10
All flaming down she on the plain was felled,
And soon her body turned to ashes cold.
I saw the fowl, that doth the light despise,
Out of her dust like to a worm arise.

---

15. This poem, written in blank verse but titled a sonnet, appeared with fourteen
similar poems in a volume called *A Theatre . . . [for] Voluptuous Worldlings,* published in
1569. These sonnets are interesting because they show Spenser's early work in the form.
Although his name does not appear in the volume, he is generally recognized as the
translator of these poems by the French poet du Bellay; these same poems appear later,
rewritten with rhymes, in Spenser's *Complaints.* The rhymed version immediately follows.
Both versions appear in Robert M. Bender and Charles L. Squier, eds., *The Sonnet* (New
York: Washington Square Press, 1965), pp. 88, 89.

The rhymed version's second quatrain is, ironically, more energetic in its enjambment than the unrhymed version.

On the other hand, it is not necessary to over-enjamb. Many poems obtain great reverberation from a flat, declarative syntax that extends in fairly long breaths. When the breaths tend to fill the individual lines, minimal enjambments can be quite shocking, with both the runovers and the residual stops creating an expressive medium whose hallmarks are attentiveness and suspense.[16]

Needless to say, in other poems with different aims and a different proportioning of the poetic elements, the treatment of the line boundary in a self-contained or stichic way will reinforce a totally different mood. David Ferry's **blank** (unrhymed) **sonnet** "Descriptive" seems to test the capacity of self-enclosed lines to suggest fluidity and gracefulness:

> Descriptive
>
> Alone, I looked down through the afternoon:
> A long lawn, a great tree, a field and a fountain.
> The whole day was full of its colors that moved
> About, above, within, and of each other,
> Like bodies in the blindnesses of love.   5
> The whole day was alive with its own creating.
> Nothing was still, would stay, and for awhile
> I looked at all this as if it were all I wanted,
> Colors and shapes, fluid as one another,
> So that the tree, which seemed one moment a tree,   10
> Seemed at another an inexhaustible fountain
> Cascading about itself in a green fall
> Of water that never fell, and the green lawn
> Was the water that never fell, running away.

With only minimal run-ons at lines 3, 7, 12, and 13, an impression of moist, fresh exuberance streams out from the general syntactic contain-

---

16. See Roy Fuller's poem "The Green Hills of Africa" (*Collected Poems, 1936–1961* [London: Andrew Deutsch, 1962], p. 64) for a good example of the effects of occasional, minimal enjambment on predominant end-stopping: the way Fuller controls the lines, playing them out in long, unbroken segments that, on two occasions in particular, run over, suggests that both control and lack of control may be deadly. Fuller's point about what has happened to innocent Africa bears out this extrapolation from form to theme.

ment. These qualities carry over to the other poems by Ferry quoted in the text.[17]

Edwin Muir's "The Gate" also has a long "breath," enjambing only mildly until the flurry of line-with-phrase counterpoint beginning at line 13—a counterpoint hinting that the safety of the castle is transient.

> We sat, two children, warm against the wall
> Outside the towering stronghold of our fathers
> That frowned its stern security down upon us.
> We could not enter there. That fortress life,
> Our safe protection, was too gross and strong   5
> For our unpracticed palates. Yet our guardians
> Cherished our innocence with gentle hands,
> (They, who had long since lost their innocence,)
> And in grave play put on a childish mask
> Over their tell-tale faces, as in shame   10
> For the rich food that plumped their lusty bodies
> And made them strange as gods. We sat that day
> With that great parapet behind us, safe
> As every day, yet outcast, safe and outcast
> As castaways thrown upon an empty shore.   15

When the present time of more mature experience in Muir's poem is unmasked as flat, the end-stopping increases along with the general stiffness and ordinariness of the meter; the hinge moment in the rhythm is the abbreviated line 21:

> Before us lay the well-worn scene, a hillock
> So small and smooth and green, it seemed intended
> For us alone and childhood, a still pond
> That opened upon no sight a quiet eye,
> A little stream that tinkled down the slope.   20
> But suddenly all seemed old
> And dull and shrunken, shut within itself
> In a sullen dream. We were outside, alone.
> And then behind us the huge gate swung open.

17. These are qualities that also carry over into Mr. Ferry's free verse, too (see "A Young Woman," in chapter 11), and into his remarkable translations of *Gilgamesh* and, more recently, Horace. See index for additional poems.

Line 21 reproduces the sudden and disturbing effect of a **reduced line** (in this case, iambic trimeter, or a line of three iambs) in a context of extension, in all the surrounding lines, to the full five feet of the pentameter weave. A vivid contrast between before and after, young and suddenly old, is implied.

Nemerov's "The Sanctuary" has far more enjambment than either Ferry's or Muir's poems, but the falls are softer, mimicking the weaving in and out of view of the swimming trout, and thus is neither divisive nor dramatic.

from "The Sanctuary"

Over a ground of slate and light gravel,
Clear water, so shallow that one can see
The numerous springs moving their mouths of sand;
And the dark trout are clearly to be seen,
Swimming this water which is color of air   5
So that the fish appear suspended nowhere and
In nothing. With a delicate bend and reflex
Of their tails the trout slowly glide
From the shadowy side into the light, so clear,
And back again into the shadows; slow   10
And so definite, like thought emerging
Into a clear place in the mind, then going back, . . .
                                     Now and again
One fish slides into the center of the pool
And hangs between the surface and the slate   15
For several minutes without moving, like
A silence in a dream. . . .

The poet pauses at *and* (line 7) rather than pushing us vigorously ahead from phrase to phrase across the line boundary between 8 and 9. In contrast to Ferry's practice in "Descriptive," Nemerov's blank verse in "The Sanctuary" keeps subtly *changing* in tempo and nudging against the linear norm *differently* each time, as a means of reflecting on the drifts and pausings of the fish (and of the mind to which the fish is being compared).

Harder end-stopping than Nemerov's can also have a soft effect. In "The Heron," Theodore Roethke applies end-stopping to a posture of careful factuality in the face of the somber apparition of the heron. The mood is an accepting one, the visual picture of the heron clear, as line and logic coincide:

The Heron

The heron stands in water where the swamp
Has deepened to the blackness of a pool,
Or balances with one leg on a hump
Of marsh grass heaped above a musk-rat hole.
He walks the shallow with an antic grace.   5
The great feet break the ridges of the sand,
The long eye notes the minnow's hiding place.
His beak is quicker than a human hand.

He jerks a frog across his bony lip,
Then points his heavy bill above the wood.   10
The wide wings flap but once to lift him up.
A single ripple starts from where he stood.

Whereas in "Moly," Thom Gunn brings to the strong end-stopping of
each couplet a coercive element that projects the stupidity of the Ho-
meric sailor now that he is turned into a beast by the witch Circe. We
return to this poem at several points later, so I give the entire text of
"Moly" here.

Moly

Nightmare of beasthood, snorting, how to wake.
I woke. What beasthood skin she made me take?

Leathery toad that ruts for days on end,
Or cringing dribbling dog, man's servile friend,

Or cat that prettily pounces on its meat,   5
Tortures it hours, then does not care to eat:

Parrot, moth, shark, wolf, crocodile, ass, flea.
What germs, what jostling mobs there were in me.

These seem like bristles, and the hide is tough.
No claw or web here: each foot ends in hoof.   10

Into what bulk has method disappeared?
Like ham, streaked. I am gross—gray, gross, flap-eared.

The pale-lashed eyes my only human feature.
My teeth tear, tear. I am the snouted creature
~

That bites through anything, root, wire, or can.   15
If I was not afraid I'd eat a man.

Oh a man's flesh already is in mine.
Hand and foot poised for risk. Buried in swine.

I root and root, you think that it is greed,
It is, but I seek out a plant I need.   20

Direct me, gods, whose changes are all holy,
To where it flickers deep in grass, the moly:

Cool flesh of magic in each leaf and shoot,
From milky flower to the black forked root.

From this fat dungeon I could rise to skin   25
And human title, putting pig within.

I push my big gray wet snout through the green,
Dreaming the flower I have never seen.

Gunn writes a constricted couplet here—even the first lines of each tend to stop hard—yet despite this he manages to surround the lines with tensile energies that work beneath the tight parallels of couplet closure (lines 12, 23, and the rhythmically risky penultimate line exhibit Gunn's variety in expressing the dumb rage of the man trapped in bestial harness). In a related way in Robert Frost's "Neither Out Far Nor In Deep," end-stopping helps satirize the closed-mindedness of the people along the shore and of beach-combing in general (Frost found the ocean sinister and stupefying). On the other hand, in the great ballad "Sir Patrick Spens," end-stopping is the vehicle of great depth of implication and passionate simplicity.

Form Follows Theme

The same flexibility obtains for run-ons in rhymed as in unrhymed poetry: *None of these effects is univocal or unchanging.* Strong enjambment can be smooth or jagged, happy or sad, emphatic or voiceless—and the same variety is enjoyed by end-stopped lines. It is only in combination with theme and its effect on the whole complex of techniques (diction, syntax, trope, etc.) that end-stopping grows boring or emphatic and the enjambment too active or just right. Even poems that end-stop so regularly that rhymes begin to accumulate are not necessarily slipshod. There is no cause to deprive ourselves of poems of the magnitude of Stevens's "The Idea of Order at Key West" merely because we must enforce some abstract proportion of enjambments to end-stops.

Finally, syntax can provide interest by varying from itself. As we've mentioned, there is an obvious link between complexity of syntax and complexity of the line-boundary tension. In addition to this pressure exerted by syntactic length on enjambment, there is also the syntax or sentence that contributes to the organization of the poem in subtle approaches to an idea. Consider how seldom poets actually use the *Helen loves Jack* formula. The few following examples of syntactic "surprise" show the flexibility poets constantly try to maintain without exploding the form. Far from it: the divergences are sometimes pleasingly faint. The long inverted conjectures in Yeats's "To a Friend Whose Work Has Come to Nothing," buried as they are in a question, are the most syntactically exotic, while the mildest enlivenings of sentence are performed by Roethke and Muir by inserting unexpected subjects and verbs; Andrew Marvell, too, varies from the *I-did* or *I-saw* formula. All four replace passive agents with active ones and the lazy personal pronouns recede into the background:

> What wond'rous Life is this I lead!
> Ripe Applies drop about my head;
> The luscious clusters of the Vine   35
> Upon my Mouth do crush their Wine;
> The nectaren, and curious Peach,
> Into my hands themselves do reach;
> Stumbling on Melons, as I pass,
> Insnar'd with Flowers, I fall on Grass.   40
> (Andrew Marvell, "The Garden")

> The plum drops pitch upon the ground,
> The nostrils widen as they pass
> The place where butternuts are found.
>   (Theodore Roethke, "The Coming of the Cold")

Long since the rust its gardens here has planned,
Flowering his armour like an autumn field.

(Edwin Muir, "The Enchanted Knight")

〰〰〰

To a Friend Whose Work Has Come to Nothing

Now all the truth is out,
Be secret and take defeat
From any brazen throat,
For how can you compete,
Being honour bred, with one   5
Who, were it proved he lies,
Were neither shamed in his own
Nor in his neighbours' eyes?
Bred to a harder thing
Than Triumph, turn away   10
And like a laughing string
Whereon mad fingers play
Amid a place of stone,
Be secret and exult,
Because of all things known   15
That is most difficult.

(William Butler Yeats)

A remarkable thing has happened in the first three excerpts above. The "flexing" of the syntax away from the *I-did* or *I-saw* formulas also produces distortions in the way things are seen to work: Other agents (nostrils, nectarines, the rust on a metal shield) supplant the central hero and do the work of feeling, movement, and change. The world *outside* the self takes over, moving toward the trope of **personification** (see chapter 5). While in Yeats's poem, the vivid brevity of the lines seems almost perverse in the face of the complex and mercurial sentence form, roughly paraphrased: *Now that X is true, / Be Y, / For how can you Z, / Being A, with one / Who, if B, / Were C neither in his own view / Nor in the view of D.* The line breaks throw out barriers against which the avidity and scorn of the speaker triumphantly hurl themselves. Yeats's poem is an example of a successfully mounted tension between simplicity of line and length and complexity of sentence-frame. Looked at more closely in light of his other work, "To a Friend Whose Work Has Come to Nothing" suggests how the preference for certain difficult sentence frames might even become a subliminal language. To estimate such a phenomenon in its full dimension, however, we need to incorporate the element of diction, which we will discuss in the next chapter.

4

Diction and Layers in Meaning

The Role of Size

The effect of syntax can be more accurately gauged if we also look at the kind of vocabulary the poet uses to build the poem and to modify what has already been built. The poem's vocabulary, or **diction,** may be either **concrete** or abstract. It may deal either with things, or with ideas, with palpable objects or with personal feelings and linguistic **abstractions** like those that pertain to mood and temperament. Running parallel to the degree of concreteness or abstractness in the diction is the tendency to be either monosyllabic and Anglo-Saxon (in the case of concrete things) or polysyllabic and Latinate (in the case of abstractions). As a rule, the more syllables in the word, the more conceptual, cerebral, conversational, and/or editorial it will tend to be. (Note that by "conversational" I imply a middle-to-high plateau of reference; it should not be considered as involving predominantly slang, dialect, or substandard grammar. Rather, the term refers to the alert diction and rhetoric of an educated person turning to serious [but not abstruse] themes and prepared to find apt and expressive comparisons for rendering such a state of mind.[1])

Conversation becomes abstract or concrete according to its syntax and its diction; diction becomes abstract or concrete according to the length of the word. The fewer the number of syllables per word, the more stubborn, objective, thing- or texture-filled the poem composed of

---

1. Examples include Sir Thomas Wyatt's satire "Myne Owne John Poynz"; Ben Jonson, "Inviting a Friend to Supper"; A. D. Hope, "Man Friday"; Elizabeth Bishop, "At the Fishhouses"; Philip Larkin, "Church Going"; Thom Gunn, "His Rooms in College"; and John Koethe, "The Realm of Ends." The last two appear in full in the book, and Wyatt's and Hope's poems are excerpted to illustrate **conversational style.**

such words will tend to be. It is this tendency toward cramming the line with active monosyllables that Pope mocks in "An Essay on Criticism," where the throng of stressed words cleverly shows how it should impede our progress:

> When Ajax strives some rock's vast weight to throw,
> The line too labours, and the words move slow;

John Milton had already illustrated the thing-filled variant of the monosyllabic line in his frequent catalogues:

> Rocks, Caves, Lakes, Fens, Bogs, Dens, and shades of death—
> A Universe of death, which God by curse
> Created evil, for evil only good;
> Where all life dies, death lives, and Nature breeds,
> Perverse, all monstrous, all prodigious things . . .   625
>
> (*Paradise Lost* II)

Later, the four elements in Milton's imagined Chaos contend in a lightly rising monosyllabic line, "Light-arm'd or heavy, sharp, smooth, swift, or slow" (II.902), while Satan is brought to his knees by thickening stresses:

>   . . . nigh founder'd on he fares,   940
> Treading the crude consistence, half on foot,
> Half flying . . .
>   . . . So eagerly the fiend
> O'er bog or steep, through strait, rough, dense, or rare,
> With head, hands, wings, or feet pursues his way,
> And swims or sinks, or wades, or creeps, or flies . . .[2]   950
>
> (*Paradise Lost* II)

One of Milton's heirs is clearly Gerard Manley Hopkins, who begins one poem with a fusillade of monosyllables: "Cloud-puffball, torn tufts, tossed pillows flaunt forth." We can hear the difference between this style

---

2. Line 950, although it alternates weak stress with strong, is heavier than the **overstressed lines** that precede because the consonants are harder to pronounce. The *ds* sound in "wades" is impeded by the voicing of the consonant *d* (the unvoiced cognate *t* in a word such as "waits" would be lighter). In addition, we must slow down over the phrases "or creeps" and "or flies" owing to the junctures between the *r* of *or* and the doubled word-initial consonant pairs *cr* and *fl*.

of forcing monosyllables one upon each other and a more conversational and discursive use of one-syllabled diction in the eleventh line of the same poem: "Man, how fast his firedint, his mark on mind, is gone!"[3] Thom Gunn also crowds some of the lines of "Moly" (see the text at the end of chapter 3) with monosyllables for mimetic effect, whether to render a sense of press and jumble ("Parrot, moth, shark, crocodile, ass, flea"), or to render mental lethargy and the struggle to comprehend what is incomprehensible ("Like ham, streaked. I am gross—gray, gross, flap-eared"). Note that both of these lines from Gunn are still audible as iambic pentameter if one reads them in context (Hopkins's lines do not attempt to be).

Not all catalogues are limited to monosyllables, of course.[4] Consider Cordelia's description of the weeds with which her father was grotesquely crowned:

> . . . he was met even now
> As mad as the vexed sea, singing aloud,
> Crowned with rank fumiter and furrow weeds,
> With hardocks, hemlock, nettles, cuckoo flow'rs,
> Darnel and all the idle weeds that grow
> In our sustaining corn.*   *life-giving wheat
>   (*King Lear* IV.iv)

But the impulse to load the poetic line leads to a diction that is still more dense both with thing and with assertion—as here Cordelia, with fascinated and unflinching care, builds up a catalogue whose profusion is horrifying. The weeds named all denote rankness; but the crowdedness of the catalogue says something worse, that many, many worthless husks readily root themselves in place of the true plant. The style itself suggests that the specifiable variety of the weeds her father Lear has put on in his mad state demean and travesty the majesty from which he has fallen just as weeds travesty (they ape, but emptily) the edible grains.

---

3. The two lines by Hopkins are from "That Nature Is a Heraclitean Fire, and of the Comfort of the Resurrection" (1888).

4. Timothy Steele is especially attentive to word-length, especially to the role two- and three-syllable words have played in iambic pentameter. See "Boundless Wealth from a Finite Store: Meter and Grammar," *Michigan Quarterly Review* (Winter 1997): 161–80.

The Diction of the Plain Style

On the other hand, monosyllabism can provide emphases that do not rely on objects, as in Hamlet's speech in V.ii about his own end, "if it be not to come, it will be now." So even when a monosyllabic line is *not* thronged with objects, traits, and textures, it may come across with considerable force, as we hear in Donne's argumentative refusal to switch places with his now more attentive lover "By being to thee then what to me thou wast."[5] The line twitches with pleasure at the tables turned. Yet more abstract is the monosyllabism Eliot perfects in the quartets, which blends mystical wisdom with conversational ease: "You must go through the way in which you are not. / And what you do not know is the only thing you know" (*East Coker* IIIb).[6] Equally forceful but more material in theme is the monosyllabism in the sestet of Auden's war sonnet, not strictly owing to things, rather to embodied generalizations: "A land laid waste, with all its young men slain."[7]

As I mentioned at the end of chapter 3's discussion of syntax, Yeats practically turns certain forms of sentence into an argumentative lexicon. He is fond of plots based on raising things to a pitch; the sentence frame is then mortised with phrases like *to such an X that Y*. Poems of his are also plotted on a ground of questions *(Why should I blame her? What could she have done? Was there another Troy? How can you compete?)* that resemble exclamations. The adverb, conjunction, and preposition *but* (meaning *just or only*; also *other than, otherwise than that which;* and even *unless, except that, which if not,* and *which not*) is very nearly Yeats's trademark: "There the king is *but as* the beggar" ("Running to Paradise"); "Time *can but make* it easier to be wise" ("The Folly of Being Comforted"—a poem in which Yeats's speaker wishes Maud Gonne would *but turn* her head in order to know the folly of the title); "Toil and grow rich, / What's that *but to lie* / With a foul witch?" ("The Witch"); "there is no deformity / *But saves us* from a dream" ("The Phases of the Moon"); "Nothing now *but comes*

---

5. John Donne, "The Prohibition," in *Major Poets of the Earlier Seventeenth Century,* edited by Barbara K. Lewalski and Andrew J. Sabol (Indianapolis: Bobbs-Merrill/Odyssey, 1973), p. 70.

6. *The Complete Poems and Plays of T. S. Eliot* (London: Faber and Faber, 1969), p. 181.

7. See the related discussion of **understressing** and **overstressing** that takes place later in this chapter (along with the full text of Auden's sonnet). This subject is continued in chapter 8.

readier to the hand" than the effort to write poems ("All Things Can Tempt Me"). Christ in Yeats's play *Calvary* repeats his passion by again climbing the hill (and climbing the cross); the First Musician speaks: "He climbs up hither *but as* a dreamer climbs. / The cross that *but exists* because he dreams it." To call these occasions "choice of diction" alone fails to account for the torque created by the extended shapes of thought imposed by their syntax; yet to align Yeats's inventions exclusively with the frame of his syntax does not entirely account for the repetitions at the level of word. The truth lies somewhere between the two.

Monosyllabic pentameter is also well suited to argument and definition, as we can hear in many of Robert Frost's poems. Sometimes the argument is simple: "'Something there is that doesn't love a wall, / That wants it down,'" says one neighbor in "Mending Wall." Frost's grasp of human foible is subtle, but all the words expressing it are plain, as is the frame of the sentence. At other times, the style of argument is almost obscure, as in the first line of another poem: "Back out of all this now too much for us." If one takes the words one by one, meaning will be clear; but the distorted colloquialism of the definition—what is *this-now-too-much-for us?*—is devious. Frost's most characteristic mode is a combination of the two, as in the speaker's comment as he watches his neighbor dig in mulishly to his position with its stubborn reliance on an old saying: "And he likes having thought of it so well / He says again, 'Good fences make good neighbors'" ("Mending Wall"). Just so, the bird in "The Wood-Pile" is careful to "say no word to tell me who he was / Who was so foolish as to think what *he* thought." The mode is built on monosyllables of reference rather than on highly textured things:

> "Home is the place where, when you have to go there,
> They have to take you in."
>   "I should have called it
> Something you somehow haven't to deserve."   120
>   ("The Death of the Hired Man")

Frost's monosyllabic style of argument is a somewhat folksy variant of an old tradition of hard probity reflected in a deceptively simple medium: "They are that that talks of going / But never gets away" ("The Sound of Trees"); "I paused and said, 'I will turn back from here, / No, I will go on farther—and we shall see'" ("The Wood-Pile"). This so-called **plain style,** albeit it with an American twist, stems from Roman prose rhetori-

---

cians as well as the poet Horace but was modified by several strong prac-
titioners in Renaissance England, notably Shakespeare and John Donne:

Nay if you read this line, remember not,   5
The hand that writ it, for I love you so,
That I in your sweet thoughts would be forgot,
If thinking on me then should make you woe.

(Shakespeare, Sonnet 71)

I cannot thinke that hee, who then lov'd most,
    Sunke so low, as to love one which did scorn . . .

(Donne, "Loves Deitie")[8]

It is this arguing *via* monosyllabic plain speech that carries through the
next two centuries after Shakespeare and Donne whenever the guise of
brooding naturalness is put on to explore deep feeling. "Tintern Abbey"
presents a monosyllabic diction in part linked to scene but more to im-
ages of the poet-narrator's own spiritual development. The diction, care-
fully paid out as one does with a fishing line when there appears to be
something nibbling it, follows a discovery that is slow to find its way
through the currents of comprehension:

And so I dare to hope   66
Though changed, no doubt, from what I was when first
I came among these hills. . . .

Nor . . .
If I should be, where I no more can hear
Thy voice, nor catch from thy wild eyes these gleams
Of past existence, wilt thou then forget. . . .   150

("Tintern Abbey")

Wordsworth maintains on the one hand his monosyllabic plain style for
an essential embodiment of his characteristically mournful thought ("The
Things which I have seen I now can see no more," as he puts it in the
"Immortality Ode"), while on the other imbedding his language in a
richer complex of abstractions ("these gleams / Of past existence" and
"the heavy and the weary weight / Of all this unintelligible world," as he
writes in "Tintern"). But unlike one of his successors in the next genera-

8. John Donne, lines 3–4 of "Loves Deitie," in *Major Poets of the Earlier Seventeenth Century*, p. 60.

tion, Alfred Lord Tennyson, Wordsworth keeps trying to reconstitute the
tenor of his earlier frame of mind, when he "gave a moral life" to "Even
the loose stones that cover the high-way . . . I saw them feel, / Or linked
them to some feeling" (*The Prelude* III.132–33).

Tennyson practices a more plangent version of plain style; his speak-
ers typically address us after the argument seems already decided and an
unalterable fate accepted:

>   . . . and though   65
> We are not now that strength which in old days
> Moved earth and heaven, that which we are, we are,
>
>   ("Ulysses")

> He is not here; but far away
>   The noise of life begins again,   10
>   And ghastly through the drizzling rain
> On the bald street breaks the blank day.
>   (*In Memoriam A. H. H.*, VII)

Wallace Stevens rejects this monosyllabic plangency of Wordsworth and
Tennyson in favor of a diction closer to the old argumentative plain style,
which he sprinkles with strokes of landscape color in "A Postcard from
the Volcano"; the italicized portion could almost have come from Tenny-
son or Frost:

> Children picking up our bones
> Will never know that these were once
> As quick as foxes on the hill;
>
> And that in autumn, when the grapes
> Made sharp air sharper by their smell   5
> These had a being, breathing frost;
>
> And least will guess that with our bones
> *We left much more, left what still is*
> *The look of things, left what we felt*
>
> *At what we saw.* The spring clouds blow   10
> Above the shuttered mansion-house,
> Beyond our gate and the windy sky
> ~

Cries out a literate despair.
We know for long the mansion's look
And what we said of it became   15

A part of what it is . . .

One could paraphrase the passage as follows: Least of all in the future will
the children who stumble upon our bones guess that the real scene before
them—"what still is / The look of things"—has been made possible by
the bones of our style. It is a style that Stevens is always trying to raise to
its highest expression ("the shuttered mansion-house," "a literate de-
spair") in order to compel it toward its pure reduction, free of trope,
driven into the tautological, indefinite monosyllable ("what we said of it
became / A part of what it is"). The simplicity of diction provides a para-
doxical difficulty of definition.

Like Wallace Stevens, the contemporary poet John Koethe uses plain
style with a preponderating ground base of monosyllabism to achieve
ends that are also more actively exploratory than Tennyson's: The heavens
above us may seem to be "the only ones there are," yet Koethe's speaker
notices that he still imagines himself looking up to them. He also remarks
that his own style of thinking, prompted in part by the sky above, is one
that like the atmosphere "must have once seemed / Clear, but which
now seems loose, strange and / Difficult to follow":

The Realm of Ends

I wish there were a state of being
Of a different kind, not comprised
And caught between the twin extremes of
Something inconceivable and something else
Untrue; between the overarching heavens   5
And the merely human. Some things are
Not to be sought after in reality, not
Even in the mind, but in a hidden region
Where the soul is free and unrestrained
And thought proceeds like weightless   10
Stars across an unseen sky.

Beyond its monosyllabic base, Koethe's diction is also noteworthy for its
neutrality, polish, and reserve; he develops a lexicon that effortlessly fends

off any unruly intrusion, without seeming to avoid any conceivable mental content or linguistic invention. It is this equanimity in the face of the obscurity of heaven that intensifies the feeling in his verse. "The Realm of Ends" concludes:

> Oh yes, I
> Realize this inner paradise is just, like
> Time, or other worlds or selves impossibly
> Remote or deep within, another intimate
> Illusion on the border of intelligence,   15
> A thing you have to touch and brush away,
> Because nothing is hidden. These heavens
> Are the only ones there are, an all-inclusive
> Frame displaying every aspect of the real
> Against an infinite night sky the thick,   20
> Dark, translucent color of obsidian. Yet
> In the wakefulness that comes towards dawn I
> Still sometimes think of myself—in a style of
> Thinking whose trajectory must have once seemed
> Clear, but which now seems loose, strange and   25
> Difficult to follow—as somehow distant from a
> Universe of merely changing things, eternal
> In the way each moment is, and free, the
> Way each star becomes increasingly
> Elusive once it crosses the meridian.   30

The poem is marked by choice as well as restraint. Koethe avoids the temptation to censor or to lyricize the language of science (*trajectory, meridian*), while actively culling and electing to employ the diction of reasonable balance in contexts that open logic to affect (he longs for a state "not comprised [defined] / And caught between . . . Something inconceivable and something else / Untrue"; he recognizes with suspicion his yearning for the inward idyll as "another intimate / Illusion on the border of intelligence"—or, as Stevens says, the poet is compelled into an expressive energy that must "resist[] the intelligence / Almost successfully"). Like the language of Stevens and, before him, Wordsworth, this language of Koethe's is at once abstract and fluent, as if polysyllables and conceptual diction had been so humanized by the surrounding plainness of the diction that the whole became a naturally expressive medium.

Plain Style as Low Style

There is a second application of plain style that began in the Renaissance;
it accommodates an impulse toward simplicity that is antilyrical in a more
stubborn and obtrusive way. The flavor of common sense lingers on the
palate. Both Wyatt and Barnaby Googe wrote in this mode; so, on occa-
sion, did Shakespeare and Donne. Sir Walter Ralegh plays wittily, in his
advice to his wastrel son, with this stolid speech of plain manners:

> The wood is that, which makes the Gallow tree,   6
> The weed is that, which stringes the Hangmans bagg,
> The wagg my pritty knave betokeneth thee.
>
> (sonnet, "Three Thinges There Bee")

We hear a less sprightly and more subdued version of this plainness when
Peter Grimes speaks to us in the poem by George Crabbe:

> And so I sat and look'd upon the stream,
> How it ran on, and felt as in a dream: 305
> But dream it was not; no!—I fix'd my eyes
> On the mid stream and saw the spirits rise;
> I saw my father on the water stand,
> And hold a thin pale boy in either hand. . . .
>
> ("The Borough")

We hear this tradition in Wordsworth, too, both when he narrates stories
of isolated folk in Crabbe-like poems such as "Michael," "The Brothers,"
"The Ruined Cottage," and "The Old Cumberland Beggar," and in his
psychological self-portraits; his poem about the leech-gatherer encom-
passes both currents:

> But now his voice to me was like a stream
> Scarce heard; nor word from word could I divide;   115
> And the whole Body of the man did seem
> Like one whom I had met with in a dream. . . .
>
> ("Resolution and Independence")

High Mixed with Low Diction

There are many poets who write in plain or low style for some poems,
high rhetoric and diction for others. Thomas Hardy sometimes rises to
elegant Romantic diction in "The Darkling Thrush":

The tangled bine-stems scored the sky 5
  Like strings of broken lyres,
And all mankind that haunted nigh
  Had sought their household fires.

But the Hardy who writes "The tangled bine-stems scored the sky" is equally capable of the burlesque diction of "The glebe cow drooled" in "Channel Firing":

  While drearisome 5
Arose the howl of wakened hounds:
The mouse let fall the altar-crumb,
The worms drew back into their mounds,

  The glebe cow drooled.

Hardy mastered the region between these extremes of diction, too. He invented nonce phrases (or **neologisms**) as Shakespeare did (see *unfaire* in Sonnet 5): Hardy's verbs *entune, outskeleton, unvision,* the participials *increeping* and *trance-lipped,* the nouns *onbearers, fender-brink, outrollings, unsuccesses,*—not to mention the many early English words and dialect terms glossed by Samuel Hynes in his edition: *gaingivings, subtrude, slovening* (being slothful), *grinterns* (compartments in a granary), *bivering* (with chattering teeth), *shrammed* (numbed), *slent* (split), *tardle* (entanglement), *caddle* (quandary), *vlankers* (fire-flakes), *lewth* (shelter).[9] The elevated diction of Hardy (in this category would also appear his personified abstractions like *purblind Doomsters, The Great Adjustment, Vast Imbecility, Crass Casualty, Dicing Time,* and mighty *Achievement* with its crushing strides) has a touch of the homemade about it, just as his lower diction has a stubborn streak of eloquence and gloomy humor. The lower diction has the advantage of imbedding us in the local while suggesting a personal attitude. The same applies to the charming "low" passage on sleep by George Gascoigne, written in **fourteener** couplets; the poet takes the analogy between sleep and death to a comic extreme at odds with the somber tone and cadence of the more typically lofty responses to this topic in the sixteenth century:

9. Thomas Hardy, *Selected Poetry,* edited with an introduction by Samuel Hynes (Oxford: Oxford University Press, 1996), pp. 253–54.

The stretching arms, the yawning breath, which I to bedward use,
Are patterns of the pangs of death, when life will me refuse:
And of my bed each sundry part in shadows doth resemble,   25
The sundry shapes of death, whose dart shall make my flesh to
    tremble.
My bed itself is like the grave, my sheets the winding sheet,
My clothes the mold which I must have, to cover me most meet:
The hungry fleas which frisk so fresh, to worms I can compare,
Which greedily shall gnaw my flesh and leave the bones full bare:[10]   30

Gascoigne's liveliness is achieved through managing the lower range of
both his diction and his details. The poet is wide awake even if his alter
ego in the poem is not; as the latter wends his way to bed, Gascoigne
wittily imagines how a yawn might be the analogue to a death-rattle,
while the fleas that devil his vividly imaged self at night ("hungry fleas
which frisk so fresh") compare with the worms that will feed on him
hereafter. Inherited ideas about sleep being the pale copy of death take
new energy from a diction of low particulars. Within Gascoigne's poem,
to be sure, occur cases of higher diction ("sundry shapes of death"), but
they are usually combined with lower ones (as the "sundry shapes" re-
lease their "dart," which "shall make [his] flesh to tremble"); the domi-
nant diction—and the sensibility implied by the descriptions—is low.

Other poets bridge less extreme polarities of each kind of diction
than Hardy's and Gascoigne's in a single poem. The **octave** of "Inniskeen
Road: July Evening" by Patrick Kavanagh is written in a plain "objec-
tive" diction that stays close to the observable realm of local place and
gesture (bicycles; a local dance; "the wink-and-elbow language of de-
light"):

The bicycles go by in twos and threes—
There's a dance in Billy Brennan's barn tonight,
And there's the half-talk code of mysteries
And the wink-and-elbow language of delight.
Half-past eight and there is not a spot   5
Upon a mile of road, no shadow thrown
That might turn out a man or woman, not
A footfall tapping secrecies of stone.

---

10. From "Gascoigne's Good Night," in *The Anchor Anthology of Sixteenth-Century
Verse,* edited by Richard S. Sylvester (New York: Doubleday/Anchor, 1974), p. 257.

while the **volta** or turn after line 8 marks a change from concrete diction
to more abstract and conversational words. The sonnet's **sestet**[11] strikes
out into a polysyllabism that is more meditative: "I have what every poet
hates in spite / Of all the solemn talk of meditation."

> I have what every poet hates in spite
> Of all the solemn talk of contemplation.   10
> Oh, Alexander Selkirk knew the plight
> Of being king and government and nation.
> A road, a mile of kingdom, I am king
> Of banks and stones and every blooming thing.

Here one has to work out the clues given by the abstractions, until one
arrives at the "answer": Like Alexander Selkirk, the prototype for Defoe's
Robinson Crusoe, Kavanagh's speaker "has" in his possession only soli-
tude. Note that "blooming" is often a slang substitute for the blasphe-
mous oath "bloody." The rural landscape may be full of flowers but it is
damned empty as far as companions go.

Philip Larkin also works his way up from sense data, literal particular-
ity, and the accompanying monosyllabism of his lists to general concepts,
like the question of religious faith and his own soul's fate in "Church
Going." And in "The Whitsun Weddings," Larkin consummates the cat-
alogue of tawdry contemporary rites in a shower of grace. In both of
these descriptive-meditative poems, the diction of the account-sheet
early on gives way to an easier, looser, and more thoughtful and conversa-
tional diction of abstraction later.

When Eleanor Wilner writes of armies as "human beetles in / their
masks," she is using a diction of deliberate particularity low in style as well
as sense; however, when she writes, of the page of history, that

> it extends and extends, the smoking cities
> scattered like open lesions
> to the periphery of sight   48
> ("Operations: Desert Shield, Desert Storm")

11. There is usually a turn in feeling, style, and/or theme between octave (the first
eight-line section of a sonnet) and sestet (the last six lines); this turn is called a volta. In
Kavanagh's poem, the volta after line 8 marks a change from concrete diction to a more
abstract and conversational diction. Many sonnets change language at the volta.

her theme is violent and her comparison unsavory but her diction is more elevated because more specialized—*lesion* (not the elegiac *wound* but also not the low *sore*). When she speaks of the castoffs of war, human as well as inert, her vocabulary is a mix of dictions, sometimes low in both senses (*junk, scraps, beetles, rotting fruit*), at other times thematically aggressive but stylistically neutral (*ashes, rising flies*) or stylistically lofty (*debris*) or otherwise removed from ordinary discourse by technicality (*lesion*). In the context of "Operations," with its profound mourning at historical repetition, diction like that of the noun *scraps* and the verbs *litter* and *expose* act to set and shape her language.

These variations are a function of the poem, of course, and depend on the nexus of expressive means Wilner can summon; one can imagine poems in which *ashes* would be the lowest diction acceptable and others in which *lesion* and *beetles* would sound too grand (or too exact). Out of context, the vocabulary of shock shocks less. This may be further evidence for the fusion effect of formal context: it is the poem that makes the dead word electric.

W. B. Yeats also needed the electricity of the chosen word. He was working to haul his poetry out of its pale and gauzy Edwardian swoon and to get free of pale moonlight and women with their clouds of hair. He appears to have felt it necessary to plunge into the mire (a favorite bit of diction for him, "mire" was redolent of the juices of life). But there is no doubting the rancorous disdain of some of his portrayals, as of the woman whom art arouses "Till her bowels are in heat" ("Under Ben Bulben"), the repellant but prophetic "lug-worm with its grey and muddy mouth" ("The Man Who Dreamed of Faeryland"), and the merchant Irish middle class, who "fumble in a greasy till" ("September 1913"); later he will personify this mercantile class he so disliked as "the raving slut / Who keeps the till" ("The Circus Animals' Desertion"). Yeats does not aim in every poem to rouse and appall us with his diction, but he learned early how to magnetize even "pretty" poems by the metal sliver of rougher, mismatched diction till it pointed everything toward the poem's true north.[12] But this is also the poet whose range of diction included such sonorous elevation as in "That dolphin-torn, that gong-

12. Many of the poems in "Words for Music Perhaps," a suite of poems spoken by his invented character Crazy Jane in Yeats's 1933 collection *The Winding Stair,* work by agitating one or two words in each brief work and making them raw.

tormented sea" across which the souls of the dead are driven in "By-
zantium."

Emily Dickinson uses two diction styles as well but modifies the ex-
tremes to suit the smaller scale of her many brief poems in **hymn meter.**
She never resorts to the catalogue in either her low or high mode—both
of her "dictions" are strict, choice, and elliptical). In "Further in Summer
than the Birds" (#1068), the diction is one of polysyllabic abstraction,
which imparts an eerie formality to the late song of the crickets:

> No Ordinance be seen
> So gradual the Grace
> A pensive Custom it becomes
> Enlarging loneliness.

While in "I heard a Fly buzz—when I died—" (#465), the diction is
simpler, the words shorter, the referents more objective (although the
second stanza where the coming of the "King" is mentioned suggests
how careful one must be with Dickinson's literalness, for this King be-
longs to unearthly royalty):

> The Eyes around—had wrung them dry—
> And Breaths were gathering firm
> For that last Onset—when the King
> Be witnessed—in the Room—

But Dickinson has other modes as well. In "My Life had stood—a
Loaded Gun" (#754), she overturns the categories we have just set up
by using an admittedly simple diction; however, it is a diction based on
abstractions (as *kill* and *die* are abstractions when applied to love and ser-
vice), and on a convoluted syntax:

> Though I than He—may longer live
> He longer must—than I—
> For I have but the power to kill,
> Without—the power to die—

The sense of this last stanza is that the Master of the gun, the "He," must
live longer than the loaded gun, the "I," if the gun is to "live" and be
used at all. But the fact is that Dickinson chose her contorted and almost
self-canceling means of expression rather than the simple paraphrase
offered above. Her choice suggests that our paraphrase may need to be

replanted in the thicket of contrasts and reservations that impede straight-forward movement through the poem. In other words, the distortion of her language is part of the distortion of feeling, the almost paralyzing allegiance, which animates the poem's speaker. Furthermore, "language" is made difficult in "My Life had stood—a Loaded Gun" by syntax (locally) and allusiveness (fundamentally)—not by difficult polysyllabic vocabulary. The poem's genuine complexity is masked by quite simple diction.

"Difficult" Diction and Etymological Style

Overt "difficulty" of vocabulary is sometimes exploited for satiric effect. John Betjeman shifts from description to snobbery in the third line below; polysyllabic diction is largely responsible for the change in tone:

> Do you know that the stucco is peeling?
> Do you know that the heart will stop?
> From those yellow Italianate arches
> Do you hear the plaster drop?   24
>
> (from "Death in Leamington")

The adjective "Italianate" is the word of an architectural historian. Clearly, in a poem where an old woman patient has died and a nurse in the shabby "home" is oblivious to the situation, the voice of the expert is tastelessly intrusive. At the same time, the intrusion is a function of distance, because the speaker's fastidious interests keep him aloof from the pathos of nurse and patient.

J. V. Cunningham moves in the opposite direction, from pedantry to direct, appealing speech:

> Despise me not,
> And be not queasy   10
> To praise somewhat:
> Verse is not easy.
>
> (from "For My Contemporaries")

The last line, so down-to-earth and colloquial, absolves the speaker of the complication of sentence and vocabulary ("Despise me not") in which he had appeared to be indulging. Really (we say to ourselves when we hear "Verse is not easy"), this fellow is all right; the excesses and punctilio were

just wrung out of him under pressure; but when he comes to, he speaks
our language.

Howard Nemerov is another poet who risks the pedantic, but, by
maintaining it against a common-speech background, he domesticates
his peculiarities of diction. In the blank sonnet "Again," the striking
choices of *mull* (dust or mold), *duff* (decaying vegetable matter), and *inter-
vale* (flat land between hills or along a river) are put into clear contexts
that flirt with explaining what these words might mean (although the
dictionary is still helpful). Meanwhile his "easy" words reserve the right
to engage in syntactic complication (for example, "The wind go ashen";
see the discussion of "Again" in chapter 3). Similarly, there is more than
one *kind* of diction play in his blank-verse "Landscape with Self-
Portrait"; even in the simpler patches (as noted in chapter 2 on line), the
syntactic allegiances blur as phrase and clause unwind:

Landscape with Self-Portrait

A shading porch, that's open to the west
Whence the weather comes, and giving on a lawn
Won from the meadow where the hay's been baled
In cubes like building blocks of dusty gold,
And further down, through trees, the streaming creek   5
With three still pools by passage work
Of rapids and rills in fretted rhythms linked;

And on the porch the life-defeated self
And reciprocating engine of reverie
Translating to time the back and forth of space,   10
The foot's escapement measuring the mind
In memories while the whole antic machine
Precesses across the floor and towards the edge
And has to be hitched back from time to time;

And there to watch the tarnished silver cloud   15
Advancing up the valley on a wind
That shudders the leaves and turns them silverside
While shadows sweep over the stubble and grass,
And sudden the heavy silver of the first
Raindrops blown slanting in and summer cold   20
And turning continuous in silver strings;

~

> And after that, the clarified serene
> Of the little of daylight that remains to make
> Distinct the details of the fading sight:
> The laddered blue on blue of the bluejay's tail,   25
> The sweeping swallows low above the swale
> Among the insect victims as they rise
> To be picked off, and peace is satisfied.

Most overt is Nemerov's intrusion, into the mild, "middle" diction in which he describes his afternoon revery, of a scientific vocabulary having to do with cogwheels and tops (*escapement; precession*)—a lexicon more technical than, say John Koethe's, more akin to John Milton's in the fondness for images out of the laboratory. Then, elsewhere in "Landscape with Self-Portrait," we find the less technical but still specialized geological term *swale*. We also hear the grammatical blurring of parts of speech and their functions: *Serene* (line 23) is an adjective acting the role of a noun, while the normally intransitive verb *shudders* (17) in Nemerov's poem takes an object ("a wind / That shudders the leaves").[13]

Among the devices that serve to normalize these occasional oddities in the diction in "Landscape with Self-Portrait" is the strong undercurrent of syntactic momentum coiling beneath momentary, mild halts of **half-meaning** (the passage begins with the lines already discussed in chapter 3 on syntax). Nemerov's stanza-long image of the mind as a top will come up again in the chapter on trope. Suffice it to say here that,

---

13. *Escapement* denotes the clock part that controls the rate and the intervals of the marking of time by the movement of a notched wheel (or escape wheel), "one tooth of which is permitted to escape from the detaining catch at a time" (*Webster's New World Dictionary of the American Language, College Edition* [New York: World Publishing, 1951; 1968]). *Precession* (definition no. 3 in *Webster's*) denotes the "effect exhibited by a spinning body, as a top, when an applied torque tends to change the direction of its rotational axis, causing the axis to describe a cone and to turn at right angles in the direction of the torque." *Swale* derives from Old Norse *svalr,* meaning cool, and denotes "a hollow, depression, or low area of land, specifically in a wet, marshy area . . . having ranker vegetation than the adjacent higher land."

These words require special knowledge; others, like *serene,* may not announce any denotative difficulty, despite the syntax shift. But the habit of dictionary reading is still recommended, providing in this case, for example, the invaluable information that because it refers to an unclouded sky, it suggests a great height (hence honorific titles such as "Serene Highness" for European royalty). For the Nemerov poem, it is crucial that we understand how physical elevation above earth is involved in the accuracy of "serene" as both adjective and noun.

despite the technical diction in places, the demeanor of the whole passage is casual, familiar, and somewhat rueful as the mind makes its uneven associative sweeps up to the "edge" of inconsequence—where the porch drops off.

Janet Lewis's severe and moving poem "In the Egyptian Museum" illustrates a mode of **style** we could call **etymological** (having to do with the origins of words); under a nearly leveled twentieth-century ease, she invokes the root meanings of selected words, *grave* (engraved), *garnered* (gathered in and stored, as with grain—a term appropriate to the burial rituals of pharaohs), and *Concéntrate* (a truncated and differently stressed past-participial modifier than its more customary twin, *cóncentrated*).

> In the Egyptian Museum
>
> Under the lucent glass,
> Closed from the living air,
> Clear in electric glare
> That does not change nor pass,
> Armlet and amulet   5
> And woven gold are laid
> Beside the turquoise braid
> With coral flowers inset.
>
> The beetle, lapis, green,
> Grave with the old device,   10
> And linen brown with spice,
> Long centuries unseen,
> And this most gracious wreath,
> Exiled from the warm hair,
> Meet now the curious stare—   15
> All talismans of death.
>
> All that the anguished mind
> Most nobly could invent,
> To one devotion bent,
> That death seem less unkind;   20
> That the degraded flesh,
> Grown spiritless and cold,
> Be housed in beaten gold,
> A rich and rigid mesh.
>
> ~

Such pain is garnered here   25
In every close-locked case,
Concentrate in this place
Year after passing year,
That, while I wait, a cry,
As from beneath the glass,   30
Pierces me with "Alas
That the beloved must die!"

A stricter form of etymological diction is practiced frequently by Milton—whose arcane vocabulary (*nocent, asperses, colure, venial, tendance*) and arcane regression to earlier applications (*science, participate, virtue, voluble, officious, devote, entire, sacred,* and *obnoxious*) are conspicuous in the challenge of their unwieldiness. Very occasionally, in a more veiled way, a modern poet like Yeats will apply the etymological touch: "Mere anarchy is loosed upon the world," in which *Mere,* taken from the Latin *merus* (unmixed or full-strength wine), means unmixed, pure—*not* the commonly understood adjective, nothing more or other than. Owing to the suggestion of strong wine, Yeats's image of *blood* in the following two lines of "The Second Coming" is driven deeper in: "The blood-dimmed tide is loosed, and everywhere / The ceremony of innocence is drowned" (see also chapter 5's discussion of trope as a feature of language enriched through punning on etymologies).

Specialized diction need not require specialized intellectual training but only a different kind of life experience or poetic ear. The latter pertains to Hopkins, whose sonnet "The Lantern Out of Doors" (reproduced in full in the "Poetry Sampler" in chapter 1) hints at the difficult style identified with this poet—the subjunctive use of the verb; the eccentric verb-phrase *to wind [the] eye after,* which Hopkins says he intends in the sense of "to weave as you look"; he is speaking of the bright and winning people one sometimes meets in life: "Death or distance soon consumes them: *wind* / What most I may eye after . . . and out of sight is out of mind."[14]

14. For a later example of Hopkins's special associations with *wind* as an active verb, see "Spelt from Sibyl's Leaves," in which the past-participial form *wound* seems to attach to light (that is, sunlight) of a diminishing, devious, or downward-going kind. Hopkins's note to "The Lantern Out of Doors" also suggests that he had pondered the phrase and deemed it accurate: "I mean that the eye winds / only in the sense that its focus or point of sight winds and that coincides with a point of the object and winds with that. For the

Life experience distinguishes the diction of other poets. Consider the sharpened particularity of Hardy's mention of "heaps of couch-grass" in "In Time of 'The Breaking of Nations'" and of Wallace Stevens's distinction between junipers and spruces in "The Snow Man" ("the junipers shagged with ice, / The spruces rough in the distant glitter"[15]). Theodore Roethke brings a wealth of garden lore to his poems; we learn, for example, that pumpkins and basswood give off scents and that rivers bear differing hues according to whether they are glacial or upland in origin. In addition to the heightened angularity of the specific diction in all the poems mentioned in this paragraph ("In Time of 'The Breaking of Nations,'" "The Snow Man," and "The Far Field"), there is the inevitable surprise as the diction in all three grades off into a vocabulary of what feels, in contrast, to be a *plainer* vocabulary of generality. This is the diction of Hardy's "War's annals" and of Roethke's "dream of journeys" (so different from water that is "yellowish-green from the mountainy upland") and of Stevens's more somber vision of the "Nothing that is not there, and the nothing that is."

Diction, Dialect, and Satiric Rhyme

Another example of a poet who shifts diction within poems is the contemporary West Indian formalist poet Derek Walcott, whose satiric poem in the vein of John Wilmot, Earl of Rochester, "The Spoiler's Return," blends official-sounding middle style (for the expression of objection to official government's contradictions)—

> All those who promise free and just debate,
> then blow up radicals to save the state . . .

—with an island patois whose range of affect includes both hilarity and despair:

---

object, a lantern passing further and further away and bearing now east now west of one right line, is truly and properly described as winding," in *Gerard Manley Hopkins: A Selection of His Poetry and Prose,* edited by W. H. Gardner (Harmondsworth: Penguin, 1953), p. 220.

15. However, according to my friend Helen Tartar, junipers don't grow in Connecticut. Stevens was probably drawn to the trisyllabic contrast of *junipers* with the monosyllabic *spruce*—not to mention their shared long *u*.

all you go bawl out, "Spoils, things ain't so bad."
This ain't the Dark Age, is just Trinidad.

Walcott's experience as a dramatist helps him to gauge the audibility of
his ironies with a fine attention to levels of diction.

Another case is that of the late eighteenth-century Scots poet Robert
Burns, who often veers between mandarin speech (in his case this was
educated London speech) and the often alien dialect of Scots. Despite the
insularity of the dialect tongue from our perspective, Burns creates effects
of pathos and surprising subtlety as he moves between the varieties and
buffer-zones of his extremes. Consider "To a Mouse." The first stanza
revels in the colloquial, the mouse described as a "Wee, sleekit, cow'rin,
tim'rous beastie" who flees away from the speaker's plough "Wi' bick-
ering brattle" (hurried scamper). The second stanza is smooth and com-
paratively abstract and polysyllabic: "I'm truly sorry man's dominion . . .
justifies that ill opinion / Which makes thee startle." Stanzas 5 and 6,
concerning the coming winter that will affect the little mouse more
harshly now that the speaker has both destroyed her home and reft her
of the growing grain to eat, abound in agricultural terms (*coulter; stibble;
cranreuch*—plough blade; stubble; hoarfrost). By contrast, the final two
stanzas (7 and 8), rise to a greater height of abstraction—or a more heav-
ily moralizing abstraction—with a corresponding increase in the inti-
macy of the mix of low diction with elevated, nondialect terms (includ-
ing the famous "The best laid schemes o' mice an' men / *Gang* oft *a-
gley*"—often go awry). What is crucial to note, however, is that the sev-
enth and eighth stanzas remain at a level of diction more receptive to
dialect than did the largely English second stanza.

Burns's more satiric "Address to the Unco [unbelievably] Guid, or
the Rigidly Righteous" creates a smooth elevation in diction at the start
of the second stanza, with its capitalized personifications "Wisdom" and
"Folly," alongside a careful staging of interruption by phrases describing
rational motive. This satiric equipoise moves easily through its routines.
Then it seems that Burns takes fire from the ease of this performance to
let in those rougher and more heartfelt phrases like *douce* (grave), *glaiket*
(giddy), and especially *donsie* (reckless)—terms that spring with the added
force of inspired precision and rollicking speed. One also finds this sec-
ond stanza extraordinary because the first and third stanzas envelope it in
folk mist. Through the mist, the more classical face of the passionate sec-
ond stanza becomes clear:

Hear me, ye venerable core,*   *company*
    As counsel for poor mortals,   10
That frequent pass douce Wisdom's door
    For glaiket Folly's portals;
I for their thoughtless, careless sakes
    Would here propone* defenses—   *to offer in excuse*
Their donsie tricks, their black mistakes,   15
    Their failings and mischances.

Burns is now speaking not in his own tongue exclusively but also in theirs to the venerable social elders, people who are rigidly righteous. But despite their cold gaze, Burns cannot help but liven his defense of those others—reckless, ordinary people—with a vocabulary that is sweet and full of feeling. Passion is only strengthened by the disparity between the two competing styles.

The poem ends with a couplet that ordinarily would sound middle-style but whose urgent rhythms belie the comparative elevation of diction and, hence, make the lines sound both low and high at one and the same time (the words opposed in meaning—and diction—are italicized):

What's *done* we partly may compute,
    But know not what's *resisted.*

This couplet reflects a residual rather than an absolute tension of diction-styles. We must imagine, not writing this pair of lines by themselves, but coming to them *through* the accumulated collisions of the previous 62 lines. With this background, we can follow the unusual tenderness emerging as dialect exhausts itself and language becomes clean and flat.

More narrowly focused throughout than Burns is, when A. E. Housman moves from higher to lower diction, it is often his rhyme-phrases that bear out and intensify the contrast:

This is for all ill-treated fellows
    Unborn and unbegot,
For them to read when they're in trouble
    And I am not.

The extremes of diction-shifting are less pronounced in Housman (who moves only from "unborn and unbegot" to the colloquially embedded "and I am not") than is the case with the rhymes of Betjeman and Cunningham. But despite his relative ease in changing from higher to lower diction, the disturbances of *feeling* hinted at in Housman's extremes are more profound. One senses that the composition of the poem brought to light a new jaggedness of self-pity and remorse at the thought of leaving the earth that had not been brought to the surface in Housman's thinking in just this way before.

No such blending is aimed at in some varieties of satiric rhyme that exploit diction-extremes. On the contrary, conspicuous opposition between the peak of one word and the trough of the second makes the accidental symmetry in the rhyme-syllables sound even more bizarre: *bathysphere/hear* (from Daryl Hine's poem "The Trout"), A. D. Hope's rhyme *undeterred/bird,* and Jonathan Swift's highly charged polarities in most of the rhymes in the tetrameter couplets of "Verses on the Death of Doctor Swift, D.S.P.D.," for example, *Writer/Mitre, his Wit decay'd / his Muse a Jade,* and—worse yet—as he humorously examines his own failings, "He's older than he would be reckon'd, / And well remembers *Charles* the Second."

In his comic rhymes in *Don Juan,* Byron puts maximum pressure on elevated polysyllabism with a style of deflation that has a low effect even when the words themselves are middling: *new one/Juan, river/Guadalquivir, Cupid/stupid, Mahogany/dog any.* Edward Lear's **limericks** are rich in unlikely rhymes often involving proper names, for example, *Marseilles/veils, Dutton/Button, up he/puppy.* Such rhymes remind us that much of the unexpectedness of good comic rhyme comes about because the words rhyme not just on syllables but *on the phrase.* In the Hine, Lear, and Hope rhymes above, for example, it is not just single words but entire phrases that conjoin to draw in the rhymes: for example, *bathysphere/cannot hear; But quickly snapt up he / Was once by a puppy; By all his years of exile undeterred / [Crusoe] Took into exile Friday and the bird.*

Rhyming on the phrase is easily grasped in the longer passage. Consider the excerpts below from the couplet poem "Man Friday" by A. D. Hope in which Hope's rhymes, like those of his forebear Alexander Pope, are strengthened by antithesis:

> from "Man Friday"
> Saved at long last through Him whose power to save
> Kept from the walking, as the watery grave,
> Crusoe returned to England and his kind,
> Proof that an unimaginative mind

And sober industry and common sense   5
May supplement the work of Providence.
He, no less providential, and no less
Inscrutably resolved to save and bless,
Eager to share his fortune with the weak
And faithful servants whom he taught to speak,   10
By all his years of exile undeterred
Took into exile Friday and the bird.
· ·
But Friday, the dark Caribbean man,
Picture his situation if you can:
The gentle savage, taught to speak and pray,
On England's Desert Island cast away,
No godlike Crusoe issuing from his cave   25
Comes with his thunderstick to slay and save;
Instead from caves of stone, as thick as trees,
More dreadful than ten thousand savages,
In their strange clothes and monstrous mats of hair,
The pale-eyed English swarm to joke and stare,   30
With endless questions round him crowd and press
Curious to see and touch his loneliness.
· ·
And yet no less than Crusoe he must find
Some shelter for the solitary mind;
Some daily occupation to contrive
To warm his wits and keep the heart alive;
Protect among the cultured, if he can,   45
The "noble savage" and the "natural man."
As Crusoe made his clothes, so he no less
Must labour to invent his nakedness. . .
· ·
Thus he piled memories against his need:
In vain! For still he found the past recede.
Try as he would, recall, relive, rehearse,   70
The cloudy images would still disperse,
Till, as in dreams, the island world he knew
Confounded the fantastic with the true,
While England, less unreal day by day,   75
The Cannibal Island, ate his past away.

Antithesis is achieved in several ways. Most obviously, Hope casts rhymes and rhyme-phrases in opposition to one another (*power to save / watery grave; common sense / work of Providence; the weak* servant / by Crusoe taken up and *taught to speak*). Hope also brings in trope to portray London as the inverse of the Caribbean island where Crusoe was cast away—the island to which, in Defoe's novel, Friday and his tribe came for ritual feasts (Friday was to have been sacrificed at one of these; Crusoe "saved" him). Now in London the houses are *caves of stone, as thick as trees* (line 27) and the eighteenth-century English with their neck scarves and waist-coats and wigs are imagined as a tribe of curious natives (lines 29–30). Unlike Crusoe, who strove to retain his culture and piety in a savage place, Friday's agon is to preserve his natural sensibility among the distortions and savagery of culture (lines 45–48) but eventually—the most extreme of Hope's inverted comparisons—England becomes a Cannibal Island and eats Friday's past away by making him forget it (lines 75–76). Not only do words shift places in Hope's doubly antithetical rhymes, so do concepts.

We might also consider how the proverbial expressions that rhyme employs can be juggled for a witty "cancellation" of the more elevated expression by a more vulgar one: "Here lies Sir Tact, a diplomatic fellow, / Whose silence was not golden, but just yellow." Timothy Steele's couplet singles out the accidental fact that two color-terms, golden and yellow, coincide on the spectrum of hues while representing proverbially opposed values—on the one hand something rare and valuable (gold), on the other something twisted, cowardly, and weak (he is only "yellow"). (See further analysis of the role of rhyme in the couplet in the discussion of stress and interval in chapter 8.)

Diction and Rhythm: Understressed and Overstressed Lines

Like rhyme, rhythm is also affected by diction. Not only does diction affect the level of particularity in the poem, it affects the tempo. The fewer the number of syllables per word, the more words there will be to make up a line—and hence the more the line will tend to be *over*stressed. On the other hand, the line composed of polysyllables will tend to be *under*stressed because polysyllabic words have fewer stresses per total number of syllables. (Note that polysyllabic words tend to have only one major stress; any secondary stresses are usually softer than the primary one.) Thus, the greater the number of syllables per word, the fewer the total of such words that can fit in one line of verse. (The relation of diction—especially as it implies word-length—and meter is discussed further in chapter 8.)

A good example of the way the longest word crowds others out is line 41 of Wordsworth's "Tintern Abbey": "Of all this unintelligible world." In context, this line illustrates other features of "polysyllabism" in metrical verse: rapidity, enjambment, and partial or unfinished syntax. Generally speaking, the use of a more abstract and elevated vocabulary of polysyllables involves a longer syntactical unit that is more rapid in execution (because fewer stresses accumulate despite the regulation number of syllables). Such a sentence will not only exceed the bounds of a single verse line but also generate a significant forward "drive" or momentum as one seeks to conclude the as-yet-unfinished grammatical sequence. Reading the Wordsworth line in context illustrates these traits:

> . . . that blessed mood,
> In which the burthen of the mystery,
> In which the heavy and the weary weight   40
> Of all this unintelligible world
> Is lightened: that serene and blessed mood,
> In which the affections gently lead us on,
> Until . . .

The half-meaning in line 41 is, in the most obvious sense, of a straightforward kind: the sentence is clearly not finished yet. But meaning can also be made by sound and nuance; note how this line's unfinished quality differs, even if only slightly, from that in the two preceding lines, where we also encounter sets of prepositional phrases complete on their own lines. And even in the context of such uniformity, line 41 is the most rapid and at the same time far more dramatic than lines 39 and 40, owing to the self-conscious exorbitance of that six-syllabled abstract word, "un-in-tel-li-gi-ble."[16]

The opposing tendencies of abstract polysyllabism and concrete monosyllabism (resulting in **understressing** and **overstressing**) can be quickly illustrated by examining two poems that manipulate the extremes. First, a poem in plain-style tetrameter quatrains by Timothy Steele:

---

16. This passage will be discussed further in chapter 8's presentation of accentual-syllabic meter.

Toward Calgary

Out over these parched, gusty plains,
Loose dirt is lifted to a sail;
Beyond wide distances, a train's
Smoke draws a horizontal trail.

Posts bear a wire, mile after mile,   5
Across deep views toward which winds roll,
That wire the only obstacle
Between the winds and the North Pole.

Here one could drive what seems an age,
Seeing no more than levelled land   10
And, on the road, slow-skidding sage
And skating shapes of wind-blown sand.

Here one could try the radio's dial
And, as the inching needle slips
Through far, infrequent static, feel   15
A stilled world at the fingertips.

And one might sense nothing but thirst
Or soundless hours in this place
Where all horizons are dispersed
Continuously into space.   20

Yet from caked, crumbly ground and rocks
The spiky purple lupines grow
And cacti shaped like tuning forks.
And some who've crossed such precincts know

The prudent heart is like these plains,   25
Where quietness has grown immense,
No landmarks rendering its terrains
Measurable to human sense,

And where, remote of any tree,
The sky is an inclusive drift   30
Of radiance chastening, endlessly,
Needless invention, needless thrift.

The poem traverses the ground from the slow and particularized line 6, which is nearly all monosyllables ("Across deep views toward which winds roll"), to the expansive rapidity of line 20, which is comparatively polysyllabic ("Continuously into space"). Relative speed, illustrated by dictional rhythms, is clearly also part of the thematic *content* of these lines. In the first case, form echoes the theme of the clouds' dense clustering and concentration, while in the second both theme and form suggest lightness and dispersal.[17]

Differing from Steele's poem in tone and topic, W. H. Auden's sonnet "But in the Evening the Oppression Lifted" also poses extremes of diction in terms of syllable count.

from *In Time of War,* XIX

But in the evening the oppression lifted;
The peaks came into focus; it had rained:
Across the lawns and cultured flowers drifted
The conversation of the highly trained.

The gardeners watched them pass and priced their shoes;   5
A chauffeur waited, reading in the drive,
For them to finish their exchange of views;
It seemed a picture of the private life.

Far off, no matter what good they intended,
The armies waited for a verbal error   10
With all the instruments for causing pain:

And on the issue of their charm depended
A land laid waste, with all its young men slain,
The women weeping, and the towns in terror.[18]

---

17. We will return to Steele's poem in the discussion of trope in chapter 5.

18. This version of the poem originally appeared in *Journey to a War* in 1939 as part of the sonnet sequence, *In Time of War,* which also included a verse commentary. Auden deleted the verse commentary, omitted six of the sonnets, and severely revised the remaining poems as "Sonnets from China" when he included the sequence in *Collected Shorter Poems, 1927–1957.* The revised version of the original Sonnet XIX (renumbered XV in the renamed "Sonnets from China") omits the adversative conjunction "But" and talks instead, in a rather unfocused time, about evening falling and the day's oppression lifting (line 1) and also sacrifices the stronger vowel rhyme of *drive* / private *life* (lines 6 and 8) for the more inert consonant rhyme on the fricative in *drive* / way to *live.*

Line 4 is rapid and ironic ("The conversation of the highly trained"), while the slower line that introduces the sestet of the sonnet uses its insistent monosyllables and frightening cadence to imply a climax that is the mirror image of Steele's sixth verse (Auden's line is: "Far off, no matter what good they intended"). His thirteenth line is still more violent in its emphases: "A land laid waste, with all its young men slain." By contrast with Auden's savagely judgmental overstressing, Steele's overstressed line ("Across deep views toward which winds roll") is depressed in affect (or emotional register) and practically monotonic.

Diction and Trope

We found in speaking of Yeats's style earlier in this chapter a pattern of syntax becoming diction and diction exhibiting features of the sentence frame. Diction can also overlap with the techniques of analogy called trope. W. H. Auden's work is characterized by a habit of abstract diction that easily turns into personification of abstract figures. Auden's Prospero praises Ariel for rescuing the "shy humiliations" from their paralysis and coaxing the "scarred rogue sorrow" down to the watering hole (in *The Sea and the Mirror*). His trick is to choose emotions not typically treated with much tenderness, like "the various envies, all of them sad" from "In Praise of Limestone," while in his great elegy "In Memory of Sigmund Freud" Auden asserts that, because Freud liberated it to be itself, "the household of Impulse mourns one dearly loved."

Diction can overlap at other points with the thickening functions of trope, as for example when repeated initial or mid-word sounds (that is, alliterations) become palpable. Alliteration resembles other devices that thicken the verbal texture; it tends to draw attention away from what words mean to hint at what are often the more or less irrational similarities in their sounds. For example, although we do not entirely ignore the meaning of the words Wallace Stevens uses in his fanciful moments, we are certainly distracted from sense to sound when he writes "Exchequering from piebald fiscs unkeyed" or "whip / In kitchen cups concupiscent curds." The exotic diction is a spoof of itself that makes the bias of Stevens's quirky narrators more prominent while depressing or obscuring *what* is being said (in the first case, paying money from gaudy, opened purses; in the second, whipping cream).

Alliteration can be used less ornamentally. In Howard Nemerov's "Writing," there are no fewer than twenty-three words that alliterate on hard *c* (that is, [k]), but even the lines with the greatest saturation of this feature (like the first, "The cursive scrawl, the squared-off characters") create by comparison with Stevens a "natural" thickening of the verbal texture. Like all poetic devices, alliteration can be given its own continuum; it can also appear toward the self-conscious end of the continuum of diction, and it can cooperate with other techniques of wordplay to increase the poem's consciousness of its medium, a phenomenon the next chapter will explore.

5

Trope and Thought

The Pressure to Compare

There is a tendency for words in the specialized fabric of the poetic line to take on more than their usual significance. It is as if, merely by being watched and listened to more closely than they might be in prose, their greater implications will begin to be felt. Thus the objects in poetry, as well as the words used to describe them, tend to be more alive with suggestion than they would otherwise be. Poems create conditions whereby the objects included in them are their own "natural metaphors" (a **metaphor** is literally a transfer of meaning; the term will designate intended comparison), and the words that render these objects readily become verbal metaphors or **tropes** (a trope is a turn of phrase; the term applies to all devices by which words come to mean twice, from pun at the complex end of the continuum to the natural metaphor called literal symbol at the other). Trope embraces all so-called **figures of thought.**

Greater metaphoric range derives from a monosyllabic and thing-based diction than from an idea-based diction, whose range is, ironically, limited to the abstract. Of course, poems that name feelings require a sturdiness in the frame and handling not required of poems that name only things; but perhaps we must rely on the skills associated with poetic sophistication (quickness, ease, and variety) even more when we move back and forth *between* feeling and thing—especially if the poem that relies on literal settings also plays with trope, or the verbal texture of resemblances.

For example, an empty winter landscape with a bird singing in it already has the makings of a commentary on the solitary poet-speaker, on that speaker's environment, on nature, on the human spirit generally, and on the possibility of hope. When a poet like Thomas Hardy furnishes this subject with further layers of elegance in sound and nuance of suggestion, as he does in "The Darkling Thrush," he is working along the grain of human association with considerable highlighting. Even when unembellished, such natural local details as Hardy's encourage easy and spontaneous transfers from thing to thought (solitude in the external realm suggests solitude within the observer's heart); when trope also comes in to embellish the literal object (the tangled stems "scored the sky / Like strings of broken lyres"), Hardy has doubled comparison away from the literal declarative plane—first, by comparing the stems to broken heavenly instruments, or lyres; next, by asserting that their torn strings rake, as well as musically score, the flat gray sheet of the sky.

To such multiple removes of comparison we can give the name **mixed trope** (not necessarily a pejorative, and frequently quiet rather than loud; consider the gentle extrusion of George Herbert's comparison between ourselves and flowers toward a third realm where both belong by virtue of the verb that suggests swimming rather then growing and dying, "We are but flowers that glide"). While to the natural objects or acts we can give the name **literal symbols.**[1] Examples of the latter include the darkling thrush from the Hardy poem, the gray tiny rocks in Muir's "Childhood," the bird singing in its sleep in Frost's sonnet, the trout in Nemerov's "The Sanctuary," the sea and the land in "The Slow Pacific Swell" by Yvor Winters, and the sleeping city in Wordsworth's sonnet "Composed upon Westminster Bridge":

> Earth has not anything to show more fair:
> Dull would he be of soul who could pass by
> A sight so touching in its majesty:
> This City now doth like a garment wear
> The beauty of the morning; silent, bare,
> Ships, towers, domes, theatres, and temples lie
> Open unto the fields, and to the sky;
> All bright and glittering in the smokeless air.
> Never did sun more beautifully steep

5

---

1. It was Christine Brooke-Rose who devised the name **literal symbol** for the literal things that achieve symbolic meaning in poetry since the Romantics. See her *Grammar of Metaphor* (London: Secker & Warburg, 1958), pp. 320–23.

In his* first splendor, valley, rock, or hill;   *its 10
Ne'er saw I, never felt, a calm so deep!
The river glideth at his own sweet will:
Dear God! the very houses seem asleep;
And all that mighty heart is lying still!

When we ask what the sleeping city is literally symbolic *of*, we begin to
realize the subtle projections of the human self who does the observing,
for the city lies down upon the folds of landscape *like* a landscape rather
than something built. It also resembles a natural scene in presenting itself
as an appealing nook for the continuation of human life. And when we
look out from within the poem's account of what is being experienced,
we note that the city's radiant appearance is in part a description of the
observing attitude, which is rapt and elated, while London's as yet distant
and unawakened calm (11) is as deep as the feeling awakened in the
viewer from his perch of privilege. The sonnet explores a literal place by
making its operative symbolism one that is based on nature.[2]

To a certain extent, we deal with literal symbols whenever we invoke
the four elements, the spaces in which we spend most our time (rooms,
cars, halls, beds), and the landscapes and thresholds about us (gardens,
shores, mountains, walls, gates, doors, highways, side-roads, toll booths).
Even the "few first flakes" of snow in Howard Nemerov's blank sonnet
"Again" are "given" to the poet as emblems of fragility and of fate by
habits of association that we share with him (see the text of the poem in
the fourth chapter's discussion of diction). That these are the *first* flakes
insures that the water isn't yet cold enough to support them (hence they
"drown"); but the implication is that, soon enough, the world will freeze
hard and so destroy us as individuals more completely than were these
"few first" cases of the doom with which we so poignantly identify our-
selves. Thus our loneliness as individuals becomes cosmic as the associa-
tions of the literal symbol ripple outward and the autumnal season be-
comes permanent winter.

Our perceptual sympathy for small objects in the distance suggests a
psychological principle true of most watchers, namely, that the fewer the

---

2. W. K. Wimsatt explores these physical and psychological transfers in "The Struc-
ture of Romantic Nature Imagery" in *The Verbal Icon: Studies in the Meaning of Poetry* (Lex-
ington: University of Kentucky Press, 1967).

numbers of things before us, the more ready we are to associate our feel-
ings with the sprinkle of items in a sparse and simplified scene. It is this
law of simplified focus and empathy to which we owe the power of
the metaphor called "literal symbol." Wordsworth follows the one ship
"with a Lover's look," preferring it to everything else in the scene (the
sonnet "With Ships the Sea Was Sprinkled Far and Nigh"). The single
lantern moving unevenly against the darkness in the Hopkins sonnet (see
the text in the "Poetry Sampler" in chapter 1) calls to mind the hand,
and then the person holding it, then the journey that man is making, and
finally the wistful flare of that person's beauty against the surrounding
darkness: such journeyings "rain against our much-thick and marsh air /
Rich beams, till death or distance buys them quite." The lantern is a **me-
tonymy** for the person holding it and a literal symbol of light in the
darkness.[3]

This law of perceptual identification evoked by simplified forms
causes us to project our sympathy more readily when we find the focal
object in a scene. Edwin Muir imagines a haunted Hector—after his de-
feat by Achilles—reliving the moments of his humiliation:

Yes, this is where I stood that day,
    Beside this sunny mound.
The walls of Troy are far away,
    And outward comes no sound.

I wait. On all the empty plain   5
    A burnished stillness lies,
Save for the chariot's tinkling hum,
    And a few distant cries.

His helmet glitters near. The world
    Slowly turns around,   10
With some new sleight compels my feet
    From the fighting ground.

I run. If I turned back again
    The earth must turn with me,
The mountains planted on the plain,   15
    The sky clamped to the sea.

~

3. **Metonymy** will be further discussed later in this chapter.

The grasses puff a little dust
    Where my footsteps fall.
I cast a shadow as I pass
    The little wayside wall.   20

The strip of grass on either hand
    Sparkles in the light . . .

                                ("Ballad of Hector in Hades")

Hector's fearful and agitated mind fixes on the strip of ground where the race takes place between himself and the eternal winner, Achilles, until this strip of unremarkable ground, dotted with low wildflowers, resonates with a more-than-ordinary significance.

The flowers do not, however, symbolize any one thing; rather, they suggest the heated anxiety of Hector's soul eager to overleap the fact of the terrible race that now, in hell, he is doomed to repeat. So the flowers come to suggest—without being actual **symbols** of—his cowardly fixation on innocent nature:

The strip of grass on either hand
    Sparkles in the light;
I only see that little space
    To the left and to the right,

And in that space our shadows run,   25
    His shadow there and mine,
The little flowers, the tiny mounds,
    The grasses frail and fine.

But narrower still and narrower!
    My course is shrunk and small,   30
Yet vast as in a deadly dream,
    And faint the Trojan wall.
The sun up in the towering sky
    Turns like a spinning ball.

The sky with all its clustered eyes   35
    Grows still with watching me,
The flowers, the mounds, the flaunting weeds
    Wheel slowly round to see.
  ~

Two shadows racing on the grass,
> Silent and so near,   40
Until his shadow falls on mine.
> And I am rid of fear.

The race is ended. Far away
> I hang and do not care,
While round bright Troy Achilles whirls   45
> A corpse with streaming hair.

("Ballad of Hector in Hades")

Although the tiny plants, flowers, and weeds do not engage any inherited system of meaning and hence do not carry acknowledged spiritual associations (unlike, say, the rose in medieval poetry, with its mystical and Christian associations with the Virgin Mary, or "coded" flowers like those listed by Ophelia in *Hamlet* IV.v—fennel [flattery], rue [regret], daisy [masking or pretense], violet [faithfulness]), nevertheless it's clear that these literal landscape details in Muir's poem are being invested with suggestive power beyond the literal. No small part of their radiant pathos lies in their paradoxical nearness to the doomed hero, who can no longer leap through his ordeal into their world of innocent self-containment.

The source of the strength to "suggest beyond" the local and literal may come, however, not so much from the elaboration of a mythic superstructure as from the care with which the immediate is seen and rendered. That hypothetical foot race between the powerful Achilles and the warrior he eventually kills is viewed from the perspective of the loser, Hector. Muir mentions in his autobiography that throughout his youth he was haunted by his cowardice when faced with a bully named Freddy Sinclair, who would wait for him after school (Muir ran from him, but couldn't get away, and the memory seemed to concentrate on the path pounded by his ineffectually running feet). This boyhood experience deepens the mature poet's evocation of Hector's terror, just as it illuminates something about the character of Achilles and his relentless pursuit of the victim.

Focus on any immediate surroundings may not automatically carry such a weight of feeling, however. Dante Gabriel Rossetti's poem "The Woodspurge" rejects background while giving us an emotional foreground of pretty strict limitation:

My hair was over in the grass,
My naked ears heard the day pass.

My eyes, wide open, had the run
Of some ten weeds to fix upon;   10
Among those few, out of the sun,
The woodspurge flowered, three cups in one.

From perfect grief there need not be
Wisdom or even memory:
One thing then learnt remains to me,—   15
The woodspurge has a cup of three.

The poem recreates a certain adolescent desperation, which is closed to comfort and aggressive toward questions, and it rather dares us to find fault with its postures. In this atmosphere of pronouncement, the little woodspurge flower gets somewhat lost. While this may well be part of the poem's charm, it does keep the flower from reverberating very far beyond itself. Contrast the final two stanzas of Muir's "Ballad of Hector in Hades": There we see the sufferer (who is both the Hector of the Homeric epic and the boyhood persona of the poet) frozen against his shadow in a tableau that nevertheless moves across a great distance. This is the distance of time, but also the distance in which the self, too, becomes mythic, objective, and pathetically small ("a corpse with streaming hair").

The Concept of the Continuum

Let's imagine again (as in the "Three Working Concepts" that introduce Part I) the constant line called a continuum that expresses some feature or relation, on which we can display the range from more to less natural examples. We can put at one extreme the natural or literal symbol—a form of expression whose exact wording is less important than the archetypal associations evoked by certain places, events, and objects. Contrast with archetypes the objects whose meanings are assigned, as hope to the anchor, or flattery to the fennel plant, or perfection to the circle. Such word-ideas would occur in the middle of the metaphoric continuum. At the other end of the continuum from literal symbol we would place the usages that bring verbal expression into the foreground and remove the literal referents into the background—in other words, the varieties of trope bound up with the techniques of mysterious likeness and echo called **pun** (wordplay stemming from likeness in sound and difference in sense).

Note that these extremes require one another. A **continuum** can be defined only by designating two poles—even if the polarities in their purest forms never occur. To speak of Hardy as a user of literal symbol, whether in one of his more ornate poems like "The Darkling Thrush," or in one of his more stolid and laconic poems like "The Walk" (see chapter 6 on rhetoric), for example, we must know whose literal symbols we believe to be more subtle than his (Yeats might provide examples, say in his poems in which a stick represents a body; age makes him "Old clothes upon old sticks to scare a bird" ["The Tower"] or "a tattered coat upon a stick" ["Sailing to Byzantium"]). Then we need to wonder whose literal symbols are so much less subtle as to flirt with being merely literal, as in Roethke's "The Heron," Oliver's "Cyclic" (late in the present chapter), and the items in many of Nemerov's poems.

A continuum also requires us to project a continuous series of minute gradations from one end to the other (eventually, these collective examples would approximate all of literary history). Usage at one end becomes more sensible by reference both to the use from which it most differs and to that which is only slightly different. Intermediate usages are definable by reference to the two cases just to each side, which exhibit greater allegiance to the extremes than does the poem they flank. Thus, the continuum helps us not just by establishing a given poem's place with respect to fairly widely removed examples but also by asking us to make minute discriminations when placed against poems it closely resembles; this latter exercise may tell us even more than the first, insofar as it asks us to weigh the most slight and shifting differences from one poem to the next rather than the most obvious ones.

Note, too, that the concept of a comparative line, or continuum, can be employed whenever the possibility for divergent style exists. Actually, we have already been using the idea of continua in presenting the six points of style (which constitute the six chapters of Part I of this guide). The method is effective in helping us to bring poems together for comparative ends. A continuum of syntax enables us to focus our attention on the varieties of sentence-form, from simple, indicative, and paratactic to hypotactic, complex, and subjunctive (hypothetical [*if-then* frames], contrary-to-fact, and optative [*if-only* frames]). Rhetoric, rhythm, and line (vis-à-vis enjambment) will also benefit from analysis by means of the continuum.

Similarly, when we try to grasp the language or vocabulary of a poem, we try to put poems along a continuum of diction, from monosyllabic, low, and plain style, to polysyllabic, high, and sophisticated. There are poems like *The Waste Land* that exhibit minute gradations along many points of the diction continuum, from low (*chemist, taxi, food in tins, C.i.f. [cost/insurance/freight paid to] London*) to high (*laquearia, the barbarous king, the young man carbuncular*). On the continuum of metaphor, we could then note how T. S. Eliot varies his diction at the "low" end to produce metaphor by making the *stony rubbish* and *frosty silence in the gardens* representative of personal and religious anguish: they are literally symbolic. At the "high" end of Eliot's diction continuum, metaphor, trope, and allusion likewise intensify the verbal elegance of the diction in the *Murmur of maternal lamentation* and *hooded hordes* and *Ionian white and gold,* in the river's tent and death by water and fear in a handful of dust and the nymphs departed; even the taxi finds a place of greater elevation than its common use and appearance warrant by means of association with the motor of the human body and the almost clinical depression of the winter dusk, as the heart waits throbbing like a taxi for some sign of ease.

Neither metaphor nor diction will account for the command of such effects if they are considered in isolation from each other. In fact, the action of Eliot's intense metaphoric implications works to dispel the bland base of his vocabulary-of-objects (desk, engine, taxi). He steers them away from the bureaucratic and industrial contexts toward archetypal settings of threat, servitude, physical reduction, and psychological despair.

For the purposes of this chapter on trope and metaphor, the literal-versus-artificial metaphoric continuum will help us to discriminate simple images from elaborate verbal tropes if we are careful whenever we discuss *one* poem to bring forward additional poems and additional examples within the poem underway, for purposes of comparison. In such a comparative context, then, the trend of any *new* verses' tendency to side with simple image (picture) or thing, on one hand, or with elaborate trope and allegory (on the other)—or to tread a movable margin somewhere in the middle range—can teach us how meaning is embodied in the individual case, to be sure. And it can also teach us how and when all the neighboring types along one continuum characteristically combine with other points of style. Further, instead of being a simple black-and-white method of contrasting examples of technique, the continua may

be blended—high diction on occasion (say in Betjeman's "Death in Lea-
mington"—see the stanza quoted in chapter 4 on diction) coinciding
with abrupt end-stopping, blunt rhymes, and a syntax on the whole
simple and declarative. Just so, in other poems, low diction can mesh with
variably subtle syntax and enjambment (see Dickinson, also in chapter 4).
Simplicity in one area does not limit us to simplicity in all.

The Continuum of Trope

Returning to the continuum of **trope,** we find **pun** at the other extreme.
In pun, overt wordplay, or double meaning, it is not so much the *thing*
that resonates with meaning as the *word* itself that is made into an object
of interest. It is as if each word could speak twice, once to denote its
meaning, then to evoke layered suggestion. The origins of words (ety-
mologies), tending as they do, early on, to be physical in reference, play
off against the subsequent application of words to emotional and mental
experience, when abstractions are formed.[4]

Parallel to the way etymologies return to root meanings and contrast
these with derived meanings is the way punning overlays the "literal
roots" with proverbial expression or turn of phrase. Literal and meta-
phorical are usually at odds but do not cancel each other out, as we see in
Alexander Pope's couplet about Queen Anne: "Here Thou, Great *Anna!*
whom three Realms obey, / Dost sometimes Counsel take—and some-
times *Tea*"[5] (*The Rape of the Lock* III, ll. 7–8). To take (or drink) tea is the
literal base of the same verb Pope applies to the insubstantial "thing,"
the counsel of the queen's advisors (she is taking or soliciting their advice).
(Note that the literal sense is listed as #13 in the *OED*[6] under "take,"
while the latter sense [take counsel; seek advice] is listed as #53, thus
coming much later in the word's history.) In another famous pairing Pope
uses "stain" in two senses, one insubstantial and hypothetical ("Or stain
her Honour"), the other substantive and literal (". . . or [stain] her new
Brocade," II.107). This use of one word to yoke two phrases across the

4. See the discussion of the **etymological style** of diction in chapter 4.
5. *Obey/Tea* is a historical rhyme, although to us the rhyme is fictitious.
6. The twelve-volume *OED* or *Oxford English Dictionary* (originally compiled by
primary editor Sir James Murray and his co-editors Bradley, Craigie, and Onions between
1897 and 1928) is the reference of choice for etymologies of words, as well as for their
history of usage since their original occurrences in English.

literal-metaphorical boundary is a variant of a figure of speech called
zeugma (yoking), one of Pope's favorite tropes in *The Rape of the Lock.*

Comparing Great with Small and Inner with Outer

As his poem's title further suggests, Pope is engaged throughout in taking
the trivial seriously, comparing the very small (a lock of hair) with the
very great (the idea of a rape that might have epic consequences); hence
the genre of the poem, **mock epic.** One important use of the contin-
uum to understand metaphor is to describe the central theme of meta-
phoric comparison according to whether the implication is literal and
implied or overt and embellished. This central theme is the approach of
the small to the great, the physical to the notional.

At the heart of metaphor is the act of providing a visible object with
implied value—in other words, making the small "large." The spray of
artificial roses on the little dancer's bodice in Elizabeth Bishop's poem
"Cirque d'Hiver" (see text in the "Poetry Sampler" in chapter 1) is a
visible object connected to the dancer in a way that comes to represent
her. The large traits suggested by the small ornament are flaws of her
character—artificiality and empty-headedness. In other poems, the large
to which the small item points may be abstract, because the force of the
small and local thing (when forcefully envisioned) so often presses out
toward meaning that is mental or spiritual. "Underneath this stone doth
lie," Ben Jonson's epitaph claims, "As much beauty as could die." The
stone is not really a literal symbol (unlike Bishop, Jonson fends off serious
attention to any locale) but a link, called **metonymy,** in which one thing
represents another closely related one: The stone represents the dead girl
beneath it, just as the words "this stone" represent the stone into
which—because he is writing an epitaph—these words are or will be
carved. (We will return to the discussion of metonymy later in this
chapter.)

William Blake spins out scores of impassioned tetrameter couplets
that insist on the justice of citing the small to implicate the great: "A
Robin Red breast in a Cage / Puts all Heaven in a Rage." Blake mean-
while suggests, by comparison with other large forces (Heaven, the Last
Judgment, God), that a mother's sorrow and individual belief are also mo-
mentous: "The Caterpillar on the Leaf / Repeats to thee thy Mother's
grief"; "The Bat that flits at close of Eve / Has left the Brain that won't

Believe."[7] Robert Burns has already shown us how the small creature (the wee cowering mouse) can lead a contrite ploughman to thoughts about the best-laid schemes of men, which are equally vulnerable to destruction. And finally, like Blake, who wrote

> The Strongest Poison ever known
> Came from Caesar's Laurel Crown.
>
> ("Auguries of Innocence," ll. 97–98)

〰〰

> How the Chimney-sweeper's cry
> Every black'ning Church appalls;   10
> And the hapless Soldier's sigh
> Runs in blood down Palace walls.
>
> ("London")

—W. B. Yeats obtains great resonance from the assumption that the flame of atrocity first kindles in the heart of a restless and unsatisfied individual. Displacements of size occur in Yeats's work on a smaller scale than they do in Blake's: the herald is reduced to his cry and the soldier to his tread. But the heart to which humanity is also reduced is so combustible (because soaked with resin) that the world can catch fire from it:

> The herald's cry, the soldier's tread
> Exhaust his glory and his might:
> Whatever flames upon the night
> Man's own resinous heart has fed.
>
> (song from the play *Resurrection*)

Yeats's abstractions are combustible, too: glory, might, and the flames of a city being burnt are given literal dimensions by the idea that human energy feeds these fires and historical dimension by the setting of the play, which is the time of Christ's crucifixion and resurrection.

To imply something great through concentration on something small, the poet must find the right objects and then the means of shifting the conception of them from one realm to another. The most common

---

7. Just as Heaven is enraged by the caged bird, the Last Judgment likewise punishes cruelty: "Kill not the moth nor Butterfly / For the Last Judgment draweth nigh" ("Auguries of Innocence").

means is comparison; even puns hold up, for a moment, the unlikely and unrelated words in distorted proximity, as in a funhouse mirror. Between wordplay at one end of the metaphor-continuum, and literal symbol at the other, we can find all the kinds of transfer (metaphor) or turn (trope) by which one thing is compared with or turned into another. Most metaphors will align themselves either with the natural or the artificial end of the continuum. When we discussed Emily Dickinson's "My Life had stood—a Loaded Gun" (#754), we said that "kill" and "die" and weaponry and explosions would be abstractions when applied to love and service. In fact, they are the abstractions more aptly called metaphors whereby the **tenor** or meaning of the comparison is implied by the action of the terms (the **vehicle**) transferred from another realm of discourse. Usually something physical and capable of being imagined by us visually (an **image**—like the loaded gun) is transferred from the literal realm over to the spiritual to imply some emotional or mental tenor, as killing and dying in the physical realm are transferred by Dickinson over to the arena where they imply devotion to a godlike master. Given the length at which Dickinson unfolds them, there is considerable coherence linking vehicle to tenor in this instance. If one were to try to represent the same complex tenorial meaning by transferring terms from gardening or card-playing or medicine, it would be harder—perhaps impossible—to suggest the same tortuous and dangerous potential for self-sacrifice as Dickinson does by impersonating a lethal weapon. We should note in passing, however, that her cast of mind made domestic decor both familiar and lethal: consider her poem beginning "A Clock stopped— / Not the Mantel's . . . An awe came on the Trinket! / The Figures hunched, with pain— / Then quivered out of Decimals— / Into Degreeless Noon—."[8] So we would place Dickinson's metaphor midway between the literal symbol and pun, perhaps leaning a bit toward the pole of artifice. (**Tenor** and **vehicle** will be discussed again below.)

Overt Comparison versus Naturalistic Suggestion

John Donne's comparison of the lovers' souls to the joined legs of a draftsman's compass in "A Valediction: Forbidding Mourning" is a selective analogy (developed for four lines as one of several tropes having to do with response to separation) more artificial than, say, Howard Nemerov's

8. #287 "A Clock stopped—."

comparison of the openings in a stream bed, made by many small springs, to "mouths of sand,"[9] Eleanor Wilner's personification of the small wind picking through the debris of the battlefield as "an indigent in search of scraps,"[10] or even Mark Strand's mixed trope comparing the lights on the bridges across Manhattan's rivers to "harps of beaded lights / that vault the rivers of New York" ("Always"). In all three, there is verisimilitude of suggestion: in the first poem, the puffs of water coming out of the earth make the sandy apertures move like mouths and support the imagery of the stream as a body so that the trout, with the delicate reflex of its tail, can remain suspended against the current, resembling what the speaker thinks of as the habit of a human being's thought.

In Wilner's poem, the personification of the wind as a little tramp lifelessly sifting through the garbage of ruin moderates the unlikelihood of the wind becoming a person by the coherence of tenor with vehicle, since "debris," "indigent," and "scraps" all come from the same realm. In the Strand example, the appearance of harps is owing to the verifiable, literal shape made by the electric lights outlining the bridge cables, and even his mixed trope ("vault the rivers") is moderated by the celestial link between the music of a harp and the vault of the night sky.

Verisimilitude and likeness in reference between such vehicles and their tenors make it possible to move from literal symbol to full-blown classical allusion, as we see in David Ferry's "Photographs from a Book," III, quoted and discussed later in this chapter, in which the fading of the flowers in the young women's hair in an Eakins's photo suddenly ages them mythically, and Ferry hears an Ovidian voice recounting the cruel entrapments of Persephone in the underworld and of Dryope with her breasts turning to tree bark.

In Donne's poem, however, there is no touch of naturalness *or* mythic transformation. The lovers are not even remotely like a compass: they aren't joined at the heads; they aren't skinny, wooden (as drafting compasses were in the Renaissance), or rigid; they aren't mathematical and exact. But they *are* like a hinged compass ("As stiffe twin compasses are two") in the one respect for which Donne chose the analogy—because movement by one "leg" produces an adjusted response from the other:

9. See the passage from Nemerov's "The Sanctuary" in chapter 3's discussion of syntax.

10. "Operations: Desert Shield, Desert Storm," l. 27. The full text of Wilner's poem appears in chapter 1's "Poetry Sampler."

If they be two, they are two so   25
　　As stiffe twin compasses are two,
Thy soule the fixt foot, makes no show
　　To move, but doth, if th' other doe.

Now although Donne is not "punning"—not drawing attention away
from sense to sound—he is engaged in comparison of a kind that is sym-
pathetic to wordplay by permitting and even encouraging far-fetched
linkages, which he rescues from absurdity by witty interpretation. Nem-
erov and Strand, on the other hand, work toward greater coincidence
between the qualities of their vehicle and the implications of their tenor.

　　Donne is also engaged in a comparison, called a **simile,** in which the
tenor is pointedly distinguished from the vehicle by the terms *like* or *as:*
"they *are* two *so / As* stiff twin compasses *are* two." The simile introduces
foreign material into the realm of the tenor. When taken to extremes in
the comparison called **epic simile,** the overt comparison is one of many
devices that provide interlude and variety in long poems. A good ex-
ample is the comparison of the sleeping Satan to mythic monsters like
Typhon and Briareos in *Paradise Lost* I.197–207 (see chapter 3 on syntax
for quotation of the passage).

　　Another sort of deliberate unnaturalness in Renaissance poetry by
Donne, Milton, and Shakespeare is the exaggerated posture. In Sonnet
31, Shakespeare exaggerates the role assigned to the beloved, whom he
imagines as the occasion for the weakening (to the point of death) of all
earlier ties and affections (which in turn function as persons).

Thou art the grave where buried love doth live,
Hung with the trophies of my lovers gon,   10
Who all their parts of me to thee did give.

　　　　　　　　　　　　　　　　　　　　　　　　　　　　(Sonnet 31)

The beloved is both a grave-site where other dead loves are collected
and the funerary place where the other supplanted lovers relinquish their
trophies formerly obtained from the speaker as love tokens. Now the *you*
possesses these trophies as decoration. This metaphor actually moves in
several stages, sometimes with an eerie rightness among the ambiguities it
creates (the *you* is alive and exercising great attraction upon the speaker).

　　Above all, we realize how uninterested in description of a naturalistic
sort Sonnet 31 is. Like Donne's, this sonnet is hardly "realistic." As Rosa-

mund Tuve points out, Renaissance poets would have been unconvinced by (and even a little mocking toward) our modern preoccupation with the local, whether the literalness that results pertains to perceptual states or to psychologically focused response.[11] Poets in the Renaissance attended, more than modern poets have done, to the illustrative, deliberative, and persuasive operations of verse. But such preferences as Donne's and ours tend to move in cycles. As there were poets before Donne who valued spontaneity above artifice, so there will be poets and readers to come after us who turn against our cultural tastes and replace artifice above authenticity.

There is, moreover, a "hidden tradition" of argument and wit concealed in ostensibly "naturalistic" poetry. Robert Frost's tableau of the white spider holding up the victim moth in "Design" is not so far removed from the so-called metaphysical wit of a poet like John Donne (see "Twicknam Garden": "that this place may thoroughly be thought / True Paradise, I have the serpent brought"). However, Donne sets out with a propensity toward idea then temporarily admits into the poem analogies and stage props to embody that idea (he mentions no spiders at Twickenham, but this doesn't prevent his speaker from being haunted by "The spider love"). Frost, on the other hand, withholds the idea which his literal objects embody until the poem's very close, concentrating instead on the impression made by moth and spider in a convincing natural landscape. In "A Valediction: Forbidding Mourning," Donne's compass makes the bond between the parting couple abstract (but no less "real" for that), whereas in "Design" Frost requires us to stare with horror at the scene he paints before we can begin to "read" it.[12]

We could also say that the difference between the sensuous intellectuality of a poem like "A Baroque Wall Fountain in the Villa Sciarra,"[13] by Richard Wilbur, and a metaphysical-deliberative poem such as "A

---

11. See Rosamund Tuve's landmark book on metaphor, *Elizabethan and Metaphysical Imagery: Renaissance Poetic and Twentieth-Century Critics* (Chicago: University of Chicago Press, 1947), especially pp. 3–26. Tuve's central argument is that we must not ascribe to Renaissance poems an ideal of sensuous immediacy with which only the twentieth-century poem is comfortable. See my annotation for Tuve in chapter 14's suggestions for further reading.

12. Frost may have been following Thomas Hardy in the plot of "Design." See the discussion of Hardy's "An August Midnight" in chapter 6 on rhetoric.

13. The poem appears in *New and Collected Poems,* by Richard Wilbur (New York: Harcourt Brace Jovanivich, 1989), pp. 271–73.

Valediction: Forbidding Mourning" by Donne, with its layering of clues upon the somewhat artificial physical object of the drafting compass, or between Wilbur's poem and Milton's "L'Allegro" and "Il Penseroso," with their landscapes like exhaustively detailed stage sets, is that Wilbur starts from and remains rooted in (and even nobly obsessed by) the total particularity of texture, vision, and association brought out in looking at the two Roman fountains. In time, he compares the two fountains to the bestial and spiritual sides of man's nature—Wilbur by no means recoils from abstraction. But he does not begin with that polarity and then conveniently or even designedly happen upon locales with statuary fountains that might illustrate it.

Primacy of the immediate scene likewise differentiates Louise Bogan's "Song for a Lyre" from George Herbert's "The Flower." Herbert's poem acknowledges and even admires the physical but readily moves beyond it to the psychological dimension:

> How fresh, O Lord, how sweet and clean
> Are thy returns! ev'n as the flowers in spring;
>   To which, besides their own demean,*   *demeanor*
> The late-past frosts tributes of pleasure bring.
>   Grief melts away   5
>   Like snow in May,
>   As if there were no such cold thing.
>
>   Who would have thought my shrivel'd heart
> Could have recover'd greennesse? It was gone
>   Quite under ground; as flowers depart   10
> To see their mother-root, when they have blown;*   *bloomed out*
>   Where they together
>   All the hard weather,
>   Dead to the world, keep house unknown.
>   . . . .
>   And now in age I bud again,
> After so many deaths I live and write;
>   I once more smell the dew and rain,
> And relish versing: O my onely light,
>   It cannot be   40
>   That I am he
>   On whom thy tempests fell all night.

We believe in the reality of the "frosts," seasonal "deaths," and "tempests," but we are not engaged in the perceptions peculiar to them. Whereas in Louise Bogan's lyric, for example, there are no psychological insights that are not, to begin with, pervasively embodied in a scene with visualizable and almost painterly focal depth (see text of "Song for a Lyre" in chapter 3). This poem's final assertion, that night belongs to and reminds her of the beloved's voice in the past, points us back from the state of recollection to the scenic markers of her autumnal mind—the leaves in throngs, the warm stream on the cold ground, the cooling stars.

Allegory and Explicit Tenor

There is a long tradition of poems with an **allegorical** bent (a tendency to cast a story about one kind of thing in terms germane to another kind—for example, a story about the growth of spiritual insight and discipline such as Spenser's *Faerie Queene,* couched in terms of chivalric quest and trial). There is usually some rationale for the choice of vehicle (as the knight's quest overlays a spiritual journey upon a geographical one). Simply put, the difference between Renaissance allegory and the modern poem with some residual impulse toward the allegorical is that in a modern poem there is greater realism of relation between the imported idea (called the **vehicle** because it carries the meaning) and the meaning itself (or **tenor**—what is represented or "held" by the vehicle or the analogy brought in for illustration). Consider the eerie setting of the contemporary poet Thom Gunn's "In Praise of Cities." The city is personified so that the tawdry glitter and physical temptations of certain districts which the speaker frequents suggest the individual and human form of a prostitute. This figure is at once a female person and a variable place—a specific shape, but present everywhere in less (or more) than human form:

> from "In Praise of Cities"
>
> Casual yet urgent in her lovemaking,
> She constantly asserts her independence:
> Suddenly turning moist pale walls upon you
> —Your own designs, peeling and unachieved—
> Or her whole darkness hunching in an alley.   5
> And all at once you enter the embrace
> Withheld by day while you solicited.

While Thom Gunn has worked to strengthen the poem with archetypes from the literary tradition, those traditions of temptation attributed to the female also help him to cloud the personal link. And this clouding is appropriate to the restless infernal beat of endless cities like London and New York where one becomes blessedly anonymous.

> She wanders lewdly, whispering her given name,
> Charing Cross Road, or Forty-Second Street:
> The longest streets, desire that never ends,   10
> Familiar and inexplicable, wearing
> Cosmetic light a fool could penetrate.
> She presses you with her hard ornaments,
> Arcades, late movie shows, the piled lit windows
> Of surplus stores. Here she is loveliest;   15
> Extreme, material, and the work of man.
>
> ("In Praise of Cities")

The structure of desire represented by Gunn's "literal allegory" deepens the aura of revulsion at what attracts us. For this feminized city, familiar to us from Baudelaire and Hart Crane, is "Extreme, material, and the work of man." Yet the icon continues to project its dangerous magic. She/it is the collective emblem of success, the contraband trophy brought back from a dangerous self-destructive foray into forbidden areas. Furthermore, as part of the allegorical cloak, Gunn has displaced onto the sinister female anatomy ("moist pale walls"), the taboo attraction a homosexual poet-sojourner would feel more spontaneously toward other men.[14]

Allegory cannot be said to work at its best on a scale any more limited than Gunn's. And yet the scale of this poem (thirty-four lines long) is inadequate to launch a successful allegory. Gunn as the poet has compressed association so that the realistic and the implied are locally meshed; the extent of local realism departs from the practice of allegorists such as Dante and Spenser. In addition, there is no "neutral" narrative line (allegory requires that there be in some sense a story, with a chronology and a dramatic arc). Nevertheless, the presence of allegory in literary history brings out an important possibility even in modern poems that fall short of it—the possibility, as Northrop Frye puts it,[15] that the events of a narra-

---

14. We will return to a discussion of **personification** at the end of the chapter.
15. See Frye's entry on allegory in the *Princeton Encyclopedia,* 1974 edition, p. 12a.

tive might "obviously and continuously refer to another simultaneous structure of events or ideas." As in allegory, so the pressure in all poetry is outward from the local toward the moral and spiritual.

In the four lines of Yeats's "Balloon of the Mind," the vehicle of metaphoric association is more "allegorical" and artificial than Gunn's city, because it seems to have been invented for purposes of illustration: The balloon does not exist in the neighborhood or the room where the poet is cautioning himself about his work. With respect to implication of locale, even Shakespeare's Sonnet 73 ("That time of yeeare [year] thou maist in me behold") is more engaged with details of a possible (autumnal) setting than is Yeats with his balloon in the wind.

But Yeats's poem may be "local" in a somewhat different way. First of all, the vehicle is more inclusive and complex than the balloon-whose-tenor-is-the-mind: this identification, after all, is already given to us in the title. The poem's vehicle is also made up of hands (the extensions of the body), balloon, and narrow shed; but to properly trace their links, we would have to account for the fact that the poem begins with a command to the hands. We break in on a gesture of impatience; thought had gotten "out of hand," as the saying goes, and the usual custodians of thought are not functioning smoothly. So the poet-speaker must jostle them into action: "Hands, do what you're bid."

> The Balloon of the Mind
>
> Hands, do what you're bid:
> Bring the balloon of the mind
> That bellies and drags in the wind
> Into its narrow shed.

Thus the tenor of this four-line vehicle is only minimally and provisionally associated with the mind; that association may be necessary but is insufficiently general. We quickly have to press on to the clues Yeats gives about the kind of temperament this vehicle of the unresponsive and disobedient subject (represented by the balloon) is supposed to carry. Yeats's balloon-mind is unwieldy; it "bellies and drags in the wind"; therefore it is a mind subject to (metaphorically considered) "currents," being light and whimsical and at best loosely moored. To control it, another faculty must be employed from elsewhere in the psyche. The hands, which bring the mind into its shed, must represent—not the body, really, but more the *active will* of the poet or thinker. Then the content of the thought that is balloonlike, or light-headed, can be imagined as the property of a mind given over to daydream or idle yearning. In its narrow shed of discipline, the energy of the daydreaming mind can be, if not quelled entirely, then corralled, made orderly and effectual. (We know from letters and anecdotes that Yeats worked hard to discipline himself to write, having himself a temptation to drift.)

"The Balloon of the Mind" is a poem of interrelatedness between tenor and vehicle as thoroughgoing as it can be short of using the same terms for both (as happens in literal symbol and metonymy). The closer the vehicle to the tenor—that is, the more numerous are the points of resemblance and continuity between the content of the thought and the terms representing the thought—then the more natural the metaphor as a result and the more it appears found rather than made. This quality of inevitability in turn will affect our sense of the speaker's naturalness and spontaneity.

Metonymy

At the other end of the metaphoric continuum from Donne's stiff twin compasses and closer to literal symbol than Yeats's equation of mind with balloon, we could place the representation of whole by part, of thing by closely related thing, or of person by his or her possessions—examples of a subclass of metaphor called **metonymy**.[16] Often persons will be represented by the objects about them, especially by their clothes. Thus attractive, elegant, or intricate clothes are suggestive of the desirability of the body beneath them ("Delight in Disorder") or of its possessor's moral balance and lack of pretention (Jonson's "Still to Be Neat" and Spenser's sonnet beginning "Fayre is my love, when her fayre golden heares, / With the loose wynd ye waving chance to marke.") Elizabeth Bishop's spray of tasteless artificial roses would figure here, too, embarrassing the circus rider in our eyes (see "Cirque d'Hiver" in chapter 1's "Poetry Sampler"). When Emily Dickinson's *hem* is touched by the maelstrom in #414, her vulnerable femininity has been threatened by a stormy force beyond her. In "Sir Patrick Spens," the ladies' gold combs and fans represent their beauty and aloofness—and also their loss, since beauty is sud-

---

16. Examples thus far include the lantern in Hopkins (see the complete poem in the "Poetry Sampler" in chapter 1), the "chimney' sweeper's cry" of exhausted misery in Blake, and the flammable "resinous heart" of Christ-like man in the Yeats poem.

denly an empty externality without the husbands who have drowned in a storm at sea. The ballad implies that these wives will no longer raise and open their fans in intimate flirtation.

When human creatures are compared to flowers, the trope is usually metaphoric, *not* metonymic ("O my luve's like a red, red rose, / That's newly sprung in June," sings Burns; and as Thomas Campion sings it, "There is a Garden in her face, / Where Roses and white Lilies grow"). Somewhat closer to the literal is Milton's Eve, who is surrounded by flowers, tends them, and is like them: "fairest unsupported flower, / From her best prop so far, and storm so nigh" (*Paradise Lost* IX.432–33). But even Milton's extension is too overt for what occurs after a time, when the flattering trope can be taken for granted, then played upon. Part of the hidden "machinery" of comparison in a poem like William Wordsworth's "Song: She Dwelt Among th' Untrodden Ways" is the unmentioned tradition of floral tribute and herbiary association with virtues (as the violet is deemed faithful):

> A Violet by a mossy stone   5
>   Half-hidden from the Eye!
> —Fair, as a star when only one
>   Is shining in the sky!

The girl who died before her time[17] was at once rude and retiring—she was not a full-blossomed, sun-drenched, cultivated flower like a rose or lily—and yet (or even because of her passive perfection) mystical and eternal—she is fair as a *star,* albeit a star visible only in the brief twilight period at dawn and dusk when none of the other major constellations is yet clear.

To the fair lady/flower analogy of European love poetry, Wordsworth adds a small footnote of local detail. He uses a fairly obvious form of metonymic link between flower and the generalized rural place (the violet beside a stone anyone might come upon near the river where the unknown girl called "Lucy" in the poem grew up) while he also clearly suggests an identity between the violet and the maid herself in a veiled,

---

17. Wordsworth's friend Coleridge took the poem as a premature epitaph for William's sister Dorothy Wordsworth (1771–1855): "Most probably in some gloomier moment he had fancied the moment in which his Sister might die," letter of 6 April 1799, quoted by Stephen Gill in his edition of *The Oxford Authors: William Wordsworth* (Oxford: Oxford University Press, 1984), p. 693.

nearly subliminal allusion to Petrarchan tradition. Then the poet uses an overt comparison (a class of metaphor called a **simile,** denoting comparisons in which the words "like" or "as" appear) between the shy but steadfast violet and the shy but steadfast star. Although the context is hereby enlarged rather drastically, the stellar enlargement is qualified by brevity and sparseness so as to preserve the violet's miniature scale.

The further apart lie the two things a poet brings together for comparison, the more transient, forced, and cerebral the resemblances between them will appear. "There are infinite things on earth," says a character in one of Borges's fictions; "any one of them may be likened to any other." The more "unique" the analogy, the less convincing; the image only one person could have dreamed up is an image that touches no one. Whereas the most persuasive comparisons are those in which the force of repeated human experience can be felt. This is why we are persuaded by Byron's analogies ("The Assyrian came down like a wolf on the fold,") and by Yeats's ("Like a long-legged fly upon the stream / Her mind moves upon silence"). But when Vladimir Mayakovsky writes that he would "gnaw out red tape like a wolf," the analogy is comparatively random and idiosyncratic (in the normal run of things, wolves aren't attracted to or caught with tape—even if the authentic bard with whom we might identify the wolf might be prepared to demolish or "gnaw out" of its bureaucratic fetters). Similarly, if we were to compare the sun rising over Paterson to an inflammation of the skin or to a squirt gun, the metaphors would tell us, at best, only that the associations of such a writer were juvenile and bizarre. Anything can, conceivably, be likened to anything else, but it is only accurate and deliberate comparison that will speak to readers beyond one's circle and time. This fact will, I hope, grant a certain longevity to the modest poem about the early dawn by Raymond Oliver, "Structures" (see the text in chapter 3).

Allusion

Poets also find it tempting to appeal to a wide audience by making allusions to large patterns of shared cultural experience. It is possible to compare ourselves (or our characters) with figures such as Buddha, Napoleon, and Jesus Christ. Such comparison will fail, however, unless we choose the right episode in that greater figure's life *for the right reason:* mere suffering does not make one Christlike, nor mere aggressiveness Napole-

onic, nor passivity Buddhalike. Apt **allusion,** however, cuts right to the
core, as when Kavanagh mentions Alexander Selkirk in "Inniskeen
Road: July Evening" to render poignant how vast he sees his shipwrecked
loneliness to be—even though it extends only over a few local farms.
Often the indirect approach to allusion and large cultural pattern is more
convincing than the direct, as in Thomas Hardy's almost casual allusion
to folklore about the animals' gift of speech at Christ's nativity in "The
Oxen"—it is, remarkably, a poem in which Christ is never mentioned.

When W. H. Auden invokes Homer in "The Shield of Achilles," he
is using allusion in two ways, both of them successful. First, in the in-set
stanzas that move to a dancing rhythm and use sparkling diction to de-
scribe images of harmony and community, Auden retells in a lyrical voice
and from a celebratory perspective the making of Achilles' new shield
from the *Iliad,* Book 18. Meanwhile, in the pentameter stanzas, in lethar-
gic meters and relentlessly drab images as well as harshly direct diction,
Auden writes his modest "answer" to Homer. Here is what the shield of
Achilles would look like if images of modern community were to be
employed: We would see concentration camps, crucifixions, rapes,
knifings, and random cruelty to dumb creatures.

> The mass and majesty of this world, all
> That carries weight and always weighs the same,
> Lay in the hands of others; they were small   40
> And could not hope for help and no help came:
> What their foes liked to do was done, their shame
> Was all the worst could wish; they lost their pride
> And died as men before their bodies died.
>
> ("The Shield of Achilles")

Ultimately, the squalor of the present infects the poem's closing view of
the past, for despite Achilles's victorious guises in the Greek epic poem
attributed to Homer, which are lightly parodied in Auden's final stanza,
he does not live long after the sack of Troy:

> The thin-lipped armorer,   60
>   Hephaestos hobbled away,
> Thetis of the shining breasts
>   Cried out in dismay

At what the god had wrought
    To please her son, the strong   65
Iron-hearted man-slaying Achilles
    Who would not live long.

This remarkable poem could have been written only by someone who had a sure command of the Greek poem and a reliable sense of which episodes from Christian history would make the best counterpoint to the classical ambience. The poem is especially interesting as a study in "large" allusion (that is, allusion to a famous work made on a large and various scale). Auden is equally ambitious in "As I Walked Out One Evening" and "Lady, Weeping at the Crossroads"—poems in which he replies to the entire ballad tradition. But in these two poems, the trick was to balance the breadth of the tradition against the intense and yet parodic localization of the requisite emotion. In the latter poem, Auden clearly delights in applying a catalogue of ballad traits to an almost coherent quest narrative without relinquishing the sense of the provisional:

Lady, weeping at the crossroads,
Would you meet your love
In the twilight with his greyhounds,
And the hawk on his glove?

Bribe the birds then on the branches,   5
Bribe them to be dumb,
Stare the hot sun out of heaven
That the night may come.

Starless are the nights of travel,
Bleak the winter wind;   10
Run with terror all before you
And regret behind.

Run until you hear the ocean's
Everlasting cry;
Deep though it may be and bitter   15
You must drink it dry.

Wear out patience in the lowest
Dungeon of the sea,
Searching through the stranded shipwrecks
For the golden key . . .   20

To the conventions of theme and attitude in the ballads—condensation, direct address, vigorous and even violent plot, the flight into nature, and a mysteriousness of fate and motive—Auden adds an imperious tone (consider the many heartless commands to *stare, push on,* then finally we must *plunge* that tiny but lethal knife of unpleasant self-knowledge into the dispirited body). The rooms and props and places are recognizable not because they are realistic but because they are symbolic:

> Push on to the world's end, pay the
> Dread guard with a kiss;
> Cross the rotten bridge that totters
> Over the abyss.
>
> There stands the deserted castle   25
> Ready to explore;
> Enter, climb the marble staircase,
> Open the locked door.
>
> Cross the silent empty ballroom,
> Doubt and danger past;   30
> Blow the cobwebs from the mirror,
> See yourself at last.
>
> Put your hand behind the wainscot,
> You have done your part;
> Find the penknife there and plunge it   35
> Into your false heart.

Auden's diction—the *penknife* and anachronistic *ballroom* and the derisory epithet *rotten* (23)—all point to the wrestling with inherited materials. The knife is the same one offered to Clerk Colvill by the witch with the beautiful face called the maid of Slane:

> Then loud, loud cried the Clerk Colvill,
>   'Ochone,* my head it pains me sair!'**   *alas **sore
> 'Then take this little pen-knife,' she said,
> 'Gin [if] from my sark* you'll cut a gare,**   *blouse ***strip for a bandage*
> I'll row* it about your lovely head   *wrap
>   And pain you'll never feel nae mair.'

~

O he has taken her little bane-knife*   *death-knife
    And from her sark he's cut a gare . . .[18]

Yet what is essential and in focus in the original ballads, such as "Clerk Colvill," "Sir Patrick Spens," "The Twa Corbies," and "Edward," shifts in Auden's poem into a disoriented rehearsal of irksome tasks. And whereas in old ballads like "The Laily Worm and the Machrel of the Sea" the repetitions and interpolations are unself-conscious, Auden is endlessly aware of repeating himself and in these redundancies of act and outcome diagnoses the weakening spirit of those who rely on stories.

Allusion must not be too enormous for the occasion, however. As a rule, when you are just starting to find your way through a poem, as reader *or* writer, it may be better not to accept the first large reference that occurs to you. Better to look for the more modest comparison, or (as in Hardy's "Oxen") approach the large subject from a side road. Still another possibility is illustrated in a brief poem, untitled, by A. E. Housman:

He, standing hushed, a pace or two apart,
    Among the bluebells of the listless plain,
Thinks, and remembers how he cleansed his heart
    And washed his hands in innocence in vain.[19]

This poem is not *about* Pontius Pilate. The allusion to Matthew 22:24 where Pilate washes his hands in water is evident but unemphatic, so that the ambiguous cowardice of the Roman governor of Judea can shed a grim light over the brief quatrain without drawing in the whole historical apparatus of the episode prior to Pilate's acquiescence in Christ's crucifixion. Housman not only "depresses" the historical contours by his controlled reticence, he exaggerates the neurosis of his protagonist, who immerses *his* hands not in water but in his victim's innocence. He thereby pollutes what is clean, just as, the metaphor implies, a seducer pollutes by experience what is untried.

18. Robert Graves, ed., *English and Scottish Ballads* (London: William Heinemann, 1957), p. 8.

19. A. E. Housman, poem XXVII from *More Poems* [1936]. I was led to study Housman's poems by reading an essay by the poet Richard Wilbur, "Round About a Poem of Housman's," on "Epitaph on an Army of Mercenaries." Wilbur's essay appears in his collection *Responses: Prose Pieces 1953–1976* (New York: Harcourt Brace Jovanovich, 1976).

We can only conjecture what this wrong in Housman's poem could
have been, although the very blurring of focus of this image (or vehicle)
of purification suggests obsessive sexual guilt. At the same time, the
sketchiness of scene and the brevity of the four-line poem forestall more
elaborate plotting. The poem hovers between biblical allusion and dram-
atized portrayal of a "third" person distinct from poet and Pilate; in light
of either, the self-accusation is obsessive.

David Ferry is adept at postponing and concentrating his allusions to
classical sources. His poems, with their carefully localized and intimately
visualized contours, do not immediately suggest the sorts of transfers by
which mythic lore might be introduced. There is in consequence often
a jolt of discontinuity when the allusion is first introduced. But Ferry
chooses his references with great care and saves them for a moment when
emotion has already built to a peak. Then there is often a twist.

from "Photographs from a Book: Six Poems" III

There is a strange, solemn, silent, graceless
Gayety in their dancing, the dancing of the young
Ladies of Philadelphia in the anxious
Saffron light of Eakins's photograph;
There in the nineteenth century, dressed in their 'Grecian'   5
Long white dresses, so many years ago,
They are dancing or standing still before the camera,
Selfhood altered to an alien poetry,
The flowers in their hair already fading;
Persephone, Dryope, Lotis, or maybe only   10
Some general Philadelphia notion of Grecian
Nymph or maiden, posing, there by the river.
"If those who suffer are to be believed,
I swear by the gods my fate is undeserved."
The light in Eakins's photograph is ancient.   15

We do not expect that the mannered pose in one of Eakins's great photo-
graphs will summon up a voice from Ovid, but there is Dryope suddenly,
turning into a tree, unable to suckle her child. In Ferry's sonnet "Grave-
yard," a son is looking at an old photograph of his now-dead father posed
in a place the son doesn't recognize.

A writing I can't read myself: the picture
Of my father, taken a couple of years
Before he died; he is sitting alone some place
I don't know; maybe one of the meetings
He took to going to, trying to keep   5
His place in the world; he is smiling a little,
Cigarette smoke drifting away; he looks
Courteous, as always, not easy to know.

("Graveyard")

The octave is almost talkative as it describes the father's lonely habits and
unspecified "meetings" (town hall? new age faith? senior citizens?). The
son can't read the writing this image represents. But during one electri-
fying moment in the sestet, the father is identified—alarmingly, and out-
side the speaker's control—with Eurydice, the woman Orpheus lost in
the underworld. Instantly after the identification with Eurydice, Ferry's
speaker has the meaning torn from him, and he "loses" his father all over
again, just as Orpheus lost Eurydice the moment he disobeyed Hermes
and looked back to see whether his beloved was still following him up
from the Underworld back into life. In the sonnet's sestet, Ferry lists the
features of the odd and seemingly unlocalized backdrop, with its dirt,
sticks, and shadows—then he recognizes the likeness in which his father
is caught:

The side of a hill, nothing but a place;
Grass, dirt, a few scattered sticks, some stones,   10
The shadow of a tree; *Eurydice,*
My father; speaking the words as they are spoken
The meaning closes itself up; a manuscript
Written in a language only the dead speak.

The loss of the father becomes a matter of the loss of the context or con-
nection by which one human being might hold another back from obliv-
ion (including the loss of the connection during life between son and
father, presumably abraded at the end). The Orpheus/Eurydice legend
illuminates the guilt and the sense of filial failure we realize must be felt—
yet which perhaps would not have been felt so poignantly had the idea
of Eurydice not fallen into the poem to irradiate the aloof, beloved father
at just that point.

Randall Jarrell alludes to the Hans Christian Andersen fairy tale about the little mermaid in his ballad, "A Soul." But the details and dialogue fragments are inventions of his own distorting of the original tale. The major "revision" Jarrell provides to the story is suggested rather than described: he identifies his persona not with the little mermaid as Andersen and his reader do, but with the prince, who hears and (noncommittally, it seems) reports the speech of the mermaid.

> It is evening. One bat dances
> Alone, where there were swallows.
> The waterlilies are shadowed
> With cattails, the cattails with willows.
>
> The moon sets; after a little 5
> The reeds sigh from the shore.
> Then silence. There is a whisper,
> "Thou art here once more."
>
> In the castle someone is singing.
> "Thou art warm and dry as the sun."
> You whisper, and laugh with joy. 10
> "Yes, here is one,"
>
> "Here is the other . . . *Legs* . . .
> And they move so?"
> I stroke the scales of your breast, and answer:
> "Yes, as you know." 15

As she is—painfully, we recall—being transformed from mermaid into human being, the small creature utters her hymn of delight curiously mingled with a longing addressed to the prince that does not promise to cease with the close of her speech and the poem:

> But you murmur, "How many years
> Thou hast wandered there above!
> Many times I had thought thee lost
> Forever, my poor love.
>
> "How many years, how many years 20
> Thou hast wandered in the air, thin air!
> Many times I had thought thee lost,
> My poor soul, forever."

She calls him her "poor soul," in the sense of the beloved bereft of her this long while. She also suggests that he is *her* soul, her higher being, drawing her forward out of a lower outward form to a higher one as well. But nothing the male speaker does in the poem would seem to warrant that kind of compliment. The speaker's view is so dominant (this is a dominance shared by perspective in most works of art) that, for much of the poem, whenever the prince is the lens, we incorrectly identify the "soul" of the title with the poor little mermaid, whose end (we know from the story) is to turn into foam on the sea.

The skewing of referent in Jarrell's title is one of its strengths, as he stubbornly deflects the mermaid's point of view, so intensely rooted in the present, onto the prince's angle of vision, with its melancholy implied foreknowledge about their eventual separation into different substance. These terms, with his focus on souls as distinct from bodies, suggest the religious perspective Jarrell invites. Hence "A Soul" is allusive in two ways, moving away from the local toward the large in two stages, once via Andersen, then by way of the Christian mystics.

The indirections of Auden, Jarrell, Housman, and Ferry suggest two features of allusion of help to the apprentice reader and writer:

1. The more one knows of the myths and literatures of the world, the more readily we can see reflections of our daily patterns in the older frames.

2. The method of allusion may be subtle or almost imperceptible, so long as the similarity is basic and deep on an imaginative level.

This latter possibility—of nuance, subtlety, and lightness-of-touch—does not make direct allusion obsolete. There may still be occasions when one wishes to layer the objective world with, say, Dantesque overtones as Eliot does in "The Burial of the Dead" in *The Waste Land* when he sees the crowd flowing over London Bridge. But there is room in our approach too for Yeats's greater immediacy of evidence and indirection of allusion: "I have met them at close of day / Coming with vivid faces / From counter or desk among gray / Eighteenth-century houses" ("Easter 1916"). Dante so saturates Yeats's thinking and development that his mode of being-in-the-world—of being a citizen and thinking of himself as a public man with an acknowledged cultural and imaginative role—already parallels the Dantesque model in a manner more natural than such a mode of belonging and representation ever was to Eliot the suffering outsider and chronicler of dislocation. We feel that Yeats is moving among the shades in broad day, whereas Eliot in *The Waste Land* (lines 60–76) must call up nightmares in order to see his. But both poets suggest the magisterial appeal of learning, urging upon others of us who write and read a comparable immersion in the arts that provide a medium for connection between people in different periods—connections that may take the form of allusion.

As a footnote to the idea of allusion, we can recognize in passing that social and economic conditions can also be alluded to. Blake often does so (see the lines from "London" above); Wordsworth is preoccupied by the jobless vagrants, hopelessly poor, who wander the land; Auden, more satirically, thinks in terms of social class, producing many small cameos of destinies bound by class, as in the revision of Sleeping Beauty in terms of a country house: "Dusty the gunrooms and the stable clocks stationary" ("The Summer Holds"). One also notes that allusion is achieved here by metonymy—the rooms and accoutrements denote the hobbies of the implied country squire.

Although I have emphasized allusion that is suggestive and indirect, a word should be said about two more overt forms of allusion—quotation and metrical borrowing. Each of the two examples below illustrates both types:

    Midwinter

We seem to be dining
Yet the salver offers
Only the unstirred flame
Of the candle whose wax
Melts over my fist   5

Beyond the cloth the gloom
Hardens the air
On which a tired head
Might strike and
Reawaken

    By day   10
A patch of snow in the yard
Flares out
    Green gravel, green
      Grave O

Oh as if a lump of radium   15
Were sending its dolor
Into the material darkness.

This poem of mine alludes deliberately to a haunting folk song called
"Green Gravel"—a phrase which Thomas Hardy conjectured was origi-
nally "Green Grave O."[20] Part of the force of the allusion to a song about
death and burial (and the wistful but hopeless gesture of dressing the dead
bride in silk) is carried by its meter, which is **amphibrachic.**[21] In contrast
to the **imagist free verse** of the poem, which resists metrical echo and
repetition, the strong triple rhythms of the folk song run in exact ⅝ mea-
sures: "Green gravel, green gravel, the grass is so green, / The fairest
young damsel that ever was seen." The melody behind the meter (D G
B, D G B, D G B, E D) is also part of the haunting authority of this song.
To counteract the pull of both melody and triple beat, I break the first
line (with its lost transposition—at least according to Hardy) in such a
way that its meter is also partly broken (line 13); line 14's unnatural pause
and stressing, "*Grave O*," then distorts and revalues the brisk and regular
original.

Julia Randall effects a similar rupture when she incorporates a line
from a passage of blank verse by Wordsworth into her **free blank verse:**

Girl in a wicker chair, a scene of the self. 'The picture
of the mind revives again,' but only the picture."[22]

Randall actually turns the Wordsworth line into triple measures at odds
with the original passage's stately melancholy:

And now, with gleams of half-extinguished thought,
With many recognitions dim and faint,   60
And somewhat of a sad perplexity,
The picture of the mind revives again . . .

("Tintern Abbey")

If we can think of meter as a language, Wordsworth's is at odds with
Randall's even though the lexicon of his original does not change. Both

20. Iona and Peter Opie, *The Singing Game* (Oxford University Press, 1985),
"Witch Dances," p. 240. The text and music to "Green Gravel" appear on pp. 239–40.
21. This and the following pair of terms about free verse are clarified in Part II.
22. *The Farewells* (Chicago: Elpenor Books, 1981), "Album Leaves, 2," p. 26.

original texts, in the variety of their evocations and in the mournful polish of all finished things, are being wrestled down to different states—made mysterious, undone, emergent—through the arduous and unsatisfied formal methods of the contemporary texts, which also (or this is the hope) haul the allusive versions back momentarily into life.

Comparison from Different Realms and Metaphoric Layers

When small is compared to large directly, without allusion to myth, literature, or history, as in James Wright's "With the Shell of a Hermit Crab," where the small crab is lifted to the context of the starry sky, the conjunction is liable to seem pathetic and extreme. But Wright has qualified effectively; the stars in the night sky deepen out into the forlornness of interstellar space, which is anything but pathetic, as the final quatrain shows:

> I reach out and flick out the light.
> Darkly I touch his fragile scars,
> So far away, so delicate,
> Stars in a wilderness of stars.   20

The scratches on the translucent abandoned carapace of the small hermit crab share with the "wilderness of stars" the comparative qualities of fragility and dereliction. *Someone* has abandoned all this, leaving behind the various disasters (including the speaker's) to run their various courses. The dead solitude of the stars thus represents and properly extends response to the battered solitude of the tiny crab.

When one thing represents another thing with which it is not usually associated—which is what occurs in many instances of metaphor—the original object is invested with a quality invisible before the comparison provided it. When not outlandish (as in Donne and the other "metaphysical" poets who delighted in the far-fetched), the unexpected but apt comparison provides a quality of evocative abstraction, of unspoken thought, and of nuanced feeling. Such is the effect of Fulke Greville's apt analogy between a top and a life driven by misfortunes to ever more frenzied attempts at distraction: "Life is a top which whipping sorrow driveth."[23] The comparison is unexpected, but thoroughly satisfying, and

---

23. From Fulke Greville, Lord Brooke's sonnet LXXXVI ("The Earth with Thunder Torn"), line 10. No longer in the *Norton Anthology,* fourth edition (see chapter 14),

requires no gloss with qualifications as Donne's metaphors often do. By contrast, Howard Nemerov's comparison of the mind to the action of a top spinning across the floor to the "edge" of what can sustain it is an example of metaphor that must be carefully evolved—almost as if the writer were searching through the file drawer as he went, trying out the optional ideas until the proper assortment of them appeared. And it is this casually indefinite demeanor and (as discussed in chapter 4's presentation on diction) the commonplace stance and diction elsewhere in the poem that work together to mask the Donneish punctilio of Nemerov's comparison.

An opera singer in James Merrill's "Matinees" flings "kisses into the furnace roaring praise" (the audience, of course). But why a furnace? Apt where only noise is concerned, the furnace suggests burning alive—and in a way adulation does consume the star. Further, awe-struck Merrill imagines himself as the stage lover of the tragic soprano, left behind "death after death" as he watches her "turn from him, restored, to fling / Kisses into the furnace roaring praise." So the singers turn from one consummation (in the fire of operatic art) to another (burning in the fires of their careers).

When metaphor is used well, the vehicle is seldom flat or single-valued; the images belonging to it have physical qualities that suggest a tenor of feeling or idea with more than one component. In fact, the vehicle of a good metaphor spins long webs of association in which complex tenorial ideas are caught. "I saw morning harden upon the wall," writes Hardy in "The Going," suggesting that as the color of the sunlight intensified, and while time passed, the observer grew alienated. (As it happens, the verb marks the moment when, unknown to him, his wife was dying.) The hardening was also a way of implying his own attention that had hardened against her, masking her departure from him. Paraphrase is (and should be) somewhat helpless to express all of what is meant by good layering of metaphor—although our job is to make the most thorough

---

this poem may be found in older anthologies such as the capacious Hebel and Hudson (*Poetry of the English Renaissance, 1509–1660*, edited by J. William Hebel and Hoyt H. Hudson [New York: Appleton-Century-Crofts, 1929; 1957], p. 129) or in the small *Quest for Reality: An Anthology of Short Poems in English*, edited by Yvor Winters and Kenneth Fields [Chicago: Swallow Press, 1969], p. 30). The sonnet also appears in the still available *English Renaissance Poetry: A Collection of Shorter Poems from Skelton to Jonson*, edited by John Williams, second edition [Fayetteville: University of Arkansas Press, 1990), p. 218.

sense we can of the swarm of meanings we encounter in the middle of the writer's way through a poem.

Some metaphors are so quiet as to seem nearly literal. Consider Louise Bogan's nuanced suggestions, often conveyed by verbs and verb-forms at the end of "Song for a Lyre" and the more puckish "Last Hill in a Vista":

> The shallow autumn stream; 10
> Softly awake, its sound
> Poured on the chilly ground . . .
>
> ("Song for a Lyre")

<div align="center">~~~~~</div>

> Last Hill in a Vista
>
> Come, let us tell the weeds in ditches
> How we are poor, who once had riches,
> And lie out in the sparse and sodden
> Pastures that the cows have trodden,
> The while an autumn night seals down 5
> The comforts of the wooden town.
>
> Come, let us counsel some cold stranger
> How we sought safety, but loved danger.
> So, with stiff walls about us, we
> Chose this more fragile boundary: 10
> Hills, where light poplars, the firm oak,
> Loosen into a little smoke.

The sound of the water in Bogan's "Song for a Lyre" is *poured* as if warm but in a stream that is too shallow to sustain itself along hard ground growing colder by the clock. The indirections are still less worked-at or contrived in the last lines of "Last Hill in a Vista" (the trees' outlines "Loosen" and become as indistinct as the smoke that twilight makes of the misty shapes of evening). One can immediately feel the collective contrast between these sorts of liminal evocations in metaphor and the more cognitive assertions in Bogan's "Memory" (memory is a common thing "that any spade may strike," see text in chapter 3).

Even further removed from nuanced literal symbolism is the sacrifice of the visual datum to a concept, as in the couplet quoted earlier by A. D. Hope about the difference between the challenge that faced Crusoe on the island and the one facing Friday back in England: "As Crusoe made

his clothes, so he no less / Must labour to invent his nakedness." Since
Friday cannot be naked now he is in England, he must "stitch" his true
and proper (mental) state of dress with ever more inward routines of dis-
guise, translation, and retreat. With these last two examples (the similes
from "Memory" and "Man Friday"), we are moving away from the more
embedded and suggestive end of the continuum of metaphor to a plainer
logic and more functional sort of illustration. Taken one step further, this
"functional" style becomes a thoroughgoing restriction in attitude that
lends itself to the two kinds of plain style we have observed in chapter 4,
the argumentative and the concrete.

Return to Plain Style

There is much to be said for the modern evolution of **plain-style** tradi-
tion, which in its concrete form selects items from a commonplace literal
scene. A good example of concrete plain style is Raymond Oliver's
"Cyclic":

> The value of those time-of-year details—
> Coffee-steam on cooler mornings, the smell
> Of coming snow, the touch of hot wood rails—
> Rose from their power suddenly to swell
> The moment to a vision, to suggest   5
> A perfect season where my thoughts could rest,
> Its essence these details on which I dwell.

Here the value of things—coffee-steam when the air turns cooler, the
smell of snow before its arrival, the feel of the wood rail heated by the
still strong sun—is measured by increased attention. The poem's speaker
(its operative sensibility, sometimes called the mask, or **persona**) is
alerted to the local and familiar details in a quickened way. The reality of
these perceptions is fresh, immediate, and liminal, that is, hinting at a
threshold before a turn. We exist in "Cyclic" during a moment of plea-
surable stasis before change, a moment of residual warmth before the ac-
tual onset of a colder season, which we can already smell in the air. The
feeling of conscious and articulate (even if momentary) well-being is
drastically controlled, however, and its resonance very subdued. These
are features of control common to the plain style.[24]

24. More will be said about the reserved tone of plain style in chapter 6 and the
discussion there on rhetoric and argument.

More ample than in Oliver's poem is the reach of the literal scene into the mental-spiritual realm in Richard Wilbur's two-quatrain autumnal, "Exeunt" (literally, "they all leave," a term often found as a stage direction in Renaissance plays):

> Piecemeal the summer dies;
> At the field's edge a daisy lives alone;
> A last shawl of burning lies
>   On a gray field-stone.

> All cries are thin and terse;
> The field has droned the summer's final mass;
> A cricket like a dwindled hearse
>   Crawls from the dry grass.

Wilbur's second stanza, with its recollection of Emily Dickinson's poem about crickets at the end of summer (her #1068, beginning "Further in Summer than the Birds"), is more heavily freighted with metaphor than his first stanza, which seems by comparison pretty straightforward. But next to Raymond Oliver's poem, the first four lines above are cushioned by metaphor for a much springier ride: The details in "Exeunt," in other words, are less reductively literal than the details in Oliver's "Cyclic." Wilbur's lines about nature's reduced fabric, "A last shawl of burning lies / On a gray field-stone," require us to look through the metaphoric veil at the physical sense datum: We feel the residual heat amid a general cooling in the air about the stone and experience its remnant warmth as a comforting version of the idea of a fine, feminine fabric that one might draw across one's shoulders. However, the shawl does not exist in the given world of the poem; it exists by analogy with what is offered as perceivable. We have gone beyond plain data flatly rendered. At the same time, the "going-beyond" in Wilbur's first stanza is less energetic than that in the second (again, this is a matter of relative values; the idea of the poem's place on a continuum will be of use in "placing" the extent of technical play in both stanzas collectively as well as in each stanza contrastively).

The literal scene in "Exeunt," with its evocations of religious funeral rites (recall Wilbur's "final mass" and the cricket like a "dwindled hearse" rather than a living insect), seems on the face of it less plain than nature appears to be in Philip Larkin's "The Trees." Larkin's plainness is deceptive, however; in his three quatrains, the trees, beginning their spring change from bud to leaf, represent to the observing intelligence some link between the natural world and the human world.

The trees are coming into leaf
Like something almost being said;
The recent buds relax and spread,
Their greenness is a kind of grief.

Is it that they are born again   5
And we grow old? No, they die, too.
Their yearly trick of looking new
Is written down in rings of grain.

("The Trees")

This human-natural link is intuitively felt, to be sure, before it is fully intelligible; it is "Like something almost being said," a simile that defeats its own specificity of technique by the vagueness of the terms (*something, almost*). The natural-human link also appears more hypothetical and casual owing to the interrogative mode ("Is it that they are born again / And we grow old?").

Alongside these features, however, Larkin has also traced the unfolding of the buds into leaves. Time accelerates. The poet telescopes days into moments in the first two stanzas, until in the third stanza the perspective is yet more advanced and year is set against year ("every May"). Nevertheless, the third and final stanza's image—the site from which the vehicle derives—is one of lush immediacy:

Yet still the unresting castles thresh
In fullgrown thickness every May.   10
Last year is dead, they seem to say,
Begin afresh, afresh, afresh.

("The Trees")

The sound of the fully leaved trees blowing in the breeze is caught by the rhyme *thresh* / *afresh,* two **onomatopoeic** words, which mimic the sound they denote, that is, they sound like what they say. In addition, *thresh* suggests the autumnal harvest that awaits the late spring growth, so a further time dimension lifts the present moment with its hopeful urgency to a more poignant level. (See chapter 6 for a discussion of the rhetoric in Larkin's poem and the dramatic effect of his deliberately mixed trope.)

Throughout Larkin's, Wilbur's, and Oliver's plain-style poems just discussed, as well as in the prior poems by Wright, Bogan, Ferry, and Wordsworth, the plain and literal present comes to represent deeper and more distant significance. Characteristic of all metaphor is a *movement from the physical toward the spiritual*. As said earlier, it is usually the local and literal that gives weight to the distal and abstract. The reverse is rarely true: In a comparison of Borges's, likening destiny to a blind camel, the goal is not a richer comprehension of camels but of destiny. We live in a world that we see through. Even in poems fairly reticent about the meanings toward which the literal picture tends as it unfolds, such as Timothy Steele's "Toward Calgary," the power of the closely observed world is such that we are prepared for the assignment of "larger meaning" later in the poem.

There are in "Toward Calgary" two overlapping events or processes that entail the work done by the perceiving intelligence on physical phenomena.[25] The poem's speaker comes to "read" and understand both the vastness and ambiguity of the distances in the Canadian Northwest and the tenuousness of the lines of communication from the "real world" (represented by the radio) to the isolated self. In the poem's middle stanza, these processes intersect in a metonymic comparison where the implication is only one degree removed from the literal facts of stillness and emptiness. Tenor and vehicle are closely aligned.

The loss of the radio signal, like the sparseness of the landscapes, marks the self's arrival at its limits or extreme point. Signals from civilization, like geological definition, grow weaker, with an inexorable rhythm, and the stasis into which the self is plunged is pointedly illuminating rather than generalizing or universal. And yet the vast uniformity of the terrain also insinuates that any one individual's response to the puniness imposed on the self by the empty land is at best nonspecific. Even—or perhaps especially—in loss, the individual is stripped of identifying particulars.

Nevertheless, unlike James Wright in the poem on the hermit crab, Steele does not end "Toward Calgary" on the realization that all distinctions must be swallowed up in such a realm. Wright moves *his* poem toward an exorbitance that releases and inflames emotion. Steele moves his toward a cautionary balance; he studies the lessons that can be drawn from the experience of leveling. And when he stretches the poem out on a more elaborate frame of association than that of the radio signal as the literal symbol of the lost self, he uses metaphors closer to the pole of artifice, where resemblances are made, not found.

25. It may help to have the poem before you. See chapter 4.

Despite Steels's artifice of "reading out" abstract meaning ("the pru-
dent heart"; the chastening "radiance") from the empty landscape, this
prudence in response to a resplendent catechism is not an arbitrary virtue.
A reflection of the vast and forbidding expanses, prudence is a trait or
talent taught by this *particular* stretch of ground as a precondition for get-
ting through it. As the message is one of reserve, so the style in which
the landscape is rendered is also reserved and contained. The realistic ele-
ment is thus still stronger in Steele than in Donne or Milton, who have
shown less interest in the exact rendering of the contours of specific
places (including emotional "places" or memories) as having numinous
significance.

Personification

That Steele's landscape can *do* things—foster intensity, chasten excess—
moves the metaphor-making in the direction of a class of trope called
personification. When the inanimate takes on the features of animal or
human life and movement, it has been person-ified. The most natural,
least artificial kinds of personification are those involving *literal* things
(one can see how personification grows out of literal symbol and meton-
ymy—recall how Wilner personifies the wind over scorched earth as "an
indigent in search of scraps"), whereas the most allegorical kinds of per-
sonification occur when abstractions act like persons. Time acts the role
of an untrustworthy scout in Shakespeare's fifth sonnet, leading summer
on to a waste country with winter close behind. But the summer then
steps down and becomes a season again in the sestet.[26] (In this regard,
recall the greater consistency of presence in the whorish city in the Thom
Gunn poem discussed above with respect to allegory, "In Praise of
Cities.")

   The ninety-fifth section of Alfred Tennyson's *In Memoriam A. H. H.*
illustrates both kinds of personification in close proximity. He further
shows how, as in Steele's "Toward Calgary," a more elaborate form of
metaphor, acting as the climax or limit of a poem, can level out the deeply
layered surrounding metaphoricity, making the "lower" stratum of trope
seem comparatively more literal.

---

26. See the text of Sonnet 5 in the "Poetry Sampler" in chapter 1.

By night we linger'd on the lawn,
    For underfoot the herb was dry;
    And genial warmth; and o'er the sky
The silvery haze of summer drawn;   4

. . . .

And bats went round in fragrant skies,
    And wheel'd or lit the filmy shapes   10
    That haunt the dusk, with ermine capes
And woolly breasts and beaded eyes;

. . . .

A hunger seized my heart; I read
    Of that glad year which once had been,
    In those fallen leaves which kept their green,
The noble letters of the dead.

And strangely on the silence broke   25
    The silent-speaking words, and strange
    Was love's dumb cry defying change
To test his worth; and strangely spoke

The faith, the vigor, bold to dwell
    On doubts that drive the coward back,   30
    And keen thro' wordy snares to track
Suggestion to her inmost cell.

. . . .

    And all at once it seem'd at last   35
The living soul* was flash'd on mine,   *of his dead friend, Arthur Henry Hallam

And mine in this* was wound, and whirl'd   *originally his
    About empyreal heights of thought,
    And came on that which is, and caught
The deep pulsations of the world,   40

Aeonian* music measuring out   *having persisted for eons
    The Steps of Time—the shocks of Chance—
    The blows of Death. At length my trance
Was cancell'd, stricken thro' with doubt.

. . . .

Till now the doubtful dusk reveal'd
    The knolls once more where, couch'd at ease,   50

> The white kine* glimmer'd, and the trees   *cattle
> Laid their dark arms about the field . . .

(In Memoriam A. H. H. XCV)

When Tennyson writes of a pastoral landscape, the local features immediately start to move beyond the literal: as if in lines 3 and 4 people and clothes were the topic rather than seasons and mists, periphrasis (or roundabout expression) suggests personification. More energetic is the personification of nature in lines 23–24, which initiates the two-stanza-long emanation of Hallam's soul. By the time we reach the white kine and the trees in line 51, it doesn't surprise us that the one glimmers while the other "Laid their dark arms about the field." With this line, we sense that we are already further into the realm of allegory than at any point in Timothy Steele's poem "Toward Calgary." But when Tennyson "rises" to the climactic insight into "Aeonian music measuring out / The steps of Time—the shock of Chance— / The blows of Death," the earlier couching kine and embracing trees (who first appear in line 15 and now return at 50) seem friendly and, relatively speaking, rather ordinary. But by the same token, Tennyson wanted to rise higher, to affirm a more binding spiritual principle in his poem than Timothy Steele's did in his— and, of course, a phrase like "Aeonian music" would have been out of place in "Toward Calgary." To accomplish the greater ascent, it was necessary to begin at a level of metaphor already closer to personification than does Steele at *his* "first plateau," when he reaches for the radio (that is, his "stilled world at the fingertips").

Two conclusions can be drawn from the comparison between Tennyson and Steele.

1. The climax of a poem can coincide with the increasing complication of the metaphors in such a way as to "level out" or nearly unmetaphorize the initial and more literal movements of trope. Put another way, the more explicit the metaphors early on in a poem, the more exaggeration is permitted (and, often, required) later in the work.

2. The poem that begins with tropes closer to literal symbol, as in "Toward Calgary," need not—in fact such a poem cannot—switch over to allegory of the majestic kind Tennyson uses at the central point of *In Memoriam* XCV. By this same rule of coherence, furthermore, a poem like *In Memoriam* XCV must "suppose" a greater metaphoricity from the outset in order to rise as high into allegorized metaphor and elevated diction as Tennyson successfully does at his peak.

The Kenning

One last example of a poem exhibiting a wide range of trope occurs in "The Mill-Race," by Anne Winters, where halfway through the poem, "Labor" is personified, makes an appearance, and speaks.[27] The very length of this poem (64 lines, some of them more than twice the length of iambic pentameter) suggests that such an appearance needed preparation. The question is whether there is something in the thirty-line preparation that makes an allegorical figure personifying Labor more presentable. Oddly enough, the metaphoricity that may or may not lead up to the figure of Labor is largely anti-allegorical. With literal setting as the foundation, Winters creates an overwhelming carousel of physical sensation to which metaphor of all kinds contributes, from the clean simile "like pale books knocked sideways" (line 4) to the overt metaphor comparing lightning to a "limpid telegraphy" (line 9). Winters is also fond of a metaphor-phrase called a **kenning,** in which two nouns joined as a compound stand for a third. Winters's examples are *stonecourse* (13, for a walk made of burial markers), *rainlight* (24, for light that is ribbed and trembling with the passage or rain over the bus window's surface), and *spittle-stream* (34, for the oblong bits of water broken by the action of a paddle wheel).

Anne Winters's title, the *mill-race,* puns on the secondary meaning of *race* as a current of water or the channel in which it runs—especially one that was built to use the water industrially. By a reverse personification, the women who spend their young days working are reduced to particles in the steady stream of a water-mill, both used for the power of others, and beaten into conformity by the action in which they are immersed.

This reduction in the human beings parallels the elevation of the entity that derives energy from their labor. Surrounding the allegorized figure of Labor, who takes life and gives back only routine ("'one day, then another. For mine are the terms,'" line 28), is Winters's increasingly sinister verbal tapestry. All the objects in the poem seem to be electric with intention: the "huge felt-edged wipers" of the bus (41); the puddles that mirror the gibberish, "in amber and crimson," of the "night signs" (43–44); the silvery shingles of the Connecticut "barn-roof" converted by a wealthy Manhattanite (53).

Threaded through the description of the welcome night as the

---

27. The full text of the poem appears in the "Poetry Sampler" in chapter 1.

women ride home are the double strands of compounds, many of them double-epithets (*felt-edged, rain-streaked, smooth-lipped* [used of a tread-mill]); some literal paired nouns (*plank-edge, office-lights*); and finally the kenninglike terms glowing with new mystery—*hire-cars* (51), *dust-demons* (62), and—the two most awful compounds—*labor-mines,* for the buildings are like shafts "running a half-mile down from the sky" (55) as if in a tall building in a huge city we are really sunk into the ground like miners in a pit; and the *curse-gift* (63) of the mill (known as Hamlet's mill[28]) that fell into the ocean and automatically, unceasingly continues to grind out everything that is salty (including our hopeless tears).

The introduction of kennings to the metaphoric pattern is one of the principal beauties of Winters's poem. To describe how she coordinates the effects of so many different kinds of metaphor, however, we need to turn to the element of rhetoric.

---

28. See Giorgio de Santillana and Herthe von Dechend, *Hamlet's Mill: An Essay on Myth and the Frame of Time* (Boston: Gambit, 1969), passim.

6

Rhetoric and Speech

Character and Distance

The more eloquent and lavish the metaphors in a poem, the more elevated one may say the rhetoric of the poem is. By **rhetoric,** I mean the attitudes and intrusions of the speaker. The terms *rhetor, orator,* and *speaker* all point to the person behind the work's so-called persona (or mask). Frequently, this rhetor or persona is a character separate from the poet; at other times, the poet speaks in his or her own voice. Whoever speaks, the illusion of directness may be another disguise. The most confiding and friendly voices are often the least trustworthy.

It is important to be able to tell the poet's voice from the poet's invented character. T. S. Eliot identifies three projections of the poetic self:

> The first voice is the voice of the poet talking to himself—or to nobody. The second is the voice of the poet addressing an audience, whether large or small. The third is the voice of the poet when he attempts to create a dramatic character speaking in verse; when he is saying, not what he would say in his own person, but only what he can say within the limits of one imaginary character addressing another imaginary character.[1]

Shakespeare uses the third voice, Alexander Pope the second, and Wallace Stevens the first. Indeed what Eliot calls the first voice of poetry comes into its own in the modern period, when writers recoil from the demands of a public demeanor and publicly and popularly approved themes.

---

1. T. S. Eliot, "The Three Voices of Poetry" [1953], in *On Poetry and Poets* (New York: Noonday/Farrar, Straus, and Giroux, 1961), p. 96.

Within each of the three voices resides a range of postures, from un-
obtrusive distance to active self-dramatization and third-person dramati-
zation. The speakers of the poems of Philip Larkin and Edwin Muir, to
name only two, tend to stand back from the evidence presented, while
the speakers of poems in the **Petrarchan sonnet** tradition (Spenser,
Wyatt, Shakespeare, Donne) exaggerate both the beloved's beauty and
their own chagrin and lovelorn obsession. The speakers of many of Rob-
ert Browning's monologues are often weaklings, like Andrea del Sarto,
and occasionally charlatans and even psychopaths (consider the Duke of
Ferrara, Caliban, Mr. Sludge, the Bishop who orders his tomb, even the
prankster Fra Lippo Lippi, who painted so delicately).

The more flamboyant the speaker of the poem, the more he or she
will tend to use **figures of speech** and metaphor, not to mention syntac-
tic forms like exclamation, invocation, repetition, command, query, en-
treaty, and curse. Exaggeration, like control, does not stop with the sen-
tence. The more self-conscious the speakers, the more elaborate also will
be diction and tropes—and the more pointed their rhetorical coordina-
tion. Even in poems where description dominates, rhetoric guides the
design. Anne Winters's "Mill-Race" (reprinted in full in the first chap-
ter's "Poetry Sampler") projects a speaker overwhelmingly receptive to
texture and minutiae. But almost at once (as noted at the end of the
previous chapter on trope) description rises into metaphor. Between pal-
ings of the church cemetery near where her bus has stopped, "oat pani-
cles sift a few bright / grains to the stonecourse" (12–13). These are rain-
drops in the shape of oval grains mysteriously shaken from nonexistent
tufts of oat. The poet is suggesting that the spectral panicles sprinkle a
kind of useless plenty (water shaped like grain) on the grave of stones
("stonecourse"): this water doesn't nourish the dead or make them bur-
geon. Also sinister is the water of the mill through which all the work-
ing people are drawn; water is the vehicle for the tenor of a stream of
female office workers (*they* are "the lucid slim sluice / falling back in a
spittle-stream from the plank-edge" [35–36]; clearly "spittle-stream"
is both visually and morally expressive, for these women have been spit
out of the machine that uses them). Once metaphor irradiates the place
and people, ascent from the voice suited to description up into a more
commanding and judgmental rhetorical positioning is not unexpected.
Even the taskmaster who orders our days speaks, "'Give me this day
your / life . . . for mine are the terms'" (26–27). The narrator likewise

intones a harsh understanding: "If there is leisure, bus-riders, it's not for you" (49). Winters's poem navigates from the first voice of the poet, brooding on a scene, to the second voice of poetry in which a voice can address an audience that grows beyond the moment of insight to many times, one of which unfolds into the moment when the voice speaks to each of us.

The voice Tennyson uses in the canto from *In Memoriam A. H. H.,* discussed at the close of the previous chapter, in which the poet summons new shapes to support the idea of the persistence of Hallam's soul, is closer than Winters's to the first voice of poetry. To be sure, it is variegated in style; Tennyson plays up and down the stylistic scale, from the literal and descriptive level to elaborate metaphor, everywhere poetically active but nowhere entirely coherent as to his belief. Rhetoric, or the authority produced by his combined styles, clearly has a different aim for Tennyson in his address to us about his thinly disguised private turmoil (as he hopes to persuade himself under cover of persuading us) than it does for Winters, whose arena is in part an evidential one—the socially and visually complex urban world, which she interprets archetypally.

But even if more concrete than Tennyson, the large-scale rhetorical shape and the many devices of eloquence in Anne Winters's poem "The Mill-Race" are more inflected by the wayward vigor of private vision than are the more carefully argued poems that follow below, in which the conditions for inwardness would seem more propitious as their solitary speakers survey their rooms:

> As in the house I sate,
> Alone and desolate,
> No creature but the fire and I,
> The chimney and the stool, I lift mine eye
> Up to the wall, 5
> And in the silent hall
> Saw nothing mine
> But some few cups and dishes shine,
> The table and the wooden stools
> Where people used to dine; 10
> A painted cloth there was,
> Wherein some ancient story wrought

A little entertained my thought,
Which light discovered through the glass.

(Thomas Traherne, "Poverty"²)

This first stanza of Traherne's poem could be circling around the beginnings of a story (line 12, about the tale embedded in the tapestry, whose archaic note suggests the Last Supper because this is a place "Where people used to dine," line 10); or Traherne could be itemizing the literal symbols of a frugal and lonely life, framing them in such a way that they could lead, in time, to greater interpreted value as their literalness deepens (lines 9 and 10 suggest such jumping-off points for a poem of literal symbolism, rooted in place). But stanza one of "Poverty" turns out to be the somewhat overspecific presentation of a setting for ruminations about virtue.[3] The setting is tangential and secondary to the meditation—unlike Anne Winters's meditation on labor, whose medium is undeniably reliant on place and time and wet, quirky weather and church stones and crowds of young women leaving work.

Traherne's treatment of such an elaborate stanza form as his fourteen lines above, which ranges from dimeter to pentameter *via* couplets (until line 9) is plain to a point the seventeenth century would view as awkward. It gives out a different impression now, something like that of George Herbert's "Artillery," so long as one does not press Traherne to duplicate Herbert's lively narrative clip.[4] To the modern sensibility, Traherne's lin-

---

2. In *Poetry of the English Renaissance 1509–1660,* edited by J. William Hebel and Hoyt H. Hudson (New York: Appleton-Century-Crofts, 1929; 1957), p. 810. Note that this anthology is the volume to which Rosamund Tuve keys all of her illustrations and arguments in *Elizabethan and Metaphysical Imagery* (see entry on Tuve in chapter 14).

3. Traherne himself strove to do without worldly goods and to study the instinctual delight of the child in warmth and open air, announcing after college that he would dress in leather (the cheapest and sturdiest clothing), eat bread, and "study felicity"; he managed to live in semiretirement for the next twelve years; his subsequent period of public life was brief, six years as chaplain to a nobleman, whom he followed into retirement for the last two years of his life. Hebel and Hudson provide a biographical sketch and stylistic capsule of Traherne on p. 1028.

4. Herbert's "Artillery" begins:

As I one evening sat before my cell,
Mee thoughts, a starre did shoot into my lap:
I rose, and shook my cloths, as knowing well
That from small fires comes oft no small mishap.

But Herbert's speaker is instantly warned not to "Expell good motions [or impulses, sent from God] from [his] brest." The speaker wittily plays on naivete and in the second stanza

gering over the wall and the few dishes that shine despite their scarcity implies that the place matters. And even if realism of place is not sustained (the poem ends on the lesson of gratitude for the little that is much: "For till his works my wealth became, / No love or peace did me inflame: / But now I have a Deity"), nevertheless during that long first movement we enter an environment more realistic than its illustrative purpose gives it leave to be. I would call the rhetorical address of Traherne's "Poverty" a divided one, the instinct for divine analogy overwhelming the attraction toward precisely visualized spareness of domestic locale. The poet in a sense makes a drama out of this division.

Using a more unified rhetorical sensibility, always opening the poem to the lived reality of the moment but never forgetting the grim lessons of fate and alienation, Thomas Hardy exercises considerable control over scene, granting both to circumstance, and to the interpretation of it, equivalent weight; the ellipsis at line 6 is Hardy's:

> An August Midnight
>
> I
>
> A shaded lamp and a waving blind,
> And the beat of a clock from a distant floor:
> On this scene enter—winged, horned, and spined—
> A longlegs, a moth, and a dumbledore*;   *bumble-bee
> While 'mid my page there idly stands   5
> A sleepy fly, that rubs its hands. . . .
>
> II
>
> Thus meet we five, in this still place,
> At this point of time, at this point in space.
> —My guests besmear my new-penned line,
> Or bang at the lamp and fall supine.   10
> 'God's humblest, they!' I muse. Yet why?
> They know Earth-secrets that know not I.

Hardy's speaker wonders at the odd confluence of destinies: here all five meet, the speaker and the creatures drawn to his light and hurting themselves—as well as smearing up the page he is writing. Hardy jollifies their

---

shows a high level of learning in his incredulity: "I, who had heard of Musique in the spheres, / But not of speech in starres, beganne to muse." In *Major Poets of the Earlier Seventeenth Century,* edited by Barbara K. Lewalski and Andrew J. Sabol (Indianapolis: Bobbs-Merrill/Odyssey, 1973), p. 325.

clumsiness so that he can turn more sharply against himself the question, why he should call these bumbling and irksome insects and spiders "humble" when they know natural secrets which he does not?[5] But the speaker does not himself take on humility, although he grants to the formerly clumsy and comically named insects a knowledge he lacks. Instead, he apportions to the creaturely world a knowledge that won't prevent them from being drowned in ink or burned alive and arrogates to himself a failure whose expression permits him to close the poem on the pronoun "I." The pride he presents as diminished returns under cover of the final line's inversion of the syntax, whose ostensible purpose, with a folksy turn, is to oblige with the required rhyme for *why*.

But finally none of these writers is actively inventing a mask in the form of another person's experience, as Frost does in the poem below— albeit a person kept by the poem at arm's length:

An Old Man's Winter Night

All out-of-doors looked darkly in at him
Through the thin frost, almost in separate stars,
That gathers on the pane in empty rooms.
What kept his eyes from giving back the gaze
Was the lamp tilted near them in his hand.   5
What kept him from remembering what it was
That brought him to that creaking room was age.
He stood with barrels round him—at a loss.
And having scared the cellar under him
In clomping here, he scared it once again   10
In clomping off—and scared the outer night,
Which has its sounds, familiar, like the roar
Of trees and crack of branches, common things,
But nothing so like beating on a box.
A light he was to no one but himself   15
Where now he sat, concerned with he knew what,
A quiet light, and then not even that.

5. Thirty-five years after Hardy's 1899 poem, Robert Frost asks his question about what steers the white moth toward the aberrant white heal-all blossom on which the white spider waits for its prey; the sonnet ("Design") answers: "What but design of darkness to appall" if design work even in something negligible? In other words, it is destiny's design to exert itself thoroughly, even down to the mistake of this normally blue flower's color, which creates the conditions for another death.

He consigned to the moon—such as she was,
So late-arising—to the broken moon,
As better than the sun in any case   20
For such a charge, his snow upon the roof,
His icicles along the wall to keep;
And slept. The log that shifted with a jolt
Once in the stove, disturbed him and he shifted,
And eased his heavy breathing, but still slept.   25
One aged man—one man—can't keep a house,
A farm, a countryside, or if he can,
It's thus he does it of a winter night.

The old man is projected as a character distinct from the author, and seen from within. These impressions are his, such as the clomping he makes, which resembles beating on a wooden box, but they cannot pierce very far beyond Frost's authorial reserve; the old man is a light "to no one but himself / Where now he sat, concerned with he knew what." His wintry mind is a private one, his memories unawakened, hope and ambition quelled. Although the character is fully open to the moment of present time, even bemused by his clatter and his own absentmindedness, he remains closed to the most intimate interpreter—himself.

How different is the genuine "third voice" in Shakespeare. Consider the visionary soliloquy as Macbeth moves to murder his guest the king:

Nature seems dead, and wicked dreams abuse
The curtained sleep. Witchcraft celebrates   50
Pale Hecate's offerings; and withered murder,
Alarumed by his sentinel, the wolf,
Whose howl's his watch, thus with his stealthy pace,
With Tarquin's ravishing strides, towards his design
Moves like a ghost. Thou sure and firm-set earth,   55
Hear not my steps which way they walk, for fear
Thy very stones prate of my whereabout
And take the present horror from the time,
Which now suits with it.

(*Macbeth* II.i)

Macbeth is here watching himself move with words, and with them alerting the audience to the sounds and movements we should imagine in the scene. Further, Macbeth tells us what would be perceptible *only* in words:

that he thinks of himself metaphorically. He personifies himself as a withered figure called "murder"; reduces his environment to a subhuman plateau (where the sentinels are wolves); and impersonates in his intentions a rapist (the legendary Tarquinius from the *Aeneid*) whose entire being reduces to the tool of his aggression[6] and the footsteps that carry him away. Macbeth is also giving shape—particularly in the line about Tarquin—to the horror his intention raises in him.

Like Shakespeare's plays, the epic poetry of Milton abounds in speeches by players whose motives alter the meaning of their words. Consider the following speech in which one character praises another:

> Thine now is all this World, thy virtue hath won
> What thy hands builded not, thy Wisdom gain'd
> With odds what War hath lost, and fully aveng'd
> Our foil* in Heav'n; here thou shalt Monarch reign. . .   *defeat 375
>
>   (*Paradise Lost* X)

It may take a late-Renaissance Puritan to quaver at the idea that "virtue" might take what others build; but no one who reads the poem can fail to be put on guard by the context, for this is Satan whose enterprise is being lauded. When we know that Satan is the addressee and that the speaker is his daughter Sin, the mother/sister of Death (for Satan was the father), then we hear a more sinister intent in "building not" and the loss of the battle (the war in heaven between Lucifer the shining and God). What is gained against odds via wisdom (here meaning guile) is paradise. Satan has succeeded in poisoning it, making it his own, and ruining the chances for the new and beautiful race of humans ever to live there.

Epic poems and full-length plays create intricate patterns of context. Brief poems must create context with greater economy. Yeats's "The Fish" is a good example of how the elements of a poem work by selective manipulation, for in eight lines we are given a plot that spurs the poet to innovation in rhetoric while the diction continues to look backward to earlier poetic conventions. "The Fish" (given in its entirety in chapter 10) presents so energetic an argument about passionate and embittering love that a mask is drawn over the visual inertia of such language as "pale tide when the moon has set" (line 2). This device could be called "dramatic syntax": a choice of syntax that is most problem-oriented, self-

---

6. This is the speech beginning with the lines about the dagger visible in the air before Macbeth.

laceratingly hypothetical, and contrary to fact. Yeats finds it appealing to argue against the impossible—to fling himself against ever more deft and touching images of the beloved's elusiveness, facing up to and even exaggerating her refusal to be caught. "The Fish" closes on a rhetorical gesture desperate and doomed, for the speaker threatens her (never a good inducement to return somebody's affection), saying that because of his work everyone will know of how he's loved and what she's done in return, "And blame you with many bitter words." The line resounds with the emptiness of the outcome.

Just as economical as Yeats, though considerably more personal and retrospective, the speaker of a poem of Donald Justice's selects moments of presence from the store of memory.

> What is it to be happy, after all? Think   5
> Of the first small joys. Think of how our parents
> Would whistle as they packed for the long summers,
> Or, busy about the usual task of parents,
>   Smile down at us suddenly for some secret reason,
>   Or simply smile, not needing any reason.   10
>   ("Sadness")

Nowhere in the stanza from Justice's "Sadness" do we encounter anything like the elevation of occasion and speech we hear in "The Fish"; Justice does without the transformative trope of Yeats. If Justice has a rhetoric—a priming of the speaker, a set of dramatic "terms"—they are those of immediate emotion—or its recollection—localized in time and quieted by diction. Even Hardy recalling his childhood in "The Self-Unseeing" is considerably more colorful. What Justice does that Hardy doesn't, however, shows in the sentence-frames—a question with a tang of that foregone quality we call "rhetorical" ("What is it to be happy, after all?"); an answer that takes the form of a command (*Think*); an indicative sentence full of hypothesis and mystery (Justice suggests that the adults had adult reasons for their inward smiling or that their lives made them happy beyond the happiness afforded by the immediate presence of their children). Rhetoric is nuanced, primarily through subtlety of syntax and implication of the governing ideas.

Rhetoric is fairly bald in this stanza by Samuel Taylor Coleridge:

> All in a hot and copper sky,   111
>   The bloody sun, at noon,

Right up above the mast did stand,
No bigger than the moon.

(The Rime of the Ancient Mariner)

By now the **common meter** stanzas and the insistent rhymes on the
even-numbered lines have begun to drone, and Coleridge tries ever more
athletic tricks within the ballad stanza's constraint: inverting and postpon-
ing the syntax; revving up the vocabulary; insisting on the atmosphere of
portent (a sun no larger than the moon is both a storm-sun and a sign of
the sun-struck sailor's near-delirium). But the cumulative effect of repeti-
tion is so strong that the variations listed are not the ones with the greatest
effect. For that we look to the departures from coincidence between sen-
tence and the metrical grid:

I moved, and could not feel my limbs: 305
I was so light—almost
I thought that I had died in sleep,
And was a blessèd ghost.

The ancient mariner cannot stray far from the ballad frame, however, and
its monotony is part of what makes his recitation fearful and compelling
to the wedding guest, who cannot break away.

At the distanced end of the continuum of rhetoric (removed as far as
possible from the mariner and Macbeth—much further than Donald Jus-
tice is), we can compare several poems in which the speakers all stand
back from what they are saying. The speaker of Raymond Oliver's "Cy-
clic" (see chapter 5) is immersed in mild physical sensation in the present
time. He moves from sense-impression to its interpretation without ever
departing from the vantage point of alert, but not inflamed, physical re-
sponse. Trope works only in the mild transfer made by the verbs "swell"
and "rest," from the body breathing to the mind absorbing. A certain
depression in the rhetorical instrument makes such minimal transfers full
of intelligent meaning. The same is true of the more elegant verses of
David Ferry in "Descriptive" and "Seen Through a Window":

Seen Through a Window

A man and a woman are sitting at a table.
It is supper time. The air is green. The walls
Are white in the green air, as rocks under water

Retain their own true color, though washed in green.
I do not know either the man or the woman,   5
Nor do I know whatever they know of each other.
Though washed in my eye they keep their own true color.

The man is all his own hunched strength, the body's
Self and strength, that bears, like weariness,
Itself upon itself, as a stone's weight   10
Bears heavily on itself to be itself.
Heavy the strength that bears the body down.
And the way he feeds is like a dreamless sleep;
The dreaming of a stone is how he feeds.

The woman's arms are plump, mottled a little   15
The flesh, like standing milk, and on one arm
A blue bruise, got in some household labor or other,
Flowering in the white. Her staring eye,
Like some bird's cry called from some deepest wood,
Says nothing of what it is but what it is.   20
Such silence is the bird's cry of a stone.

Ferry's shift from detail to interpretation is not a radical one—the membrane between them is permeable to the plain and responsive "middle" diction and the contained examples of metonymy. The naive fluencies of Ferry's formulations make perceived realities into emblems of that reality, for example, "washed in my eye," "a dreamless sleep; / The dreaming of a stone," and a cry that "called from some deepest wood." Furthermore, the atmosphere of the poem is one of concentration. We are trying to see through and into those lives we glimpse through a window, penetrating beyond the obvious despite having only the obvious to base our insight upon. We are trying to keep hypnotically present before our eyes the scene we saw only momentarily, painstakingly reconstructing details that may not have reached us consciously at all. In fact, there is a curiously psychoanalytic component to the poem, as if we were struggling to recover repressed memory. The speaker's tenacity of focus in the face of descriptive alternatives alerts us to the controlling rhetoric.

Consider Ferry's second stanza. The passage works by a carefully staged succession of variations and verbatim repetitions but in a style so resistant to overflow or exuberance that it gives the impression of making exclusions. We recall one of the cardinal rules of writing, that *good poetry*

fends off. It resists the claims of the many **periphrases** that mill about in
any experience of composition. There is at least one ready, and predict-
able, word that is deliberately *not* chosen by David Ferry for inclusion in
"Seen Through a Window"—and that is the word *gravity.* Note instead
how he explores his own fresh and hard-earned way of getting at the idea
behind that word in lines 11 to 15. Meanwhile, rhetorical focus allows
him to risk magisterial metaphors of radical replacements between noun
and noun: "The dreaming of a stone is how he feeds"; "Her staring eye /
Like some bird's cry"; "Such silence is the bird's cry of a stone." The
radical metaphorical equations are made powerful and viable by a rhetori-
cal effect of distance—almost the speaker's removal from our field of view.

Ferry is more ambitious in his poem than Oliver in his. Although
there is in Raymond Oliver's brief poem a relaxed, precisely observant,
and intelligent well-being, the poem's ambitions are small. It aims to sense
and smell and take in and brood but not to think. In it the persona's
"standing back" is absorbed but not contemplative. In Ferry, the angle of
penetration is more acute. In either case, what results is a specificity that is
deliberate and necessarily transient. (Timothy Steele's "Toward Calgary"
employs abstractions more moralizing, not to mention techniques more
self-conscious and "literary" than Oliver and Ferry—but only just: with
Tennyson, Donne, or Wordsworth as authors for comparison, Steele's re-
semblance to Oliver and Ferry will inevitably become more pro-
nounced.)

By contrast with these three plain-style poets—still at the "dis-
tanced" end of the rhetorical continuum but moving slightly toward the
"engaged" pole of active dramatization—we can revisit "The Trees," by
Philip Larkin (see chapter 5). This is a poem in which the first-person
pronoun is entirely hidden; this is not true of Ferry's "Seen Through a
Window" or Oliver's "Cyclic," although one necessarily registers how
reserved those "I's" sound, compared with, say, Wordsworth's or Mac-
beth's. Furthermore, in Larkin's poem there is a rigorously concise at-
tempt to render impressions that are being made by seasonal change upon
someone with idiosyncratic response-patterns. The rhetorical, or persua-
sive, method Larkin employs is that of understatement made prominent
by metaphor. Throughout the poem, in the human realm, something is
"almost being said," while in the arboreal realm, there is cyclical change
and fullness that is never quite matched from the human perspective (al-
though the possibility of comparable human divination is hinted at: recall
"Last year is dead, they seem to say, / Begin afresh, afresh, afresh").

Here in the last stanza, diction, metaphor, and rhetoric all expand the small boundary of the poem to a surprising and moving degree. But we never learn what the speaker had been grieving over, nor what, exactly, it must mean for him to view the trees (in a daring **mixed trope,** in which the vehicle touches three divergent realms) as "unresting castles" threshing the air. What threshes grain is a flail; what might thresh the field of the air is a leafy tree branch; castles have no role to play in this transfer. If a poet of Larkin's long discipline elects such a misfit metaphor, it must be for some consciously dramatic effect, as if he had decided, there at the turn into the third and final stanza of "The Trees," to propose something outlandish and top-heavy about these beautiful apparitions by leaving behind in his poem—refusing to fend off from it—the weird conjunction of harvest with architecture in the tropes. More important is the fact that this decision overbalances the poem just before a more daring invention at its close, the verbatim repetition of that command charged with emotional yearning ("Begin afresh, afresh, afresh"). The one extravagance (castles threshing) makes us less resistant to his persona's precarious readiness to start passionately over, which in a more somber context might have flirted with the callow and sentimental.

But Larkin's poem is not exclusively "about" this sleight-of-hand with trope, diction, and rhetorical stance. It is also "about" the themes raised by both of the subject-terms (people and trees) *as reflections of* the feelings implied by the transfers only clumsily hidden by the technical sleight-of-hand. The poem plays out a small drama of resistance to aging, then release from anxiety about it. The achievement in emotional terms is deceptively slight, just as the artistic deftness masks itself most in appearing to be maladroit.

A third poem from the "distanced" end of the rhetorical continuum is Janet Lewis's "In the Egyptian Museum." Unlike Steele and Larkin, Lewis finally, at the climax of feeling and insight in the fourth stanza, permits the use of the first-person pronoun "I." It is the contrast between this personal eruption and the general mode elsewhere that makes the announcement of this "I" so compelling; the first twenty-eight lines are restrained and formal, spoken in an "objective" diction and from an almost "official" posture (see full text of the poem in chapter 4). At times, it seems as if a museum guide were speaking. Of course, this official voice soon begins to warm toward the mummified woman buried with her gems and ornaments. In the second stanza, phrases like "most gracious" and "warm hair" betray the loosening of the posture of objectivity, so that the third stanza can turn effortlessly from details toward their emotional significance—a turn only increased sympathy would have enabled. The movement from outside observation to fellow feeling is completed when the realization of the love and devotion this dead woman's consort must have felt toward her opens into universally experienced emotion. Lewis's speaker responds in anguish not only to the particular way loss was addressed in Egyptian death rites but to the pain of losing the beloved *ever*, anywhere, in any age. Janet Lewis's speaker begins in one rhetorical mode and moves over into another, more engaged, more particularized, more inflexible, devoted, and extreme.

Dramatic Extremes

We see here a curious corollary to our widespread assumption that objectivity permits greater range: it also provides less excitement. Whereas the virtue of the dramatic poem, as Richard Wilbur has said, "is that, while it may not represent the whole self of the poet, it can (like the love song, hymn, or curse) give free expression to some one compelling mood or attitude." Sometimes, Wilbur adds, we need to "yield utterly to a feeling or idea," however partial the result may be in mirroring the complete and complex thought processes in all the poet's (or the persona's) moods.[7] Janet Lewis's "In the Egyptian Museum" is a good example of the way the ironic-meditative-objective speaker can be suddenly seized and transformed into a unified, impassioned sensibility responding to *one* idea in *one* moment. Despite its restrained build-up, the climax of the poem is an utter yielding to sorrow.

Moving toward greater emphasis on the first-person speaker, there are poems of transparent self-presentation like Hardy's "The Walk"—

You did not walk with me
Of late to the hill-top tree
    By the gated ways,
    As in earlier days;
    You were weak and lame,   5
    So you never came,
And I went alone, and I did not mind,
Not thinking of you as left behind.
    ~

7. Richard Wilbur, "On My Own Work" (1966), in *Responses: Prose Pieces 1953–1976* (New York: Harcourt Brace Jovanovich, 1976), p. 122.

I walked up there to-day
Just in the former way;   10
    Surveyed around
    The familiar ground
    By myself again:
    What difference, then?
Only that underlying sense   15
Of the look of a room on returning thence.[8]

The poem does not seem dramatized at all. Plain, unemphatic, seemingly unembellished, the very restraint of the speaking voice can become absolute in its power to move us. The same is true of the following haiku by Buson:

A sudden chill—
in our room my dead wife's
comb, underfoot.[9]

In both Hardy and Buson, the speaker's wife has recently died. Neither describes the dead woman or the bedroom; neither names any feeling beyond the most fleeting one. Yet both poems draw their energies from holding clearly in view (while refraining from exploring) those very images and circumstances that soon sink indelibly into the mind. To imagine moving through these poems as they are being made and testing the proscribed threshold of past reference is to feel the threshold give, even as one withholds the particulars. Such reticence can be useful as a model in avoiding overassertion.

Then there are poems like "Tintern Abbey," "The Slow Pacific Swell," and "The Fish," by Elizabeth Bishop in which the poet-speakers persuasively elevate their past experiences. In the Wordsworth and Yvor Winters poems, elevation is achieved by the swells and falls of rhetoric and the majesty of landscape; in Bishop's poem, the method of elevation is a particularity so extreme as to become elegiac (the barnacles near the tiny white sea-lice that also infest the venerable fish the speaker once caught appear as "fine rosettes of lime"). These three poems would be called self-dramatizing. In each, a past experience becomes more mo-

8. Thom Gunn draws attention to the laconic demeanor of this poem in his essay "Hardy and the Ballads" (1972) in *The Occasions of Poetry* (London: Faber & Faber, 1982).
9. Buson, in *Japanese Poetry,* translated by Lucien Stryk and Takahashi (New York: Penguin, 1979).

mentous upon present review and interpretation; each assumes that the experience of an individual in a natural setting is meaningful and that the particular individual he or she in fact happens to be is equipped to speak convincingly about it. Yvor Winters speaks about the alien dimension of the ocean, which he comes to understand only after being nearly drowned by it.

> The Slow Pacific Swell
>
> Far out of sight forever stands the sea,
> Bounding the land with pale tranquillity.
> When a small child, I watched it from a hill
> At thirty miles or more. The vision still
> Lies in the eye, soft blue and far away: 5
> The rain has washed the dust from April day;
> Paint-brush and lupine lie against the ground;
> The wind above the hill-top has the sound
> Of distant water in unbroken sky;
> Dark and precise the little steamers ply—   10
> Firm in direction they seem not to stir.
> That is illusion. The artificer
> Of quiet, distance holds me in a vise
> And holds the ocean steady to my eyes.

Winters toys with the fiction of all descriptive and meditative poetry, that time can be rolled backward to the point before awareness took shape. The first verse paragraph suggests a benign world in which blurry pastel images from land and ocean criss-cross one another in their innocence. But the voice of (subsequent) wisdom reminds the self (who seems still to be sunk in a dream of childhood) that the pastel vision and toylike fixedness of painted ships on the painted ocean "is illusion." Then he proceeds to explain what the ocean is truly like.

> Once when I rounded Flattery, the sea   15
> Hove its loose weight like sand to tangle me
> Upon the washing deck, to crush the hull;
> Subsiding, dragged flesh at the bone. The skull
> Felt the retreating wash of dreaming hair.
> Half drenched in dissolution, I lay bare.   20
> I scarcely pulled myself erect; I came
> Back slowly, slowly knew myself the same.

That was the ocean. From the ship we saw
Gray whales for miles: the long sweep of the jaw,
The blunt head plunging clean above the wave.   25
And one rose in a tent of sea and gave
A darkening shudder; water fell away;
The whale stood shining, and then sank in spray.

This second movement of "The Slow Pacific Swell" provides two actions
in parallel. One is a near escape from the massive crumpling of the water
that nearly drags the speaker overboard (15–22). The second is the marvel
of the huge pod of whales along which they travel, one of which breaches
nearby (23–27). The perspective we adopt in reading as if we were writ-
ing allows us to fathom how the guise of self is put on, so that one "plays"
oneself, regards the impression one's experience is making in words, *and,*
while this happens, limits the signals of self-regard in favor of techniques
of rhetorical transparency. The voice of wisdom is thus, understandably,
more transparent, less worked-at, than the original innocent voice:

A landsman, I. The sea is but a sound.
I would be near it on a sandy mound,   30
And hear the steady rushing of the deep
While I lay stinging in the sand with sleep.
I have lived inland long. The land is numb.
It stands beneath the feet, and one may come
Walking securely, till the sea extends   35
Its limber margin, and precision ends.
By night a chaos of commingling power,
The whole Pacific hovers hour by hour.
The slow Pacific swell stirs on the sand,
Sleeping to sink away, withdrawing land,   40
Heaving and wrinkled in the moon, and blind;
Or gathers seaward, ebbing out of mind.

The transparency of this final verse paragraph of Yvor Winters's "The
Slow Pacific Swell" is achieved by great craft. The adjective *wrinkled* alerts
us to the deeper actions of trope animating the passage; it is a term often
used by Melville in describing the forehead of the white whale Moby-
Dick and points to the embodiment of the ocean as a being like the
whales that swim in it. So although the rhetorical "position" of the
speaker is quieter once he has alerted us to his resolve to remain land-

bound (29–30), these are studied thoughts, not impromptu ones, and the atmosphere of directness is a delicate ruse.

When the dramatic experiment with the second voice of poetry becomes a matter of overtly and flamboyantly playing roles, with sustained exaggeration, we no longer feel that a person is speaking as it were "personally" to us, rather that the person is speaking with general artifice to a multitude. The *kind* of multitude (social, political, theatrical, what have you) depends on the poet. The satire beginning "Myne Owne John Poynz," by Sir Thomas Wyatt is devised as a letter but is clearly intended to be overheard by the English court that has denied the speaker automatic preferment.

> My Poynz, I cannot frame me* tune to fayne,**   *my **pretense
> To cloke the trothe for praisse withowt desart,*   *if not deserved by truth 20
> Of them that lyst all vice for to retayne.
> I cannot honour them that settes their part
>   With Venus and Baccus all theire lyf long;
>   Nor holld my pece of them allthoo I smart.*   *am stung
> I cannot crowche nor knelle to do so grete á wrong,   25
>   To worship them, lyke gode on erthe alone,
> That ar as wollffes thes sely* lambes among.   *blessed and simple

Wyatt's speaker is defending his own modesty and lauding his independence of spirit in terms redolent of disappointment and rancor. His retreat is a form of **hyperbole** or exaggeration called **meiosis** (except that instead of inflating oneself, one deprecates oneself). Both are devices that aim to persuade an audience of the justice of one's pose—because, that is, one has been driven into the inflation or deprecation by evident and pressing circumstances.

Meiosis can be sustained at a pitch of invention far exceeding Wyatt's, when the object is to satirize. W. H. Auden's poem addressing the ballad tradition in Freudian terms persistently uses the pose and tropes of reduction; it is as if the modernity of the outlook Auden wanted to impersonate here made it necessary for him to undercut and mock any emotion that seemed absolute:

> Cross the silent empty ballroom,
> Doubt and danger past;   30
> Blow the cobwebs from the mirror,
> See yourself at last.
> ~

Put your hand behind the wainscot,
You have done your part;
Find the penknife there and plunge it   35
Into your false heart.

("Lady, Weeping at the Crossroads")

Although the death will be decisive, the weapon (even if borrowed) is derisory. This message may well be true of Auden's poetics as a whole: he seems to be attracted to unveilings that discourage us. When Robert Herrick employs satiric meiosis to portray another, as in his epigram on his former maidservant, the feeling is considerably more humane: "In this little urn is laid / Prudence Baldwin, once my maid, / From whose happy spark here let / Spring the purple violet." And even in poems no one would be tempted to call gentle, a certain agreement about the purpose of meiosis or reduction serves to keep the wit both wicked and reasonable:

Tho' secure of our hearts, yet confoundedly sick
If they were not his own by finessing and trick;
He cast off his friends as a huntsman his pack,
For he knew when he pleased he could whistle them back.

Oliver Goldsmith's satire of the vain actor Garrick implies that there is a vulnerable quality in the manoeuvres the actor went through to keep himself interested in the way people admired him. This foible is one the poet makes touching through the self-consciousness of each "turn" (for example, Garrick is perfectly secure about our devotion but "sick" and hence insecure at the same time; he sends his chums packing in order to whistle them back). Garrick's friendship with the poet must be rugged enough for the sting of Goldsmith's portrayal to be canceled by the slavishness of the author's affection, he being one of the pack.

For the most part, our period more admires the quiet than the overt satiric poem. A tendency in postwar poetry in this country, aptly traced by Paul Breslin in *The Psycho-Political Muse*,[10] is psychological surrealism, a movement in which the poet can retreat from confession (as well as engagement) behind a screen of numinous objects and dimly symbolic gestures. Meiosis is taken to new extremes as inadequacy, uncertainty, and loss are not so much probed as celebrated. Mark Strand is the figure

10. Paul Breslin, *The Psycho-Political Muse: American Poetry since the Fifties* (Chicago: University of Chicago Press, 1987).

who draws most successfully on the "recessive" example of European writers like Zbigniew Herbert from Poland and Carlos Drummond de Andrade from Brazil—both writers who translate very well into English (Strand himself has translated Drummond de Andrade). One reason for the ease of carry-over into English is the clarity of the diction and the retreat from both formal and allusive complexity. It is as if ideas of some density could not be contained in language from which affect and nuance have been removed. Strand's long poem *Dark Harbor* abounds in moments of uncertain hovering that nevertheless seem to give him the impetus to exult. Even the suspicion that his words have been said for him by another, that he is thus not the author of his own work, provides Strand with a frisson of dreadful delight: "Tell me," he pleads, framing the line to come in such a way that we know the answer contradicts him, "That what I have said has not been said for me" (VIII). Inadequacy becomes a key to deeper poetic insight, reaching beyond the mere poem. Loss is seen as gain and diminishment can be viewed as a possession: "the loss that is continuous / Will be all yours and will only increase" (VI).

> XV
>
> What light is this that says the air is golden,
> That even the green trees can be saved
> For a moment and look bejeweled,
>
> That my hand, as I lift it over the shade
> Of my body, becomes a flame pointing the way   5
> To a world from which no one returns, yet towards
>
> Which everyone travels? The sheen of the possible
> Is adjusting itself to a change of venue: the look
> Of farewell, the sun dipping under the clouds,
>
> Faltering at the serrated edge of the mountains,   10
> Then going quickly. And the new place, the night,
> Spacious, empty, a tomb of lights, turning away,
>
> And going under, becoming what no one remembers.
>
> *(Dark Harbor)*

On the edge of humor yet resisting the presentation of self, Strand in his long poem of celebration and farewell offers a new and fresher version of the lyric of deprivation that begins in the oddly satiric bent of late twentieth-century surrealism.

One feature that quiets satire down and makes it available for more lyrical purposes is the retreat from an audience. Seemingly more personal than Wyatt, Auden, and Goldsmith by virtue of the reduced scale of his address (and unlike these, he does not anticipate being overheard by king, swain, scholar, actor, or playgoer), James Merrill dramatizes his noontide anomie in a domestic play involving his five senses:

> NOON finds me faced by a small troop of furies
> They are my senses shrill and ominous
> *We who were trained* they cry *to do your pleasure*
> *are kept like children   Is this fair to us*
>
> *Dear ones* I say bending to kiss their faces   5
> *trust me   One day you'll understand   Meanwhile*
> *suppose we think of things to raise our spirits*
> and leading the two easiest to beguile
>
> into the kitchen feed them shots of Bourbon
> Their brother who loves Brahms conceives a wish   10
> for gems from L'Africana played at volumes
> that make the dwarf palm shudder in its dish
>
> The pale one with your eyes restively flashing
> takes in the dock the ashen Sound the sky
> The fingers of the eldest brush my features   15
> *But you are smiling* she says coldly   *Why*
>
> (from "From the Cupola," poem 6)

His "small troop of furies" resent being disciplined like children rather than indulged as equals. Merrill bends to them as a mother might, even kissing their faces and (using the patronizing plural of the first-person pronoun) promising to "think of things to raise our spirits." Mollifying the senses of taste and smell with alcohol (the pun on "spirits" creates a jolly ripple), acceding to hearing's wish for loudly played symphonic music, and putting sight into a trance before the picture window, the speaker of Merrill's witty poem isn't entirely able to counter the aggressive-erotic address of the fifth, the sense of touch (whom he considers the eldest):

> The fingers of the eldest brush my features   15
> *But you are smiling* she says coldly   *Why*

It is not just dialogue that makes Merrill's poem dramatic: Enormous concentration also moves his final quatrain beyond description. Aptness is achieved in part by the sort of work that goes on behind the scenes (perhaps before the poem even begins)—in the entire conception. Merrill has invoked an older mode of conceiving of the human body and its psychology that we recognize as un-contemporary. It more closely approximates the kind of thinking that makes possible Andrew Marvell's dialogue between his body and his soul. Merrill, too, personifies his sensuous faculties and implies the existence of a potent mental realm—the realm *he* impersonates—in a drama whereby the first four senses are progressively exhausted until the fifth sense remains on the stage all by herself. Then, unlike the others, she appropriates the right to speak. It is an electrifying moment. Weird, even upsetting, it shifts the poem away from mild amusements surrounded by monologues onto an intimacy of exchange that is taboo (though about this unpleasant debauch Merrill's "From the Cupola" is ominously silent).

It is easy to see the links between these habits of self-dramatization and the speech of an invented character whose historical idiosyncrasies are different from the poet's. The latter is called a **dramatic monologue.** Thom Gunn's poem in end-stopped couplets, "Moly," is spoken by a character whose appetites and standards are pointedly other than the poet's and ours. Not only has the speaker been turned (he realizes gradually) into a sow, he is also one of Odysseus's sailors, adrift in a cultural landscape (Circe's island) far from ours where Gunn imagines the bestial and the human are closer together than we might think. (Indeed, this approach is taken to devastating extremes in Gunn's sequence of poems about the nuclear age, *Misanthropos* [1967].)[11] In the *Misanthropos* poems and in "Moly," Gunn hypothesizes speakers who have crossed over some threshold difficult for us to imagine.

In such dramatically displaced monologues, there is a sense of uncertainty in approaching the new world's boundaries. "Andrea del Sarto," by Robert Browning, is a monologue by a "historical" figure (a Renaissance painter), whom we hear rather than watch. We follow his attempts to work and to reconcile himself to his wife's infidelities just as we feel her attractiveness as it moves him aesthetically and demoralizes him humanly.

---

11. *Misanthropos* is also worth studying as the record of a poet raised in accentual-syllabic meters working to transform himself into a free-verse poet by first loosening the bond of regular accent, then shifting over to syllabics of odd-numbered count (his favorite seems to be the seven-syllable line). See the samples below in the section on syllabics in chapter 10 of Part II.

Browning places the poem's sensibility in a specific past place on a specific afternoon of work, but owing to the selectivity of vision by which we shed self-consciousness when we are deeply imbedded in our experience, del Sarto at the same time acts with minimal props.

The much briefer lyric by Louise Bogan, "Cassandra," takes the voice of passion a step further than does the compromised del Sarto in Browning or the slow-to-emerge "I" in Janet Lewis's poem. Like Thom Gunn in "Moly," Bogan has embodied an extreme that feels uncompromising and absolute in the speech of this tormented "third voice"—neither the poet herself nor the poet speaking in public but a third person from a world well beyond that of these first two representatives. In "Cassandra," the prophetess herself delivers a brief but complex monologue expressing her excruciating weariness with her own unwilled gift—since she is never believed. But she is also curiously "neutral" in the face of her own suffering and her helpless exclusion from life, order, community, sanity, and calm:

Cassandra

To me, one silly task is like another.
I bare the shambling tricks of lust and pride.
This flesh will never give a child its mother,—
Song, like a wing, tears through my breast, my side,
And madness chooses out my voice again,   5
Again. I am the chosen no hand saves:
The shrieking heaven lifted over men,
Not the dumb earth, wherein they set their graves.

Bogan's biographer has suggested that Cassandra's knowledge (which is never believed) represents "that part of the psyche which drives the conscious mind to recognize truths it is reluctant to accept."[12] This assertion aptly reminds us that all our dramas and myths are in part self-projections, even those we know to have a social dimension. Because we accept the persuasive voice of feeling, however, we accede to the most daring improbabilities: Cassandra sees herself "projected" upon the sky from which come storms and portents ("the shrieking heaven"), although she would rather be the more limited and even personal "dumb earth" beneath.

12. Elizabeth Frank, *Louise Bogan: A Portrait* (New York: Columbia University Press, 1985), p. 113.

As mentioned earlier, poems spoken by highly rhetorical and self-dramatizing personas are frequently also presenting an ironic or double argument, that is, a logical organization of matter that is perverse or contradictory. In "Cassandra," the world of the Greek imagination is revealed as cruel, doomed, and short-lived. Obviously, a distortion, and not one shared by the makers of such works as the *Iliad* and the *Oresteia,* which are saturated with other preoccupations—honor in the former, revenge in the latter. Even within one work like the *Iliad* there is variety of view, with Homeric characters like Patroklos tending to attract images suggesting the shadowy presence of the larger hero, Achilles; Menelaus promoting those suggesting sexual rivalry. Then again, as "Ballad of Hector in Hades" indicates (quoted above in chapter 5), it's tempting for a different sort of reader of the Greek psyche (in this instance, the Scots poet Edwin Muir) to predict how Hector's cowardice might obsessively contort the psychological scene.

Another highly self-dramatizing monologue is Shakespeare's "Noe Longer Mourne for Me When I Am Dead" (Sonnet 71). This time we hear, not the speech of a "third" character, but the ever more intemperate address of a figure claiming kinship with that "second self" of the poet speaking to others. This poet-speaker attempts to convince his lover of the strength of his passion by rejecting earthly fame. But there is an under-plot that starts kindling the rhetorical facade of the poem until it threatens to burn away. What flames up about the high-minded if sometimes luridly expressed legacy to his beloved (recall those vile worms he imagines dwelling with him after he dies) is a complaint at his own treatment by the world—presumably, the *literary* world:

> O if (I say) you looke upon this verse,
> When I (perhaps) compounded am with clay,   10
> Do not so much as my poore name reherse;
> But let your love even with my life decay.
> Least* the wise world should looke into your mone**   *lest **moan
> And mocke you with me after I am gon.

Shakespeare's speaker urges his lover to forget him, yet the instructions he gives on the social risks of remembering somebody like himself are wittily memorable. The combined stress falls on the wish to be unforgettable.

The arguments of many ballads, on the other hand, are simpler, based on narrative line or plot—telling a story in sequence. "Maid's Song," by

Julia Randall parodies the simple declarative style of such ballads, presenting a "third" character, the ruined maid, almost incapable of saying (let alone interpreting) her sorrow. All she can do is rehearse the cryptic events as they enter her consciousness.

Maid's Song

I wept on cypress knees,
I made a coat of moss,
I took the glowing worm
And hid him from the grass.

The river moved but once,   5
I could not plant my foot,
I'd mouths about my arm.
At last my love went out.

Hers is a form of "mad song," like Ophelia's in *Hamlet* or the macabre *Kindertotenlieder* of Rückert set to music by Mahler. We could call it a metaphysical ballad. Julia Randall's speaker comes from the engaged end of the rhetorical continuum, although the diction and syntax are reductively simple; one might want to call them "deprived"—compare the relative jauntiness of the quatrains of Roethke's "My Papa's Waltz." Randall's "Maid's Song" exhibits a stoppage in expressiveness in part owing to the poem's peculiar rhythm, a rhythm in turn created by the succumbing of each line to the meter.

7

Rhythm as Combination

Real rhythm as it plays against abstract meter is one of the devices that makes a poem's (and a poet's) voice identifiable. The difference between slowness experienced as peaceful, and slowness experienced as lethargic, is produced by the rhythm of the diction, syntax, etc., as they course (or meander) through the metrical line. The same is true for the difference between the various *effects* of rapidity, which can be experienced either as jagged, or as wittily swift. More specific to the writing and hearing of lines of **accentual-syllabic** poems (poems that count both **accents**—or speech stresses—and syllables), the poetic **rhythm** may be defined as the accommodation of one's individual voice in its natural scope (from how that voice sounds when idly conversing to how that voice sounds when grieving) to the abstract, or automatic, metrical norm. This metrical norm is assumed, for most of the history of poetry in English, to be iambic, moving from an unstressed to a stressed syllable (the word "ássúmed," for example, is a natural **iamb**—where the [o] marks an unstressed syllable and the virgule [/], a speech stress). Note that these marks are relevant only to speech, not to meter; a different set of signs will be helpful when we talk about metrical prosody. The iambic alternation of stressed and unstressed or slack syllables tends to be the habit of spoken English and of English prose—although these are not necessarily the same phenomenon, as can be seen by comparing your most recent essay with the style of your last conversation with a friend; hence it is all the more remarkable that iambic alternation should prove to be the ground base of both.

The meter is merely the grid over which the human voice moves as it weaves its thought. Owing to the fact that meter is constant and invariable (because it is abstract), any *actual* line of metrical verse is necessarily a deviation from the norm, even if there are no odd or reversed feet.

In their collaborative essay on the metrical contract, W. K. Wimsatt and Monroe Beardsley write:

> There is no line so regular (so evenly alternating weak and strong) that it does not show some tension. It is practically impossible to write an English line that will not in some way buck against the meter. Insofar as the line does approximate the condition of complete submission, it is most likely a tame line, a weak line.[1]

Speech stress (accent) and meter are, says James McAuley, "constantly pulling against one another even when they cooperate"; meter's role is

> to provide a fixed schema, across which the endless variety of stress fluctuations can play as one line succeeds another. Our experience of a line of verse is therefore . . . essentially *dual:* comprising a simultaneous recognition on the one hand of the constant metrical pattern (with its occasional variations by substitution of feet), and on the other of the actual stress-profile of the line as natural speech would require.[2]

McAuley goes on to affirm that the two experiences, of meter and of variation in a spoken line of accentual-syllabic verse, are linked together—"mated":

> they are not *radically* distinct since meter is rooted in stress. But they are not identical, and a true feeling for verse depends on appreciating the difference. (p. 31)

Meter also acts as a limit and in that sense as a second kind of norm for speech rhythms to approach, mimic, and mildly diverge from. It can designate some variations as acceptable, others as unacceptable. Most of these "rules" are extensions of speech habits, as for example the rule that one cannot speak English for more than four syllables without providing some sort of interim stress to one or another syllable. Frost's line from

---

1. Monroe C. Beardsley and W. K. Wimsatt, "The Concept of Meter: An Exercise in Abstraction" [1959], in W. K. Wimsatt, *Hateful Contraries: Studies in Literature and Criticism* (Lexington: University of Kentucky Press, 1965), p. 140.

2. James McAuley, *Versification: A Short Introduction* (East Lansing: Michigan State University Press, 1966), pp. 31, 32.

"The Death of the Hired Man" presents six weak monosyllables in a row; none is typically stressed strongly in speech, but strong stress will have to fall somewhere before the fifth syllable (probably on the fourth): "Back out of all this now."[3]

Another rule relates to reversal of stress (in an iambic poem, this reversal is called a **trochaic inversion** or **substitution** of a strong syllable where one expects a weak one, and of a weak syllable where a strong is indicated by the iambic meter, as in "An Old Man's Winter Night" in chapter 6, where the out-of-doors looks in through the frosty window *ALmost in SEParate STARS*—the **trochee** *ALmost* is the mirror image of an iamb). Trochaic inversion is generally heard or felt as unacceptably awkward when it occurs in the second foot of a poem ("The lawn *SPRINKler* did not go on today") but acceptable and even common when the beginning of a line coincides with a slight pause ("*SPRINKle* the lawn, since I will not be home"), or after a midline caesura ("I will not be home: *SPRINKle* the lawn").

But although meter can be said to exact obedience to certain rules, these rules have come down from habits of speech and hence should be thought of as no more than diagnostic tools or as part of a shared framework or limit in poetry. The task at the start of any apprenticeship to poetry lies in mastering its rudiments. Once meter is mastered, the real work of hearing and making rhythm can begin. (More will be said about the weaving of speech with meter to create rhythm in Part II, "The Elements, Controlled in Time.")

When viewed properly, rhythm is the complex interweaving of all of the techniques we have considered thus far. Instead of looking at rhythm as a mechanical exercise with slack and stressed syllables, let us consider it as the final end of the poet's craft and define it as the accommodation of the poet's own sound—his or her argument, rhetorical postures, tropes, diction, along with that poet's syntax—to the constraints and relaxations of the accentual-syllabic line. All verse—even free verse, if it is well crafted—addresses the formal line in its feints and recoils from large and sonorous utterance. Everyone who reads poetry seriously, and everyone who writes it, is involved in tracing the gestures through which traditional elements are counterpointed against the maker's own unique forms of energy and experiment.

---

3. The adverb *Back* might seem more strongly stressed than the other monosyllables here, yet notice what happens in the sentence *he RACED back HOME*.

PART II

The Elements, Controlled in Time

The primary concepts we need for the movement of verse in time are:

1. the syllable (or smallest pronounceable portion of an individual word);

2. rules for syllable articulation and stress (in Greek, length of vowel within a syllable marks the meter, whereas in English, speech-stress and non-stress are the alternatives of focus);

3. provision for the intervals between focal syllables (in English, intervals are measured in terms either of nonstressed syllables or implied nonstresses).

English is a language that counts both speech-stress and numbers of syllables and has accordingly experienced several metrical histories, the first largely accentual, the second accentual-syllabic. The dividing line between its two main periods was drawn by Geoffrey Chaucer, who imported the decasyllabic line from French and Italian poetry into the primarily accentual landscape of English verse.[1] The blend resulted in iambic pentameter verse, which has more than just ten syllables. It has five divi-

---

1. John Hollander, "Romantic Verse Form and the Metrical Contract" [1965] in *Romanticism and Consciousness: Essays in Criticism,* edited by Harold Bloom, pp. 189–90 (New York: W. W. Norton, 1970).

sions of two syllables each, each division (or foot) formed of a weak, then a strong syllable. Iambic pentameter preserves the heavy stress features that were native, stretching them out temporally with greater syllabic regularity and lightness than had been the case.

Chaucer is a milestone in a second sense because, during the time since he wrote, English progressively lost most of its endings. This made it different from the Romance languages in radically reducing the number of rhymes and making those rhymes that remained more masculine than they had been. In other words, line endings became more emphatic, too. Blank verse becomes a possibility only when the line-endings regularize and harden.

This sketch would suggest starting with accentual verse to follow the history of verse in English. But because accentual-syllabism has predominated from Chaucer's time to the beginning of this century, and so forms the core of contributions made by writers in English to the fund of formal verse, I prefer to begin with accentual-syllabic poetry, then look at the relation of meter to rhyme and stanza. I shall then take up variant forms: first, accentual verse and varieties of syllabic verse, then free verse, in brief, after that.

8

Accentual-Syllabic Meter:
The Role of Stress and Interval

Accent and Stress

Meter and **scansion** and the accompanying terminology are shorthand for the way certain poetic traditions measure both their method of counting and the basis on which syllables within the poems differ. In the lines of verse in English of primary concern here, syllables differ according to whether they coincide with the pre-established beats (these are metrically accented syllables) or not (in this case, they are metrically unaccented). Furthermore, verse in English typically counts both the line's length in terms of syllables and the number of **accents** or patterned beats, so that the speech **stresses** that become accented (metrically expected) become so at **intervals;** these intervals are defined by the set recurrence of syllables that are not stressed in speech.

The term **accentual-syllabic verse** (as mentioned in chapter 7's discussion of rhythm) describes lines of verse adhering to a constant pattern of alternation of which the **iambic** line (weak-strong, weak-strong, etc.) is the most common case, as in **dimeters** (two-foot lines) like Thomas Hardy's: "Her fringes brushed / His garment's hem," Richard Wilbur's **trimeter** (three- foot) lines, "That music growing harsh," and the **tetrameter** (four-foot) lines of Emily Dickinson ("How short it takes to make a Bride," #461), Andrew Marvell ("A Plume of agèd Trees does wave"[1]), and Oliver Goldsmith ("To hide her shame from every eye").

This alternation is also heard in longer lines such as Spenser's "You stop my toung, and teach my heart to speake," Shakespeare's "The sad

---

1. Andrew Marvell, "Upon the Hill and Grove at *Bill-borow*," in *Major Poets of the Earlier Seventeenth Century,* edited by Barbara K. Lewalski and Andrew J. Sabol (Indianapolis: Bobbs-Merrill/Odyssey, 1973), p. 1131.

account of forbemonèd mone," and Wordsworth's "And nettles rot and adders sun themselves."[2] Lines longer than this last group of three **pentameters** (five iambs each), while unusual, are expected in some stanzas like the **Spenserean stanza,** which ends with a six-measure iambic line or **hexameter** (as in lines from Shelley's "Adonais," "The life can burn in blood, even while the heart may break" and "A light of laughing flowers along the grass is spread"). Seven-measure lines, or **fourteeners,** are more difficult to manage because they tend to break into the alternating 4–3–4–3 pattern of **common meter,** as in the Civil War song beginning "John Brown's body lies a' mouldering in the grave."

Another kind of line is **syllabic.** Some metrists like Daryl Hine can't help thinking in Alexandrines (12-syllabled lines, borrowed from French, with lighter stresses than iambic hexameter); Hine prefers Racine to Shakespeare, he writes,

> Which may explain why I am writing in a metre
> So alien to English, the Alexandrine. . . .[3]

The syllabic (as distinct from any accentual-syllabic) meter of the Alexandrine partly suspends the issue of stress. Not so the iambic lines of six **measures.** Sometimes, hexameters and even seven-measure lines will occur in the blank verse of writers like Wallace Stevens and Mark Strand. Clearly, theirs is a kind of blank verse that stretches easily, in its conversational and meditative amble, beyond five measures, as in Stevens's seven-measure line about Penelope, "She has composed, so long, a self with

---

2. A backward or grave accent [`] is used to indicate the voicing of the suffix. Marvell's *A G-èd* is two syllables, not one; Shakespeare's *for-be-MON-èd* is four syllables, not three. The practice of articulating endings has fallen off since the eighteenth century, but it was common in the medieval and Renaissance periods as it gave poets another means to "buffer" strongly stressed syllables (it also increased the fund of end-rhymes for those who did not object to **light rhyme**—rhyming on unstressed syllables). Since then, poets have not only had to work harder to rhyme, but they have also had to rely more on monosyllabic speech particles to mediate as prefixes and suffixes once did. See the discussion below for the role of monosyllabic particles in scansion and **pronunciation** in chapter 13's "Poetic Terms."

3. Daryl Hine, "February: Valentine's Day," *Academic Festival Overtures* (New York: Atheneum, 1985), p. 79, where (as in French) the unstressed final syllables (like the last in *metre*) aren't sounded. Hine's 200-page poem is composed entirely in Alexandrines.

which to welcome him,"[4] and Strand's line in fourteeners, "An understanding that remains unfinished, unentire" (*Dark Harbor* xxxii).[5]

Except for the last three examples (two from poems primarily iambic pentameter that cast up longer lines and one from Hine's poem in Alexandrines, in which stress is light), there is constant handling of the **stresses** in the poems from which the lines mentioned thus far in this chapter are taken (two in the dimeters, three in the trimeters, and so on), while the **accents** (anticipated stresses) occur at stipulated and repeating intervals. These intervals are bridged by syllables the language does not stress.

Our aim is to get into the habit of hearing this anticipated alternation of accent with nonaccent (the terms of an abstract meter), in order finally to move beyond isolated features of the meter to those qualities of language, including speech-stress and nonstress, that work together with other points of style to create **rhythm** as defined in chapter 7. There is no doubt that meter and metrical issues can be exaggerated if they are not referred to diction, syntax, and the nuance of meaning.

But without looking closely at meter *by itself* as one starts learning to read and write poetry, it's harder to be certain of one's ability to hear and write metrically. Both activities—working in a metrical mode and hearing the modes in works written by others—require some attention to regularity. Both also require a taste for variation from the merely automatic. Only after one identifies the abstract pattern (of metrically accented and unaccented syllables) can one gauge and thus appreciate the living variations in the pattern (coming from actual speech stresses), which make for meaning and interest.

Even when one starts to learn to scan (or make a visual graph of) a poem's meter, one should realize that *a line cannot be scanned out of context*. All we can do is to mark the syllables as stressed [/] or unstressed [°] in ordinary speech. Distinguishing stressed from unstressed syllables—while

---

4. Wallace Stevens, *Collected Poems* (New York: Alfred A. Knopf, 1954), p. 521. See two other iambic lines by Stevens extruded into hexameters: "Of life and spring and of the lustrous inundations" (*CP*, p. 125) and "It is a choice of the commodious adjective" (*CP*, p. 475).

5. Note that a speech stress falls on the prefix of *únentire* because Strand's neologism is focused on the negative tilt of the prefix, picked up from *unfinished*. See other examples of **elective stress** from *Hamlet* and *Paradise Lost* later in this chapter, in which meaning places stress on prefixes and other speech particles not typically stressed in speech.

being crucial to the eventual forming of a metrical expectation—does not add up to scanning the lines. Even a traffic ticket (*Yŏu múst páy ĭn tén dáys*) or a recipe (*Crúsh thĕ ánchŏvĭĕs tŏ å páste*) can be marked according to whether each syllable is stressed or not. Prose and nonmetrical poems can also be divided into **slack** (unstressed) and stressed **syllables.**

Determining speech stress is the first step in scanning a poem. The method is fairly straightforward and the rule of thumb is the same for prose and poetry of all kinds:

1. Monosyllabic nouns, adjectives, adverbs, and "strong" verbs are stressed wherever they occur. Verbs used as auxiliaries and those I have called **non-verbs** (see chapter 12) may or may not be stressed, depending on the semantic context. The many monosyllabic speech particles (articles, conjunctions, prepositions, and pronouns) are usually unstressed.

2. Bisyllabic words have one stressed and one unstressed syllable (exceptions, with two equally strong stresses, tend to be nursery words like *Mama,* interjections like *Amen,* and compounds like *hamstrung, hipbone, birdbath, touchstone, handrail, blue-green, hailstones,* and *Cream-bowl;* Milton, who used the last, also devised the suggestive *Crop-full* for the cream-fed "Lubber Fiend" in "L'Allegro," ll. 106–13).

3. Polysyllables have one main stress and a variable number of unstressed syllables; sometimes it helps to use the dictionary where polysyllabic words are concerned, because scansion makes one over-stress the secondary syllables (Dickinson's *un-CER-tain* has one stressed syllable, so (despite being twice as long) does Wordsworth's *un-in-TEL-li-gi-ble*).[6] Some polysyllables appear with secondary stresses in American but not British usage: *àp-pre-HÉN-sion, còn-ver-SÁ-tion,* while many lack second-

---

6. If there is a true secondary stress, we could mark it with a secondary stress mark [\ ]—not to be confused with the backwards or grave accent [`], which alerts the reader to voiced suffixes (see note 2). Thus:

      \ / / o o   / / o
    Preheat oven to three-fifty

But it may be best to understress polysyllables in scansion, accounting only for dominant stress. To compensate for this restraint, our method of graphing will account visually for what Harold Whitehall calls "secondary" and "reduced secondary" stresses relative to "zero" stress. See Whitehall's article on "The English Language," which introduces *Webster's New World Dictionary* (Cleveland: World Publishing, 1968), in particular his discussion of the syllable and the concept of stress—as well as the basic grammatical features of English (pp. xvii–xxv).

aries in either country: *e-QUIV-o-cal, U-nis-on, re-GARD-less-ly, un-INT-ter-est-ed, me-RID-i-en.*

The other piece of the scansion puzzle is the **derived meter**—the abstract pattern of our expectations. Only when a poem is known fairly well can one theorize about its meter—and even after forming some statistical picture of the poem, expectations must be linked to actual words that possess, when spoken aloud, stressed and slack (or unstressed) syllables. Then a scansion of the line may be completed by deciding what model it approximates. Quite simply, at this point, we are no longer hearing individual lines alone—we are registering our hearing of the entire poem and resolving it into its basic pattern.

Scansion

Various symbols might be used to graph a scansion of an accentual-syllabic poem, but whatever symbols are employed, there are two requirements, following from the basic law of scansion, which is first in the following list:

1. A line should not be scanned out of context (without the context, one can only mark the stressed and unstressed syllables). See rule 4 below.
2. A scansion must have at least three symbols (two to register expectation of accent and nonaccent and one to show where the actual speech-stresses fall).
3. Basic metrical expectation does not change. Even when there are **substituted feet,** say a trochee where one expects an iamb, neither the poem nor the metrical **foot** becomes trochaic. (Moreover, the trochee in an iambic poem is a different animal than a trochee in a trochaic poem.)

Two additional rules, to be discussed later in the chapter, can nevertheless be mentioned here:

4. **Context makes meter.** This corollary to the first rule is especially pertinent with lines that do not immediately suggest their metrical allegiance.
5. **Meaning makes stress.** Some lines can be spoken, that is, properly stressed, only when we make decisions about ambiguous syllables (many will be monosyllables).

Following rule 2, I have adopted Vladimir Nabokov's three-symbol scansion because, after we provide the metrical context by indicating what metrical expectations a given poem arouses, his account gives the most coherent visual reflection of the requirements; and it allows us to register the influence of expectation on unstressed syllables.[7] For expectation, Nabokov uses the classical short, or **breve** [∪], and long, or **macron** [−]. For actual speech stresses, a primary stress mark is used [∕]. Thus an iamb in a real line of poetry (for example, the word *above* in this line from Wordsworth:"Where leafless oaks towered high above") would be sketched [∪ −́].[8]

I've said that three signs are necessary to scan a line of accentual-syllabic poetry. Now let us apply these signs. Consider two lines of perfectly regular iambic pentameter, one by Tennyson, "To strive, to seek, to find, and not to yield" (from "Ulysses") and one by Nemerov, "In cubes like building blocks of dusty gold" (from "Landscape with Self-Portrait"). This is how one might scan them using, first, the abstract "mapping" of iambic feet [∪ −]—

$$\left|\begin{array}{c}∪ \ \ −\\ \text{To strive}\end{array}\right|\begin{array}{c}∪ \ \ −\\ \text{to seek}\end{array}\left|\begin{array}{c}∪ −\\ \text{to find}\end{array}\right|\begin{array}{c}∪ \ \ −\\ \text{and not}\end{array}\left|\begin{array}{c}∪ \ −\\ \text{to yield}\end{array}\right|^{9}$$

$$\left|\begin{array}{c}∪ \ \ −\\ \text{In cubes}\end{array}\right|\begin{array}{c}∪ \ \ \ −\\ \text{like build}\end{array}\left|\begin{array}{c}∪ \ \ \ −\\ \text{ing blocks}\end{array}\right|\begin{array}{c}∪ − \\ \text{of dust}\end{array}\left|\begin{array}{c}∪ −\\ \text{y gold}\end{array}\right|$$

—then the strokes of the syllables that are actually stressed [∕]; note that the [∘] is no longer used, because the unstressed syllables are already articulated (counted as separate units) by the marks of anticipated non-accent (breves [∪]):

$$\left|\begin{array}{c}∪ \ \ ∕\\ \text{To strive}\end{array}\right|\begin{array}{c}∪ \ \ ∕\\ \text{to seek}\end{array}\left|\begin{array}{c}∪ \ ∕\\ \text{to find}\end{array}\right|\begin{array}{c}∪ \ \ \ ∕\\ \text{and not}\end{array}\left|\begin{array}{c}∪ \ ∕\\ \text{to yield}\end{array}\right|$$

$$\left|\begin{array}{c}∪ \ \ ∕\\ \text{In cubes}\end{array}\right|\begin{array}{c}∪ \ \ \ ∕\\ \text{like build}\end{array}\left|\begin{array}{c}∪ \ \ \ ∕\\ \text{ing blocks}\end{array}\right|\begin{array}{c}∪ \ ∕\\ \text{of dust}\end{array}\left|\begin{array}{c}∪ ∕\\ \text{y gold}\end{array}\right|$$

But the scansions suggest that these lines sound quite similar, when in fact the first line is loud and heavy, and the second line is at once loose

---

7. Vladimir Nabokov, *Notes on Prosody and Abram Gannibal* (Princeton, NJ: Princeton/Bollingen Series, 1964).

8. The curved line beneath a word, an elision mark [‿], shows that two syllables have been collapsed into one. The process is called **elision** (literally, a "striking out").

9. I follow James McAuley in omitting punctuation when writing out a line of scansion. See his *Versification: A Short Introduction* (East Lansing: Michigan State University Press, 1966), p. 4.

and brisk. What do we do to symbolize differences our signs don't distinguish?

Main Line-Stress

In order to register the residual conviction of the difference in overall weight between the Tennyson and the Nemerov lines, we could use another sign to mark the stresses that rise above the foot-stresses—in other words, **main line-stresses.** These can be marked with an [x]. This mark must not be used in abundance, since the point is to record only a subtle pressure added by meaning to terms already strongly stressed:

$$
\begin{array}{ccccc}
 & & & & \text{x} \\
\cup \;/ & \cup \;/ & \cup \;/ & \cup \qquad/ & \cup \;/ \\
\mid \text{To strive} \mid & \text{to seek} \mid & \text{to find} \mid & \text{and not} \mid & \text{to yield} \mid
\end{array}
$$

$$
\begin{array}{ccccc}
 & \text{x} & & & \text{x} \\
\cup \;/ & \cup \;/ & \cup \quad/ & \cup \;/ & \cup \;/ \\
\mid \text{In cubes} \mid & \text{like build} \mid & \text{ing blocks} \mid & \text{of dust} \mid & \text{y gold} \mid
\end{array}
$$

Adding main line-stresses to the scansion already performed allows us to focus on the dramatic pressure Tennyson reserves for the last term in the series, and the most important one—even if he has negated it ("not to yield"); "yield" is still positioned so as to insist on a subliminal loosening of one's hold on life. Whereas in Nemerov's line one hears the more common propensity toward symmetrical anchoring by crucial stresses that is especially conducive to antithesis (which Nemerov is not using here) and to adjective-noun pairing (which he is).

Scansion and Syntax

We may still feel that the cadence and tempo of the two lines have not been given adequate visual distinction. Let's recall the **caesura** or cut between different units of syntax. The strongest cut will be made between the end of one sentence and the beginning of another; weaker caesuras occur when clauses end midline, next, when phrases emphatically end and new ones begin on a single line. When we look at the way the syntax of these two lines unfolds, we note that Nemerov's sequence of prepositional phrases modifying "hay" from the previous line is evenly derived, one phrase slipping effortlessly out of another: The cubes are like building blocks; the building blocks are of a dusty gold color (see complete text of "Landscape with Self-Portrait" on pp. 127–28). Even if there are three different phrases, they link easily together in a series. Hence we cannot hear a caesural pause anywhere in the line.

In Tennyson's line, by contrast, the caesuras are significant. Recall the poem's occasion: Ulysses is about to set out for the final journey, the one that will take him beyond the pillars of Hercules. The atmosphere of "Ulysses" is one of grandiose self-sacrifice amid romanticized inklings of death ("the deep / Moans round with many voices," Ulysses says; but he is not particularly concerned with portents—so long as they lead to expressions of beautiful fluency as he exhorts his sailors to go with him "beyond the sunset, and the baths / Of all the western stars," even if "It may be that the gulfs will wash us down").

> Death closes all; but something ere the end,
> Some work of noble note, may yet be done,
> Not unbecoming men that strove with gods.
> The lights begin to twinkle from the rocks;
> The long day wanes; the slow moon climbs; the deep   55
> Moans round with many voices. Come, my friends.
> 'Tis not too late to seek a newer world.
> Push off, and sitting well in order smite
> The sounding furrows; for my purpose holds
> To sail beyond the sunset, and the baths   60
> Of all the western stars, until I die.
> It may be that the gulfs will wash us down;
> It may be we shall touch the Happy Isles,
> And see the great Achilles, whom we knew.
> Though much is taken, much abides; and though   65
> We are not now that strength which in old days
> Moved earth and heaven, that which we are we are,
> One equal temper of heroic hearts,
> Made weak by time and fate, but strong in will
> To strive, to seek, to find, and not to yield.   70

In such a death-saturated setting, the heady idea of yielding is everywhere implicit. Consequently, when Ulysses claims that they are all still capable of heroic acts, we hear a summons to collective suicide as well. Accordingly, Tennyson brackets together yielding with nonyielding in one phrase, making either option ambiguous: Syntax permits and the **prosody** or voiced rhythm supports a harmony between release and its mirror, resistance (the two contradictory impulses that drive Tennyson's

Ulysses through the rhetorical currents of the poem). Adding the syntactic junctures to the metrical ones, the line would be scanned as follows:

$$
\overset{\cup}{\mid \text{To}} \ \overset{/}{\text{strive}} \ \| \ \overset{\cup}{\text{to}} \ \overset{/}{\text{seek}} \ \| \ \overset{\cup}{\text{to}} \ \overset{/}{\text{find}} \ \| \ \overset{\cup}{\text{and}} \ \overset{/}{\text{not}} \ \mid \ \overset{\cup}{\text{to}} \ \overset{\overset{\text{x}}{/}}{\text{yield}} \ \mid {}^{10}
$$

The complete scansion can now record the curious *logical* hitch in this line: that we have reached the goal *three times* before we go through the middle of the struggle. Ulysses and his men, having already *found* the end or source, must stiffen themselves in order *not to yield* along the way. Indeed, it is the not-yielding that requires the largest syntactic breath— double that of either uninflected striving or seeking, let alone of simple finding. And it is in this last phrase, "and not to yield," that we locate the greatest emphasis (main line-stress), which counteracts the many "arrivals," set off by caesuras, in the first three feet of this poem's dramatic last line.

Looking only at the caesuras and main line-stressing in the last two lines will illustrate these tensions from another perspective:

$$
\Big\{\text{Made weak by time and fate}\Big\} \Big\{\text{but strong in will}\Big\}
$$

$$
\Big\{\text{To strive to seek to find}\Big\} \Big\{\text{and not to YIELD}\Big\}{}^{11}
$$

To set off the segments of lines logically while retaining prominent line-stresses in this way may also help us to see the spatial relation between the rhymes and alliterations we half-consciously hear (*weak/seek, fate/ find/strive, weak/will, will/yield*) as well as the logical contrasts, for example, *weak versus strong, fate versus will, will versus yield,* and *strive versus yield.* (Similar binding effects can be found in Milton's blank verse, as noted in chapter 2's discussion of syntax.)

---

10. When foot and caesura coincide, only the double line for the caesura is used, but at the same height as a foot-division bar. When caesuras occur midfoot, they are shown by shorter parallel lines.

11. I would argue *against* a main line-stress on *find* because the series is not yet over; the fact that another phrase will follow the third **infinitive** (or the potential form of any verb, beginning with *to*) bears stress forward toward the final item in the rising arc of achievement implied, first by striving and seeking, next by finding, and finally, because finding neither satisfies nor impedes us, by . . . whatever will ensue to cap the series.

Beyond Iambic Meter

What of other metrical feet? In the same iambic tetrameter poem quoted earlier, a trochaic foot audible in the phrase / -*blast from* / in line 1 (from which the title is taken), "A whirl-blast from behind the hill," would be sketched [∪ –]. But the metrical assumption (that we are "in" an iambic poem) remains the same; hence the actual fall of the stress must work *counter* to our expectation, and indeed Wordsworth's line metrically imitates the surprise and deranging force of the gale:[12]

$$ \mid \overset{∪}{A\ whirl} \mid \overset{/}{blast\ from} \mid \overset{∪/}{behind} \mid \overset{∪/}{the\ hill} \mid $$

Nabokov's system registers the lengths to which spoken language goes (or does not go) to counteract regularity. A trochee in an iambic line can be disruptive; a trochee in a **trochaic** line, on the other hand, is perfectly normal and would be sketched [– ∪]. Speech-stress coincides with awaited accent here. Consider any of the feet in these lines from Samuel Johnson's trochaic "Short Song of Congratulation": "Lavish of your Grandsires guineas, . . . What are acres? What are houses?" Cecil Alexander's majestic carol is also regularly trochaic: "Once in royal David's city." Somewhat more whimsically, Wordsworth patters along in "To the Small Celandrine": "Pansies, lilies, kingcups, daisies, / Let them live upon their praises." Similarly, all the feet, including the last (defective) foot, in Auden's title-line bring stress into coincidence with accent: "Lay your sleeping head my love." All of these are perfectly straightforward trochaic feet that make themselves heard just where one expects trochaic feet to be.

Based on a sense of the coherence of the stress-pattern across a number of lines, one can derive an estimate of the poem's meter. This derived meter will fall into one of two categories: it will be either a two-syllabled meter or a three-syllabled meter. It will be either rising to its strongest stress or falling from it (hence the terms **rising meter** and **falling meter**). The two rising feet are the iamb (abstractly sketched [∪ –]) and the **anapest** [∪∪ –]. The two falling feet are the trochee (abstractly sketched [– ∪]) and the **dactyl** [– ∪∪]. But only the iamb and the trochee have proven consistently metrically viable in English, since whole poems are

---

12. Nabokov (who, to provide audible examples for non-Russian-readers, excerpts only English *tetrameters*—not our poetic tradition's strongest suit, but the primary mode in Russian poetry) quotes the Wordsworth poem in *Notes on Prosody*, p. 62.

written in them. The "triple" feet, dactyls, anapests, and **amphibrachs** [∪ – ∪], provide special cases, whose restrictions have made them rare throughout accentual-syllabic writing in English—*except* for literature in the nineteenth century, when a huge burst of experiment in all three triple measures took place. Chapter 13's "Poetic Terms" gives several examples of each type. Poems such as Longfellow's "Evangeline" abound in lines that prove the rule that dactyls are top-heavy in English and conducive to filler: "Faint was the air with the odorous breath of magnolia blossoms." A consistent procession of anapests also sounds lurching—in a way even excellent metrists have trouble controlling, for example, Sidney Lanier: "I have waked, I have come, my beloved! I might not abide: / I have come ere the dawn, O beloved, my live-oaks, to hide / In your gospelling glooms" ("Hymns of the Marshes"). Or it may be that we have lost the ear receptive to serious use of either dactyl or anapest.

The amphibrach has a strong life in nursery rhyme and ballad: "Farewell and adieu to you, fair Spanish Ladies" and "O where hae ye been ^ Lord Randal, my son?" are largely amphibrachic, although the occasional anapestic line is encountered in both.[13] For example, "But we hope in a short time to see you again"; "I hae been to the wild ^ wood; mother, ^ mak my bed soon, / For I'm weary wi hunting, and fain wald lie down."

The tendency is for triple feet (amphibrach, anapest, and dactyl) to blend into each other just as iambs can blend with trochees. And just as there is a preference for iambs in our perception of alternating stresses, there may also be a slight preference for amphibrachs among triple feet:

I have fine moulds for cooks, and fine cutting knives,
Axes for butchers, and fine glasses for wives;
Med'cines for rats to shorten their lives,
What lack you? What buy you? Come hither to me.

I have rollingpins, battledores, washbowls, and broom,   5
Wild beasts and puppets, sent from beyond Rome;
Fine gay and strange garlands, for bride and for groom,
What lack you, fair maidens? Come hither to me.[14]

---

13. W. H. Auden and John Garrett, eds., *The Poet's Tongue* (London: G. Bell & Sons, 1935), "Lord Randal" I.101; "Farewell Fair Spanish Ladies," II.20.

The caret [^] indicates an assumed unstressed syllable.

14. Thomas Newbery (fl. 1563), in *Children's Verse*, edited by Iona and Peter Opie (New York & Oxford: Oxford University Press, 1973), p. 15.

Of these eight lines by Thomas Newbery, three are amphibrachic (4, 7, 8), three dactylic (2, 3, 6), and only two anapestic (1, 5).

Contrasted with folk poems like those above, literary poems based on the amphibrach tend to be either more inflexible (for example, Robert Browning's: "No seeing our skiff / Arrive about noon from Amalfi, / — Our fisher arrive, / And pitch down his basket before us, / All trembling alive / With pink and grey jellies, your sea-fruit" ["The Englishman in Italy"]; Rudyard Kipling's comic amphibrachs in "Seal Lullaby" are also strictly observed: "Where billow meets billow, there soft be thy pillow; / Ah, weary wee flapperling, curl at thy ease!"[15]). Or the literary amphibrachs tap a vein of folk vigor, as in John Clare's poem about autumn, the season that is boiling and burning and flaming up everywhere: "The ground parched and cracked is like overbaked bread. . . . The fallow fields glitter like water indeed. . . . Burning hot is the ground, liquid gold is the air; / Whoever looks round sees eternity there."[16] The literary amphibrachs by Charles Dalmon suffer from non sequitur—one pretty line about the sea next to one about a fuchsia tree—and repetition (*awaken*, a natural amphibrach, appears three times in one line), but the lines themselves are often moving: "O what if the fowler my blackbird has taken? . . . And sing to me out of my red fuchsia tree!"[17]

This lean toward inflexibility or roughness in the literary use of the amphibrach may be the accidental reason why the anapest has had more play and why, instead of being the dominant rhythm, amphibrachs have been supposed merely as alternatives in poems taken as anapestic, as in William Cowper's "Poplar Field":

> The poplars are fell'd; farewell to the shade,
> And the whispering sound of the cool colonnade!
> The winds play no longer and sing in the leaves,
> Nor Ouse* on his bosom their image receives.   *a river

The only anapestic line is the second; the other three are amphibrachic. Yet this was in its time a compelling example (for an appreciative audi-

15. Kipling, "Seal Lullaby," in *Animal Poems,* edited by John Hollander (New York: Knopf/Everyman, 1994), p. 186.

16. John Clare, "Autumn," in Auden and Garrett, eds., *The Poet's Tongue,* I.142–43.

17. Dalmon, in Auden and Garrett, eds., *The Poet's Tongue,* I.100.

ence that included poets like Wordsworth) of the anapest's suitability for elegiac themes.[18]

Overstressing and Understressing in Iambic Pentameter

Truly nonviable are the **spondee** [− −], the **pyrrhic** [∪∪], the **cretic** [− ∪ −], and the **bacchius** [∪ − −], which appear in English accentual-syllabic poems *only* to substitute in a foot rather than to determine the operative meter. Two of these feet, the pyrrhic and the spondee, have never (even in classical prosody) been used for anything but substitution. Thus, because they are not viable as basic meters, when they appear in English poems, they are sometimes called "false pyrrhics" (in an iambic poem in our system, this would be sketched [∪ −]), and "false spondees" [∪ −]:

| ∪ / | ∪ / | ∪ − | ∪ / | ∪ / |
| Nor torne | the worde | that from | my mouthe | is gone |

(Wyatt)

| ∪ / | ∪ / ‖ ∪ / | ∪ − | ∪ / |
| You frame | my thoughts ‖ and fash | ion me | within |

(Spenser)

| / ∪ | ∪ / ‖ ∪ − | / ∪ / | ∪ − |
| Came lov | ers home ‖ from this | great fes | tival |

(Marlowe)

| ∪ / | ∪ / | ∪ / | ∪ − | ∪ / |
| My brain | I'll prove | the fe | male to | my soul |

(Shakespeare)

| ∪ / | ∪ − | ∪ / | ∪ − | ∪ / |
| Excite | ments of | my reas | on ‖ and | my blood |

(Shakespeare)

| ∪ / | ∪ / | ∪ − | ∪ / | ∪ / |
| And Lil | ies blaz | ing on | the reg | al Shield |

(Pope)

18. See again "Romantic Verse Form and the Metrical Contract," in *Romanticism and Consciousness: Essays in Criticism*, edited by Harold Bloom, pp. 191–93 (New York: W. W. Norton, 1970), where Hollander reminds us of the enormous fad in elegiac anapestic tetrameters in the late eighteenth and early nineteenth centuries.

| Of all | this un | intel | ligib | le world |

(Wordsworth)

| The wear | iness ‖ the fev | er ‖ and | the fret |

(Keats)

| And strug | gling through | its er | ror with | vain strife |

(Shelley)

| I say | the wood | within | is the | dark wood |

(Justice)

"False pyrrhics" or unstressed iambs occur in the third foot of Wyatt's line, in the fourth in the line from Spenser, and in feet 2 and 4 of the Wordsworth, Keats, Shelley, and second Shakespeare lines—a common symmetrical pattern of coasting over weaker syllables in iambic pentameter poems in all centuries but the eighteenth.[19] Nabokov's graphing helps to differentiate the weak syllable in a weak place [U] from a weak syllable in a strong place [−] and thereby register the mild disappointment at expecting stress and hearing none. (Nabokov calls this "scudding," which motivated him to give the "false pyrrhic" or unstressed iamb the clunky soubriquet "a scud.") The unstressed iambic feet lighten and loosen and make more dreamlike this line from "Frost at Midnight":

| Heard on | ly in | the tran | ces of | the blast |

(Coleridge)

19. Poets in the eighteenth century favored third-foot pyrrhics in their iambic pentameters, which emphasize the habit of balance and of splitting every phrase and idea and line in two, for example, Pope's "His swelling Waters, and altérnate Tydes" ("Windsor-Forest" 334); "Who rules in Cornwall, or who rules in Berks" (trans. of Horace Ep.I.v.104); "The mossie Fountaines and the Green Retreats!" ("Summer" 72) (the above quotations from John Butt, ed., *The Poems of Alexander Pope* [1963] (New Haven: Yale University Press, 1969).

With regard to pyrrhics (understressed iambs), see Herbert Lanz, *The Physical Basis of Rime: An Essay on the Aesthetics of Sound* (Stanford University Press, 1931), pp. 211–34 for graphs contrasting the habits of Milton, Pope, Goethe, Kleist, and Shelley. In the iambic pentameter of Shelley, Lanz finds twice as many symmetrical pyrrhics (that is, in both foot 2 and foot 4) as in the pentameter couplets of Pope, where the full complement of five stresses is the norm. To this fact Lanz attributes the greater heaviness of Pope compared with the iambic verse of the Romantic poets.

The reverse—a slight overstressing, or "false spondee"—opens both Coleridge's line above and another Wordsworth line below; note again how Nabokov's scansion makes visible the unexpectedness of the extra strong stress:

```
    /    /        U /  U  /  U  /    U /
| Dear God ‖ the ver| y hous| es seem | asleep |
```

However, the initial overstressing in these two lines is felt differently; the Coleridge line is less emphatic than that of Wordsworth, who plays out the remainder of the line with alternating speech stresses. "False spondees" and "false pyrrhics" create, respectively, the slow overstressing and rapid understressing discussed in chapter 4. It is not uncommon to find the pyrrhic and the spondee in close succession,[20] sometimes for violent effect, as in the lines below:

```
  U  /  U     _    U   /      U   /   U /
| Excus| ing thy | sins more | than thy | sins are |[21]
```

(Shakespeare)

```
  U  /   U _    U    /       U   /   U  /
| A bring| er of | new things ‖ and vile | it were |
```

(Tennyson)

```
  U _    U   /   U_    U  /    U  \
| as a | dark fus| illade | of ket| tledrums |
```

(Derek Walcott)

Walcott, irritated by the racket in his hotel on New Year's Eve, underscores the spondee in foot two with another pyrrhic in foot three; altogether, this line's aggressive syllables (including the first syllable of *KÉT-tle-drùms*) are thrown into higher relief by the two unstressed iambic feet—or pyrrhics. In the same poem ("The Hotel Normandie Pool"), Walcott calls his alter-ego, the Roman poet Ovid in exile on the Black Sea

```
  U /    U   /  U  _      U  /    U   /
| a fleck | of spit| tle from | the she-| wolf's tooth |
```

---

20. The pyrrhic-spondee combination, as Charles Hartman once pointed out to me, simulates the classical Greek foot of four syllables, the "rising Ionic" [UU − −]. Although this "foot" is not recognized in scansion in English, and thus not available to us as a pattern for substitution in a poem of two-syllabled feet, the reference to the Ionic gives visual shape to a crucial counterpoint to the iambic expectation.

21. Meaning makes stress on the second "thy," whereas the meaning-stress on the first "sins" withholds stress from the first "thy." The gist is that one is forgiven for one's sins before one can be singled out as an individual sinner.

The pyrrhic is separated from the spondee by an iamb. The possible tightening from the delayed *off-ON,* pyrrhic-spondee combination is exchanged for a much stronger sort of effect, since the iamb-spondee pair produces three strongly stressed syllables in a row, *SHE-WOLF'S TOOTH* (the founders of Rome, the twin orphans Romulus and Remus, were suckled by a wolf). The pyrrhic third foot produces a little pocket of air in the line before this series of stresses. The "scudded foot" also sets off the two main line-stresses, in the second and fifth feet—

$$
\left| \begin{array}{c} \cup \ \diagup \\ \text{a fleck} \end{array} \right| \begin{array}{c} \cup \ \diagup \\ \text{of spit} \end{array} \left| \begin{array}{c} \text{x} \\ \cup \ \diagup \\ \text{tle from} \end{array} \right| \begin{array}{c} \cup \ \diagup \\ \text{the she-} \end{array} \left| \begin{array}{c} \diagup \quad \text{x} \\ \cup \ \diagup \\ \text{wolf's tooth} \end{array} \right|
$$

But these two main line-stresses are not produced solely by the meter—they are produced by aggressive diction (*spittle, tooth*) and clever metonymy: Ovid, who was banished by Augustus, stands in the same relation to the vast Roman empire of 8 A.D. as a random fleck of spit fallen from the fang of the wolf-mother who rejected him would stand to her more active imperial predations (say, the conquest of the Germanic peoples then underway). In other words, Rome had bigger game in mind than Ovid. Like the Roman poet, Walcott's persona feels isolated both racially and culturally; on behalf of Ovid, a far more sweet-natured individual, this persona also seems driven by disgust at the figures of power. Walcott's prosody supports his savage diction to dramatize this theme of bitterness—but almost in an unselective way (this is one of numbers of lines with the same prosodic features—four lines later, Walcott writes that the sands "are stained with sewage from each tín-shácked Róme"). Thus there's a sense that his formal embodiments of resentment become almost reflexively aggressive.

Gentleness offsets aggressiveness in "The Hotel Normandie Pool" when Ovid speaks:

> Then Ovid said, "When I was first exiled,
> I missed my language as your tongue needs salt,
> in every watery shape I saw my child . . .

Even when Ovid looks into the water, the laws of optics recoil from him

> "till, on a tablet smooth as a pool's skin,
> I made reflections that, in many ways,
> were even stronger than their origin."

The pyrrhic-spondee combination in *as a POOL'S SKIN* is softer than the other examples from Walcott, just as his meter opens to reversals (*EX-iled* in the fifth foot of the first line above) softened by **light rhyme** (with "child"). The play between harsh and regressive voices makes the prosody in Walcott more flexible.

Wyatt also stretches the iambic line by pairing one pyrrhic-spondee combination with *two* trochaic substitutions in the fourth line. Out of a possible five iambs, four are variant feet:

> Myne owne John Poynz, sins ye delight to know
> The cause why that homeward I me drawe,
> And fle the presse of courtes wher soo they goo,
> Rather than to lyve thrall, under the awe
> Of lordly lokes, wrappid within my cloke . . .   5
>
> (Satire I, Myne owne John Poynz)

$$| \overset{\text{/}}{\underset{\text{Rather}}{\cup} -} | \underset{\text{than to}}{\cup -} | \overset{\text{/}}{\underset{\text{lyve}}{\cup}} \underset{\text{thrall}}{\diagup} \| \overset{\text{/}}{\underset{\text{under}}{\cup} -} | \underset{\text{the}}{\cup} \underset{\text{awe}}{\diagup} | \qquad 4$$

Because the trochaic substitutions occur following natural caesuras (the cuts or pauses imposed by syntax), we're never tempted to defect to any rival metrical norm; the iamb is still the pattern against which we register the counterpoint of speech-stressing. But the line is awkward, rough, uneasy. It may not be necessary, even for dramatic effect when lambasting social corruption, to be as rambunctious as Wyatt when he strains against the iambic frame.

Louise Bogan's dramatic address to the sonnet form keeps the line— even with two caesuras in the middles of the iambic feet—manageable in its variations. The key to such management is our ability to hear the iambic pentameter model under the surface (this we could not quite do with the Wyatt above):

$$| \overset{\text{/}}{\underset{\text{Now}}{\cup}} \| \underset{\text{you}}{-} | \underset{\text{great stan}}{\cup \diagup} | \underset{\text{za}}{\cup} \| \underset{\text{you}}{-} | \underset{\text{hero}}{\cup \diagup} | \underset{\text{ic mould}}{\cup \diagup} | \qquad 1$$

$$| \overset{\text{/}}{\underset{\text{Bend to}}{\cup} -} | \underset{\text{my will}}{\cup \diagup} \| \underset{\text{for I}}{\cup -} | \underset{\text{must give}}{\cup \diagup} | \underset{\text{you love}}{\cup \diagup} | \qquad 2$$

Bogan's variations are muscular and her midline pauses are striking, but over them all she has stretched the air of deliberate control, as the poet-speaker tries the pretty outrageous tactic of writing a poem of seduction and subjugation to the sonnet tradition itself. The third feet are pallid or understressed, but they are still iambs and register the tug of metrical expectation. Meter moves the voice at both pronouns because we are at strong places with no near competition for stress (unlike the case in the last foot of the second line and in the first foot of the first line, where "you" is entirely overshadowed by the nearby "love" and the even more peremptory "Now," which creates a reversed foot, or trochee).

Every modulation of the pattern is thus an occasion for proving her excellence as a poet in a "man's field" (Sidney, Drayton, Shakespeare, Campion) and as a twentieth-century poet in a world where the values of the Renaissance lyric can be grasped only in a blurred way. Part of Bogan's achievement here is to have insisted that the sonnet must answer to rather more profound ideas about love and sexual passion than we find in most of the sonnets (even Shakespeare's—with a few exceptions: #94, #116, and #138). Bogan wants to insist on greater *psychological* seriousness and complexity as she, too, exaggerates the pain of longing; what sets her poem apart is that she also implies the pain of satiety—or perhaps "saturation" is the better term for that mood of paralysis in mannerism that can come with obsessive erotic love. She sees herself as a woman on a frieze, punished by the existence of the gestures to which she actively yields.

Elective Stress

It is this punishing experience which Bogan treats almost entirely by means of rhythm in "Single Sonnet," which is surely one of the slipperiest and slowest of pentameter poems in this form. If we wonder why the option of pyrrhic feet (or understressed iambs) does not provide greater lightness or quickening, we have to acknowledge the role of overstressing throughout in reducing the possibility of movement. Heavy monosyllabic nouns for heavy substances do some of the coercion: "No stone, slate, metal, under or above / Earth." Feeling as well as rhythm is made ponderous and wrenching. But monosyllables normally not stressed are also brought out by the argument: "Too long, as ocean bed bears up the ocean, / As earth's core bears the earth, have *I* born *THIS*." What we might call **elective stress** grows dominant here and in the final couplet to draw the antagonists of passion into an embrace: "Staunch meter, great song, it is *YOURS,* at length, / To prove how stronger *YOU* are than *MY* strength." Meaning does not, however, make stress on every pronoun that is normally lightly stressed.[22]

22. Shakespeare also enjoyed the technique of pronouns antithetically deployed; as in Bogan's poem, the device helped produce an atmosphere of both solemnity and dread

In contrast to *over*stressing, the wrenching effect of trochees, and prominent elective stress of weak monosyllables, *under*stressed feet can lighten even the heavily stressed ones in their neighborhood. The pyrrhic-spondee combination (or spondee-pyrrhic—see the second line below) can produce far subtler, smoother, and more lightly melancholy music than what we've just heard in Walcott, Shakespeare, and Bogan. Consider the refrain lines from Spenser's "Prothalamium" (bridal song):

$$\left|\; \overset{\cup}{\text{Against}}\overset{/}{} \;\middle|\; \text{the}\,\overset{\cup}{\text{brid}}\overset{/}{}\middle|\overset{\cup}{\text{ale}}\,\overset{/}{\text{day}} \;\middle\|\; \overset{\cup}{\text{which}}\,\overset{\_}{\text{is}} \;\middle|\; \overset{\cup}{\text{not}}\,\overset{/}{\text{long}} \;\middle|\right.$$

$$\left|\; \overset{/}{\text{Sweete}}\,\overset{\cup}{\text{Themmes}} \;\middle\|\; \overset{\cup}{\text{runne}}\,\overset{/}{\text{soft}}\middle|\overset{\cup}{\text{ly}} \;\middle\|\; \overset{\_}{\text{till}} \;\middle|\; \overset{\cup}{\text{I}}\,\overset{/}{\text{end}} \;\middle|\; \overset{\cup}{\text{my}}\,\overset{\_}{\text{Song}} \;\middle|\right.$$

The pyrrhic following the second spondee further softens Spenser's effect in the refrain above. In the following lines, by Coleridge, note how pyrrhic-spondee pairs produce an abundance and languor very different from either Bogan's elusive dance with destructive love or the more aggressive tactics of Walcott on exile before that:

The frost performs its secret ministry,
Unhelped by any wind. The owlet's cry
Came loud—and hark, again! loud as before.
The inmates of my cottage, all at rest,
Have left me to that solitude, which suits   5
Abstruser musings: save that at my side
My cradled infant slumbers peacefully.
'Tis calm indeed! so calm, that it disturbs
And vexes meditation with its strange
And extreme silentness. Sea, hill, and wood,   10
This populous village! Sea, and hill, and wood,

---

involving the two players. See Sonnet 71 for an example of how meaning makes stress on the personal pronouns *I, me,* and *you, your.* In fact, meaning makes such enormous stress on these pronouns that the last line is almost made into a tetrameter by them:

$$\left|\; \overset{\cup}{\text{Least}}\,\overset{\_}{\text{the}} \;\middle|\; \overset{\cup}{\text{wise}}\,\overset{/}{\text{world}} \;\middle|\; \overset{\cup}{\text{should}}\,\overset{/}{\text{looke}} \;\middle|\overset{\cup}{\text{in}}\overset{/}{\text{to}} \;\middle|\; \overset{\cup}{\text{your}}\,\overset{/}{\text{mone,}} \;\middle|\right.$$

$$\left|\; \overset{\cup}{\text{And}}\,\overset{/}{\text{mocke}} \;\middle|\; \underset{\text{x}}{\overset{\cup}{\text{you}}} \;\middle\|\; \overset{\cup}{\text{with}} \;\middle|\; \underset{\text{x}}{\overset{\_}{\text{me}}} \;\middle\|\; \overset{\cup}{\text{af}}\middle|\overset{/}{\text{ter}}\,\overset{\cup}{\text{I}} \;\middle|\; \overset{\cup}{\text{am}}\,\overset{/}{\text{gon}} \;\middle|\right.$$

The incipient tetrameter would be anapestic and would split where phrase ends: | *And mock you* ‖ *with me* ‖ *after I* | *am gone* |. As in Louise Bogan's poem, many syntactic phrases lie in tension with the feet—this, too, creates metrical strain.

With all the numberless goings-on of life,
Inaudible as dreams! the thin blue flame
Lies on my low-burnt fire, and quivers not;
Only that film, which fluttered on the grate,   15
Still flutters there, the sole unquiet thing.

("Frost at Midnight")

Coleridge's music, so much lighter than Walcott's and Bogan's, moves gingerly among the items the speaker names, as if superstitious that the magical moment might otherwise disappear. Note the state of trance in which he recurs to "sea, hill, and wood" (10), adding more space and shifting the foot-stress pattern in line 11 so that the terms assume more terrain; the added nonstress in the second foot has the effect in context of an additional retard:

$$\mid\ \overset{\cup\quad /}{\text{This pop}}\mid\overset{\cup\ \cup\quad /}{\text{ulous vil}}\mid\overset{\cup}{\text{lage}}\ \parallel\ \overset{/}{\text{Sea}}\ \parallel\ \overset{\cup\quad /}{\text{and hill}}\ \parallel\ \overset{\cup\quad /}{\text{and wood}}\ \mid$$

This very solicitude about naming, however, anchors Coleridge to a verse texture of stronger borders than other blank-verse poets depend on:

I have been studying how I may compare
This prison where I live unto the world;
And for because the world is populous,
And here is not a creature but myself,
I cannot do it; yet I'll hammer it out.
My brain I'll prove the female to my soul,
My soul the father; and these two beget
A generation of still-breeding thoughts,
And these same thoughts people this little world.

(*Richard II* V.v)

From no one line here do we derive the vantage to predict how the next will open itself out; whether in his syntax, tropes, or diction, Shakespeare's Richard casts out an unfathomed line, often giving us the eerie sense we experience grammatically in German during that interval before we haul up the main verb.

Variable Stress

Almost any soliloquy from one of the tragedies presents verse of forward drive equal to that in *Richard II,* and of equal variability of stress-alternation and enjambment. Consider the end of the soliloquy by Ham-

let beginning "How all occasions do inform against me"; he is worried
about his want of resolve to carry through with the murder of his vile
uncle Claudius in the face of the courage of an entire army blithely has-
tening off to kill and die. Note especially how the thought that seems to
end with the appalling death-sleep rises up twice again, once fighting for
a plot, next covering it with a tomb ("I . . . have a father killed" means
he has "a father [, who has been] killed"):

> How stand I then,
> That have a father killed, a mother stained,
> Excitements of my reason and my blood,
> And let all sleep, while to my shame I see
> The imminent death of twenty thousand men
> That for a fantasy and trick of fame
> Go to their graves like beds, fight for a plot
> Whereon the numbers cannot try the cause,
> Which is not tomb enough and continent
> To hide the slain? O, from this time forth,
> My thoughts be bloody, or be nothing worth!

(*Hamlet* IV.iv)

The final pronouncement, in which Hamlet tries to spur himself to kill
his uncle, who is now his stepfather, may be stiff and unconvincing. Both
Prince Hamlet and King Richard may be less effective at facing the pres-
ent task than in imagining other worlds (Richard thinks of nations like
manikins, Hamlet of the soldiers fighting over a postage stamp of land).
But whatever the flaws on which the blank verse snags, there is no deny-
ing a larger orchestration in the speeches just quoted than we hear in the
lyrics and meditations of the other poets whose pentameters are exam-
ined in this chapter. Looking back at Coleridge from a Shakespearean
perspective, it seems a world of great delicacy and reserve, almost as if
one were using mirrors to look around the corners of human experience:

| And ex | treme sil | entness ‖ | Sea ‖ hill ‖ | and wood | 10

| This pop | ulous vil | lage ‖ Sea ‖ | and hill ‖ | and wood | 11

| Inaud | ible | as dreams ‖ | the thin | blue flame | 13

| Lies on | my low | burnt fire ‖ | and quiv | ers not | 14

Like his friend and contemporary Wordsworth, and like Frost and Nemerov in our period, Coleridge uses many conversational pyrrhics to lighten and at the same time concentrate the weight of a mind drifting among its objects.

Learning to Scan

To practice the three-sign scansion system outlined thus far, consider the following exercises; all are based on iambic pentameter poems in the text:

1. After typing it out triple-spaced, divide Raymond Oliver's poem "Structures" into iambic feet. Using the two-tiered method of scansion, map the two signs of constant iambic expectation over the available syllables. Then mark actual stresses. In two or three sentences at the bottom of the page, describe the effect produced by the meter and the metrical variations in lines 4 and 5 ("As when a line ends with a comma—stressed, / Slightly, but showing that the sense runs on"). Recall the relation between caesuras in the meter and the building blocks of syntax (phrase, clause, and full sentence), and note also how pointedly Oliver focuses *thematically* on the rhythm his own lines embody, for his central illustration about the colors of the dawn sky. Ask how prosodic form follows theme in these two lines.

2. Type out, in triple-spaced form, and divide into iambic feet W. H. Auden's sonnet beginning with the line "But in the evening the oppression lifted." Map expected meter over the available syllables, bearing in mind the possibility of an extra unstressed syllable at the ends of iambic lines. Then mark actual speech stresses. Look up the stressing of the polysyllables *conversation, instruments,* and *chauffeur* in a good dictionary. On a separate sheet, quote the *least* stressed line, then the *most* stressed (recall the discussion of monosyllabic versus polysyllabic diction). In two or three sentences, explain what purposes are served by **understressing** and **overstressing.**

3. Prepare for scansion lines 15 through 28 of Yvor Winters's couplet meditation, "The Slow Pacific Swell." Divide into iambic feet. Use the two-tiered method; map expected meter over available syllables and then actual speech stresses—wherever they fall. Describe two points in this passage at which metrical form (trochaic inversion and spondees in particular) mirrors what is being said.

4. If a fourth scansion exercise is desired, look at Sir Walter Ralegh's sonnet beginning "Three thinges there bee." After scanning the poem,

ponder the tension between the meter and the **rhythm** in the final line, in which the father prays that "Wee part not with thee at this meeting day."

These exercises treat poems which keep to a fairly regular iambic measure, so that the variations stand out and become meaningful. But it is also the reader's task to figure out how the meaning of the rhythmical ups and downs supports the meaning of the words.

Deriving the Meter: How Context Makes Meter

Although one cannot scan a line out of context, a line that *sounds* more or less like iambic pentameter may very well *be* iambic pentameter. But some lines do not give unambiguous evidence about their metrical mode: "And mock you with me after I am gone" (Shakespeare); "Wee part not with thee at this meeting day" (Ralegh); "Young Vane, and others who called Milton friend" (Wordsworth); "And some words played between us to and fro" (Hardy). These four lines contain ten syllables apiece, but none proceeds along a clear course; the first and second might be amphibrachic [$\cup - \cup$], the third might be anapestic, the fourth might be iambic. But all these identifications are wrong.

Only the complete poetic context makes a meter. The decasyllabic lines above all make a different impression on the ear when heard alone than they do when revealed against their complete prosodic (or rhythmic) background. Only within this complete context can we "resolve" the lines against a patterned expectation. The same is true of the following lines-in-isolation:

> Must I show outright
>
> > (Bogan)
>
> O Solitude! where are thy charms?
>
> > (Cowper)
>
> Push on to the world's end, pay the
>
> > (Auden)
>
> Sunke so low, as to love one which did scorn.
>
> > (Donne)

Possibilities for background meter hover in the air not unlike what occurs with the **half-meaning** in lines that enjamb (see chapter 2). Just as temporary and often incorrect meanings appear when we hover at one line before it runs over to the next line, so discordant meters suggest themselves when we dwell on lines as isolated units. In context, these lines resolve, Bogan's against dimeter quatrains in "The Daemon," Auden's against trochaic **common meter** quatrains[23] in "Lady, Weeping at the Crossroads," Cowper's against anapestic trimeter,[24] and Donne's against the contentious rhymed iambic pentameter of "Loves Deitie."

The line earlier from Hardy's "Neutral Tones," *could* fit in the mold of iambic pentameter, / *And some* / *words played* / *between* / *us to* / *and fro* /, but this line appears in a poem sprinkled with "triple feet"—feet with three syllables (the most common *substituted* triple foot in a language with an iambic base, like English, is the **anapest** [∪∪–], weak-weak-strong):

Your eyes on me were as eyes that rove   5
Over tedious riddles of years ago;
And some words played between us to and fro
    On which lost the more by our love.

In addition, **responsion** helps us confirm the meter, inasmuch as the *other* third lines in each quatrain of "Neutral Tones" are more clearly anapestic than line 7: "And a few leaves lay on the starving sod"; "And a grin of bitterness swept thereby"; and "Your face, and the God-curst sun, and a tree." In their company, line 7 finds its proper mode, for it is actually an anapestic four-measure line (or tetrameter—each stanza concluded by a trimeter) in which iambs act to soften the unpleasant and quasi-comic effect of the so-called anapestic gallop:

23. Common meter quatrains rhyme $a^4b^3a^4b^3$. The numbers refer to line length in numbers of feet, the letters to the rhyme-pairs; thus, a quatrain alternating rhyming tetrameters with rhyming trimeters. The *kind* of metrical foot must be supplied verbally—as here, "trochaic."

24. Cowper, "Verses Supposed to Be Written by Alexander Selkirk, During His Solitary Abode in the Island of Juan Fernandez":

I am monarch of all I survey,
    My right there is none to dispute;
From the center all round to the sea,
    I am lord of the fowl and the brute.
O Solitude! where are the charms   5
    That sages have seen in thy face?
Better dwell in the midst of alarms,
    Than reign in this horrible place.

$$\text{| \underset{\text{And}}{\breve{U}} \underset{\text{some}}{\breve{U}} \underset{\text{words}}{\acute{/}} | \underset{\text{played}}{\overset{/}{\breve{U}}} \underset{\text{be}}{\breve{U}} \underset{\text{tween}}{\acute{/}} | \underset{\text{us}}{\breve{U}} \underset{\text{to}}{\acute{/}} \underset{\text{and}}{\breve{U}} \underset{\text{fro}}{\acute{/}} |}^{25}$$

Putting the argument from the other direction, there are lines that have the requisite number of syllables for iambic pentameter (ten, or, with room for one triple foot—say an anapest midway every so often, or an extra syllable at the end—eleven), but which out of context do not make their metrical adherence plain: "Young Vane, and others who called Milton friend" (the complete text of "Great Men have been among us" appears on p. 29). Against an anapestic background (recall Goldsmith's "With no reason on earth to go out of his way, / He turned and he varied full ten times a day"), Wordsworth's line could be heard, perhaps with additional pausing after the caesura—that point so conducive to shifts in tempo—as a four-measure line with three syllables per metrical unit, or foot:

$$\text{| \overset{/}{\underset{\text{Young}}{\breve{U}}} \underset{\text{Vane}}{\acute{/}} \| \underset{\wedge}{} \underset{\text{and}}{\breve{U}} \underset{\text{oth}}{\acute{/}} | \underset{\text{ers}}{\breve{U}} \underset{\text{who}}{\breve{U}} \underset{\text{called}}{\acute{/}} | \overset{/}{\underset{\text{Mil}}{\breve{U}}} \underset{\text{ton}}{\breve{U}} \underset{\text{friend}}{\acute{/}} |}$$

But the anapestic trail is a false one. The strongly iambic context throughout Wordsworth's sonnet turns the ambiguous middle of the line iambic, too, like a magnet directing the iron filings all one way:

$$\text{| \underset{\text{The}}{\breve{U}} \underset{\text{lat}}{\acute{/}} | \underset{\text{er}}{\breve{U}} \underset{\text{Sid}}{\acute{/}} | \underset{\text{ney}}{\breve{U}} \| \underset{\text{Mar}}{\acute{/}} | \underset{\text{vell}}{\breve{U}} \| \underset{\text{Har}}{\acute{/}} | \underset{\text{rington}}{\breve{U}} \underset{}{-} |}$$

$$\text{| \overset{/}{\underset{\text{Young}}{\breve{U}}} \underset{\text{Vane}}{\acute{/}} \| \underset{\text{and}}{\breve{U}} \underset{\text{oth}}{\acute{/}} | \underset{\text{ers}}{\breve{U}} \underset{\text{who}}{-} \| \overset{/}{\underset{\text{called}}{\breve{U}}} \underset{\text{Mil}}{\acute{/}} | \underset{\text{ton}}{\breve{U}} \underset{\text{friend}}{\acute{/}} |}$$

$$\text{| \underset{\text{These}}{\breve{U}} \underset{\text{mor}}{\acute{/}} | \underset{\text{alists}}{\breve{U}-} | \underset{\text{could}}{\breve{U}} \underset{\text{act}}{\acute{/}} | \underset{\text{and}}{\breve{U}} \underset{\text{com}}{-} | \underset{\text{prehend}}{\breve{U}\acute{/}} |}$$ 5

The rhyme at the end of line 5 brings in the more unambiguously iambic rhythm of the entire fifth line as a test of iambic choice in line 4. Note

25. Note that *played* is a monosyllabic verb and hence receives stress wherever it appears (even if it muddies our explanatory pattern!).

The metrical context in Hardy's "Neutral Tones," which creates the expectation of anapests in particular and triple feet in general, makes the anapestic second foot [*played between*] an *overstressed* anapest [$\breve{U}\breve{U}\acute{/}$]. Although the poem is still anapestic (with the liberal interspersing of iambs that make anapests bearable), this second foot can also be thought of as a substituted cretic foot, or "false cretic," impersonating the classical foot with a strong-weak-strong pattern [$-\breve{U}-$]. Recall the discussion of "false" pyrrhics and spondees above. Note that in all three "false" feet, expectation is not changed; thus, in most of the poems we have observed, the metrical accents still conform to iamb or anapest.

that the speech-stressing of 4 remains the same in these two scansions of Wordsworth's line about young Vane. Only our picture of the derived meter shifts, depending on perceived context.

How Form Follows Theme in Blank Verse

We might look at further examples of lines that are hard to place metrically: "Arcades, late movie shows, the piled lit windows" (Gunn, "In Praise of Cities"); "I said, 'A line will take us hours maybe'" (Yeats, "Adam's Curse"); "Some boy too far from town to learn baseball" (Frost, "Birches"); "Of well-sealed, antiseptic samples of cloud" (Anthony Hecht, "The Venetian Vespers"); "by echo alone. Still, the point of style" (Nemerov, "Writing"); "Go; for thy stay, not free, absents thee more" (Milton). The last two examples seem rough and hard to place because they involve so many different pieces of syntax—almost as if in the latter Adam were blurting out his judgment, tripping over himself, interrupting with clauses and phrases; while in the former, there is the possibility of double allegiance (as the words *alone* and *still* in the Nemerov line about the bat promise to modify the same noun—but do not). Any lines of verse in which syntax shifts to extremes will be more preoccupied with achieving the sense than with accommodating the meter to regular pentameter; the overriding impression in the Milton line is one of struggle-against, not alignment-with.

Does this struggle mean that these lines of verse are poorly written and ineffectual? Not if one looks at the relevant context within which the effect is made. Nemerov is weaving his way through an array of comparisons between the tracks of skaters, the invisible vectors guiding the bat through blackness, and the paths between stars as astronomers once traced them. Because he is thinking of the idea that, like blade-marks on ice, the constellations make shapes (of archer and fish and crab), he assumes that someone must have drawn these shapes. And in this "drawing," there are loops, returns, and, as the poet himself says, a kind of miraculous flexible threshold of hesitation where the God who draws us all paused with his pen in the air—a pause which the poet imitates with his dexterous navigation of the nine line boundaries encompassed by the passage, as if *they* were the blank spaces between the stars, where the imagination momentarily pauses before making the next connection; we should particularly note the hovering enjambments from lines 6 through 15:

Writing

The cursive scrawl, the squared-off characters,
these by themselves delight, even without
a meaning, in a foreign language, in
Chinese, for instance, or when skaters curve
all day across the lake, scoring their white   5
records in ice. Being intelligible,
these winding ways with their audacities
and delicate hesitations, they become
miraculous, so intimately, out there
at the pen's point or brush's tip, do world   10
and spirit wed. The small bones of the wrist
balance against great skeletons of stars
exactly; the blind bat surveys his way
by echo alone. Still, the point of style
is character. The universe induces   15
a different tremor in every hand, from the
check-forger's to that of the Emperor
Hui Tsung, who called his own calligraphy
the 'Slender Gold.' A nervous man
writes nervously of a nervous world, and so on.   20

Miraculous. It is as though the world
were a great writing. Having said so much,
let us allow there is more to the world
than writing: continental faults are not
bare convoluted fissures in the brain.   25
Not only must the skaters soon go home;
also the hard inscription of their skates
is scored across the open water, which long
remembers nothing, neither wind nor wake.

It is as if the poet were waiting, with his own pen in the air, just where
his poem sheers off into emptiness—an emptiness falling both at the line
boundaries, and at that precipice right in the middle of the line (and of
the foot):

```
     ⏑ /    ⏑ _   /́          /       ⏑ /      ⏑ /
 | by e | cho a | lone ‖ Still ‖ the point | of style |
```

These syntactical breaks, or **caesuras** (marked by double vertical lines), may or may not coincide with the boundaries of the metrical unit, or foot. When they do not, it is usually the implied syntax that commands the tempo; but when the foot-division is the same as the syntactical break, the tempo isn't noticeably affected.[26] But note in Nemerov's line 14 how jagged is the long caesura in the middle of the third foot. In part, the jaggedness is also the result of the odd placement of the pyrrhic-spondee combination relative to the abrupt ending of the sentence in the middle of the line: / *cho a* / *lone.* // *Still,* /. The halting in this line's prosody has a "meaning" specific to the terms of the poem "Writing": It imitates the halting in the creative intelligence of God-the-maker, and of his mortal substitute, the metaphor-maker, who draws his curling diagram between the bat, the skaters, and the stars.

As for the excessive syntactic divisions in the Milton line, we must remember that Book IX of *Paradise Lost* is 1,190 lines long and that line 372 is not only the most densely stressed but also the most broken in syntax. The context for the variations at the end of Adam's speech here is therefore a background of cumulative smoothness, amplitude, and parallel. So when Adam finally gives Eve permission to garden apart from him, he does so in a way that mirrors his demoralization, and unwillingness to see her go from him, by the prosodic ungainliness of his concession. We noted the pattern of caesuras in chapter 2's presentation of syntax; now we can supply the line's complete scansion:

$$
\begin{array}{ccccc}
\text{x} & & \text{x} & / & \text{x} \\
/ & & & / & / \\
\cup & \_ & \cup \; \underline{/} & \cup \; \underline{/} & \cup \; \underline{/} & \cup \; \underline{/} \\
\mid \text{Go} \parallel \text{for} \mid \text{thy stay} \parallel \text{not free} \parallel \text{absents} \mid \text{thee more.} \mid
\end{array}
$$

As in the Nemerov line, here in Milton's the most obtrusive gap occurs midfoot, after "Go"; it is also this command that participates in the tug-of-war of wrenched stress (the first-foot trochee), overstressing (foot three), and the additional discord in the main line-stresses—all boiling about Adam as in some distress he veers between the idea of Eve's going and the wish that she stay, mentally rejecting the mixed blessing of her beloved presence in case of her active will's absence. Hence, there is a sense of reaching the limit of disorganization for the iambic pentameter

---

26. Even when the new unit of syntax begins with a trochee: This is a common and acceptable place for a substitution or reversal of stress (see Nemerov's fifth line in "Writing" above, when a new phrase starts with the natural trochee *scoring*).

line, even if, all the while, alongside discord is the well-managed tight-
ening of all Adam's disciplined beliefs.

Uncertain Syllables

Consider another series of rocky and ill-at-ease iambic feet, these from a
poem that was composed before the iambic line had quite settled itself in
literate use:[27]

> She that me lerneth to love and suffre,   5
> And will that my truth and lustes negligence
> Be rayned by reason, shame and reverence . . .
> ("The longe love, that in my thought doeth harbar")[28]

When we listen to Wyatt, we hear an indisputably interesting poet but
one who in some of his work wrote with no real interest in anything like
a minimal threshold for accentual-syllabic meter (only five of this sonnet's
fourteen lines are audibly metrical—assuming the metrical model to be
iambic pentameter—and some lines such as 12 are positively unruly); in
line 4 the speaker blushes, and perhaps the look on his face (line 3) also
reveals his infatuation:

> The longe love, that in my thought doeth harbar
> And in myn hert doeth kepe his residence,
> Into my face preseth with bolde pretence,
> And therin campeth, spreding his baner.
> She that me lerneth to love and suffre,   5
> And will that my trust and lustes negligence
> Be rayned by reason, shame and reverence,
> With his hardines* taketh displeasur.   *boldness
> Wherewithall, unto the hertes forrest he fleith,
> Leving his entreprise with payn and cry,   10
> And ther him hideth and not appereth.
> What may I do when my maister fereth

27. This is the view of John Thompson, who discusses the great divide between
Wyatt and Surrey in *The Founding of English Meter* (New York: Columbia University
Press, 1966).

28. Richard Sylvester, ed., *The Anchor Anthology of Sixteenth-Century Poetry* (New
York: Doubleday/Anchor, 1974), p. 130.

But in the feld with him to lyve and dye?
For goode is the liff, ending faithfully.[29]

Wyatt comes out of the more syllabically based Romance tradition (see chapter 10). However, when his "opposite number," Henry Howard, Earl of Surrey, revises Wyatt and cleans up everything in Wyatt's work, the result, while it kept the way open for the next century of dramatic experiment with iambic pentameter,[30] is often flat. We find Surrey's "improved" and metrical version of the Petrarchan sonnet, first rendered by Wyatt, to suffer not only from melodrama in the tropes, but also from a metronome in the rhythm:

> But she that tawght me love and suffre paine,
> My doubtfull hope and eke* my hote desire   *also
> With shamefast clooke* to shadow and refrayne . . .[31]   *may be a misprint
>   for looke

Despite the increase in military trappings by Surrey (he speaks of a captive breast and arming to fight, while Wyatt spoke of the heart's harbor and the gay banner of its temporary residence), there is less poetic ferocity than we heard in Wyatt's more subdued, smooth, and rhetorically subtle text. Metrical "correctness," which leads Surrey to pile one closed pentameter line upon another, does not insure good poetry (and the Surrey versions of many Wyatt works seem padded out—note the frequency of doubled phrases linked by *and*), just as metrical "incorrectness" does not absolutely diminish a fine poem, although it makes the job riskier (we noted this feature in Wyatt earlier). Of course, meter that always limps and lurches may irk the reader and distract the writer at the wrong moment. The middle ground may yield greater success—lines, that is to say, in which neither is the variation so wild as to cancel out the background music of metrical expectation, nor the metrical ground base so rigid as to

---

29. Wyatt's trope comparing the self to a vassal and the heart to a lord (love) who takes then quits the field of war, is the type of **Petrarchan** exaggeration on which Emily Dickinson draws to such eerie effect when she likens her abject life to a loaded gun (#754), which can only kill but not die. See above, p. 125.

30. See Howard Baker, "The Formation of the Heroic Medium," in *Elizabethan Poetry,* edited by Paul J. Alpers (see the entry in chapter 14's "Annotated Bibliography of Further Reading").

31. In Sylvester, ed., *Sixteenth-Century Poetry,* p. 185.

silence all departures from the alternation of stressed and unstressed syllables.

How Meaning Makes Stress

We don't need a metrical context to hear how meaning can make—and shift—stress. Consider the title of Frost's poem, "Mending Wall." If we put a stronger stress on *mend* than on *wall,* then we assume that *mending* is a participial adjective modifying *wall:* The wall must be mending itself, or be a wall by which we mend (as a wailing wall is a wall by which we grieve). None of these meanings makes much sense, particularly in light of the plot of the poem, in which two country people come together once a year to mend the wall between their properties. They are *mending WALL,* and the participial noun (or gerund) *mending* takes as its object the more heavily stressed *WALL.*

Arbitration by meaning is often just as necessary in verse as it was in the title of Frost's poem in helping us to speak the lines. One of the effects that creates a special music in metrical verse that can't be obtained in free verse comes from the use of weak syllables where one expected strong ones. There are two ways in which such "weakness" can occur, through a sprinkling of monosyllabic speech particles that don't normally carry strong stress and through the unstressed portions of polysyllabic words. In the monosyllabic line, furthermore, often it is the meaning that makes the stress.

The Role of Monosyllables

One of the ways the monosyllabic speech particles, pronouns, and connectives achieve a prominence sufficient to make stress is by catchphrase, parallel, and antithesis. This is why we stress both *fro* and *to* in Hardy's line from "Neutral Tones"; and how John Donne magnetizes so many of the monosyllables in "I dare not move my dimme eyes any way" into feet of equal stress (note also the effect of the examples of the letter *m* that surround—and nearly coax into equivalence with them—the word *my* in foot 3); and why we grant to the word *of* a meaning-status that is uncharacteristic in David Ferry's line from "Descriptive," which lists all the adverbial prepositions to describe the way colors slide over their shapes on a summer's day:

$$\left| \begin{array}{c} \cup \; / \\ \text{About} \end{array} \right\| \begin{array}{c} \cup / \\ \text{above} \end{array} \right\| \begin{array}{c} \cup \; / \\ \text{within} \end{array} \right\| \begin{array}{c} \cup \; / \\ \text{and of} \end{array} \right\| \begin{array}{c} \cup \; / \; \cup \\ \text{each other} \end{array} \right|$$

It is because meaning makes stress that we wrestle certain monosyllabic lines *away* from automatic iambic pentameter stress:

$$
\begin{array}{cccccc}
/ & & \text{x} & & & \text{x} \\
\cup \quad \_ & \cup \quad / & \cup\ / & \cup & \_ & \cup\ / \\
\end{array}
$$

| They that | have powre | to hurt ‖ and will | doe none |

"They" receives stress because it is the designation of the group being defined: This class of individuals . . . is praiseworthy; they "rightly do inherrit heavens graces" (later in the poem, they will be contrasted with "Others" who do not). "Powre" and "doe" receive main line-stresses because these words define the major antithesis: Capable of harming because they are heroically attractive, nevertheless they will do no harm by using the power of their beauty *for* power.

Sonnet 94

They that have powre to hurt and will doe none,
That do not doe the thing they most do showe,
Who, moving others, are themselves as stone,
Unmoovèd, could,★ and to temptation slow: ★*cold*
They rightly do inherrit heavens graces,   5
And husband natures ritches from expence,
They are the Lords and owners of their faces,
Others, but stewards of their excellence:
The sommers flowre is to the sommer sweet,
Though to it selfe, it onely live and die,   10
But if that flowre with base infection meete,
The basest weed out-braves his dignity:
    For sweetest things turn sowrest by their deedes,
    Lillies that fester, smell far worse than weeds.

The second line of the same sonnet continues in the monosyllabic style of the first—a style that requires us to detect the role of meaning in making stress:

$$
\begin{array}{ccccc}
& \text{x} & & & \text{x} \\
\cup \quad \_ & \cup\ / & \cup\ / & \cup\ / & \cup\ / \\
\end{array}
$$

| That do | not doe | the thing | they most | do showe |

There are two grammatical modes for "do" in line 2: auxiliary (or supporting) verb and main, transitive verb (which can take an object). In the first foot, *do* is an auxiliary; hence this is an understressed iamb, or pyrrhic foot. The second "do" (spelled *doe*) is a primary verb of action, hence its coincidence with a main foot-stress is satisfying in a way the first foot was not. This second "do" shares the main line-stressing with "showe" because the central contradiction (a paraphrase of the idea in line 1) is that these restrained yet powerful individuals admirably refuse to enact and carry out the kind of threat which their beings exhibit as possibility (that is, they show a capacity to trap others, but they will not *do* what they *show* by enacting it). This power, as we find when we read further, is the seductive power of physical beauty and noble accomplishment to entice others to fall in love—this is the "hurt" which these natural aristocrats refuse to make others suffer; they refuse to act in a seductive manner. (It's clear from the laboriousness of paraphrase that the poem condenses complex notions into a small area by means of these variably stressed monosyllables and the abstractions they join.)

A final example, from Ralegh: the end of the sonnet giving advice to his wastrel son to mend his ways (before his sins and the gallows platform and the noose "meet all in one place," for "when they meet, it makes the timber rott, / It fretts the halter, and it choakes the childe"). The meter in this poem of Ralegh's is regular to the point of singsong—until the final line:

> Three thinges there bee that prosper up apace
> And flourish, whilest they growe a sunder farr,
> But on a day, they meet all in one place,
> And when they meet, they one an other marr;
> And they bee theise, the wood, the weede, the wagg.   5
> The wood is that, which makes the Gallow tree,
> The weed is that, which stringes the Hangmans bagg,
> The wagg my pritty knave betokeneth thee.
> Marke well deare boy whilest theise assemble not,   10
> Green springs the tree, hempe growes, the wagg is wilde,
> But when they meet, it makes the timber rott,
> It fretts the halter, and it choakes the childe.
>   Then bless thee, and beware, and lett us praye,
>   Wee part not with thee at this meeting day.

The wrenching of rhythm in Ralegh's prayer that

| ˘ ́ | ˘ _ | ˘ _ ‖ ˘ ́ | ˘ ́ |
| Wee part | not with | thee ‖ at | this meet | ing day |

reinforces the irony in his imagery about objects that "meet" only to "part" the child from his life and the father from the child. So it is fitting that the sturdy iambic checks-and-balances wobble a bit in line 14. (The demonstrative adjective *this* in the fourth foot may be stressed, but I have not done so. Readers should choose in the context of the meaning of the entire **sestet**.)

It is because meaning can make stress that we permit even a prefix such as *un-* to be lifted by well-managed antithesis out of its unstressed background:

$$\overset{\cup}{\text{Posses}}\overset{\diagup}{}\big|\overset{\cup}{\text{sing}}\overset{\diagup}{\text{what}}\big|\overset{\cup}{\text{we}}\overset{\diagup}{\text{still}}\big|\overset{\cup}{\text{were}}\overset{\diagup}{\text{un}}\big|\overset{\cup}{\text{possessed}}\overset{\diagup}{}\overset{\cup}{\text{by}}\big|$$

(Frost, "The Gift Outright")

Note that this kind of "retrieval" of stress for a syllable by its nature unstressed is accomplished by meaning—not by the variable music of parallel we hear in such lines as

$$\big|\overset{\cup}{\text{Unhous}}\overset{\diagup}{\text{eled}}\ \|\ \overset{\text{—}\cup}{\text{dis}}\big|\overset{\diagup}{\text{appoint}}\big|\overset{\cup}{\text{ed}}\ \|\ \overset{\text{—}}{\text{un}}\big|\overset{\cup\diagup}{\text{aneled}}\big|$$

(*Hamlet* I.v)

The appealing lift of the Shakespeare line comes precisely because the second and third of the three negative prefixes fall—without being stressed—into strong places, with weak stress on either side (so there is no competition for the comparative metrical difference they exhibit). When Christ speaks of grace in Milton's epic, relieved that mankind will be saved by it, he relishes the generosity of its arrival—that it

$$\big|\overset{\cup}{\text{Comes}}\overset{\diagup}{\text{un}}\big|\overset{\cup\diagup}{\text{prevent}}\big|\overset{\cup}{\text{ed}}\ \|\ \overset{\text{—}\cup}{\text{un}}\big|\overset{\diagup}{\text{implor'd}}\ \|\ \overset{\cup}{\text{unsought}}\overset{\diagup}{}\big|$$

(*Paradise Lost* III.231)

In this line we perceive three values or grades of "un-stress"; added to the two kinds in *Hamlet* (weak syllable in a weak place; weak syllable in a strong place), is the first negative prefix *un-* in a strong place but following a trochaic downbeat on "Comes," with which *un-* shares a near-rhyme as well. So there is some magnetism about the first prefix that can carry over into an uncharacteristically strong stress on the second syllable of the line.

Milton provides further examples of prefix parallel:[32]

---

32. W. K. Wimsatt suggests the first two in *The Verbal Icon: Studies in the Meaning of Poetry* (Lexington: University of Kentucky Press, 1967), pp. 155–56; I give these, and add a line from *Paradise Regained,* but use our method of scansion.

| Ŭnres | pited ‖ unpit | ied ‖ un | reprievéd |

(*Paradise Lost* II.185)

| Unshak | en ‖ un | sedúced ‖ unter | rified |

(*Paradise Lost* V.899)

| Unhum | bl'd ‖ un | repent | ant ‖ un | reform'd |

(*Paradise Regained* III.429)

The first and last lines' fourth feet and the second line's second foot flirt with stress even though they're weak, simply because they fall in strong places. Nothing short of this pleasurable accident of placement, and with it the blurring of some of the monotony of parallel, might carry off the illusion of greater importance for these prefixes. But at the same time, however grand the rhetorical scale, metrical usage is straightforward. It's clear that in "The Gift Outright" Frost is making a rhythmically far more contentious point with his **neologism,** *UN-pos-SESSED,* and the meaning-stress on *UN-,* which contrasts with the positive verb *possessed.*[33]

Mimetic and Antimimetic Meter

Part One stressed the many kinds of cooperation between form and theme. One of the clearest functions of the rhythm of a poem is to support the theme and demeanor of the style. How crookedly the king expresses his crookedness as a leader in *2 Henry IV:*

33. Jon Stallworthy recognizes the need to stress this prefix in his scansion of "The Gift Outright" in the *Norton,* 4th ed. (pp. lxvi–lxvii), but he unfortunately also insists on stressing the *un-* of *unenhanced* in line 15 ("But still unstoried, artless, unenhanced"), not because of its meaning but only because it falls in a strong place, while he doesn't stress the *un-* of *unstoried* in that same line, because it does not. He then overdoes a bit the stress on *we* and *she* in lines 10 and 16, even encouraging it in 9 (it may be enough, for the struggle between *us/we* and our country [*her/she*], to insist upon the pronouns' meaning-stresses in five of the poem's 16 lines: 1, 2, 3, 5, and 8). I think I might also want to redivide the feet in line 14,

| To the | land ‖ vague | ly re | aliz | ing westward |

and try to urge the parallel of the final amphibrach here with like trisyllabic feet to end 11 and 10, where Stallworthy has six feet—he puts the eleventh syllables into feet of single unstressed syllables. (The minimal norm for a foot is a single stressed syllable.)

> God knows, my son,
> By what bypaths and indirect crooked ways
> I met this crown.

(IV.v)

In the middle line, the verse slithers and veers and trips up on syllables that are either additional (foot four) or apparently so (see the stretch of nonstresses that reach from the fifth to the eighth syllables; the seventh syllable is extra):

$$| \;\overset{}{\underset{By\ what}{\cup\quad /}}\; | \;\overset{/}{\underset{bypaths}{\cup\ \backslash}}\; \| \;\overset{}{\underset{and\ in}{\cup\quad -}}\; | \;\overset{/}{\underset{direct\ crook}{\cup\cup\quad /}}\,|\overset{}{\underset{ed\ ways}{\cup\quad /}}\; |$$

Form and theme are clearly aligned; rhythm almost derails as the ideas and implied recollections in the line seek expressive form for their content.

Shakespeare is also capable of framing the most devious and complex ideas in the most straightforward meters, speaking straight when he means crooked, as in the definitions of love in Sonnet 116: "love is not love / Which alters when it alteration finds." The words *say* alteration, but the meters do not mimic it. We could call this a reverse case of imitation, for the point is that love does not thus alter with conditions.

Edwin Muir shows in "Childhood" how the most regular iambic pentameter—even when it is end-stopped and rounded out by rhyme—can conform to an effect of breathless enchantment.

> Often he wondered what new shores were there.
> In thought he saw the still light on the sand,   10
> The shallow water clear in tranquil air,
> And walked through it in joy from strand to strand.

An impression of great, if serene, excitement is created by the poet's careful resistance to the expected **inversion** ("shores *there were*") at the end of line 9; by Muir's ingenuities of description masked by a fairly commonplace diction (I am always struck by the idea that the *sand* and not the water is reflecting the light in line 10); and by the parallelism of phrases whose adjectives are also metrically parallel (*shallow water/tranquil air*), which suggests that air and water are almost identical dream-substances. The poem's final stanza is a small masterpiece of evocation in which the imaginative dimension is sublimely wakeful, while the metrical means stand in shadow:

Grey tiny rocks slept round him where he lay,
　　Moveless as they, more still as evening came,
The grasses threw straight shadows far away,
　　And from the house his mother called his name.   20

("Childhood")

Recession of technique in the rhyme, stanza frame, and gently varied iambic meters (a recession Muir practices with great skill) permit the advance of vivid description, mild personifications (note the sleeping rocks and the grasses that throw shadows), and psychologically accurate plot resolution (as evening falls and from the perfected world of his day the child is gathered into the necessary creature comfort of the parents' sphere).

A too-regular iambic pentameter line is, of course, susceptible to parody. Pope mocks the patness of alternating measures, suggesting that the meter promotes patness of idea: "*Let Spades be Trumps!* she said, and Trumps they were" (*Rape of the Lock* III.46). To name is a task that confers great power on the namer—except when the setting is a card game rather than the cosmic void over which the divinity broods in Genesis 1:3, when God commanded, "Let there be light: and there was light."

Just short of parody are the many occasions when deliberately sluggish use of regular meters enhances serious themes. The American poet Edwin Arlington Robinson writes almost exclusively on this knife edge between simplicity and unconscious self-parody, often falling into the latter; his speaker is walking about in patches, diffident about asking for help:

　　　　　He was cold,   25
And old, and hungry; but the worst of it
Was a forlorn familiar consciousness
That he had failed again. There was a time
When he had fancied, if worst came to worst,
And he could do no more, that he might ask   30
Of whom he would. But once had been enough,
And soon there would be nothing more to ask.
He was himself, and he had lost the speed
He started with, and he was left behind.
There was no mystery, no tragedy;   35
And if they found him lying on his back

> Stone dead there some sharp morning, as they might,—
> Well, once upon a time there was a man . . .
>
> ("Captain Craig")

This is **plain style** muzzy from regularity and made mildly monotonous by a rhetorical disposition to proffer the loose blank-verse frame as a warrant for repetition. Robinson's Captain Craig keeps whipping himself up (as at the end of lines 31, 32, 34, and 35) to the same plateaus of previously expressed feeling, without much change in the voice's register.

More elegant (or at least self-conscious) is the sluggishness of Shakespeare's "Lov's not Times foole, though rosie lips and cheeks / Within his bending sickles compasse come" (Sonnet 116, 9–10): The tenth line imitates the inexorable, slow sweep of the scythe cutting a swath through beautiful faces and lives. How does it imitate? by nesting the dense possessives within the alternating meter (*his bending sickles compass*). "O how shall summers hunny breath hold out, / Against the wrackfull siedge of battring dayes" (Sonnet 65, 5–6): The sixth line imitates the bludgeoning effect of time imagined as a device for battering down stone walls. How does it imitate? by collecting within the metrical web words difficult to pronounce singly (*wrackfull*) or together (*wrackfull siedge of battring*).

Again just short of parody, other lines that mimic honesty. After Agincourt in *Henry V* the victorious king (the son of Henry IV) reads out the long roll of French dead beside the list that shows minimal loss of British life, choosing the most regular of meters for expressing his direct and un-crooked devices:

> When, without stratagem,
> But in plain shock and even play of battle,
> Was ever known so great and little loss
> On one part and on th' other?
>
> (IV.viii)

The overstressing on the phrase "plain shock" supports the hardness of the encounter; the regular meter in that line and the next also indicates Henry's grateful incredulity that the inevitable military encounter could have resulted in so much lost on the enemy's side, so little on his own.

Not a little of the imitative plainness of Henry's lines derives from the use of monosyllables that require the contribution of meaning. Most monosyllabic lines of iambic pentameter require us to interpret the stressing-potential of many of the words. When Vittoria in John Webster's *The White Devil* says to Ludovico "Thou hast too good a face to be a hangeman," all the monosyllables except for *a* and *to* are candidates for a major line-stress (sharing that place with a main line-stress on *hange-*). Similarly, Lear's monosyllabic line early in Act One, "Who is it that can tell me who I am?" (*King Lear* I.iv), asks the actor to choose a stress-pattern. Is Lear primarily issuing a challenge to Goneril or a chaffing rejoinder to the Fool's irritating riddles? We must all, like actors, try to imagine where in the line to strike so as to be true to the gruffness of the scene with Goneril and still properly foreshadow the remainder of this gruelling play in which bareness and plainness, foolishness and madness, treachery and loyalty, encounter such vicissitudes of definition. Above all, the line cannot be read with arbitrary alternation of meter—we hear in the background but must reject as a sensible interpretation the merely metrical reading of the line: *Who IS it THAT can TELL me WHO I AM?*

Monosyllabism is a subtle technique because it requires a speaking choice that runs somewhat counter to absolute regularity. After Lady Macbeth scolds him for being like the cat in the adage who wants the fish but not wet paws, "Letting 'I dare not' wait upon 'I would,'" Macbeth retorts defensively, "I dare do all that may become a man" (I.vii). *Dare, do, all,* and *man* are all clearly candidates for main line-stressing, but a choice must be made whereby main line-stress on *dare* removes the option from *do,* and main line-stress on *do* reduces the possibility for *all.* (I would favor putting main line-stress on *all* and *man.*)

Metrical **form follows theme** in innumerable ways, often by producing sounds that are like the sound of what is described—like the line in "Birches" describing the fall of the shells of ice from the tree branches: "Shattering and avalanching on the snow-crust." (Indeed, "Birches" is a treasure of mimetic lines of iambic pentameter—that is, lines that imitate their themes by their forms.) Reversed stress frequently imitates some torque or tension in the action, as in John Marston's lines describing the galley-slave who all day long "Tugges at his oare against the stubburne wave, / Straining his rugged veines" (*The Malcontent* III.i). The tug and strain against the oars is expressed by the trochaic inversions in the first foot of each line (the galley slave sleeps at last, but the malcontent cannot). Michael Drayton's line about a sudden wind storm is sped rather than slowed by the trochaic inversion: "Quicker than thought, from East to West that ran" (The Moone-Calfe," line 658). Why is Drayton's line quick and the lines by Marston somewhat swollen? The rest of the lines offer one clue, in the heavy habit of adjective-noun combinations in the one, and the preference for an easily finished cliche in the other (for example, "from East to West"); furthermore, Drayton's subject and verb are reserved for the end of the line ("that [namely, that wind] ran"), whereas Marston effectively finishes the sentence at the beginning of the first line, adding only (slower) descriptive phrases thereafter.

Similar metrical imitations of content about clumsiness, speed, and arduous mental work, are performed by means of rhythms that are clumsy, or slow then fast, or irregular and difficult; the lines in question below are by Alan Stephens, Howard Nemerov, and Thom Gunn, and devices to watch are spondees (and any pyrrhics), inversion of metrical foot, and extra syllables:

| Slow ‖ frail ‖ ungain|ly ‖ set | for the | long run |³⁴

| The few | first flakes | come hur | r y i ng in | to drown |

| Unev|enly ‖ grad|ually ‖ and | with dif|ficulty |

Gunn's line is itself so uneven and difficult that its scansion is by no means straightforward. This is a case where the writer of wide experience and significant accomplishment pushes at the boundaries of a form, even

---

34. From a sonnet sequence, "Running at Hendry's," by Alan Stephens:

    Heron Totem

Up the long beach, a flock of sanderlings
Will swoop past a ridge of ocean roaring near
(Their white chests flashing), tilt and disappear,
Or pelicans line up, dark, heavy things,
And form one body with a dozen wings   5
Approaching me head-on, or godwits flare
Warm cinnamon wing-linings on the gray air
When they veer off in the big flocks winter brings.
I love them all, and most this homely one:
Color of driftwood, among the bustlers, the wary   10
Swervers, he leans inquiringly, and waits.
Slow, frail, ungainly, set for the long run,
Silent with hope, by nature solitary
He picks his spot, stands still, and concentrates.

·

crossing beyond into the world of the un-formed, in a way we might not be pleased to imitate. Note, however, that the lines on either side of line 20 are quite well-mannered from a metrical point of view.

His Rooms in College

All through the damp morning he works, he reads.
The papers of his students are interrupted
Still by the raw fury, the awkward sadness
His marriage has become. The young serious voices
Are drowned by her remembered piteous wail   5
'Discovering' the one unfaithfulness
He never did commit.
                              Be more specific.
What do they have ahead of them, poor dears,
This kind of thing?
                              Today no supervisions;
But though he meant these hours for his research   10
He takes a book, not even in his 'field,'
And some note touches him, he goes on reading
Hours long into the afternoon from which
The same low river fog has never lifted.
If every now and then he raises his eyes   15
And stares at winter lawns below, each time
He sees their hard blurred slopes the less. He reads,
He reads, until the chapel clock strikes five,
And suddenly discovers that the book,
Unevenly, gradually, and with difficulty,   20
Has all along been showing him its mind
(Like no one ever met at a dinner party),
And his attention has become prolonged
To the quiet passion with which he in return
Has given himself completely to the book.   25
He looks out at the darkened lawns, surprised
Less by the loss of grief than by the trust.

                                                    (Thom Gunn)

The poem as a whole is a model of approach to and retreat from extremes, rhetorical as well as metrical.

In a passage from James Merrill's "An Urban Convalescence," only three of the eight lines are clearly iambic pentameter. Of the remaining ones, the seventy-first, seventy-second, and seventy-sixth are metrically misleading. Lines 71 and 75 could come from different poems. The speaker has just used the phrase "the sickness of our time" to describe the habit of yanking old buildings down to put up tasteless new monstrosities, and the metrical liberties are a reaction against the cliche he hears himself using:

> There are certain phrases which to use in a poem
> Is like rubbing silver with quicksilver. Bright
> But facile, the glamour deadens overnight.
> For instance, how "the sickness of our time"
>
> Enhances, then debases, what I feel.   75
> At my desk, I swallow in a glass of water
> No longer cordial, scarcely wet, a pill
> They told me not to take until much later.

But the lines that most diverge are buffered by less irregular modulations until the iambic pentameter norm is reasserted. Thus the irregularity follows from and illustrates the theme of revulsion at pat formula: Merrill clearly felt that asserting revulsion in regular iambs would enhance his feeling only momentarily before debasing it.

In another poem, Merrill also employs meter to suggest a hitch or stumble in the speaker's composure as he describes the disturbing effect of the sense of sight in his poem personifying the five senses (see full text on p. 207); the chief technique that affords this derailment is the tension between the metrical groupings—

$$| \text{ The pale } | \text{ one } \| \text{ with } | \text{ your eyes } | \text{ restive} | \text{ly flashing } |$$

—and the syntactical groupings:

$$\{\text{The pale one}\} \, \{\text{with your eyes}\} \, \{\text{restively flashing}\}$$

Another source of tension occurs because the sentence shifts from speaking about the pale one in the third person to referring to that "one" in the second person ("your eyes"). Tensions make the line seem to veer off into falling rhythm. It is harder than, say, in the line from *King Lear* ("Who is it that can tell me who I am?"), to continue to hear the tick-tock of the meter behind the words, *The PALE one WITH your EYES restIVEly FLASHing.* The rhythm imitates an uncertainty both in the identity of this allegorized "pale one," and in the feelings of the self who speaks, as if he didn't know quite where to look.

In sum, poems must behave metrically if one is to hear a meter at work; but they must not behave *too* metrically or the poem becomes dry. That there are small insurrections here and there throughout the best poems means we have to remain alert to the reading process, so as to anticipate those sudden plunges into thwart, unruly currents, and the equally necessary movements of gradual ebbing and retreat.

A Word about Word Order

Another way in which meter coordinates with the other elements of poetry is in suggesting boundaries for normal word order to strike against. In his discourse on meter, George Gascoigne offers us two versions of one idea:

I understand your meaning by your eye.

Your meaning I understand by your eye.[35]

Although they use the very same words, the latter he calls "neyther true nor pleasant" because metrical expectation (which we presumably derive from the first line in his example) makes us skew the word *un-der-STAND* so that in the second line it reads *un-DER-stand*. Presumably an unnatural stress would also fall on *I*. Both are clearly contrary to natural intonation, and this is Gascoigne's point.

But what of the order within the two sentences? Not only is the second line rhythmically pretty close to prose, it is syntactically inverted. The first line is normal s-v-o sentence order *and* has the advantage of being metrical, which together secure the line as the most orderly ("true") and the most rhythmically pleasant. But there is another possible rendering of the same words:

By your eye I understand your meaning.

Sentence order is inverted, to be sure, but the syllables follow an easy alternation of stressed with unstressed, suggesting a version of the pattern in the normative line, "I understand your meaning by your eye." If this

35. Sylvester, ed., *Sixteenth-Century Poetry*, p. 322.

is still the preferred line (preventing Gascoigne from supposing a third option), it may be that in our revision trochees rather than iambs alternate, and further, that we end with an unstressed ending (no great matter in Shakespeare's blank verse, but a sticking point when one is trying to rhyme, as Gascoigne typically does). But even in blank verse, he does not permit feminine endings (of the 1,181 lines in *The Stele Glas* only four end with an additional syllable, though some do end with understressed iambic feet).

More crucial for Gascoigne, I think, is his aversion to any but normal sentence order. He was the spokesman for regular sentence order and strong, English monosyllables—the building blocks of a version of plain style that bogged down in a closed line. It became **stichic.** As a model for the newcomer, the plain line has much to teach, but a thousand lines of it makes heavy going.

There are any number of lines in poems by others, however, that would sound much *less* natural in regular sentence order:

To bend with apples the mossed cottage trees

(Keats)

And in fowle weder at my booke to sitt

(Wyatt)

Whose woods these are I think I know

(Frost)

Of his bones are coral made

(Shakespeare)

Trees, where you sit, shall crowd into a shade

(Pope)

But we hope in a short time to see you again

(traditional)

How with this rage shall beautie hold a plea

(Shakespeare)

Came lovers home from this great festival

(Marlowe)

My brain I'll prove the female to my soul*

(Shakespeare)

That for a fantasy and trick of fame
Go to their graves like beds. . .*

(Shakespeare)

. . . the open water, which long
remembers nothing, neither wind nor wake*

(Nemerov)

With ships the sea was sprinkled far and nigh

(Wordsworth)

A light of laughing flowers along the grass is spread

(Shelley)

Syntactic inversions in the examples above (all but the first five from the present chapter) are fairly mild, and the lines are often memorable. Not all the inversions are made for the purposes of rhyming (the asterisked lines appear in works of blank verse). But even those that are rhymed (Shelley's, or Ariel's line from *The Tempest*) show a sensitivity to the roughness of alternative arrangements of the same words. And finally, the majority of these lines could not be offered in s-v-o syntactical order without disrupting the meter.

The issue of word order brings us back to central concerns about the role of meter. While slippery as a concept, meter can easily be felt as a silent limit within the enormous varieties of lines written both in it and, to some degree, against it. For meter is a limit that affects and controls while enlarging the scope of elements of verse like the line and sentence. A sentence to all appearances bland can become taut with power, when it enjambs, writing itself *against* the meter. Correlatively, the line can grow in expressive energy when it stands out briefly above the residual patterning. **Rhyme** is a device that highlights this process, and to it we now turn.

9

Stanza and Rhyme: The Role of Echo

Symmetry versus Alternation

The **couplet** is the earliest and most obvious rhymed form in English, connected to songs and rounds, to riddle, and to nursery and jumping rhymes. The popular base of the couplet links it with brevity and striking diction on one hand and, on the other, with the use of rhyme to anchor the lines in time. Further, the function of rhyme in the late Middle Ages in England was, at least in part, to take up the mnemonic (or memory-stimulating) function of Teutonic alliteration. Borrowed from the Latin hymns as well as the profaner work of the Goliard poets who wrote in Latin, rhyme was the spur that kept the lines trotting along in pairs. Mirroring accentual meters with their strong central breaks, the rhymes often fell at the line ends *and* after the midline caesura (this technique is called **leonine verse**), as can be heard in the following two examples from the thirteenth-century *Carmina Burana* or songs of wandering students. The first is a drinking song, the second a love lyric:

> bibit pauper et e*GROTUS*   bibit exul et ig*NOTUS*
> bibit puer bibit *CANUS*   bibit presul et de*CANUS*
>
> . . . .
>
> bibit ista bibit *ILLE*   bibunt centum bibunt *MILLE*
>
> > (*Carmina Burana* 175)[1]
>
> suspice flos *FLOREM*   quia flos designat *AMOREM*
> illo de *FLORE*   nimio sum captus *AMORE*
>
> > (*Carmina Burana* 147)

---

1. In K. P. Harrington, ed., *Medieval Latin* [1925] (Chicago: University of Chicago Press, 1962). Further examples of **leonine verse** appear in chapter 13's "Poetic Terms."

The rhymes above are really examples of likeness of ending. **Like endings** (*homoeoteleuton*) are a feature of grammar whereby identical suffixes carry identical noun cases or verb conjugations. The like endings denote parallels of meaning owing to the words' role in the sentence (only the same parts of speech will acquire the same inflections, or endings, to show case and function). The use of like endings instead of pure rhyme occurs when the roles of prose and verse are in flux. In the history of English poetry, rhyme takes over when alliteration leaves off, with the result that rhyming demotes poetry yet further into the popular realm, while Latin prose remains the medium of cultivation. Alliteration will be discussed in the next chapter, on accentual verse and syllabics.

Early ballads in English depend on rhyme in something of the same way late-medieval Latin verse does, rhyming as often as possible for ease of recall. Here the shepherds come to the stable to worship Jesus:

Haill, litill tine mop*	*tiny baby
Of our crede Thou art crop.*	*head
I would drink on thy cop,*	*from thy cup
Litill daystarne.*	*day star
Haill! Put forth thy dall!*	*hand
I bring thee but a ball:	
Have and play thee withall,	
And go to the tenis.	

(The Second Shepherd's Play VIII, mid-fourteenth century)

Consider also Geoffrey Chaucer's translation of *The Romance of the Rose*, with its decisive rhymes on **feminine** (unstressed) **endings:**

For Narcisus, shortly to telle,	
By aventure com to that welle	
To reste him in the shadowing	155
A day whanne he com fro hunting.	
This Narcisus had suffred paines,	
For renning alday in the plaines,	
And was for thurst in gret distresse	
Of heet, and of his werinesse	160
That hadde his breth almost binomen,*	*taken away
Whanne he was to that welle ycomen . . .	

Three of the five rhyme-sets are based on endings, and one of the two exceptions (*paines/plaines*) rhymes on a root-plus-plural-ending combination.

But after the fourteenth century, when root words emerged from the wrapping paper of their endings, leonine verse disappears and phenomena like alternating **rhyme** appear. Above all, English now offers far fewer rhymes. And now, words must rhyme on roots, not endings, thus creating auditory resemblances between words much further apart in meaning.[2]

The **ballads** do not exploit the distance in meaning between the rhyme words as later couplet writers will do. But these stories-in-verse from the late Middle Ages onward do establish a new poetic unit—the clustering of lines called a **stanza,** particularly the four-line stanza, or quatrain. Capable of indefinite repetition and contained by four-beat lines, the ballads simplify certain formulas well adapted to short-line stanza form. The **refrain** is the most recognizable device—an identical line in the fourth or last place which announces that the stanza has ended. One could vary the refrain line slightly for dramatic effect, introducing a "small but telling substitution at some crucial spot" (called "incremental repetition").[3] This device allowed the singer to tease out similarities, then produce a huge detour, as in the fourth (refrain) lines of "Barbara Allen": "Send word for Barbara Allan," "For a sight of Barbara Allan," "And it's all for Barbara Allan," "Cried 'Woe to Barbara Allan,'" and at the end, this more striking change, in *her* voice: "'I'll die for him tomorrow.'" Simplified rhymes are also typical of the ballads in general, along with a

---

2. W. K. Wimsatt suggests that poetry differs from prose in the same way modern rhyme differs from likeness of ending. In his searching and acute essays collected as *The Verbal Icon,* Wimsatt does more than any modern poet with the possible exception of W. H. Auden to open the treasure-box of prosody, trope, and stylistic technique to the reader and writer of poetry. The relative difficulty with Auden's insights is that they are scattered throughout his criticism and, even then, more a matter of brilliant hint than pointed exposition.

The essays in Wimsatt's *The Verbal Icon* of particular relevance to the style of the couplet are "One Relation of Rhyme to Reason," "Rhetoric and Poems" (on Alexander Pope), and "Verbal Style: Logical and Counterlogical." See *The Verbal Icon: Studies in the Meaning of Poetry* (Lexington: University of Kentucky Press, 1967).

3. Albert B. Friedman's paraphrase of the device ("incremental repetition"), which F. B. Grummere formulated in 1907 (*Princeton Encyclopedia,* 1974 ed., p. 382b).

syntax anchored on noun and verb rather than on adjective and noun. Clause is favored over phrase and action over quality.[4]

In ballads we note as well holdovers from leonine verse that aid the memory: In addition to verbatim closing refrains, ballads typically use intermediate repetitions of phrases ("the fitt of the tree" and "the machrel of the sea" from "The Laily Worm"), many bare category-phrases (for example, "his hawk, his hound, and his lady fair," from "The Twa Corbies"), and juxtapositions between generalizable realms; these **juxtapositions** are focused on proverbial oppositions like health and illness, youth and age, love and greed, constancy and betrayal, innocence and guile. Whereas literary poets, as Alan Bold points out, depend on "the unexpected phrase, the ingenious rhyme, the contrived figures of speech, . . . oral poets must depend on formulas."[5] Magical numbers, obligatory epithets (fair, foul, etc.), and what Bold calls "nuncupative testaments" (oral wills) are among the ballad formulas.

Simplicity of means is made compelling by the atmosphere of immediate speech, frequent dialogue, and the dramatic arc of the stories whose unfolding is implied. The plots were meant to be recognizable and thus could be amplified at will; as a result, their thematic ingredients were as unambiguous as their forms were pared down and serviceable. Bold calls the ballads "schematic story-containers sturdy enough to retain their basic shape despite repeated usage by different people."[6] But at the same time, the ballads seem planted in uncertainty and omission. The poet Thom Gunn describes as follows the ballad "The Laily Worm": this poem's "images and narrative move us even though we do not understand their original force. It makes a completely satisfying whole as we have it, yet it is filled with mystery." Among the ciphers of mystery in the "Laily Worm" Gunn lists "the directness of the utterance," the "seeming arbitrariness" of the tale, and "the brutality of the action."[7] Omission counts

4. Clausal versus phrasal **modes** are defined by Josephine Miles in *Eras and Modes in English Poetry* [1964] (Westport, CT: Greenwood Press, 1976), pp. 1–19, 100–123, and 203–48.

5. Alan Bold, *The Ballad* (London: Methuen, 1979), p. 14.

6. Bold may be simplifying somewhat. Roger D. Abrahams and George Foss show how much distortion and imperfect transmission occurred in balladry, particularly when the songs crossed the Atlantic. See their *Anglo-American Folksong Style* (Englewood Cliffs, NJ: Prentice-Hall, 1968), pp. 1–82 *passim*.

7. Thom Gunn, "Hardy and the Ballads," in his *Occasions of Poetry: Essays in Criticism and Autobiography* (London: Faber & Faber, 1982), p. 85.

so heavily in the structure and function of the ballads that even "bare situations" are "of such intensity that their implications are very wide."

Ballads and the Rule of Two

Several elements of style support the intensity of the ballads; directness of rhetoric is balanced by withholding of information, and simplicity of diction by ambiguity of referent (Gunn suggests we never discover why the king decides to send Sir Patrick Spens to sea[8]). Bareness of means figures also in the lengths and rhythms of the ballad lines. These poems did not use the full array of meters. The metrical norm in the ballad is a stress pattern alternating strong with weak syllables—but with surprisingly little exact alternation, as befits both the musical context for most of the ballads and the oral dimension of their transmission (hence openness to variation at every line). Triple measures are liberally used, as we hear in "Sir Patrick Spens" and "As You Came from the Holy Land of Walsinghame" (see the texts for both in chapter 10). Furthermore, many would argue that the ballad is built on a two-stress, alternating unit (a unit Derek Attridge convincingly illustrates as essential to English verse[9]).

The ballad **rule of two,** as we might call it, pertains to alternation at the level of syllables (weak versus strong) and at the level of foot-clusters. If we imagine each weak-strong pair of syllables as a unit, we find alternations in strength across the four parts of the line, each part centered on a beat, **S** W **S** W, for example: *The* **KING** *sits* **IN** *DumFERling* **TOWN.** The second and fourth main beats are comparatively weak, while the first and third are comparatively strong. The rule of two obtains even in the

---

8. Stanzas usually omitted from anthologies suggest that Spens is sent to Norway:

To Norraway, to Norraway,
To Norraway o'er the faem.*   *foam
The King's daughter of Norraway,
'Tis I must bring her hame.

See Robert Graves, ed., *English and Scottish Ballads* (London: William Heinemann, 1957), p. 18. The granddaughter of Alexander III of Scotland, called the maid of Norway, was brought back across the North Sea to marry Prince Edward of England but died in the Orkney islands. See Frances Mary Hendry, *Quest for a Maid* (New York: Farrar Straus Giroux, 1988) for a dramatization of the Patrick Spens ballad.

9. In fact, to get to pentameter from a two-stress or four-stress line, it was, Attridge thinks, necessary to diverge radically and counterintuitively from a basic dipodic convention antedating literary poems. See *The Rhythms of English Poetry* (London: Longman, 1982), chapter five *passim*.

apparent trimeter or three-stress lines of earlier rhyming poetry. These trimeters contain what Attridge calls a suppressed fourth beat (which he would illustrate with a bracketed [B]), for example:

    B   B **B**   [B]
But nothinge it availed   25

    B   B   **B**   [B]
To call Philip againe,

          B   B   **B**   [B]
Whom Gib our cat hath slaine.

  B   B   **B** [B]
Gib, I saye, our cat

  B   B   **B**   [B]
Worrowid★ her on that   ★*crammed herself*

  B   B   **B**   [B]
Which I loved best: 30

  B   B   **B**   [B]
It can not be exprest

  B   B **B**   [B]
My sorrowfull hevinesse . . .[10]

                             (John Skelton, "Philip Sparrow")

The mechanism that provides the **unrealized** fourth **beat** is the expectation of equivalent time (**isochrony**) between the beats, which we have heard at work in other ways in the chapter above.

Unrealized Beats in Ballad Quatrains

The presumptions about these echo-beats, or unwritten stresses, are:

1. The basic rule is two beats divided by one or more offbeats (unstressed syllables); tetrameter (four-beat) lines being a doubled echo of the basic two-beat group.

2. Just as rhyme is stronger than prerhyme,[11] and the closing of a parenthesis stronger than its opening, the echo of a line caps and com-

---

10. The automatic super-stress on -*nesse* rather than on *heav-* comes about owing to context. One would not be tempted thus to stress Skelton's line 32 if it were the first in the poem.

11. The term "prerhyme" for the first occurrence of a syllable that will be rhymed upon is Barbara Herrnstein Smith's. See *Poetic Closure: A Study of How Poems End* (Chicago: University of Chicago Press, 1968), p. 72.

pletes its initial sounding (thus it need not be uttered entire, in the second instance, to be operative; this, says Attridge, is the reason why 4-3-4-3 **ballad meter** stanzas feel so symmetrical[12]).

3. Another rule for perceived symmetry in a three-beat line is that the first and third beats of each four-beat sequence are dominant.

4. The third item of the four-item sequence is the strongest, whether beats in a four-stress line, or lines in a quatrain:

>   /   \\   /   \\
> Ride a cock-horse to Banbury Cross
>   /   \\   /   \\
> To see a fine lady upon a white horse;
>   /   \\   /   \\
> **Rings on her fingers and bells on her toes,**
>   /   \\   /   \\
> She shall have music wherever she goes.

(traditional)

>   〰〰
>   /   \\   /   \\
> Hard is her heart as flint or stone,
>   /   \\   /   \\
> She laughs to see me pale; [B]
>   /   \\   /   \\
> **And merry as a grig* is grown,**   **cricket*
>   /   \\   /   \\
> And brisk as bottled ale. [B]

(John Gay)[13]

The most heavily stressed syllable in each stanza is the third stress in the third line (*bells* and *grig*).

The primacy of the four-beat line is also an audible feature of Emily Dickinson's #423; here is the last of its three quatrains:

> The manner of the chil ^ dren—
> Who weary of the Day— [B]
> Themself—the noisy Play ^ thing
> They cannot put away— [B]

The odd-numbered lines, particularly the stanza's third line, which acts as a pivot, shift effortlessly (with no sense of departure from the four-beat norm) from four realized beats to three. (Note the stanza-central stress on *Play-*, the third stress in line three of Dickinson's quatrain.) We con-

---

12. See Attridge, *The Rhythms of English Poetry*, chapter 4.3.
13. The examples are Attridge's, *The Rhythms of English Poetry*, pp. 82–83 and 89.

tinue to hear the fourth beats in the lines of secondary weight, which we complete according to the rule of two.

The Literary Stanza

The three stanzas quoted above trace an arc that is increasingly literary. This means that the three stanzas are decreasingly like songs. Song as chant, as John Hollander points out,[14] is more important in literary history than song as *chanson*, or song as sung. The true ballads, with all their devices designed to promote memorability, give way to quatrains ornamented with descriptive texture and striking but not easily memorized diction. Compared with the movement of the early ballads, eighteenth-century poems in ballad or common measure (4-3-4-3 stanzas rhyming *abab*) fatten the stanza with adjectives while exaggerating the regularity of stress-to-nonstress alternations:

> King Edward saw the ruddy streaks
>   of light eclipse the gray;
> And heard the raven's croaking throat
>   proclaim the fated day.

(Thomas Chatterton)[15]

The weak-strong alternation is monotonous; so is the pairing of bisyllabic adjectives with monosyllabic nouns. By the time we get to the rhyme, the fire in the line gutters out, its energy diverted elsewhere.

Some eighteenth-century poets dropped the rhymes, which made the stanzas less palpable. It would seem that one obvious fact about the metrical stanza is the organization of its materials by means of rhyme. Any other fashion of grouping lines that does not use rhyme will not register, in English, as inevitably stanzaic (that is, will not have the authority, contour, or coherence of a stanza, but rather of a verse paragraph, whose closure is ideally logical and expressive rather than evenly numbered and coincident in sound). William Collins's unrhymed Horatian quatrains in his "Ode to Evening" do not cohere in lines of four but run on past stanza breaks (the first sentence is twenty lines long). Because Collins uses pentameter rather than tetrameters in the first two lines of

---

14. See Hollander's entry on song in the *Princeton Encyclopedia*, 1974 ed., p. 781a.
15. Chatterton is quoted by Josephine Miles, *Eras and Modes in English Poetry*, pp. 104–5.

each four-line segment, their length, in the absence of rhyme, may diffuse stanza shape even further:

> Now air is hushed, save where the weak-eyed bat
> With short shrill shriek flits by on leathern wing,   10
>   Or where the beetle winds
>   His small but sullen horn,
> As oft he rises midst the twilight path,
> Against the pilgrim borne in heedless hum . . .

Contrast Collins's with Andrew Marvell's poem, "An Horatian Ode: Upon Cromwell's Return from Ireland," in which stanzas mark clauses with definite terminal points; the $a^4a^4b^3b^3$ scheme shapes the terminal points.[16] Marvell is speaking of the double edge of Cromwell's sword, for while it is so potent as to frighten the dead, it can never be laid aside:

> Beside the force it has to fright
> The spirits of the shady night,
>   The same arts that did gain
>   A power must it maintain.   120

Rhyme is the feature signaling the parallels and closings more quietly established by the meter as it balances idea.

The Rules of Rhyme

Should a stanza contain only *one* rhyme linking two or more of a stanza's line ends, that rhyme must occur in the final line, otherwise the sense of closure will not be satisfied. Yet another perceptual threshold under the conditions just described makes it necessary to have the line that forms the line pair fairly close by.

> Between two dreams,
> bloody and rare,
> my heartways cross.
> A shade hangs there.

> (Julia Randall, "Adam's Dream")

---

16. The Collins-Marvell contrast is Philip Hobsbaum's, but he thinks of the Collins poem stanzaically, which I cannot, quite. See Hobsbaum, *Metre, Rhythm and Verse* (London: Routledge, 1996), p. 133.

No more than one unrhymed line ending may intervene without a breakdown of the symmetrical tensions that make any stanza satisfying and complete; the iambic tetrameter "In Memoriam" quatrain (*abba*), intruding a couplet between the *a* rhymes, is often closer to a visual than an auditory unit.

Assuming letters for rhymes, these minimal thresholds for rhyme would be framed as follows:

1. *abxb* If only one rhyme sounds in a stanza, it must appear in the last line.

2. *abxyb* is not a viable stanza because too many freelance lines intervene.

Rhyme can be either strict alternating (for example, *abab*), irregular alternating, or interspersed (*abcbac*), or adjacent (in couplets, for example, *aabbcc*, and so forth). Some rhyme schemes bring together alternating with adjacent rhyme, for example, **rhyme royal,** a seven-line stanza useful for both narratives and verse meditation (*ababbcc*).

Rhyme sounds can be full (exact) or near (rhyming either final vowel or final consonant—or the consonant envelope and not the vowel). Some effect of rhyme can be gained—but is insufficient for the final line—by "rhyming" stress, that is, providing a feminine or masculine ending to match with the paired line ending. By the same token, the effect of rhyme is diminished when the last, rhyming syllables are unequally stressed. Philip Hobsbaum labels near rhymes (for which he uses Wilfred Owen's term **pararhyme**) with percentages (rhymes that are unequally stressed earn a ¼). Here is an example from a poem by Owen (a Welsh poet who was killed in World War I); I have extended Hobsbaum's mode of calculation to account for the fuller feminine rhymes on multisyllabic words in Byron and Auden (where maximum rhyme, as for example Auden's *interior/superior* and *Duke of Wellington/Duke Ellington,* would earn a 2). In a vein more pure and grim than theirs, Owen's speaker addresses an enemy soldier who is his mirror image:

Courage was mine, and I had mystery,	*a*	30
Wisdom was mine, and I had mastery:	1½ *a*	
To miss the march of this retreating world	*b*	
Into vain citadels that are not walled.	¾ *b*	
Then, when much blood had clogged their chariot-wheels,	*c*	
I would go up and wash them from sweet wells,	¾ *c*	35

Even with truths that lie too deep for taint.   *d*
I would have poured my spirit without stint   ¾ *d*
But not through wounds . . .

A half-rhyme in Hobsbaum's system would be *bar/fire,* a quarter-rhyme *ón/órgan,* and an eighth-rhyme merely a metrical symmetry (for example, *réal/súit*). But the poems by Philip Larkin and Peter Porter, from which the last near rhymes are taken, do not register major advances in stanza formation. As Hobsbaum says, "it is the less distinctive verse forms that have the longest cycles of employment."

Heterometric Rhymes

Not only simplicity but parallelism in the lines that end in rhymes (isometric rhymes) makes for longevity. Heterometric lines (lines metrically dissimilar, particularly when adjacent) produce comic works, as in many of Edward Lear's couplets: "Our sieve ain't big. / But we don't care a button! we don't care a fig!" Rhymes also haul up at the end of the lyrics (or "patter-songs") of W. S. Gilbert, not to mention the myriad less polished types:

> And the grease spots on Mary's doll dress don't seem to come out,
>   and we can't think how they got there;
> Unless it was when we bought that Macassar oil, because she has
>   real hair.
>
>   (Juliana Horatia Ewing)[17]

Owing to the opposing stress pattern, the rhyme of *hair* with *got there* would earn only half a Hobsbaum point. Thomas Hood used **heterometric rhymes** in his more sophisticated portrait, "Our Village":

> And Mrs. Brown, in domestic economy not to be a bit behind her
>   betters,
> Lets her house to a milliner, a watch-maker, a rat-catcher, a cobler,
>   lives in it herself, and it's the post-office for letters.
> . . . .
> There's fifty-five private houses, let alone barns and workshops, and
>   pigstyes, and poultry huts, and such-like sheds;

---

17. In Iona and Peter Opie, eds., *The Oxford Book of Children's Verse* (Oxford and New York: Oxford University Press, 1973), pp. 258–59.

With plenty of public houses*—two Foxes, one Green Man, three
Bunch of Grapes, one Crown, and six King's Heads.   *taverns

Heterometric lines with rhymes both irregularly dispersed as well as
strictly alternating occur in much serious verse, including Milton's *Samson
Agonistes,* Arnold's "Dover Beach," and many irregular or Pindaric odes,
such as Wordsworth's "Intimations Ode" and George Herbert's "The
Flower." The stanza of Elizabeth Bishop's "Cirque d'Hiver" is based on a
simple variation of the heroic quatrain (see the full text in chapter 1's
"Poetry Sampler"). While the first three and last lines are iambic pentam-
eter, the fourth line is iambic trimeter; it rhymes with the second and last
lines, $abxb^3b$. The stanza pattern is like a quatrain with a hitch in it just
prior to the return of the pattern with the last line—a variation common
in music to clinch the ending.

Closure in the Bishop stanzas is enhanced by verbatim repetition in
the rhymes (in all stanzas but the penultimate—again employing, as in
the entire rhyme scheme, that variation-near-the-end, whereby the re-
turn to the norm at the close sounds more satisfying). The penultimate
stanza is further varied from the norm by enjambment between lines 15
and 16 ("that pierces both her body and her soul // and goes through his
. . ."), and by exaggerated cuts in the syntax (it's the stanza in which the
most activity is concentrated—cantering, bowing, clicking, stopping,
looking). When the last stanza stretches its lines out again, they do so in
willful non sequitur (the dancer does *x;* the horse is more intelligent;
horse and speaker face each other, then his eye is like a star, etc.). But
conversational provisos ("the more," "rather," "'Well'") support the
return from active gesture to a demeanor beguiled by affection. Con-
versational ease also undergirds the naturalness of the nominally simple
rhymes on *far,* which is first couched in an adverbial phrase of value judg-
ment (the horse is more intelligent *by far*), and in the last line of the poem
forms part of a modest concessive phrase, "'Well, we have *come this far.*'"
To a degree, Bishop is not rhyming on the word but **rhyming on the
phrase.**

Another poem already examined, Richard Wilbur's "Exeunt" (see
chap. 5, p. 179), leans on the technique of rhyme more heavily than
Bishop does. First, Wilbur's diction is active everywhere and flexes its
muscles in the rhymes (*terse/hearse*). Then we encounter complication in
metaphors attaching to Wilbur's relatively simple rhymes, such as *dies/
lies,* for the thing that *lies* is delicacy itself: "A last shawl of burning lies /

On a gray field-stone." Thus the rather fundamental-sounding rhyme of *stone* with *alone* is made ineffable by the tropes in *other* lines. Further, Wilbur personifies the daisy in the line with the prerhyme—the stanza's only pentameter line, "At the field's edge a daisy lines alone"—thus stimulating the complexity of the stanzaic frame, $a^3b^5a^4b^3$. The fact of metrical assortment in the lines is not itself the *cause* of elaboration; the poem's quatrain shape and the dominance of monosyllabic rhymes should streamline the stanzas. But trope, active predication in the syntax, nimbly self-conscious diction, and a careful application of metrical drag (in the form of syllables long in **quantity**—spondees [*field-stone, dry grass*], reversed feet [*Crawls from*], and defective feet [| *A last* | ^ *shawl* | *of burn* | *ing lies* |]) increase the interest of what happens in every corner of the poem—a fact that slows our passage through it. Wilbur's treatment of this stanza of his would *not* make it suitable for a narrative, or for passing along to others as the ballad stanzas were. By contrast, Bishop's "Cirque d'Hiver" stanza might more easily teach itself to an audience as a frame for narrative extension.

Extrapolation of the stanza beyond the quatrain often results in curiosities such as the somewhat tortuous stanza in Lowell's "Mr. Edwards and the Spider" (see chap. 2, pp. 60–61) or the appealing stanzas of Herbert's "The Flower" (whose short lines—for example, "It cannot be / That I am he / On whom thy tempests fell all night"—nicely compress into his base-line, tetrameter). Extrapolation can also result in nonrepeating stanzaic forms, as in Abraham Cowley's "Ode upon Doctor Harvey," Dryden's "A Song for St. Cecilia's Day," and Coleridge's "Dejection Ode." But for heavy service, the simpler stanzas have worked better, such as the **Burns stanza** that builds on a tetrameter ballad quatrain and interjects a couplet in dimeters (see "Tam Samson's Elegy" in chapter 13's "Poetic Terms").

Ottava Rima

Another good repeating stanza is the rhymed eight-liner, or **ottava rima** (*ababablcc*), a staple with Byron and Yeats. The latter made ottava rima work for him in a particularly revealing way. Yeats essentially reoriented a stanza that Byron had devoted to comic purposes by slowing it down for meditation. Even when he was in a contemplative mood, Byron's ottava rima stanzas are brisk:

An infant when it gazes on a light,
    A child the moment when it drains the breast,
A devotee when soars the Host in sight,
    An Arab with a stranger for a guest,
A sailor when the prize has struck* in fight,   **lowered its flag; surrendered*
    A miser filling his most hoarded chest,
Feel rapture; but not such true joy are reaping
As they who watch o'er what they love while sleeping.
                                          (*Don Juan* Canto II.196)

Yeats alters the eight-line ottava rima stanza somewhat, using both the conventional *ababab cc* form in "The Gyres," "Among School Children," and "Coole and Ballylee 1931," and two further rhyme patterns that combine couplets with envelope-quatrains. The first of these types is *aabbcddc*—the rhyme scheme of the eight-line stanzas in "A Prayer for My Daughter," "The Tower, II," and "Byzantium," and another that resembles the pattern of the octave in a Petrarchan sonnet, *abbaabba* or the seven-line pattern of rhyme royal, *ababbcc;* this variant, with more rhymes than the Petrarchan, *abbacddc,* is used by Yeats in "A Dialogue of Self and Soul," "In Pity for Man's Darkening Thought," and "After Long Silence." The first (couplet-plus-envelope-quatrain) ottava rima variant is illustrated below:

An intellectual hatred is the worst,
So let her think opinions are accursed.
Have I not seen the loveliest woman born   60
Out of the mouth of Plenty's horn,
Because of her opinionated mind
Barter that horn and every good
By quiet natures understood
For an old bellows full of angry wind?   65
                           ("A Prayer for My Daughter")

The most telling change in the ottava rima stanza inherited from Byron is Yeats's introduction of **reduced lines;** in each stanza of "A Prayer for My Daughter" and "The Tower, II," the fourth, sixth, and seventh lines are tetrameter, not pentameter). This envelope of reduced lines is carried to dramatic extremes in "Byzantium":

At midnight on the Emperor's pavement flit   25
Flames that no faggot feeds, nor steel has lit,
Nor storm disturbs, flames begotten of flame,
Where blood-begotten spirits come
And all complexities of fury leave,
Dying into a dance,   30
An agony of trance,
An agony of flame that cannot singe a sleeve.

The pressure toward reduction from pentameter (the first three lines) and tetrameter (the fourth line) to trimeter in the sixth and seventh may not be as radical as it looks, for the three-stress lines can be heard against the rule of two: We can, that is, still hear an unspoken *fourth* beat in each of the short lines above, and in the most memorable of the reduced passages in the poem: "Those images that yet [B] / Fresh images beget. [B]" Nevertheless, Yeats puts the climax of his ottava rima stanza (lines 6 and 7) under the pressure of radical abbreviation.

Thinking in Stanzas

To think properly about what stanzas like Byron's and Yeats's actually do, however, it's necessary to step back a moment from the idea of this poetic object—the stanza—as a completed thing in front of us (a product whose rationale can be hypothesized after the fact)—and to imagine the *writing* of a poem in stanzas. Think how Byron is trying to make more universal an episode somewhat doomed in personal terms (in Canto II, Haidee has just yielded to Juan and watches him sleeping); the manic humor of the libertine hero is momentarily absent. Yeats is working in two different modes above, the first stubbornly plain style with an editorial axe to grind against Maud Gonne's crippling political mania; to this end, a hint of the conversational ("an intellectual hatred is the worst") blends with the proverbial ("mouth of Plenty's horn"; "an old bellows"). In the second stanza (from "Byzantium"), the poet directs the energy of the stanza into the stasis of the two most greatly reduced lines: Spirits, in an almost purgatorial way, are here purging themselves of their fleshly memories. The short lines image the point of greatest torment.

So when we ask, 'What advantage does a stanza intrinsically furnish?' we can think of responses that address the poem's immediate as well as general aims. What is it, after all, that the writer wishes to do when the idea of writing the poem in stanzas presents itself? Create a frame of euphony and order for a narrative that (in Byron's case) is mixed and comic and, for meditative lyrics (in Yeats's case), to build a repeating sequence strong enough to bear a great argument that goes on between the terms of action and those of art. If we wonder what is achieved by putting together the materials we find between the white spaces that separate stanzas—and doing this at regular intervals—we can speculate that syntactic and narrative coherence is framed by this shape and recollected by the rhymes.

There are larger questions to ask: What is the attraction of echoing? Yeats clearly needed rhyme, to attach his voice to the springs of the demotic and folk rhythms. Every practicing poet carries about the echo tradition, after all, derived from ballads, songs, and nursery rhymes. It is this communion that authors, on the threshold of conceiving a work, intuitively turn to the stanza *for*. First, we are looking for an echo of an oral form within a written one. The great ballads like "Lord Randal" and "Barbara Allen" were not first written down, then set to song—rather the inverse. They were created *to* melodies and only later transcribed apart from their music. In the same way, the aura of the song that must once have been sung animates the lyrics of Wyatt and Burns and recurs in the less vigorous, somewhat more saccharine tradition of songs such as those composed by Thomas Moore:

> Believe me, if all those endearing young charms,
>   Which I gaze on so fondly today,
> Were to change by tomorrow, and fleet in my arms,
>   Like fairy-gifts fading away,
>
> Thou would'st still be ador'd, as this moment thou art,   5
>   Let thy loveliness fade as it will,
> And around the dear ruin, each wish of my heart
>   Would entwine itself verdantly still.

The musical setting to Tom Moore's song remedies any anapestic clumsiness by its *largo* use of waltz time.

Although the poems later poets write may not be designed for singing, we can be moved by the desire to create words as plain and poignant as the words for texts that are. When Coleridge is both exceedingly plain and dramatic at one and the same time, he probably has in mind this world of words enmeshed in music:

> The body of my brother's son   341
> Stood by me, knee to knee.
> The body and I pulled at one rope,
> But he said nought to me.

("The Ancient Mariner")

Auden is similarly drawn to the profound affect of the ballad, turning the theme of urban loneliness away from the static lyric that might be spoken by a solitary individual into a dynamic narrative of the psychologically wounded; his ballads, "As I Walked Out One Evening," "Miss Gee," "Victor," and "Lady, Weeping at the Crossroads," all bring to bear on modern neurosis some of the form's grim, archaic poignancy.

Metaphysical Ballads

Simplicity and concentration of act and idea—these lie at one end of the continuum of the stanza. The sentences meet the line ends with a clang as of a great bell even when the words are not rhetorically inclined. (Although her stanza is five lines and not four, Bishop approaches the ballad in her frugality and control.) Julia Randall has evolved a species of metaphysical ballad, more dense than Bishop, yet not absolutely relinquishing the opportunity to echo the song. These ballads are half-literary, half-ditty, carried along by a kind of crooning under-melody in which the grotesque and self-lacerating subjects in Yeats, Dickinson, Blake, and Roethke have been transmuted by Randall into her own, sometimes metaphorically turbid, artifacts of expression.

> And I lay down, a beast, to die
> And rose up seven years ago
> In the poplar fields of home.   30
> There the streams go out and in,
> All the men are common men,
> The blackbird whistles in the corn.
> Touch me. It is mine.

("Boundbrook")

After their ballad qualities, the next most striking feature of Randall's metaphysical lyrics is their resistance to headwork and argument. The realm to which her poems point is curiously intermittent, never wholly possessed.

At the other end of the stanzaic continuum lie restless, syntactically demanding, enjambing, and intellectually muscular stanzas like Wilbur's, Lowell's, or this group of syntactically complicated couplets by J. V. Cunningham, whose linear and rhyming patterns are almost too light for the occasion. Cunningham's poem is also metaphysical in its content, which proceeds by extremes (flesh versus spirit):

> You that undertake this story
> For his life nor death be sorry
> Who the Absolute so loved   5
> Motion to its zero moved,
> Till immobile in that chill
> Fury hardened in the will,
> And the trivial, bestial flesh
> In its jacket ceased to thresh,   10
> And the soul none dare forgive
> Quiet lay, and ceased to live.

("With a Copy of Swift's Works")

Rather than relying on the rhymes and validating the poem through them, one feels that Cunningham only pulls them in as he passes—even writing the poem *past* the rhymes. Thought (as expressed in sentence) does not lie down with line.

Modern Rhyme and Syntactic Clash

Line and sentence are often at odds (and fruitfully so). To the degree that the sentences enjamb, the lines are absorbed. So, too, stanza and sentence are also potentially antagonistic. To the degree that the sentences enjamb, the stanza is skewed. Just as line, to be audible, coincides with syntax, so—if stanza is to be audible—the sentence-frame should match up with the stanza parts. J. W. Johnson distinguishes two kinds of ancient lyric, the stichic (which demarcated lines of equal length and was recited) and the melic, which used phrases of varying length or movement for singing.[18] The two traditions in modern English do not quite mesh with these, but the distinction throws a clearer light on the English differences. Stanzas in English have combined features from both stichic and melic

---

18. J. W. Johnson, "Lyric," *The New Princeton Encyclopedia of Poetry and Poetics*, 1993 ed., edited by Alex Preminger and T. V. F. Brogan (Princeton, NJ: Princeton University Press, 1993), p. 717a.

lyrics in the symmetrical ballad stanzas. Whereas in the stanzas of irregular lines the melic principle of variety is observed along with the principle of repetition, on the whole, meter remains constant.[19]

But English lines have been incalculably altered by one feature unique to it. As Wimsatt points out, English changed in the fourteenth century from being a language whose rhymes acquiesced to logical parallel to being a language that *resists* logical parallel when its poets rhyme. Wimsatt judges Chaucer to be closer to prose than Alexander Pope is, because the fourteenth-century poet had so many endings that were rhymed on—for the nouns alone there were a score of endings and few nouns with none. As a result, as we see in the lines from his version of *The Romance of the Rose* above, Chaucer's rhymes tend to be limited to identical parts of speech (by the device called **like ending**). By contrast, Alexander Pope, writing three hundred years after Chaucer, "perforce rhymed words differing more widely in meaning."[20]

Wimsatt makes the further point that it is not sounds that rhyme but meanings (or the single-syllabled meaning-nuggets linguists call "morphemes"), which now clash under the cover of likeness. What comes together in the technique we call rhyme are not so much aural signifiers as semantic ones with subtle syntactical identities, for it is Wimsatt's view that "words have no character as rhymes until they become points in a syntactic succession" (p. 156). Auditory chiming lags in importance well behind the structural clash of morphemes.

In the couplets of Pope, in particular, Wimsatt believes the disparity between the auditory resemblance and the logical divergence—a divergence in both function (syntax) and meaning (root)—is exploited with unparalleled cleverness. The accidental nature of the chiming-together of root syllables is accommodated to parallels (and their logical mirror, antitheses) by many architectonic devices. Among these are two rhetorical devices Wimsatt thinks have an unusually strong hold over Pope. **Zeugma** (literally, "yoking") is one device Pope uses to create double-

---

19. An exception in a literary poem would be Philip Sidney's "When to My Deadly Pleasure," in which all the lines have the form $-\cup\cup-\cup--$:

As you, alas, my sun bends.
Thus do I fall, to rise thus;
Thus do I die, to live thus;
Changed to a change, I change not.
Thus may I not be from you.   30

20. Wimsatt, "One Relation of Rhyme to Reason," *The Verbal Icon,* p. 157.

ness. It permits one word (the "yoke" word, like *go* or *lose*) to link two meanings, one material (to run like a watch; to lose one's necklace), one spiritual (to proceed in an orderly argument; to lose one's heart or fall in love):

> 'Tis with our Judgments as our Watches, none
> Go just *alike,* yet each believes his own.   10
>
>   (*An Essay on Criticism*)

> Or lose her Heart, or Necklace, at a Ball
>
>   (*The Rape of the Lock* II.109)

Another example: Pope suggests a material denotation for the verb *take* with regard to *Treats* but a more abstract meaning for *give* relative to *Assignations* (meetings); the sense is that she gives permission to her suitor to meet with her secretly:

> While Nymphs take Treats or Assignations give
>
>   (*The Rape of the Lock* III.169)

Pope's second device, far more complex, is called **chiasmus** (literally, "crossing," as with an *X*, or Greek *chi*), whereby two neighboring lines are made into thought-segments that match up in reverse order in the second line. Wimsatt gives an example from Andrew Marvell:

> And your quaint honor[1] turn to dust[2],
> And into ashes[2'] all my lust[1'].

If we connect both of the related terms (1 with 1', 2 with 2'), we sketch the *chi* or *X* that gives this balancing device its name. But most of Wimsatt's examples of chiasmus are chosen from the master of this sleight-of-hand, Pope:

> Whether the nymph shall break[1] Diana's law[2],
> Or some frail China jar[2'] receive a flaw.[1']

Rhyming on the Phrase

Both zeugma and chiasmus, but particularly the latter, knit up the rhyme words in phrases that are subjected to subtle counterbalancing. *Dust* and *lust* and *law* and *flaw* are not merely *words* that rhyme, but small parts of larger, countermatching line-segments (clauses and phrases), which come together with a closure in sound that contradicts the contrast in meaning:

receive a flaw logically parallels not the authority of *law* with which *flaw* rhymes, but the peril that someone might *break* it, and *Diana's law* parallels not the phrase it rhymes with but that other breakable entity, a *China jar.* One notes, too, how chiasmus, like zeugma, involves punning between material and spiritual levels of meaning. For "Diana's law" is female virtue, perhaps more literally a virgin's maidenhead, which can be broken as irremediably as delicate China: no mending can ever bring either the body's tissue or the fine porcelain—let alone the woman's reputation—back to its state of pristine wholeness. And yet the juxtaposition of woman to vase is no sooner argued than subverted. Pope displaces his harsh strictures unsymmetrically affecting sexual behavior onto the plateau of objects—a plateau on which, ironically, men and women are reduced to ciphers mutually trivializing. This is a world where instead of wars there are cards played and instead of rape the cutting of locks of hair. It's clear why Pope found tropes of uneven comparison useful and how rhyme knits such figures into apparent symmetry within the couplet.

It's also clear how much less pointed the prerhymes are than the rhymes in the second lines. Consider the phrases of which each rhyme is a part:

> Avoid *Extreams;* and shun the Fault of such,
> Who still are pleas'd *too little,* or *too much.*
>
> (*An Essay on Criticism* [1711], 384–85)

> So much they scorn the Crowd, that if the Throng
> By *Chance* go right, they *purposely* go wrong.
>
> (426–27)

> Some valuing those of their own *Side,* or *Mind,*
> Still make themselves the measure of Mankind.
>
> (452–53)

> *Good-Nature* and *Good-Sense* must ever join;
> To Err is *Humane;* to Forgive, *Divine.*
>
> (524–25)

> All seems Infected that th' Infected spy,
> As all looks yellow to the Jaundic'd Eye.
>
> (558–59)

The last couplet is particularly interesting because it may well be the first example of the phrase "Jaundic'd eye" for the distorting effects of envy (only "jaundiced look" appears in the *OED* with this metaphorical application prior to Pope's poem, and up until the end of the seventeenth century only the material application—literal visual distortion owing to the ailment of jaundice—had been used). A phrase new to use (like "a Jaundic'd eye") achieves currency by solidly falling at the very place in a couplet (the second rhyme) where concentration by phrase memorably occurs.

This is a device Pope perfects in time. Twenty years after *An Essay on Criticism* (from which I quoted above), he publishes the four *Moral Epistles* (1731–35); in these four poems he is yet more receptive to the appeal of catchphrase and proverbial expressions by others and from the culture at large. Here is a sampler from the third of his four "moral essays" on the evils of riches, the "Epistle to Bathurst"; note the liberal use of allegorized and travestied figures (Nature, Gold, Reason; Sappho). The borrowed expressions are *italicized:*

What Nature wants, commodious Gold bestows,
'Tis thus we eat *the bread another sows.*

(*Epistle to Bathurst* 21–22)

Had Colepepper's whole wealth been hops and hogs,
Could he himself have *sent it to the dogs?*

(53–54)

Yet, to be just to these poor men of pelf,
Each does but hate *his Neighbour as himself;*

(109–10)

Why she and Sappho raise a monstrous sum?
Alas! they fear a man will *cost a plum.*[21]

(123–24)

Ask we what makes one keep, and one bestow?
That P O W ' R who bids the Ocean *ebb and flow,*
Bids seed-time, harvest, equal course maintain,
Thro' reconcil'd extremes of *drought and rain.*

(165–69)

---

21. One of J. V. Cunningham's epigrams perfects the ideas in this couplet of Pope's—using the same proverbial ease, but now in *both* the second hemistichs: "You wonder why Drab *sells her love for gold?* / To have the means *to buy it when she's old.*"

Not so his Son, he mark'd this oversight,
And then mistook reverse of *wrong for right*.

(199–200)

In heaps, like Ambergrise, a stink it lies,
But well-dispers'd, is *Incense to the Skies*.

(235–36)

Who copies Your's, or O X F O R D ' S better part,
To ease th' oppress'd, and raise *the sinking heart?*

(243–44)

What late he call'd a Blessing, now was Wit,
And God's good Providence, *a lucky Hit*.

(377–78)

Resolve me, Reason, which of these is worse,
Want with a full, or *with an empty purse?*

(319–20)

Not all of the couplets above represent Pope at his best. Some have more density, wit, and closure than others. But they have in common this characteristic of rhyming on the phrase—which may help other writers to imitate the Popean couplet more successfully by suggesting one model for the way it is put together.

The mechanism by which all the couplets quoted thus far are resolved involves the gradual coming-on of cliche, or proverbial expression. We don't know whether the first or the second line in these couplet was the harder for Pope to write, but it is plain to hear how the second lines are often buoyed up by pieces of language imported, with slight or no overt changes, from ordinary discourse—except, of course, in those cases where the device of coming-upon-cliche has proven so effective that Pope became responsible for making the apt phrases he was the first to form into rhymes so inevitable they seemed to have been already in common use (for example, "To Err is *Humane;* to Forgive, *Divine*").

Couplets in Narratives

A further observation about the couplet is that, despite the forces that work to close the poem after each one, these rhymed units are additive. As Barbara Herrnstein Smith aptly points out, couplets are something like iambs because they present themselves as units that need to be added up in order to form a larger whole. This is especially true of couplets with narrative rather than epigrammatic force, as in these couplets from Byron's "Epistle from Mr. Murray to Dr. Polidori":

> Dear Doctor, I have read your play,
> Which is a good one in its way,
> Purges the eyes, and moves the bowels,
> And drenches handkerchiefs like towels
> With tears that, in a flux of grief,
> Afford hysterical relief
> To shattered nerves and quickened pulses,
> Which your catastrophe convulses.
> . . . .
> I write in haste; excuse each blunder;
> The coaches through the street so thunder . . .

Of course, enjambing syntax creates a headlong momentum that carries us well beyond the individual couplets; Pope needed the varieties of pause surrounding his lines to stem this forward tide.

Derek Walcott's extended monologue by the rogue of Laventille, a satiric gadfly who calls himself "Bedbug the First," eager to make the powerful itch, has significantly less forward momentum than Byron's lines:

> The shark, racing the shadow of the shark   25
> across clear coral rocks, does make them dark—
> that is my premonition of the scene
> of what passing over this Caribbean.
> . . . .
> Lock off your tears, you casting pearls of grief
> on a duck's back, a waxen dasheen leaf,
> the slime crab's carapace is waterproof
> and those with hearing aids turn off the truth,   50
> and their dark glasses let you criticize
> your own presumptuous image in their eyes.
> . . . .
> All those who promise free and just debate,
> then blow up radicals to save the state,   70
> who allow, in democracy's defense,

a parliament of spiked heads on a fence,
all you go bawl out, "Spoils, things ain't so bad."
This ain't the Dark Age, is just Trinidad.

("The Spoiler's Return")

Walcott's couplets close much more than Byron's—although closure is counteracted both by the rhetorical energy of the Spoiler and by his Trinidadian patois, which runs against the metrical norm (as in the decasyllabic line "of what passing over this Caribbean").

However, when narrative quiets the pull of couplet wit in order to coast more rapidly over the rhymes, then sentence and passage become more commanding than the line—so much so that even the lines from Byron's "Epistle" above might seem comparatively epigrammatic. The final movements in A. D. Hope's "Man Friday," using devices so different from this poem's first part, provide cases of rhyme made small, streamlined for speed:

Brushed, barbered, hatted, trousered and baptized,
He looked, if not completely civilized,
What came increasingly to be the case:
An upper servant, conscious of his place,
Friendly but not familiar in address   85
And prompt to please, without obsequiousness,
Adept to dress, to shave, to carve, to pour
And skilled to open or refuse the door,
To keep on terms with housekeeper and cook,
But quell the maids and footmen with a look.   90

. . . .

Yet as the years of exile came and went,
Though first he grew resigned and then content,   110
Had you observed him close, you might surprise
A stranger looking through the servant's eyes.
Some colouring of speech, some glint of pride,
Not born of hope, for hope long since had died,
Not even desire, scarce memory at last,   115
Preserved that stubborn vestige of the past.

It happened once that man and master made
A trip together on affairs of trade;

A ship reported foundered in the Downs
Brought them to visit several seaport towns.   120
At one of these, Great Yarmouth or King's Lynn,
Their business done, they baited★ at an inn,   ★*stopped for food*
And in the night were haunted by the roar
Of a wild wind and tide against the shore.
Crusoe soon slept again, but Friday lay   125
Awake and listening till the dawn of day.
For the first time in all his exiled years
The thunder of the ocean filled his ears;
And that tremendous voice so long unheard
Released and filled and drew him, till he stirred   130
And left the house and passed the town, to reach
At last the dunes and rocks and open beach:
Pale, bare and gleaming in the break of day
A sweep of new-washed sand around the bay,
And spindrift driving up the bluffs like smoke,   135
As the long combers reared their crests and broke.
There in the sand beside him Friday saw
A single naked footprint on the shore.
His heart stood still, for as he stared, he knew
The foot that made it never had worn shoe   140
And, at a glance, that no such walker could
Have been a man of European blood.
From such a footprint once he could describe
If not the owner's name, at least his tribe,
And tell his purpose as men read a face   145
And still his skill sufficed to know the race;
For this was such a print as long ago
He too had made and taught his eyes to know.
There could be no mistake. Awhile he stood
Staring at that grey German Ocean's flood;   150
And suddenly he saw those shores again
Where Orinoco pours into the main,
And, stunned with an incredible surmise,
Heard in his native tongue once more the cries
Of spirits silent now for many a day;   155
And all his years of exile fell away.
~

The sun was nearly to the height before
Crusoe arrived hallooing at the shore,
Followed the footprints to the beach and found
The clothes and shoes and thought his servant drowned.   160
Much grieved he sought him up and down the bay
But never guessed, when later in the day
They found the body drifting in the foam,
That Friday had been rescued and gone home.

                                                                                                (A. D. Hope)

Despite the many showers of Popean wit and pointed antithesis (in Hope's lines 81, 88, 112, 145, and 163–64), the working unit has shifted from the couplet to the paragraph—a shift made possible only by calming the rhymes into unselfconsciousness, placing weight on event. A crucial irony looms large in the poem, but it is dispersed throughout the subtleties of the circumstance, such that only by recovering his memory of his earlier native understanding and then flinging himself toward the Atlantic and drowning can Friday "go home." Hope is now rhyming more like Muir and the balladeers than like Alexander Pope, Byron—or even himself, in the lines from "Man Friday" quoted in chapter 4 on diction. His stylistic switch emphasizes how the elements in narrative require swiftness and an even surface, while those that make up satire, irony, and wit rely on traction and resistance within the line.

A final word about **rhyming on the phrase** would allow for its function in stanzas with alternating rhymes, such as Lewis Carroll's "Mad Gardener's Song":

He thought he saw a Buffalo
    Upon the Chimney-Piece;
He looked again, and found it was
His sister's Husband's Niece.
. . . .
He thought he saw a Rattlesnake
    That questioned him in Greek:
He looked again, and found it was
    The Middle of Next Week.
. . . .
He thought he saw a Garden-Door
    That opened with a key:

He looked again, and found it was
A Double Rule of Three.[22]

The clue to Carroll's wit in these quatrains is the rhyming on a semantically nonsymmetrical phrase. The nouns by themselves will remain inscrutable without some aid from colloquial and metaphoric usage. Carroll is also exploiting the pleasurable discontinuities that emerge from rhyming concrete with abstract terms.

Carroll and Pope and Byron sport their rhymes rather like certain feathered creatures do with their fighting crests; they clearly enjoy flaunting the bright plumage and daring their opponents to match their skill in keeping the game going. But rhyme need not be so extravagant nor the stanzaic units so stichic as those of the first two in order to connect us as writers with the deep and not entirely rational currents of poetry in rhyme. Mild enjambment and near-rhyme (as in Owen) may yield results more natural, that is, closer to one's own speaking voice. It is also worth examining the career of W. B. Yeats for a radiant example of a modern pure-rhymer's way of crafting stanzas that make the intricacies they embody sound spontaneous and seem transparent.

22. In Opie, *The Oxford Book of Children's Verse*, pp. 250–51.

10

Further Rhythms in English—Counted Forms: Accentual Verse and Syllabic Verse (Including Haiku)

At the Threshold between Forms

Accentual verse counts stresses, with deliberate variation of syllables before and after the stressed syllables. This form has been favored in partially inflected languages with no articles and few freely occurring monosyllables, where the syntactic preference is for nouns and noun-compounds. **Syllabic verse** counts syllables at the expense of stresses. In a sense, syllabic verse began with the Greeks writing lines dismembered into morphological segments.[1] A syllabic meter draws attention away from stress in two ways: by a substitute and more comprehensive number system and by equalizing the differences between the stressing and non-stressing of words when written (though in speech these differences remain great). Particles and connectives (articles, pronouns, prepositions, and conjunctions)—not to mention polysyllables—play a larger role in syllabic verse than in accentual: They lighten stress and dissipate the thematic weight of words on which it falls. Thus accentual verse seems the quintessentially spoken meter and syllabic verse the written. Like sun and moon, accentual verse and syllabic verse circle each other over terrain once disputed between them, but now occupied by two hybrids, accentual-syllabic verse and free verse.

It may be harder to hear accentual verse and syllabic verse in a period when the ear is attuned to the mixture of rhythms available in **free verse**—particularly when free verse is casually devised and overlaps at so many points with prose. But I should like in this chapter to examine these two earlier counted verse forms that have such a curious background in

---

1. Although the classical writers superimposed on these articulated syllables the yet more difficult idea of vowel **quantity.**

English—because their presence is from time to time powerfully felt, also because an understanding of their music shaped the poetry we know, and finally because the *withholdings* of pattern that form the basis for their two rhythms can open a world of variety both delicate and eloquent to readers engaged with the writing of poems.

The presence of verse forms other than **accentual-syllabics** (verse that balances a steady alternation of stresses in a network of strictly alternating non-stresses) has already emerged in the previous chapters on meter and stanza, which from time to time presented poems from more recent periods whose metrics were troubling. Not only were the metrics troubling, but they were so in ways that hinted at alternatives to accentual-syllabic measures as well as to **dipodic** meters. There were a number of examples of poems that do not give immediate and unambiguous evidence about their metrical mode. One such poem is Yeats's "The Wild Swans at Coole." Consider his line "Under the October twilight the water," with its eleven syllables. The line sounds as if it could be a thwarted line of iambic pentameter with too many trochees—or even a pentameter in **trochaic meter**. But in reading this line against all the others it matches in the five stanzas of "The Wild Swans at Coole," one wonders whether iambic tetrameter might not have been intended (as in the poem's twenty-seventh line, "Among what rushes will they build")? Yet this possibility of iambic tetrameter is canceled by the matching-lines from the other stanzas, in which any putative iambic feet are so ruffled and obscured by multiple additional syllables that Yeats's prosody at many points sounds more like **accentual verse** than accentual-syllabic: "All's changed since I, hearing at twilight," "Companionable streams or climb the air," and "I saw, before I had well finished." If only one of these five lines sounds especially like iambic tetrameter, it's unlikely that this (or any) accentual-syllabic norm is at work, although *some* form of symmetry is clearly assumed.[2]

In passing, it is important to note that Yeats can be perfectly presentable and even highly symmetrical in accentual-syllabic lines when he chooses: "I stared upon his blood-bedabbled breast / And sang my malediction with the rest" ("Her Vision in the Wood"); "Where none has

---

2. The name for the expectation of equivalence between two or more corresponding lines in a metrical whole is **responsion**. See *The New Princeton Encyclopedia of Poetry and Poetics,* edited by Alex Preminger and T. V. F. Brogan (Princeton, NJ: Princeton University Press, 1993), p. 1045a.

reigned that lacked a name and fame / Or out of folly into folly came"
("Coole and Ballylee, 1931"). Thus when he elects *not* to write with
equal attention to syllables, stresses, and their intervals, we must conclude
that he is attempting a different sort of music:

> The Witch
>
> Toil and grow rich
> What's that but to lie
> With a foul witch
> And after, drained dry,
> To be brought   5
> To the chamber where
> Lies one long sought
> With despair.

"The Witch" slides in and out of focus. Too many lines have more than
two stresses for the whole to feel solely accentual (we tuck the extra
stresses in "Lies one long sought" and in "And after, drained dry" back
into a dimeter perspective with a mix of trochaic reversal, overstressed
iamb, regular iamb, and overstressed anapest—terms belonging to accen-
tual-syllabic **scansion**). But then there are lines like "With despair," in
which there seem too few stresses let alone syllables for securing an ac-
centual-syllabic dimeter pattern. Here we find ourselves *equalizing* (add-
ing to or subtracting from) stress count and **interval** (an interval is
formed by the unstressed syllables that fall between stressed syllables).
Two obvious pair-lines in the Yeats poem are *TOIL and GROW RICH*
(1) and *WITH a FOUL WITCH* (3). The more evident trochee-spondee
line 1 has a spillover effect on the four syllables of line 3, and in the grip
of this pairing, after placing stress on the normally unstressed preposition
With, we make other rhythmical adjustments. In line 2, for example,
"What's that but to lie," there is a tendency to hurry up the syllables be-
tween the stressed *that* and the stressed *lie* so as to equalize the unstressed
interval, reducing the time given to nonstress down to one syllable rather
than the two that stand there. We do not elide the words *but* and *to*; in-
stead we allow the increase in nonstresses to coast by as a substitution—
an anapest for an iamb—rhythmically taking up the same time in the
line. Time has been evened out. By the same principle that works in
"The Witch" fairly automatically, namely isochrony, the poem's aberrant
eighth line is filled out, doubly, causing adjustment to both stress and

interval (*WITH* ^ *deSPAIR*), to equal the first and third lines. Time has again been equalized but now by adding syllables to make up an interval equivalent to the norm heard in the majority of lines.

It is the principle of **isochrony**, or equalized interval between stresses, that controls the different mediating syllables in Yeats's "The Witch." So we still, somehow, come out with a dimeter—or try to, even if all we are given to work with are two weaks and a strong. The point would be that the assumption of accentual-syllabic meter is more power-ful and automatic than the possibility of accentual meter; at the merest inkling we resume this mode:

> The horse that comes from the road,   45
> The rider, the birds that range
> From cloud to tumbling cloud,
> Minute by minute they change;
> A shadow of cloud on the stream
> Changes minute by minute;   50
> A horse-hoof slides on the brim,
> And a horse plashes within it.

> ("Easter 1916")

So even if there is only one line (47) in the excerpt from "Easter 1916" where we detect the return of accentual-syllabic conformity, this return is enough to disturb that deliberate *im*balance necessary for producing the "cadential lilt" (Nabokov's fine phrase for the unequal rhythm of accen-tual verse), which Yeats has so carefully built up. Because we cannot ig-nore the rhythm of alternation, however, and because an accentual poem must consciously count every stress, particularly for subject terms (like *horse* and *hoof* in line 51), we cannot hear this excerpt as purely accentual. The first four syllables of line 51 are absorbed back into an iambic pattern, the first two syllables being regular (*a horse-*), the second pair producing an overstressed iamb (*-hoof slides*).

Derek Attridge has the rather brilliant notion that, like many ballads, Yeats's "Easter 1916" has an "unrealised fourth beat" whose nonbeing acts as background or buffer in suspending the stress possibilities in any one line.[3] I find this idea so captivating that it's hard to get it out of my mind whenever I read the poem. But I still wonder whether Attridge

---

3. Derek Attridge, *The Rhythms of English Poetry* (London: Longman, 1982), pp. 326–27.

hasn't given a curious explanation for a phenomenon more widespread than the turning of three-stress into four-stress lines, as he sees it: namely, the spontaneous bent of modern familiar English to equalize stress intervals both upwards (adding unspoken syllables) and downwards (contracting or speeding over syllables heard as excessive). We may owe our inkling of added length to isochrony's adjustment of intervals rather than to extra feet or the fully functioning stresses that Attridge marks with his phantom beat [B].

      B   B   B   [B]
And a horse plashes within it

Instead of Attridge's graphing, a provision for what he calls **implied offbeats** (missing unstressed syllables) might better record the line's rhythm:

And a horse ^   ^ plashes within it[4]

In a third poem, "Long-legged Fly," Yeats takes up his most precarious position at that far limit of accentual-syllabism before the prosody must move out into authentic accentualism.

> Our master Caesar is in the tent   5
> Where the maps are spread,
> His eyes fixed upon nothing,
> A hand under his head.
> *Like a long-legged fly upon the stream,*
> *His mind moves upon silence.*   10

One need only recognize the different weight given to the identical preposition *upon* in lines 9 and 10 to realize that some notion of compensation is at work in the meter. In the case of "Long-legged Fly," the meter assumed is the basis of the ballad stanza, which alternates four-stress with three-stress lines (see **hymn meter**, where ballad meter is also discussed).

The Irregular Ballad

Other poems composed centuries before Yeats's also come to mind as presenting enough "normalcy" to be nearly accentual-syllabic. Indeed, they are rather more normal than this poem of Yeats's, but with too much

---

4. Recall that carets [^] designate assumed additional unaccented syllables in accentual-syllabic poems: They hold the time constant between metrical accents. This time-holding function does not exist in either accentual or syllabic verse. See chapter 8.

irregularity to result in clear resolution against the norm. Many of the old ballads fall into this category, where a background of prevailingly regular feet highlights the lines that don't "square up":

The king sits in Dumferling toune,
    Drinking the blude-reid wine:
"O whar will I get guid sailor,
    To sail this schip of mine."

Up and spak an eldern knicht,   5
    Sat at the king's richt kne:
"Sir Patrick Spens is the best sailor
    That sails upon the se."

The king has written a braid* letter   *fine
    And signd it wi his hand,   10
And sent it to Sir Patrick Spens,
    Was walking on the sand.

The first line that Sir Patrick red,
    A loud lauch lauched he;
The next line that Sir Patrick red,   15
    The teir blinded his ee.

"O wha is this has don this deid,
    This ill deid don to me,
To send me out this time o' the yeir,
    To sail upon the sea!   20

"Mak hast, mak haste, my mirry men all,
    Our guid schip sails the morne":
"O say na sae*, my master deir,   *so
    For I feir a deadlie storme.

"Late late yestreen I saw the new moone,   25
    Wi the auld moone in hir arme,
And I feir, I feir, my dear master,
    That we will cum to harme."

O our Scots nobles wer richt laith*   *very unwilling
    To weet their cork-heild schoone*:   *shoes 30
Bot lang owre a'* the play wer playd,   *long before ever
    Thair hats they swam aboone.*   *swam above them

~

O lang, lang may their ladies sit,
    Wi thair fans into their hand,
Or eir they se Sir Patrick Spens   35
    Cum sailing to the land.

O lang, lang may the ladies stand,
    Wi thair gold kems in thair hair,
Waiting for thair ain deir lords,
    For they'll se thame na mair.   40

                          ("Sir Patrick Spens")

Lines 3, "'O whar will I get guid sailor,'" 16, "The teir blinded his ee,"
and 40, "For they'll se thame na mair," all create dissonance when the
poem is assumed to be subordinated to accentual-syllabic expectations,
the first of which is that exceptions such as line 3 in "Sir Patrick Spens"
must not outnumber the obedient metrical feet, and the second that
meaning must not waver too long over alternative stressings, as line 40
seems to make the reader do: *For they'll SE thame na MAIR; For THEY'LL
se THAME na MAIR; For THEY'LL se THAME na mair; For THEY'LL
SE thame na mair.* Many of the peculiar lines can be regularized only if the
reader/listener (or sayer/singer) provides some additional breathing stops
while curtailing others. Line 40 also illustrates the discomfort created by
an accentual-syllabic assumption, because we must do violence to speech
stress and ignore the primacy of the word *se* [see]. Furthermore, one
notes that the speech stresses on the word *master* fit comfortably into the
ballad's twenty-third line, "'O say na sae, my master deir,'" but anything
but comfortably into line 27, "'And I feir, I feir, my dear master.'"

The same ambiguities abound in one of the most moving of the later
ballads of the Elizabethan period, which places domestic bereavement
under the sign of sacred fire, "As You Came from the Holy Land of Wal-
singhame"; I quote from the version of Sir Walter Ralegh.[5] This ballad,
which alternates four-stress with some two-stress and other three-stress
lines, is devised as a dialogue between an unsuspecting traveler and a
speaker obsessed with his bereavement, who, rather like the ancient mar-
iner, compels his hearers to listen to his entire saga:

5. Richard Sylvester, ed., *The Anchor Anthology of Sixteenth-Century Verse* (New
York: Doubleday/Anchor, 1974), pp. 335–36. Walsinghame was a famous medieval
shrine in Norfolk that was destroyed in 1538.

As you came from the holy land
　　Of Walsinghame,
Mett you not with my true love
　　By the way as you came?

How shall I know your trew love   5
　　That have mett many one,
As I went to the holy lande
　　That have come, that have gone?

She is neyther whyte nor browne
　　Butt as the heavens fayre,   10
There is none hathe a forme so divine
　　In the earth or the ayre.

Such an one did I meet, good Sir
　　Suche an Angelyke face,
Who lyke a queene, lyke a nymph, did appere   15
　　By her gate, by her grace.

She hath lefte me here all alone,
　　All allone as unknowne,
Who somtymes did me lead with her selfe,
　　And me lovde as her owne.   20

Whats the cause that she leaves you alone
　　And a new waye doth take;
Who loved you once as her owne
　　And her joy did you make?

I have lovde her all my youth,   25
　　Butt now ould, as you see,
Love lykes not the fallyng frute
　　From the wythered tree.

Know that love is a careless chylld
　　And forgets promyse paste,   30
He is blynd, he is deaff when he lyste*   *when he wishes
　　And in faythe never faste.
~

His desyre is a dureless contente*   *brief satisfaction
    And a trustless joye,
He is wonn with a world of despayre   35
    And is lost with a toye.

Of women kynde suche indeed is the love,
    Or the word Love abused,
Under which many chyldysh desyres
    And conceytes are excusde.   40

Butt true Love is a durable fyre
    In the mynde ever burnynge;
Never sycke, never ould, never dead,
    From itt selfe never turnynge.

We devise a symmetrical norm for this poem, or a norm that is at least balanced enough to show that the following are lines that *should* match, but to the modern ear, they fall awry of audible symmetry: lines 29, "Know that Love is a careless chylld"; 27, "Love lykes not the fallyng frute"; 25, "I have lovde her all my youth"; and 36, "Of women kynde suche indeed is the love." And the even-numbered lines are even harder to hear as patterned—whether accentually, accentual-syllabically, or even syllabically—because there is symmetry in none of the obvious methods of control: (1) patterning and numbers of stresses; (2) stress-plus-interval; (3) syllable count and pronunciation. The clear relation to time missing from the two ballad texts printed above, however, would have been supplied by the songs to which they were sung. Extra syllables and beats could, like missing ones, be indefinitely supplied by the minstrel or mimicked by the scribe as Ralegh does in "Walsinghame." Whether they are principally folk products or literary efforts, the Scottish and English ballads before the eighteenth century assume the melody to regularize shifting oral production of the words.[6]

---

6. See Bertrand Bronson's collections, the four-volume *Traditional Tunes of the Child Ballads* (Princeton, NJ: Princeton University Press, 1959–72) and *The Singing Tradition of Child's Popular Ballads* (Princeton, NJ: Princeton University Press, 1976). Francis James Child (1825–96), while a professor of English at Harvard, made the first comprehensive collections of *English and Scottish Popular Ballads* and their multiple variants in volumes that appeared between 1882 and 1898.

Podic Verse

Lewis Turco gives the name "podic verse" to the folk poems that stand midway between accentual and accentual-syllabic verse.[7] His examples of **dipodic** or two-stress lines (for him, a subclass of podic verse) come from nursery rhymes like

> Old Mother Goose,
> When she wanted to wander,
> Rode through the air
> On a very fine gander.

But such sing-songs fall into a much more strictly regulated pattern than *written* examples do; indeed, "Old Mother Goose" is pretty clearly dactylic, with missing slack syllables navigated by instinctive equalization of the interval between stresses—that is, **isochrony**. / *OLD Mother* / *GOOSE, When she* / *WANTed to* / *WANder,* ^ / *RODE through the* / *AIR On a* / *VERy fine* / *GANder* ^ /. Indeed, the dactylic rhythmical thump is so strong that it "demotes" strong stresses to secondary status (*fine; Mother*).

More convincing examples of **podic free verse**, as we might relabel it, would come from poems not designed for dancing or singing, in which the syllables vary in number within the line, and in which the stresses are shiftier. John Skelton, who composed "Philip Sparrow" from 1505 to 1507, uses a more primitive two-stress verse than does the author of the subsequent example, Sir Thomas Wyatt, who lived from 1503 to 1542:

> from "Philip Sparrow"
> The estrige, that will eate
> An horshowe so great,
> In the stede of meate,   480
> Such fervent heat
> His stomacke doth freat;*   *fret, gnaw
> He can not well fly,

7. See Attridge, *Rhythms of English Poetry*, chaps. 4 and 7 *passim*, and Lewis Turco, *The New Book of Forms: A Handbook of Poetics* (Hanover: University Press of New England, 1986), pp. 20–23.

Nor singe tunably,
Yet at a braide★   ★*for a whim* 485
He hath well assaide★   ★*attempted*
To solfe above ela★ . . .   ★*sing above high C*
. . . .
The best that we can,   491
To make him our belman,
And let him ring the bellis★;   ★*bells*
He can do nothing ellis★.   ★*else*

Note that in the first two and last three lines the numbers of stressed
syllables increases, but to the ear (and eye) of original readers, these "sec-
ondaries" did not detract from the stresses on the words of chief impor-
tance: *estrige* (ostrich), *eate; horshowe, great; best, can; make, belman; ring,
bellis; do* and *ellis*. The dipodic example from Wyatt may well have been
given a musical accompaniment, but its literary complexity and rhythmic
shifting are significant and serve to distinguish his from the more monot-
onous forms of earlier English carol:

from "My Lute and I"

Nought may prevaill
To wepe or waill: 10
Pitie doth faill
    In you, Alas!
Morning or mone,★   ★*moon (with play on "moan")*
Complaint or none,
It is all one,
    As in this case.   15
. . . .
No Tigres hert   25
Is so pervert,
Withoute desert
    To reke his Ire;
And you me kill
For my good will: 30

Lo, how I spill*   *perish
For my desire![8]

Contrast modern examples of uneven rhythm given in a frame of counted accents but with no apparent regularity of intervals between. When there is no regularity in the numbers, real or implied, of slack or unstressed syllables between insistently stressed syllables, the poem might be accentual. For instance, this quatrain is from a sonnet by Gerard Manley Hopkins, "Duns Scotus's Oxford"; Hopkins is addressing, and describing, the town:

> Thou hast a base and brickish skirt there, sours   5
> That neighbour-nature thy grey beauty is grounded
> Best in; graceless growth, thou hast confounded
> Rural rural keeping—folks, flocks, and flowers.

When we read the Hopkins stanza against the lines from Wyatt's "My Lute and I" or from Skelton's earlier poem "Philip Sparrow," those poems sound more regular and contained, and Hopkins's more alien. Even if Hopkins's poem were to be broken into shorter segments (*THOU* hast a *BASE* and *BRICK*ish, *That NEIGH*bour-*NA*ture thy *GREY*) no recurrent patterns occur such as we hear in Skelton ("Such fervent heat / His stomach doth freat") and Wyatt ("Morning or mone, / Complaint or none").

A poem more recent than theirs might bring into higher relief the contrast with Hopkins. Consider these lines from Elizabeth Bishop's "Filling Station": "It has a cement porch / behind the pumps, and on it / a set of crushed and grease- / impregnated wickerwork." Certainly, they present unevenness of rhythmical effect. But for one thing there is no generous and expandable store of unstressed syllables, as we would need in order to argue that Bishop's was an accentual poem, nor does she consistently stress heavily at the start of each line (another feature of accentualism). In addition, the two lines following those just quoted fall back into iambic trimeter (with an amphibrach [∪ − ∪] to lengthen the last iamb). This makes us supply an understood unstressed "breath" before *on,* in order to make an understressed iamb of it [^ −]: " ^ on the wicker sofa, / a dirty dog, quite comfy," and correlatively to suppress the extra

8. Kenneth Muir, ed., *Collected Poems of Sir Thomas Wyatt* (Cambridge: Harvard University Press, 1949), pp. 37–38.

stress on *quite* (or at least excuse it as a permitted intensification). Stress-parallel coupled with syllable-parallel between *sofa* and *comfy* tugs the lines back into a nonaccentual prosody that is accentual-syllabic. Bishop's "Filling Station" moves against the background of iambic trimeter just as Yeats's "The Fish," quoted later in this chapter, moves against iambic tetrameter.

Fully fledged accentual verse does not invoke the idea of interval in this way. Coming back to Hopkins's "Duns Scotus's Oxford" and placing it against a background like Bishop's, Wyatt's, Skelton's, or Yeats's poems is like hearing poetry in a different language—an experience that puts attention on words in clumps and knots rather than on their sequences either in sentences *or* in lines. The units of Hopkins's **mode** are more abbreviated than the lines in which they function—again suggesting an analogy with accentual verse, in which each line is broken at least once, into two partial units (the **hemistichs,** each of which has a different rhythmical pattern[9]). It is a "language" (as I am calling this strange rhythm of Hopkins's) that also slips free of the primary feature separating what poets write from prose; playing more loosely than do Bishop, Skelton, and Wyatt with the threshold of the line, it smuggles into the poem more ambiguities of syntax (through **half-meaning** and compression, as in "Thou hast a . . . skirt . . . [which] sours / That nature"; and through enjambment-fragments like the syllable *sours* at the end of line 5, the beginning of a clause most of which is propelled forward into line 6; and the leftover syllables *Best in,* part of the clause begun in line 6, "That . . . nature [which] thy . . . beauty is grounded / Best in"[10]).

9. See Donald G. Scragg, "The Nature of Old English Verse," in *The Cambridge Companion to Old English Literature,* edited by Malcolm Godden and Michael Lapidge, p. 61 (New York: Cambridge University Press, 1991); and Howell D. Chickering, Jr., *'Beowulf,' A Dual-Language Edition* (Garden City, NY: Anchor/Doubleday, 1977), p. 33ff. Chickering also sketches in the way some hemistiches are naturally filled by certain grammatical constructions—the so-called Type A rhythmic pattern, for example [/ ∪ / ∪], with its heavy trochaic inclination, accommodates several common plural patterns like infinitive-plus-verb, *wealdan moston,* to wield they were able, and subject-plus-verb, *beornas feollon,* the warriors fell, or adjective-plus-noun, *lathe gystas,* hateful strangers (p. 34).

10. The leftover phrase, *Best in,* is called a *rejet* (something that is sprung back) in French prosody; whereas a short segment like that on Hopkins's line 5 enjambing into line 6, *sours,* is called a *contre-rejet* (a counter-sprung syllable). These phrases describing line juncture will be familiar to readers of poet-prosodist John Hollander's essay "'Sense Variously Drawn Out': On English Enjambment" (1973) in his collection of essays on prosody, *Vision and Resonance: Two Senses of Poetic Form* (New Haven: Yale University Press, 1975).

Over against Hopkins's enjambments, which like all enjambments pit syntax against line, stand his end-rhymes (*sours/flowers* and *grounded/confounded*) and numerous alliterations, all of which reassert the line against the pull of the sentence, the alliterations also confirming the role of stress and the preference for frontal beats (as in Hopkins's natural **trochees** *brickish* and *beauty, neighbour* and *nature, grounded* and *graceless*). Accentual verse also favors strong frontal beats, alliteration, and a constant tension between the fit of phrase into the verses and the syntax blending apposition with unfixed word order (see the entry on Fred C. Robinson's study of apposition in chapter 14).

Furthermore, accentual verse presents to us now one other overwhelming difficulty, that the modern writer and reader lack any background for making temporal sense of the free variety in unstressed syllables. The auditory setting for accentual verse, with its accompaniment by the singer, once provided this context—particularly the kind of monodic music that permits *rubato,* or stolen rhythm, for lengthening out some verses when need be, say for purposes of suspense.[11] In place of regularity of total syllable-count in the poetry most familiar to us (the accentual-syllabic poetry that developed with Chaucer, the first poet to blend the accentual insistence of English with the continental ten-syllable line), preliterary traditions of bard and court skald as well as some kinds of post-Gregorian antiphonal song established accentual verse upon the analogy of freely or indefinitely **expandable time** between *all* the syllables.

The Boundaries of Isochrony

Expandable time in accentual verse is the opposite of the equalizing of time (or **isochrony**), which holds true only when there is an effort to make the measures even. Whenever we use an **elision** mark to shorten a

---

The driving of a new unit of syntax forward toward a new line is stronger the more necessary the new unit is to the meaning of the sentence underway. Adjective and descriptive phrases that are tacked on after the fact seldom provide much counter-springing back to the last line *or* forward momentum to the next line. See the discussion of the *rejet* in Milton's *Paradise Lost* IX.372 in chapter 8 and of *contre-rejet* in Raymond Oliver's "Structures" on p. 78 above. Hopkins's *contre-rejet* at the end of line 5 and his *rejet* at the start of line 6 are imbedded in and crucial to his energetic translation of descriptions into predications, claims, and subordinating syntax.

11. Donald Scragg points out that lines 1408–21 of *Beowulf,* after the monstrous mother of the slain monster Grendel has attacked the shining hall, contain the smallest number of (stressed) syllables "that the meter will allow, the performer slowing down his

word and decrease the number of "extra" syllables, or a caret to hold the place of missing syllables, we are obeying the principle of isochrony, equalizing (*iso-*) the time interval (*chronos*) between the stresses. Isochrony can also be stretched a bit to cover those poems (like Yeats's and the ballads) Turco would call "podic," that is, ones which fall midway between accentual and accentual-syllabic poems. But in poems governed by isochrony, the intervals between accents (where stress is expected to fall) are heard in the same conformation; that is, the same number of unaccented *tocks* will be supplied by the maker and the audience between the *ticks* of the syllables that fall in the slots held for major accent: "By word, ^ sign, or touch" (David Ferry, "At a Low Bar"); "I stroke the scales of your breast, and answer: / ^ 'Yes, ^ as you know'" (Randall Jarrell, "A Soul").[12] Too many *tocks* will, correlatively, be quickened, as Yeats demonstrates by inserting anapests into every line but the fourth and sixth of "The Fish," and as Frost does throughout "The Strong Are Saying Nothing" (both of which are accentual-syllabic poems):

The Fish

Although you hide in the ebb and flow
Of the pale tide when the moon has set,
The people of coming days will know
About the casting of my net,
And how you have leaped times out of mind   5
Over the little silver cords,
And think that you were hard and unkind,
And blame you with many bitter words.

~~~~~~

The Strong Are Saying Nothing

The soil now gets a rumpling soft and damp,
And small regard to the future of any weed.

---

recitation to give his audience plenty of time to absorb" the horrific details of the bleak landscape as Beowulf and Hrothgar follow her to her den. See "The Nature of Old English Verse," p. 62. In other words, the singer is *expected* to expand the time between stresses.

12. See footnote 4 regarding the significance of the carets [^] in a poetic line.

The final flat of the hoe's approval stamp
Is reserved for the bed of a few selected seed.

There is seldom more than a man to a harrowed piece. 5
Men work alone, their lots plowed far apart,
One stringing a chain of seed in an open crease,
And another stumbling after a halting cart.

To the fresh and black of the squares of early mold
The leafless bloom of a plum is fresh and white; 10
Though there's more than a doubt if the weather is not too cold
For the bees to come and serve its beauty aright.

Wind goes from farm to farm in wave on wave,
But carries no cry of what is hoped to be.
There may be little or much beyond the grave, 15
But the strong are saying nothing until they see.

Anapests fall naturally and conversationally in the two iambic poems
above (even though Frost is more chatty than Yeats). Thus we do not
hear even Frost's fourth or eleventh line as aberrant or disorienting.

Consider, too, the considerably less regular poem by Tennyson often
cited in the context of equalized interval, "Break, Break, Break," which
we are encouraged to hear as three-measure (or trimeter) anapestic ^ ^
Break, ^ ^ *Break,* ^ ^ *Break* because of the pattern of the surrounding
lines (for example, "That he shouts with his sister at play" and *On thy
cold,* ^ *gray stones,* ^ *O sea*). Edward Lear also exploits isochrony in the
anapestic **common meter** of "The Jumblies"; the "far and few" line,
although it has but six syllables, approximates the normative line of
twelve syllables for a tetrameter composed of anapests:

Far and few, far and few,
   Are the lands where the Jumblies live;
Their heads are green, and their hands are blue, 15
And they went to sea in a sieve.[13]

   ^ ^ Far ^ and few, ^ ^ far ^ and few

---

13. Edward Lear, *A Book of Nonsense* [1846] (New York: Knopf, 1992), p. 80.

Expandable Time in Accentual Verse

By contrast with poems like Edward Lear's, in which intervening syllables
are provided by the reader when they do not exist on the page, true ac-
centual poems such as Auden features in his book-length verse drama *The
Age of Anxiety* (1944–46) typically ignore the accumulations of syllables
that are not stressed:

> High were those headlands; the eagles promised
> Life without lawyers. Our long convoy
> Turned away northward as tireless gulls
> Wove over water webs of brightness
> And sad sound. The insensible ocean,
> Miles without mind, moaned all around our
> Limited laughter, and below our songs
> Were deaf deeps, denes* of unaffection . . .   *dunes*
>
> (from Emble's speech in *The Age of Anxiety* I)

Note how "frontal" the speech stresses are, occurring early in the lines,
but also with a minimum of speech particles to soften the hard-stress
effect. This is typical of accentual verse. Consider also how this effect
is centered on the primacy of the noun and the adjective; inactive and
nonsubject terms aren't stressed; furthermore, the poem seems to get by
without too many of these uncounted syntactic bridges. Auden glides
over the stresses in his bisyllabic connectives *without* and *over* and in the
adverb *away*, but one doesn't feel that anything important has been
slighted. (Auden formalizes these nonstresses by placing them all in a
gradually expanding web in the first four lines, where they occur as ana-
logues for the initial unstressed pair of monosyllables, *were those;* also,
until line 4, these uncounted bisyllables don't participate in any of the
major alliterations—and even in line 4 the *v* and *r* of *over* are secondary
to the structural alliterations on *w* and *b*: "Wove over water webs of
brightness.") The other, genuinely unaccented syllables are often clus-
tered in polysyllabic words; Auden's glut of polysyllables is befitting of
his imitation of a verse form that flourished while English still carried
long inflections.

A word about the "free" occurrence of some stresses in Auden: in
his withholding of central stress from normally stressed but noncentral
vocabulary in *The Age of Anxiety,* Auden may also be imitating medieval
English. The medievalist and translator Marie Borroff says that even rela-

tively late Middle English verse with an accentual base shares the traits just noted. Her argument is an ingenious one. She asserts that a regular iambic poem such as Robert Frost's familiar "Stopping by Woods on a Snowy Evening" would have to be "translated" to approximate the metrical understanding of the *Pearl* poet (the late fourteenth-century writer to whom is also attributed the Arthurian verse romance, *Sir Gawain and the Green Knight*).

One change she would make in Frost's second stanza involves inserting an anapest among the iambs (a change Frost himself was fond of, to judge from poems like "The Strong Are Saying Nothing"—see the text of the poem quoted earlier in this chapter). The second and more important change, however, is to retract what Borroff calls "chief position" and what we have called expectation of stress or strong metrical position from words that are not "chief syllables," or primary carriers of meaning, such as the stressed root-morphemes of nouns and verbs. "In the original," as she points out, Frost lets "three prepositions, *without, between,* and, most important, *of,* occupy chief position." (His lines in question are "To stop without a farmhouse near," "Between the woods and frozen lake," and "The darkest evening of the year.") In demoting connectives to secondary-stress rank, Borroff imitates the habit, which the *Pearl* poet shares with early strong-stress poets, of giving metrical primacy in the form of major stress to chief carriers of meaning and enhancing these latter with alliteration. Thus she adds the word *harness* (which Frost uses later on in his poem) to alliterate with *horse* and imports a substitute for *snowy*—*wintry*—that pairs alliteratively with *woods,* "and, less perceptibly, *never* and *near.*"

Here is the stanza Frost begins with the line "My little horse must think it queer" revised by Marie Borroff according to fourteenth-century accentual metrical practices:

My horse in harness must think it queer   5
To stop with never a farmhouse near
'Twixt wintry woods and frozen lake
On the darkest night of all the year.

While the result may not replace Frost's poem in our affections, and indeed seems to fall back into a kind of folk cant in matters of diction and symbolism (as in *'Twixt, never a,* and *of all the*), the "translation" does bring before us the signal fact, that Frost's music in the poem is often largely a matter of promoting stress on a "soft" lexicon.

This promotion is exactly what Gerard Manley Hopkins does *not* do; Borroff quotes a stanza from Hopkins's "Inversnaid," in four-stress lines, to illustrate a modern poem that approaches *Pearl* both in respect of syllabic freedom and with regard to the suppression of stress on connectives and the linking of strong words by alliteration (for example, *coop* and *comb, fleece* and *foam,* and *low* and *lake*):

> This darksome burn,* horseback brown,   *little stream
> His rollrock highroad roaring down,
> In coop* and in comb the fleece of his foam   *hollow
> Flutes and low to the lake falls home.[14]   4

One result of the refusal to "promote" stress and of the prominence of alliterating nouns in Hopkins and Auden is what Harvey Gross calls "consonantal clang."[15] And another danger to which Auden in this unparalleled modern experiment in accentual verse, *The Age of Anxiety,* enthusiastically succumbs is that of Gross's "unearned significance," due to the alliterative line's fondness for gnomic utterance (pithy compression) as well as its tendency toward purely accidental associations of words. The free association produced by the need to alliterate only one consonant (so much easier than rhyming—and excitingly less conducive to rational bonds) is also a less guarded and manageable formal habit than rhyme, because it is less syntactically relevant.[16] Hence the pithy quality we observe in accentual poetry *of any period* tends to be thwarted by the randomness of the many inventions in an atmosphere that is (to some hearers, at least) dissonant.

Accentual Verse and the Two-Stress Unit

Accentual verse may be easiest to compose into an authentic, living prosody when four conditions are met: a fixed number of stresses occurring in unfixed places, but with a preference for downbeats; the variable expansion of the unaccented syllables; relaxed alliteration; and short lines, as in this two-stress ballad:

---

14. See Marie Borroff, *Pearl: A New Verse Translation* (New York: W. W. Norton, 1977), pp. 32–33.

15. Harvey Gross, *Sound and Form in Modern Poetry: A Study of Prosody from Thomas Hardy to Robert Lowell* (Ann Arbor: University of Michigan Press, 1964), p. 157.

16. See chapter 9 for more about the "logic" of rhyming relative to the frame of the sentence.

I sing of a maiden
That is makeles★:   ★*matchless*
King of alle kinges
To here sone she ches★.   ★*chose*

He cam also stille
Ther his moder was,
As dew in Aprille
That fallith on the grass.

To read this poem and its display of strong stresses in the proper historical garb, we might display the lines the way poems are in Old English. This two-stress medieval ballad uses a line that comprises one-half of the original Anglo-Saxon poem's line. The model had originally been a *four*-stress line divided into two symmetrical half-lines, or **hemistichs**, with a syntactical pause honored by all modern editors with a midline space, as follows:

I sing of a maiden	That is makeles;
King of all kinges	To here son she ches.
He cam also stille	Ther his moder was,
As dew in Aprille	That fallith on the grass.

Except for alliterating (which it avoids), the poem now visually resembles the rhythmic form it takes: the accentual line.

The Anglo-Saxon alliterative model underscored its stresses with three alliterations on the same initial consonant, two in the first half-line, or hemistich, one in the second. There was also an inviting sense that sentence should not coincide with line. Unfortunately, it is impossible to quote comprehensible examples from *Beowulf*, whose language must be learned. But the stress-profile and shape of the hemistichs might be clear nevertheless; this passage describes the secret waste land, thick with wolves and washed with icy water, where Grendel's mother lives:

Hie dygel lond
warigeath[17] wulfhleothu,   windige naessas,
frecne fengelad,   thaer fyrgenstream

---

17. Both the Old English letter known as the *thorn* (at the end of *warigeath*), and the letter *eth* (in *wulfhleothu*) have been transcribed in this passage with the letters *th*.

under naessa genipu   nither gewiteth,   1360
flod under foldan.[18]

〰〰〰

"In a secret land
they dwell, among wild fells, wolf-slopes,
windy headlands where a waterfall
hurtles down through the mist into darkness   1360
under the fells.[19]

〰〰〰

A secret land they guard,   high wolf-country,
windy cliffs,   a dangerous way
twisting through fens,   where a mountain torrent
plunges down crags   under darkness of hills,   1360
the flood under the earth.[20]

Although neither translation captures the binding effect of the alliteration, both versions convey a sense of the way the original twists syntactically through the sequence of lines, and the second further suggests how the phrases clump together, observing the midline pause.

Some Middle-English poems, whose words are only a few layers removed from those in our own lexicon, still preserve something of the strong-stress rhythm and syntactical vigor of *Beowulf.* For example, *Piers Plowman:*

Sutthe that Satan   missaide thus foule
Lucifer for hus lesinges,   leve ich non other

18. George Jack, *"Beowulf": A Student Edition* (Oxford: Clarendon Press, 1994), pp. 109–10.

19. Marijane Osborn, *"Beowulf": A Verse Translation with Treasures of the Ancient North,* with an introduction by Fred C. Robinson (Berkeley, CA: University of California Press; London: Robert Springer/Pentangle Press, 1983), p. 50. Osborn does not use a space-gap midline. She inserts quotation marks to remind us that Hrothgar, king of the Danes, is describing the habitat of Grendel and his mother.

20. More literal than Marijane Osborn, Howell Chickering's translation is at this point off by a hemistich from the original for a line or two before catching up in line 1359. *"Beowulf": A Dual-Language Edition,* p. 127.

Bote our Lord atte last   lieres here rebuke[21]

The modern three- and four-stress imitations of accentual verse would seem less successful than the two-stress. This fact may point more to the difficulty of accustoming the ear to an earlier kind of prosody than to inherent weakness in the four-stress form. However one accounts for it, the two-stress line winds up being easiest for the writer to maintain while furnishing control over what readers hear. That is to say, the most viable norm may be the two-stress accentual line with clusters of from one to four unstressed syllables. This is a pattern that permits the poet to insist on the sum of stresses as well as to withhold stress *seriatim* from any number of syllables belonging to words of less importance, some of which may well have full stress. Some lines from Eliot's "Ash Wednesday" (1930) embody this verse form's greatest strength in enforcing a binary distinction between stressed syllables belonging to primary "subject" terms, on one hand, and all the other grades and degrees of stress, down to zero, on the other. Eliot clearly has in mind a devotional litany (which outlines the speaker's need while it describes the divinity's powers) when he invokes the Virgin as *Lady of silences,* the *single rose,* or the *Rose of memory*—lines rhythmically as different from one another as possible while retaining the two-beat pattern. Note the difference between the troublesome two-stressed bisyllabic word *horse-hoof* in "Easter 1916" (discussed earlier in this chapter) and the clear demotion of stress on *give* in *life-giving* in Eliot's line "exhausted and life-giving" in "Ash-Wednesday."

The Auden lines that follow also allow us, as Eliot's do, to adjust to an unmetrical music. After a while, we grow alert to the need to appreciate the lines as separate rhythmic entities. The "music" of this accentual form becomes more audible as one gives oneself time to get used to the gravity-shift in moving from line to line, always taking care to give the languorous, unstressed syllables room to trail off. Eliot's *Rose of forgetfulness* may be compared with Auden's *Sweetly, dangerously* for the adroit refusal of either poet to place secondary stresses anywhere in polysyllabic

---

21. To illustrate the conjunction of couplets with traits of strong-stress meter, I have suggested printing the lines of "I Sing of a Maiden" in four-stress form, just as I've reinserted the spaces for caesuras into *Piers Plowman* here. As usual, I quote from the anthology compiled by Norman Holmes Pearson and the ubiquitous and learned poet W. H. Auden.

words. The Auden lines come from his lovely invocation to Ariel in the 1944 homage to *The Tempest,* called *The Sea and the Mirror:*

> from "Prospero to Ariel"
>
> Sweetly, dangerously,
> Out of the sour
> And shiftless water,
> Lucidly out
> Of the dozing tree,
> Entrancing, rebuking
> The raging heart
> With a smoother song
> Than this rough world,
> Unfeeling god.

Auden's poem is evidence of a poetic urge much different from Eliot's, whose lines sound comparatively stiffened by their mood of sad reverence. By contrast, the address to Ariel generously but feistily argues a view of godhood as adversarial. Without Prospero's shipwreck and stalled spiritual state, there is no need for a local rescuer; without rough Caliban, no compensatory enchantment. Auden's use of accentual verse is, to be sure, a *tour de force*—an occasion of delighted and unabashed showing-off. But the poetry is also an example of how what is, for the most part, a moribund trunk in a dead language, grows new limbs when submerged in fresh diction and syntax.

Dimeter versus Two-Stress

Two-stress lines of accentual verse may differ by only a syllable or two from lines of accentual-syllabic meter. To grasp the auditory difference a few syllables make in breaking up the alignments of alternating meters like iambs, it would be helpful to play some accentual-syllabic dimeters against the more accentual model of the poems just quoted. For the effect of this contrast, return to "The Witch" at the beginning of this chapter, recall too the invocation to Ariel by Auden just quoted, then examine the following excerpts from a little narrative by Thomas Hardy:

> from "Side by Side"
>
> So there sat they,
> The estranged two,

Thrust in one pew
By chance that day. 4

. . . .

Her fringes brushed
His garment's hem
As the harmonies rushed
Through each of them: 20
Her lips could be heard
In the creed and psalms,
And their fingers neared
At the giving of alms.
And women and men, 25
The matins ended,
By looks commended
Them, joined again.
Quickly said she,
"Don't undeceive them— 30
Better thus leave them:"
"Quite so," said he.

Slight words!—the last
Between them said,
Those two, once wed, 35
Who had not stood fast.
Diverse their ways
From the western door,
To meet no more
In their span of days. 40

For all the liberties Hardy takes in straining the metrical mode (the
strange sentence-split in lines 27–28, the **neologism** in 30, the three
strong stresses in a row following the two weak syllables, [∪∪ / / /], in
line 36), his poem is accentual-syllabic and Yeats's "The Witch" and
Auden's Ariel poem are not.

Syllabic Verse

The accentual line, which counts only stressed syllables, controls the
voice so as to suspend and expand time rather than equalizing it between
the strongly marked stresses. In accentual, or "strong-stress" meter,

we find ourselves picking our way across the weave of secondary syllables, careful not to ignore the unstressed ones that provide the passive warp of all the patterns. It is curious that syllabic verse has something of the same effect. By deliberately deregulating or making random the number and arrangement of strongly stressed syllables, poetry written in **syllabics** tends to brood over each syllable as a unit of meaning, or **morpheme**, rather than insisting on black-or-white stress-allegiance from each.

To suspend or disperse stress in the way English must when it turns to a syllabic line creates an unnatural equability, a tone of enforced ease. A double consciousness is created: we are, at one and the same time, alert to sense (including many of the elements of verse we have studied—line, syntax, diction, trope, rhetoric, and natural stress-melody) and to something that runs against sense, namely, the syllable.

To the extent that English is a language poetically marked by stress, syllabification is secondary in the formation of both metrical boundary and duration; even pitch is more emphatic and spontaneous than syllable. In French, by contrast, which has shown itself so hospitable to syllabics, pitch, length, and stress are not the determining features of the syllables; instead, the primary determinants are kinds of juncture between syllables (the silent e or "*e atone*," which is counted as a syllable when the following word in a poem begins with a consonant) and the number of the syllables themselves (the most significant being the eight-syllable or octosyllabic line, and the twelve-syllable Alexandrine, which divides into two groups of six syllables each). Even Charles Baudelaire, so modern in his preoccupation with the swarming city, its depravity and psychological exhaustion, upheld the elegant and unnatural (because purely "written") laws of syllabification and caesural division half-way through the line. In the following line from "La Beauté" (1857), the *e* that concludes the verb *trône* is articulated as one of six syllables even though it would not have been pronounced; it is "voiced" only on the page:

Je trône dans l'azur ‖ comme un sphinx incompris[22]

Baudelaire's is a line that would turn amphibrachic [∪ − ∪],

22. "I reign in the azure like a sphinx, beyond all understanding." In *Baudelaire: Selected Verse,* edited and translated by Francis Scarfe, p. 27 (Harmondsworth: Penguin, 1964).

Je TRÔNE dans
I REIGN in

    l'aZUR comme
    the BLUE like

        un SPHINX in-
        a SPHINX un-

            comPRIS
            exPLAINED

if stress and ordinary pronunciation were not restrained by the intellectual patterning. For the native reader, the hint that the *e* of *trône* would take up time—would occur *in* time—is enough to touch off that restraint and to soften and redistribute stress across the line.

Historically, Romance languages have freely distributed their stresses except at the ends of lines and hemistichs (since medial caesuras divide lines of classical French verse into two half-lines, and the final syllable of each is stressed); furthermore, metrical accent and speech stress need not coincide. Thus, except for the last syllable of each hemistich in French, there is greater *evenness* of articulation in the uttering of syllables in non-Germanic than in Germanic tongues like English.[23]

Thus, despite the similarity mentioned above, namely, that both accentual verse and syllabic verse draw attention to syllables of depressed or withheld accent, the number of these syllables is fixed in syllabic verse, and the music created by the avoidance of strong stress is much lighter and less coercive than that in accentual poems. For many non-French-speakers, indeed, the rigors to which the syllabic line has been subjected are more subtle than any translation can render because the shadow of artifice and archaism is energetically drawn across the formal surface of poems, even when the subject matter is decadent and anarchic.

Syllabic verse in English would seem to have the following characteristics. It keeps constant (or varies regularly or in recurring patterns) the number of syllables per line. Unlike accentual-syllabic verse, however, syllabic verse deliberately avoids the arrangement of stresses at regular intervals. And unlike accentual verse (or strong-stress meter), syllabic verse draws attention and expectation away from the total number of stresses

---

23. See Tatiana Fotitch's article on "Romance Prosody" in the *Princeton Encyclopedia*, 1974 ed., p. 713. Clive Scott's article on "French Prosody" in the 1993 edition is more difficult for the nonlinguist to grasp.

per line. In a syllabic poem—or at least in modern syllabic poetry in En-
glish—the stresses deliberately vary in position and frequency. In accen-
tual verse, the nonstresses deliberately vary both in position and fre-
quency. Thus, syllabic verse is in one sense the contradiction or mirror
image of accentualism. Like it, though, syllabic verse defines itself against
a background of accentual-syllabic English meters.

We might set the closing lines of Shakespeare's Sonnet 73, which
abide by an iambic pentameter norm while forcefully varying it,

> Consum'd with that which it was nurrisht by.
> This thou pereiv'st, which makes thy love more strong,
> To love that well, which thou must leave ere long   14

against these ten-syllable lines in **syllabics**:

> She comes over the lawn, the young heiress,
> from her early walk in her garden-wood
> (Elizabeth Daryush, "Still-Life")

It may be that *any* line of ten syllables can be contorted so as to fit an
iambic pentameter scansion; still, the lines above by Elizabeth Daryush
(daughter of the noted poet and metrist Robert Bridges) do not announce
themselves as sharing in the same meter as Shakespeare's. Neither do
these lines by W. H. Auden:

> the remotest miserable duchy
> . . . .
> the bright circle of his recognition
> . . . .
> and weeping anarchic Aphrodite
> (Auden, "In Memory of Sigmund Freud")

Even were we to assume that Auden were taking wide liberties with an
accentual-syllabic norm, the total number and placement of stresses vary
in such a way that we do not know where the stresses are *not* falling, and
at which metrical intervals they are failing to do so. There is—except for
the falling rhythm in the last two syllables of each line—no meter behind
the variations, only variations that resemble the normal rhythms of prose.

Syllable Count

As Daryush points out in her 1934 note on syllabic meters,[24] and as J. V. Cunningham also notes, syllabic verse comes into its own in English when an odd (rather than even) number of syllables is used. The reason is clear: to help the writer avoid falling into one of the two habitual binary meters, iambs or trochees. Cunningham's account is succinct: Syllabic verse is, like the accentual, an old tradition in English; it accounts for the decasyllabic line of Wyatt and Donne:

> So, if I dream I have you, I have you [Donne, "Elegy X"]

and sometimes of Sidney:

> If you hear that they seem my heart to move
> > [*Astrophel and Stella* 91]

"observing only number (with some regard to the accent)," as Sidney himself describes it. In the modern tradition it has these rules: the syllabification is that of ordinary educated speech, not of careful enunciation, and elision is optional. Final unaccented syllables count. And there is a negative principle, testifying to the power of traditional meter, that no succession of lines should establish the expectation of a repetitive stress pattern. Consequently, verses of seven or nine syllables are best.[25]

Nine syllables could, of course, just as readily fall into an alternating pattern, *IF you DREAM you HAVE this, IS it TRUE?* But presumably the poet of syllabics, eager to institute a subtler music, would not *repeat* such an alternation in successive lines. Furthermore, nine-syllable lines usually provide four stresses but sometimes five, while seven-syllable lines vary between three and four. This variation keeps the rhythms flexible. The following is the close of a poem called "Reading During Marriage," in which the husband is reading a Russian novel while the wife reads fiction by Elizabeth Bowen:

---

24. Included in her *Collected Poems,* with an introduction by Donald Davie (Manchester: Carcanet New Press, 1976).

25. "How Shall the Poem Be Written?" (1967), *The Collected Essays of J. V. Cunningham* (Chicago: Swallow Press, 1976), pp. 260–61.

Mortally tired but nothing
wasted I see the fair sweep
(as you depart the carriage   30
wheel scoring her muff with snow)
of my face in your regard:

this no older than I am,
that no longer discouraged.[26]

Beginning with three speech stresses in line 28 and four in 29, the numbers alternate to the end without falling at the same distance from the other stresses in any case.

Cunningham limits his own syllabic poems to seven and nine syllables. Elizabeth Daryush is master of the five-syllable line; she also employs rhyme. But she also has a number of finely precarious decasyllabic sonnets. Neither of these poets varies the syllable count once the poem begins.

Both Marianne Moore and W. H. Auden do. Moore also rhymes. She is perhaps the least approachable of syllabists, because her prosody is the hardest to hear. Of course, her typography (with indentations staggered in retreat from the left-hand margin) often tips us off that we might anticipate a pattern-in-progress—it even lets us, in briefer lines, *count* the pattern—but not, I think, enabling her lines to speak always as syntactic units, let alone as aural ones. In "An Egyptian Pulled Glass Bottle in the Shape of a Fish," Moore's syllable count is 5 6 12 15, and her rhyme scheme is *aabb* (with a falling off in rhyme-clarity in stanza two):

Here we have thirst
and patience, from the first,
    and art, as in a wave held up for us to see
    in its essential perpendicularity:

not brittle but   5
intense—the spectrum, that
    spectacular and nimble animal the fish,
    whose scales turn aside the sun's sword by their polish.

The only two lines we hear as equivalent in syllabic length are the first and fifth. Lines 2 and 6, which might have come within haling distance of each other, spin off into different orbits owing to the radical syntactic splits in 6—three syntax cuts in six syllables. The twelve- and fifteen-syllable lines are too remote because of their length, even if they did have any rhythmic contours in common (but they clearly don't—see lines 3 and 7), for us to hear them as syllabically equal.

Thom Gunn's Syllabics

Syllabically easier to hear than Marianne Moore, and far more contained in his stanzaic norms than she is, Thom Gunn uses the seven-syllable line in a score of poems, beginning with the well-known "My Sad Captains." The poem is interesting because Gunn does not seem to make his medium flexible until the poem is half over:

> One by one they appear in   1
> the darkness: a few friends and
> a few with historical
> names. How late they start to shine!
>
> . . . .
>
> True, they are not at rest yet,
> but now that they are indeed
> apart, winnowed from failures,   15
> they withdraw to an orbit
> and turn with disinterested
> hard energy, like the stars.

Harvey Gross says of the poem that "Count of syllables will not, by itself, provide sufficient rhythmic interest; in Gunn's poem a forceful syntax, a variable number of stresses (from two to four), and the phrasing of the line endings overlay the seven-syllable pattern."[27] About the second half of the poem, Gross is correct, for here the lines are enjambed less fitfully. Also, the cresting effect of phrasings like "rest yet" (13) and "are indeed" (14) brightens the line-boundaries and secures both the *sense* of the lines just passed, as well as their *movement on* to the next ones. But there is not much line-boundary grace in the second and fourth lines—"friends, and / a few," "historical / names. How." And the second stanza as a whole

27. *Sound and Form in Modern Poetry*, p. 35.

disintegrates into prose that has been counted, then cut-and-pasted over
a grid of seven-syllable lines. Lines 13 through 18 in the third stanza,
however, affirm the poet's emerging control over the syllabic form, using
minimal enjambment with quiet point ("disinterested / hard energy"),
and, as Gross commented, shifting stress around deftly.

Gunn matures in his command over the seven-syllable line in the six
years between *My Sad Captains* (1961) and *Misanthropos* (1967). When
Gunn came to Northwestern in 1981, I asked him why he had devoted
so much of his energy to syllabics. He said that he had begun to write
syllabics because he was too afraid to write free verse; syllabics seemed
safer. But he said it took him a long time before he felt he had mastered
what syllabics had to teach. One result of Gunn's long sojourn with these
forms is that he has, in reality, expanded what syllabics in poetry at the
present time *can* express. *Misanthropos* is a poetic sequence remarkable
both for its dazzling formal control and for the grimness of its vision and
the fierce authenticity of its expressed distaste for humanity. Something
of the same grimace is felt in "Moly," albeit softened by Homeric irreality.
One of the speakers in *Misanthropos*—or one of the many forms of pee-
vish revulsion taken on by the central sensibility in the poem—grows
uncertain of his role when he wears dark glasses: Is he real or a strange
kind of shadow like "an armed angel among men"? He perceives the true
outlines of the world more perfectly:

> The coarse   10
> menace of line was deepened,
> and light was slightly impure.
>
> Yet as I lingered there was,
> I noticed, continual
> and faint, an indecision,   15
> a hunger in the senses.
> I would devour the thin wail
> of foghorns, or abandon
>
> my whole self time after time
> to the chipped glossy surface   20
> of some doorjamb, for instance,
> cramming my nail with its grime,
> stroking humps where colorless
> paint had filled faults to substance.
> ~

I was presence without full   25
being; but from the corner,
in the mere fact of movement,
was I entering the role
of spy or spied on, master
or the world's abject servant?   30

("Misanthropos" VII)

Note that the end-consonant rhymes of "My Sad Captains" have been
replaced by a more ambitious pattern of end-consonant and interior
rhymes sprinkled throughout a stanza. We can't help registering at some
level the humming undersong of the letter *n* in lines 13 through 18, and
the bitter creak of hard consonants including hard *c,* or [k], and *g* in 21
through 24[28]—not to mention the chronic and subtle vowel alliterations
there, often of unstressed vowels (notice how the short *a* travels through
after/jamb/cramming/-stance, just as the swallowed *e,* or schwa, threads its
way through the last stanza's *pres*e*nce,* mov*e*ment, serv*a*nt, not to mention
the frequent *the*).

Thom Gunn's acts of stylistic thickening in this particular poem sug-
gest the tentative means at the speaker's disposal to achieve his desperate
aim of putting on weight and dimension as he slides into shadow. The
syllabic frame is also exploited for its naturally more tentative way of as-
serting even appalling notions. Another poem from the sequence well
illustrates the advantage of this form over accentual-syllabism for preserv-
ing, between exaggerations in the themes and their prosodic expression,
an eerie envelope of suspended affect:

A serving man. Curled my hair,   1
Wore gloves in my cap. I served
all degrees and both sexes.

. . . .

No passer-by could resist   8
the fragrant impulse nodding
upon my smile.

. . . .

28. Note the quantity of plosives, too, as many of the consonants involved (*g, t, d,*
and hard *c*) become more energetic when they take word-initial positions. Contrast the
plosive hard *c* in *colorless* with the unflexed hard *c* in *stroking*).

Needing me, needing me, "Quick!"
they would call: I came gladly.
Even as I served them sweets   15
I served myself a trencher
of human flesh in some dark
sour pantry, and munched from it.

My diet, now, is berries,
water, and the gristle of   20
rodents. I brought myself here,
widening the solitude
till it was absolute. But
at times I am ravenous.

("Misanthropos," IX)

It is as if the syllabic form, the brevity of the line and the niceness of the
diction, made orderly what threatens to tip the balance into the sensa-
tional and grotesque. The risk of psychological derailment makes the ele-
ments of control more fragile while also making them stand out *as* formal
controls. *Misanthropos* remains one of the foremost examples of syllabic
verse in modern poetry in English.

Alcaics as a Syllabic Form

Alcaics are a stanza form used by classical writers (the Latin poet Horace
in particular). The stanza has four lines of 11, 11, 9, and 10 syllables
respectively. The meter is dactylic with spondees early in the lines and
trochees woven in later; the first two lines of each stanza end with ris-
ing, iambic, or masculine stresses, the second pair with falling, trochaic,
or feminine end-stress (see **masculine** and **feminine line endings** in
chapter 13's "Poetic Terms"). Here is a sample of my own:

    After Frost at Midnight

                "Heard only in the trances of the blast"
                         —Coleridge

    Moon rise, and no one wakened to notice how
    Savage or hard the trances can sound from here
        Where light picks out the deeper patches
      Darkened by wind as if wind were knowledge.

    ~

Scraps rustle, stuck to a frozen canal where in   5
Summer, or later, there would be fragrances
    Moved upward, felt by us as living,
    Mingled with flecks of the chimney vapor.

Easy to think the cosmos grows poisonous
Or worse, while we improve: individuals   10
    Marked out, despite our forlorn virtue
    Eagerly wishing for nothing over.

This is a verse form which the ear may not pick up and whose stanzaic shape may remain hypothetical. But the lines that match do achieve a symmetry by **responsion**, for example, the fourth lines:

DARKened by WIND as if WIND were KNOWledge

EAGerly WISHing for NOTHing Over

In order to create lines that end in unstressed syllables, Alcaic quatrains in English seem to require enjambment; their lines are frequently bridged by normally unstressed connectives and prepositions. Despite the difficulty of hearing the Alcaic quatrain, its strict yet alien meter insists on falling rhythms or feminine endings, which accounts for two features that give Alcaics their contradictory appeal—their closing on content-terms at once rueful and ironic (the end-terms in a **sestina** have a similar range and cause) and their reliance on connectives that tend to extrude thought and statement beyond clipped declaration. A syntax of dependant clauses is almost inevitable in English, and such a syntax, alongside qualities like irony and rue, promotes exploration of the **conversational style**.

The Syllabics of Cunningham and Daryush

J. V. Cunningham's poems in nines and sevens also evade audibility as *numbers,* although the seven-syllable line can almost be checked visually. Here is an example of each, from Cunningham's 1963 collection, *To What Strangers, What Welcome;* first, syllabics in nines:

A half hour for coffee, and at night
An hour or so of unspoken speech,
Hemming a summer dress as the tide
Turns at the right time.
~

> Must it be sin,
> This consummation of who knows what?   5
> This sharp cry at entrance, one, and twice?
> This unfulfilled fulfillment?
>   Something
> That happens because it must happen.
> We live in the given. Consequence,
> And lack of consequence, both fail us.   10
> Good is what we can do with evil.

A small masterpiece of understatement, Cunningham's poem traverses perilous ground in treating the man's sexual insistence against the woman, and his subsequent grudging self-castigation, with a sense of guarded exhilaration. To read this last line, so poisonously smug, is like hearing one of the damned confess relief at being in hell. The poem's tonalities, which move back and forth between confession and excuse, are as much the result of the syllabic limitation as they are of the dry and withering diction.

Cunningham's most ambitious syllabic poem risks longer words in a briefer line and the barest minimum of detail; yet the implications open into the growth and death of ghostly companions who stand in for—and stand in the way of—the solitary, alcoholic speaker:

> You have here no otherness,
> Unaddressed correspondent,
> No gaunt clavicles, no hair
> Of bushy intimacy.
> You are not, and I write here   5
> The name of no signature
> To the unsaid—a letter
> At midnight, a memorial
> And occupation of time.
> I'll not summon you, or feel   10
> In the alert dream the give
> And stay of flesh, the tactile
> Conspiracy.
>   The snow falls
> With its inveterate meaning,
> And I follow the barbed wire   15

To trough, to barn, to the house,
To what strangers, what welcome
In the late blizzard of time.

On the highway cars flashing,
Occasional and random   20
As pain gone without symptom,
And fear drifts with the North Wind.
We neither give nor receive:
The unfinished drink
Left on the table, the sleep   25
Alcoholic and final
In the mute exile of time.

More than Thom Gunn in the syllabic sevens quoted earlier, Cunning-
ham in these poems from *To What Strangers, What Welcome* plants himself,
rhythmically and imaginatively, within each line. Whereas Gunn needs
the borders of the six-line stanzas to limit the uneasy phrases stretching
toward their syntax, Cunningham acknowledges each syllabic threshold
as a syntactic limit as well, even though he can enjamb beyond it. This
stylistic compact, however, by means of its ease within stiff limits, con-
veys a sense of profound psychological revulsion.

With the poetry of Elizabeth Daryush we at last encounter syllabic
verse that we can hear as syllabically metered. At first, she seems to be
writing an older metered lyric:

If there's no ruling,
only lot's empire,
what is sorrow's lyre?
Why should danger sing?

Why should poverty   5
Be a fluted stream?
Why should trouble seem
the drums, the glory-

fifes of ocean-shows?—
Why should the world ring,   10
if time has no strong
or rightful tuning,
only random blows?

Clearly, Daryush must recoil with deliberation from the accentual or ca-
dential norm; thus I find the music of her rhymed syllabic fives in the
untitled poem above somewhat forced. But in her decasyllabic (ten-
syllable) sonnets like the incomparable "Drought" (given below), Dary-
ush manages what no one else yet has: She audibly rhymes (thus she pre-
serves the lines as units) without hauling back into accentual-syllabic time
the lines that the rhymes complete.

> Drought
>
> The shadeless elms, the poplars shimmerless
> Have yellowed, dropped their flaccid leaves a full
> Two months before their time; the alder-pool
> Is a black miry swamp, ploughed by the press
> Of tortured, thirsty cattle; or look where   5
> Once would a spreading line of verdure show
> The river's lush umbrageous path, that now
> Is a white hard road, hedged with willows bare.
>
> Autumn will flush no harvest in these fields
> Failed of slow Nature's sober, ripening clime,   10
> Nor winter in these woods brighten with rime
> Red berry, brown nut, her late-lavished yields
>
> To bird and beast: the blighted copse they rob
> Already of its last lean hip and cob.

Here, too, I think we can almost hear the long, cool, unemphatic syllabic
tens as individual units. We might also note the delicate twisting and oc-
casional inversion of the thread of the sentence as the thoughtfully ex-
tended clauses lapse from one line into another (see especially lines 5
through 7). The poet's sorrow is mirrored in a style that probes here and
there, almost as if sleep-walking (not yet given over to despair), for any
scrap of hope in an environment that is unmerciful and dry.

Syllabics in Other Languages (Haiku)

Of the syllabic poems in other languages, it is the Japanese forms, the
five-line **tanka** and the seventeen-syllable **haiku**, that have proven the
most appealing to the English-speaking public, primarily through
the efforts of Marcel Revon in France and T. E. Hulme, Ezra Pound, and
the Imagists in England. "On the model of haiku," says Earl Miner in his

article on this form in the *Princeton Encyclopedia,* 1974 edition, "Pound devised a 'form of superposition,' or use of a vivid image in combination with a more discursive or less vivid passage" (p. 334). This technique has, he notes, had an incalculable and pervasive effect on modern poetry, affecting the work of Frost, Pound, Stevens, and Yeats. (I would add William Carlos Williams to Miner's list.) Haiku in English is thus one of those forms that, like the sonnet, has both a prosodic evolution and an intellectual history. Like the sonnet, which moved from the Petrarchan atmosphere of passionate exaggerations expressed in figures of formal containment, to religious poetry (Donne), nature description (Wordsworth), and finally political themes (Auden), the haiku abides by certain strict rules for its formal boundaries while promoting reverberations of an absolute and universal feeling; **imagism** continues these trends.

Haiku resembles the sonnet in one final sense: Each has, built into its accepted pattern, a hitch, or leap, that takes us from one context to another. In the sonnet, this hitch occurs at the **volta** or turn between lines 8 and 9, where some fundamental divergence in the argument occurs. Paul Fussell believes that the *volta* of a sonnet permits the speakers to change their mind, turn the idea around the other way, move (but effortlessly) from one side of a position to another—it is something like "the actions of inhaling and exhaling."[29] One often finds a shift from abstract to highly concrete in moving from octave to sestet—even in a Shakespearean sonnet (see Sonnet 94).

Similarly in the haiku, either after the fifth syllable or the twelfth, there is felt to be a separation between the small and local on one hand, the cosmic, or spiritual, on the other. In addition, in a haiku the time of year should be suggested along with, or by means of, a clear picture that arouses emotion and prompts deeper insight. Babette Deutsch translates as follows the haiku based on the Buddhist proverb, "The fallen flower never returns to the branch; the broken mirror never again reflects":

> The falling flower
> I saw drift back to the branch
> Was a butterfly.[30]

---

29. Paul Fussell, *Poetic Meter and Poetic Form* (New York: Random House, 1965), p. 120.

30. Babette Deutsch, "Haiku," *Poetry Handbook: A Dictionary of Terms* (New York: Grosset & Dunlop, 1962), pp. 59–60.

Babette Deutsch's haiku keeps the syllabic form we have been taught to expect, a 5, 7, 5 distribution of seventeen syllables (deployed into three separate lines in English translations). The following versions from the Japanese by Lucien Stryk are not syllabically exact but suggest the thematic features as well as the moment of insight or *satori* that comes in the space between one line and the other two:

> White butterfly
> darting among pinks—
> whose spirit?
>
> (Shiki)

> Nights are getting cold . . .
> Not a single insect now
> attacks the candle.
>
> (Shiki)

> Autumn—
> even the birds
> and clouds look old.
>
> (Basho)

> Deer in rain—
> three cries,
> then heard no more.
>
> (Buson)

> A sudden chill—
> in our room my dead wife's
> comb, underfoot.
>
> (Buson)

> Piled for burning,
> brushwood
> starts to bud.
>
> (Boncho)

One of Pound's imitations, called "Ts'ai Chi'h," captures the feeling of Japanese haiku without reproducing its syllabic regularity:

The petals fall in the fountain,
　　　　the orange-colored rose-leaves,
Their ochre clings to the stone.

It is easy to feel how the brevity of this form and the way the poems pause over the lapidary syllables can focus the attention with incomparable force on the single sense perception until it reverberates with meaning. It is the same care Stevens and Carlos Williams use in their imagist (but not syllabic) poems, "Anecdote of the Jar," and "Poem." In each poem we leap from the bland simplicity of the things to the enormity of the ideas by means of an uncanny and almost deprived plainness in the poetic style (Stevens "composing" the naturally disordered extensional world by placing a jar on the hill in Tennessee; Carlos Williams beholding the precarious surefootedness of the cat so as to suggest equivalent feats by the poem). Both poems teeter on the edge of nothingness. To this precarious trait the half-heard order of the syllabic poem adds a sense of deliberation and temporary rescue among shifting emphases. It is a form well suited to moments of threshold and moods of uncertainty, which writers of free verse have also explored.

11

Further Rhythms in English—Non-Counted Forms: The Four Freedoms of Free Verse

The First Freedom: Podic or Sprung Free Verse

The last chapter discussed two poetic modes in which stress is not sym-
metrically placed—the modes of accentual verse (with its preference for
strong beats early in word and line) and of syllabic poems. We also looked
at verse that fits neither, but seems to fall midway between accentual-
syllabic poems and those clearly accentual. These kinds of verse have been
called **podic** (or "footed") although they decline both meter (or division
into feet) and continuity of stress. Whereas nursery rhymes and counting
songs use unambiguous stresses and equally unambiguous depression of
weaker stresses (as in "Ride a cock-horse to Banbury Cross"), many lines
both folk and literary skirt clear stress choices. I would reserve for these
outlying poems, including some of Yeats's poems, Matthew Arnold's
"Rugby Chapel," not to mention the work of Hopkins, the name **podic
free verse**.[1] Some critics follow Hopkins and call this kind of verse
sprung, that is suspended between accentual and accentual-syllabic.[2]

---

1. I would differ with Lewis Turco who in *The New Book of Forms: A Handbook of
Poetics* (Hanover: University Press of New England, 1986) includes, under **podic**, verse
that is clearly triple in its measures. What distinguishes metrical from podic verse is the
former's ability to equalize the intervals of time (**isochrony**). If we equalize, we are obey-
ing a rule of repeating meter, as in the dactyls of the nursery rhyme "Old Mother Goose,
when she wanted to wander, etc." (Turco, pp. 21–22 and 36–38). See the discussion of
equalizing in chapter 10.
2. Philip Hobsbaum, *Metre, Rhythm and Verse* (London: Routledge, 1996), pp.
158–59 and 163, identifies some iambic pentameter sonnets as "sprung," even (in John
Berryman's case) "buckled," but he does not immediately link sprung rhythm to experi-
ments in free verse.

What makes it appealing to give this variety of verse a name more specific than "free" is the echo of regularity involving stresses and a fondness (evocative of accentual verse) for **trochaic meter.** Hopkins's poetry, as well as John Donne's, frequently wavers across the boundary between accentualism and accentual-syllabism. (In their work, strength of stress so dominates and deranges the rhythm that the syllabic model is not apropos. Whereas Sir Thomas Wyatt's verse—when it strikes us as irregular—is more in the syllabic vein than the accentual; see his sonnet beginning "The longe love that in my thought doeth harbor" in chapter 8.)

But by far the most striking podic or sprung free verse is that which is limited in total number of stresses to between two and four per line. Furthermore, this type is often rhymed. "The Witch" and "Easter 1916" (see the texts in chapter 10) are examples. Because no one metrical foot is dominant, neither can be easily scanned absent ingenious handling of many disobedient feet. The dimeters of "The Witch" never release us from the pull of the interval the way accentual meters do. Yet if one were to ask why the poem could not be imitating one of the triple measures, with occasional binary feet, we would have to rely on our sense that the poem keeps to this side of a crucial perceptual boundary: It does not *feel* triple as, say, the same poet's "The Lake Isle of Innisfree" does (for example, "Dropping from the veils of the morning to where the cricket sings") or his "The Pity of Love":

> The cold wet winds ever blowing,
> And the shadowy hazel grove
> Where mouse-grey waters are flowing.

Triple feet are clearly at the core of both these poems. But in "Easter 1916" no sense of the triple stands out above the double. There is no consistent model, that is, to govern isochrony. To equalize stress, we must know how many unstressed syllables fall into the intervals. On the other hand, Yeats shows no unfailing habit of indefinitely expanding the number of syllables between stresses, which would indicate a purely accentual poem.

These ambiguities are more pleasing when the lines are brief enough for us to test expectation against stress count, as well as to count intervening syllables and even the total number of syllables per line. (Like syllabic poems, accentual poems encourage us to be aware how many syllables are implicated even in the suspension of stress between main beats.[3])

Note, too, that both of the Yeats examples of podic or sprung free verse are rhymed. Rhyme is another force for measure, and it gives the auditory signal for line ending, setting the lines as units apart from each other. Podic free verse without rhyme, such as Arnold's "Rugby Chapel," creates an extrametrical tension between line and strong enjambment:

> Thunder crashes from rock
> To rock, the cataracts reply,
> Lightnings sizzle our eyes.
> Roaring torrents have breach'd
> The track, the stream-bed descends   95
> In the place where the wayfarer once
> Planted his footstep . . .

By no stretch is "Rugby Chapel" free of meter, but it does not remain in any of the three metrical patterns for long, either. Many lines have three beats but not at reliable intervals. On the other hand, there is a temptation to hear more than three stresses in the ninety-second line, which would negate the accentual option. Brevity of line, however, and stress that falls early seem to help Arnold manage the rhythmical margin this verse uneasily treads.

Brevity and an indefinite sprinkling of unstressed monosyllables in a gentler but still strongly enjambing sprung free verse poem by David Ferry likewise helps the poem balance on a rhythmical margin; the sentence is fragmentary until it is reversed by a prayer in the last two lines:

> A Young Woman
>
> That she, with such gifts given,
> In the abundance and grace
>
> Of her youth and sweetness,
> As if in a garden, walking,
>
> ~

---

3. In fact, prosodists of Old English have identified a half-dozen patterns for the **hemistich**, which allows for over seventy combinations in whole lines. Types E and D are the most densely stressed [/ / \ ∪ and / \ ∪ /] and Type B is the airiest [∪ ∪ / ∪ /]. But extra unstressed syllables can be added, making [/ ∪ \ ∪ ∪ /] a variant of [/ \ ∪ /] (Type E). See Howell D. Chickering, Jr., *"Beowulf": A Dual-Language Edition* (Garden City, NY: Anchor/Doubleday, 1977), p. 30.

In a summer of freshness   5
And of the wind lifting

And falling in a lavishing
Of light and penultimate

Shadow, that she should falter
At all through this phase,   10

Pressing, with hand outstretched,
The surface of the future,

As one who is blind presses
The surface of darkness,

Of corridor, or wall,   15
For any assurance at all,

May she be blessed
In this faltering forward.

Sprung free verse like Ferry's and Elizabeth Bishop's (in "The Fish" and "Filling Station") would seem to rely both on brevity of line and on a uniformity that flirts with the effect, in English, of syllabics, in which some receding norm provides a frame for minutely varying rhythmic adjustments. Ferry's "A Young Woman" is doubly appropriate because his syntax, so indefinite in its aim, holds the poem as a winch, well-locked, holds a steely cable. The more freedoms a poem engages, the more rigorous must be the hidden tools of control.

The Second Freedom: Free Blank Verse

I have borrowed from Philip Hobsbaum the useful if apparently contradictory phrase **free blank verse.** Recalling chapter 8's discussion of accentual-syllabic meter and the variety of devices iambic feet in pentameter lines employ to escape monotony, we realize how much liberty comes with the form. Unrhymed pentameter requires a more muscular syntax to achieve the enjambments its want of rhyme requires. In Shakespeare's time trochaic reversal and supernumerary unstressed syllables were common. In Milton's, caesural pause escalates in placement and frequency—both shorter units of syntax and greater complexity and involution (and blatant interruption) abound in *Paradise Lost*. Pope explores the saturation of the iambic line, as well as the basic counterlogical fact that the lines don't split evenly. While ten syllables can evenly divide into five syllables per hemistich, one of these sets of five (the first) will contain only two stresses, while the second hemistich has three. Wordsworth makes blank verse subtle rather than dramatic, showing later poets how to describe and feel; his primary trick is to understress the line. Robert Frost leans on the limits by reversing feet in the "wrong" places (feet two and five) and by anapests so numerous he flirts with revision of the base meter. Overstressing is available throughout prosodic history but more typical of dramatic poetry. In discursive poems, words that steer the rhetoric of argument are often overstressed, while in descriptive poetry, overstressing thickens the material texture of scene and response.

This thumbnail review brings us to the brink of the twentieth century. Unrhymed iambic pentameter has a second life in the modern period in the enormously evocative and influential poems of T. S. Eliot. The iambic base of Eliot's verse is obvious—"parasitic" on blank verse, Yvor Winters called Eliot's reliance on the rhythms, shape, and tonalities of blank verse.[4] Hobsbaum's view is kinder, in that he traces the Renaissance dramatists John Webster's and John Ford's influence on Eliot's iambs: "What appears often to be, in Webster, a loose and sometimes broken-backed blank verse is, with surprisingly little alteration, transferred by Eliot into his own brand of free verse."[5]

The work of Wallace Stevens also explores the loosened iambs of an often stricter free blank verse (see chapter 8's discussion of meter). The American poets Mark Strand and Donald Justice have also mastered free blank verse (see the excerpt from Strand's *Dark Harbor* on p. 206). Here is an example of Justice's work in this mode:

A Man of 1794

And like a discarded statue, propped up in a cart,
He is borne along toward the page allotted to him in history.

To open his heavy-lidded eyes now would be merely
To familiarize himself with the banal and destined route.

~

4. Yvor Winters faults Eliot for "limp" rhythms that wanly reflect limpness of spirit—yet another example for Winters of the "fallacy of imitative form," by which "form succumbs to the raw material of the poem." See his *Primitivism and Decadence: A Study of American Experimental Poetry* [1937], reprinted in *In Defense of Reason* (Athens, OH: Swallow Press/Ohio University Press, 1987), p. 22.
5. Hobsbaum, *Metre, Rhythm and Verse*, p. 99.

He is aware of the mockery of the streets,   5
But does not understand it. It hardly occurs to him

That what they fear is that he might yet address them
And call them back to their inflamed duty.

But this he cannot do; the broken jaw prevents speech.
Today he will not accuse the accusers; it is perhaps all that saves
    them.   10

Meanwhile his head rocks back and forth loosely on his chest
With each new jolt and lurch of the endless-seeming street:

Impossible to resist this idiot shaking.
—But it is hard after all to sympathize

With a man formerly so immaculate,   15
Who, after a single night of ambiguous confinement,

Lets go all pride of appearance. Nevertheless,
Under the soiled jabot,* beneath the stained blue coat, *French for neck frill

Are the principles nothing has shaken. Rousseau was right,
Of that he is still convinced: *Man is naturally good!*   20

And in the moment before the blade eases his pain
He thinks perhaps of his dog or of the woods at Choissy,

Some thought in any case of a perfectly trivial nature,
As though already he were possessed of a sweet, indefinite leisure.

The man of the title is the French lawyer who supported the king's execu-
tion and then tried to moderate the excesses of the Right. He has been
tortured and is now being taken to the guillotine in a cart. The date falls
in the second year of the Reign of Terror (the king and queen are already
dead); now in 1794 there are mass executions—far more severe than
Robespierre himself ordered—in which are carried away also Danton,
St. Just, even the chemist Lavoisier. "He is aware of the mockery of the
streets / But does not understand," writes Justice, using a **metonymy** of
place for persons that suits with his statesman's reductive thinking.[6] The
man's accusers are assumed to be just barely in control of the carnage they

6. Yeats invokes the same metonymy to describe how Maud Gonne inflamed the
ignorant: She "hurled the little streets upon the great" ("No Second Troy").

commit (or have committed for them); old habits of class obedience are not broken overnight. They fear Robespierre might scold them back into a subservience that might save him, but the only subservience is the one to grooming, which used to separate him from themselves and now provides an object of derision. Neither the protagonist nor his ancillary tormentors along the route can take the full measure of the Terror.

Veering off from knowledge on both sides, Justice's poem veers off from iambic pentameter as well, while planting a few lines to steady the departures (for example, ll. 5, 6, 8, 12, 14, 21). Line 8 is an especially interesting echo of formal devices like the voiced suffix to regularize the pentameter: *And **CALL** them **BACK** to **their** in-**FLAME**-ed **DU**ty.*[7] But the other lines given as analogues to iambic pentameter are looser, forming a bridge to the least patterned lines (1, 9, 15, 16, 24). In these last lines, the poet creates rhythms contrary to the frame of iambic pentameter that still never entirely lose their ground base in the iamb. The indirections in Justice's forms take us far from consequences to the profound ignorance on both sides of the Terror. The poem's theme is thus the idiot persistence of codes despite the ironies that should undermine them. Nevertheless, the poem's last line makes a breathtaking stretch beyond both the iambic base and the irreconcilable class war with seven measures, two of them anapests and the final one a flurry of unstressed syllables called a third paeon ($\cup\cup-\cup$). Furthermore, the sweep of the line is also the expression of a theme that is tentative and unfinished, thus counteracting the logic that hems the poem in and which demands that death—the most definite event—supervene. The free blank verse of Justice, like that of Eliot and Stevens, embraces and indulges ambiguities and meditative restraints as different as can be from the next form of freedom we shall discuss.

The Third Freedom: Biblical Free Verse

The third mode of freedom in verse aligns the poem with a mode of incantation familiar from the Hebrew Bible as translated into English in

7. When he read "A Man of 1794" at Northwestern in October of 1997, Justice himself did not read "inflamed" as trisyllabic. As he spoke it, the line in which it appears used the more irregular final-foot trochee reminiscent of Frost. Whatever the articulation of the last foot, however, the third foot is understressed. I have left "their" lowercased to indicate its weakness relative to the other strongly stressed syllables. But the word appears

1611 by scholars for King James of England (and called the King James Version). As noted in Part I, Hebrew verse emphasized units of syntax that fall in parallels like **isocolon** and **anaphora.** So this could also be called "syntactical free verse," though it is more commonly known as **biblical free verse.** Verbatim repetitions and alliterations echo the parallels of grammar; oppositions and antitheses also abound. Catalogues are frequent, and a structure of presentation connected to celebration and **ode.** In addition, the Bible in the King James Version imbedded in the literary imagination of both England and America for almost three hundred years a kind of rhythm that involved alternation. As Karl Shapiro and Robert Beum explain this rhythm, it is based on the **verset:**

> Originally a French term, but adopted by English writers, for the kind of prose that most closely resembles verse (for example, some of the Tyndale and Authorized Version Psalms; parts of Macpherson's Ossian). In a verset every other stressed syllable is a strong, usually a primary, stress:
>
> \ / \ / \ / \
> He shall feed me in a green pasture, and lead me forth beside
>
> / /
> the waters of comfort.[8]

The charismatic character of poems in versets, or biblical free verse, stems from the long line, which another writer notes may be actually several lines of print, collecting in "a powerful rhythmic surge corresponding roughly to one outpouring of breath from full lungs."[9] The French writers who perfected the verset include Claudel, St.-John Perse, and Charles Péguy. German poets of versets include Friedrich Hölderlin (*Hyperion*) and Friedrich Nietzsche (*Also Sprach Zarathustra*). In English, the KJV Psalms, the Song of Songs and many passages in the Prophets, particularly Isaiah may be consulted. The passages early in chapter 2 on line may also be "scanned" in the alternating stress of the verset:

---

in bold because it falls into a metrically strong place in the third iambic foot—if we assume that this is a line of iambic pentameter.

8. Karl Shapiro and Robert Beum, *A Prosody Handbook* (New York: Harper & Row, 1965), p. 201.

9. John Simon, in the *Princeton Encyclopedia*, 1974 ed., p. 890b.

$$\overset{/}{\text{Sing}}, \overset{\backslash}{\text{O heavens}}; \text{and be } \overset{/}{\text{joyful}}, \overset{\backslash}{\text{O earth}}; \text{and break } \overset{/}{\text{forth}}$$

$$\text{into } \overset{\backslash}{\text{singing}}, \overset{/}{\text{O mountains}}.$$

(Isaiah 49:13)

The alternation between strong and still stronger main stresses is never absolute, but the pattern in the verset is firm enough to suggest a rhythm running underneath the accumulations and balances of the grammar.

A further set of characteristics links the long free-verse line to the Bible, and that is the language of the sublime setting, the landscape cosmic and majestic, the wonders persisting in time, the emotions elevated and rapturous (or their opposite—desperate and extreme).[10] The line stretching from James Thomson's nature descriptive poetry to William Blake is clear. Here is Blake's hero Los surveying the "land of death eternal" that lies around the mythic city he calls Golgonooza:

> The Vegetative Universe opens like a flower from the Earth's center
> In which is Eternity. It expands in stars to the Mundane Shell   35
> And there it meets eternity again, both within and without,
> And the abstract Voids between the Stars are the Satanic Wheels.
> There is the Cave, the Rock, the Tree, the Lake of Udan Adan,
> The Forest and the Marsh and the Pits of bitumen deadly,
> The Rocks of solid fire, the Ice valleys, the plains   40
> Of burning sand, the rivers, cataracts & Lakes of Fire,
> The Islands of the fiery Lakes, the Trees of Malice, Revenge
> And black Anxiety, and the Cities of the Salamandrine men . . .

(Jerusalem, plate 13)[11]

We can see the elements of biblical free verse common to Blake and Walt Whitman: prophetic catalogues; visionary authority and the massive breath the poet must take to utter it; instead of enjambment or rhyming, as Miles notes, an *internally* modulated line (with the alternating strengths of the main stresses characteristic of the verset); and a habit of accumulat-

---

10. See Josephine Miles's chapters on "The Sublime Poem" and "The Sublimity of Blake" in *Eras and Modes in English Poetry* [1964] (Westport, CT: Greenwood Press, 1976) for an exhaustive accounting of the features of sublime eighteenth-century English poetry and its progressive shifts up to and including Blake's prophetic books.

11. Geoffrey Keynes, ed., William Blake, *Complete Writings* (London: Oxford University Press, 1969), pp. 633–34.

ing quality, based on the noun phrase (rather than the verb) and internally onomatopoeic.

The sublime free-verse poem's internal patterning of sound is in large part reliant on a piling up of qualities in which personal response is interwoven with physical description. Here is Whitman:

    /   \\   /   \\
Sea-lettuce, vast lichens, strange flowers and seeds, the thick

    /   \\   /
    tangle, openings, and pink turf

. . . .

  /   \\   /   /   /   \\
sluggish existences grazing there suspended, or slowly crawling

    /   \\
    close to the bottom . . .

("The World Below the Brine")

Everything strange and wondrous is celebrated in Whitman, especially as the crowding of perceptions designates a state of response with which he can identify his inmost impulses.

Anne Winters's "Mill-Race" is squarely in the biblical free-verse mode. Consider how the verset alternations illuminate the shape of her exceedingly long lines:

    /   \\   /   \\   /
But we won't (says the bus-rider, slumped, to herself). Nothing's

    /   \\   /   /   \\   /
left over, really, from labor. They've taken it all for the mill-race.

       \\
    Even now,   40

    /   \\   /   \\
as the driver flicks off the huge felt-edged wipers,

     /   \\   /
the rain slackening, lifting, labor

  /   \\   /   \\
lengthens itself along Broadway. Fresh puddles

  /   \\   /   \\
mirror in amber and crimson the night signs . . .

The marking of verset-alternation is intended to suggest rather than codify a pattern that acts to keep the lines together as individual units—

whatever forces may be in the syntax that make the lines run over from line to line.

Also like Blake and Whitman, Louise Bogan, in her biblical free-verse poem (which appears in chapter 2) "Baroque Comment," deliberately rejects the active syntax of her more typical poems to explore fragmentary syntax that is unusually tense with syntactical awareness. The "baroque" of her title not only identifies the style of sculpture and ornament but also refers, I think, to the most characteristic device in continental baroque poetry, **asyndeton,** or the omission of conjunctions, articles, and pronouns from a piled-up catalogue (the word for the baroque catalogue in German is "word-heap," *Worthäuffung*).[12] Bogan plays with many of the devices of the sublime mode, including multiple **epithets** ("kelp-disordered beaches," "weather-bleached hair"), participial and compounding sentence structure ("pale and laurel chosen as noble and enduring," "The turned eyes and the opened mouth of love"), an irregular ode-like line, and anaphora (*The x, the y, the z; From a, From b, From c,* etc.).[13]

The Fourth Freedom: Imagist Free Verse

If biblical free verse, dependant on invocation and catalogue, phrasal accumulation and texture, admiration and terror, could be condensed into its minim, that residue would be the **imagist free-verse** poem. This is a poem necessarily short both in line and in total number of words whose aim is the turning of a single impression into a perfectly polished verbal expression—something like what Marianne Moore does (albeit in syllabics) in her poem "An Egyptian Pulled Glass Bottle in the Shape of a Fish" (see chapter 10). The enjambment of Moore's syllabic verse is accentuated in the free verse of poets like Eleanor Wilner (see her free-verse political poem "Operations: Desert Shield, Desert Storm" in the "Poetry Sampler" in chapter 1). The primary rhythmical device in this fourth type of free verse is the subphrasal cut—the use of the line break to register both closure and interruption of what cannot yet be closed. These subtle-

---

12. See Lowry Nelson under "Baroque" in the *Princeton Encyclopedia,* 1974 ed., p. 122.

13. Robert Pinsky is also masterful at the "word-heaping" of biblical free verse. See his poems "Shirt" and "The Figured Wheel" in his new and selected volume *The Figured Wheel* (New York: Farrar, Straus, Giroux, 1997).

ties of punctuation-by-line have been amply examined by Charles O. Hartman in his book on free verse. His examples—the most striking are from Bogan, Moore, and Carlos Williams—fall partly under other freedoms than the fourth, but he is impeccable in reading the function of line boundary in the making of free verse. Those who wish to pursue the last freedom are encouraged to look both at Hartman's examples and at the work of the few modern poets who have written free verse both biblical-sublime and imagist: Ezra Pound, A. R. Ammons, and James Schuyler.

What makes imagist free verse so admirable—and so difficult—is the deceptive ease of expression alongside the apparent casualness of the lineation. Louise Bogan, who published fewer than a half-dozen nonmetrical poems in her lifetime, nevertheless closed her career with one of the great extended imagist free-verse lyrics, "After the Persian":

> from "After the Persian"
>
> I
>
> I do not wish to know
> The depths of your terrible jungle:
> From what nest your leopard leaps
> Or what sterile lianas are at once your serpents' disguise and home.
>
> I am the dweller on the temperate threshold,   5
> The strip of corn and vine,
> Where all is translucence (the light!),
> Liquidity, and the sound of water.
> Here the days pass under shade
> And the nights have the waxing and the waning moon.   10
> Here the moths take flight at evening;
> Here at morning the dove whistles and the pigeons coo.
> Here, as night comes on, the fireflies wink and snap
> Close to the cool ground,
> Shining in a profusion   15
> Celestial or marine.
>
> Here it is never wholly dark but always wholly green,
> And the day stains with what seems to be more than the sun
> What may be more than my flesh.   20

II
I have wept with the spring storm;
Burned with the brutal summer.
Now, hearing the wind and the twanging bow-strings,
I know what winter brings.

The hunt sweeps out upon the plain   5
And the garden darkens.
They will bring the trophies home
To bleed and perish
Beside the trellis and the lattices,
Beside the fountain, still flinging diamond water,   10
Beside the pool
(Which is eight-sided, like my heart).
. . . .
V
Goodbye, goodbye!
There was so much to love, I could not love it all;
I could not love it enough.

Some things I overlooked, and some I could not find.
Let the crystal clasp them   5
When you drink your wine, in autumn.

(Louise Bogan)

The controlling dimension in "After the Persian" is personal experience
of beauty (and its transience). Bogan's choice of this mode of free verse is
symbolic of her letting go of the poetic medium; the work is a gesture of
relinquishment to others of the rich, contradictory, and intricate emo-
tions and visions of life. Those who live after her she blesses with a spec-
tral toast, in autumn.

Other poets are at their best in briefer free-verse lyrics. William Car-
los Williams, A. R. Ammons,[14] Ezra Pound under Chinese influence,
and Wallace Stevens with his surreal badinage in *Harmonium* eschew the
orotund prophecies, elaborate parallels, and massive catalogues that flood
the lines of biblical free verse. Stevens, as reticent about the literal experi-

14. See my study of the imagistic, syntactically splintered free-verse poetry of A. R.
Ammons. Mary Kinzie, *The Cure of Poetry in an Age of Prose: Moral Essays on the Poet's
Calling* (Chicago: University of Chicago Press, 1993), pp. 105–9.

ences that give his poems vigor as Louise Bogan was, displays a rueful, hectic playfulness and a chronic metaphysical drift that few poets of the immediate lyric have so effectively combined.

> Fabliau of Florida
>
> Barque of phosphor
> On the palmy beach,
>
> Move outward into heaven,
> Into the alabasters
> And night blues.   5
>
> Foam and cloud are one,
> Sultry moon-monsters
> Are dissolving.
>
> Fill your black hull
> With white moonlight.   10
>
> There will never be an end
> To this droning of the surf.

Even Stevens's title, *fabliau* or the fable suggestive of things bawdy, when followed by the odd mix of moon-monsters and the ghostly ship made of glints from the moon and water ("barque of phosphor") points to the theme of distance and longing. Yet when the black hull fills with moonlight, the heart is dissatisfied and the surf returns to a "drone." As often as not, poems like Stevens's evaporate into their own delicacy. It takes a wise head to limit the use of the form to occasions of the greatest probability of accuracy, or of greatest need (as John Morris does in "The Unburied," discussed in the next chapter). No other form so readily flies into pieces as imagist free verse does. But when it is done well, no other form so perfectly reflects insight into the moments that must pass.

PART III

Writing in Form

> "'Form' is regarded not as a neat mould to be filled, but rather as a
> sieve to catch certain kinds of material."
> —Theodore Roethke

I imagine many of you believe, as I do myself (in a qualified way), that
poetic form can easily strangle ideas. At the start, nothing seems more
true: You are beleaguered at every turn by the wrong word in the right
place—you need a trochaic noun in place of the monosyllabic ones that
occur to you, you need flat rather than abstract diction (or vice versa),
you need a rhyme with such limiting pair-words as *ocean* or *loom,* or you
need a syntactic gambit that will stretch for several lines. Soon enough
you come to view form as inhibiting your expression.

Poets are always trying to do everything at once; this is the challenge
of the craft. Rather than making the job easier, form seems to make it
fiendishly hard. But one may be strangled sooner by ease than by form.
Dead-ends may occur more readily owing to naivete—or to impa-
tience—than through knowledge and application. The French poet Paul
Valéry says that the writing of regular verses may destroy "an infinite
number of fine possibilities"; but he adds that "at the same time it sug-
gests a multitude of distant and totally unexpected thoughts." I'm in-

clined to agree that poetic forms trigger infinitely more ideas than they destroy. More than this, forms offer a type of training that keeps bringing the writer close to the hot core of language: It puts pressure on the poet to think beyond words automatically given by the self. In this sense also form acts to keep out of poetry what would chill or muddy it.

Form also provides variety, which liberates us from repetition. Rather than strictness, forms offer extraordinary surprise—different ways of sounding and different ways of conceiving of the total shape of an utterance. Who is not relieved at the chance to sound new? To put one's thought into a different frame—to impose fresh aims on one's train of association—may well rescue us from the habitual qualities of selfhood that make writing all too predictable (especially to the writer). Unformed stream of consciousness may finally not take us anywhere; after all, not every cluster of intimate associations is coherent.

So it may be that, even if we are not crazy about the exercise, there is a lot to be gained by thinking in certain directions, using certain language (while giving up other kinds), and furnishing ourselves with a knowledge of certain syntactic options. We learn, above all, how *we* sound when inhabiting a new syntax, a new argument, or a new line. To explore forms methodically may save time, too, moving us through ideas it might take years to stumble upon in the normal course of things, while also providing the exposure so helpful in the future, when, long after the experimental phase, we experience that far-off desire to write something for which that very form, explored in the past, is the perfect spur. Then, it may happen that the poem (unborn as yet) can try on rhetorical and formal shape and imagine itself as a religious sonnet or a symbolic stanzaic narrative, as a blank-verse apology or an ode or a lament. When a poet has read widely, this part of the creative process is sped up and simplified. It is clearer which form will suit when you have used many. During the period of composition, when bits of language and a sense of direction start cooperating, the poet can test these new gleanings against the store of poetic shapes already experienced from within.

12

Exercises for Beginning and Advanced Writers

The most effective way to think oneself through a poetic form is to try to write in it. The following exercises (or their variants) have been staples in my teaching. They can be adjusted up or down in complexity and (of course) rearranged according to topic and restriction. The first four poetic exercises are directed toward the formal beginner, while the ten poems in the following section are designed for the writer who is further along. In every case, it is assumed that the resulting poems will be in iambic meter.

About writing in iambics: The best preparation for experiment with accentual-syllabic lines is to read. Read poems written in iambic feet. Read poems in the stanza forms suggested in the fourteen exercises below. Also read iambic poems that tackle some of the themes stipulated for *your* draft—poems that show the same **rhetoric**, **mode**, and methods of handling idea and **passage**. Because a metrical line is both a pattern of sound and part of a series of sentences, it helps to have at hand several models for mixing the two. And because a metrical line is both a segment of a logical sequence and a coordination of the varieties of word patterning and suggestion encompassed by the concepts of **diction** and **trope** that affect the words' length and sound, one can never divide the theme from the form. Form follows theme, to be sure, but theme is also sparked by certain forms.

There is no absolute way of knowing when you are ready to write. To begin with, I recommend reading until the light of your own idea begins to dawn; then follow it as long as it shines. When your own draft gutters out, go back to different poems by others until the way back into your own poem is shown to you. For those uncertain about composing metrically, it helps to read one's own work aloud—perhaps read it to somebody else—then read one of the poems in the same form from your group of personal favorites, then return to the draft, then to a different poem from the tradition. (When reading aloud, by the way, *read slowly.*) The more one refers to the poems one has come to know for guidance and echo, the more likely that in time a new turning will appear. Memorizing the work of others can speed the process.

Sample Exercises—Starting Out

Exercise I: Descriptive Quatrains

1. *Form:* A 300-word prose draft, followed by a poem that should have a minimum of four quatrains of **long meter** (iambic tetrameter) rhyming either *abab* or *abxb*.

2. *Theme:* Someone (or something) seen through a window. You can be looking in or looking out.

3. *Method:* Once the prose reflects your best response to the theme of glimpsing something whose meaning takes time to unfold, you can look through the prose for phrases and comparisons worth keeping and begin to devise a tetrameter poem that takes this prose to a higher plane. Even after many passes through the prose as it is being drafted, you may expect to discover much more to discard when you try to take the prose over into the rhymed stanzas of long meter. The prose-draft approach (which I recommend later for the blank verse poem) can become a useful preliminary for any poetic mode in which plainness plays a role—as it did for both Ben Jonson and W. B. Yeats, who drafted prose "preliminaries").

4. *Restrictions:* Keep a maximum of one adjective per quatrain (this includes participial adjectives, formed from verbs, ending in *-ing* or *-ed*). Use only **literal symbols**—objects literally present in the scene, though chosen for their ability to hint at meanings beyond themselves. (See the sections after the exercises on literal symbol and cliche p. 375ff.)

5. *Read:* David Ferry, "Seen Through a Window" (pp. 196–97).

6. *Consider* the way Ferry sorts through observations even as he makes them, performing careful adjustments upon his spare diction and simple, declarative syntax as his speaker tries to uncover the impression that, after he had looked only briefly at the man and woman in the kitchen, sank so deeply into his mind that it practically has no shape; the subaqueous green of the air and the shrill cry of the solitary bird are the **vehicles** he devises for the **tenor** that is part oppression and part realization for the

gazed-upon and the gazer too. Your details and surfaces of the world glimpsed through a window should be as gingerly handled, to keep the exact meanings beneath the rough image from disappearing.

Exercise II: Sonnet of Dramatized Description

1. *Form:* Iambic pentameter sonnet using either the Petrarchan rhyme scheme (*abbaabba | cdcdcd*) or the Shakespearean (*abab cdcd | efef gg;* the colophon represents the volta—see no. 3 below).

2. *Theme:* An old photograph.

3. *Method:* The goal of this exercise is to adapt the essentially descriptive bias of the theme to the dramatic frame of the sonnet with its built-in shift in argument between the **octave** and the **sestet**. This shift, called a **volta**, can mark any of a number of turns both logical and metaphoric. One can move from general ideas in the octave to specific instances in the sestet, from an octave in the past to a sestet in the present, from plain to complex diction and/or syntax. And, of course, any of these shifts can be inverted, so that one moves instead from complex to plain, present to past, and specific to general. (See sonnets other than those discussed below in the "List of Poems by Form.")

Like the poem you prepared for "Exercise I: Descriptive Quatrains," this poem is in part an exercise in selecting the right details, which also entails rejecting the superfluous ones. Because a sonnet is so brief, every detail that appears must have the flexibility to mean beyond itself.

4. *Restriction:* Try to include at least one sentence that takes more than two lines.

5. *Read:* David Ferry's third poem from "Six Photographs from a Book" (p. 169), John N. Morris's "The Unburied" (later in this chapter), and Donald Justice's sonnet about his boyhood:

My South: On the Porch

There used to be a way the sunlight caught
The cocoons of caterpillars in the pecans.
A boy's shadow would lengthen to a man's
Across the yard then, slowly. And if you thought
Some sleepy god had dreamed it all up—well,   5
There was my grandfather, Lincoln-tall and solemn,
Tapping his pipe out on a white-flaked column,

Carefully, carefully, as though it were his job.
And we would watch the pipe-stars as they fell.[1]
As for the quiet, the same train always broke it.   10
Then the great silver watch rose from his pocket
For us to check the hour, the dark fob
Dangling the watch between us like the moon.
It would be evening soon then, very soon.

6. *Consider* how detail is experienced rather than explained in Justice's sonnet, until the speaker is in the poem as its lens without needing to refer to himself as "I." See lines 4–5 where the boy whose shadow lengthens in the late afternoon light approaches the porch where the grandfather raises up before him and the other children the moon of the watch and the stars of the tobacco embers as the train rattles off into the future, leaving all of this behind. Without referring to the photographic process, Justice's "My South: On the Porch" creates a mental snapshot—a moment in which the meaning of the past has been caught, a precipitated and compact particle of time.

Consider, too, how memory by its nature defines an alteration the writer must reverse until what has hardened into the routine or the quaint can be thawed and released into the river again.

Exercise III: Couplet Narrative

1. *Form:* Write a minimum of ten heroic (iambic pentameter) couplets (twenty lines rhyming *aa bb cc,* etc.).

2. *Theme:* Retelling of or a sequel to a famous tale from the Brothers Grimm, Hans Christian Andersen, Greek myth, or the Bible (KJV).

3. *Method:* Your version of whatever tale you choose to retell should be differently stressed or weighted than in the original. Like the theme in Exercise XII described below, in which a minor or secondary character suddenly stands at center stage, Exercise III also moves in the direction of realigning assumed interpretations. In this couplet poem you might also wonder about "missing" moments in well-known narratives, such as

---

1. The volta in Justice's poem is late, and the rhyme scheme from 5 through 12 unorthodox. However, the details are luminous and the diction sparkling, and the child's consciousness of adult mystery is both coherent and evocative; the first nine lines make up one progression of deeply linked visual recollections, to which this sonnet's last five lines act as dramatic continuation and climax.

the childhood of Dido, later queen of Carthage, or the missing story of Lolita's marriage in the novel by Vladimir Nabokov, or an unmentioned encounter in the life of Christ, say with Barabbas when both were still at liberty, or the missing scene might take the form of a conversation between Jesus and his mother. The new scene might be an act left out of *Hamlet,* one tracking the hero abroad once he leaves Denmark mid-play, or a major revision such as Eleanor Wilner performs in the title poem of her 1989 volume *Sarah's Choice,* in which the poet supposes that Sarah and not Abraham has been commanded by Yahweh to sacrifice her only son Isaac.

Your goal is to think about the idea at the center of inherited material; one way to focus on it is by an irreverence toward the original that allows you to skew or displace its symmetries. In consequence, what is assumed or given (called the *donnée*) can be seen afresh (even when the re-vision is critical of the original).

4. *Restriction:* At least half of the rhyme-pairs must be made up of different parts of speech (that is, nouns cannot be rhymed with nouns, or verbs with verbs; but a noun with a verb or a verb with an adjective is fine). This requirement will jostle the lines into different syntactic patterns, thus avoiding redundant s-v-o (subject-verb-object) sentences.

5. *Read:* Review the discussion of **allusion** in chapter 5's presentation on trope. For examples of retellings, look at Muir's "Ballad of Hector in Hades" and "The Enchanted Knight," Gunn's "Moly," Auden's "Lady, Weeping at the Crossroads," and Hine's "Bluebeard's Wife" (all in the text), as well as Bogan's "Medusa," Eliot's "Journey of the Magi," and A. D. Hope's "Man Friday." The Eliot and Bogan poems are in the *Norton* (4th edition). A. D. Hope's couplet narrative "Man Friday," which takes up the tale from the perspective of Friday's suffering where the saga of Daniel Defoe's *Robinson Crusoe* leaves off, provides ample evidence of the smoothness and momentum of the couplet form (see chapter 4, pp. 134–35, and chapter 9, pp. 286–88).

6. *Consider* Hope's methods of softening the couplet's **stichic** tendency. In the excerpts from "Man Friday" in chapter 4, lines 4–6, 7ff., 22, 41, 47–48, 70, 72, and 75–77 all exhibit sentence frames that stand out against—and often run on from—the framework of iambic pentameter lines. In the excerpts from "Man Friday" given in chapter 9, lines 82, 111, and 114–15 are also worth study in regard to syntactic variety as it plays off of line; in these cases, variety provides **tension** against the **coincidence** between meter and line.

Exercise IV: Blank Verse Meditation

1. *Form:* A 300- to 600-word prose draft, followed by a minimum of twenty lines of **blank verse** (unrhymed iambic pentameter with occasional—and necessary—**enjambment**).

2. *Theme:* Someone in your family looks at the season. (Note that this exercise was discussed in "The Enchantment of the Work," on page 7).

3. *Method:* The relation here of prose to poem is more intimate than it was in "Exercise I: Descriptive Quatrains," where the rhymed tetrameter cohered in quatrains. In the present exercise, the aim is to incorporate some of the digressiveness of prose into the three-part out/in/out organization resembling that in the works listed in the readings in no. 5, that is, first the description of a scene, which then triggers a meditation on something in the speaker's experience, which finally enables the speaker to return to the initial scene with a sense of resolution or renewed understanding. The poem should close with a reference to the place where the poem began, which has been implicitly altered by the meditation that intervenes.

4. *Restriction:* Avoid more than two **end-stopped** lines in sequence.

5. *Read:* Coleridge, "Frost at Midnight," Wordsworth, "Tintern Abbey," Larkin, "Church Going," Gunn, "His Rooms in College, and Nemerov, "Landscape with Self-Portrait" (the last two are in the text).

6. *Considerations:* Like the writers of fiction who provide smooth and comprehensible prose as they speak through speechless characters (objects, animals, children, or individuals in extreme situations), the poet's job is one of sympathetic insight into minds that rebuff the attention. Using the bridge of language, the imaginative writer articulates the thought of those who, it may be, neither understand themselves nor speak coherently about what they experience.

To take on the "translation" of the sensibility of some near relation requires facing the habit on the part of what is most familiar to slip out of one's grasp. It also permits us to get *ourselves* out of the picture, or to write about self from a disengaged or even unflattering angle.

Further Exercises for Advancement

Exercise V: Trimeter Mad Song

1. *Form:* Write seven stanzas of iambic trimeter rhyming *abxb*.

2. *Theme:* Song either of an innocent being or someone driven mad.

3. *Method:* At the heart of this exercise is the attempt to think and speak through another character or **persona**; this type of poem is called a **dramatic monologue**. The projection of oneself into the world of another being can lead to the mythic realm without requiring the naming of the principal figures. Try combining the idea of the mad song with the different personalities of Medea, the little match girl, Ariadne, or the princess who was silent in the Grimm brothers' tale of the seven swans—but refrain from giving name or title.

One can be mad owing to circumstance, as were Shakespeare's Ophelia and Bogan's Cassandra, or on the other hand mad in a way that has more to do with temperament, as was the case with Ajax, Lady Macbeth, and the young wife (played by Harriet Andersson) in Ingmar Bergman's film "Through a Glass Darkly."

Short of clinical dementia are the torments described in the poems of great literary innovators like Emily Dickinson ("I Felt a funeral, in my Brain" #280), Bogan ("'Come, Sleep, . . .'"), and Sylvia Plath ("Elm"). The figures projected by such poems might also be taken up as speakers for your monologue.

4. *Restrictions:* Use at least one sentence in the **subjunctive** or hypothetical **mood**, as in Dickinson's stanza-long sentence beginning "So set its Sun in Thee" (p. 79) or Yeats's relative clause with its implied *if/then* hypothesis in the subjunctive ("Who, were it proved he lies, / Were [then] neither shamed in his own / Nor in his neighbours' eyes" ["To a Friend Whose Work Has Come to Nothing," p. 109]).

5. *Read:* In addition to the works mentioned in no. 3 on method above, look at Louise Bogan, "Cassandra" (p. 209), Julia Randall, "Maid's Song" (p. 211), and William Blake's *Songs of Innocence and Experience.*

6. *Consider* the trimeter poems by Robert Herrick, Emily Dickinson, W. B. Yeats, and David Ferry in the text to bring to mind the muscularities of **syntax** by which the constriction of the trimeter line can be dissolved while retaining the rhythmical tautness of this brief iambic linear unit. The Herrick poem "A Conjuration, to Electra" (p. 66) proceeds in parallel phrases beginning with the preposition *By*—locutions that might be instrumental (by means of: "By these soft Tods of wool") or geographical ("By all the tinctures *there*"; "By [something located near the] Dewes and drisling Raine") but which in lines 19 and 20 yield the correct sense of prepositional use—the listing of tokens in an oath ("By Time, that hastens on / Things to perfection . . . O my Electra! be / In love with none but me"). Herrick's phrases are parallel in orientation to the **imper-**

ative verb *Be,* but varied within each phrase by changing syntactic extenders, including both noun and verb clauses. The poem rhymes as couplets, but the thematic-syntactic units are sometimes as long as six lines.

Yeats accomplishes a yet more complex recovery of rhymed trimeter in the quatrains of "To a Friend Whose Work Has Come to Nothing," in which sentences run on past the four-line rhyming units (the poem *rhymes* in quatrains, but does not *think in* stanzas or insist on space breaks between rhymed units, either—the **passage** overruns the stanza).

Dickinson's trimeters in the two-quatrain **short meter** poem "To One denied to drink" (#490) and in the trimeters mixed with **dimeters** of the six-line "So set its Sun in Thee" show a further tightening of syntax within a more tightly coiled stanzaic frame.

Herrick shows ways to vary parallel syntax, while both Dickinson and Yeats exhibit the advantages of planning a twist *in advance of* the start of the poem—a twist that involves **hypotaxis**.

Exercise VI: Ballad of Metamorphosis

1. *Form:* Six stanzas of **common meter** rhyming *abxb.*

2. *Theme:* A protagonist of whom the speaker is fond is changing or has been changed into something living, but inhuman.

3. *Method:* Try to focus the attention on an unstable or partial insight on the part of either the main character who is changing or the companions who observe but cannot explain the disappearance. The most efficient method of describing a baffling or inchoate experience is through comparison, or **trope**, whose terms are clear even if this theme, by definition, engages perception that is ambiguous or uncertain. Recall the poem by James Merrill beginning "NOON finds me faced by a small troop of furies" (p. 207); the "senses" (already an abstraction from immediate perception) are further removed from the moment by **personification** as bored children whom the speaker, in the role of parent, must amuse. So Merrill creates an entire dramatic situation unfolding at some remove from the tenor—for he is really speaking about someone whose senses are in revolt, who is deviled by conflicting and exorbitant demands. It is a state in which satisfaction only feeds a stronger fire of balked erotic desire. However, because the actors are such complex and controlled projections, the moment of greatest excitation in the tenor is rendered with great coolness in the vehicle, as touch torments the protago-

nist: "The fingers of the eldest brush my features / *But you are smiling* she says coldly   *Why.*"

4. *Restriction:* To frame the uncertain dimensions of the threshold into another realm, try starting the poem with either of the phrases "Never before" or "Always" in the first line.

5. *Read:* For examples of handling this topic, see the *Metamorphoses* of the Latin poet Ovid, in which four realms (the material, animal, human, and divine) blend inextricably—but always from the human perspective. See also Richard Wilbur, "Merlin Enthralled," in which Merlin has been changed by the enchantress Nimue into part of the natural world—the woods which Arthur and Gawen can see but don't recognize as holding the dispersed spirit of the magician Merlin. Muir's "The Enchanted Knight" in chapter 5 also draws on this theme (adding a touch of horror from the ballad of the "Twa Corbies"). Recall as well the quality of desolation in the ballads "As You Came from the Holy Land of Walsinghame" and "The Laily Worm and the Machrel of the Sea."

6. *Consider* what enchantment might be a metaphor *for.* Rather than an end in itself in a story whose twists are transparent, ask whether the plot of metamorphosis might not readily pertain to more ordinary lives. Our understanding of who we are and the stage we've reached at any given moment is constantly shifting before it reaches the point of articulation. In some ways, the persons we used to be are out of our reach as if they were women who had turned into trees, the bark covering up their mouths; just so, there coils and separates underfoot, regardless of our precautions, the unreliable ground of the future. Anything might break through.

Exercise VII: Linked Form Using Lines by Another

1. *Form:* Write a pantoum, triolet, villanelle, glosa, or other **linked form**, in which some or all of the repeated lines are by another hand.

2. *Theme:* A poem in conversation with the writer whose lines you incorporate. Or you might choose a topic from the list in no. 2 of "Exercise XIV: Sestina of Early Intuition."

3. *Method:* Inasmuch as our task initially is to sound like others before trying to create an original composition, this verbatim quotation of others' lines within a linked poem of our own encourages an active absorption and reflection of some model of style. When the model's style sounds in some way antiquated, there is the challenge of negotiating between

the older style and a more colloquial one; one aim of this stylistic friction might be to create a context within which the lines by another could sound almost natural.

4. *Restriction:* The poem should use iambic lines of equivalent length, either tetrameter or pentameter; thus the poem from which you borrow should be either tetrameter or pentameter.

5. *Read:* Poems in the entry on **linked forms** in chapter 13.

6. *Consider:* In an effort to create a colloquial plateau on which you and the earlier writer(s) might meet, consider several ways of flexing the exercise. First, by combining lines from different periods in the same poem (Coleridge's "Quietly shining to the quiet Moon," from "Frost at Midnight," for example, with, say, Stevens's "Even if what she sang was what she heard," from "The Idea of Order at Key West," and George Gascoigne's gaze "Which follows fancy dazzled by desire" like a moth drawn toward a candle from the sonnet "For That He Looked Not upon Her"). Or combine the unbroken utterance of Donne's "I dare not move my dimme eyes any way" with the broken drama of Browning's "You understand me: I'm a beast, I know" from "Fra Lippo Lippi" or with the embedded significations in Hamlet's comment to his mother over the body of Polonius, whom he has killed, saying that heaven saw fit "To punish me with this and this with me," *Hamlet* III.iv. Second, by slightly altering the original (instead of the last line of Shakespeare's sonnet 73, "To love that well, which thou must leave ere long," a more colloquial variant with a metrical twist across the middle three feet of the pentameter line, "Or love well what I must leave before long").

Exercise VIII: Table-Talk in Heroic Quatrains

1. *Form:* Write a minimum of four stanzas of **heroic quatrains** (iambic pentameter) rhyming *abab*.

2. *Theme:* Table-talk (or *obiter dicta* or "-ana" poems, as in Dickensiana or Holmesiana); the loose thoughts or casual hints dropped by an eminent person in conversation and collected by a friend.[2] Eminence can precede print culture; you can imagine the conversation of figures such as Hipparchus (the first astronomer) or the Egyptian queen Hatshepsut just as you may that of the Latin poet of familiar address, Horace, or Sir

---

2. See J. A. Cuddon, *A Dictionary of Literary Terms and Literary Theory,* 3d rev. ed. (Cambridge: Basil Blackwell, 1991), under "table-talk."

Philip Sidney or Blaise Pascal or Jonathan Swift or Lady Mary Wortley Montagu or Christina Rossetti—though the earlier persons may call for more invention on your part. Or take a modern figure—like the ambitious Katherine Mansfield or Leo Szilard, the first atomic physicist to realize the bomb could be built (he went to European leaders to spur world opinion against its building). Ask how character changes conversation.

3. *Method:* Experiment with sensibilities from another country, century, or discipline—artists or leaders familiar to you whose tricks of style and cast of mind you are curious about and then come to know well. As you mimic the main character's way of approaching the world, try placing it against a new (perhaps more modern) context. While doing so, write *against* the language of your chosen protagonist by a second and more secretive diction, described in no. 4 below.

4. *Restrictions:* Choose one of the following techniques:

(a) Use four of the following Scandinavian loan words: *axle, dregs, skill, clasp, droop, glitter, skulk, want, muggy, sly, ugly, wrong* (look each up first[3]); or

(b) Use four pairs of mirror words. Comic examples such as *flog/golf, straw/warts, parts/strap,* and *knits/stink* may prove unwieldy, imposing thematic directions difficult to control. But other pairings might be easier to contain while coinciding more accurately with the diction contrast at the poem's center: *ward/draw, room/moor, evil/live, liar/rail, edit/tide, wolf/flow.*

(c) Use either **etymological style** or **adnomination**—two devices that bring out the shape and logic of word formation. The goal in imposing such restrictions is to teach oneself the transparency of style afforded by a superimposed rather than directly expressive restraint.

5. *Read:* Edwin Arlington Robinson's dramatic monologue (which echoes Ben Jon's "Inviting a Friend to Supper") in which the playwright has Shakespeare to supper; it's called "Ben Jonson Entertains a Man from Stratford" (from Robinson's 1910 volume *The Man Against the Sky*). See also Auden's long epistolary poem *Letter to Lord Byron* and Browning's monologues, which are formed to make idle perambulations around historically timely ideas and personalities, for example, "The Bishop Orders His Tomb at Saint Praxed's Church," "Andrea del Sarto," "Fra Lippo

---

3. The same end (the nonevident structural and linguistic linking between words) could be served by drawing upon a lexicon loaned to English from Hindi or French. See Cuddon's *Dictionary of Literary Terms* under "loan words."

Lippi," "The Grammarian's Funeral," "How It Strikes a Contemporary," and "Abt Vogler." More recently, the American poet Richard Howard has revived the poem of "cultural gossip," beginning with his volume *Untitled Subjects* (monologues by those who knew the eminent) and continuing through *Two-Part Inventions* (in which heroic artists who never met are drawn together) and the poems based on the personalities imaged by the French photographer Nadar in *Misgivings*.

6. *Consider* the role the heroic stanza with its rhymes might play in sharpening the edge of pithy comment while providing colloquial release; the poems of the Canadian Daryl Hine rank with the American James Merrill's and the English Auden's in exhibiting the possibilities of fresh and uncoerced diction within a frame of lines whose ends are tipped with darts of rhyme.

Exercise IX: Epigram of Condemnation

1. *Form:* Write an **epigram** that consists of two end-stopped heroic (iambic pentameter) couplets, rhyming *aa bb*.

2. *Theme:* You are disgusted with the shabby behavior of someone of your acquaintance.

3. *Method:* Epigrams require both discursive clarity, or succinctness, and multiple layering of the point. To this combined end, **rhyming on the phrase** may prove helpful. Choose rhymes that have the additional feature of suggesting **allusion** to another realm of experience than that described. For example, if you are lambasting a spendthrift, you might select a rhyme-phrase like "drain the cup," which could perversely suggest the many chalices in the story of the Crucifixion in the Gospels, including the cup of suffering that Jesus asks his father to have taken from him in Gethsemane (Mark 14:36). If one is to rhyme on *drain the cup,* one must work toward it through the first or "prerhyme" that represents the form of wastrel behavior one most dislikes—as here the rough cruelty of male bonding is reflected in the phrase that means to support one's team, *hold up the side:*

> Large at the bar, the boys hold the side up,
> Roaring with laughter as they drain the cup.

Now a spendthrift wastes what he drinks while Christ transformed the suffering he endured to the dregs. But the one action might compel the other, as the story of Christ invariably sets a lone sufferer against a bullying crowd; I have tried to work backwards in the second couplet from the crowd's desire to get behind the mask of innocence:

> Large at the bar, the boys hold the side up,
> Roaring with laughter as they drain the cup
> And pricking each other on to that fierce task
> Of finding life and tearing off its mask.

More freedom might be afforded by a rhyme-phrase whose evocations are more distant, whose style is more "familiar": *drain the cup* might be moderated to *drain the glass* or *tip the cup* and thus bring into play different ranges of suggestion and colloquial possibility.

5. *Read:* For a crash course in rhyme wit in the short poem, the poems of three poets are particularly recommended: Alexander Pope (even his long poems teach lessons in the epigram), J. V. Cunningham (of additional interest owing to his imitation of the savage epigrams of the Latin poet Martial), and James Merrill (especially the volume whose clever modesty of title—*First Poems*—belies its lavishness of invention).

6. *Consider* the role played by the poem's speaker. You are free in this regard: The speaker need not be yourself in every particular. Indeed, what might the poem sound like if those you condemn were to speak their own epigram of condemnation of you?

Exercise X: Couplets in Praise of Place

1. *Form:* Write nine heroic couplets; enjambment permitted.

2. *Theme:* Praise of a gracious home OR praise of a setting or environment.

3. *Method:* Instead of composing in couplet-units, you might explore the composition of **passages** that happen to rhyme *aa bb cc*, etc. You can be somewhat less pointed in your use of rhyming on the phrase than you were in "Exercise IX: Epigram of Condemnation."

4. *Restriction:* Create one example of **syntactic inversion.**

5. *Read:* Jonson, "To Penshurst," Carew, "To Saxham," and Yeats, "Meditations in Time of Civil War." Marvell also has two noteworthy "gracious home" poems, "Upon the Hill and Grove at *Bill-borow*" and "Upon Appleton House, To My Lord Fairfax."[4] If you prefer "praise of

---

4. In *Major Poets of the Earlier Seventeenth Century,* edited by Barbara K. Lewalski and Andrew J. Sabol (Indianapolis: Bobbs-Merrill/Odyssey, 1973), pp. 1130–33 and 1133–60.

a setting" as a theme, see Philip Larkin's "Church Going"; Auden's "In Praise of Limestone" is an example of the more abstract "praise of an environment" topic, which overlaps still more closely than does Larkin or Yeats with **anatomy** and with **ode** (discussed in chapter 11).

6. *Considerations:* As the previous poem asks you to start with revulsion, this exercise begins with an attitude of approval and celebration. You are also being urged to move beyond the so-called lyric "I" into a world in which social cohesion is implied along with a link between society and nature.

Exercise XI: Dialogue in Nonce Stanzas

1. *Form:* Invent your own stanza of at least five lines and write five or more stanzas in this form; one line should be iambic pentameter, one trimeter, and the others a mix of trimeter, tetrameter, and pentameter.

2. *Theme:* Dialogue between opposing principles (like mind and soul, or brain and body) in the guise of creatures and/or things (frog and lily-pad, aspen and stream,[5] pen and paper, clapper and bell—although your possibilities are not limited to these thematic pairs.

3. *Method:* Give voice to the opposites or complements you most strongly believe in and embody the opposition in the working of opposing temperaments (perhaps imagining the spiritual and psychological tension between persons of your acquaintance—though you must give them the form of animals, shapes, or things).

4. *Restrictions:* A minimum of three lines in each five- to six-line stanza (and four lines in seven- to eight-line stanzas) should rhyme. This proviso includes—of necessity—the last line in each stanza (see chapter 9 on stanza for the reasons for last-line rhyme). You must try to find a way to suggest different style of mind within identical frame of stanza. Syntax and diction can be varied for immediate distinguishing moves. See "Exercise XII: Sonnets of Secondary Characters," no. 6, and "Exercise XIV: Sestina of Early Intuition," no. 6, for further discussion of syntactic variation.

5. *Read:* Marvell's dialogue poems, Richard Wilbur's "The Aspen and the Stream," and Louise Bogan's "Summer Wish." For rhymed stan-

---

5. After the Richard Wilbur poem "The Aspen and the Stream," in *New and Collected Poems* (San Diego, CA: Harcourt Brace Jovanovich, 1988).

zas with uneven line lengths (**heterometric rhyme**), see the work of the Renaissance poets.

6. *Consider* the work of the great writers of dialogue, the confrontational dialogues of Plato; the imbedded situational dialogues of the Renaissance dramatists; the dazzling encoded dialogues in the fiction of Ernest Hemingway; the cerebral dialogues in the major novels of Thomas Mann; the dialogue-novels of Ivy Compton-Burnett; the unattributed dialogue-play in the novels of Iris Murdoch. All of these writers see ways to immerse the self in the play of intercourse with others.

Exercise XII: Sonnets of Secondary Characters

1. *Form:* Two sonnets in linked sequence. Revisit your efforts in "Exercise II: Sonnet of Dramatized Description" and compose now two sonnets in the other form, the one you did not take up earlier. The "linking" means that the last line of the first sonnet (Exercise II) should be the first line of sonnet (a) here; the last line of sonnet (a) (Exercise XII) then becomes the first line of sonnet (b).

2. *Theme:* You are a secondary character in a famous story (like Sancho Panza, Joseph of Nazareth, Calypso, Telemachus, Karenin, Rosamund Vincy, Patroklos, Grete Samsa, Inspector Japp, King Claudius).

3. *Method:* Unlike the earlier sonnet exercise whose theme was descriptive, this sonnet is a dramatic monologue that requires the building (before the poem opens) of a platform of personality based on a recognizable literary work from which to open an occasion. This occasion will be momentous for your minor character—though it may have been overlooked by the major actors in the play. Telemachus, for example, is so slighted by his father that almost any moment in the middle of the Homeric poem would find Odysseus *not* thinking about his son. The son's perspective is therefore liberated from contact with (even if haunted by) the indifference of his father. To consider Telemachus for this exercise would thus offer numerous points in the father's experience for a simultaneous meditation by his son: on Nausicaa, say, who is not much older then the boy, or on the visit to the dead in the underworld, or on the adventure of the sirens, with his father, racked by the longing awakened by their song, lashed to the mast of the ship.

4. *Restrictions:* Avoid adjectives. The sonnets should attempt the spare lucidity of unembellished declaration, using comparison (trope) as your fallback for rendering physical texture and emotional impression.

5. *Read:* The character sketches, some of them sonnet-portraits, of the Tilbury Town folk created by Edwin Arlington Robinson; Reuben Bright and Richard Cory and Luke Havergal and Mr. Flood are as isolated by their experience as if they were supporting actors in a production with no main stars. See also the many portraits in Auden's sonnet sequences *In Time of War* (aka "Sonnets from China") and "The Quest."

6. *Consider* how despite the prohibition against adjectives you carry with you in this exercise, syntax might be made to work to your advantage. Even if you decide to remain with simple declaration, avoiding extension either by addition (**parataxis**) or subordination (**hypotaxis**), the choice of starting-point for the sentence can suggest large displacements. In a poem to be spoken by Telemachus, for example, beginning with "I" moves you in a direction more tedious in its claims than would beginning with "My father." If the son is imagining his father among the sirens or on Circe's island, you might begin the poem with a different pronominal referent (*she* or *they*) in the subject position: "They heard my father singing out his grief," or

> She watches him behind her bovine lashes
> As his legs widen into flanks and hide.

Note then the suppleness to be obtained from hypotaxis, the hypothetical or **subjunctive mood**, and syntactic inversion:

> Had he looked back on us from the wind's distance
> As it wailed the women and the years
> Between . . .

The sentence now requires a concluding "then" clause, either direct

> Had he looked back on us from the wind's distance
> As it wailed the women and the years
> Between, he might have made out a resistance
> To homecoming like his own, to fears . . .

or contrary-to-fact

> He would not have believed in our resistance
> To his return . . .

The perspective of this one minor character allows a writer to imagine that of the more famous one—Penelope, whose responses the son might fold into his own.

Exercise XIII: Ottava Rima Vision

1. *Form:* Write three or more Yeatsian **ottava rima** stanzas (eight-line pentameter stanzas with two **reduced lines,** rhyming *aabbcd²d²c*).

2. *Theme:* A moment of fierce, *collective* attention to some uplifting, visionary, or simply appalling phenomenon—a migration of birds or butterflies; a sports or entertainment spectacle; a tornado or seiche; a political demonstration; or a human disaster.

3. *Method:* Think of each stanza as a **passage** or paragraph with its own climax and closure and the poem as a whole as an argument or drama in three acts. You might use an out/in/out arrangement as in "Exercise IV: Blank Verse Meditation" or arrange your materials in a dramatic arc created by the action's development, crisis, and interpretation or aftermath (*dénouement*).

4. *Restrictions:* Use only images, no abstractions.

5. *Read:* Edwin Muir, one of the first individuals to be psychoanalyzed in Great Britain in the late 1920s, has written powerfully about many of his visionary dreams; see his poems "Adam's Dream," "The Brothers," the second of his two poems entitled "Horses," and "The Return." Read also the ottava rima poems by Yeats discussed in chapter 9 on stanza, paying particular attention to how he begins, argues, and resolves his works. For theme, see also Auden's "The Shield of Achilles" and T. S. Eliot's first and fourth quartets, "Burnt Norton" and "Little Gidding."

6. *Consider* how the limits of the self-expressive lyric are exceeded in the great "public" poems of Yeats, Muir, Eliot, and Auden, yet how each finds a way to maintain great musicality; none of the four resorts to prosaic flatness or rhetorical harangue. Although poetry is a capacious medium, it cannot contain much literal prose. Put another way, it needs the minimal threshold of music before the first of its doors can open.

Exercise XIV: Sestina of Early Intuition

1. *Form:* Write a **sestina**[6] using trochaic nouns for end-words.

2. *Theme:* Write either about (a) the first inklings of a disease; a suspi-

---

6. The **sestina** is a poem of thirty-nine lines, based on a six-line stanza, all of which end with six identical words (with a three-line envoi or send-off). The pattern of repetitions (see chapter 13) is intricately interleaved.

cion; a provocative insight; a new affection; or (b) choose from the fol-
lowing topics from the classroom, some of them drawing on the work—
prose and poetry—of writers such as John Ashbery, Louise Bogan, Ben
Jonson, Andrew Marvell, Hans Christian Andersen, Elizabeth Bishop,
Richard Wilbur, and poets in other languages (Montale, Rilke, Horace,
Sappho):

> You return to the house you lived in as a child.
> You have come to a house in a cave of trees.
> Someone speaking from beyond the grave.
> The beloved is lost.
> Rules for a children's game.
> Description of a child's plaything.
> The death of a small creature.
> Your own epitaph; an epitaph for your best friend.
> Reading a book containing somebody else's notes in the margins.[7]
> Instructions to the architect.
> A note for the postman.
> A day in the life of a poet whose work you admire.
> What your death will be like.
> The uses of one particular beautiful thing.
> Objects for some time neglected.
> You are floating on your back in the water.
> The world underneath this world.
> Someone speaking from the deck of the ship in the bottle.
> Waking before dawn.
> A nightmare lesson or quest.
> Reading an old poem of yours.
> Journey around your room.
> The appeal of miniatures (the young cucumber on the vine; the
>   Battersea box; one of the Thorne Rooms; the ottavo volume;
>   the bee as frost approaches).
> Compose a prayer to a divinity in whom your speaker believes.
> Win in love what you don't want or can't use.

---

7. The most interesting responses to this exercise were: (1) reading a poem by
Wordsworth and only gradually recognizing the marginalia as your own; (2) reading your
mother's copy of Henry James's *The Portrait of a Lady;* (3) fervent marginal comments in a
second-hand Bible.

Spiritual q-and-a questionnaire (for example, "Did you seek love?").

Walking around [in] a poem by Marvell, Herbert, or Campion.

Monologue by a person of the opposite sex.

Your earliest memory.

Trying to get lost.

Farewell to a bad habit.

A view from a window or rooftop.

To be sung on the water.

Verses to accompany a gift.

Ode to a remarkable animal.

The person you were two years ago writes about one of the big subjects (or one of the small ones—say, a scattering of salt on the stove).

Being asked to recall a moment of true happiness.

Inviting a friend to supper.

How to do something by hand (W. D. Snodgrass has written a poem about regraduating the lute; Howard Nemerov writes about playing baroque keyboard music, "Playing the Inventions"; Adrienne Rich often writes of domestic tasks like quiltmaking).

Mentally searching for something you've lost.

Dramatic monologues to be spoken by: the one-eared cat; the dissipated princess; the insurance agent; the orphan; the athletics instructor; the crime writer; the miller's daughter; the third son; the man without qualities; the girl with a limp; the knight of the doleful countenance; the grandmother of the tyrant; he who gets slapped; the log in the plane-saw; the spinning top; the worn shoe; the pair of glasses; the dusty mirror.

3. *Method:* In your sestina, play with the contrast between the frequent **end-stopping** of lines, which suggests persuasion and definiteness of demeanor, and the indefinite quality of the intuitions of the theme. If you have chosen one of the other topics, experiment with the ways diction, syntax, and trope can loosen the tightness of the end-stopping lines. Try to avoid complete **coincidence** between simplicity on all levels.

4. *Restrictions:* First, choose at least two abstract terms as end words and four nouns of increasing particularity. Second, speak in the third-

person about yourself from the perspective of somebody else—a parent, sibling, teacher, partner, friend, or antagonist.

5. *Read:* Auden's "Paysage Moralisé," Daryl Hine's sestina "The Destruction of Sodom," and the poems listed in chapter 13 under "sestina" and in the article by John Frederick Nims in chapter 14.

6. *Consider* how one or more of the thematic exercises listed in no. 2 above would benefit from a dramatic hitch or wrinkle: *but why does that sky look so odd?* or from a grammatical subtext (repeating a root word several ways, for example, *concentrated, central, concentric, decenter*). Also pertinent is the hidden constraint—depriving yourself of certain vowels, like the French novelist Georges Perec, or deciding to shift main vowels every few lines as Daryl Hine does in "Vowel Movements," for example, "Primitive physics a sophisticated fiction" and "Monotony the awful drawback of my song"; Strand in *Dark Harbor* XXIV opens one of his lines to the large melody of vowel passage when he says of the weather, "When it's really an aura or odor or even an air / of uncertainty"; Pope's line from the *Essay on Criticism* is a famous instance of vowel alliteration, or assonance: "Though oft the ear the open vowels tire"—a line that is anything but tiring.

Syntax can also provide ingenious perspectives and side-chutes (recall the suggestions in no. 6 of "Exercise XII: Sonnets of Secondary Characters"). To start a poem (as Auden does) with a "But" ("But in the evening the oppression lifted"), requires some sense of an earlier condition or belief to which the present is contrasted, and to which it will persist in referring. Altogether different from declaration is the pressure exerted on the poem's shape by an adversative or tag of supposition to launch the subjunctive mood. Start the poem with "If" or "Although," as a means (if nothing else) of making flat declarative syntax less available.[8] David Ferry's sprung free-verse poem "A Young Woman" begins with a "that" clause; the poem fulfills itself in unfolding the hypothesis of the young woman's growth as she (and we) move forward in time from the crux created by syntax. Perhaps the descriptive preoccupations that may plague the beginner will also be lightened with the help of more complex sentences and the ideas they kindle.

---

8. Questions and commands may also be helpful to the same end. Furthermore, one wants to avoid becoming a writer for whom the exclamation point is either impossible or chronic.

A Note on Non-Verbs

Syntax can also alert us to certain pitfalls. The following verbs tend to perform limited or specialized work in sentences. The **intransitive verbs**, which do not take direct objects, congregate in the "weakest" column. Among these, the **copulas** (or linking verbs) promote sentences that are like equations, in which the verbs equate nouns with other nouns and adjectives. Even when the verbs are **transitive** and do (or can) take direct objects, the verbs in columns 2 and 3 often provide merely more indirect means of loading a sentence with texture and description.

On occasion, one *wants* to avail oneself of these verbs and of the syntactical structures that attend them—for example, in the flat reaches of the **plain style**. But one should be alert to any exclusive dependency on them. Not only do they cause many a sentence to clog, owing to their colorlessness and their habit of making the description top-heavy, but they also displace the class of transitive verbs that contribute to the most active variety of comparison: the verb-**metaphor**.

Note also that many of the monosyllabic verbs on these lists are not ordinarily strongly stressed. Even those that are, like *give, lend, find, keep,* or *leave,* may not be used in their "strong" senses but rather as substitutes, once-removed, for *is, are,* and other forms of the verb *to be.*

1. WEAK	2. WEAKER	3. WEAKEST
hold	have	be
carry	contain	seem
lend	keep	become
make	leave (with)	grow
give	see	lie/lay
find	own	remain
allow		stay
do		stand
		rest
		wait
		prove

Note that verbs such as *grow* and *stand* are to be understood in their intransitive rather than their transitive roles—I do not consider *grow* in a sentence like "She intends to grow Kentucky wonder-beans" to be a **non-verb**, but in "The sky grows dark," it is. Similarly, "would you stand

the broom in the corner" is a transitive case of a verb that can also—
all too often—remain intransitive (for example, "she stands moody by
the open door"). Even when *grow* and *stand* can take direct objects, these
and the other verbs like *lie* with its past tense, *lay,* often provide merely
more subtle means of loading a sentence with adjectives of mood and
texture.

To test the extremes of possibility with regard to verbs and verb-
use, imagine your examples on the continuum of **diction**. At the ornate
extreme, there is often a tendency for poets to crowd the elevated diction
into the standing elements of syntax—nouns, adjectives, and adverbs. At
the extreme of simplified diction, the more the strong verb with its ar-
guing connectives (conjunctions) will stand out. This latter type may also
extract greater liveliness of *effect* from verbs that, in a more ornate poem,
among the textures and nuances of perception, would be stunned by
overload.

Hence some of the verbs on the list above—in the proper context—
may actually be capable of great power (a good example is the use of *do*
in Shakespeare's 94th sonnet, discussed in chapter 8). On the other hand,
a much "stronger" transitive verb than any in the octave of Shakespeare's
sonnet (or on the list above) may prove relatively inert in the actual poem
(note how strong verbs disappear against the more aggressive patterns of
pun and antithesis in the couplets of Pope and in the monotonous vio-
lence of Byron's "Darkness," pp. 92–93).

Diction and **trope** can also be flexed in exercises. Sprinkled
throughout the sample assignments above are comments about abstract
and concrete words (certain proportions permitted or proscribed): To
know that you will be balancing your accumulating particulars against an
abstraction gives the poem underway a grounding from which to view
those emerging details with second sight.

Exclusions to the Exercises and the Challenge of Free Verse

Two of the poems in each group of exercises above are in repeatable stan-
zas (such as one or more of the kinds of **hymn meter, heroic couplets,**
and, for meditative subjects, **heroic** or pentameter **quatrains**). The or-
der of exercises is variable and can lead from unrhymed to rhymed forms,
or vice versa. Some of my colleagues have been successful starting with
blank verse because it feels less artificial than stanzaic forms.

I agree that blank verse can feel more natural in its mimicry of ordinary discourse, but blank verse also risks flatness. I have been more successful beginning with shorter-line stanzas—say, **common meter**—and ending with a shift away from rhyme to unrhymed blank verse.

By the time of this final exercise in blank verse, writers experience first a release from the constraint of the stanza; second, they recognize the need to make the sentences work harder than may have been required to do in rhymed forms.[9] Blank verse goes well with syntax (and thought) that is more energetic, various, and lengthy. It is then an easy step to experiment with lines that not only do not rhyme but which do not repeat a metrical unit; **syllabic verse** is one example, **accentual verse** another.

The advantages of syllabic and accentual verses is that they provide a framework or limit, unlike **free verse**, which uses no frame but the typographic line. **Podic** or sprung free verse, **free blank verse**, and **biblical free verse** also offer that helpful frame of quasi-rhythmical expectation (different in each) and even of syntactic, metaphoric, and thematic expectation (for the biblical-sublime), which give the apprentice writer and reader some hand-holds. But **imagist free verse** resists any of these patterns of recurrence, anchoring itself instead in brevity and breathtaking stasis. The challenge in imagist free verse is to provide good and sound reasons for breaking each line. Free verse proper must face one central choice from the start: Will line breaks be coincident with syntactic closure or enjamb across incomplete phrases, clauses, and/or sentences? Because the line of free verse (in any form) should not duplicate itself, either numerically or syntactically, each line subtly counteracts

---

9. Rhymed stanzas can often seem, in respect to syntax and rhyme, rather bland:

The race is ended. Far away
    I hang and do not care,
While round bright Troy Achilles whirls
    A corpse with streaming hair.

This stanza from Muir's "Ballad of Hector in Hades" is not showy in its style. But the hypothesis of the stanza is electrifying, and a bit of that lightning runs through it from the fourth line above (see the complete poem in chapter 5's discussion of trope). In other words, the stanza embodies a complex thought in its plot and organization of image, while the poet permits the carefully managed syntax to recede (this phenomenon is known as **recession of technique**).

its neighbors while intensely asserting its own reason for being in the
shape it is:

   Objet

Dear child, why
Is it still, along the pillow—
This hand of yours half
Open on the brightness
Thrown by the lamp,   5
Anemone in
Water the current
Once passed through?

In sleep you answer
That life catches   10
Against the edge
Of its own likeness,
Vein ever blue
In the body's
Marble drift.   15

"Objet" (the French for *object* that suggests *art* object) was a deliberate
attempt to write in the abbreviated imagist mode, playing minute pauses
against suggested continuity. The tenors of the tropes whose vehicles are
an anemone breathing in the current and the veins in a block of sculpted
marble both point (from opposite ends) to a sleeping threshold between
flexible flesh and frozen form. Dramatically, the poem turns on a sublimi-
nal loss of the child when sleep draws the living being away. I was con-
scious also of trying to remove myself from the sentence so as to leave the
parts of speech free to follow a mild but pervasive personification (see
lines 3–5).

The poem "Objet" in places is pretty, but I'm afraid it's neither as
comprehensive in feeling nor as various in device as the poem against
which I wrote it, by the late John N. Morris:

   The Unburied

My dear, who are they years ago
By that weedy river? He has lost
Something and she
Is helping him to find it.

They are only a day   5
Old together. They do not know
The river flows. The time
They will have lost
Closes about them.

Look! It shines before them,   10
What they are looking for.
This is taking years.
If only we could guide them!

No. Though we know who they are
Who are wandering there,   15
The dangerous years
Ago rising about them,

We know we must leave them alone.
For a time thus shall we protect them:
For a time they are wandering there,   20
Though they are lost to us,
Us who are lost to us,
Lost in recollection.

Time and again Morris returns to the pictured image, and as we peer into
it we grow cognizant of peering into the same depths of time that en-
trance the figures in the photograph as they search for something lost. To
reflect the varying moods of his own queries about losing and being lost,
the poet moves toward the enjambing line breaks with at least a half-
dozen tempos (line-boundaries 2-3, 5-6, 7-8, 14-15, and 16-17 illustrate
the range of Morris's momentum). Philip Hobsbaum suggests that lines
of free verse connect in bursts of alternating energy, much as metrical
feet do, one line providing "thrust" (a concept implying both stress and
thought), the next, recoil from thrust.[10] This idea helps us concentrate on
the need for an extrametrical dimension in free-verse form—to give each
line a reason for being that is not dependent on repetition. Typically, I
leave free verse for later on, except in rare cases when beginners reach
some sophistication early in their apprenticeship. I would measure so-

10. Philip Hobsbaum, *Metre, Rhythm and Verse* (London: Routledge, 1996), pp.
115–20.

phistication by a working grasp of the free-verse techniques just discussed.

The Passage, Not the Line

Like the need to have good reasons for breaking lines, we also need to write poems in **passages** and not just lines. There is a danger particularly in blank verse (*not* the free variety) that young writers will simply cut-and-paste: It is all too tempting to generate long skeins of fairly regular iambic matter and snip it whenever five feet have passed. (Actually, writers of some renown have been guilty of cutting-and-pasting, too; see Robert Lowell's early, formal verse.) Now, "passage" is a loose idea, and it may be easier to recommend than to teach newcomers what is entailed in animating the shape of a passage so that it can arch above the individually well-behaved parts. The animating energy may depend on syntax, but it can't entirely be reduced to it; the origin is more a matter of mental coherence. Let me share a splendid example I recently came upon.

Alfred Harbage contrasts a drab passage of blank verse with a far brighter one. Both are spoken by wives who want their husbands to usurp the throne. First, here is Harbage's choice of a poor passage (Eleanor speaking to Duke Humphrey in *2 Henry VI* I.ii), written in the early 1590s:

> Why droops my lord like over-ripened corn
> Hanging the head at Ceres' plenteous load?
> Why doth the great Duke Humphrey knit his brows,
> As frowning at the favors of the world?
> Why are thine eyes fixed to the sullen earth,   5
> Gazing on that which seems to dim thy sight?
> What seest thou there? King Henry's diadem,
> Enchased with all the honors of the world?
> If so, gaze on and grovel on thy face
> Until thy head be circled with the same.   10
> Put forth thy hand, reach at the glorious gold.
> What, is't too short? I'll lengthen it with mine.

End-stopping is so prominent that, as Harbage says, these lines are "simply couplets with the rhymes omitted."[11] Along with end-stopping

---

11. Alfred Harbage, "Shakespeare's Technique," in Harbage, ed., *William Shakespeare: The Complete Works* (Baltimore: Penguin, 1969), p. 37.

comes the hyper-regularity of the iambic pentameter: The **stresses** of spoken speech never stand out against **line**.

Harbage contrasts Lady Macbeth's masterful advice to her husband, written fifteen years later:

> Your face, my Thane, is as a book where men   60
> May read strange matters. To beguile the time,
> Look like the time; bear welcome in your eye,
> Your hand, your tongue; look like th' innocent flower,
> But be the serpent under't. He that's coming
> Must be provided for; and you shall put   65
> This night's great business into my dispatch,
> Which shall to all our nights and days to come
> Give solely sovereign sway and masterdom.
>
> (*Macbeth* I.v)

Notice how stress veers from midline to the extremes, as if Lady Macbeth wanted to turn her husband's gaze in all directions *but* inward. Harbage's commentary on the form is apt: "Although closed off with a rhyme, these lines show no trace of the couplet-making habit since the unit of thought is neither the line nor the pair of lines *but the whole speech* as in the way of a paragraph; and the iambic beat is sufficiently irregular to be unobtrusive" (my emphasis). I would adjust the terms somewhat, calling the pentameter not "irregular" but muscular in its variations—including the subtle forward tug of metaphor from future to past and day to night and flower to grave, as well as the backward reach of each idea to its first suggestion. The most intriguing vantage point is the end of 65 with "put" alliterated with "provided" and, like it, susceptible of linkage with the work of the hand; "he that's coming" is going to be "provided" for by being "put" somewhere out of the way—into that lady's dark working where he can be dispatched from life. The passage from 61 to 68 is full of rhythmical veerings and suspicious halts, until the artificial rhetoric and soothing lilt of the final couplet. True metrical irregularity does occur elsewhere in *Macbeth,* as in the king's conversations with the witches and apparitions in IV.i, in which Macbeth's sentences start and stop frequently, breaking up the lines with a series of shudders. But here, in I.v, the meter strengthens the sinister counterpoint of the desperate woman who can act only through a husband who is too weak for the smile of treachery.

Dramatic verse is, on one level, better behaved than written verse, because it must be capable of being spoken (alternative stress-patterns cannot equivocally compete). But owing to its commitment to extreme states rather than to bland or delicate ones, dramatic verse is, on another level, given to greater extremes of emphasis. Shakespeare as dramatist is thus a dubious mentor for the narrative or meditative poet, to the extent that he encourages magniloquence and exaggeration *in the moment,* in a way too easy to divorce from the dense context of evolving action in a play.

Dramatic verse designed to be acted must therefore be studied with care; what may sound "natural" in a tragedy by Shakespeare may be overly loud in the silence of a meditation. Narrative verse as in the ballads (which tell stories and employ simplicity of diction and directness of syntax) and expository verse (that orders and sets forth a worldview shared with others, as in Donne's *Anniversaries* or the kind of poem that instructs in a skill or which argues about astronomy, or consciousness, like the great expository poems of Milton and Wordsworth) are also **modes** that may require study and imitation, to fathom their working from within. Whenever poetic means adapt to discursive themes, some formulas will be required to move us between passages; the treatment of the line must lend itself both to statement and to idea—and to the means of maneuvering between them, none of the three proving to be the medium most attractive to the writer of lyric (the poem of intense—and condensed—occasion). Some who have always thought of poetry as limited to the lyric mode at first may find it hard to hear the flexible wit behind the techniques in Alexander Pope. But when the features of the balanced satiric couplet are made clear (the close observation of types in society and government, with a particular fondness for revealing flaws; the application of devices of contrast, which rely on noun-adjective doubling and, except for the middle foot of the favored pentameter line, which often remains unstressed, an iambic saturation that favors bisyllabic words), it is not difficult to take pleasure in following Pope's model and imitating his decorum—and even to find uses for the subtle comedy of his derogations:

Inspir'd when living, and bequeath'd in Death

And Legislators seem to think in stone

Grove nods at grove, each alley has a brother,
And half the platform just reflects the other.

~~~~

A solemn Sacrifice, performed in State,
You drink by measure, and to minutes eat.

Clearly, one doesn't always want to sound like Pope. But his verse is a store of rhetorical treasures from which young writers can learn a great deal, including the ability to imagine how forms and themes based on a balance of contraries might blend. Yet more useful is the working ethos of a writer who assumes that every detail of place, dress, hobby, conversation, and gesture, reveals a moral dimension. Many a budding political journalist would benefit from looking through the eyes of Pope.[12]

Literal Symbol versus Cliche

One of the most difficult lessons the beginning writer faces is one that is not always easy to teach. This lesson has to do not merely with cliches of language, but with **cliches** of thought and feeling. As a first step toward helping others grasp why cliches are bad, it helps to know that the French verb *clicher* means to stamp in metal, to make a metal mold or stereotype; something that has been *cliché* has been stamped in a rigid and repeating form, one just like the next.

But now the harder lesson comes, because there is usually a good reason why countless users of language have been drawn to cliches, that is, because to begin with they were fresh, pointed expressions; they gave the same satisfaction as when a carpenter's hammer hit the nail on the head and the nail drove straight down into the wood. Cliches always experience an aboriginal moment when the words all fall right, perhaps especially when they are slightly twisted, as for example in such phrases as Auden's "the age of anxiety," which requires that we know there was earlier an "age of reason" and, before that, an "age of gold." Some cliches may require us to think an idea through, as for example "the exception that proves the rule," for the phrase doesn't simply give us all the right to

---

12. Further discussion of the **passage** can be found in chapter 3 on syntax, in the section on "The Sentence and the Pentameter Passage," starting on p. 97, and in chapter 9 on stanza and rhyme, in the section called "Thinking in Stanzas" that begins on p. 276.

break rules.[13] The cliche "to go to the dogs" meant to go to destruction because only table leavings were thrown to the dogs; if you went to the dogs, you were offal to be snapped up by them. (If you threw the dog a bone, you also silenced him, which is why distraught Rosalind in *As You Like It* I.iii says she has "Not one [word] to throw at a dog.") Pope gives the cliche a further twist when he imagines a wealthy man translating his money into "hops and hogs," then *sending* these to the dogs (see the couplets from the "Epistle to Bathurst" in chapter 9).

To turn a cliche, however, one must examine it and get behind it. Study of word origins is also helpful, not just to interpret puns in poetry, but to reach back to and draw on the material and active sources of the language's many borrowings. A phrase such as "forlorn hope," for example, with the plangent adjective derived from the German for "lost" (*verloren*), has accidentally connected itself to the abstraction "hope." Fowler explains the process as one of misreading a Dutch word, *hoop* (in English, heap): "The forlorn hope is the devoted or lost band [of soldiers], those who sacrifice themselves in leading the attack."[14] As in many of the thematic materials of poetry, notably trope and diction, the movement of cliche is often from the physical to the spiritual and abstract, as "forlorn hope" shows. Knowing the origin of a cliche allows you to use both plateaus of signification at the same time.

Cliches of Feeling

More difficult to recognize when you are first starting out are cliches of feeling. These include all the assumptions that generalize feeling as they whisper incontrovertible truths from the inmost self. I have in mind such cliches of emotion as the idea that spontaneous reactions are the most trustworthy; that problems should be shared; that trying is more important than succeeding; that everyone is a winner; that the old regret not being young; that the outward reflects the inward; that beauty is some-

---

13. "'Special leave is given for men to be out of barracks tonight till 11 p.m.' 'The exception proves the rule' means that this special leave implies a rule requiring men, except when an exception is made, to be in earlier. The value of this in interpreting statutes is plain. 'A rule is not proved by exceptions unless the exceptions themselves lead one to infer a rule' (Lord Atkin)." H. W. Fowler, *A Dictionary of Modern English Usage,* 2d ed., revised by Sir Ernest Gowers (New York and Oxford: Oxford University Press, 1965), entry on "exception," p. 176.

14. Ibid., "forlorn hope," p. 208.

how "correct"; that appetite is finally natural or healthy, and so forth. Not all these assumptions sort well together—if everyone is a .winner, how can beauty be a measure of the good? Vladimir Nabokov suggests that cliches of feeling (to which he gives the collective term *poshlust*) are the basis of advertising, even for periods before that marketplace term or the practice was widespread.[15] Cliches of feeling degenerate easily into platitude, a quasi-profound truism accompanied by a rush of self-satisfied warmth. Consider an assertion like the following, "Death is sad and life is good." Dullness of mind is here matched by the sloppiness of the feeling, and both are imaged in the patness of the expression. Logically, the terms are nearly tautological (life/good). Thematically, the statement is an example of sentimentality, or *Kitsch* (literally something painted or tricked out; by extension, *Kitsch* is suffused with sentimentality and linked to moral corruption). In Milan Kundera's novel *The Unbearable Lightness of Being* (1984), an artist named Sabrina struggles against the *Kitsch* produced by communism, only to recognize that she is susceptible to it as well:

> All her life she had proclaimed kitsch her enemy. But hadn't she in fact been carrying it with her? Her kitsch was her image of home, all peace, harmony, and ruled by a loving mother and wise father. It was an image that took shape within her after the death of her parents. The less her life resembled that sweetest of dreams, the more sensitive she was to its magic, and more than once she shed tears when the ungrateful daughter in a sentimental film embraced the neglected father as the windows of the happy family's house shone out into the dying day. [translated by Michael Henry Heim]

The best advice one can give a new writer is to work against the grain of *Kitsch*. Whereas sentimentality and cliche trap the writer in one groove and narrow the range of association, experience keeps changing. We don't always want to respond even to commonplace events in the same conventional way. Blankets are not always comforting, nor flowers delicate or (worse) wilted, nor are knives necessarily ominous. See Elizabeth Bishop's lines about Robinson's Crusoe's beloved knife (Crusoe himself is speaking):

15. See the second chapter of Nabokov's monograph on the Russian prose writer Nikolai Gogol, entitled *Gogol* (New York: New Directions, 1944).

The knife there on the shelf—
it reeked of meaning like a crucifix.
It lived. How many years did I
beg it, implore it, not to break?
I knew each nick and scratch by heart,
the bluish blade, the broken tip,
the lines of wood-grain on the handle.

("Crusoe in England")

What we can call **literal symbols**, like the knife in Bishop's poem, are always specific before they are general, but because they take on larger, possible archetypal significance, we call them literal details that are symbolic as well.

The Voice of the Object

In fact, the focus on the radiantly clear object permits the poet to perform the writer's two central tasks simultaneously—to describe the world, and to interpret it. To show the general interpretation imbedded in what is literal and specific, it is necessary for the writer to render clearly what is near at hand and to make the poem the record of the exact physical state of the **persona** or perceiving consciousness. The writer should try to *get out of the way* of the experience she or he is trying to embody, while never taking the eye from its communication. This means carefully screening any automatic vocabulary that presents itself (recall David Ferry's disciplined resistance to the obvious term "gravity" in "Seen Through a Window" above pp. 196–97). Vocabulary that is automatic is often temporary in the mind, holding a place in the shape of your statement until the right language is found. This padding, space-holding behavior describes the language that will occur to almost anyone, given your subject, hence it will never cease to be part of that endless social filler (of conventionally approved metaphor) which is language in unselective common use. That is, cliche.

Trying to Be True

In respect to themes, a poet must also labor to be true. Poems do not always have to be heavy and dead-serious, and yet, something must be touched by the poem that can be touched in no other way. J. V. Cunningham thinks this effort is analogous to playing chess, not because of its rules, but because of the deep intellectual design, which the rules make possible.

> The player is not free to erect what structures he pleases within the rules of the game. If he chooses to be whimsical, there are consequences that must be dealt with. If he moves his pieces merely to accomplish a pretty design, an apparent pattern, he moves to disaster. The poet, too, has an opponent. His opponent is experience. The nature and quality of the game the two of them play will depend not only on his own skill but also on the adroitness and resourcefulness of his opposing experience. If experience is simple, unseasoned, without depth, the poet may have an easy time of it but the game suffers; it lacks depth and interest. And if the opponent is dishonest, if he throws away a queen to extricate the poet from a difficult spot, the game will be shoddy and not worth playing. There are poems that are praised for their order, simplicity, and charm that so far as I can see represent a victory over nothing at all.[16]

My experience confirms the accuracy of Cunningham's comparison; at their best, the forms of the game—poetry's rules—permit maximum complexity of idea and feeling under the guise of economy and smoothness. The ease that results is that of tension, deftness, and speed, not stasis. Ease, too, must be learned.

---

16. J. V. Cunningham, *Collected Essays* (Chicago: Swallow Press, 1960), pp. 138–39.

13

Poetic Terms

What is unique in this book are a number of concepts not strictly prosodic or stylistic that suggest an ambitious framework for understanding style. The idea of looking at the poem from within is the first of these. The **continuum,** another concept imbedded in my approach, is so basic to the process of thought it could be applied anywhere, I should think, even in a paper on philosophy or history. **Recession of technique** is my term for the habit of managing all the parts that feed into a coordinated skill, but seizing strongly on only one or two for the effect; piano and painting are skills in which recession of technique is also prominent.

Such analytic concepts help make sense of some of the more familiar elements of poetic practice, which I also define in the dictionary that follows. To grasp the approach of this book visually, I have included the following graphic schema and grouped the essential terms in relation to the **line,** which is the beginning and end point of **verse.** When line is viewed as the carrier of sense, it relates to issues of syntax, meaning, parity, and contrast—the elements of relation and resemblance. These groupings appear on the left. When **line** is viewed as the carrier of sound, it relates to the terms of interval, stress, echo, and stanzaic shape—the elements controlled in time. Note that not all the terms in the chapter appear in the scheme, while a few appear more than once, usually with a shift in application.

When an analytical concept refers to both the idea of the elements of resemblance and to their movement in time, it appears in the middle of the "analytical" column.

My stress on **syntax** is uncharacteristic of literary study now, but will, I hope, prove helpful to the new poet and reader inasmuch as sentence carries so much of the total proportion of meanings in language, not to mention offering so much real variety (and economy) to those who keep it in mind. With respect to **trope,** my assumption that poetry starts with the thing and moves to the thought helps us focus both on the material world and also on how we are to stand in relation to the considerable universe of **abstraction.** The rhetoric of weakness, incapacity, and loss (or **meiosis,** the opposite of **hyperbole**) suggests both a main thread in modern poetics and an opportunity to try on a mask—just to see what speaking through a mask of deprivation rather than accomplishment would allow us to say. The idea of **expandable time,** as a countermeasure to equalized time (**isochrony**), I hope will go some way in making accentual meter clear, while elective stress, the way **meaning makes stress,** and the way **context makes meter** are helpful concepts for getting to the heart of **rhythm** (the way natural speech cooperates with abstract meters). Other concepts (such as literal symbol; logic and counterlogic in rhymes; dipodic verse and unrealized beats; and a three-sign scansion) are borrowed from writers on this topic. My assignment of four freedoms to free verse is an outgrowth of the thought of many others. I have benefitted not only from their work but from the example of the poets, who have contributed to our understanding of the subtle and multifarious art of the poem. Annotations on these forerunners appear in chapter 14. It will be clear throughout how much I owe to them.[1]

---

1. Not every term discussed in the text of earlier chapters is given an entry here. Consult the index for further direction.

The Elements of Poetry

LINE

anaphora
antithesis
end-stopping
enjambment
half-meaning
inversion
isomorphism
juxtaposition
law of simplified focus
lineation
overstressed line
understressed line
verse
word order

SYNTAX

absolute construction	Hebrew verse	juxtaposition
apposition	hyperbaton	like endings
caesura	hypotaxis; parataxis	morphology
clause	indicative mood	passage
compound sentence	imperative mood	phrase
copula	infinitive	rhyming on the phrase
declarative sentence	interrogative sentence	sentence
epithet	intransitive verb	subjunctive mood
fragment	inversion (syntactic)	tag
half-meaning	isocolon	transitive verb

DICTION

abstraction	etymological style	overstressed line
adnomination	high style	plain style
alliteration	kenning	pronunciation
cliche	mixed diction	pun
concrete diction	monosyllabism	understressed line
conversational style	neologism	word order
epithet	onomatopoeia	

TROPE

adnomination	imagism	persona
allegory	kenning	personification
alliteration	law of simplified focus	pun
allusion	literal symbol	simile
epic simile	metaphor	symbol
etymological style	metonymy	tenor
figures of thought	mixed trope	vehicle
image	onomatopoeia	zeugma

RHETORIC AND MODE

adynaton	conversational style	meiosis
allusion	dramatic monologue	mock epic
anaphora	epigram	ode
anatomy	figures of speech	periphrasis
antithesis	high style	persona
aporia	hyperbole	Petrarchan mode
Augustan mode	imagism	plain style
ballad	incremental repetition	rhyming on the phrase
blason	inversion	tag
chiasmus	isocolon	volta
cliche	juxtaposition	zeugma

ANALYTICAL CONCEPTS

coincidence
continuum
passage

etymological style

form follows theme
half-meaning
isomorphism
law of simplified focus

mode
recession of technique
rhyming on the phrase

tension
threshold

METER AND PROSODY

accent
accentual verse
accentual-syllabic
amphibrach
anapest
biblical free verse
blank verse
caesura
chiasmus
dactyl
derived meter
dimeter
dipodic verse
elective stress
elision
expandable time
foot
fourteeners

free blank verse
free verse
Hebrew verse
hemistich
hexameter
iambic pentameter
imagist free verse
implied offbeat
intervals
inversion (metrical)
isochrony
main line-stress
meter
offbeat
overstressed line
pentameter
podic free verse (sprung)
pronunciation

pyrrhic foot
quantity
reduced line
rule of two
scansion
spondee
stichic
stress
substitution
syllabics
tetrameter
trimeter
triple and double meter
trochaic inversion
understressed line
unrealized beat
verset
word order

STANZA AND RHYME

accentual verse
alliteration
ballad
Burns stanza
chiasmus
common meter
couplet
dipodic verse
end-stopping
enjambment
haiku
heroic couplet
hymn meter

incremental repetition
leonine verse
linked forms
  glosa
  pantoum
  triolet
  villanelle
light rhyme
like endings
limerick
long meter
octave
ode
ottava rima

pararhyme
quatrain
reduced line
refrain
rhyme royal
rhyming on the phrase
sestet
sestina
short meter
sonnet
Spenserean stanza
stichic
strophic
volta

LINE

accentual verse
accentual-syllabic verse
blank verse
elective stress
end-stopping
enjambment
free verse
heterometric rhyme
main line-stress
overstressed line
stichic
strophic
syllabics
understressed line
verset
word order

context makes meter
derived meter
elective stress

expandable time

meaning makes stress

rule of two

Absolute Construction A free-floating phrase or clause suspended alongside the main sentence-frame rather than linking up to part of it. "[T]here are clerkes," writes Ben Jonson, "The skie not falling, thinke we may have larkes" ("Inviting a Friend to Supper"); "The skie not falling" is an absolute clause amounting to the proviso, *as long as the sky doesn't fall*. These constructions embed verbs in present- and past-participial adjectives. Auden's line "Doubt and danger [being] past," in "Lady, Weeping at the Crossroads," is an example of the absolute, or suspended grammatical clause:

> Cross the silent empty ballroom,
> Doubt and danger past;   30
> Blow the cobwebs from the mirror,
> See yourself at last.

Despite their disconnection, absolute constructions (related to the ablative absolute of Latin SYNTAX) have more logical urgency than APPOSITION, which is triggered by, and refers back to, a noun in the "home" sentence.[2] Hardy ("The Going") hides the disconnected quality of his absolute construction "No soul foreseeing" (that is, nobody being able to foresee the wife's imminent death) by rhyming the present-participial ending of the absolute term "foreseeing" (a verb acting as an adjective) with the present-participial gerund (or verb acting as a noun) "fleeing": "O you could not know / That such swift fleeing, / No soul foreseeing— / Not even I—would undo me so!" See also the crucial information (in italics here) provided in an absolute phrase by Timothy Steele in "Toward Calgary": "*That wire [being] the only obstacle* / Between the winds and the North Pole." Like PARATAXIS, absolute constructions favor linear play with JUXTAPOSITION.

Abstraction Theoretical, general, or immaterial properties or ideas; the inverse of particularity of detail. Both of these semantic features of language can affect the shape of words (MORPHOLOGY) and thus the sound and style of poems. See DICTION and METAPHOR.

Accent The expectation of patterned metrical emphasis in a verse line. Accent and nonaccent are determined during our reading and describe the average behavior of the syllables throughout a poem. Typi-

---

2. BOLDFACED SMALL CAPITALS are used for terms defined elsewhere in this dictionary.

cally, in ACCENTUAL-SYLLABIC poetry, combinations such as weak/
strong [∪ −] win out over the occasional unusual pattern such as
[− ∪] or [− −]. See STRESS. For examples, see EXPANDABLE TIME,
also KENNING.

Accentual-Syllabic Verse Poems that count both metrical accents and
the syllables between them, thus controlling the intervals at which
the expected accents fall:

> the HEAVing SPEECH of AIR, a SUMmer SOUND
>
> 〰〰
>
> I WAKE and FEEL the FELL of DARK, not DAY
>
> 〰〰
>
> Still FLUTters THERE, the SOLE unQUIet THING
>
> 〰〰
>
> Here LIVing TEApots STAND, an ARM held OUT

Note that not all accentual-syllabic verse alternates weak and strong
syllables so evenly:

> with FRETty CHERvil, LOOK, and FRESH WIND SHAKES
>
> 〰〰
>
> WINE BOTtles of a CLEAR SEA WATer BLUE
>
> 〰〰
>
> HAD COLEPEPpers WHOLE WEALTH been HOPS and
>   HOGS
>
> 〰〰
>
> AS when a LINE ENDS with a COMma—STRESSED
>
> 〰〰
>
> LONG FALlen WIDE. You can SEE how it WAS

Although the lines above are all **iambic pentameters,** their
rhythms differ widely.

Accentual Verse A variant metrical form that prevailed in early English
verse. Also called strong-stress meter. It insisted on regularity only in
total numbers of accents (or speech stresses) per line. Further, it in-
sisted on *ir*regularity of numbers and placement of unstressed syl-
lables, to the end of creating different rhythms in each half-line or

HEMISTICH. The strong stresses (known as "lifts") were highlighted by three ALLITERATIONS, two in the first hemistich, and one at the beginning of the second. The occurrence of stressing early in words and in the lines created a strongly trochaic tendency and a marked preference for nouns over verbs.

Few poets in the modern period have attempted serious work in strict accentual verse, Auden being the major exception. Seamus Heaney (b. 1939) experiments successfully with a line of two stresses in *North* (1975). For examples beyond those in chapter 10, see EX-PANDABLE TIME. See also KENNING, TROCHAIC METER, and MODE.

Adnomination A repetitive device whereby a poet elaborates in differ-ent words the kind of morpheme (or linguistic unit of meaning) called a "root." Adnomination has the effect of punning when many of its variant members have, over time, acquired meanings different from the roots. Milton uses this device when he puns on the word *tempt* by half-hiding it in *temptation* and *tempted* (which do not drive the meaning far from home), and *attempt* (which does). See ANAPH-ORA and ETYMOLOGICAL STYLE.

Adversatives Conjunctions which begin oppositional clauses. Ex-amples: *although, but,* and *yet,* or phrases that act as conjunctions such as *in spite of* and *no matter.* Lord Byron uses an adversative in "Oh pleasure! you're indeed a pleasant thing, / *Although* one must be damned for you, no doubt" (*Don Juan* I.119). Auden provides an-other example: "*no matter* what good they intended, / The armies waited for a verbal error" (from the sonnet beginning with another adversative, "But in the evening the oppression lifted").

Adynaton The figure of excess or bragging (the opposite of APORIA). For examples, see HYPERBOLE.

Allegory An extended metaphor that ranges from more to less artificial kinds of poetic plot and example. One end of the continuum of alle-gory occurs in the late medieval and Renaissance tradition of casting a story about one thing in terms germane to another kind (for ex-ample, Spenser's use of allegory in *The Faerie Queene* casts the narra-tive about the growth of spiritual insight in terms of a chivalric quest). The other extreme conforms to modern poetical use, in which there is usually greater realism joining the imported idea (or vehicle) with

the meaning itself (tenor). Consider the PERSONIFICATION of the
city in Thom Gunn's "In Praise of Cities," and of the rocking-chair
emblem of distracted self in stanza two of Nemerov's "Landscape
with Self-Portrait." An allegorical bent moves the poem from local
associations and literal meanings outward to moral or spiritual associ-
ations. Arnold, not content with the general metaphor "the sea of
life," extends it so that we human beings become islands in that sea
"with echoing straits between us thrown," sensing the "enclasping
flow" of that broad water that acts as our "endless bounds" (in "Do-
ver Beach"). Yeats's use of an unruly balloon to represent human
thought is a more contained example of the tendency toward alle-
gory ("The Balloon of the Mind"). Strictly speaking, however, alle-
gory is an *extended* rather than contained form. See TROPE, META-
PHOR, TENOR, and VEHICLE.

Alliteration Repetition of the same sounds to bind or balance—usually
initial sounds, and usually consonants. Tennyson overdoes it in the
iambic TETRAMETER line "On the bald street breaks the blank day,"
whereas Gascoigne's alliteration is light and charming: "The hungry
fleas which frisk so fresh." Constant or uniform alliteration on identi-
cal sounds, though favored in ACCENTUAL VERSE, is less attractive to
many poets than a mix of alliterating consonants both medial and
initial, as in Donald Justice's line from "My South: On the Porch"
about the grandfather who is "Tapping his pipe out on the white-
flaked column." Each of the three alliterating consonants, *t, p,* and
hard *c* [k], appear both within and at the beginning of a word to
produce an auditory scheme for holding the changeable vowels that
is both crisp and subtle.

No letter or sound commands only one tone of voice. Allitera-
tion on the letter *f* may suggest not friskiness but aggressive pain,
as in Yeats's "Byzantium": "Flames that no faggot feeds . . . flames
begotten of flame"; Yeats then underscores the *f*-alliterations by
rhyming twice on this consonant's voiced version (*v*): "And all com-
plexities of fury leave . . . An agony of flame that cannot singe a
sleeve."

The longer the line and the passage, the more ample the setting
for alliteration; for example, the *f, h,* and short *a* sounds repeat in
Milton's lines already quoted:

> Hell heard th'insufferable noise, Hell saw
> Heav'n ruining from Heav'n, and would have fled
> Affrighted, but strict Fate had cast too deep
> Her dark foundations, and too fast had bound.   870
>
> (*Paradise Lost* VI)

Note that the binding by alliteration here applies to content about what comes unbound when the angels war; the theme of dissolution touches a style marked by symmetry and order. (See **TENSION**.) See also the streamlined and deliberate use of hard *c* [*k*] in the first six lines of "Writing," by Howard Nemerov. By contrast, alliteration exaggerates only savagery when Milton describes the followers of Bacchus tearing the singer Orpheus apart; the word *barbarous* may be the seed that scatters forth the sounds of both *b* and *r* as the poet asks his muse, Urania, to

> . . . drive far off the barbarous dissonance
> Of *Bacchus* and his Revellers, the Race
> Of that wild Rout that tore the *Thracian* Bard★   ★*that is, Orpheus*
> In *Rhodope,* where Woods and Rocks had Ears   35
> To rapture . . .
>
> (*Paradise Lost* VII)

The sound of the words *Rhodope* and *rapture* maintain the pattern, since *p* and *b* are identical except for voicing.

Rhymed verse produces more condensed alliteration, sometimes linked with **ANTITHESIS**: Both initial and medial (middle) alliteration on *w* occurs in Sonnet 30: "And with old woes new waile my deare times waste." The arresting and rhythmically retarding effect of repeating consonants is also audible in Spenser's hexameter: "The feeble flocks in field refuse their former foode." See also **ASSONANCE**.

Allusion A form of **TROPE** in which the literal referents in a work (images, persons, plot) suggest analogies with well-known myths or stories, ranging from direct to less direct forms of reference. In "The Oxen," Hardy makes a homely but still indirect allusion to the story of Christ's birth from the Gospel of Luke, while Auden alludes directly and explicitly to Homer's *Iliad* in "The Shield of Achilles." Less explicit are Auden's formal and thematic allusions to the entire ballad tradition in "Lady, Weeping at the Crossroads." Eleanor Wilner alludes to multiple works in "Operations: Desert Storm, Desert

Shield," pointedly retelling the *Antigone* in modern dress. More knotted allusion appears in the excerpt from James Schuyler's "A Few Days" in chapter 2; this is the passage where the speaker puzzles over a quotation left unexplained in the poem, "Who said, 'Only / health is beautiful'? There's truth in the old saw." Schuyler suggests that the phrase is a familiar adage (or *saw*). But the source is a saying in German by the expounder of Romanticism Friedrich von Schlegel (1772–1829) who thus stipulated a certain pure subject matter and form for German poetry: *"Nur Gesundheit ist liebenswurdig,"* "Only health is worth one's affection" (with a colloquial echo of being charming, friendly, or kind). Schlegel's meaning is not Schuyler's, since the latter's poem was written by someone who came and went in the shadow of sickness and who took delight in a few days of ease; Schuyler's is the instinct of gratitude, not aesthetic pronouncement.[3]

Allusion may occur in several stages, a second opening beneath the first, as in David Ferry's sonnet "Graveyard" (p. 170), in which the sudden eruption of the name of Orpheus's lost beloved (*"Eurydice"*) is instantly paired with the father's (*"Eurydice, / My father"*). The conjunction between the two at the entrance to the Underworld reminds us that Aeneas in Virgil's *Aeneid* VI encounters his father Anchises in the Elysian Fields and that they recognize one another and speak. Contrary to Anchises's eloquent discourse on the nature of universal spirit, however, the father in Ferry's poem is speechless, "not easy to know," having lost his place in the world.

Compared with Schuyler's ambiguous Schlegel allusion (touched lightly, because with a knowledge of more personal burdens) and with Ferry's doubly-masked classical allusions, those of Edwin Muir

---

3. If we look further into the possible context of Schuyler's source, allusion trebles in complexity. As Joanie MacArthur pointed out to me, Schuyler may have found this adage in Wallace Stevens's 1942 essay "The Noble Rider and the Sound of Words" (in Stevens's *The Necessary Angel: Essays on Reality and the Imagination* [New York: Vintage, 1951], p. 17), where Stevens is discussing the narrowness and madness of the spirit that mistrusts and negates art, putting into one category the radio comedians who "regard the public use of words of more than two syllables as funny" and Søren Kierkegaard (1813–55), who believes poetry is unjust to men because it insists on keeping sickness out; Stevens then disapprovingly quotes Kierkegaard who disapprovingly quotes Schlegel. In the fashion of the double negative, Stevens's casting in a poor light the Dane's anti-aesthetic bent is equivalent to his agreeing with the artistic impulse described by Schlegel—one that connects health and wholeness with aiming at a higher reality.

are more in the nature of a threshold over which, once marked, one readily passes. Muir alludes to a famous poem by Keats, "La Belle Dame Sans Merci," in "The Enchanted Knight"—a direct verbal allusion—whereas in "The Horses," Muir alludes more glancingly to an indefinite or nonexistent event (but an omnipresent fear)—the nuclear holocaust.[4] If a CONTINUUM reached from indirect to direct allusion, I should place "Lady, Weeping at the Crossroads" at the indirect end and "The Enchanted Knight" at the other, direct end, with Hardy's "The Oxen," Muir's "Horses," Wilner's poem, "The Shield of Achilles" by Auden, and Schuyler's "A Few Days" (in that order) in between. But if the continuum of allusion were to reach from simple to complex, I would put Schuyler's quotation from Schlegel (for all its verbatim directness) at the extreme pole. At the simple end would appear Hardy's "The Oxen" or perhaps Muir's "Horses."

Amphibrach (literally *two-armed*) A metrical foot in which the arms of two weak syllables clasp a strong stress [$\cup - \cup$], the amphibrach is found as an end-of-the-line substitution in iambic poems (see "They are the Lords and owners of their faces," from Shakespeare's Sonnet 94). The amphibrach is seldom used in the modern period for entire poems, owing to its comical lurch, but examples are found in certain nursery rhymes like the COMMON METER quatrains of "The Hunting of the Snark," by Charles L. Dodgson (Lewis Carroll) [1832–98]; when the Baker faints,

> They roused him with muffins—they roused him with ice—
>   They roused him with mustard and cress—
> They roused him with jam and judicious advice—
>   They set him conundrums to guess.   4
>
>   (Fit the Third)

And with regard to the Jubjub bird in the same poem:

> "You boil it in sawdust: you salt it in glue:
>   You condense it with locusts and tape:
> Still keeping one principal object in view—   95
>   To preserve its symmetrical shape."
>
>   (Fit the Fifth)

---

4. Muir, "The Horses," *Norton Anthology of Poetry,* 3d ed., 992.

Note that the last (weak) syllable suggested by the form [∪ − ∪] is lacking at the ends of Carroll's lines.

In the next example, only the odd-numbered lines conclude with the third unstressed syllable of the amphibrachic foot. Winthrop Mackworth Praed (1802–39) carries off the amphibrach with a light spirit in the TRIMETERS of "Good–Night to the Season"; here he is satirizing Parliament:

> The breaches, and battles, and blunders,
> Performed by the Commons and Peers;
> The Marquis's eloquent thunders,
> The Baronet's eloquent ears.

But for serious verse, the amphibrach seldom comes out well. An exception can be found in Algernon Charles Swinburne's (1837–1909) "By the North Sea," whose even-numbered lines dispense with the last weak syllable:

> Far flickers the flight of the swallows,
>> Far flutters the weft of the grass
> Spun dense over desolate hollows
>> More pale than the clouds as they pass.

John Betjeman is somewhat more barbed in "Death in Leamington":

> But Nurse was alone with her own little soul,
>> And the things were alone with theirs.

Like the other triple feet, the amphibrach can easily slide into one of its neighbor rhythms. Note Betjeman's shift from amphibrachs to ANAPESTS in the last line above.

Anapest A metrical foot of two weak syllables followed by one stressed syllable. An anapest is marked [∪ ∪ −] and often called a rising foot because it rises toward a strong syllable. It is not especially viable in English except for comic verse, owing to its hiccup or "gallop":

> "Though I travel *incog*.* From the Land of Fog   *short for* incognito
>> And Mist I am come to proffer
> My crown and my sceptre to lay at your feet;
> It is not every day in the week you may meet,
>> Fair Maid, with a Prince's offer.[5]

---

5. *Satan in Search of a Wife* (1831), II.x, from Charles Lamb, *The Complete Works in Prose and Verse,* edited by R. H. Shepherd (London: Chatto & Windus, 1875), p. 747.

The LEONINE RHYME in line 1 reinforces the jouncing anapestic gait. However, John Hollander argues a nonsatiric tradition of elegiac tetrameters from Cowper to Shelley.[6] The Victorians were fond of anapests and the other triple meters, AMPHIBRACHS and DACTYLS, for longer narratives: "They had fasten'd the door of his cell. ^ 'O mother!' I heard ^ him cry / . . . / 'Do you think I was scared by the bones? ^ I kiss'd 'em, I buried 'em all / . . . / But I charge you ^ never to say that I laid him in holy ^ ground' / . . . / Do you think that I care for *my* soul if my boy ^ be gone to the fire?'" (Tennyson, "Rizpah"). Note the metrical compression of the anapests into IAMBS to heighten immediacy; this effect can be shown by a caret [^] to register an offbeat or implied unstressed syllable between articulated syllables.

Anapests can be too regular; Browning uses hyper-regular anapestic tetrameter couplets in *Saul:*

"Oh, the wild joys of living! the leaping from rock up to rock,   70
The strong rending of boughs from the fir-tree, the cool silver
   shock
Of the plunge in a pool's living water, the hunt of the bear,
And the sultriness showing the lion is couched in his lair.[7]

But other nineteenth-century poets avoid the seduction of the "anapestic gallop"; among them are Swinburne ("Hymn to Proserpine": "'Thou hast conquered, O pale Galilean; the world has grown grey from thy breath; / We have drunken of things ^ LeTHEan, and fed on the fullness of death'"); William Morris (1834–96) (see Morris's *The Story of Sigurd the Volsung:* "And he hung down his head as he spake it, and was silent a little ^ space; / And when it was lifted again there was fear in the Dwarf ^ -King's face"—the nominal seven measures here and in the next example break into groupings of four and three, much as COMMON METER does); and Thomas Hardy (in poems like "Afterwards": "When the Present has latched ^ its postern behind ^ my tremulous stay / . . . / Will this thought rise on

6. See John Hollander's essay, "Romantic Verse Form and the Metrical Contract" [1965], in *Romanticism and Consciousness: Essays in Criticism,* edited by Harold Bloom, pp. 189–90 (New York: W. W. Norton, 1970).

7. Jacob Korg, ed., *The Poetry of Robert Browning* (Indianapolis: Bobbs-Merrill, 1971), pp. 278–79.

those who will meet ∧ my face ∧ no more, / ' ∧ ∧ He was one who had an eye for such mys ∧ teries'?").[8] Twentieth-century writers tend to avoid anapests—or reserve them for comic or conversational ends, or both, as Frost does; note the rolling gait of his anapestic tetrameter couplets in "Blueberries."

A few contemporary poets have written with great success in anapests. Consider metrical master Daryl Hine's book-length autobiographical poem *In and Out* (1975), composed in anapestic trimeter, for example, "Are the sins of the flesh so important?" Anapests appear more typically in iambic poems, particularly in the modern period where conversational ease and naturalness are esteemed, and, although a stricter alternation of iambic feet might be considered fussy, unvarying triple meters seem comic. Anapests now tend to vary iambs rather than providing the central meter. See Robert Frost's "The Strong Are Saying Nothing" in chapter 10.

Anaphora The repetition of the same word or words at the beginning of successive clauses or phrases:

> *Never* did sun more beautifully steep
> In his first splendor valley, rock, or hill;   10
> *Ne'er* saw I, *never* felt, a calm so deep!
>
> (Wordsworth, "Composed Upon Westminster Bridge")

As an organizing structure, anaphora secures the sense of each line by encouraging comparison between it and other lines beginning with the same words, while also drawing attention to the larger enumerative sequence. Litanies and psalms use anaphora, as do poets like Christopher Smart (1722–71) in *Jubilate Agno,* T. S. Eliot in section V of *The Waste Land,* and Louise Bogan in "Baroque Comment" and "After the Persian." Elizabeth Bishop's poem entitled "Anaphora" (from *North and South,* 1946) does not use the device but does refer to a comparable idea—that each day begins in the same way. See also ISOMORPHISM, ISOCOLON, and FIGURES OF SPEECH.

Anastrophe The reversal of parts of a sentence. See examples under SYNTACTIC INVERSION.

---

8. In the context of the other lines of anapestic pentameter in "Afterwards," this line of Hardy's would be stressed as follows:

∧ ∧ HE was one WHO had an EYE for such MYS ∧ terIES

Anatomy (literally a *cutting up*) Any exhaustive analysis or account that works by analogy with the human body—it becomes a coherent shape only when all the parts are named and fitted together. A Renaissance example is the pair of poems John Donne composed from 1610 to 1612, called the "Anniversaries," the first of which is actually called an "anatomie," which surveys scientific as well as spiritual knowledge. Auden's *The Sea and the Mirror* (1950) gives an anatomy of possible poetic and rhetorical forms, turning on the poet's responses to the characters and scenes in Shakespeare's *The Tempest.*

We might stretch this term to embrace contemporary poems such as Timothy Steele's "Of Friendship" and "Of Culture" (*Uncertainties and Rest,* 1979) and Les A. Murray's "Equanimity," "First Essay on Interest," and "Quintets for Robert Morley" (the latter on the advantages of membership in an obese elite; see *The Vernacular Republic,* 1982); Robert Pinsky's poem "Shirt" (from *The Want Bone,* 1990) anatomizes one item of clothing by its parts, gliding from catalogue to narrative while implying the moral cost of any industry (the poem turns on the catastrophe of the 1911 Triangle Shirtwaist Factory fire).

Antithesis Contrasting ideas made sharp by words of pointedly different meaning in neighboring phrases. Louise Bogan's speaker in "Last Hill in a Vista" wants to counsel some cold stranger "How we sought safety, but loved danger," antithesis here suggesting a divided emotional state. Hebrew verse often uses this and other devices that play off of parallelism: "they shall beat their swords into plowshares and their spears into pruning hooks" (Isaiah 2:4); "Or ever the silver cord be loosed, or the golden bowl be broken" (Ecclesiastes 12:6). Alexander Pope typically embeds antitheses in his couplet rhymes and the extended phrases of which his end-rhymes are part: the goddess Dulness encourages mediocre poets: "Let others aim: 'Tis yours to shake the soul / With Thunder rumbling from the mustard bowl" (*The Dunciad* II.225–26). See also HYPERBOLE, ISOMORPHISM, JUXTAPOSITION, and RHYMING ON THE PHRASE.

Aporia The figure of anxiety, indecisiveness, and doubt (its opposite is ADYNATON). See examples under HYPERBOLE.

Apposition The drawing-near of juxtaposed assertions in a sentence. Words or phrases are said to be in apposition to other nouns or modifiers when they explain or elaborate them. An appositional phrase occurs immediately after the word it modifies and is typically set off by commas. For example, the middle phrase in the following sentence, "Poetry, the art of resemblance controlled in time, is the fundamental form of literature," falls in apposition to "Poetry," the term it defines. A verse example occurs in Samuel Johnson's tribute to Dr. Robert Levet:

Well tried through many a varying year,   5
    See LEVET to the grave descend;
Officious, innocent, sincere,
    Of ev'ry friendless name the friend.

Lines 5, 7, and 8 all contain phrases that link up in apposition to the proper noun "LEVET" in line 6. See the appositions also in Bogan's invocation to the beloved in "To Be Sung on the Water": "Beautiful, my delight, / Pass . . ." [that is, the beloved, "my delight," is "Beautiful"]; in David Ferry's comment about a photograph, "A writing I can't read myself: the picture [of my father]"; and in Janet Lewis's paraphrase of the mummy case, made of "beaten gold, [which is] / A rich and rigid mesh." Apposition can thus substitute for forms of the verb *to be* and in this way be useful in introducing TROPE. See COPULA.

Note that apposition refers to syntactic grouping while JUXTA-POSITION refers to physical placement in the verse passage; both involve logical linkage and the potential for thematic contrast. See also ABSOLUTE CONSTRUCTION.

Assonance Repetition of medial vowels in words that begin and end on different consonants; more generally, alliteration on vowels. For example, the short *a* sound, which is repeated in *cast, fast,* and *have* in the first Milton excerpt given under ALLITERATION. The latter term, however, can be used for repetition of both consonants and vowels.

Asyndeton (literally *unconnected*) Omission of conjunctions and other connectives so as to heap many assertions or qualities upon each other in a short time; for example, Gunn's catalogue, "Parrot, moth, wolf, crocodile, ass, flea," and Bogan's "Mask, weapon, urn; the ordered strings." A device also associated with baroque poetry in Europe.

Augustan Poetry Augusta was the name given to London by the Romans in honor of the emperor Augustus during the height of his imperial expansion. "Augustan" denotes the early eighteenth-century writers, during England's great imperial expansion, whose models and ethos were Roman—that is, urbane in tone and rhetorically complex while laying claim to directness and even simplicity of character.

Bacchius A substituted metrical foot in accentual-syllabic poetry that consists of one unstressed syllable followed by two stressed syllables [∪ – –]. Technically, it is not a viable foot for the metrical line in English because it is never used for an entire poem.

Ballad A poem in repeated rhyming stanzas that tells a story. It may be sung to familiar melodies. Most famous are the Scottish ballads, which project an atmosphere of eerie solitude and forlorn violence.

Ballad Meter and **Ballad Stanza** Generally, the meter of ballads is alternating and the ballad stanza is a 4 × 4 quatrain (four lines of four beats or stresses each), but many variations and irregularities occur in true folk ballads, so that triple rhythms and a 4-3-4-3 quatrain (tetrameter alternating with trimeter) can sometimes predominate. See COMMON METER (discussed under HYMN METER), DIPODIC VERSE, and the RULE OF TWO.

Biblical Free Verse (also called syntactical free verse) A poetic style, tending to sublime themes, with long lines that break according to closure in phrase and clause. See **HEBREW VERSE** and **VERSET**.

Blank Sonnet Like the rhymed sonnet, a poem in fourteen lines, typically in iambic pentameter. Unlike the true sonnet, however, it is not rhymed, and the argumentative shift usually registered at the volta is either missing or considerably subdued. The reason for retaining the term "sonnet" at all may be that this form has imprinted itself in the minds of poets as the essential shape of lyric utterance, hence something to cling to even when its full shaping mechanisms cannot be employed. Robert Lowell wrote more than 360 blank sonnets in his volume *History* (1973) as a means of keeping the channels open for ideas that he would want to treat at greater length, once his dry spell was over. See SONNET.

Blank Verse Unrhymed iambic pentameter lines (five iambs per line), with occasional—and necessary—ENJAMBMENT. The "blank" denotes absence of rhyme. Blank verse is used in place of rhyming stanzas in Shakespeare's major plays, in epics like Milton's *Paradise Lost* and Wordsworth's *The Prelude,* and as a central form in modern poetry by Stevens and Frost. Opposed in influence and structure to the folk rhythms of DIPODIC VERSE. See also FREE BLANK VERSE.

Breve The symbol [∪] used to denote an expected nonaccent in a scansion graph. An anticipated accented syllable is marked by a [−], called a macron. Actual speech stress is marked by a slash [/]. See SCANSION.

Burns Stanza A six-line stanza based on four rhyming tetrameters (the *a* lines) with two iambic dimeters after the third and fourth lines of the tetrameter quatrain: aaa^4b^2ab.

Now safe the stately sawmont★ sail,	★*salmon*
And trouts bedropp'd wi' crimson hail★,	★*sprinkled markings*
And eels, weel-ken'd★ for souple† tail,	★*well known* †*supple*
And geds★ for greed,	★*pike*
Since, dark in Death's fish-creel we wail	35
Tam Samson's dead!	
Rejoice ye birring paitricks a'★;	★*whirring partridges all*
Ye cookie★ muircocks, crowsely craw†;	★*cocky* †*crossly caw*
Ye maukins, cock your fud—fu' braw[9]	40
Withouten dread;	
Your mortal fae★ is now awa;	★*foe*
Tam Samson's dead!	

("Tam Samson's Elegy")

Attridge believes the fundamental four-square tetrameter frame (which he renders "4 × 4") is "realized" in the Burns stanza, while at the same time being "extended to create an effect of suspension or prolongation."[10] See also DIPODIC VERSE, HETEROMETRIC RHYME, and REDUCED LINE.

9. You hares, flaunt your scuts bravely.
10. Derek Attridge, *The Rhythms of English Poetry* (London & New York: Longman, 1982), p. 86.

Cadential Verse (from *cadence,* literally *falling* when applied to speech)
A term for the fall of the voice in speaking that has been applied
(1) to ACCENTUAL VERSE—Vladimir Nabokov and others use it as
synonymous with accentual verse, because it counts only the fall of
the accents and reminds us of the prominence there of FALLING ME-
TER—and (2) to FREE VERSE, because the term can be stretched to
apply loosely to any rhythmic (a euphemism for informal) quality of
speech—see Paul Fussell (*Princeton Encyclopedia,* 1974 ed., entry on
"Free Verse") and Karl Shapiro.[11] The present text uses cadential
verse as an expressive variant for accentual verse. See chapter 10 on
variant rhythms in English.

Caesura (literally *a cut*) A break or pause within a line of metrical verse
caused by an interruption in the sentence form (or **syntax;** indicated
in scansion by parallel bars). This line by Milton comprises three cae-
suras: "Go; ‖ for thy stay, ‖ not free, ‖ absents thee more." Caesuras
may or may not coincide with the divisions between metrical feet.
When they coincide, the line slows down; when they do not, the
line speeds up and/or moves in jagged spurts, as in Milton's line
and in Raymond Oliver's "As when a line ends with a comma—
stressed. . . ."

Chiasmus A balancing device (literally a *crossing*) whereby neighboring
lines are made into thought-segments that match up in reverse order
in the second line. For example, in *The Dunciad* Pope uses chiasmus
highlighted by rhyme words that are subjected to subtle counterbal-
ancing:
    The vapour mild[1] o'er each Committee[2] crept[1];
    Unfinished Treaties[2'] in each Office slept[1'].
The things filmed by dullness and lethargy[2] match up crosswise, as
do the acts of sleep and numbing[1].[12]
    Robert Alter also points out a multiple chiasmus in 2 Samuel
22:5–6, in which the speaker (the poet David) describes being near
death (note that only new lines are capitalized):

11. Karl Shapiro and Robert Beum, *A Prosody Handbook* (New York: Harper &
Row, 1965).
12. The graphing (though not the example) is W. K. Wimsatt's, "One Relation of
Rhyme to Reason" [1944], in Wimsatt, *The Verbal Icon: Studies in the Meaning of Poetry*
(Lexington: University of Kentucky Press, 1954), p. 162.

> For there encompassed me[1] the breakers of death,[2]
>   the rivers of destruction[2'] terrified me.[1']
> The cords of Sheol[2"] surrounded me,[1"]
>   there greeted me[1'''] the snares of death.[2'''][13]

Choriamb The classical metrist's term for a four-syllable foot that creates an envelope of weak syllables within strong ones $[-\cup\cup-]$. In our system of iambic scansion, the choriamb would be heard as a TRO-CHEE followed by an IAMB $[\acute{\cup}-]$ $[\cup\acute{-}]$.

Clause A syntactically dependent unit in which a subject and verb occur. It can either coincide with the line, as in "While I lay stinging in the sand with sleep" (Yvor Winters, "The Slow Pacific Swell") or "That ar as wollffes thes sely lambes among" (Sir Thomas Wyatt, "Myne Owne John Poynz"); or clause may diverge syntactically from the line-unit, as in David Ferry's "Seen Through a Window": "as rocks under water / Retain their own true color." The consequences of both COINCIDENCE and TENSION between sentence and line are discussed throughout Part I. See also SYNTAX and MODE.

Cliche (literally, *stamped in metal*) A phrase with a mass-produced feeling, used automatically and with unvarying sense. The best expressions are never far removed from that pithy exactness that can release into general use and become cliched. Herbert's description in "The Flower" borders on the predictable but never collapses into it, per-haps because his impulse is to worship God's patterns in natural things rather than to describe merely pretty or interesting scenes; thus the detail is always underlit by another kind of radiance.

Often the CONVERSATIONAL STYLE plays off of cliche (as in John Koethe's work) without itself becoming stale.

Coincidence The coordination of different stylistic elements, as in the simultaneous closure of SYNTAX and LINE. Simple or symmetrical syntax can also coincide with regular METER and simple DICTION for an overall effect of deliberate flatness as in, say, Edwin Muir's poems, in which, nevertheless, astonishing themes and ambitious TROPES

---

13. I have applied Wimsatt's method of graphing the components in chiasmus to Robert Alter's translation from 2 Samuel 22. See Robert Alter's "Ancient Hebrew Poetry," in *The Literary Guide to the Bible,* edited by Robert Alter and Frank Kermode, pp. 611–24 (Cambridge, MA: Harvard University Press, 1987), p. 613.

are used. Theme and trope would thus be *in tension* with plain diction and meter, rather than coinciding with them at the same level of experiment. See RECESSION OF TECHNIQUE and TENSION.

Common Meter The stanzaic foundation of the Scottish and English ballads, composed of lines of tetrameter alternating with trimeter (4-3-4-3). Compared with it, the tetrameter quatrain seems "long" and a 3-3-4-3 quatrain "short." See HYMN METER for examples of all three types.

Compound Sentence A sentence that contains two complete sentences. They are often joined together by conjunctions as in Frost's "There may be little or much beyond the grave, / But the strong are saying nothing until they see." A semicolon can also connect the two parts of a compound sentence, as in this line by Auden: "The peaks came into focus; it had rained."

Concrete Diction The opposite of ABSTRACTION in the selection of nouns and the actions and traits attributed to them. See DICTION and MONOSYLLABISM.

Context Makes Meter See SCANSION RULES.

Continuum An imagined constant line that expresses some feature of relation in a poem; defined by the naming of two poles and by positing a series of gradations between the extremes at each end. For example, a continuum of TROPE could range from more to less natural forms of comparison. A continuum could equally be imagined starting with the likeness implied by such devices as juxtaposition and ending with stated likeness (as in a SIMILE). In either case, one would place at the more natural end the LITERAL SYMBOLS, in which the form of expression in words is less important than the progressively more profound associations evoked by certain places, events, and objects (the bird in Hardy's "The Darkling Thrush" and the city in Wordsworth's "Composed upon Westminster Bridge" and Keats's swelling gourd in the ode "To Autumn"). In the middle we would place SYMBOLS whose literal status is vaguer than the meaning symbolized, like the fish that represents the beloved woman in Yeats's "The Fish" and the lilac-bush in Whitman's long elegy for President Lincoln. At the other extreme from Wordsworth, Keats, and Hardy would come usages that bring verbal expression into the foreground and remove the literal referents into the background, as in a pun (see Pope's comparison of two meanings for stain: "Or stain her Honour, or her new Brocade"). By comparing minute gradations of difference between the two extremes on such a continuum, it is possible to compare the way trope functions in individual poems and in different poets' work.

The concept of the continuum can be applied for all the elements of poems (SYNTAX would distinguish varieties of sentence from simple PARATAXIS to HYPOTAXIS; DICTION would contrast PLAIN STYLE versus elevated style, and so forth). Because it requires comparison between texts, styles, poets, and periods, the continuum is a concept essential in a writer's apprenticeship to the poetic tradition.

Conversational Style The use of cerebral and conceptual diction, rather than either blunt or oratorical address. Conversation in verse can range from a middle to high plateau of reference. Rather than employing slang, dialect, or substandard grammar to achieve a relaxed mood of speech and thought, the conversational style consists of crisp diction and self-conscious, but not overbearing, rhetoric to express the thoughts of an educated person turning to (or stumbling upon) serious themes, unafraid of leaving the commonplace behind and meditating on abstract ideas. See Auden's "In Praise of Limestone," Thom Gunn's "His Rooms in College," and John Koethe, "The Realm of Ends" (the last two in the text) for examples. For its time, Arthur Hugh Clough's *Amours de Voyage* (in **DACTYLS**) also exhibited a conversation idiom and a meditative middle style. See **DICTION**.

Copula (literally, *a coupler*) A verb form that links other parts of speech, such as nouns, pronouns, and adjectives, as if with an equals sign, for example, *He is a prince.* Commonly called a "linking verb." See **APPOSITION, NON-VERB,** and **SYNTAX**; also **TROPE**.

Couplet A set of two lines which act as a unit in a poem, either by an *aa bb* rhyme scheme or by the poet's decision to group pairs of lines together on the printed page. The couplet form encourages devices of balance and close contrast, such as **JUXTAPOSITION** and **ANTITHESIS**. Couplets have been used for poems divergent in style—for the briefest poems (see Matthew Prior's [1664–1721] **EPIGRAM** from *Sol-*

omon: "From Earth all came, to Earth must all return; / Frail as the Cord, and brittle as the Urn"), and for the most extended mock epics, narrations, and meditations (such as George Chapman's [1559?–1634?] translations of Homer, Alexander Pope's *The Rape of the Lock,* Yvor Winters's "The Slow Pacific Swell," and A. D. Hope's "Man Friday"). Robert Frost wrote a number of his sonnets in couplets. Also see **RHYME** and **ISOMORPHISM**.

Cretic A metrically inviable foot for standard accentual-syllabic verse but imported from classical prosody for substitutions. A cretic foot consists of one accented syllable, one unaccented syllable, followed by another accented syllable [– ∪ –].

Dactyl A metrical foot consisting of one accented syllable, followed by two unaccented syllables [– ∪∪]. Often called a falling foot because it ends in an unaccented syllable, thus falling from strong to weak. Although popular with nineteenth-century writers (see Swinburne in particular—for example, this line from an Aristophanes translation, "Lift up your minds unto us that are deathless, and dateless the date of our being"; also Tennyson's opening line from "The Voyage of Maeldune," "I was the chief of the race—he had stricken my father ^ dead—"), restriction to dactyls creates unintentionally comic effects, such as Tennyson's line, later in the poem: "Blossom and blossom, and promise of blossom, but never a fruit!" and Henry Wadsworth Longfellow's (1807–82) breathless "To the Driving Cloud": "Lo! the big thunder-canoe, ^ that steadily breasts the Missouri's / Merciless current!" Thomas Hardy's "The Voice" features lines hardly better, perhaps owing to their monotonous execution: "Woman much missed, how you call to me, call to me, / Saying that now you are not as you were." (Note the freedom in the final feet to dispense with one or both unstressed syllables.) The dactyl, being unsuited for the ground base, appears typically only for purposes of substitution in **TROCHAIC METER** poems. Exceptions to these strictures appear in Arthur Hugh Clough's long epistolary poem *Amours de Voyage:*

> Is it contemptible, Eustace—I'm perfectly ready to think so,—
> Is it,—the horrible pleasure of pleasing inferior people?

(I.xi)

> So, I have seen a man killed! An experience that, among others!

(II.vii)

It may be that Clough is unusual in his knack of making the dactyl amenable to conversational ease; to illustrate how deftly he lands on words not always open to stress (*this, that, one, will, be*)—which means also withholding stress from some words (*thing, entering, day*)—I divide several lines into their component dactyls. His hero Claude is nervously excited that he seems to be

        Fusing with
            this thing and
                that, entering
                    into all
                        sorts of re-
                            lations,
    Tying I
        know not what
            ties, which what-
                ever they
                    are, I know
                        one thing,   230
    Will, and must,
        woe is me,
            be one day
                painfully
                    broken,—
    Broken with
        painful re-
            morses, with
                shrinkings of
                    soul and re-
                        lenting,
    Foolish de-
        lays, ^ more
            Foolish e-
                vasions, most
                    foolish re-
                        newals.

                                   (*Amours de Voyage* I.xii[14])

14. *The Poems of Arthur Hugh Clough,* edited by A. L. P. Norrington (London: Oxford University Press, 1968), p. 184.

See also FALLING METER.

Declaration The gesture of stating, claiming, or announcing to a clearly defined audience, thus leading to elevation in style or at least to self-consciously public speech (see RHETORIC). The term can also refer to a type of sentence that states the facts. See DECLARATIVE SENTENCE.

Declarative Sentence A simple sentence formed by adding a verb to a subject ("Jesus wept"), or by adding additional terms to the subject-verb combination (as in Wright's double verbs-with-adverbs, "I reach out and flick out the light" and the double modifiers in "Darkly I touch his fragile scars."). Sentences that declare are markedly different from interrogative sentences, which ask a question.

Declarative sentences can also be compounded by the union of shorter declarative sentences or by adding parallel phrases or clauses to the declaration, as in Jarrell's "I stroke the scales *of your breast*" ("A Soul), Bogan's "we sought safety *but loved danger*" ("Last Hill in a Vista") or the more complex lines from her "Single Sonnet": "Too long as ocean bed bears up the ocean, / As earth's core bears the ocean, have I borne this." See also INDICATIVE MOOD, SYNTAX, and TRANSITIVE VERB.

Derived Meter (1) the meter of a poem, which we infer from a complete reading of it; (2) the abstract pattern of expectation in a scansion graph. See SCANSION.

Diction Style viewed from the perspective of word formation (morphology), word length, and suggestive complexity. PLAIN STYLE (also called "low" style) at one end of the continuum of diction employs concrete words, refers to things, objects, and feelings, and tends to be monosyllabic and have Germanic etymological origins ("the thin blue flame / Lies on my low-burnt fire"). By contrast, when Thomas Traherne (1637–74) speaks of his "unexperienced infancy," or Yeats remarks of a woman he cared for "an intellectual hatred is the worst," they are using a judgmental, editorial diction far removed from Coleridge's simple objects in "Frost at Midnight." More abstract diction, referring to cerebral, conceptual, or conversational subjects, tends to be polysyllabic and of Latin origin: Nemerov's speaker calls his mind a *reciprocating engine of reverie* in "Landscape with Self-Portrait." Raymond Oliver surrounds his concrete details in "Cyclic" with middle-style abstractions, *value, power, moment, vision,* and *essence.* "High" style as a form of rhetoric often employs elevated diction to suggest a refined mode of argument and description and a leisurely, sometimes involuted mode of thought (as in PERIPHRASIS). See also HYPERBOLE for more examples of high and low diction and EPITHET, KENNING, and PERIPHRASIS for examples of stylized diction.

When high or middle diction combines with low, we say the diction is MIXED. Burns illustrates one possibility of mixed diction, blending standard English with Scots dialect in "Address to the Unco Guid, or the Rigidly Righteous": "Their donsie tricks, their black mistakes," where *donsie* means *reckless*. In the Nemerov poem just quoted, the speaker compares his reveries to the movements of a top; there is a deliberate TENSION between the language of engineering and a low, more concrete style:

. . . the whole antic machine
Precesses across the floor towards the edge
And has to be hitched back from time to time.

This lower-style last line is entirely monosyllabic, suggesting how diction as a syllabic limit also foreshadows a poem's themes by affecting word-length, which in turn affects rhythm (because a line filled with monosyllabic particles moves on the whole more slowly than a line filled with polysyllables). Also see LITERAL SYMBOL, OVERSTRESSED LINE, and UNDERSTRESSED LINE.

Dimeter A verse line consisting of two feet: "It said, *Why not?* / It said, *Once more*." See MEASURE.

Dipodic Verse Term given by some metrists (who call it the underlying rhythm of English poetry) to a pair of rhythmic units with a dominant stress on the first of each pair.[15] The term draws attention away from the metrical foot and toward the uniform spacing-out of pairs of rhythmical clusters, whether two, three, or more offbeats (unstressed syllables) intervene. Dipodic verses may combine in pairs in nursery rhymes—

/   \   /   \
Ride a cock-horse to Banbury Cross
/   \   /   \
To see a fine Lady upon a white horse

where "secondary" stress marks [\ ] stand above the relatively *weaker* stresses on the second and fourth beats. Or dipodic verse may appear

15. See Attridge, *The Rhythms of English Poetry,* chaps. 4 and 7, *passim.*

in two-stress lines with (again) a hierarchical preference for the first beat—

> from "For the Bed at Kelmscott":

The wind's on the wold
And the night is a-cold,
And Thames runs chill
Twixt mead and hill

. . . .

I am old and have seen
Many things that have been,
Both grief and peace,
And wane and increase.

(William Morris, 1834–96)

Dipodic verse is opposed to accentual-syllabic rhythms—which means, particularly in the modern period, BLANK VERSE. See also HYMN METER and the RULE OF TWO.

Dramatic Monologue The speech of an invented character whose historical idiosyncrasies are different from the poet's. See PERSONA for examples.

Elective Stress The stress made by meaning on ordinarily unstressed syllables (including prefixes). The stresses on *not* and *thee* in the last line of Ralegh's sonnet "Three Thinges There Bee" ("We part not with thee at this meeting day") must be insistent in their meaning to overcome the habitual alternation of weak with strong stresses, which might, programmatically metered, produce a logical garble like *We **PART** not **WITH** thee **AT** this **MEET**ing **DAY***. Such a line is only metrical as a metronome might be. See SCANSION RULES.

Elision (literally, a *striking out*) The collapse of two syllables into one; marked by a curved line [___] beneath a word in scanning a poem. The most common elisions are the most effortless and involve the blurring of lightly aspirated consonants rather than hard ones (*today* and *compass* will seldom be elided, while *we will* and *ever* and *over* easily become *we'll, e'er,* and *o'er*—in speech, if not in spelling). Elision was needed when poets felt an impropriety in substituting anapests for iambs—so they shortened the words to keep the feet iambic. Many elisions are natural, as for example pronouncing the *-tion* in *despera-*

tion as one syllable instead of two, and words like *iron* and *flower* as monosyllables (although they need not be). The same variability obtains for polysyllables like *indifference,* which may be elided to a trisyllabic word with the metrical form of an amphibrach (weak-strong-weak), or which may be fully articulated, as when J. V. Cunningham disdains to "Flaunt a presumptuous innocence. / I have preferred *in-DIF-fer-ence*." See also PRONUNCIATION.

End-stopping Convergence between the line-boundary and the end of a syntactical unit. For example, the last three lines in Louise Bogan's poem, "The Daemon" stop at the ends of sentences:
> Must I speak to the lot
> Who little bore?   10
> It said *Why not?*
> It said *Once more.*

See also STICHIC.

Enjambment The linked continuation of phrase or clause across the line boundary, creating a certain "tugging" effect. See also BLANK VERSE and TENSION. Examples of verse passages that enjamb can be found under the following headings: ALLITERATION, HYPOTAXIS, PODIC FREE VERSE, SUBJUNCTIVE MOOD, and TENSION. The passages illustrating the ODE and the Landor poem under HYPERBOLE fall in the middle between enjambment and END-STOPPING. See also index under *rejet*.

Epic Simile A lengthy and dramatic comparison in epic poems such as the *Iliad* and *Paradise Lost* that suspends the action in order to give the background for an event, or provide a unique flavoring to one of many similar episodes. For example, to vary the myriad encounters between warriors in hand-to-hand combat, Homer provides analogies not only for the swelling of the war fever (often compared to natural disasters) and the ferocity of the blows (like crashing waves of surf, *Iliad* IV.422–27), but for the cruelty of some warriors (Patroklos drives a spear up through Thestor's jaw like a fisherman who drags a fish roughly out against a rock by a glittering bronze hook—his spear, *Iliad* XV.405–10; Patroklos and Sarpedon leap down from their chariots and face each other like beaked vultures who go at each other with their claws, screaming shrilly, *Iliad* XVI.428–30) and also for the eerie balance of might (Hector and Achilles can no more gain

on each other than can runners in a dream, *Iliad* XXII.199–202).
Epic similes in the *Iliad* also provide an opportunity for the poet to
mourn the waste of so many young men (see the comparison of
Euphorbus in *Iliad* XVI.52–60 to a slip of an olive tree, tended lov-
ingly by a farmer, as it weathers blasts of wind and breaks into blos-
som yet is eventually uprooted and leveled by an even stronger tem-
pest); the comparison also dramatizes the woeful shifting of fortunes
in equally matched combat. Further, as Richard Lattimore points
out, epic simile provides "the most natural and frequently used . . .
escape from the heroic" (my emphasis); he cites the description of a mo-
ment in the middle of a morning of uninterrupted fighting when, in
a very different world, another sort of man can stop what he is doing:

> But at that time when the woodcutter makes ready his supper
> in the wooded glens of the mountains, when his arms and
>   hands have grown weary
> from cutting down the tall trees, and his heart has had enough
>   of it,
> and the longing for food and for sweet wine takes hold of his
>   senses;
> at that time the Danaans★ by their manhood broke the   ★*Greeks*
>   battalions.
>
> (*Iliad* XI.86–90)[16]

The Greeks fight on, breaking vigorously through the Trojan ranks,
with never a thought of supper.

In a spirit of greater psychological vulnerability, Milton presents
Satan from an unusual domestic angle, first catching sight of Eve:

> As one who long in populous City pent,   445
> Where Houses thick and Sewers annoy the Air,
> Forth issuing on a Summer's Morn to breathe
> Among the pleasant Villages and Farms
> Adjoin'd, from each thing met conceives delight,
>
> . . . .
>
> Such Pleasure took the Serpent to behold   455
> This Flow'ry Plat, the sweet recess of *Eve*
> Thus early, thus alone . . .
>
> (*Paradise Lost* IX)

---

16. *The "Iliad" of Homer,* translated and with an introduction by Richard Lattimore
(Chicago: University of Chicago Press, 1951), p. 43.

Milton has also adjusted the material of Homeric simile to his own brand of religious allegory as Sin and her son Death "snuff'd the smell / Of mortal change on Earth" owing to their hero Satan's success and are emboldened to build a bridge from hell to earth:

> As when a flock
> Of ravenous Fowl, though many a League remote,
> Against the day of Battle, to a Field,   275
> Where Armies lie encampt, come flying, lur'd
> With scene of living Carcasses design'd
> For death, the following day, in bloody fight.
> So scented the grim Feature*, and upturn'd   *creature
> His Nostril wide into the murky air . . .   280
>
> (*Paradise Lost* X)

Note the code phrases above that announce the similes, *as one . . . such was* and *as when . . . so also*.

In later poems the epic simile is occasionally varied by moving the VEHICLE closer to the abstract TENOR, as in this excerpt on the ruling passion by Pope; the "young disease" is the germ of mortality; the tags of epic simile are italicized here:

> *As* Man, perhaps, the moment of his breath,
> Receives the lurking principle of death;
> The young disease, that must subdue at length,   135
> Grows with his growth, and strengthens with his strength:
> *So,* cast and mingled with his very frame,
> The Mind's disease, its ruling Passion came;
> Each vital humour, which should feed the whole,
> Soon flows to this, in body and in soul.   140
>
> (*An Essay on Man* II)

Another variation of epic simile makes the formula of comparison less obvious than the *just as/so also* form, and brings the tenor and vehicle close together on the side of the *vehicle;* Wordsworth's *Prelude* provides many examples of comparison between detail of setting in the similitude (the vehicle) and similarly embedded observation about the period of time (or tenor) in general:

> *As* one who hangs down-bending from the side
> Of a slow-moving Boat, upon the breast
> Of a still water, solacing himself
> With such discoveries as his eye can make,   250
> Beneath him, in the bottom of the deeps,

Sees many beauteous sights, weeds, fishes, flowers,
Grots, pebbles, roots of trees, and fancies more,
Yet often is perplexed, and cannot part
The shadow from the substance, rocks and sky,   255
Mountains and clouds, from that which is indeed
The region, and the things which there abide
In their own dwelling; now is crossed by gleam
Of his own image, by a sunbeam now,
And motions that are sent he knows not whence,   260
Impediments that make his task more sweet;
—*Such* pleasant office have we long pursued
Incumbent o'er the surface of past time
With like success . . .

                                                        (*The Prelude* IV)

Important to note is the turn of the tenor not simply toward the mi-
nutiae of perception but also toward the composition of the poem,
whose meanderings the poet and the reader (*we,* line 262) may ob-
serve unfolding in front of our eyes. Thus the epic simile in Words-
worth becomes—not an interlude or device to flavor another sort of
narrative—but the core of his poem about the growth of the poet's
mind. Form becomes theme.[17]

Epigram A brief clever saying in either succinct prose (like the emperor
Augustus's "More haste, less speed" or the historian Livy's "We can
endure neither our evils nor their cures") or in verses often marked
by pointed rhymes: "Like many of the Upper Class / He liked the
Sound of Broken Glass" (Hilaire Belloc, 1870–1953). Donne's lines
from "Lovers Infinitenesse" show a sonnet-like worrying of a clever
point: "Thou canst not every day give me thy heart, / If thou canst
give it, then thou never gavest it: / Loves riddles are, that though thy
heart depart, / It stayes at home, and thou with losing savest it"; and
Marvell, speaking of the vicious circle created by one use of force, in
a style more plain and stern: "The same *Arts* that did *gain* / A *Pow'r*

17. For further discussion of the transfer of content and setting from vehicle to
tenor, see W. K. Wimsatt, "The Structure of Romantic Nature Imagery," in *The Verbal
Icon,* pp. 104–16.

must it *maintain*" ("An Horatian Ode upon Cromwell's Return from Ireland"). See also RHYMING ON THE PHRASE.

Epithet A descriptive word or phrase attached to a name or a thing, for example Homer's *wily* Odysseus, *shining* Athena, Zeus *the thunderer.* Often the epithets are multiple: *wine-dark* sea, *strong-wheeled* chariot, *fair-cheeked* Briseis, *swift-footed* Achilleus, *flowing-haired* Achaians, *eleven-cubit-long* spear. Auden performs homage as well as parody in "The Shield of Achilles" when he applies double epithets to physical quirks ("The *thin-lipped* armorer, / Hephaistos") and when he pairs formulaic epithets for the hero to suggest his primal coldness of temper ("The strong, / *Iron-hearted man-slaying* Achilles, / Who would not live long").

Double epithets may be coded metaphors (*wine-dark, Iron-hearted*) and thus resemble the KENNING. Yeats's "blood-begotten spirits" in "Byzantium" encode the somber moment of crossing over from life to death. In descriptive poetry, the multiple epithet provides condensation, richness of texture, and sometimes even dramatic subtlety; the former are evident in Louise Bogan's "Baroque Comment," where we encounter "kelp-disordered beaches" and foreheads under "weather-bleached hair," the latter in a poem by Leigh Hunt (1784–1859) where man addresses the fish as "You strange, *astonished-looking, angle-faced, / Dreary-mouthed,* gaping[18] wretches of the sea" and the fish calls the man "*Long-useless-finned,* haired, upright, unwet, slow!" ("The Fish, the Man and the Spirit"). On occasion, as in Hunt's poem, multiple epithet is descriptive shorthand (recall "the *wink-and-elbow* language of delight" in Kavanagh's "Inniskeen Road: July Evening"), but just as often the description embedded in a double epithet opens out into psychological portrayal: consider Macbeth's request to the "sure and *firm-set* earth" in II.i that it "hear not" his steps; Macbeth attributes to earth a quality that would support his own stealth and diminish any likelihood that the murder he is going to commit might shake the ground he treads.

---

18. *Gaping* denotes not looking but opening the mouth hungrily, just as it does in *Romeo and Juliet,* act II, where Romeo's "young affection" for Juliet replaces the old for Rosaline: "Now old desire doth in his deathbed lie, / And young affection *gapes* to be his heir."

Equalized Time The literal meaning of ISOCHRONY. See also its opposite, EXPANDABLE TIME.

Etymological Style A style of diction, ranging from more to less natural, that returns to root meanings of selected words. Since words generally originate to describe material objects or states and only later acquire spiritual connotations, the reference to origins uncovers the physical base of many abstractions. A natural example might be Janet Lewis's use of *garner* to refer to both the gathering-in of objects or ideas (the modern application) and to its original association with the harvest and storage of grain, as by pharaohs in ancient Egypt ("In the Egyptian Museum"). Frost in his sonnet "Design" uses *appall* in the same dual way, both etymologically (to make pale or white) and conversationally (to shock and chasten). At the same time, he plays with a serious aim upon the antithesis of dark and light, asking what else could have motivated the white spider and the white moth to converge on this unnaturally white heal-all (which is ordinarily blue) if not a dark plan: "What but design of darkness to appall . . . ?" Darkness has made light its servant, just as Frost's speaker's progressive horror makes his light play on etymology open to darker ideas.

Milton's importation of the word *nocent* (harmful) into *Paradise Lost* IX.186 would place him at the other extreme of the continuum as a less natural and more self-conscious user of etymology, since this word has no modern overlay of meaning. Yeats's choice of *mere* to describe *anarchy* in "The Second Coming" (from the Latin *merus,* or unmixed wine) falls in the middle between the two extremes because the disparity between modern colloquialism and the original source of the word is greater than in Lewis, but the emphasis on archaism is less pronounced than in Milton. See ADNOMINATION and PUN.

Etymology The origin and history of a word, beginning with material denotation and gradually acquiring less material, even spiritual, connotations.

Expandable Time The flexible and indefinite lengthening of unstressed syllables between stresses in ACCENTUAL VERSE; for example, two lines from *Sir Gawain and the Green Knight* use the same meter but whose variety of unstressed syllables produce different rhythms: *The **WALLE** wod in* [went into] *the **WAT**er **WOND**erly*

DEPE (787) and *And thus he BOURDed* [jested] *aYAYN with MONy a blythe LAGHter* (1217).[19]

Comparable to the effect of *rubato* (or "stolen time") in music, expandable time is the opposite of ISOCHRONY, which *equalizes* the intervals between stresses in ACCENTUAL-SYLLABIC VERSE.

Falling Meter Refers to metrical feet that begin with (or fall from) strongly stressed syllables and end with weakly stressed ones. See AC-CENTUAL VERSE, DACTYL, and TROCHEE; see also RISING METER.

Feminine Line Ending A line that ends with an unstressed syllable. This is not sexist nomenclature; its origin (from Provencal) is purely grammatical.[20] See FALLING METER.

Figures of Speech These are the classical devices of rhetoric and grammar for arresting the attention and steering the audience, including devices of repetition, parallel, and contrast. See ANAPHORA, ANTITHESIS, ISOCOLON, and SYNTACTIC INVERSION.

Figures of Thought These are the classical devices of comparison and implication, collectively called TROPES, whereby words acquire both literal and symbolic signification, including LITERAL SYMBOL, METONYMY, METAPHOR, and SIMILE.

Foot A repeating unit of prosody in accentual-syllabic verse, consisting of accented and unaccented syllables. See SCANSION.

19. Marie Borroff's translation of the two lines does not preserve the accentual cadences exactly:

The **WALL** went in the **WAT**er **WOND**rous **DEEP**

Thus **JEST**ed in **ANS**wer that **GENT**le **KNIGHT**

See Borroff, *Sir Gawain and the Green Knight* (New York: Norton, 1967), pp. 59, 61.

20. As John Frederick Nims points out: "In Provencal the masculine words for *beautiful, white,* and *fresh* are *bel, blanc,* and *fresc;* the feminine forms are *bela, blancha,* and *frescha,* accented on the first syllable. If a masculine rhyming word ended a line of poetry, that line would end with an accent (masculine rhyme); if a feminine word ended it, it would end with an unaccented syllable (feminine rhyme)" (Nims, "Our Many Meters," in *Meter in English: A Critical Engagement,* edited by David Baker [Fayetteville: University of Arkansas Press, 1996], pp. 171–72).

Form Follows Theme The idea that semantic and logical meaning is imitated by one of the six elements or (more typically) by some combination of them. See also COINCIDENCE and MODE.

Fourteeners Couplets consisting of two rhymed lines of seven iambic feet each, often made up from, and breaking back into, a tetrameter (four-measure) line and trimeter (three-measure) line. Two such lines have the effect of a COMMON METER stanza rhyming *abxb*. Examples: Gascoigne's "The hungry fleas which frisk so fresh, to worms I can compare, / Which greedily shall gnaw my flesh and leave the bones full bare," and Wordsworth's "Star Gazers": "The silver Moon with all her vales, and Hills of mightiest fame, / Do they betray us when they're seen? and are they but a name?" Both are fourteener couplets that sound like quatrains of common meter.

Occasionally, fourteeners are so flexible that the jog-trot of common meter is no longer heard. This is the case with George Chapman's (1559?–1634) translation of the *Iliad*. In the following passage from Book XVIII, where, still unarmed and prevented from fighting to avenge Patroklos until his mother Thetis returns with new armor for him, Achilleus appears in a divine haze to frighten the Trojans; his voice is compared to a trumpet:

> And forth the wall he stept and stood, nor brake the precept
>   given
> By his great mother (mixt in fight), but sent abroad his voice
> Which Pallas farre off ecchoed—who did betwixt them hoise★   ★*raise*
> Shrill Tumult to a toplesse height. And as a voice is heard
> With emulous affection, when any towne is spher'd★   ★*surrounded* 185
> With siege of such a foe as kils men's minds, and for the towne
> Makes sound his trumpet: so the voice from Thetis' issue
>   throwne
> Won emulously th'eares of all. His brazen voice once heard,
> The minds of all were startl'd so, they yeelded; and so feard
> The fair-man'd horses that they flew backe and their chariots
>   turn'd.[21]   190

The fourteener heard as a line is achieved by techniques based (as the editor Nicoll points out on pp. xii–xiv) on a variable CAESURA (see

21. *Chapman's Homer*, edited by Allardyce Nicoll (Princeton NJ: Princeton/Bollingen, 1967), vol. 1, p. 377.

lines 186–89) and frequent sets of consecutive strong stresses (as in *SO FEARD, FAIR-MAN'D HORses,* and *FLEW BACK.* Line 190 is a particularly good example of a *whole,* that is, rhythmically unbroken fourteener.

Fragment See SENTENCE FRAGMENT.

Free Blank Verse Verse that still exhibits the length and alternation of weak with strong syllables prominent in BLANK VERSE, but with significant loosening of the IAMBIC PENTAMETER model, as in these lines by Mark Strand in *Dark Harbor,* VIII:

> Tell me that I have not lived in vain, that the stars
> Will not die, that things will stay as they are,
> That what I have seen will last, that I was not born
> Into change, that what I have said has not been said for me.

See also VERSET.

Free Verse Poetry without any set meter; lines may break either when the unit of syntax is complete or midway through the syntactic unit (phrase, clause, or sentence). Types are PODIC FREE VERSE (sprung rhythm), FREE BLANK VERSE, IMAGIST FREE VERSE, and VERSET (biblical or sublime free verse). As an attitude toward theme, free verse appears well-suited for an exploration of uncertainties and the indefinite zone between more vividly seen alternatives. See the free blank verse of Eliot's fourth quartet, "Little Gidding Ia," where even the season is qualified by being called a *midwinter* spring, and where the soul like a tree sends up sap that cannot reach all the way to the bracts of the tree because the weather veers so "between melting and freezing."

Grammar The combined structures in a language for generating sentences (SYNTAX) and for forming words (MORPHOLOGY).

Haiku Poetry of Japanese origin; it is a syllabic form in seventeen syllables that occur in English translations in three lines of 5, 7, and 5 syllables respectively, in which a sharply etched visual scene or seasonal detail is used to suggest some ineffable condition, as in this attempt of mine:

> The orchard dying—
> Trunks badged with disease lean down,
> Tranquil in their thirst.

At one point in any haiku comes a "hinge moment" where larger meanings are suggested and the commonplace present time is open to other forms of time; this moment may be linked to *satori,* or insight. (In the example above, the hinge occurs at the break between syllables 5 and 6.)

Half-Meaning The "provisional," or partial meaning created by an enjambed line (as in Kavanagh's "I have what every poet has in spite"), in addition to the "whole" meaning of the sentence (". . . in spite / Of all the solemn talk"). Sometimes half-meaning is as mild as the hovering dominance of one MAIN LINE-STRESS over a second one that brings larger context into view; this is true of our temptation to stress BORN in Larkin's line in "The Trees," when we need to stress THEY: "Is it that THEY are born again / And WE grow old?" But other cases of half-meaning present a more unsettling ambiguity about syntactic role, as in Elizabeth Daryush's "The blighted copse they rob"; we may take *copse* for the sentence's subject modified by a relative clause, "[which] they rob." We would expect a main verb to follow. But owing to SYNTACTIC INVERSION, *copse* is the direct object of the verb *rob,* and *they* the sentence's subject. The sense is that, before autumn can mow down the fields or winter lay its stylish coating of frost on each bright berry, the distorted forces of summer have already stripped the body of earth: "The blighted copse they rob / Already of its last lean hip and cob" ("Drought"). These half-meanings may also counteract or clash with the meaning of the completed sentence.

Hebrew Verse Poetry whose ordering principles are syntactic and rhetorical rather than strictly prosodic; it is characterized by coincidence of line with grammatical unit, frequent ISOCOLON, or parallelism of opening phrases (TAGS) and balancing of ideas:

> Have you entered into the springs of the sea
> or walked in the recesses of the deep?
> Have the gates of death been revealed to you,
> or have you seen the gates of deep darkness?

(Job 38:16–17)

See ANTITHESIS, BIBLICAL FREE VERSE, CHIASMUS, and VERSET.

Hemistich One of the two half-lines in a line of strong-stress or ACCENTUAL VERSE, comprised of two "lifts" (or strongly stressed syllables) and two or more unstressed syllables in a half-dozen variable patterns. The first hemistich has two lifts that alliterate with the first lift in the second half-line (called the "major stave").

Heroic Couplet Iambic pentameter rhyming couplet, called "heroic" owing to the subject matter of the verse for which it was first used, translations of the Greek and Roman dactylic hexameter epics whose themes were the acts of warrior heroes. Heroic scale also character-ized the long poems of Pope (the MOCK EPICs *The Rape of the Lock* and *The Dunciad*), in which the basic unit was the couplet. See RHYME.

Heroic Quatrain Iambic pentameter stanza with alternating *abab* rhymes. The "heroic" comes from the iambic pentameter line, asso-ciated with translations of epic, but which had also emerged in the sixteenth century as the medium of one of England's greatest indige-nous literary forms, the poetic drama.

Heterometric Rhyme Rhyme concluding lines that do not have the same metrical length. Often comic, satiric, or lugubrious, as in these lines from Alfred Lord Tennyson:

> Here are cool mosses deep,
> And thro' the moss the ivies creep,
> And in the stream the long-leaved flowers weep,   55
> And from the craggy ledge the poppy hangs in sleep.
>
> ("The Lotos-Eaters")

But heterometric rhyme is capable of subtler usages, as these couplets from Donald Justice's meditative-descriptive poem "Anonymous Drawing" show:

> Meanwhile the petty lord who must have paid
> For the artist's trip up from Perugia, for the horse, for the boy,
>   for everything here, in fact, has been delayed,
> Kept too long by his steward, perhaps, discussing
> Some business concerning the estate, or fussing
> Over the details of his impeccable toilet   15
> With a manservant whose opinion is that any alteration at all
>   would spoil it.

Many ODE stanzas employ heterometric rhyme. The implied obverse of uneven lines that rhyme are even ones, hence "isometric rhyme."

Hexameter A line with six measures or feet. The length is associated with Greek and Latin epic poetry, in both of which the basic meter is the DACTYL; see also QUANTITY. In English poetry, the iamb is more prevalent, as in Keats's "With hair blown back, and wings put crosswise on their breasts" and "Or may I never leave my grave among the dead" ("The Eve of St. Agnes," in SPENSEREAN STANZAS); Coventry Patmore (1823–96), "Where the religious walls have hid the bright reproof" ("Legem Tuam Dilexi"); and William Butler Yeats, "A mist that is like blown snow is sweeping over all" ("Meditations in Time of Civil War").

Hymn Meter Formal designation of stanza forms used for Protestant hymns, all of which refer to quatrains using alternating rhyme. Folk poetry lies in the background, and hymn writers built their four-square structures upon it. Although preference for quatrains fell off in popularity during the high Renaissance, it was revived in the late seventeenth and eighteenth centuries (see Samuel Johnson's [1709–84] "On the Death of Dr. Robert Levet," the poems of Thomas Gray [1716–71] and William Collins [1721–59], also the *Lyrical Ballads* [1789] of Wordsworth and Coleridge). Emily Dickinson wrote most of her 1,775 poems in hymn meter. Hardy, Housman, Muir, Auden, and Larkin are notable poets of hymn and ballad measures.

    The four major types are (1) COMMON METER, also called BALLAD METER (alternating lines of tetrameter and trimeter, rhyming *abab* or *abxb*):

> The King sits in Dumferling toune,
> > Drinking the blude-reid wine:
> "O whar will I get guid sailor,
> > To sail this schip of mine."   4

(traditional)

~~~~~~

> I wait. On all the empty plain   5
> > A burnished stillness lies,
> Save for the chariot's tinkling hum,
> > And a few distant cries.

(Edwin Muir)

~~~~~~

Put your hand behind the wainscot,
You have done your part;
Find the penknife there and plunge it
Into your false heart.   35
(W. H. Auden)

(2) SHORT METER (a trimeter quatrain whose third line stretches out
into a tetrameter line, the stanza rhyming $a^3b^3a^4b^3$)—
Hickory dickory dock,
The mouse ran up the clock,.
The clock struck one, the mouse ran down,
Hickory dickory dock.

(traditional)

The Heart asks Pleasure—first—
And then—Excuse from Pain—
And then—those little Anodynes
That deaden suffering—

(Emily Dickinson)

I look into my glass,
And view my wasting skin,
And say, "Would God it came to pass
My heart had shrunk as thin!"

(Thomas Hardy)

(3) and the third major type is LONG METER (a tetrameter quatrain
rhyming *abab* or *abxb* or sometimes in couplets, *aa bb*):
Our plesance★ heir is all vaneglory,   ★*pleasure* 5
This fals warld is bot transitory,
The flesche is brukle,★ the Fend is sle;†   ★*brittle* †*Fiend is sly*
Timor mortis conturbat me.★   ★*The fear of death distresses me*
(William Dunbar, 1460–1520)

The cracked glass fuses at a touch,
The wound heals over, and is set
In the whole flesh, and is not much
Quite to remember or forget.   4

. . . .
And while she lives, the unwise, heady
Dream, ever denied and driven,
Will one day find her bosom ready,—   15
That never thought to be forgiven.
                                    (Bogan, "The Changed Woman")

Common meter (or ballad meter) is thought by some (including
Derek Attridge) to be the normative or basic stanza in English be-
cause it is based on the normative line—the tetrameter (or—viewed
from the perspective of **STRESS**—a pair of **DIPODIC LINES**). The fact
that, in common or ballad meter, the second and fourth lines have
three rather than *four* stresses is countered by Attridge by positing the
existence of an "unrealised beat"; further, owing to the lesser impor-
tance of the second and fourth compared with the first and third
beats, the reduction is felt as acceptable. Short meter is also able to
satisfy us because the length of the third line mirrors its dominance:
Even if it sometimes does not rhyme, *the third line is the most important
of the four lines in a ballad stanza (common meter)*. (Note, however, that
although there are four beats—realized or not—in each ballad line,
it's always the third beat that takes the most weight.) It is for these
reasons that some ballads waver back and forth between what we per-
ceive as short meter and what we hear as common meter, or even
add two lines to a quatrain here or there—because the basic continu-
ity (which is dipodic, with a preference for the first and third beats
and third—or longest—line) is understood:

"I was but seven year aull
    Fan my mider she did dee,
My father marred the a* warst woman   *very 25
    The wardle* did ever see.   *world

"She changed me to the layely worm*   *hideous dragon
    That layes att the fitt of the tree,
An my sister Messry
    To the makrell of the sea.   30

"And every Saterday att noon
    The machrell comes to me,
An she takes my layle head,
    An layes it on her knee,

An kames it weth a siller kame,*   *silver comb* 35
   An washes it in the sea.

                                 ("The Laily Worm and the Machrel of the Sea")

So, too, Muir has a six-line ballad "quatrain" in his "Ballad of Hector in Hades" (see p. 146). See DIPODIC VERSE, RULE OF TWO, and UN-REALIZED BEAT.

Hyperbaton An interruption in a sentence by an ABSOLUTE CON-STRUCTION, APPOSITION, or other expletive material. See examples under SYNTACTIC INVERSION.

Hyperbole An exaggerated inflation for rhetorical effect, not meant to be taken literally. The parallel technique of exaggerated deflation, modesty, or self-abasement, is called MEIOSIS. Subtypes of hyperbole and meiosis include ADYNATON (comparison to something impossible, for example, Auden's "I'l love you dear, I'll love you, / Till China and Africa meet ["As I Walked Out One Evening"]); and APORIA (the rhetorical figure of expressive doubt or misgiving—the speaker is unable to find the words for the occasion: "How—I didn't know any / word for it—how 'unlikely'" (Bishop, "In the Waiting Room"). Self-deprecation and even aporia can be transposed against eloquence as in Milton's wondering whether "answerable style I can obtain / Of my Celestial Patroness [that is, his muse Urania]" (*PL* IX.20) or in Walter Savage Landor's (1775–1864) clever quatrains about aesthetic self-disgust:

   Dull is my verse: not even thou
      Who movest many cares away
  From this lone breast and weary brow,
      Canst make, as once, its fountain play;
  No, nor those gentle words that now   5
      Support my heart to hear thee say:
  "The bird upon its lowly bough
      Sings sweetest at the close of day."

Landor's gestures of melancholy meiosis disclose fretful pride more than a fundamental change of heart about the writing; he may *feel* dull (and there is no doubt he whines), but when his speaker can command verses so supple and ingenious, he doesn't persuade us of dullness. The lines from Mark Strand under FREE BLANK VERSE illustrate an eloquent contemporary version of doubt and misgiving.

Poets may also exaggerate in diction, upwards to the sublime mode ("The City now doth, like a garment, wear / The beauty of the morning") or downwards to the world of muck and muddle where Wallace Stevens's man on the dump beats his tin lard pail and the Thames of T. S. Eliot is littered and rank. Of course, the modern poet may also be exultant at surviving her traffic with dreck, as Bogan shows when she celebrates the "sparse and sodden / Pastures that the cows have trodden" in "Last Hill in a Vista." This is a poem that bursts free of its echoes of Bogan's model—Yeats's gloomier meiosis in his diction of impure ditch and mire and blood.

Hypotaxis (literally *lesser frame*) The logical dependence of one clause upon another in complex subordination. Hypotactic sentences can be created by descriptive subordination, as in Roethke's "The heron stands in water where the swamp / has deepened to the blackness of a pool." From such straightforward clausal extension, hypotaxis can move to more argumentative or debating complication of syntax. At the complex end of the syntactic continuum, Shakespeare's Sonnet 71 would serve as an example of an extended series of concessive and qualifying hypotactic clauses to argue a point; note that lines 1–4 of the poem still acknowledge mild "break" at the line-closes.

Noe Longer mourne for me when I am dead,
Than you shall heare the surly sullen bell
Give warning to the world that I am fled
From this vile world, with vildest* worms to dwell.   *vilest

When complex subordination occurs with more jagged lines and breaking of lines, a sense of disorder is created, as in Yeats's "To a Friend Whose Work Has Come to Nothing" (see p. 109).

Iamb The basic foot of accentual-syllabic poetry in English: a weak syllable followed by a strong; it is abstractly sketched [∪ –].

Iambic Pentameter Accentual-syllabic binary prosody, defined as an unaccented syllable followed by an accented (weak-strong / weak-strong, etc.) in a line consisting of ten syllables. The most common pattern in accentual-syllabic verse in English, as in Frost's line "The soil now gets a rumpling soft and damp." See also BLANK VERSE.

Image Something physical that is capable of being imagined visually, an image can also function as a frame for trope in the form of a metaphor. In this way, a recurrent physical or visual motif can become a figure of thought (or TROPE) and a concrete verbal reference the vehicle of a metaphor. Consider the plausibly literal image of the driver fooling with the radio dial in "Toward Calgary," which comes to represent the speaker's recognitions about prudence and self-control. See LITERAL SYMBOL.

Imagism A poetic movement in the early twentieth century that advocated brevity and sharply drawn visual detail. Imagism also produced resonant feeling from its skillful cameos of objects, scenes, and human gestures. The term can extend to earlier poetry of concentrated visual effects such as one finds in Walt Whitman's (1819–92) poems, for example, "Cavalry Crossing a Ford": "A line in long array . . . their arms flash in the sun . . . Behold the silvery river . . . Some emerge on the opposite bank, others are just entering the ford— while, / Scarlet and blue and snowy white, / The guidon [signal] flags flutter gayly in the wind" (in the *Norton* 4th ed., p. 972), or in James Thomson's (1700–1748) *The Seasons* as birds collect fur, hair, and twigs for their nests: "often, from the careless Back / Of Herds and Flocks, a thousand tugging Bills / Pluck Hair and Wool; and oft, when unobserv'd, / Steal from the Barn a Straw" ("Spring"). See IMAGIST FREE VERSE.

Imagist Free Verse One of four types of FREE VERSE, favored by the high modernists, who were led by Ezra Pound, in which IMAGISM correlates with brevity of word, idea, and line.

Imperative A form of sentence in which commands are given, using verbs stripped of personal pronouns (although the subject-pronoun *you* is understood). See IMPERATIVE MOOD.

Imperative Mood When the verb in a sentence is used to express commands, we say it is in the imperative mood. All imperatives are assumed to occur in the present tense, even if they imply acts that must be completed in the future. Adam in Book IX of *Paradise Lost* says to Eve "Go," giving as a reason that when she stays under coercion she is more distant from him than if she had left him. *Go* is a verb in the imperative mood. So is Hope's urging that the reader imagine poor Friday in London, "*Picture* his situation if you can" ("Man Friday"). Verbs of command are also prevalent in Auden's "Lady, Weeping at the Crossroads": *Bribe the birds, Wear out patience, Cross the rotten bridge, Climb the . . . staircase, Cross the . . . ballroom, Find the penknife, Plunge it;* the poem moves through time and space in the imperative mood. Contrast with these commands the habit of DECLARATION of verbs in the INDICATIVE MOOD and with the hypotheses of the SUBJUNC-TIVE MOOD.

Implied Offbeat The unstressed syllable a listener reflexively supplies between stressed syllables or between one unstressed syllable and a stress to equalize the interval between stresses in a metrical poem:

> Hink ^ ^ spink ^ the pud ^ dings stink
> The fat ^ begins ^ to fry
> Nobody at home, ^ but jumping ^ Joan
> Father, ^ mother, and I[22]

Most nursery rhymes are organized rhythmically by the unspoken offbeat (indicated by a caret). See also ISOCHRONY (equalized time) and UNREALIZED BEAT.

Indicative Mood A form of sentence based on statements about things as they are (it *indicates* them) rather than as they might be. Contrasts with the more hypothetically bent SUBJUNCTIVE MOOD. Unlike these others, however, indicative verbs can occur in any tense, from present and future to past, past-perfect, and future-perfect. All DE-CLARATIVE SENTENCES are in the indicative, but may be either simple, compound, or complex. See SYNTAX.

Infinitive (literally, *unconfined, unlimited*) The simple or uninflected form of a verb, expressing being or movement without reference to person or tense; given in English with the preposition *to* as in *to be, to fly, to sleep, to write*. The final line of Tennyson's "Ulysses" comprises a series of infinitives: "To strive, to seek, to find, and not to yield"; so does Hamlet's soliloquy in III.i with its periodic reference to abstract states: "To be, or not to be . . . To die, to sleep— / To sleep—per-chance to dream." Hamlet's indecision is mirrored by the indefinite shape of his formulations about actions, with no actors, and no time.

---

22. *The Nursery Rhymes of England,* edited by James Orchard Halliwell (London: The Percy Society, 1842), p. 87.

Intervals The pattern created by the metrical expectation of nonaccents that alternate with accents (English verse typically counts both the line's length in terms of the number of accents or beats and the interval between these beats). The intervals are defined by the set recurrence of syllables that are not stressed in speech.

Intransitive Verb A verb that does not take an object, used to describe a condition or the progress of a state. Fosters more descriptive themes than sentences with TRANSITIVE VERBS, by means of which agents (subjects) perform acts upon or make changes in objects of the action. Compared with the "equation" of *a* with *b* in sentences based on intransitives (for example, "the alder-pool *is* a black miry swamp" [Elizabeth Daryush]), sentences with transitive verbs provide a second, subtler means of making TROPES, as in Yeats's wild swans, who "paddle in the cold / Companionable streams or *climb* the air." See COPULA and NON-VERB.

Inversion See METRICAL INVERSION; SYNTACTIC INVERSION.

Ionic See RISING IONIC.

Isochrony (literally *equalized time*) The rhythmic organization of speech into equal intervals of time that occurs only in ACCENTUAL-SYLLABIC VERSE. Isochrony operates in such a way that the distance between stressed syllables is held constant in speech regardless of the number of syllables between them; unstressed syllables between stresses are either lengthened (by supplying IMPLIED OFFBEATS) or shortened in timing (by a species of metrical elision) in order to keep the intervals isochronous, or temporally equivalent. The opposite of EXPANDABLE TIME.

Isocolon The repetition of the same phrase-, sentence-, or clausal-frame on successive occasions. A feature of prose that sometimes coincides in both prose and poetry with ANAPHORA, as in Cassius's fretful and hectic speeches, in which he tries to implicate Caesar in the omens that surround that leader; Cassius addresses the credulous Casca:

> But if you would consider the true cause—
> Why all these fires, why all these gliding ghosts.
> Why birds and beasts, [depart] from quality and kind;

> Why old men, fools, and children calculate;
> Why all these things change from their ordinance . . .
>
> (*Julius Caesar* I.iii)

Cassius concludes that heaven wished to make the time seem monstrous to warn all Rome against this man. The repeating phrases that question the weird events also specify why they should frighten the listener.

Isometric Rhyme See HETEROMETRIC RHYME.

Isomorphism In poetry, the instinctive granting of equivalent weight to equivalent forms (primarily, the equivalent weight given to *lines*). This equivalence in substance between any two line-units in a poem results from the fact that each line represents an auditory and/or thematic unit of meaning. Upon this instinctive equivalence are built many rhetorical structures of repetition and balance. Some poems formally exploit a balanced equivalence. See Yeats's "A Drinking Song," in which the material act of drinking the substance of the wine is paralleled to the spiritual act of drinking in the beloved's appearance: "I lift the glass to my mouth, / I look at you and I sigh." In free-verse poems, the absence of formal balance and continuity can still foster isomorphic links, so strong is the psychological expectation of meaning deriving from JUXTAPOSITION. Donald Justice underscores this expectation with rhyme (see HETEROMETRIC RHYME) just as the Bible does with parallelism (see example under **HEBREW VERSE**). See also **ANAPHORA**, **ANTITHESIS**, and **COUPLET**.

Juxtaposition Conspicuous joining of comparable, even if contrasting, terms. For example, in the lines from "A Drinking Song," quoted in the entry on ISOMORPHISM above, Yeats implies not just a temporal link but also an emotional parallel between the two actions described. Elizabeth Bishop juxtaposes a line describing the face of the circus horse with one noting his role in holding up his companion figure in "Cirque d'Hiver": "His eyes are glossy black. / He bears a little dancer on his back." Rhyme supports the cause-effect relation between the expression in the horse's eyes and the unflattering burden on his back. However, the contrast and contradiction that results from juxtaposition in neighboring lines, can also result in what seems like non sequitur (disconnected observation) as in Auden's "The Fall of Rome":

In a lonely field the rain
Lashes an abandoned train;
Outlaws fill the mountain caves.

But discontinuity stemming from these juxtapositions disappears on consideration: postindustrial debris—the giant limbs and cradles of abandoned machines (or useless ideas)—can indeed suggest the likelihood of aberrant social behavior. See also ANTITHESIS, APPOSITION, ISOMORPHISM, COUPLET.

Kenning A metaphorical name made up of two substitute nouns in a compound phrase, for example, *whale-road* for sea, *sea-steed* for ship, *bone-house* for body, *sword-storm* for war, sea-robe (*mere-hraegl*) for sail. The object in kennings is periphrastic—to sidestep the obvious name in preference to an indirect, evocative one. A passage from George Darley's (1795–1846) *Ethelstan; or the Battle of Brunaburgh* illustrates the habit of noun substitution characteristic of kennings:

O'er the wild gannet's bath
Come the Norse coursers!
O'er the whale's inheritance
Gloriously steering!
With beaked heads peering,
Deep-plunging, high-rearing . . .

The curious expressions "gannet's bath" and "whale's inheritance" are kennings referring to the sea; the "Norse coursers" are Norse ships with their prows like "beaked heads." (Poets of the kenning do not trouble about MIXED TROPE, as here Darley compares the ships to horses but then gives them the traits of birds.) Note how the doubling of nouns suggests to Darley the doubling of epithets ("Deep-plunging"; later his sea-steeds are "Creamy-neck'd" and "pitchy-ribb'd"). Antique authority for double EPITHETS would come from Homer; closer in time, the AUGUSTAN poet Alexander Pope employs such descriptive periphrases as "Sea-born Brothers" to refer to England's rivers, supposedly born of Oceanus and Tethys ("Windsor-Forest" 337). In the same poem also occurs one of Pope's most famous periphrastic inventions, revealing fish under the riddling phrase "Scaly Breed" ("Windsor-Forest" 139), which he alters to "Finny Prey" in *The Rape of the Lock* I.26. In another example of "elegant variation," Pope wittily substitutes "*China's* Earth" for tea when the card players stop for refreshment in *The Rape's* canto three:

> From silver Spouts the grateful Liquors glide,
> While *China's* Earth receives the smoking Tyde.   110

Pope's energy is primarily descriptive and in judgment satiric. By contrast, the minor poet George Darley's bent is celebratory and narrative—he tries, with some success, to render Anglo-Saxon rhythms and diction; even if his poem has an antiquated style, Darley deploys it with zest. The diction of Seamus Heaney (b. 1939) is considerably more ingenious; he domesticates the alien themes of Anglo-Saxon poetry by launching one epic substitution: Instead of recorded territorial aggression (battle, mythic voyages, teamwork) whose setting is the sea, Heaney writes of the slow and violent prehistoric ages represented by the icy north-European bog. "Earth-pantry, bone-vault, / sun-bank," he calls the bog that embalms whatever falls into it; it is at once archaic tomb and garbage tip, treating man and weapon to the same rapacious humbling: "Insatiable bride. / Sword-swallower." [23] Other use of the kenning may, like Heaney's, also permit meditation rather than formula (for examples see the close of chapter 5, on trope). See also EPITHET and PERIPHRASIS.

Law of Simplified Focus Our spontaneous identification with a single object in a stylized landscape. (Many LITERAL SYMBOLS prompt us to identify with them.) Occasionally, attention on one focal object will veer over to focus on a random or residual detail (as the shadow of Achilles in Edwin Muir's "Ballad of Hector in Hades" shifts to the flowers and wayside dust, which Hector finds himself staring at as he runs). Under pressure, the idle detail becomes meaningful. Poems that begin in profusion (like many of Philip Larkin's descriptive-meditative poems) must learn to cull, from the distractions, the concentrated gaze of understanding. For this more intense gaze, in the end, metaphor is preferable to description.

Leonine Verse The poetic technique in Romanesque Latin of two-syllabled rhyming at line ends and after a midline caesura, creating the effect of a couplet in one line instead of two. The rhyme is based on word endings and thus tends to implicate the same parts of speech with identical syntactic functions. This technique was originally used by the Goliard poets:

---

23. Seamus Heaney, "Kinship," from the volume *North* (1975), included in his *Poems 1965–1975* (New York: Farrar Straus Giroux, 1980), pp. 195–206.

*"Florem Flora **TENE**," tua vox cantus philo**MENE**.*
*Oscula des **FLORI**, rubeo flos convenit **ORI**.*
*Flos in pic**TURA** non est flos, immo fig**URA**;*
*Qui pingit **FLOREM** non pingit floris od**OREM**.*

(Carmina Burana 147)

Peter Abelard (1079–1142) also uses the Leonine rhymes in his lament:

Hebet sidus laeti visus
Cordis nubilo.
Tepet oris mei risus
Carens jubilo.

Nine of the twelve words rhyme, with alliteration and stress-contour binding *Carens* to *Cordis*. Thus *mei* and *laeti* are the only words not woven into the tight leonine pattern—though their final syllables do rhyme.

Leonine rhyme was used in early ballads in English which also rhyme often, for ease of recall, as in these lines from Richard Rolle (d. 1349): "My sange is in *SIHTING* [sighing], My life is in *LANG-INGE* [longing], / Till I thee se, my *KING,* So fair in thy *SHINING.*"[24]

Edward Lear uses leonine rhyme in "The Owl and the Pussycat": "They took some *HONEY* and plenty of *MONEY*. . . . They dined on *MINCE* and slices of *QUINCE.*" Charles Carryl (1841–1920) also used leonine rhyme: "It's nobody's *HABIT* to ride on a *RABBIT.*"[25] Kipling has one triple leonine rhyme in "Seal Lullaby" (the other lines are end-rhymed): "Where *BILLOW* meets *BILLOW,* there soft be thy *PILLOW.*"

Light Rhyme The rhyme of a syllable stressed in speech, such as *well,* with a secondary or unstressed syllable, such as the *-le* in *peaceable.* The game is heavier when *alloys* rhymes with *boys* (as in Auden's *Letter to Lord Byron*) or *some* rhymes with *random* (Philip Larkin, "Church

---

24. The excerpt from the *Carmina Burana* appears in K. P. Harrington, ed., *Medieval Latin* [1925] (Chicago: University of Chicago Press, 1962). The lines from Rolle appear in R. T. Davies, ed., *Medieval English Lyrics* (Evanston, IL: Northwestern University Press, 1964). The lines attributed to Abelard appear in P. S. Allen, ed., *Medieval Latin Lyrics* (Chicago: University of Chicago Press, 1931).

25. Carryl, in Iona and Peter Opie, eds., *The Oxford Book of Children's Verse* (Oxford and New York: Oxford University Press, 1973), p. 306.

Going") or when Robert Bridges rhymes *paw* with *outlaw*,[26] for Lar-
kin rhymes two *un*stressed syllables, while Bridges rhymes the
weaker syllable of a bisyllabic word formed of two words equally
stressed when free-standing (*out* and *law*). Meter is further ruffled
when Larkin brings together (in "Church Going") the last syllable of
reverence (which coincides with a strong metrical place in the iambic
line) and the last syllable of *silence* (which is supernumerary). The rule
would be that natural TROCHEES (like *silence* and *random*) create
greater metrical tension when they rhyme with syllables that yield to
iambic meter (like **RE**-*ver*-**ence**).

Like Endings (*homoeoteleuton*) A feature of grammar which denotes par-
allels of meaning owing to the words' role in the sentence. Only the
same parts of speech will acquire the same inflections or endings to
show case and function, as Chaucer does in the many nouns ending
in -*nesse* and -*ioun* (like *discrecioun/divisioun* in *The Knight's Tale,* ll.
1799–80, and in the following pair of excerpts. In the first, the Wife
of Bath argues that in the Epistles St. Paul does not tell her she could
marry but once:

> But of no nombre mencioun made he,
> Of bigamye, or of octogamye;
> Why sholde men speke of it vileynye?★   ★*reproachfully*
> > (Chaucer, "The Wife of Bath's Prologue," lines 32–34)

Note that there are additional unstressed syllables at the ends of lines
33 and 34 (the articulated -*e*), and at the ends of each of the following
four lines, which rhyme on endings; it makes great mischief, says the
Wife of Bath,

> To wedde a povre womman, for costage★;   ★*expense*
> And if that she be riche, of heigh parage,★   ★*descent* 250
> Thanne seistow★ that it is a tormentrie   ★*do you see*
> To suffre hire★ pride and hire malencolie.   ★*her*

Use of like endings instead of either pure rhyme or rhyme on root-
syllables (or *no* rhyme as in Greek and Latin poetry) occurs when

---

26. "Within the peach-clad walls the old outlaw, / The Roman wolf, scratches with
privy paw." James McAuley quotes the Bridges lines in his *Versification: A Short Introduction*
(Michigan State University Press, 1966), p. 17.

the roles of prose and verse are in flux. See RHYME and LEONINE VERSE.

Linked Form Poem in which entire lines repeat in thematic and substantive form, with progressive shifts in meaning, rather than echoically, as in a REFRAIN. When the lines are by another writer, as in the four-line text used as an epigraph in the glosa and deployed one each at the ends of the glosa's four stanzas, the reverberations of irony and layering increase. Linked forms may be either indefinite in length, like the glosa and pantoum, or of fixed shape and length, like the villanelle and the triolet.

The villanelle, literally rustic or pastoral, is a complex 19-line French form in tercets with a final quatrain, in which the first and third lines repeat throughout as refrains, coming together again in the final couplet; a rhyme scheme of *aba* is maintained. Dylan Thomas's "Do Not Go Gentle" is the most familiar, although Elizabeth Bishop's "One Art" may be among the best examples of the villanelle in English.

The triolet is a brief (not additive), eight-line stanza form, which, like the sonnet, is complete after one instance. The triolet has only two rhymes, five distinct lines, and two lines (the first and second) that repeat verbatim, creating three identical A lines and 2 identical B lines in the brief span of eight. The aim is to mask the artifice of the frame with a naturalness of speech and feeling, as in this example of Hardy's:

> At a Hasty Wedding
>
> If hours be years the twain are blest,
> For now they solace swift desire
> By bonds of every bond the best,
> If hours be years. The twain are blest
> Do eastern stars slope never west,   5
> Nor pallid ashes follow fire:
> If hours be years the twain are blest,
> For now they solace swift desire.

Best for the triolet are repeating lines which can lend double allegiance to the sentences that precede and come after (see line 4). Occasionally, as in "Birds at Winter Nightfall," Hardy splits the one-sentence line "Around the house the flakes fly faster" into three

syntactic groups, a leftover (or *rejet*), a short exclamation, and a pre-
view of the next line: "... berries are gone / From holly and
cotonea-aster / *Around the house. The flakes fly!—faster* / Shutting in-
doors that crumb-outcaster / We used to see. . . ." So many divisions
in a poem of so few lines may detract from naturalness and draw too
much attention to the stitches holding the poem's seams together.

Of the indefinitely long linked forms, the glosa is less demanding
than the pantoum. Its four stanzas are limited only by metrical sym-
metry with the four-line excerpt (often printed as an EPIGRAM) and
by the requirement of placing one of the lines of this borrowed poem
at the end of each of the stanzas in turn. The stanzas need not rhyme,
nor need they be of equal numbers of lines. The glosa is the only
linked form mentioned here that stipulates borrowing, although the
other three may also employ it.

The pantoum is another interlinked-chain poem whose length is
indefinite; it begins and ends with the same line and creates a pattern
in which the second and fourth lines of each stanza serve as the first
and second lines of the next:

Plague Summer

Homage to Albert Camus

The leaden heat beats down on the deadening drum
The dusty town rolls out, wave after wave
Stifling the sea and in delirium
Plunging alike the foolish and the grave.

The dusty town rolls out, wave after wave,   5
An evening like a golden-reddish shroud,
Plunging alike the foolish and the grave
Into the alien vacuum of a crowd

Which evening like a golden-reddish shroud
Tints with its lurid climate of soft smoke.   10
Into the alien vacuum of the crowd
Fear passes with the knife beneath its cloak,

Tints, with its lurid climate of soft smoke
—Is it the drumming of extinguished souls?
Fear passes with the scythe beneath its cloak,   15
Hooding from our gaze its empty holes.
~

Is it the drumming of unnumbered souls
Timed to the eerie whistling of the plague
Hooding from our gaze its flashing coals
We hear now from a distance, horrible and vague?   20

    Timed to the eerie whistling of the plague
    Stifling the sea, and in delirium,
    We hear now from a distance, horrible and vague,
    The leaden heat beat down on the deadened drum.[27]
This poem was helped considerably by dwelling on and varying
phrases by Camus.

    Like the SESTINA and the SONNET, linked forms ask poets to pay
homage to repetitive technique until its chimes and echoes become
quiet—or familiar—enough to speak for themselves.

Limerick Comic poem alternating trimeter and dimeter triple measures
(anapests and amphibrachs) in the following five-line stanzaic pat-
tern: $a^3a^3b^2b^2a^3$—

    There was an old person of China,
    Whose daughters were Jiska and Dinah,
    Amelia and Fluffy, Olivia and Chuffy,
    And all of them settled in China.

    There was a young lady of Greenwich,
    Whose garments were border'd with Spinach;
    But a large spotty Calf, bit her shawl quite in half,
    Which alarmed that young lady of Greenwich.[28]
Edward Lear (1812–88) typically presents his limericks with both *"b"*
rhymes together on the same four-beat line. His limericks thus com-
bine into SHORT METER.

Line The primary formal unit in poetry; the medium of expression po-
etry has and prose lacks. Lines are either end-stopped to coincide
with syntax or enjambed into the next line.

---

27. Mary Kinzie, "Plague Summer," *Summers of Vietnam and Other Poems* (Riverdale,
NY: Sheep Meadow, 1990), p. 100.
28. Edward Lear, *A Book of Nonsense* [1846] (New York: Knopf, 1992), pp. 174
and 204.

Lineation The technique of making lines of verse that involves also the rationale for breaking the lines, whether by closure (coming to the end of the phrase, clause, or sentence at the end of the line) or by enjambment (continuing the sentence beyond the line boundary, into the next line). The SHORT METER stanza of Hardy enjambs its lines more than the short meter of Dickinson (these examples appear under HYMN METER). See also the lists of examples under END-STOPPING and ENJAMBMENT.

Literal Symbol Natural objects or acts which become symbolic in context but whose tenor is left implicit. This term, coined by Christine Brooke-Rose, derives from the idea of comparison and implies pressure on material things to yield immaterial meanings. Examples include the shallow autumn stream in Bogan's Song for a Lyre," the wayside flower in "Ballad of Hector in Hades," the smell of the sun-warmed wood in "Cyclic," the chimney and cups of Traherne's "Poverty" (all examples from the text), as well as the Hardyesque hawks and falcons in Auden's poems, which turn the tiny countryside into a map.[29] When one thing or place or moment begins to resonate with meaning beyond itself, as happens in the emergence of the literal symbol, the exact signification is never easy to pin down. What we can say is that the given scene is invested with a quality that was invisible before the specialized lens of the poet began to make its verbal record. This is the case in the poem about an arctic glacier in summer in Stephen Spender's "Polar Expedition" where the wet flood of the summer thaw on the ice and permafrost creates a loudly echoing expanse; half the world "Became a ship with a deep keel, the booming floes / And icebergs with their little birds," and the tundra with its "burnish of bees."[30] Building upon literal symbol, the Spender poem contains other tropes within it (the metaphor of the ice-sheet that "Became a ship" and the cluster of whirring, brownish-golden bees' wings like the polished boss ["burnish"] on a shield). But the locale itself is never reduced to any of these passing

---

29. See Auden's poems beginning "Consider this and in our time" (1930) and "O love the interest itself" (1932), in *The English Auden,* edited by Edward Mendelson (New York: Random House, 1978).

30. Spender's poem appears in *Hero's Way: Contemporary Poems in the Mythic Tradition,* edited by John Alexander Allen (Englewood Cliffs, NJ: Prentice-Hall, 1971), p. 69.

metaphors. Further, the tenor of the whole only begins to take shape when we register the oddity, remoteness, and monotony of this frigid world, and the "burnish" and celebratory glee of Spender's description of it. In other words, one cannot say the poem presents the antarctic as a literal symbol of some single abstract idea.

Long Meter A quatrain of tetrameter. The "long" derives from the assumed norm for the quatrain as a **BALLAD STANZA** or sung measure of **COMMON METER** that alternates tetrameter with trimeter. See examples in **HYMN METER**.

Macron The symbol [−], used in scanning a line to denote an expected accented syllable. A nonaccent is marked with a breve [∪]. For example, the marking for an expected iambic foot would be [∪ −]. Actual speech stress is then marked with a slash [/]. See **SCANSION** and **BREVE**.

Main Line–Stress In a scansion graph, the speech stress that rises above the foot-stresses. Main line-stress is marked with an [x] and is never used in abundance; usually there is only one main stress per line. See also **SCANSION**.

Masculine Line Ending A line that ends with a stressed syllable. This is not sexist nomenclature—see the argument under **FEMININE LINE ENDING**.

Meaning Makes Stress See **SCANSION RULES**.

Measure The term for a kind of metrical foot regardless of the length of the line (for example, trochaic, iambic) or for a length of line regardless of the meter of that line (for example, **DIMETER** means "two-measure," **TRIMETER** "three-measure," and so forth). A complete description of any poem's accentual-syllabic form draws on both senses of measure. See **ANAPEST, IAMB, METER,** and **TROCHEE**.

Meiosis A form of exaggeration which deprecates the thing described, thus an extreme or outlandish lessening for rhetorical effect. See examples under **HYPERBOLE**.

Metaphor A transfer of meaning in which one thing is explained by being changed either into another thing or into an emotion or idea.

The originating scene, situation, object, or state is the TENOR (or part of the tenor), but until the entire illustration is unfolded, we often cannot know what the whole tenor could be. In an oversimplified metaphor such as *the fire of love,* the condition that needs defining—in part the *meaning*—is love; but as this is an experience that can be imagined many ways, the vehicle of fire actually alters the tenor by the idea of burning (which may be painful as well as exhilarating). The actual state is more precise than the mere ABSTRACTION with which we began (that is, *love*) and is fathomed and enriched by moving through a hypothetical process that cannot, literally, affect an abstract idea.

Edwin Muir describes the time of innocence in late childhood by means of a landscape. In it, there is "a still pond / That opened upon no sight a quiet eye" ("The Gate"). Within the generalized link between setting (vehicle) and idea (tenor) Muir has inserted a secondary site that we would expect to carry with it some emotional signification. Now, this eye does not *mean* innocence; it does point to the way a limpid, dreamy, clear-eyed patience accompanies that poised period in the child's maturation before the gates of sensual desire unexpectedly swing open. Unlike the action of detail in an ALLEGORY, in which each item stands for a discrete idea, a metaphor such as Muir's does not supply the meaning before we have explored the atmosphere; allegory by contrast typically turns attention away from the material circumstance as soon as the moral of the connection can be assumed (as a pond in Spenser or Bunyan might represent a danger to the soul, the slough of failure, the temptation to dally or digress, or a focus on personal vanity).

Like allegory, but without its inevitably judgmental perspective, metaphor employs the physical to suggest the spiritual, thus reversing the bent of languages, historically, away from things toward thoughts.[31] On occasion, thoughts represented as abstractions behave more like beings in an embodied material realm than like ideas, owing to metaphorical implication (this is the reverse of PERSONIFICA-TION). For example, the noun *chance* in Louise Bogan's line "From loud sound and still chance" ("Baroque Comment") acts much like

---

31. It is this traveling of the bent of language across the current of metaphor that PUN exploits.

the physically denotative noun *sound* to suggest all the savagery of instinct and mutation, all the desolation of eons without civilization. In other words, *sound* represents all the animals and primitive humans who made the sounds and *chance* the vacant periods of predation, disaster, and extinction. Looked at from the perspective of the habit of allegory and that of personification, Bogan's metaphoric abstractions would fall in the middle; the movement from left to right would be one of increasingly cerebral invention:

PERSONIFICATION	METAPHORIC ABSTRACTION	ALLEGORY

Poems that might exemplify the two extremes might be Wordsworth's "Composed upon Westminster Bridge" at the personification end and Gunn's "In Praise of Cities" for an (abbreviated version of) allegory. For the place of metaphor among the other forms of comparison, see CONTINUUM and TROPE.

Meter A normative and abstract idea of how the line of verse should behave. Meter is based on the formal auditory structure of a language. Hence in Greek, quantity (or length of vowel) determines the way syllables measure within metrical feet, but in English degrees of STRESS (relative emphasis given to some syllables in preference to others) perform this function. Meter as a term discriminates the stress-contour of verse from that of prose. Stresses can be marked in prose, but prose cannot be scanned (metrically graphed—see SCANSION).

Meter is the fixed, or notional, grid above a line, which is constantly pulling against the line's actual patterns of stress and emphasis. Since English verse typically counts both the line's length in terms of syllables and the number of accents or beats, the speech stresses generally become regular and expected by conforming to patterns that schematize accents and intervals between accents. In order to estimate a particular poem's meter, or scan a line of accentual-syllabic verse, the syllables are divided into either two-syllable or three-syllable units of stressed and unstressed syllables. Each foot in a meter either rises to its strongest beat or falls from it (hence the terms RISING METER and FALLING METER). Rising meters are the iamb [∪−] and the anapest [∪∪−]. The trochee [−∪] and the dactyl [−∪∪]

are forms of falling meter. Since metrically viable feet in English consist of at least (but no more than) one strong beat, variant feet such as the spondee [– –], the pyrrhic [∪∪], the cretic [– ∪ –], and the bacchius [∪ – –] can only be used as substitutions in accentual-syllabic verse.

Metonymy A subclass of trope in which one thing represents another closely related one. A whole can be represented by a part or a person can be represented by his or her possessions. For example, the ladies' gold combs and fans in "Sir Patrick Spens," stanzas 9 and 10, represent both their beauty and their loss. Less flattering is the spray of artificial roses on the bodice of the little clockwork dancer in Elizabeth Bishop's "Cirque d'Hiver." The lantern in Hopkins's sonnet in the "Poetry Sampler" in chapter 1 represents the radiant being who holds the lantern. The bicycles in "Inniskeen Road: July Evening" by Patrick Kavanagh represent the cyclists going to the country dance. More active is the trope in the metonymy of chariot for Achilles in "Ballad of Hector in Hades": all is still "Save for the chariot's tinkling hum, / And a few distant cries." See also LITERAL SYMBOL and TROPE.

Metrical Inversion A reversal of the expected metrical foot. The most common inversion is a bisyllabic foot stressed as a TROCHEE [∪́ –] when we expect an iamb [∪ –́]. See TROCHAIC INVERSION.

Mixed Trope Multiple layers of comparison; these can alienate metaphor so far from the literal declarative plane that the terms of the VEHICLE compete for attention with the sense that is intended (the TENOR).

    Mixed metaphor can be justified by extreme occasions. The speaker of "As You Came from the Holy Land of Walsinghame" shifts suddenly from the image of a candle flame to that of a terminally ill person. The shift is warranted, indirectly, by the suggestion that the speaker, although sick with longing, is afire with an emotion that makes him feel immortal. Illogic of trope bends to the logic of character also when Enobarbus uses mixed trope to express his sense of estrangement from his life and physical person (he is dying of grief for having abandoned the failed general Antony): He implores the moon to poison him ("the poisonous damp of night disponge [squeeze out] upon me"), then to break him into pieces:

Throw my heart
Against the flint and hardness of my fault,
Which, being dried with grief, will break to powder,
And finish all foul thoughts.

(Antony and Cleopatra IV.ix)

See also JUXTAPOSITION.

Mock Epic A poetic genre which makes what is trivial grandiose, in order to satirize behavior.

Mode The combination of syntax with rhythm, theme, and line. Josephine Miles defines mode (which she somewhat loosely calls "the selective use of the elements and structures of language"[32]) to include the poem's thematic range when themes are understood as channeling the DICTION and prosody (as in what she calls the "sublime" poem, with its syntactically expansive, descriptive base and STICHIC organization). She includes under mode the SYNTAX when this is understood to control and be controlled by diction and theme (the "clausal" mode is richer in verbs and, thus, action). Thus RHETORIC or the sound and range of the voice speaking the poem can be read as a coordination in style produced by the general features of the poem's mode.

Miles's two primary (and mutually exclusive) modes are the clausal or "predicative" whose exemplars are the BALLAD STANZA and the sinuous argumentative rhymed stanza of Donne; clausal poetry has more strong verbs and more subordination of clause than does "phrasal" poetry, the mode of physical quality and descriptive feeling, whose sentence structures are both more noun-based and more exclamatory. Spenser's sonnets and pastoral poems, Milton's epics, and *The Prelude* of Wordsworth represent this phrasal or line-oriented mode.

Monosyllabism Diction which consists mostly of words with one or two syllables: "I do not think that they will sing to me" (says Eliot's Prufrock). Monosyllabic words tend to be of Anglo-Saxon origin and describe concrete things: "They lard their lean books with the fat of others' works" (Richard Burton, 1577–1640); "Eye of newt,

---

32. Josephine Miles, *Eras and Modes in English Poetry* [1964] (Westport, CT: Greenwood Press, 1976), p. ix.

and toe of frog, / Wool of bat, and tongue of dog" (*Macbeth* IV.i.14–
15). The fewer the number of syllables per word, the more stubborn,
objective, thing- or texture-filled the poem composed of such words
will tend to be. But words of one syllable may also be words of refer-
ence and argument, rather than particulars (both Donne and Frost
exploit this more cerebral kind of monosyllabism). Milton, too,
achieves a persuasive simplicity through monosyllabism when Adam
asks the angel Raphael to reveal to him who his maker is so that he
might know "From whom I have that thus I move and live, / And
feel that I am happier than I know" (*Paradise Lost* VIII.281–82). Yet
more dramatic is Peter Grimes's agitated misery in Crabbe's "The
Borough": "But dream it was not;—no!—I fixed my eyes / On the
mid stream" where he sees his father holding by the hand two pale
(murdered) apprentices. But whether dramatic and particular, or log-
ical and argumentative, the monosyllabic line will have more stresses:
Those at the mercy of crowds "Could not hope for help and no help
came" (Auden, "The Shield of Achilles"). See also OVERSTRESSED
LINE.

Mood The attribute of verb use that depends on the speaker's attitude
toward the action or state expressed and which entails choice in verb
conjugation and tense. If the sentence describes a matter of fact, the
verb is in the INDICATIVE MOOD and can occur in any tense ("Bliss
was it in that dawn to be alive" [Wordsworth]; "The time they will
have lost / Closes about them" [John N. Morris]). If the sentence
expresses a supposition or a condition contrary to fact, the verb is in
the SUBJUNCTIVE MOOD, which typically involves present and past
(in statements hypothetical or contrary to fact—for example, Mac-
beth's "I dare do all that may become a man") and subjunctive past
and future (in hopeful or speculative constructions—for example,
Yeats's "were it proved he lies" or Bardolph's fond wish to be with
Falstaff (though he be dead), "Would I were with him, wheresome'er
he is," *Henry V* II.iii). When the sentence is a command, the verb is
in the IMPERATIVE MOOD and uses the present tense ("Let my people
go"; "Stare, stare in the basin"; "Look like the time; bear welcome
in your eye").

Morpheme Linguistic term for the smallest carrier of meaning in a
word. The term alerts us to the rules by which a language forms
words (with prefix, suffix, and vowel shift) upon roots. See DICTION.

Morphology (literally, *the study of forms*) The linguistic study of word formation apart from a word's function in the sentence (**SYNTAX**). Together, the two fields of study constitute grammar.

Neologism A new word; the protean habit of poetry to regenerate language with new combinations of prefix with root words; with shifts between transitive and intransitive verb usage; with loan words from other languages and disciplines such as physics; and with bona fide new words. Attention to pattern should not blind us to the need for freshening from techniques like neologism; at the same time, newness is inevitably related to the tendency of formerly new language to grow stale.[33]

Affixing a negative prefix is a popular means to extend the lexicon. Thom Gunn crafts a neologism to describe failed hopes in a shabby urban reality that represents them: "Your own designs, peeling and *unachieved*" ("In Praise of Cities"). W. H. Auden presents the sinister birds who eye us in "The Fall of Rome" as "*Unendowed* with wealth or pity." Leigh Hunt coins *unwet* to cap the insulting description of man by fish: "Long-useless-finned, haired, upright, *unwet*, slow!" ("The Fish, the Man and the Spirit"). A fertile area for new coinings is also provided by the kenning, as Anne Winters shows in her new combined forms *stonecourse* and *rainlight* in "The Mill-Race." See **ADNOMINATION** and **ETYMOLOGICAL STYLE**.

Non-verb A verb that, whether **TRANSITIVE** or **INTRANSITIVE**, does no real work in the sentence. Like the **COPULA**, the non-verb invites in description to surround (or even smother) the nouns in a sentence; see the lines from Keats's "The Eve of St. Agnes" (p. 93) and Spenser's *Faerie Queene* (under **SPENSEREAN STANZA** below).

Octave The first eight lines of a sonnet considered as a unit. See **SESTET**, **SONNET**, and **VOLTA**.

Ode A poem in praise of nature (birds are popular subjects), public figures, or important events (cf. Marvell's "An Horatian Ode: Upon Cromwell's Return from Ireland"). In addition to conventions of theme, odes often urge a rhetoric of direct address to some person or idea (Keats has an "Ode to Psyche," Robert Pinsky [b. 1940] a poem

---

33. For more about **neologism,** see Brogan and Preminger, eds., *Princeton Encyclopedia,* 1993 ed., under "lexis."

entitled "Ode to Meaning"). Finally, ode stanzas (which rhyme in English) are often in HETEROMETRIC RHYME—see Herbert's "The Flower," Lowell's "Mr. Edwards and the Spider," and "Ode to a Dressmaker's Dummy," by Donald Justice:

> How like the terrified,
> Shy figure of a bride
> You stood there then, without your clothes,   15
> Drawn up into
> So classic and so strict a pose
> Almost, it seemed, the little attic grew
> Dark with the first charmed night of the honeymoon.
> Or was it only some obscure   20
> Shape of my mother's youth I saw in you,
> There where the rude shadows of the afternoon
> Crept up your ankles and you stood
> Hiding your sex as best you could?—
> Prim ghost the evening light shone through.   25

See also ANATOMY.

Offbeat Term used by Attridge and other metrists to refer to the unstressed syllables between strong beats. See IMPLIED OFFBEAT.

Onomatopoeia Imitation of theme by a poem's sound—usually a local effect of the sounds of certain words rather than general effects of the larger rhythm and syntax, for example, *slither, crash, boom, whisper, crisp.* Opinions about effect (and affect) differ, of course. Some writers associate sibilance (repeated *s* sounds) with a sweet or affectionate signification, for example, although for the most part sibilance to my ear produces a grating and unsavory effect. Imitations of animal sounds have national idiosyncrasies (*der Kikeriki* in German is *cockadoodledoo* in English) as well as historical tics (like the English nightingale's *iug iug, chuk chuk,* or *yoog yoog;* the plover's *pu we* (or *pewit*); or the owl's cry, which Coleridge (like Shakespeare) transcribes as *Tu—whit—tu—whoo,* but which Thomas Nash [1567–1601] heard as *ta witta woo*).[34]

34. Shakespeare's owl (winter) answers the cuckoo (spring) in *Love's Labor's Lost* (V.ii); Coleridge's owl can be heard in his poem *Christabel,* and Thomas Nash's in "Spring, the sweet spring"; for John Skelton's nightingale, see "In Praise of Isabel Pennell" (the latter in Walter de la Mare, ed., *Come Hither: A Collection of Rhymes and Poems for the Young of All Ages* [New York: Alfred A. Knopf, 1957], p. 35—de la Mare himself heard the

Ottava Rima Eight-line stanza of iambic pentameter rhyming *abababcc;* employed by Byron for narratives and by Yeats (with many variations) for the meditative lyric.

Overstressed Line A line which consists primarily of monosyllables and, since each word carries a stress, has more stressed syllables than a regular iambic line. Because overstressing, with its extra syllables, slows down the rhythm of a line, the diction can work along with appropriate trope and syntax for a heavily dramatic effect. Hopkins thickens his overstressing with ASYNDETON in the line that overstresses against an iambic norm, "Cloud puffball, torn tufts, tossed pillows flaunt forth." Yeats emphasizes his frustration with his hands and mind by thinking in emphatic groups of slightly unmanageable monosyllables in "Hands, do what you're bid." Wyatt overstresses in an argumentative use of monosyllabism in "Stond Whoso List": "In hidden place, / So lette my dayes forthe passe . . . That . . ." ALLITERATION and dialect also thicken diction and support overstressing. See UNDERSTRESSED LINE.

Pararhyme Welsh poet Wildred Owen's term for envelope rhyme that varies only the intermediate vowel between repeating consonants: *rid/red, stuns/stones, stir/star, shores/shares, groined/groaned, spilled/ spoiled, seeds/sides.* Both W. H. Auden and Daryl Hine widely explore the subtleties of pararhymes in their poems.

Parataxis (literally *equivalent frame*) The joining of one simple declarative sentence to another in parallel series, usually with a conjunction (*and, or, nor, but, yet,* or *for*). Blake's lines "I will not cease from Mental Flight / Nor shall my sword sleep in my hand" provide an example. See also the quotation by Auden under COMPOUND SENTENCE. The adjective form is "paratactic."

Passage A series of lines in a poem (analogous to a paragraph in prose) in which theme is woven with the six elements of verse so as to produce a logically and rhetorically coherent sequence. The term is used in preference to STANZA either in nonstanzaic poems, such as BLANK VERSE and FREE VERSE, or in those stanzaic poems in which the blocks of thought are either longer or shorter than the repeating

---

nightingale singing *yoog yoog*). T. S. Eliot may be using Thomas Nash's transcription of its song (*iug iug*) in *The Waste Land* II.

stanza shell. (In blank verse, we sometimes speak of "verse para-
graphs"; if they possess the coherence of theme and style we have
designated, they would also be passages.) While it may happen that
neither stanza nor line boundary are observed in those segments of a
poem described by the term, the close of a passage typically coincides
with completeness, or closure, in the syntax.

Short stanzas like QUATRAINS tend to clump together, coral-like,
into larger passages, while longer stanzas like the SPENSEREAN and
OTTAVA RIMA and ODE stanzas might break into two or more smaller
passages (although if every stanza in a poem of longer stanzas broke
into multiple logical segments, the passage would undermine the
shape of the stanza).

Pentameter Five-measure lines. This is one of the two most prevalent
line lengths in English verse; the second is DIPODIC VERSE. See
BLANK VERSE and IAMBIC PENTAMETER.

Periphrasis Roundabout speech. In prose its effect is often comic in its
entanglement: "[T]he play is running yet—a fact that may render
strange the failure to be deeply conscious of which two persons in
the audience were guilty" (Henry James).[35] In poetry that focuses on
an image subjected to comparison, periphrasis is easier to control.
The roundabout form of Frost's style in "An Old Man's Winter
Night" mirrors his theme, that the man's age dims his memory:
"What kept him from remembering what it was / That brought him
to that creaking room was age." Indirection of thought is shown by
the indirection of Frost's sentence. Hardy makes a virtue of his speak-
er's hesitation in "Neutral Tones" in describing the wan and insin-
cere smile of the woman about to part from him: "The smile on your
mouth was the deadest thing / Alive enough to have strength to die."
Here periphrasis takes a riddling form, starting from the assumption
that a smile can be a thing capable of life or death. (See also METON-
YMY.) Metaphor, too, can be periphrastic in order to render the
growth of one idea out of another. For example, instead of *bronze
flowers,* already hardened into the ornamental frieze, Louise Bogan
describes how tendril and petal bend into artistic shapes: "The flower

35. From the short story "Broken Wings" (1900) in *Henry James's Stories of Writers
and Artists,* edited by F. O. Matthiessen (New York: New Directions, n.d.), p. 320.

at last in bronze, stretched backward, or curled within" ("Baroque Comment").

Raymond Oliver periphrastically avoids naming any colors in "Structures," yet the poem is rich with the hues he implies, including all the minute gradations of dawn-light from twilit charcoal through dusky lilac to blazing gold (the clear gold of sunrise being the *more* that is *coming* in his line asserting "That more is coming than one could have known"). Sometimes the avoidance of naming becomes "elegant variation" (as in Pope's *finny Tribe* for *fish* or the many names James devises for himself in *The American Scene* [1907], for example *the visionary tourist, the shuddering pilgrim,* and *the restless analyst*—terms not far removed from Wallace Stevens's terms for Crispin in "The Comedian as the Letter C" [1923], *the affectionate emigrant, connoisseur of elemental fate, magister of a single room,* and *prickling realist*). See EPITHET and KENNING.

Persona (literally *mask*) The rhetorical pose that the speaker invents and speaks through. It can be different from what we might expect the poet's own rhetorical and intellectual position to be. See the many personas Shakespeare and Donne assume in their sonnets. More dramatic still is the gambit of taking the persona of a famous character: Bogan speaks through Cassandra, Tennyson through Ulysses, Muir through a cowardly Hector, Nemerov through Conrad's Marlow (in "Runes"), and Auden through Caliban, Prospero, and Ariel (in *The Sea and the Mirror*). Poems in which a freestanding character speaks or thinks are called dramatic monologues.

Personification A class of trope in which the inanimate takes on features of animate or human life and movement, for example, "Gray tiny rocks slept round him where he lay" (Muir, "Childhood"), in which the stones suggest tiny animals, and "a stone's in the midst of all," in which Yeats projects on the unmoving stone features of an essentially Irish malaise—the paralyzed state of being worn out by commitment to chronic upheaval.

Personification can emerge from a natural comparison between literal things, as in literal symbols and metonymy, or from more allegorical dramatizations that personify the abstract. At the allegorical end of the personification continuum we find Wordsworth's rendering of the city of London as a human body wearing a garment of air and light in "Composed upon Westminster Bridge." Personification of a more psychologically driven kind occurs in Bogan's "Cassandra" where the prophetess speaks not of herself in the subject-position, but of an abstract noun (*madness*), as she wails "Madness chooses out my voice again," thus treating the term not as an idea but as an aggressive force that invades her. Similarly, the distraught hero in Muir's "Ballad of Hector in Hades" imagines that "The sky with all its clustered eyes / Grows still with watching me"; personification reveals at once the hero's keen vision of the planets in a vast sky at this moment of his ordeal and his paranoia about being exposed to universal view.

Personification can both animate the inanimate world and stiffen the animate world back into an abstraction, as when Macbeth reduces himself in II.i to "withered murder," his anticipated act having become the rigid mask he wears. At the opposite extreme is personification that is overtly animistic, whereby the material world becomes intricately alive with motive and gesture; this happens when Gerard Manley Hopkins describes the silken radiating lines of light (*trambeams*) from a candle as they *truckle at the eye* (timidly lower and disappear—themselves like shy eyes) when the observer's eye is entirely open ("The Candle Indoors"). Compared with such an enlivening of the physical and perceptual world as in Hopkins's poem, the personification of Muir's "The grasses puff a little dust" in the Hector poem is pretty mild, seeming more a sleight of SYNTAX (by turning an intransitive verb—one that does not take an object—into a transitive one) than a fully enacted TROPE. See graph for METAPHOR.

Petrarchan Descriptive term derived from the poetry and practice of Italian writer Petrarch (Francesco Petrarca, 1304–74), who invested a set of brief love-lyrics based on complex rhyme schemes (the SONNET) with aspects of religious devotion and metaphysical association. Exaggerations are typical, both in feeling (the lover driven to extremes) and in figures of speech like paradox and ANTITHESIS (burning and freezing at the same time; loving another, thus hating oneself) and rhetorical devices like the catalogue of charms (the *blason,* employing formulas for praising the parts of the body from head to toe)—all of these techniques teasing out the illusion of exhaustiveness in the short span of the sonnet's fourteen lines. Sir Thomas Wyatt translated many of Petrarch's sonnets:

I fynde no peace and all my warre is done,
I fere and hope, I burne and freise like yse;
I fley above the wynde yet can I not arrise,
And noght★ I have and all the worold I seson.†   ★*nothing* †*seize on*
That loseth nor locketh[36] holdeth me in prison   5
And holdeth me not, yet can I scape nowise;
Nor letteth me lyve nor dye at my devise,★   ★*by my own choice*
And yet of deth it gyveth me occasion.★   ★*yet it kills me*
Withouten Iyen, I se, and withoute tong I plain,[37]
I desire to perisshe, and yet I aske helthe,   10
I love an othre, and thus I hate my selfe,
I fede me in sorrowe and laughe in all my pain,
Likewise displeaseth me boeth deth and lyffe,
And my delite is causer of this stryff.[38]

Phrase A coherent group of words (not containing both a subject and verb) that act together. A phrase can either coincide with the line unit (as in Bogan's line "Beautiful, my delight" from "To Be Sung on the Water") or diverge from the line and enjamb (as in "Never that chill / Resonant heart" from her double sonnet "Fifteenth Farewell").

Plain Style A style characterized by monosyllabism, direct statement, and unadorned speech, sometimes in the guise of brooding naturalness, often put on to explore deep feeling. The style has been called "Drab Style" (C. S. Lewis's term) to refer to the seemingly antipoetical and antilyrical, and definitely anti-Spenserean, diction of Renaissance poets such as Wyatt, Googe, and Donne, and later of Crabbe. But plain style also embraces the lucid simplicity of the conversational poems of Ben Jonson and of much of the work of Wordsworth, just as it appealed to writers like Thomas Hardy, Edwin Muir, Robert Frost, Donald Justice, and Philip Larkin. It is most commonly writ-

---

36. Something that neither releases nor locks me up nor holds me in prison.
37. Without eyes I see, and without tongue I lament.
38. And the one in whom I delight causes me all this torment, or strife. Wyatt's poem appears in *The Anchor Anthology of Sixteenth-Century Verse,* edited by Richard S. Sylvester (Garden City, NY: Anchor/Doubleday, 1974), p. 135.

ten in iambic pentameter. See DICTION and HYPERBOLE for examples.

Podic Free Verse (literally, *footed*) A type of verse that falls midway between ACCENTUAL and ACCENTUAL-SYLLABIC meter. Matthew Arnold's "Rugby Chapel" is a good example of verse that is neither three-stress (hence indulgent, like all accentual poems, toward the effect of seemingly random nonstresses intervening between the stresses), nor able to equalize the interval between stresses as either binary meters (iambs or trochees) or triple meters (strictly anapestic or dactylic or amphibrachic) would do. But there is an overall preference for TROCHAIC METER (see lines 1, 3, 6, 13):

> Coldly, sadly descends
> The autumn-evening. The field
> Strewn with its dank yellow drifts
> Of wither'd leaves, and the elms,
> Fade into dimness apace,   5
> Silent;—hardly a shout
> From a few boys late at their play!
> The lights come out in the street,
> In the school-room windows;—but cold,
> Solemn, unlighted, austere,   10
> Through the gathering darkness, arise
> The chapel-walls, in whose bound
> Thou, my father! art laid.

Podic free verse is sometimes called SPRUNG VERSE.

Pronunciation The rule of normal speech for a historical period, which affects rhythms as well as rhymes. An example of the latter occurs in Pope's couplet, "Here thou, Great ANNA, whom three realms obey, / Dost sometimes counsel take, and sometimes tea." Because *obey* and *tea* no longer share a vowel, the OED should be consulted whenever there is uncertainty about historical rhyming.

In the Renaissance, variability obtained where past participles were concerned; sometimes they were voiced (pronounced as an additional syllable on the model of *mint-ed*), but in words we have since elided, for example, *banished, buried, inflamed*. Shakespeare used the *-ed* suffix both ways in some of the same passages, for example, when the lovers hear that Romeo has been banished from Verona; both he and Juliet play upon the word. Here is a sampler of Romeo's lines:

There is no world without Verona walls,
But purgatory, torture, hell itself.
Hence banishèd is* banished from the world,   *means
And world's exile is death. Then banishèd
Is death mistermed   20

. . . .

Hadst thou no poison mixed, no sharp-ground knife,
No sudden mean of death, though ne-er so mean,   45
But 'banishèd' to kill me—'banishèd'?

(Romeo and Juliet II.iii.)

Line 18 presents the suffix as both voiced and unvoiced. Similarly, the poet toys with trisyllabic "burièd" and bisyllabic "buried" in Sonnet 31, lines 4 ("And all those friends which I thought burièd") and 9 ("Thou art the grave where buried love doth lie").

Variability in the pronunciation of polysyllables does not disappear with the Renaissance, nor is the more recent poet always the one who elides or slurs the word. Edwin Arlington Robinson says each of the four syllables in *spir-i-tu-al*, fitting them into the available strong-weak strong-weak positions in feet 3 through 5 of his blank-verse line: "When we have earned our spiritual ears" ("Captain Craig"). Milton, by contrast, elides the same four syllables into three—and even then he employs an anapest in the third foot: "Millions of spiritual Creatures walk the Earth / Unseen, both when we wake, and when we sleep" (*Paradise Lost* IV.676–77). When John Berryman's Henry wonders in the Dream Songs, "When will indifference come," he uses a colloquial elision of *indifference* into three syllables, yet it is the same word Eliot stretches into four syllables in one of the more overtly pentameter lines in *The Waste Land,* "And makes a welcome of in-**DIF**-fer-**ence**." Articulation does not always produce identical meters, however. Cowper's poem on Alexander Selkirk puts the unambiguous stress on the second syllable at the peak of am amphibrach (in-**DIF**-fer-ence): "The beasts, that roam over the plain, / My form with indifference see" ("Verses Supposed to Be Written by Alexander Selkirk, During His Solitary Abode in the Island of Juan Fernandez").

Vowel pronunciation also affects rhyme; the OED should be consulted when there is uncertainty about historical rhyming (consider Byron's rhyme in *Don Juan* I.50 between *child, wild,* and *toiled*). See also **ALLITERATION, ELISION, NEOLOGISM,** and **QUANTITY.**

Prosody Derived from the Greek word for accent and often used as the category for all effects of poetic sound. More strictly, the study of versification, that is, the auditory logic or rhythmic style of a poem when viewed as the interaction of the other elements of style with the poem's meter.

Pun (from *puntiglio,* fine point) Humorous use of like-sounding words with different meanings (usually owing to different derivations), as when mad Lear in IV.vi, seeing blind Gloucester, says "No eyes in your head, nor no money in your purse? Your eyes are in a heavy case, your purse in a light." The English word *case* has two possible sources, *casus* (meaning example, situation, facts, plight) and *capsa* (from *capere;* meaning container, chest, sheath, box). Lear thus puns on *case.* So does Pope in *Rape of the Lock* when his empty-headed Sir Plume "first the Snuff-box open'd, then the [legal] Case" (IV.126). James Merrill's use of *cordial* in its etymological sense of medicine that stimulates the heart allows him to mix in two of its later meanings— to describe something that is abstractly friendly or affectionate and something that is as literal as the sticky alcoholic liqueur called a cordial (an identification supported in that water is the referent): "I swallow in a glass of water / No longer cordial, scarcely wet, a pill / They told me not to take until much later" ("An Urban Convalescence"). See ETYMOLOGICAL STYLE.

Pyrrhic Foot A substituted foot of two unaccented syllables and denoted as [∪∪] in classical metrics. Pyrrhic feet in accentual-syllabic verse in English are sometimes called "false pyrrhics" because one syllable of each foot will have a slightly stronger stress than the other, even if the stronger syllable is weaker than other speech stresses in the surrounding line. In our system of scanning iambic lines by expectation, the pyrrhic foot would be marked as an expected iamb but with no slash for a speech stress: [∪−].

Quantity The length of the vowel in classical prosody, in which metrical feet were determined by longs and shorts rather than by stressed and unstressed syllables. Although the concept has been replaced by syllable and stress in poetry in English, length of the vowel is still often palpable. In Wilbur's "Exeunt," the *i* in both *cricket* and *dwindled* is short relative to the long *i* in *dry* and the almost drawling long vowels in *shawl* (stanza 1) and its echo in the second stanza, *crawls:* "A cricket like a dwindled hearse / Crawls from the dry grass." Owing to play between the length and brevity of vowels, the lines' tempo is affected.

Note that tempo derived from the length of time the words take is affected by the behavior of consonants, too; Wilbur's *dw* consonant combination in *dwindled* takes longer to say that the *gr* in *grass*. To determine which exerts greater force in determining length, the retarding effect of consonants or vowels, contrast the first foot of Shakespeare's line with the last: "Sap checkt with frost and lustie leav's quite gon" (Sonnet 5). Both are overstressed iambs (or false spondees), but foot 1 even with its short vowels is longer than the fifth, owing to consonant thickening. See ACCENTUAL-SYLLABIC VERSE.

Quatrain A four-line rhyming stanza. Lines may be any length (usually trimeter to pentameter) and of any measure (iambic, amphibrachic, etc.).

Recession of Technique The intentional avoidance of one element or several elements of style in the interests of strengthening the effect of another element. For example, the use of drab or unremarkable technique, such as flat rhyme and no trope in the Scottish ballads, allows for the emergence of other emphases. Avoidance of the image (trope) in the ballads emphasizes the role of passion, instinct, and terror, and highlights the clean edges of narrated actions. But words such as "passion," "instinct," and "terror" are examples of language that would *not* be used in these poems (see ABSTRACTION and DICTION). On the other hand, in lyrics with a lexicon and handling of TROPE that are more self-reflective, other techniques must recede; in order that some words achieve the status of tropes, it may be necessary for the poet to depress the symbolic texture of the surrounding vocabulary to the level of what Donald Davie calls "fiduciary symbols"—words as direct counters, without suggested nuance.[39] In Muir's "The Enchanted Knight," for example, the word "blackening" in the line "In the bare wood below the blackening hill" stands out as metaphoric and not merely descriptive like the rest of the language. The hill is blackening because the farmer's plow is turn-

39. Donald Davie, *Articulate Energy: An Inquiry into the Syntax of English Poetry* (London: Routledge & Kegan Paul, 1955), pp. 122–35.

ing over the soil. By extension, the agricultural world is encroaching on the eerie close of the knight's gothic world—something like death's shadow is also implied. Much work is done by this one "turn" on "blackening" while the rest of the line (and the stanza) stays still.

Receding technique does not mean flatness in a pejorative sense, but rather the general control of all the apparently receding elements that makes a subtle change like Muir's "blackening" metaphor, powerful.

Reduced Line An abbreviated line in an accentual-syllabic poem, such as Muir's single trimeter line (line 20) in a poem ("The Gate") whose other twenty-three lines are iambic pentameter: The effect is dramatic and provocative. Reduced lines can also recur as part of a stanzaic pattern, and therefore usually rhyme, as in the stanza identified with Robert Burns; in many tetrameter ballads that, like Keats's "La Belle Dame Sans Merci," end with dimeter lines; and in poems like the following by Walter de la Mare:

> The dusk was still, with dew a-falling,
> I saw the Dog-star bleak and grim,
> I saw a slim brown rat of Norway
> Creep over him.

> ("John Mouldy"[40])

Reduced lines can share some of the features of the REFRAIN in closing off stanzas, while retaining, as de la Mare's reductions do, the ability to form bonds with run-on lines; thus enjambment pitches the stanza forward and the reduced line acts as a sudden brake. Thomas Wyatt and George Herbert are masters of the tempo shifts obtained from such reductions. See **BURNS STANZA** and **HETEROMETRIC RHYME**.

Refrain Repeating phrase, line, or stanza in a poem of many stanzas, such as the ballad, to give closure in passing. Often nonsensical (*Fol de rol O; With a heigh and a nonny*), refrains can also be abstruse (as in Dunbar's Latin refrain in "Lament for the Makaris," *Timor mortis conturbat me*—the fear of death distresses me). A refrain can be identical—as in Thomas Dekker's (1570?–1632) "Cradle Song," each stanza ending "Rock them, rock them, lullaby," Burns's "Tam Sam-

---

40. In Opie, eds., *Oxford Book of Children's Verse*, p. 326.

son's Elegy," each final dimeter line of which is "Tam Samson's dead,"
and Edward Lear's "The Jumblies," "And they went to sea in a
Sieve"—or subtly varied, in a device called "incremental repetition,"
which keeps a frame with subtle changes, as in the final lines of Ten-
nyson's "Sweet and Low" ("While my little one, while my pretty
one, sleeps"; "Sleep, my little one, sleep, my pretty one, sleep")[41]
and in the final line of each stanza in Ralegh's 78-line trimeter poem
"The Lie":

> Say to the Court it glowes,
>> and shines like rotten wood,
> Say to the Church it showes
>> whats good, and doth no good.   10
> If Church and Court reply,
>> then give them both the lie.*   *say they lie
>
> Tell Potentates they live
>> acting by others action,
> Not loved unless they give,   15
>> not strong but by affection.
> If Potentates reply,
>> give Potentates the lie.

Incremental repetition in the refrain is less argumentatively presented
in this brief lyric by Charles Lamb:

> She Is Going
>
> For their older sister's hair
> Martha does a wreath prepare
> Or bridal rose, ornate and gay:
> To-morrow is the wedding day:
>> She is going.   5
>
> Mary, youngest of the three,
> Laughing idler, full of glee,
> Arm in arm does fondly chain her,
> Thinking, poor trifler, to detain her—
>> But she's going.   10

---

41. The poems by Dekker, Lear, and Tennyson appear in *The Oxford Book of Chil-
dren's Verse,* pp. 17, 187–89, and 213.

Vex not, maidens, nor regret
Thus to part with Margaret.
Charms like yours can never stay
Long within doors; and one day
          You'll be going.[42]   15

The refrain in Lamb's poem is half the length of the trochaic tetrame-
ter of the main stanza, suggesting the poignant force of a refrain line
that is simultaneously reduced as a gathering point for and commen-
tary upon what comes before. See also **HETEROMETRIC RHYME** and
REDUCED LINE.

Responsion Equivalence between matching lines in metrically match-
ing stanzas.

Rhetoric The art and style of persuasion when referred to speech gener-
ally rather than writing or poetry exclusively. One way to think of
rhetoric involves the implied presence of a speaker (or a **PERSONA**
through whom the writer both projects and filters the ideas and "ges-
tures" of a poem). The imagined speaker puts pressure on the poem's
language to mirror the skewing of experience at the critical moment
he or she has reached. The poetic **MODE** known as a dramatic mono-
logue is the result.

The second way rhetoric relates to poetry is through the cate-
gory of persuasive devices used to convince, teach, impress, or goad
the listener. When we become aware of being worked on, rhetoric
is what we call the sense of influence. Pertinent devices include the
FIGURES OF SPEECH.

A third angle from which to view rhetoric would ask us to look
for evidence of spoken speech standing out above the kind of speech
we think of as written. Syntax is generally smoother, and trope and
diction simpler in poems where the participation of rhetoric is
strong—although complex intentions can produce more intricate
designs (see **CONVERSATIONAL STYLE, DICTION,** and **HYPERBOLE**).

Rhyme The agreement of two metrically accented syllables and their
terminal consonants. Rhymes can either be subtle (overshadowed by
syntax) or definite. Some end-stopped satiric rhymes such as Shake-
speare's *deedes/weeds* (Sonnet 94) and Daryl Hine's *bathysphere/hear*

42. Lamb, *The Complete Works,* p. 723.

(from "The Trout") call attention to themselves and can also imply an ironic comparison between the two rhyming words. The irony is increased when the rhymes are lengthened out into phrases, as in Pope's rhyme between *British Queen* and *charming Indian screen,* or Byron's *serious matter* and *soda-water.* Compared with these elaborations, a rhyme such as Dickinson's *Grass/Mass* sounds somewhat more modest. More modest still are the rhymes of root-words with endings (for example, -*ing* with *sing*), although sometimes the device (called LIGHT RHYME) is moving (as when John Bunyan defends his authorship of *Pilgrim's Progress:* "It came from mine own heart, so to my head, / And thence into my fingers trickled"[43]).

Rhyme can be **(1) adjacent** (in couplets, *aabbcc,* etc.), or **(2) alternating** (as in the *abab* BALLAD STANZA), or **(3) interspersed** (as in the more complex schemes of poems like Herbert's "Flower," in which rhyme is further imbalanced by heterometric lines—Herbert's scheme is $a^4b^5a^4b^5c^2c^2b^4$). The letters stand for the final rhyme sound, comprising a vowel and any subsequent consonants; the superscript numbers stand for metrical length, or number of feet. When the letters are uppercased, an end-word is repeated verbatim (see SESTINA).

See also LIGHT RHYME, RHYMING ON THE PHRASE, and HETEROMETRIC RHYME.

Rhyming on the Phrase Like simple rhyme, this is a technique that adds to the closure of the line unit. It is produced by throwing the weight forward from the first occurrence of rhyme sound (the "pre-rhyme," which may be weaker, or attached to a less remarkable word) to a second or subsequent occurrence of the rhyme by means of phrases that have a colloquial ring. The rhyming words are placed at the end of the catchphrases. For example, recall the rhyme Merrill uses in "From the Cupola," *ominous/fair to us,* where rhyming on the phrase allows both pathos and wit ("They are my senses shrill and ominous. . . . *Kept like children Is this fair to us*"). The pre-rhyme of a couplet from Pope's *An Essay on Man* II.269–70 ("golden views") denotes the alchemist's hope of making gold from lead; it is far less colloquial and easy to grasp than the second rhyme, connecting the

---

43. Bunyan's couplet appears in de la Mare, ed., *Come Hither: A Collection of Rhymes and Poems,* p. 616, where the editor notes that "trickled" is trisyllabic: *trick-le-ed.*

poet with his muse: The theme is that everyone has some illusory comfort, "The starving chemist, in his golden views / Supremely blest, the poet in his muse." (Note how the ENJAMBMENT propels sense forward from the more obscure HALF-MEANING in the pre-rhyme line to the resolved and more familiar whole.) Auden rhymes on identical sounds but in what sound like different dialects when in *Letter to Lord Byron* II he rhymes *to hold the baby for us* with *to chat with Set and Horus*. Byron had even called attention to the device by putting one such rhymed-on phrase in quotation marks; Juan is reading the witty and sometimes obscene poet Martial in an edition where the offensive passages are removed from the text but collected (punningly "marshaled") in an *appendix* ("Which saves, in fact, the trouble of an *index*"):

> For there we have them all "at one fell swoop,"
>> Instead of being scattered through the pages;
> They stand forth marshaled in a handsome troop,
>> To meet the ingenuous youth of future ages,
> Till some less rigid editor shall stoop
>> To call them back into their separate cages,
> Instead of standing staring all together,
>> Like garden gods—and not so decent either.

(Don Juan I.45)

All the lines except 5 and 8 conclude in rhymes on ready-to-hand colloquial phrases.

Children's rhymes often provide intricate comic phrases:

> What is the rhyme for *porringer*⋆?   ⋆*bowl for child's porridge*
> The King he had a daughter fair
> And gave the Prince of Orange her.[44]

Here the distance in meaning between the rhyme-terms and the tortuous syntactic inversion by which the terms are postponed to the end add to the pleasant accident of the likeness in sound.

Accident plays no apparent part in Yeats's rhymes-on-the-phrase in "A Prayer for My Daughter": "Have I not seen the loveliest woman born / Out of the mouth of Plenty's horn." The rhyme sounds are contained in *born* and *horn,* but the rhyme sense reaches

---

44. Halliwell, ed., *The Nursery Rhymes of England*, p. 10. The note indicates that this rhyme was written in 1641 when the eldest daughter of Charles I married the Prince of Orange.

back nearly through the full extent of both lines, making the lovely woman rhyme in shape and concept with the curving harvest horn.

Rhyme Royal A pentameter stanza of seven lines rhyming *ababbcc* typically employed for narrative poems such as Sackville's *A Mirrour for Magistrates* (1555) and later for poems in a meditative vein (Wordsworth's "Resolution and Independence" [1807]). Auden used rhyme royal for his sprightly epistolary epic, *Letter to Lord Byron* (1936).

Rhythm The accommodation of the poet's individual voice in its natural scope to the constraints and relaxations of the accentual-syllabic line. A particular poem or line's rhythm is created by variation from or adherence to the anticipated alternation of accent with nonaccent. Qualities of diction (including speech-stress and nonstress, monosyllabism and polysyllabism), along with the other elements of style, also effect the rhythm. See PROSODY.

Rising Ionic The classical metrist's term for a combination of pyrrhic with spondaic feet. In our scansion, the rising ionic would be sketched [∪ −][∪ −].

Rising Meter Refers to metric feet that end with (or rise to) strongly stressed syllables following weakly stressed ones. See ANAPEST and IAMB.

Rule of Two My phrase for the assumption (made by prosodists such as Attridge) of the doubled two-stress unit (or tetrameter line) as the basic line of English verse. In any two-part unit of rhythm, the first beat will be perceived as stronger (primary) and the second beat or stress as weaker. The strongest beat in a four-stress line is the third, and the third line of a quatrain is the strongest of the four lines. (These are inductive conclusions about perception of rhythm by speakers of English rather than rules stipulated by makers or critics.) See BALLAD METER, DIPODIC VERSE, HYMN METER and UNREALIZED BEAT.

Scansion The visual graph of a poem's meter, taking into account the number of accents, the expected intervals between metrical accents, and the actual speech-stresses of the spoken words.

    Step One: *Determining Stress:* (1) Polysyllables have one major stress; secondary stresses as well as nonstresses that are one syllable away from a neighboring primary stress in word or line can coincide with metrical **ACCENT** (expected stress). (2) Bisyllabic words have one stressed and one unstressed syllable. (3) Monosyllabic words of content are always stressed, but articles, prepositions, pronouns, and conjunctions are not stressed as a rule.

Step Two: *Deriving Meter:* We derive the meter and the type of metrical **FOOT** by examining the pattern of stressed and unstressed syllables that a reading of the entire poem persuades us is operative. The meter of a poem will be constant, and the foot-lengths will be consistent.

Step Three: Metrical *expectation is mapped* over the available syllables, then *actual speech stresses are marked.* **MAIN LINE-STRESSES,** which rise above all the other syllables stressed in speech, help give each line of metrical verse its own unique stress contour (another case in which meaning makes stress—see below).

Scansion Rules Assumptions on which a system of scansion is based. Our assumptions are:

1. *Lines cannot be scanned out of context.*

2. *A scansion system requires at least three signs,* two for expectation of accent and nonaccent; a third for actual speech stress. We use [∪ −] for metrical expectation in an iambic foot, and [/] for an actual speech stress, which typically occurs in those places where the metrical pattern leads us to expect stress, namely places marked with a **macron** [−]. **Main line-stress** can also be marked [x].

3. *Metrical expectation remains constant,* even when feet other than the basic metrical foot are substituted. The **DERIVED METER** is a generalized result of recognizing patterns in the poem (see **SCANSION**). The substitution of one of more trochees or anapests does not make an iambic line suddenly trochaic or anapestic (although anapests are such powerful magnets that they soon take over).

4. *Context makes meter.* Some lines that sound like pentameter out of context are tetrameter in context; some lines that sound tetrametric become trimeters when read in place. The rhythmic contours of some lines are frankly baffling absent surrounding lines.

5. *Meaning makes stress.* The making of stress by meaning becomes pertinent with ordinarily unstressed monosyllables. Weak syllables (even prefixes) earn their place (so long as they also fall in strong places) by forming part of rhetorical emphases such as parallel,

antithesis, and catchphrase or proverbial expression. See ELECTIVE
STRESS. Chapter 8 contains sample scansion exercises.

Sentence A complete syntactical unit consisting of a subject and verb.
The normal order is subject-verb-object (s-v-o); any other sequence
inverts the sentence. WORD ORDER also affects and is affected by
meter. See also SYNTAX and SYNTACTIC INVERSION.

Sentence Fragment A broken-off and incomplete sentence, missing
either a subject or a verb, or comprising a dependent without a main
clause. Although fragments usually create a disjointed impression,
some poets can join together fragments to create a deft and layered
effect—but still without forming a complete sentence:

> Rather, like shards and straw upon the course ground
> Of little worth when found,—
> Rubble in gardens, it and stones alike,
> That any spade may strike.
>
> (Bogan, "Memory")

David Ferry's "A Young Woman" is a sixteen-line fragment; see
the discussion under SYNTAX.

Sestet The last six lines of a SONNET as a unit, following the first eight
lines, or octave. Between the last line of the octave and the first line
of the sestet, a volta, or shift in mood, attitude, or meaning usually
occurs.

Sestina (literally *six-rhymed*) A poem of thirty-nine lines based on a
stanza of six lines whose end words (nouns with a trochaic form or
ending, for example, *country, disturbance, mountain, sorrow, coffee, river*)
repeat verbatim in each of the following stanzas. The pattern of repe-
tition is *ABCDEF, FAEBDC, CFDABE, ECBFAD, DEACFB,
BDFECA*, where each capital letter represents an end-word. The
seventh stanza (called an envoi or send-off) uses all six end-words,
three of these embedded earlier in the lines (*ECA*) the other three at
line ends (*BDF*).

If one asks why poets would be drawn to such an elaborate
scheme, one would look to the period in the late medieval period
when Provencal poets like Arnaut Daniel (fl. 1200) and those in the
other Romance languages, which are so fertile in rhymes, explored
rigorous stanzaic patterns as a means of giving the work greater trac-

tion. As my trope of progressive grip suggests, the traction provided by such redundancy also threw out sparks as it ground away at the familiar, recurrent sounds and identical parts of speech. The trick was to rescue the poem from its imposed stasis, both semantic and syntactic, by subtle interpolations of phrase that shifted the meanings, or turned concrete terms abstract (and vice versa).

In modern English the sestina's most engaging practitioners are either those who, like Auden, are at home in rhetorical variety (see the poems beginning "We have brought you, they said, a map of the country" and "Hearing of harvests rotting in the valleys") or who, like Elizabeth Bishop, can successfully bear the risk of repeating the commonplace terms in a commonplace realm while sustaining the aura of wonder as nouns change shape with other nouns (see Bishop's "A Miracle for Breakfast" and "Sestina" ("September rain falls on the house"). See also LINKED FORMS.

Short Meter A quatrain of three trimeter and one tetrameter line (3-3-4-3) that, measured against common meter (tetrameter alternating with trimeter in a 4-3-4-3 stanza), comes up short by one foot—or one stress—in the first line. Owing to the greater weight given to the third stress or the third line in any sequence of four, however, the short meter stanza operates within the scope of the RULE OF TWO. See examples under HYMN METER, also UNREALIZED BEAT.

Simile A class of trope in which vehicle and tenor appear together; the tenor is logically demanded because simile always uses one of the grammatical formulas that signal comparison. Appearing between the tenor and the vehicle will be either the connective term *like* (for phrases) or *as* (for clauses). The term to be explained is often left unembellished while the comparative term (brought in from a different realm) assumes the main burden of description and interpretation. Burns's simile, "my luve's like a red, red rose," has become typical of similes that compare women to flowers. As in METAPHOR, the vehicle is often "objective" while the tenor is variously spiritual (in Burns's poem, the woman comes to represent everything that is light, melodious, symmetrical, and long-lasting; this composite tenor is the sum or residue of all the comparisons).

Because metaphor need not designate the tenor, however, and the simile must, the comparison using *like* or *as* may tend toward being more explanatory (even didactic, as in the EPIC SIMILE, the most expansive form of the simile).

Even when things only are compared in a simile, the tenor often grows ethereal as it takes on some of the fluency of the vehicle, as in this line by Harold Monro (1879–1932): "The fresh air moves like water around a boat."[45] The diction is simple and uniform but the idea of the mild current rippling around the stationary vessel is subtle and evocative of an extended scene—and of the feeling with which it is viewed. Similarly, in Milton's description of the clouds before the great flood, "now the thick'n'd Sky / Like a dark Ceiling stood" (*Paradise Lost* XI.742–43), the reduction of the sky to the proportions of a room aptly renders the lowering atmosphere. To think of the cramped room as one looks toward the storm keeps both ideas in play.

Some similes throw all the weight onto the imported comparative term, so that we move away from the literal or experiential starting point into more fanciful terrain. Wallace Stevens suggests the pathos of mutability by imagining in some future time how children might pick up the bones of those of us who used to live here, but grieves lest they "never know that these were once / As quick as foxes on the hill" (p. 117), *quick* implying both being rapid (like the small fox) and being alive with the same nimbleness such instinctual creatures possess. David Ferry's simile is more ambitious in its overlay of comparisons, though he, too, argues from the material (bodies) to the abstract (a rapturous swirl of sensuous color): "The whole day was full of its colors that moved / About, within, and of each other, / Like bodies in the blindnesses of love." Elizabeth Bishop's Crusoe speaks more aggressively, moving the simile further from the literal end of the continuum of trope by bringing in a religious SYMBOL whose range of suggestion is both stipulated by dogma (embedded in narrative and liturgy) and also spontaneously suggested to a speaker familiar with such signs: "The knife there on the shelf— / It reeked of meaning like a crucifix" ("Crusoe in England"). For simile's relation to other forms of comparison, see TROPE.

45. Walter de la Mare, ed., *Come Hither: A Collection of Rhymes and Poems for the Young of All Ages;* Monro's poem appears on p. 9.

Slack Syllables In prose and nonmetrical poems, the unstressed syllables in the spoken language (as opposed to natural speech stresses).

Sonnet A fourteen-line poem, first popular during the fourteenth to seventeenth centuries, with an intricate rhyme scheme and a built-in propensity to shift viewpoint, tempo, or topic at the **VOLTA** or turn between lines 8 and 9 or before the final couplet. The two major rhyme patterns are the Petrarchan, with an octave rhyming *abbaabba* and a sestet rhyming *cdcdcd,* and the Shakespearean model of three quatrains of alternating rhyme, *abab cdcd efef,* plus a couplet, *gg.* The advantage of Shakespeare's sonnet form in English, a language that is poor in rhymes, is the ability to change rhyme sounds frequently. Sonnets are typically in iambic pentameter.

Note that even when many are strung together in cycles, sonnets are considered poems rather than stanzas in a poem. In Sidney's *Astrophil and Stella* and Auden's "Sonnets from China," each sonnet is a complete poem. See also **PETRARCHAN** mode.

Spenserean Stanza A nine-line iambic pentameter stanza with a hexameter (six-foot line) in line 9, rhyming *ababbcbcc⁶*. The stanza is used for narrative and descriptive poems. See Spenser's *Faerie Queene:*

> And more, to lulle him in his slumber soft,
> A trickling streame from high rock rumbling downe
> And ever-drizling raine upon the loft,★   ★*upon the air*
> Mixt with a murmuring winde, much like the sowne★   ★*sound*
> Of swarming bees, did cast him in a swowne.★   ★*swoon*
> No other noyse, nor peoples troublous cryes,
> As still are wont t'annoy the walled towne,
> Might there be heard; but carelesse Quiet lyes
> Wrapt in eternall silence farre from enemyes.

> (*FQ* I.i.41)

See also Shelley's "Adonais," Keats's "Eve of St. Agnes," as well as Daryl Hine's "Bluebeard's Wife" in the present volume.

Spondee A metrical foot consisting of two stressed syllables and classically denoted as $[--]$. However, because the two accents are never exactly equal in stress, the foot is sometimes called a "false spondee" and marked preferably as $[\cup\,\acute{-}]$ or $[\acute{-}\,\cup]$ in a **SCANSION** grid, depending on whether the basic binary foot of the poem is the **IAMB** or the **TROCHEE**. Spondees rely on a diction of monosyllables and create an **OVERSTRESSED LINE**.

Sprung Verse A term devised by Gerard Manley Hopkins for the blend of accentual with accentual-syllabic meters. See **PODIC FREE VERSE**.

Stanza (literally *station, room, stopping-place*) A group of three or more lines, usually with a fixed rhyme scheme, which is repeated more than once. Stanzas are used additively, unlike a one-time pattern of rhymed lines such as the sonnet, which is complete in fourteen lines. In Byron's *Don Juan* and Spenser's "Epithalamium," each stanza is part of a larger whole and is not meant to stand on its own. See examples of the various ballad quatrains under **HYMN METER**. The sonnet and the various stanzas (ottava rima, rhyme royal, Spenserean) also have their own entries.

Stanzaic Poetry A term that addresses the clustering of lines into larger units that repeat in identical form. The opposite of **STICHIC**.

Stichic (from *stichos,* meaning *row* or *line*) Line-bound, self-consciously end-stopped lines in which there is marked coincidence between grammar and line. (The opposite tendency, by which a larger frame takes precedence over a smaller, could be called either stanzaic or syntactic.) The term "stichic" is not necessarily pejorative and can be used effectively, as in Wallace Stevens's great blank-verse poem "The Idea of Order at Key West." See **STANZA** and **SYNTAX**.

Stress The pressure provided by speech on at least one syllable in a word. Not to be confused with accent or the *expectation* of stress created by rhythm in a poem. Stress is indicated by a slash in our system of scansion; accent is indicated by the macron, as in the iamb *I dare* in Donne's line "I dare not move my dimme eyes any way." *Dare* falls in the place of a metrical accent [$-$] and is given a stress because it is a strong verb ordinarily stressed in speech [/], hence the phrase *I dare* from the iambic pentameter line is scanned [$\cup \overset{/}{-}$] .

Strophic Organized in strophes, or stanzas, rather than in lines; the opposite of **STICHIC**.

Subjunctive Mood Grammatical term for a sentence that reflects the hypothetical possibilities of the language. Forms of hypothesis, using linked constructions such as *if/then, so/that, when/then),* also extend to optative (or hopeful) constructions (*would that* and *if only*) and the contrary-to-fact statement. The verbs in the hopeful constructions are often subjunctive masked as **INDICATIVE** future tense and might depend upon a statement with a present-tense verb: "there are clerkes," says Ben Jonson to persuade his friend to come to dinner, "The skie not falling, thinke we may have larkes," using the auxiliary of the potential subjunctive, the present-tense *may*, with the infinitive (uninflected verb form) *have*, to suggest a hopeful attitude toward the future. Throughout the poem Jonson employs several forms of subjunctive that imply a future, from predictive to hopeful, to seal his promise:

> No simple word,
> That shall be utter'd at our mirthfull boord,*   *table
> Shall make us sad next morning: or affright
> The libertie, that wee'll enjoy to night.

("Inviting a Friend to Supper")

The gist of Jonson's invitation is: If you will come, I promise you will be fed and entertained well, and there will be nobody to tattle tomorrow about any verbal excesses we indulge in tonight. The promissory verbs are in the subjunctive (hypothetical) mood, even though their tense seems future-indicative. Auxiliary (assisting) verbs are often the signs of subjunctive mood; words to watch are *may, might, should, would, could,* and *let*.

In other cases, subjunctive verbs have an immediately recognizable form different from the indicative—for example when Othello is haunted by contrary-to-fact past possibilities, which he might have borne better than Desdemona's supposed infidelity (the subjunctive verbs in both the conjectural and main clauses are in italics): "*Had it pleased* [that is, if it had pleased] heaven / To try me with affliction, *had they rained* / All kinds of sores and shames on my bare head . . . *I should have found* in some place of my soul / A drop of patience" (*Othello the Moor of Venice*, IV.ii). The sestet in Frost's "On a Bird Singing in Its Sleep" reverses the hypothetical order of "if/then" to stress a conclusion, given first, that leads to a negated (hence impossible, or contrary-to-fact) hypothesis, which comes last; the negated verb, *had made it,* is in the subjunctive "mood" (see p. 22).

Browning's dramatic speaker Bishop Blougram exults as he harangues his literary guest Gigadibs in outlandish similes and florid hypotheses about faith (which he calls "perpetual unbelief"). The

subjunctives (which are set in italics and boldface italics here for illus-
tration) slide into and fold back into one another like Chinese boxes:

How *you'd exult **if I could put*** you back
Six hundred years, *blot out* cosmogony,
Geology, ethnology, what not, 680
(Greek endings, each the little passing bell
That signifies some faith's about to die),
And *set* you square with Genesis again—
When such a Traveller *told* you his last news,
He *saw* the top of Ararat 685
But *did not climb* there since 't was getting dusk
And robber-bands infest the mountain's foot!
How should you feel, I ask, in such an age,
How act?

("Bishop Blougram's Apology")

Blougram asks Gigadibs in effect, what if a traveler who had been
there at the flood told you the hypothetical fact that he saw the top
of Ararat, where Noah's ark came to rest, but was not in a mood to
climb it? The entire passage is in the subjunctive. Note how the pas-
sage is tightened across a dozen lines by the hypothetical and subordi-
nating syntax. See **HYPOTAXIS**.

Substituted Feet Metrical unit in which the expected stress pattern is
replaced by a different kind of foot. The most common substitutions
are the spondee and the anapest where one expects iambs, and a third
substitution, which takes the form of reversal of stress; see **METRICAL
INVERSION** and **TROCHAIC INVERSION**.

Syllabics Verse form that counts the total numbers of syllables. More
popular in lightly stressed tongues (such as French), than in English.

Symbol A type of metaphor in which only the vehicle is given and the
tenor or signification is general and archetypal. A symbol can have a
specific vehicle (like the crucifix—although its meanings are mul-
tiple and, in some ways, contradictory: suffering, sacrifice, redemp-
tion, resurrection, transfiguration, promise of an afterlife) or a more
generalized vehicle, like a reef (which either protects the island or
destroys the ship). When the provenance of a symbol is stipulated in
one direction, we say the objective vehicle is an "emblem" (as an

anchor is an emblem of hope or a skeleton of mortality—emblems don't expand or become more complex by association based on their vehicles but rather rely on cultural knowledge to draw the right associations—say religious ones—to complete their tenors.

To symbolize a spiritual presence, poets will often introduce birds into their work. Like Keats's nightingale and Hardy's darkling thrush, the bird in Frost's sonnet "On a Bird Singing in Its Sleep" is a symbol of the poet's soul at the same time remaining the naturalistic and literal bird. What dictates the extent of naturalism is the amount of episode. The more episode and description in the poem, the more literal will be the base of the symbols. Thus Frost's bird is more literally symbolic than Keats's nightingale, some of whose meanings derive from the Bible and literary history. See also the kind of invention called a LITERAL SYMBOL, whose tenor evolves gradually and stays specific to the poem rather than being immediately recognizable and fit for all places. By contrast a METAPHOR usually compares two things or provides an indefinite vehicle (fire, water, earth) with its temporary, open-ended tenor (the fire of jealousy or of love, the water that kills or quenches, the earth of bloom or burial). See also TROPE.

Syntactic Inversion Contortion or reversal of sentence order that makes the disturbed order itself "marked" or significant to the meaning: "Give money me, take friendship whoso list." Here George Gascoigne mimics the freedom of classical languages to rearrange the sentence (owing to its grammatical inflections that identify syntactic roles). Milton was also fond of taking the risk of inversion with its classical flavoring: "Me [to me], of these / Nor skilled or studious, higher argument / Remains" (*Paradise Lost* IX.41–43); "Him [the serpent] after long debate, irresolute / Of thoughts revolved, his [Satan's] final sentence chose" (*PL* IX.87–88). Pope also mocked the balanced epic formulas in "Beaux banish beaux and coaches coaches drive" (*Rape of the Lock* I.102) and "'Gainst Pallas [Athena], Mars; Latona [that is, against Latona], Hermes arms" (V.47). Context helps tell the subject (sons) from the object (fields) of the verb *divide* in Goldsmith's inverted sentence: "Those fenceless fields the sons of wealth divide" ("The Deserted Village," 307). In Muir's line, "Long since the rust its gardens here has planned," the inversion of object with verb emphasizes the antagonistic link between the garden and the PERSONIFICATION of the rust as it parodies living "gardens" with its corrosive lace-work.

Mild inversion of syntax is common in rhymes for children. Consider the poem by Jane Taylor (1783–1824) beginning "Twinkle, twinkle, little star":

> When the blazing sun is gone,   5
> When he nothing shines upon . . .

More ambitious is the postponement of the main verb by an auxiliary—*doth* (for *does*), used for its expletive grace—in this cautionary poem by Isaac Watts (1674–1748):

> How doth the little busy bee
>   Improve each shining hour,
> And gather honey all the day
>   From every opening flower.
>
> ("Against Idleness and Mischief")[46]

This is the poem Alice tries to remember in the labyrinth when she has grown too large to move, but "the words did not come the same as they used to do":

> How doth the little crocodile
>   Improve his shining tail,
> And pour the waters of the Nile
>   On every golden scale![47]

The words don't come the same, but the shape of the sentence's inversion does, and this is what misleads her.

Both inversion (which in a sentence is also called ANASTROPHE) and interruption of the s-v-o sentence order (also called HYPERBATON) act in tension with the unfolding line. Wordsworth's "Composed upon Westminster Bridge" abounds in inversions that run counter to closure ("Dull would he be of soul who could pass by . . ."; "This City now doth, like a garment, wear . . ."; "Never did sun more beautifully steep . . ."—the last a pattern completed by successive inversions, "steep / In his first splendour, valley, rock or hill"). More self-conscious is Louise Bogan's question halted by hyperbaton in her poem "Rhyme," "What laid, I said, / My being waste?" (that

46. Opie, eds., *Oxford Book of Children's Verse*, pp. 123 and 49.

47. *Alice's Adventures in Wonderland* (1865), *The Complete Illustrated Lewis Carroll*, illustrated by John Tenniel, introduction by Alexander Woollcott (New York: Gallery/ W. G. Smith, 1991), p. 26.

is, what laid waste to my being?). Her poem in free verse, "Baroque
Comment" postpones by anastrophe the main nouns that are her
fragment's subjects until the second verse paragraph; the first five
lines are all displacements of her theme, kept in uneasy suspense. In
A. D. Hope's "Man Friday," lines 7–12 provide good examples of
both anastrophe (line 11) and hyperbaton (all the lines between 7 and
12 interrupt the s-v kernel "He . . . took"):

> He, no less providential, and no less
> Inscrutably resolved to save and bless,
> Eager to share his fortune with the weak
> And faithful servants whom he taught to speak,   10
> By all his years of exile undeterred,
> Took into exile Friday and the bird.

A related technique is that of deploying complex syntax across many
lines; such partial containment within the individual lines, like syn-
tactic inversion, often projects uncertainty or struggle:

> He consigned to the moon—such as she was,
> So late-arising—to the broken moon,
> As better than the sun in any case
> For such a charge, his snow upon the roof,
> His icicles along the wall to keep;
> And slept.
>
> (Frost, "An Old Man's Winter Night")

Robert Browning also makes maximum use of suspension in his
verse-novel composed of dramatic monologues, *The Ring and the
Book*. See also PASSAGE, SYNTAX, and WORD ORDER.

Syntax (literally *collective arrangement*) The way the basic components of
a sentence are arranged, connected according to phrases and clauses,
and extended to other sentences. The continuum of syntax is graphed
on pp. 46–47. It begins with the simplest units (themselves only frag-
ments of sentences), the phrase ("Unsafe at any speed") and clause
("Because it's there"), moves to the simple declarative sentence ("I
am a kind of burr"), then to a compound sentence ("I am a kind
of burr; I shall stick," *Measure for Measure* IV.iii), and on to the two
main varieties of complex subordinating sentence, the descriptive
("they came into a land / In which it seemèd always afternoon"
(Tennyson, "The Lotos-Eaters") and the argumentative ("If this be

error, and upon me proved, / I never writ, nor no man ever loved,"
Sonnet 116).

As one of the major determinants of poetic shape, syntax is im-
plicated at many points in a poem's thought, although some poems
put more pressure on it than others. One example of greater pressure
is David Ferry's "A Young Woman," which begins not with the
young woman as agent moving through her modifiers and com-
manding her verbs, but with a provision for reversal. More even than
the syntax in Ferry's poem, what is inverted and left incomplete is the
entire hopeful enterprise of youth: "That she, with such gifts
given. . . ." The ambiguity of this first clause stretches past the mid-
point of the poem, where it finally takes on a verb ("That she . . .
should falter"). But the clause never takes its place in a sentence: It
remains a dependent clause with no main clause to complete it. We
can imagine many ways to complete Ferry's sentence—*that she should
falter . . . is expected, . . . would be sad, . . . would only make her more
beautiful,* etc.), but these alternatives hover indefinitely over the
young woman's thematically and syntactically spellbound progress.

Syntax may either coincide with or diverge from line; it may be
simple or complex, in the indicative or subjunctive (hypothetical)
mood. Capable of enormous variety, the ordering of the sentence is
also that element of style which adheres most closely to logic, and
which therefore borders most nearly on the world of prose. "Loose
dirt is lifted to a sail," writes Timothy Steele in "Toward Calgary,"
employing a complete declarative sentence on one closed line; the
diction (*dirt;* the fact that it's *loose*) supports the sentence's matter-
of-factness. Still, syntax may be employed in poetry so as to suggest
connection to rationality, yet be undermined by other elements.
Trope operates in Steele to transform the observable data into a per-
ceptual fantasy: when the dirt rises it *is lifted* on- or *into a sail,* as if the
entire landscape were being driven like a vessel before a swift wind.
The illusion of objective fact is progressively dispersed in the poem,
which meditates on definite but indirect virtues like prudence and
quietness. See **DICTION** and **TROPE**.

Tag The formula phrase repeated in order to introduce successive lines
of parallel clauses in **HEBREW VERSE** and other religious poems. See
ANAPHORA and **ISOCOLON**.

Tanka A poetic form of Japanese origin; a poem of five lines and thirty-one syllables, lines 1 and 3 having five syllables, lines 2, 4, and 5 with seven syllables. As in HAIKU, the strict limitation in syllables promotes economy and poise.

Tenor The meaning of a metaphor; what is represented or "held" by the vehicle or physical image in a comparison. Metaphor must always state its vehicle because this is the object or physical embodiment that carries the meaning, but may leave its tenor implicit. (The reverse is impossible, for a tenor without a vehicle is only an abstraction.) The closer the vehicle is to the tenor, the more natural the comparison; conversely, the further apart they are, the more cerebral and artificial their connection. On occasion, a poem will explicitly name both its vehicle and its tenor, as in Shakespeare's Sonnet 73 ("That time of yeeare thou maist in me behold, / When yellow leaves, or none or few doe hange / Upon those boughs . . ."). See METAPHOR and VE-HICLE.

Tension Pull, or tugging, which occurs either when syntax works against and diverges from line, or when other elements of style work against each other. For example, in Samuel Taylor Coleridge's and Emily Dickinson's brief stanzas, line often makes one shape and sentence another:

> I moved, and could not feel my limbs: 305
> I was so light—almost
> I thought that I had died in sleep
> And was a blessed ghost.
>
> ("The Rime of the Ancient Mariner")

> And though the Woe you have Today
> Be larger—As the Sea
> Exceeds its Unremembered Drop—
> They're Water—equally—
>
> (#660)

Syntax and line are in tension. Not all poems employ tension (let alone any one sort of tension), although some seem to require it, especially poems with both lyrical and intellectual impulse, such as the work of Stevens, whose metaphysical aims are subjected to a kind of verbal swoon, and Auden, whose enormous musical variety jars

against his sometimes austere dogmas. Milton's work is also made
muscular by the tension between dramatic episode and complex
rhetoric.

Note, too, that even when one form of tension predominates (as
that of line with syntax in the Dickinson stanza above), other tensions
can support this dominant one (as the theme of emotional tension
and imbalance links the two seasons of the speaker's grief). For ten-
sion to work in some areas, in other words, COINCIDENCE is required
in others. See RECESSION OF TECHNIQUE.

Tetrameter A verse line consisting of four feet; most commonly either
iambic ("My little horse must think it queer") or trochaic ("But to
see her was to love her"); however, amphibrachs and anapests prolif-
erate in ballads and imitations of folk poetry (for example, "His
hounds they lie down at his feet ^ ^ [B] ^ " and "The Assyrian
came down like a wolf on the fold."). The most significant body of
iambic tetrameter lyric poetry in English may be that of Andrew
Marvell, who also used the tetrameter couplet for his poems descrip-
tive of place, as did Thomas Carew in "To Saxham" (1640) and John
Dyer in "Grongar Hill" (1726); Sir Walter Scott also used rhymed
tetrameter for many of his narratives (although Scott was overfond of
triple feet). And the form has often fulfilled a contrastive function,
too: Shakespeare gives the commentator Gower in *Pericles* speeches
in tetrameter couplets that differ profoundly from the blank verse
spoken by the other characters. See also BALLAD STANZA and the
RULE OF TWO.

Threshold Boundary between the more limiting shapes and meanings
stemming from the elements in isolation and the work of the ele-
ments in overlap. Examples include HALF-MEANING, which bridges
the authority of sentence and line and Brooke-Rose's concept of the
LITERAL SYMBOL, which bridges the pull of the given and the nuance
of the implied, as in the many shabby and domestic landscapes of
Yeats, Muir, and Nemerov, through which we glimpse archetypal
worlds both debased and sublime. Threshold is also broached when
forms are deflected from their conventional usage, as when blank
verse loosens into free blank verse (as in the work of Stevens and
Eliot), or when a poet like Marianne Moore veers back from her
purely syllabic norm to an alternation of weak with strong syllables

in an accentual-syllabic pattern (see the end of "An Egyptian Pulled Glass Bottle in the Shape of a Fish").

In a larger sense, threshold also refers to the condition of all verse when it is underway, poised on the edge of the known, about to disappear into its own transgressions and eruptions—the most effective and lasting transgressions being those which, like Shakespeare's and Yeats's, have taken in the most nourishment from models outside their evolved habits.

Transitive Verb A verb that transmits an action to a consequence, moving usually from an agent to an object. The relation is schematically given as s-v-o (subject-verb-object), for example, "Samson cut his hair." Not all active verbs can take objects, so they are grouped with copulas and the verbs of being and feeling I call "non-verbs" under the heading of "intransitive" (that is, un-transmitting). An example of an intransitive verb of action would be "The temple fell." A transitive verb of a related action in an s-v-o sentence would be "Samson pulled down the temple." Transitive verbs enable the poet to work through both plot and mode (including trope) at the level of the sentence. See further examples under INTRANSITIVE VERBS; see also MODE and SYNTAX.

Trimeter A verse-line consisting of three feet; most commonly anapestic ("In the old Presbyterian College," from Daryl Hine's epic autobiography *In and Out*) or iambic (as in Hardy's "I look into my glass").

Triolet See LINKED FORM.

Triple Meter A metrical foot of three syllables, typically used for ballads and nonsense rhymes. The primary feet are ANAPESTS, DACTYLS, and AMPHIBRACHS.

Trochaic Inversion (also called TROCHAIC SUBSTITUTION) A trochee in place of an iamb in an iambic poem. This reversal of expected stress—a metrical foot of a strong syllable followed by a weak—must work to overcome the weak-strong expectation characteristic of the iambic line. At the same time, iambic lines will grow dull without some metrical inversion. The most common place for trochaic inversion to fall is after a line break or a midline caesura; the trochees are in boldface type:

Now all is done, **have what** shall have no end

(Sonnet 110)

wwwww

They that have powre to hurt, and will doe none
. . . .
They are the Lords and owners of their faces,
Others, but stewards of their excellence
. . . .
Lillies that fester, smell far worse than weeds.

(Sonnet 94)

wwwww

Into my face **preseth** with bolde pretence
. . . .
Leving his entreprise with payn and cry

(Wyatt, "The Longe Love, that in My Thought Doeth Harbar")

wwwww

or when skaters curve
all day across the lake, **scoring** their white
records in ice.

(Nemerov, "Writing")

wwwww

And these same thoughts **people** this little world.

(*Richard II* V.v)

wwwww

The log that shifted with a jolt
Once in the stove, disturbed him and he shifted

(Frost, "An Old Man's Winter Night")

These last lines from Frost suggest how trochaic inversion may be used mimetically; the reversal of stress imitates the shifting of the logs in the fireplace and the flurry of imbalance—in fire and in the sleeper's dream—that results.

But trochaic inversion that does not follow a caesura is perceived as wrenched and should be reserved for dramatic occasions, or at least be used judiciously:

A boy too far from town to learn **baseball**

(Frost, "Birches")

~~~~~

All through the damp **morning** he works, he reads

<div align="right">(Gunn, "His Rooms in College")</div>

~~~~~

Wee part not with **thee at** this meeting day.

(Ralegh, "Three Thinges There Bee")

On occasion, even trochees that follow the caesura can be used to create a deliberate metrical hitch to support the difficulty of the logic:

> Let me not to the marriage of true mindes
> Admit impediments, **love is** not love
> Which alters when it alteration finds

(Sonnet 116)

Trochaic Meter The mirror image of iambic meter, hence often tending to become indistinguishable from it. Memorable exceptions occur in trochaic tetrameter, such as Longfellow's *Song of Hiawatha*, where the shadowed half of the moon is explained as follows:

> Once a warrior, very angry,
> Seized his grandmother, and threw her
> Up into the sky at midnight;
> Right against the moon he threw her;
> 'Tis her body that you see there.

This poem's curious sing-song, which I label the "*Hiawatha* syndrome" to caution new writers as to its pitfalls, is also capable of great power, but must be read in longer passages. The poem is (according to Auden) Longfellow's attempt to render the heroic meters of Nordic poetry into English. Shakespeare's song of Juno and Ceres from *The Tempest* IV.i uses a catalogue dense with qualities to offset the monotony of the trochaic chant:

> Earthes increase, foison plenty,
> Barns and garners never empty,
> Vines with clustering bunches growing,
> Plants with goodly burthen bowing . . .

Trochaic lines can be tightened by leaving off the final unstressed syllables, as in Auden's poem beginning "Lay your sleeping head, my love," or by alternating masculine with feminine endings, as Thomas

Campion (1567–1620) does in "Rose-Cheekt Laura"; imagine the
first syllable—*The*—receiving a stress and *dull* not receiving one:

> The dull notes we sing
> Discords neede for helps to grace them;   10
> Only beauwty purely living
> Knows no discord.

Few are the poets who have made pure trochaic tetrameters convinc-
ing, though Burns does so with the help of variable syntax (and ac-
companying caesuras) in "Ae fond kiss, and then we sever":

> Who shall say that Fortune grieves him   5
> While the star of hope she leaves him?
>
> . . . .
>
> Had we never lov'd sae blindly,
> Never met—or never parted—
> We had ne'er been broken-hearted.

Trochaic Substitution Another way of phrasing the occurrence of a
trochee when the meter is iambic. The term TROCHAIC INVERSION
is preferable because it does not suggest that another kind of meter
has been put in place of the basic iambic meter.

Trochee A binary accentual-syllabic foot, abstractly sketched [– ◡].
The meter it makes is called "trochaic."

Trope (literally *a turn*) The element of poetry that includes all forms of
comparison and transfer of meaning by means of which language
means doubly. Since the late Middle Ages, trope has been associated
with figures of thought rather than figures of speech (the latter am-
plify and create novel patterns using conventional meanings of
words—these devices include ANAPHORA, ANTITHESIS, ASYNDE-
TON [removal of conjunctions between successive clauses], ISOCO-
LON, PUN, and ZEUGMA). But rather than being completely separate,
figures of thought connect with these figures of speech at the point
where words achieve the greatest physicality owing to meter and
rhyme and the layered doubleness of meaning known as pun. A con-
tinuum of trope could be imagined that stresses the role of material
reference, from the LITERAL SYMBOL whose sole operative trait is
resonant physical presence in the poem's scene, through the midstage
METAPHOR, which must mention the vehicle of meaning but need
not mention the tenor that is implied, through SIMILE, which men-

tions both, to pun, which exploits the literalness of reference buried
in many words that have opened, somewhere during their history, to
ABSTRACTION. The continuum below moves between extremes of
thing (on the left) to *word* (on the right):

LITERAL SYMBOL AND
          METONYMY   METAPHOR   SIMILE   PUN

In pun it is not the *thing* that means twice, but the *word* for the thing.
At the other extreme, with literal symbol, time is the force that makes
the thing mean twice—once immediately, then progressively.

In general, trope's comparisons change the literal and figurative
meanings of words relative to each other. It features comparisons that
are stated (as in similes) and those framed by copulas ("I am a cam-
era"), but is not limited to these; trope includes all the syntactical and
rhetorical possibilities of suggestion. Christine Brooke-Rose names
these by syntax but also describes them by rhetorical affiliation in *A
Grammar of Metaphor,* for example the "genitive link," whereby an
idea flames up like a thing, as in *the fire of love,* or one thing bursts out
of a second, like Ben Belitt's trope of *a talon of ash* representing the
greatest heat in a painting;[48] the metaphor called "simple replace-
ment," in which the noun we expect—say "Prayer" in the George
Herbert poem of that name—is then called "Exalted Manna" and
"The Milky Way" instead (note that a simple replacement metaphor
can appear in the syntactic form called **APPOSITION**); and the "verb
metaphor," as when the falcon *towered* in the air in *Macbeth* II.iv.[49]

Metaphor occurs near the middle of the continuum of compari-
son below, dividing tropes of material participation (literal symbol),
partial representation (that is, parts for the whole, or **METONYMY**),
and the resonance of traditional plots and characters seen from the
perspective of a local scene or set of events (**ALLUSION**), from more

48. In "Double Poem of the World's Burning," in *Possessions: Selected Poems 1938–
1985,* by Ben Belitt (Boston: David R. Godine, 1986).
49. This play is rich in metaphors that transfer to unusual nouns the actions of unac-
customed verbs; night should "scarf up the tender eye of pitiful day," in III.ii, and in II.ii
Macbeth thinks that, rather than being cleaned by water, his hand will "incarnadine"
(make red, because guilty of Duncan's murder) "the multitudinous seas" in which he
anxiously thinks of plunging it. Note the freedom within this verb metaphor to create
new words; see **NEOLOGISM**.

stylized embodiments of likeness, beginning with those of shared sympathy (**SYMBOL** and archetype) and proceeding through the more overtly stipulated comparisons, to the right:

				SYMBOL			
LITERAL				AND			
SYMBOL	METONYMY	ALLUSION	METAPHOR	ARCHETYPE	SIMILE	EMBLEM	ALLEGORY
|	|	|	|	|	|	|	|

The easiest item to grasp is the **LITERAL SYMBOL** because it is primarily literal before a hint of symbolic representation can show itself. Examples would include the wayside flower in Muir's "Ballad of Hector in Hades" no less than the handkerchief of Desdemona, which begins as a literal object that only in time comes to represent a travestied love-token and the blotched virtue of the woman from whom it is deviously stolen by Iago. The key to the literal symbol is its literal onset, and only eventual signification, which can glide over into metonymy (the handkerchief representing the women who owned it, the courtier to whom it was supposedly given, the shortsightedness of Iago's wife, who obtained it, the destructive credulity of Othello, and/or the malevolence of Iago himself): But in the moment of its origins, the literal symbol is self-identical.

METONYMY comprises both possession, or vertical linking (the combs of the forlorn ladies waiting for their drowned lords in "Sir Patrick Spens," which represent the ladies who wear them) and lateral association (like that between the group and the single member—one leaf representing a treeful, one drop a deluge, one tantrum a spate of them, one beggar a rabble, one citizen a town, one king a country ruled by monarchy). **ALLUSION** follows literal symbol and metonymy because its effectiveness is often dependent on inexplicit suggestion rather than direct naming of the desired evocation. **MET-APHOR** and **SYMBOL** (with its related background of archetype) also bridge the continuum by remaining necessarily rooted in the need for objective counters but open to traditional associations that, in simile, emblem, and allegory, employ greater economy and stylization of means. Individual entries on each of the tropes will provide further examples. See also **PERSONIFICATION**.

Understressed Line A line composed of polysyllables that has fewer speech stresses than a normal iambic line (each polysyllabic word tending to have only one major stress; secondary stresses are usually softer than the primary one): "Familiar and inexplicable, wearing" (Thom Gunn, "In Praise of Cities"); "And had the inspiration to de-sist" (Robert Frost, "On a Bird Singing in its Sleep"). Understressing also usually corresponds to longer syntactical units that are rapid in execution (because fewer stresses fall on the extra syllables):

> Being intelligible,
> these winding ways with their audacities
> and delicate hesitations, they become
> miraculous, so intimately, out there
> at the pen's point or brush's tip, do world   10
> and spirit wed.

(Howard Nemerov, "Writing")

So the polysyllabic, conversational sentence will not only exceed the bounds of a single verse line, it will also generate a forward "drive" or momentum. See **OVERSTRESSED LINE**.

Unrealized Beat Term for the unspoken fourth beat in the even-numbered lines of **COMMON METER**:

> Dingle, dingle, doo ^ sey;
>   The cat's ^ in the well ^ [B]
> The dog's away to Bellingen
>   To buy the bairn a bell[50] ^ [B]

or in longer stanzas that build upon the 4-3-4-3 stress profile of common meter:

> It fell upon a high holiday
> And the very first day of the year ^ [B]
> Little Mattie Groves to church did go
> God's holy word to hear ^ [B]
> God's holy word to hear ^ [B]

("Mattie Groves")[51]

The jingle illustrating **IMPLIED OFFBEAT** also uses unrealized fourth beats in the even-numbered lines, before which one supplies the two intervening offbeats needed to maintain the triple rhythm:

> Hink ^ ^ spink ^ the pud ^ dings stink
> The fat ^ begins ^ to fry ^ ^ [B]

50. Halliwell, ed., *The Nursery Rhymes of England,* p. 87.
51. Roger D. Abrahams and George Foss, *Anglo-American Folksong Style* (Engle-wood Cliffs, NJ: Prentice-Hall, 1968), p. 38.

Nobody at home, ∧ but jump ∧ ing Joan
Father, ∧ mother, and I[52] ∧ ∧ [B]

It is not only folk rhymes like these which leave the fourth beats implied; more literary poems in trimeter, SHORT METER, and common meter rely on our supplying the unrealized beat. Emily Dickinson's short-meter quatrains clearly show the effect of HYMN METERS (see her "The Heart asks Pleasure—first—," #536 and "To One denied to drink," #490). Rudyard Kipling's "The Way Through the Woods" illustrates the compensation that occurs in the trimeter lines:

It is underneath the coppice and heath
And the thin anemones[53] ∧ [B]

Christina Rossetti's poem beginning "In the bleak midwinter" stretches out words like *midwinter* and *iron,* to make room for implied offbeats and add an extra (unrealized) beat, when it is sung to the "Cranham" melody of composer Gustav Holst (1874–1934); a preference for trochees places unusual stress on *In,* the *-ter* of *midwinter,* and the first syllable of *ago:*

In the bleak midwin ∧ ter
Frosty wind made moan ∧ [B]
Earth stood hard as i ∧ ron
Water like a stone ∧ [B]
Snow had fallen, snow on snow   5
Snow ∧ on ∧ snow ∧ [B]
In the bleak midwin ∧ ter
Long ∧ a ∧ go ∧ [B]

It's worth noting that the poem is sung to a regular four-beat measure, even though there is only one line that is tetrameter (line 5) and one line with only two speech stresses (line 8).[54]

Vehicle The part of trope that is transferred from another realm of discourse in order to give clarification of the tenor, or which acts as the literal ground from which the figurative idea emerges (as in literal symbol). As an imported idea, the vehicle carries the meaning by revealing, through an aspect of the object described, a feature in the more abstract tenor that might not have been apparent before. In

52. Halliwell, ed., *The Nursery Rhymes of England,* p. 87.
53. Opie, eds., *Oxford Book of Children's Verse,* p. 323.
54. *Carols for Christmas,* compiled and arranged by David Willcocks (New York: The Metropolitan Museum and Henry Holt, 1983), p. 48.

Thom Gunn's *Misanthropos* VII, we encounter not just a literal setting but a gesture of abandoning oneself to it. Thus the vehicle is both material detail and an act of participation on the part of the speaker, who runs his hand over the crusty surfaces of his life,

> the chipped glossy surface   20
> of some doorjamb, for instance,
> cramming my nail with its grime,
> stroking humps where colorless
> paint had filled faults to substance.
>
> I was presence without full   25
> being . . .

The tenor which the speaker derives from his vehicle is the idea that he himself is a kind of filler. We might also observe that the vehicle is thematically "low" (grime and old paint) while the tenor derived from it is "high" (that is, substantiality of being). See LITERAL SYMBOL and TENSION.

Verse Literally, a *turn* that creates a line. Often implies metrical lines and occasionally some conventional features of theme when the poem is viewed as formulaic. However, verse can also be a useful term when attention is being called to a work that employs the LINE, whether metrical or free.

Verset (literally *biblical verse*) A form of writing in long lines with underlying rhythmic alternations between the strong beats and the even stronger ones. Biblical verse also typically uses syntax to shape lines. See HEBREW VERSE and FREE VERSE.

Volta (literally, a *turn*) The change in direction of argument in a sonnet that occurs between the octave and sestet.

Word Order A syntactic trait that makes us focus on conventional sentence order. Some poems use normal word order in such a way that the metrical and stanzaic conventions they undertake seem validated (see PLAIN STYLE). Variation from the norm is most striking when the order of words is not constrained either by the need to rhyme (as it is in Clough's "Old things need not be therefore true"[55]) or by the requirement of exact meter (as it is in the inverted placement of the

---

55. Norrington, ed., *The Poems of Arthur Hugh Clough*, p. 89.

pronoun *I* and auxiliary verbs in two lines from Hardy's "In Tenebris III," in DACTYLS: "Confident I in her watching and ward through the blackening heather"; "Then might the Voice that is law have said 'Cease!' and the ending have come."

But when nothing is seemingly gained by the variation, the unexpected word sequence is revealing, as in Bogan's "wet with a dead million leaves" ("Baroque Comment"), in which the poet visibly refuses the more colloquial exaggeration in favor of a phrase in which the excess of number is still linked with the leaves' living forms. More far-fetched reversals and interruptions abound in the six-volume *faux*-antique blank verse epic *The Dawn in Britain* (1906), by Charles M. Doughty:

> And when those all, in the king's ship, had spoiled;
> They Cloten, did, on thwart row-bank compel,
> To drag an oar . . .

("Bladyn's Song of Cloten")

The effect of the displacements (consistent throughout Doughty's poem) is to render the ethos of archaic Britons as harsh and coercive; every action is arduous and thwarted in a way the sentence order imitates.

Consider also the second line of Shakespeare's Sonnet 73:

> That time of yeeare thou maist in me behold,
> When yellow leaves, or none, or few doe hange
> Upon those boughes which shake against the could . . .

The series is less logical and sequential, but perhaps truer to both a perceptual law (we thought there were none left, but when we look more closely, yes, a few still remain), and perhaps also to a psychological one (is it not more withering—more shameful—to have a few remnants of living matter clinging about, than to be dramatically bald?). See also SYNTACTIC INVERSION.

Zeugma (literally, *yoke*) A figure of speech that uses one word to yoke two phrases. The second stanza of the parodied Isaac Watts poem in Alice's version contains the simplest zeugma in the sixth line, which shares with line 5 the subject-pronoun *he:*

How cheerfully he seems to grin,   5
   How neatly spreads his claws,
And welcomes little fishes in,
   With gently smiling jaws![56]

Both uses are direct. Shakespeare also yokes two ideas with a single verb-plus-object phrase *lends them,* both of whose applications are abstract, in the chorus that opens the second act of *Romeo and Juliet:* "But passion lends them power, time means, to meet." In Sonnet 76, however, abstract is yoked to particular when the speaker asserts that "you and love are still my argument" or theme. This FIGURE OF SPEECH becomes more potent with greater disparity between the ideas and things brought together.

    Zeugma at its strongest can also yoke words or phrases across the literal-metaphorical boundary (thus illustrating how figures of speech might overlap with FIGURES OF THOUGHT). Pope suggests with his zeugma in the *Imitations of Horace* (*Ep.II.ii* 217) that we can imagine vice as a weapon directed against the sinner: it's unfortunate, he says, that good satire makes "Men only feel the Smart, but not the Vice"; the yoking term is feel, as in feel the pain of. Similarly, in "Epistle to Bathurst" Pope yokes the idea of deprivation that is concrete (want with an empty purse) to deprivation that is intellectual and moral: "Resolve me, Reason, which of these is worse, / Want with a full, or with an empty purse" (319–20).

---

56. *The Complete Illustrated Lewis Carroll,* p. 26.

14

Annotated Bibliography of Further Reading

The following is a partial list of the anthologies of poetry and the handbooks, articles, and books about poetry and prosody that I have found useful in writing, teaching, and thinking about poetry. After each entry I have added a brief description of its most appealing features. You will notice a preference for the work of poets about poetry. Poets who are articulate about the craft of verse are among the best expositors.[1]

I. Anthologies

Allen, Donald M., ed. *The New American Poetry*. New York: Grove Press, 1960.
  Concentrates on the postwar period from 1945 to 1960 and presents the work of poets who identified themselves with antiformalist movements or waves, often associated with fugitive publications and little magazines (*Yugen, Neon, Kulchur, Big Table*, etc.): the most prominent groups were the Black Mountain school (Olson, Duncan) and the experimental city poets from New York (like Frank O'Hara, LeRoi Jones, and Gilbert Sorrentino) and San Francisco (the "Beats" Kerouac, Corso, Ginsberg). John Ashbery, James Schuyler, Denise Levertov, and Gary Snyder are also represented. An anthology that awakened many readers and would-be writers to another sort of pos-

---

1. W. H. Auden is exemplary, even in his eccentricity. (See my discussion of some of the many volumes edited by him.) Another poet, F. T. Prince, has looked closely at Milton's prosody in a way that sheds light on prosody in general; see *The Italian Element in Milton's Verse* (1954). Poets John Frederick Nims and J. V. Cunningham are also acute when they write about verse; and I have already mentioned Charles O. Hartman and Timothy Steele in connection with meter and rhythm (see chapter 8 on accentual-syllabic meter).

sibility for writing—one in which the poet slips free of intention and gets a little lost in the culture. The "Statements on Poetics" at the back are as lively and disorienting as the free-verse selections.

Allen, John Alexander, ed. *Hero's Way: Contemporary Poems in the Mythic Tradition*. Englewood Cliffs, NJ: Prentice-Hall, 1971.

As in de la Mare's anthology, the most engaging feature of Allen's lies in the categories devised for experience, which resemble those of Ignatian meditation and spiritual autobiography: "Stagnation," "The Meeting," "The Call," "The Road of Trials," "Conflict," "Atonement," and "Rescue," arrayed under larger headings from Freudian and comparative analysis: "The Lady," "The Double," "The Beast," "The Father," "The Boon." Many now-lesser-known poets of mid-century are represented, and the poems Allen has culled are less impressive on occasion than their aptness in embodying the myth—not to mention the light they shed on the poems lying to either side. He never employs only the obvious connections. That Bogan's "Medusa" appears under "stagnation" is less surprising than the fact that Frost's "Neither Out Far Nor In Deep" shows up there too. Eliot's "Marina" is not in "The Lady" but "The Boon." Instead of being printed under "Loss," Hardy's "The Voice" ("Woman much missed . . . When you had changed from the one who was all to me") occurs in "Intimations" along with "Lorelei," by Sylvia Plath, Eliot's "La Figlia Che Piange," and Barbara Howes's "City Afternoon" with its "whinnying of Venetian blinds." Allen exhibits such ingenuity and tact in assigning poems to his categories that he makes this anthology as rich in analysis as many another more discursive study with a mythic orientation.

Allison, Alexander W., Herbert Barrows, Caesar R. Blake, Arthur J. Carr, Arthur M. Eastman, and Hubert M. English, Jr., eds. *Norton Anthology of Poetry*. Third edition. New York: W. W. Norton, 1983.

The most capacious one-volume anthology of poetry in English from the Middle Ages to the 1960s. Many long narrative and meditative poems are reprinted in their entirety, including Chaucer's Pardoner's and Nun's Priest's tales, Marlowe's *Hero and Leander,* Dryden's *Mac Flecknoe,* Pope's *Rape of the Lock,* the entire first epistle of the *Essay on Man,* and *Epistle to Arbuthnot,* 119 stanzas from *Don Juan,* and the whole (perhaps not entirely necessary) *Rubaiyat of Omar Khayam.* Included is an ample representation of the Romantics' longer poems. On the other hand, Marvell's *Upon Appleton House* and some representation of Auden's and Stevens's longer works are wanting; and the selection is patchy on the second half of the twentieth century. *See also* Margaret Ferguson.

Auden, W. H., and John Garrett, eds. *The Poet's Tongue.* Two volumes in one edition. London: G. Bell & Sons, 1935.

An anthology that aims to discourage the idea that all poetry is serious or written by famous persons. Accordingly, the poems are all anonymous and arranged alphabetically according to the letter with which the poem or excerpt begins (so "The first day of Christmas" is followed by Marvell's "The forward youth that would appear," which is followed by Blunden's "The hop-poles stand in cones"; "We're all in the dumps" is preceded by "Weep you no more, sad fountains"). So long as it be memorable speech, "the audible spoken word and cadence" to which we surrender ("as we do when talking to an intimate friend"), poetry can be about anything and need not engage only great themes: "First, one must overcome the prejudice that poetry is uplift," and next that it provides escape.

As Richard Davenport-Hines points out, this assortment of lyrics, skipping and nursery rhymes, drinking songs, and ballads, not to mention swatches of narratives and dramatic verse, is a "hard-headed celebration of the power of the spoken word for semi-literate people," which secondarily serves as a "tribute to the local cultures" being erased by factories and highways.[2] Once one gets past a certain unease, it is pleasant to read poems chosen only for the pleasure they give to two men with eclectic tastes and arranged with no attention to context. Auden has clearly been influenced by Walter de la Mare (see below) in the making of this anthology.

Auden, W. H., and Norman Holmes Pearson, eds. *Poets of the English Language* (New York: Viking/Penguin, 1950; 1978), 5 vols., I. *Medieval and Renaissance Poets, Langland to Spenser;* II. *Elizabethan and Jacobean Poets, Marlowe to Marvell;* III. *Restoration and Augustan Poets, Milton to Goldsmith;* IV. *Romantic Poets, Blake to Poe;* V. *Victorian and Edwardian Poets, Tennyson to Yeats.*

Editions and biographical capsules for each poet. Auden and Pearson have also devised helpful timelines linking the dates of poems to cultural and historical events. The selections are original and revealing—there are far more long works than in any other available an-

2. Richard Davenport-Hines, *Auden* (New York: Pantheon, 1995), pp. 138–39.

thology—and the editors have not been cowed by the distinction between verse and drama: medieval mystery and shepherd's plays and scenes from Jacobean dramas and all of *Antony and Cleopatra* are presented as crucial examples of poetic invention. Auden wrote the introductions to all five volumes. The anthology of choice for poets.

Bate, Walter Jackson, and David Perkins, eds. *British and American Poets, Chaucer to the Present.* New York: Harcourt Brace Jovanovich, 1986. Half the length of the latest *Norton,* the Bate and Perkins anthology at 1,048 pages still amply represents most of the poets one needs to have ready to hand—with the painful exception of Louise Bogan. On the plus side is the selection of Eliot's "Burnt Norton" from *Four Quartets* and Lowell's great political poem "Waking Early Sunday Morning." The selections result, for the most part, in arguable presentations of each poet's strengths and development. But the high point of the volume is the editing—the headnotes in particular—which reveals the work of alert and sensitive readers. The entry on T. S. Eliot begins, "A shy, sheltered, bird-watching, and bookish child . . ."; the editors also acutely discriminate Eliot's later efforts from his earlier work: "The most important stylistic development in *Four Quartets* was the use of discursive speech, the language of meditation and generalization that had been excluded from *The Waste Land.*" Since we tend to think of *The Waste Land* as indefinitely capacious, this exclusion is worth noting. The editors' understanding of Yeats's blend of symbolism and nationalism is acute. The representation of Auden is succinct about the enormous complexity of this poet's impulses: "He showed how this age of economic and political breakdown [in the 1930s] engendered utopian, apocalyptic, and elegiac states of mind, and he understood the longing of the period for a strong leader . . . Uniting Freudian with Marxist insights, he described, for example, the wealthy bourgeoisie as subject to neurotic death wishes. . . . Essentially Auden was a moralist, and his lyrics enacted a process of formulating moral judgments or of reluctantly accepting moral truths." Such insightful judgments will provide readers with a starting place for argument—even if one disagrees.

Bate and Perkins have added an invaluable essay on "Reading Poetry Aloud" that acts as a cure for the two chronic errors in the audible reading of verse, sing-song and reading as if verse were prose ("the way most Shakespearean actors have tended to recite since the 1940s"). The editors advocate a version of *rubato* on the vowel of each end-word and "extravagant" observation of pauses, on the theory that "Silence never makes a mistake."

Carruth, Hayden, ed. *The Voice That Is Great Within Us: American Poetry of the Twentieth Century.* New York: Bantam, 1970.

A fascinating anthology, chosen by a poet with an independent view of things and the energy to read outside the mainstream. In addition to bringing out lesser-known and forgotten poets, he puts a new accent on Kenneth Patchen, Yvor Winters, Adrienne Rich, Stanley Kunitz, and Louis Zukofsky. Informative and opinionated headnotes on each poet.

Davies, R. T., ed. *Medieval English Lyrics.* Evanston: Northwestern University Press, 1964.

Puts conveniently in one place many of the carols and lyrics that bridge the period during which the accentual base of English was shifting over to accentual-syllabic meter.

de la Mare, Walter, ed. *Come Hither: A Collection of Rhymes and Poems for the Young of All Ages.* 1923; rev. ed. 1928. New York: Alfred A. Knopf, 1957.

Extends the appreciation of the short lyric in the direction of songs and rhymes from many obscure sources. The poet de la Mare provides a stylish introduction (in a secret room, where he found his first book of poems, "The wings of the flies shone like glass in its shafts of light") and 200 pages of beguiling notes (as this, on the prosody of Chaucer: "If every dotted letter [*sonne,* sun; *floures,* flowers; *renne,* run] is made a syllable of, his rhythm will flow like water over bright green waterweed"). *Come Hither* is organized under eccentric headings that proceed from a country boyhood—when de la Mare claims to have read Alice Meynell (1847–1922) by the light of a glow-worm and to have formed on good evidence his unshaken belief in magic (one of the sections is titled "Elphin, Ouph and Fay"). But even the "Garden" chapter that closes the volume, like the "Summer: Greenwood: Solitude" section midway, is eerier than its bland title suggests. A delightful anthology that may need to be encountered at an early age (as W. H. Auden did).

Ferguson, Margaret, Jon Stallworthy, and Mary Jo Salter, eds. *Norton Anthology of Poetry.* Fourth edition. New York: W. W. Norton, 1996.

When the *Norton* was revised recently, many numerical injustices were corrected, but earlier gaps remain and earlier strengths are weakened. There is more poetry by women, by late twentieth-century writers, and by members of racial minorities. There are some poets new to me whom I am glad to know (Allen Curnow, b. 1911, from New Zealand; R. S. Thomas, b. 1913, from Wales; and Peter Kane Dufault, b. 1923, from the United States). But correction has brought in too much filler; of the 140 new poets, not more than a dozen are notable artists—among whom I am pleased to see John Gay (1685–1732), Trumbull Stickney (1874–1904), Norman Nicholson (1914–87), Eleanor Wilner, and Derek Mahon (b. 1941). But for every new gem (say by Isabella Whitney [fl. 1567–73]), we must pay with mediocrities (by Aemilia Lanyer [1569–1645] and Margaret Cavendish [1623–73] and Anna Laetitia Barbauld [1743–1825]). Much that was valuable has also been removed (for every poet now better represented, like Philip Larkin or James Merrill, there are three who are less well represented, whether because poor poems were added and/or left behind (both are true of the Marianne Moore and Randall Jarrell selections) or because too many good poems were removed (Edwin Muir, James Wright, Patrick Kavanagh, Roy Fuller, Derek Walcott, and even Elizabeth Bishop suffer by excision). Many good poets are underrepresented, too (Louise Bogan, James Schuyler, Robert Penn Warren [1905–89], Daryl Hine, and W. S. Merwin [b. 1927]). And wasn't it time to get a different Eliot quartet into this anthology?

Anthology making is perhaps always thankless. But with the possible exception of a handful of new poets and the newly revised notes for the poetry through the Renaissance, in which one can see Margaret Ferguson's hand, the greater length of the fourth edition signals a diminution in literary breadth and risk since the third. It does not, finally, seem to have been put togethers by *readers*.

Fields, Kenneth: *See* Yvor Winters.

Lewalski, Barbara K., and Andrew J. Sabol, eds. *Major Poets of the Earlier Seventeenth Century*. Indianapolis: Bobbs-Merrill/Odyssey, 1973.

Contains the work of Donne, Herbert, Vaughan, Crashaw, Jonson, Herrick, and Marvell, with the original spelling and orthography.

Nims, John Frederick, ed. *Harper Anthology of Poetry*. New York: Harper & Row, 1981.

Although it appears to be assembled along the lines of the *Norton* anthologies, Nims's anthology predates them, being the expansion of tastes and examples represented in his earlier introduction to poetry called *Western Wind* (New York: Random House, 1974). Although eight hundred pages shorter than the fourth *Norton,* and unfortunately short on blank verse, it has an excellent section on prosody and informative biographical headnotes for each poet.

Norton Anthology of Poetry: See Allison, Barrows, et al. and Margaret Ferguson.

Opie, Iona and Peter, eds. *The Oxford Nursery Rhyme Book* (1955), *The Oxford Book of Children's Verse* (1973), and *The Singing Game* (1985), all published by Oxford University Press.

The Opies are interested not only in the songs and jingles written by single authors (these are to be found in *The Oxford Book of Children's Verse*) but also in the anonymous and endlessly changing rhymes and chants that circulate among schoolchildren (*The Singing Game* records the twentieth-century variants from playgrounds all over England during the past fifty years, including the tunes and descriptions of the rings and running associated with the words). Throughout the Opies' work runs the strong thread of respect for the folk tradition that children keep alive and for the ways in which this tradition keeps getting language right by saying it wrong. Consider a rhyme from the category the Opies call "Chinese Counting" or nonsense counting; they take their version with two exceptions (they use "briar thorn" instead of "apple thorn" and "Wire" instead of "Wine") from Halliwell's collection for the Percy Society of 1842; I quote from the latter:

> Intery, mintery, cutery-corn,
> Apple seed and apple thorn;
> Wine, brier, limber-lock,
> Five geese in a flock,
> Sit and sing by a spring,
> O-U-T, in again.

As the Opies display each variant alongside many others, the counting and game-playing rituals grow clearer; meanwhile, the primary linguistic logic of the rhymes remains constant, based as they are on the obedience of mysterious syllables to rules of symmetry and even, though foggily, rules of grammar, for example:

> One-ery, two-ery, ickery, Ann,
> Phillisy, phollisy, Nicholas John,
> Quever, quaver, Irish Mary,
> Stickerum, stackerum, buck.

Ennity, feenity, fickety, feg,
El, del, domen, egg,
Irky, birky, story, rock,
An, tan, toosh, Jock.

(*The Oxford Nursery Rhyme Book,* p. 111)

One sees how the third line of "Intery, mintery" changed from "Wine" to "Wire," because the habit of interior rhyme early in the lines has been set by the kind of poem it is ("El, del," "Irky, birky," "Quever, quaver," not to mention such dactylic phrases as "Intery, mintery," "Hickety, pickety," and "Phillisy, phollisy")—a habit which attracts *wine* into *wire* to pair with *brier.*

Sylvester, Richard, ed. *The Anchor Anthology of Sixteenth-Century Verse.* Garden City, NJ: Doubleday/Anchor, 1974.

Ample selections from Drab Age (C. S. Lewis's term) poets Wyatt, Gascoigne, and Sackville, but it also has all of Skelton's *Philip Sparrow* (as does the Auden/Pearson anthology), Spenser's *Amoretti,* Sidney's *Astrophil and Stella,* twenty pages of Campion lyrics, and the work of the minor sonneteers.

Winters, Yvor, and Kenneth Fields, eds. *Quest for Reality: An Anthology of Short Poems in English.* Chicago: Swallow Press, 1969.

Every poem in this small anthology that stresses the finer minor lyrics primarily from the Renaissance and Edwardian periods turns out to have great staying power. (The central strength comes from the plain style.) The book has the feeling of a breviary—like something one would take into battle.

II. Handbooks

Beum, Robert: *See* Karl Shapiro.

Brogan, T. V. F.: *See* Alex Preminger.

Cuddon, J. A. *A Dictionary of Literary Terms and Literary Theory.* 3d rev. ed. Oxford: Basil Blackwell, 1991.

The best single-author dictionary—literate, quirky, and comprehensive. Preferable to the *Princeton* for brevity, range of entries, and freshness of literary example, although naturally no competitor to the *Princeton* in the latter's articles on national literatures and poetic and prosodic concepts. For starters, consult Cuddon's entries on literary epiphenomena such as "allegory" (which discusses how to transform a fable into an allegory), "author, death of," "ghost story," "grand

guignol," "Grand Tour," "langue and parole," "literary forger-
ies," "literary prizes," "Living Newspaper," "loan words," "psycho-
babble," "sigmatism" (excessive use of the letter *s*), and "table-talk."
Especially good are the articles on realism (poetic and fictive), on
children's literature, and on the conceit.

Deutsch, Babette. *Poetry Handbook: A Dictionary of Terms.* New York:
Grosset and Dunlap, 1957; 1962.

Workmanlike handbook with excellent entries on meter, the ode,
the rondeau and roundel, verbal texture, and rhyme.

Fussell, Paul. *Poetic Meter and Poetic Form.* New York: Random House,
1965.

A good first introduction to issues of style through history. Fussell
pays close attention to the sonnet.

Groden, Michael, and Martin Kreiswirth, eds. *The Johns Hopkins Guide
to Literary Theory and Criticism.* Baltimore, MD: The Johns Hopkins
University Press, 1994.

As a reference to accompany the *Princeton Encyclopedia of Poetry and
Poetics,* this guide provides useful background on critics and on theo-
retical as well as literary movements, particularly since the eighteenth
century. Entries on Eco and Empson, Dryden and Derrida, Kristeva
and Kierkegaard, Susan Sontag and Sainte-Beuve rub shoulders with
entries on the Moscow-Tartu School, the Cambridge Ritualists, and
Biblical Midrash and Medieval Commentary in this informative and
eclectic mix. A few artists such as Horace, Dante, Friedrich Hölder-
lin, Henry James, and Wallace Stevens are featured, but only from the
perspective of their thought *about* art. Of special note are the entry on
"History of Ideas" with its provisos about vitality as measured by a
theory's stimulation of "fruitful objections" and its final paragraph
about the future of an idea, and the volume's introductory essay, both
by Richard Macksey, the Johns Hopkins scholar who has facilitated
so much critical exchange in the past three decades; the introduction,
with Macksey's fine discrimination of the thirteen angles from which
literary phenomena can be approached, stands with the M. H.
Abrams essay on the four main theories of poetry in the *Princeton* as
a necessary preamble for anyone thinking about the aim and purpose
of art. Both essays insist on a wider context for examining the two
most prevalent modern biases about art, that it expresses only the
writer's feelings and that it expresses only the culture in which the
writer is imbedded.

Hollander, John. *Rhyme's Reason: A Guide to English Verse.* New Haven: Yale University Press, 1981.

A brief (52-page) survey of verse with examples written by Hollander himself to explain while they imitate. For example, the two refrain lines in his villanelle discuss refrain and repetition: "The repetitions build the villanelle" and "This form with two refrains in parallel." The explanatory aim limits one's sense of what a form might accomplish if paired with the appropriate themes and artistic urgency, but within its limits the book is helpful. The best discussions are of the least familiar forms—classical meters and the attempts to render quantity in English.

Howell, W. S. *Logic and Rhetoric in England 1500–1700.* Princeton: Princeton University Press, 1956.

Long out of print, this is a treasure of information about all the major figures of speech and figures of thought during the period when education encouraged discrimination of the two. *See also* Rosamund Tuve in "IV. Critical Volumes on Poetry, Prosody, and Style" below.

Johns Hopkins Guide: See Michael Groden.

Longman Dictionary: See Jack Myers.

Myers, Jack, and Michael Simms, eds. *Longman Dictionary of Poetic Terms.* New York & London: Longman, 1989. Briefer and more schematic than the *Princeton* but with a useful admixture of cinematic and theoretical terms as well as categories of judgment (such as "cliche"). Excellent appendices listing devices and forms.

Preminger, Alex, with Frank J. Warnke and O. B. Hardison, Jr., eds. *Princeton Encyclopedia of Poetry and Poetics.* Enlarged ed. Princeton: Princeton University Press, 1965; 1974.

The definitive handbook of terms, with excellent articles on features such as diction and the various tropes as well as containing surveys of national literatures. Especially recommended is Meyer H. Abrams's instructive essay on the changes in the assumed purposes of poetry, filed under "Poetry, Theories of."

The new edition of the *Princeton* (1993), edited by Preminger and T. V. F. Brogan, is an extensive tome (1,383 pages—500 pages longer than the 1974 edition) with many articles added on new critical movements and extensive revision of older topics to adjust for broader inclusion of national and subnational literatures. The impression in many of the articles now is of an eclecticism that can lead to want of focus; the overview does not always resolve into a view.

For many topics, I have been drawn back to earlier articles (by John Hollander, Paul Fussell, and others) in the 1965 and 1974 editions. However, the articles on topics from linguistics and syntax in the 1993 volume are outstanding.

Princeton Encyclopedia: See Alex Preminger.

Shapiro, Karl, and Robert Beum. *A Prosody Handbook.* New York: Harper & Row, 1965.

The first handbook I turn to when I am in doubt about a term or about how a poem sounds. Poet-scholar Karl Shapiro's learning in matters of rhythm is prodigious.

Turco, Lewis. *The New Book of Forms: A Handbook of Poetics.* Hanover: University Press of New England, 1986.

Although he may overdo the obscurer forms, Turco is a mine of information on the stanza, particularly Welsh rhymed forms.

III. Essays and Essay Collections

Abrams, M. H. "Poetry, Theories of": *See* Alex Preminger in "II. Handbooks" above.

Alpers, Paul J., ed. *Elizabethan Poetry: Modern Essays in Criticism.* New York: Oxford University Press, 1967.

In addition to Howard Baker and L. C. Knights, authors include Rosamund Tuve, William Empson, I. A. Richards, Yvor Winters, and T. S. Eliot. An anthology on nondramatic English verse with insights for the practicing reader/writer.

Baker, David, ed. *Meter in English: A Critical Engagement.* Fayetteville: University Arkansas Press, 1996.

Although flawed by its focus on an uneven essay on meter by Robert Wallace, this anthology of responses by various writers contains, in addition to the essay by John Frederick Nims mentioned below, interesting pieces by Charles O. Hartman, Margaret Holley, and Timothy Steele.

Baker, Howard. "The Formation of the Heroic Medium," from his *Induction to Tragedy* [1939]. Baton Rouge: Louisiana State University Press, 1939.

On the development of blank verse from Chaucer to Shakespeare as a direct result of—because it was also a prime facilitator of—the evolution of the psychological hero in dramatic tragedy. In Alpers, ed., *Elizabethan Poetry,* pp. 126–68.

Burke, Kenneth. "Four Master Tropes." In *A Grammar of Motives* [1945]. Berkeley: University of California Press, 1968.

An essay that prompts us to reassess the implication of indirect representation in literature. A helpful addition to the articles on trope, metaphor, synecdoche, metonymy, symbol, icon, image, and emblem in the *Princeton Encyclopedia*.

————. "On Musicality in Verse," In *The Philosophy of Literary Form*. Rev. ed. New York: Vintage, 1957.

The best available treatment, keyed to passages of verse, of the function of alliteration (including concealed and acrostic alliterations on cognate consonants $n/d/th$, $n/t/th$, $m/b/v$, and $m/p/f$) in creating a subliminal coherence of texture.

Chatman, Seymour, and Samuel R. Levin eds. *Essays on the Language of Literature*. Boston: Houghton Mifflin, 1967.

The most wide-ranging anthology on the language as distinct from the themes and structures of literary works; includes the work of linguists (Jakobson), grammarians (Brooke-Rose), literary critics (Beardsley and Wimsatt; Miles; Richards; Tuve), and representatives of classical theoretical movements (for example, Mukarovsky and the Prague School).

Gunn, Thom. "Hardy and the Ballads" (1972). In *The Occasions of Poetry, Essays in Criticism and Autobiography*, by Thom Gunn. London: Faber & Faber, 1982.

New look at poems that combine suppression and simplicity to provide depth of implication. Revealing discussion of the English "reflective" ballads (for example, "As You Came from the Holy Land of Walsinghame") as contrasted with poems from the more encoded and mysterious Scottish tradition (for example, "The Laily Worm and the Machrel of the Sea"); the above as preamble to studying Hardy's sensibility in poems such as "The Walk," "Near Lanivet," and "During Wind and Rain."

Hollander, John. "Romantic Verse Form and the Metrical Contract" [1954]. In *Romanticism and Consciousness: Essays in Criticism,* edited by Harold Bloom. New York: W. W. Norton, 1970.

On meter as an emblem of mode: how the choice of different meters becomes linked, by convention, to the choice of mode (the combination of theme with syntax and expressive attitude). Especially revealing on the elegiac use (and, as it were, the elegiac *hearing*) of anapestic tetrameter in the eighteenth and nineteenth centuries.

Hollander differentiates metrical evolutions from metrical crises during which the terms of the metrical "contracts" are redrawn. A succinct and compelling argument with examples still fresh after many years.

Hope, A. D. "The Discursive Mode: Reflections on the Ecology of Poetry." In *The Cave and the Spring: Essays on Poetry.* Chicago: University of Chicago Press, 1970.
An engaging argument for the virtues of the "middle style"—primary among them, the role of teaching young poets "the exercise and management of their craft" while ensuring that the literary ecology (as his central metaphor has it) remains in balance.

Knights, L. C. "Shakespeare's Sonnets," from his *Explorations* [1946]. London: Chatto and Windus, 1946.
An ambitious reading of the sonnets as paralleling Shakespeare's blank verse in the dramas. In Alpers, ed., *Elizabethan Poetry,* pp. 274–98.

Koethe, John. "Contrary Impulses: The Tension Between Poetry and Theory." *Critical Inquiry* 18.1 (Autumn 1991).
The poet and philosopher John Koethe surveys the contemporary poetry scene through the lens of its intellectual ambitions. Especially good on the work of John Ashbery.

Macksey, Richard. Essay on the thirteen critical questions. *See* Michael Groden in "II. Handbooks" above.

Murphy, Francis, ed. *Discussions of Poetry: Form and Structure.* Boston: D.C. Heath, 1964.
Contains essays by Kenneth Burke, William Empson, J. C. Cunningham, Josephine Miles, and W. K. Wimsatt; a strong consideration of parallelism in Walt Whitman's poetry by Gay Wilson Allen, and a cautionary essay on experiment in American poetry from the mid-thirties by Yvor Winters.

Nims, John Frederick. "Our Many Meters: Strength in Diversity." In *Meter in English,* edited by David Baker.
Nims witheringly argues that iambics are hardly the only meter in English, that "feminine ending" is not in the least sexist, and that "anacrusis" has a specific meaning. One by one, the weak propositions of Mr. Wallace are exposed and discarded under a steady accumulation of scholarship and examples drawn from a long career of reading verse. Meter is defined aptly as the collection of "arterial systems through which the lifeblood of poetry flows."

———. "The Sestina." In *A Local Habitation: Essays on Poetry*. Ann Arbor: University of Michigan Press/"Poets on Poetry," 1985.

A wide-ranging treatment of the sestina since the late medieval period, which includes sensitive discussion of Arnaut Daniel's and Dante's poems in the form (and translations by Nims himself and Leslie Fiedler), as well as the somewhat more hidden life of the sestina in Auden's *The Orators,* Eliot's "Dry Salvages," and in the little-known work of Weldon Kees, Howard Nemerov, and (most surprising and moving) Malcolm Lowry's "Sestina in Cantina," about which Nims writes as follows: "The six end-words are the *dawning* and *sunset* of the drunkard; the *prison* of his compulsion (as well as his actual jail); the *ocean* of possible freedom and escape; the distorting *mirrors* in which the victim sees himself and his world; and the *horrors* of his existence. As in most good sestinas, the words are ambivalent: If dawn and ocean suggest purity and health, they also suggest hangovers and nausea."

Steele, Timothy. "Boundless Wealth from a Finite Store: Meter and Grammar." *Michigan Quarterly Review* (Winter 1997).

Excellent if technical look at the convergence between meter (place in the iambic line), syntax (including doubling in noun-adjective pairs), and the grammatical shape of words (bisyllabic, trisyllabic, etc.). Particularly suggestive about why pentameters are hard for students to write.

IV. Critical Volumes on Poetry, Prosody, and Style

Attridge, Derek. *The Rhythms of English Poetry*. London: Longman, 1982.

The most sophisticated blending of linguistics with aesthetics, with several striking and unignorable hypotheses about the habit of stress and the role of interval, especially in poems in which absent metrical patterns are still residual (as are tetrameters in many trimeter poems).

Auden, W. H. *The Dyer's Hand* [1962]. New York: Vintage, 1989.

One of the sunniest and widest-ranging of critics, the major twentieth-century poet and intellectual W. H. Auden is also the author of succinct, bold, and interesting prose—interesting even when he leaves poetry proper for subjects like opera, religion, and parable. Contains one of the best essays ever written on Franz Kafka, "The I Without a Self."

Baker, William E. *Syntax in English Poetry 1870–1930*. Berkeley: University of California Press, 1967.

Helpful look at the great shift from Victorian and Edwardian rhetorical elaboration in Robert Browning and others to the more compressed implications of syntax in symbolist poetry.

Barfield, Owen. *Poetic Diction: A Study in Meaning* [1928]. Middletown, CT: Wesleyan University Press, 1973.

With a fervent spirit, the late Mr. Barfield argues on behalf of the deep grounding in metaphor by which we recognize not only strong poetic periods but strong individual artists. Close studies of poetic productions such as Milton's that emerged when the silent reading of poetry on the page was added to (and eventually replaced) the hearing of poetry in hall or inn or on stage.

Bogan, Louise. *A Poet's Alphabet: Reflections on the Literary Art and Vocation,* edited by Robert Phelps and Ruth Limmer. New York: McGraw-Hill, 1970.

Bogan mastered the art of brevity and reverberation in her literary journalism. Especially pertinent for those interested both in her work and in prosody and tone are her essays on Yeats, Frost, Pound, and the poetry of the Greeks.

Borroff, Marie. *Language and the Poet: Verbal Artistry in Frost, Stevens, and Moore*. Chicago: University of Chicago Press, 1979.

Written by the noted medievalist and translator, this volume contains superior essays on Marianne Moore and the emphases and exclusions of "promotional prose." The material on Wallace Stevens is also thoughtful.

Brooke-Rose, Christine. *A Grammar of Metaphor*. London: Secker & Warburg, 1958.

Thorough and eye-opening, Brooke-Rose examines the way sentences create metaphors—by "simple replacement" of one noun by another, by verbs from a realm not governed by the sentence's subject or object, by the "genitive link" (for example, the fire of love), and by the appearance of literal things that take on symbolic resonance ("literal symbols").

Bruns, Gerald L. *Modern Poetry and the Idea of Language*. New Haven: Yale University Press, 1974.

Suggestive history of one dialectic, between poetic language as substantive and hermetic, and language as transparent and Orphic.

Burckhardt, Sigurd. *Shakespearean Meanings.* Princeton: Princeton University Press, 1968.

The most intellectually challenging readings of Shakespeare as an artist.

Cunningham, J. V. *The Collected Essays of J. V. Cunningham.* Chicago: Swallow Press, 1976.

Steeped in Elizabethan and Jacobean poetry, the poet-scholar J. V. Cunningham also exhibits the pertinacity of the lover of a certain kind of pure and plain minor verse—a taste shared by the better-known poet-critic Yvor Winters.

Davie, Donald. *Purity of Diction in English Verse.* London: Routledge & Kegan Paul, 1952; 1967. And *Articulate Energy: An Inquiry into the Syntax of English Poetry.* London: Routledge & Kegan Paul, 1955.

Two books that take a rigorous view of the idiosyncratic nature of the rhetoric and syntax of verse and single out the role of both narrative and of trope and textured image in forming the authentic "syntax" or language of poetic articulation. *Purity of Diction* lays stress on minor eighteenth-century verse while *Articulate Energy* branches out into modern poetry; in the latter, Davie writes well on the syntax of Eliot's *Four Quartets.*

Eliot, T. S. *Selected Essays* [1950]. New York: Harcourt, Brace & World, 1964.

The literary journalism of T. S. Eliot has exerted an incalculable influence over critics and poets alike, particularly in increasing the popularity of certain lesser-known Renaissance poets and dramatists. Also worth studying are the essays on Dante and the pieces on the role and right demeanor of the poet ("Tradition and the Individual Talent," 1919, and "The Function of Criticism," 1923). Although there is a side of Eliot that is overly decorous and severe, he can often surprise us with his enthusiasms (as for music hall performers like Marie Lloyd) and his pronouncements (such as that we should attempt to read medieval poetry in Italian before we have learned Italian).

Gross, Harvey. *Sound and Form in Modern Poetry: A Study of Prosody from Thomas Hardy to Robert Lowell.* Ann Arbor: University Michigan Press, 1964; 1968.

Excellent survey with good treatment of the work of individual poets. Gross may be most helpful in treating poetry that does not lie in the main metrical tradition, such as Ezra Pound's.

Hartman, Charles O. *Free Verse: An Essay on Prosody*. Princeton: Princeton University Press, 1980.

Nimble and compelling argument about the line of verse as the sluice controlling the waters of free verse. To be read against the bracing history of free verse by Timothy Steele, *Missing Measures*.

Hobsbaum, Philip. *Metre, Rhythm and Verse Form*. London & New York: Routledge, 1996.

Inventive, brisk, and the product of long synthesizing. Hobsbaum's ingenious concepts include the mutual modification in free verse of lines of thrust and lines of receipt of thrust (analogous to thesis [raising] and arsis [lowering] in meter); the fractioning of rhyme (for example, three-quarter rhyme, half-rhyme, one-quarter rhyme); and "free blank verse." Contains the best explanation I have read of Hopkins's sprung rhythm.

McAuley, James. *Versification: A Short Introduction*. East Lansing: Michigan State University Press, 1966.

The best short introduction to prosody, featuring careful audition, clear explanation, and pertinent examples.

Miles, Josephine. *Eras and Modes in English Poetry* [1964]. Westport, CT: Greenwood Press, 1976.

In a clear prose and with engaging breadth of citation, Miles argues the relation between sentence-type, metaphor, sound, and theme in poetry in English. Her major distinction, between the "phrasal" and the "clausal" modes, carries over persuasively into her discussion of sublime modes versus predicative modes like the ballad. Major chapters devoted to Blake as a sublime poet; the school of Donne; Dryden; and Yeats.

Nabokov, Vladimir. *Notes on Prosody and Abram Gannibal*. Princeton, NJ: Princeton University Press/Bollingen, 1964.

In this appendix to his translation of Pushkin, Nabokov contrasts the prosody of Russian with English tetrameters. To discuss the prominent prosodic feature of the Russian language (understressing), Nabokov evolves his own intelligent system of scansion, which registers expectation consistently, whatever the actual pattern of speech. Although the terminology is quirky (*scuds, reverse tilted scuds, duplex tilts*, etc.), this study is invaluable.

Perloff, Marjorie. *The Poetics of Indeterminacy* [1981]. Evanston: Northwestern University Press, 1983.

An inventive, clear, and sympathetic reading of modernist poets and poetics, based on syntax, rhetoric, and mode.

Pinsky, Robert. *The Situation of Poetry: Contemporary Poetry and Its Traditions*. Princeton: Princeton University Press, 1976.
Written by an excellent poet-critic, these essays are drawn from his omnibus reviews of the 1970s and record a discriminating series of responses to the diction and the rhetoric of the day.

Robinson, Fred C. *"Beowulf" and the Appositive Style*. Knoxville: University of Tennessee Press, 1985.
A monograph of roughly eighty pages that explains a highly stylized accentual poem's syntax in terms that reveal much about the layering of meaning in poetry and language as a whole.

Smith, Barbara Herrnstein. *Poetic Closure: A Study of How Poems End*. Chicago: University of Chicago Press, 1968.
A study of the features that produce the sense of an ending in varieties of verse, from couplets and stanzaic poems to blank verse and free verse. *Poetic Closure* is lucid and insightful in grasping formal distinctions (for example, "in closing itself, the couplet does not necessarily close the structure of which it is a part," that is, a succession of closed couplets function rather like lines than like the two-line poems they also mimic). Smith is also acute in discriminating modes; lyric, for example, differs from dramatic or narrative verse in being "the representation not of an action or chronicle . . . but of an utterance. Lyrics can't end in death, though they may (and often do) end in references to death." Written by a critic sympathetic to the thought process of the poet.

Steele, Timothy. *Missing Measures: Modern Poetry and the Revolt Against Meter*. Fayetteville: University Arkansas Press, 1990.
A reading of twentieth-century poetic experiment as marked by a huge misunderstanding about the prosodic oddity of free verse. Steele shows one writer after another mistaking outmoded diction for meter itself. This informative account can be read (for contrast) alongside Hartman's book on free verse's prosodic controls.

Stein, Arnold. *Answerable Style: Essays on "Paradise Lost."* Seattle: University of Washington Press, 1953.
An estimable and compelling work of literary criticism—and literary meditation. Written from an understanding of the precariousness of the poetic artist's creation. Indeed, in Stein's view one of the implica-

tions of the style Milton called "answerable" is that it should put him in a position to be "answerable to the as yet *unattempted*."

Thompson, John. *The Founding of English Metre*. New York: Columbia University Press, 1966.

Takes us through the Drab Age that spans the period from Wyatt to Sidney. Thompson is particularly good in writing about the changes Surrey and Tottel made in Wyatt's "irregular" syllables for the *Miscellany* of 1557.

Tuve, Rosamund. *Elizabethan and Metaphysical Imagery: Renaissance Poetic and Twentieth-Century Critics*. Chicago: University of Chicago Press, 1947, especially pp. 3–26.

Tuve's central argument is that we must not ascribe to Renaissance poems an ideal of sensuous immediacy with which the twentieth-century poem is comfortable. She points out that this false ascription can only come of not reading *all* of a Renaissance poem: "the nature of the imagery and the intention of a poem are indissolubly connected. *Only the rest of the poem can tell us why the image is there;* and unless we know that (in our partial way), we shall only lump together images that are really very different" (p. 21, my emphasis). That is, because they seem to us to have the same feeling, sensuous origins, or texture, we might incorrectly assume that the images serve the same intellectual and strategic aims. Tuve exhaustively examines the nonsensuous horizon of metaphors in Renaissance poems.

Vendler, Helen. *On Extended Wings: Wallace Stevens's Longer Poems*. Cambridge: Harvard University Press, 1969.

Although focused on Stevens's poems, this study raises many issues related to producing long poems in any period—particularly periodic and ratiocinative structures. Can profitably be studied alongside Smith's *Poetic Closure* and Marie Borroff's *Language and the Poet*.

Wimsatt, W. K. *The Verbal Icon: Studies in the Meaning of Poetry*. Lexington: University of Kentucky Press, 1967.

Of particular interest are the essays on rhyme, "One Relation of Rhyme to Reason" and on "image" as both experience and trope, "The Structure of Romantic Nature Imagery." The last named can profitably be read along with Rosamund Tuve's *Elizabethan and Metaphysical Imagery*.

LIST OF POEMS BY FORM

A poem's form can be categorized in several ways:
- **mode**—by thematic identification with a recognized mode such as the lyric or the epic
- **stanza**—by the type of stanza and frequency of rhyme
- **line**—according to the rhythm and reach of each line.

The categories often overlap: a poem can be at once a lyric (mode), rhymed in quatrains (stanza), and written in anapestic tetrameter (line). The poems identified as dramatic, lyric, and narrative, therefore, sometimes have other lives to live when one thinks about their paragraphing and lineation. Similarly, for a complete identification, even a sonnet needs to be designated by line and rhetorical mode.

The following list provides two or three examples from the text for each category. The examples in "Mode" and "Line" are arranged alphabetically, while those of "Stanza and Rhyme" are arranged in order of increasing length and complexity of stanza.

Mode

dramatic
Robert Browning, "Bishop Blougram's Apology"
William Cowper, "Verses Supposed to Be Written by Alexander Selkirk, During His Solitary Abode in the Island of Juan Fernandez"
Randall Jarrell, "A Soul"

lyric
Louise Bogan, "Song for a Lyre"
Christina Rossetti, "In the Bleak Midwinter"
W. B. Yeats, "Byzantium"

narrative
ballad and tale
Samuel Taylor Coleridge, *The Rime of the Ancient Mariner*
A. D. Hope, "Man Friday"
traditional, "The Laily Worm and the Machrel of the Sea"
epic
Chapman's Homer
George Gordon, Lord Byron, *Don Juan*
John Milton, *Paradise Lost*

meditation
   Samuel Taylor Coleridge, "Frost at Midnight"
   Thom Gunn, "His Rooms in College"
   Eleanor Wilner, "Operations: Desert Shield, Desert Storm"

Stanza and Rhyme

couplets
   dimeter
   Richard Rolle, "A Song of Love for Jesus"
   Sir Thomas Wyatt, "My Lute and I"
   trimeter
   Robert Herrick, "A Conjuration, to Electra"
   John Skelton, "Philip Sparrow"
   tetrameter
   William Blake, "Auguries of Innocence"
   Oliver Goldsmith, "Retaliation"
   George Gordon, Lord Byron, "Epistle from Mr. Murray to Dr. Polidori"
   pentameter (or "heroic") couplets
   Thom Gunn, "Moly"
   Ben Jonson, "Inviting a Friend to Supper"
   Alexander Pope, "Epistle to Bathurst"
quatrains with alternating rhymes
   dimeter
   J. V. Cunningham, "For My Contemporaries"
   Thomas Hardy, "Side by Side"
   Julia Randall, "Adam's Dream"
   trimeter
   Julia Randall, "Maid's Song"
   Theodore Roethke, "My Papa's Waltz"
   W. B. Yeats, "To a Friend Whose Work Has Come to Nothing"
   common meter (also called "ballad meter")
   Robert Burns, "Address to the Unco Guid, or Rigidly Righteous"
   Thomas Hardy, "The Oxen"
   Edwin Muir, "Ballad of Hector in Hades"
   short meter
   Emily Dickinson, #536 "The Heart asks Pleasure—first—"
   Edward Lear, limerick ("There was an old person of China")
   traditional, "Hickory dickory dock"
   long meter
   Samuel Johnson, "On the Death of Dr. Robert Levet"
   Timothy Steele, "Toward Calgary"
   W. B. Yeats, "The Fish"
   In Memoriam stanza (iambic tetrameter abba)
   W. H. Auden, "The Fall of Rome"
   Edward Herbert, 1st Baron Herbert of Cherbury, "An Ode upon the Question
      Moved, Whether Love Should Continue Forever?"
   Philip Larkin, "The Trees"

iambic pentameter (or "heroic") quatrains
   Thomas Gray, "Elegy Written in a Country Church-Yard"
   George Herbert, "Artillery"
   James Merrill, "From the Cupola"
quatrains extended or varied
   trimeter base
      W. H. Auden, "A Walk After Dark"
      Janet Lewis, "In the Egyptian Museum"
      Sir Walter Ralegh, "The Lie"
   tetrameter base
      Robert Burns, "Tam Samson's Elegy" (Burns stanza)
      Thomas Hardy, "At Castle Boterel"
      Andrew Marvell, "An Horatian Ode: Upon Cromwell's Return from Ireland"
   pentameter base
      Elizabeth Bishop, "Cirque d'Hiver"
      Donald Justice, "Sadness"
      Philip Larkin, "Home Is So Sad"
sonnet
   W. H. Auden, *In Time of War* XIX ("But in the evening the oppression lifted")
   William Shakespeare, Sonnet 94 ("They that have powre to hurt and will doe
      none")
   Sir Thomas Wyatt, "I fynde no peace and all my warre is done"
rhyme royal
   W. H. Auden, "The Shield of Achilles" & *Letter to Lord Byron*
   Thomas Sackville, *A Mirrour for Magistrates*
   William Wordsworth, "Resolution and Independence"
ottava rima
   George Gordon, Lord Byron, *Don Juan*
   W. B. Yeats, "Byzantium"
   W. B. Yeats, "A Prayer for My Daughter"
Spenserean stanza
   Daryl Hine, "Bluebeard's Wife"
   John Keats, "The Eve of St. Agnes"
   Edmund Spenser, *The Faerie Queene*
Irregular (or Pindaric) ode
   Donald Justice, "Ode to a Dressmaker's Dummy"
   Robert Lowell, "Mr. Edwards and the Spider"
   Thomas Traherne, "Poverty"

Line

accentual (unrhymed)
   W. H. Auden, *The Age of Anxiety*
   Beowulf (tenth century)
   "I Sing of a Maiden" (fifteenth century; rhymed)
accentual-syllabic
   amphibrachic (rhymed)
      Charles Dodgson (Lewis Carroll), "The Hunting of the Snark"

Winthrop Mackworth Praed, "Good-Night to the Season"
Algernon Charles Swinburne, "By the North Sea"
anapestic
  rhymed
    Edward Lear, "The Jumblies"
    Thomas Moore, "Believe Me if All Those Endearing Young Charms"
  blank (unrhymed)
    Daryl Hine, *In and Out*
dactylic
  rhymed
    Thomas Hardy, "The Self-Unseeing"
    traditional, "Hink, spink, the puddings stink"
  blank (unrhymed)
    Arthur Hugh Clough, *Amours de Voyage*
iambic
  rhymed
    Emily Dickinson, "'Tis good—the looking back on Grief" (#660)
    Edwin Muir, "The Enchanted Knight"
    Sir Thomas Wyatt, "Satire I" ("Myne owne John Poynz")
  blank (unrhymed)
    (tetrameter) Wallace Stevens, "A Postcard from the Volcano"
    (pentameter—so-called "blank verse")
      Robert Frost, "An Old Man's Winter Night"
      William Wordsworth, *The Prelude*
  trochaic (rhymed)
  W. H. Auden, "Lady, Weeping at the Crossroads"
  Robert Burns, "Ae Fond Kiss"
  William Wordsworth, "To the Small Celandrine"
free verse
  biblical free verse
  William Blake, *Jerusalem*
  Walt Whitman, "The World Below the Brine"
  Anne Winters, "The Mill-Race"
  free blank verse
  David Ferry, "Seen Through a Window"
  Donald Justice, "A Man of 1794"
  Mark Strand, *Dark Harbor* XV
  podic or sprung free verse
  Matthew Arnold, "Rugby Chapel"
  Gerard Manley Hopkins, "Duns Scotus's Oxford"
  W. B. Yeats, "Long-legged Fly"
  imagist free verse
    end-stopped
    Ezra Pound, "Ts'ai Chi'h"
    Wallace Stevens, "The American Sublime"
    James Wright, "Lying in a Hammock at William Duffy's Farm in Pine Island, Minnesota"

enjambed
John N. Morris, "The Unburied"
Sylvia Plath, "Edge"
James Schuyler, "A Few Days"

syllabic verses
Alexandrine
Daryl Hine, *Academic Festival Overtures*
Haiku
Babette Deutsch, haiku "The falling flower"
Varied Syllabic Count
Marianne Moore, "An Egyptian Pulled Glass Bottle in the Shape of a Fish"
7-syllable Line
Thom Gunn, *Misanthropos* VII and IX
9-syllable Line
J. V. Cunningham, "A half hour for coffee, and at night"
10-syllable Line
Elizabeth Daryush, "Drought"

AUTHOR AND TITLE INDEX

Poems and authors discussed or referred to but not quoted in the text are listed in the Subject Index.

Abelard, Peter (1079–1142)
"Lament," 421
"Adam's Dream" (Randall), 270
"Address to the Unco Guid, or the Rigidly Righteous" (Burns), 133
"Ae fond kiss, and then we sever" (Burns), 475
"After Frost at Midnight" (Kinzie), 322–23
"After the Persian" (Bogan), 341–42
"Again" (Nemerov), 96
"Against Idleness and Mischief" (Watts), 467
Age of Anxiety, The (Auden), 306
Alice's Adventures in Wonderland (Carroll), 467, 482
"American Sublime, The" (Stevens), 54
Amours de Voyage (Clough), 402, 403
"Anonymous Drawing" (Justice), 417
Antony and Cleopatra (Shakespeare), 439
Arnold, Matthew (1822–88)
"Dover Beach," 15, 17
"Rugby Chapel," 332
"Artillery" (Herbert), 190
Ashbery, John (b. 1927)
"Melodic Trains," 54
"As You Came from the Holy Land of Walsinghame" (ballad), 297–98
"At a Hasty Wedding" (Hardy), 431
"At a Low Bar" (Ferry), 63

Auden, W. H. (1907–73)
The Age of Anxiety, 306
"But in the Evening the Oppression Lifted" (*In Time of War*, XIX), 139
"The Fall of Rome," 72, 427
"Lady, Weeping at the Crossroads," 166, 167
"Prospero to Ariel," 312
"The Shield of Achilles," 165–66
"A Walk After Dark," 73
"August Midnight, An" (Hardy), 191
"Autumn—" (Basho), 328

"Ballad of Hector in Hades" (Muir), 145–47
"Balloon of the Mind" (Yeats), 161
"Baroque Comment" (Bogan), 58
Basho (1644–94)
"Autumn—," 328
"Believe Me if All Those Endearing Young Charms" (Moore), 277
Beowulf, 309–10
Betjeman, John (1906–84)
"Death in Leamington," 126
Bishop, Elizabeth (1911–79)
"Cirque d'Hiver," 42–43
"Crusoe in England," 378
"Filling Station," 301
"Bishop Blougram's Apology" (Browning), 465

Blake, William (1757–1827)
   "Auguries of Innocence," 153
   Jerusalem, 338
   "London," 153
"Bluebeard's Wife" (Hine), 95
Bogan, Louise (1897–1970)
   "After the Persian," 341–42
   "Baroque Comment," 58
   "Cassandra," 209
   "The Changed Woman," 420–21
   "The Daemon," 62
   "Last Hill in a Vista," 177
   "Memory," 91
   "Single Sonnet," 30
   "Song for a Lyre," 89
   "Summer Wish," 54
   "To Be Sung on the Water," 76
Boncho (?–1714)
   "Piled for burning," 328
"Borough, The" (Crabbe), 120
"Boundbrook" (Randall), 278
"Bristowe Tragedie, The" (Chatterton),
   269
Browning, Robert (1812–89)
   "Bishop Blougram's Apology," 465
   "The Englishman in Italy," 228
   Saul, 392
Burns, Robert (1759–96)
   "Address to the Unco Guid, or the Rig-
      idly Righteous," 133
   "Ae fond kiss, and then we sever," 475
   "Tam Samson's Elegy," 397
Buson (1715–83)
   "Deer in rain—," 328
   "A sudden chill—," 328
"But in the Evening the Oppression
   Lifted" (Auden), 139
Byron, George Gordon, Lord
   (1788–1824)
   "Darkness," 92
   Don Juan, 275, 456
   "Epistle from Mr. Murray to Dr. Poli-
      dori," 285
"By the North Sea" (Swinburne), 391
"Byzantium" (Yeats), 276

Campion, Thomas (1567–1620)
   "Rose-Cheekt Laura," 475

Canterbury Tales (Chaucer), 430
"Captain Craig" (Robinson), 253–54
Carmina Burana (songs), 429
Carroll, Lewis (1832–98)
   Alice's Adventures in Wonderland, 467, 482
   "The Hunting of the Snark," 390
   "Mad Gardener's Song," 288–89
"Cassandra" (Bogan), 209
"Cavalry Crossing a Ford" (Whitman),
   423
"Changed Woman, The" (Bogan),
   420–21
"Channel Firing" (Hardy), 121
Chatterton, Thomas (1752–70)
   "The Bristowe Tragedie," 269
Chaucer, Geoffrey (1343?–1400)
   Canterbury Tales, 430
   The Romance of the Rose, 263
"Childhood" (Muir), 252, 253
"Cirque d'Hiver" (Bishop), 42–43
"Clerk Colvill" (anonymous/traditional),
   167–68
"Clock stopped—, A" (#287) (Dickin-
   son), 153
Clough, Arthur Hugh (1819–61)
   Amours de Voyage, 402, 403
Coleridge, Samuel Taylor (1772–
   1834)
   "Dejection: An Ode," 86
   "Frost at Midnight," 235–36
   The Rime of the Ancient Mariner, 195–96,
      278, 470
Collins, William (1721–59)
   "Ode to Evening," 270
"Coming of the Cold, The" (Roethke),
   108
"Composed upon Westminster Bridge"
   (Wordsworth), 143–44, 393
"Conjuration, to Electra, A" (Herrick),
   66
Cowper, William (1731–1800)
   "Poplar Field," 228
   "Verses Supposed to Be Written by
      Alexander Selkirk, During His
      Solitary Abode in the Island of
      Juan Fernandez," 240
Crabbe, George (1754–1832)
   "The Borough," 120

"Crusoe in England" (Bishop), 378
Cunningham, J. V. (1911–85)
   "For My Contemporaries," 126
   "A half hour for coffee and at night,"
     323–24
   "With a Copy of Swift's Works," 279
   "You have here no otherness," 324–25
"Cyclic" (Oliver), 178

"Daemon, The" (Bogan), 62
Dark Harbor (Strand), 206
"Darkling Thrush, The" (Hardy), 85, 121
"Darkness" (Byron), 92
Darley, George (1795–1846)
   Ethelstan; or the Battle of Brunaburgh, 427
Daryush, Elizabeth (1887–1977)
   "Drought," 326
   "If there's no ruling," 325
Dawn in Britain, The (Doughty), 481
"Death of the Hired Man, The" (Frost),
   115
"Deer in rain—" (Buson), 328
"Dejection: An Ode" (Coleridge), 86
de la Mare, Walter (1873–1956)
   "John Mouldy," 452
"Delight in Disorder" (Herrick), 67
"Descriptive" (Ferry), 103
Deutsch, Babette (1895–1982)
   "The fallen flower," 327
Dickinson, Emily (1830–86)
   "A Clock stopped—" (#287), 153
   "Further in Summer than the Birds"
     (#1068), 125
   "The Heart asks Pleasure—first—"
     (#536), 419
   "I heard a Fly buzz—when I died—"
     (#465), 125
   "The Months have ends—the Years—
     a knot" (#423), 267
   "My Life had stood—a Loaded Gun"
     (#754), 125
   "So set its Sun in Thee" (#808), 79
   "'Tis good—the looking back on
     Grief—" (#660), 24–25
Dodgson, Charles L. *See* Carroll, Lewis
"Dolls' Wash, The" (Ewing), 272
Don Juan (Byron), 275, 456
Donne, John (1572–1631)

"Lovers Infinitenesse," 410
"A Valediction: Forbidding Mourning,"
   156
Doughty, Charles M. (1843–1926)
   The Dawn in Britain, 481
"Dover Beach" (Arnold), 15, 17
"Drinking Song, A" (Yeats), 64
"Drought" (Daryush), 326
"Dull Is My Verse" (Landor), 421
Dunbar, William (1460–1520)
   "Lament for the Makaris," 419
Dunciad, The (Pope), 398
"Duns Scotus's Oxford" (Hopkins), 301

"Easter 1916" (Yeats), 172, 293
"Edge" (Plath), 56
"Egyptian Pulled Glass Bottle in the
   Shape of a Fish, An" (Moore), 318
"Elegy Written in a Country Church-
   Yard" (Gray), 71
"Enchanted Knight, The" (Muir), 69
"Englishman in Italy, The" (Browning),
   228
"Epistle from Mr. Murray to
   Dr. Polidori" (Byron), 285
"Epistle to Bathurst" (Pope), 283–84
Essay on Criticism, An (Pope), 282
Essay on Man, An (Pope), 409
Ethelstan; or the Battle of Brunaburgh
   (Darley), 427
"Eve of St. Agnes, The" (Keats), 93
Ewing, Juliana Horatia (1841–85)
   "The Dolls' Wash," 272
"Exeunt" (Wilbur), 179

"Fabliau of Florida" (Stevens), 343
Faerie Queene, The (Spenser), 462
"fallen flower, The" (Deutsch), 327
"Fall of Rome, The" (Auden), 72, 427
Ferry, David (b. 1924)
   "At a Low Bar," 63
   "Descriptive," 103
   "Graveyard," 170
   "Photographs from a Book: Six Po-
     ems," 169
   "Seen Through a Window," 196–97
   "A Young Woman," 332–33
"Few Days, A" (Schuyler), 55

"Filling Station" (Bishop), 301
"Fish, The" (Yeats), 304
"Flower, The" (Herbert), 158
"For My Contemporaries" (Cunningham), 126
"For the Bed at Kelmscott" (Morris), 406
"From the Cupola" (Merrill), 207
Frost, Robert (1874–1963)
   "The Death of the Hired Man," 115
   "An Old Man's Winter Night," 192–93
   "On a Bird Singing in Its Sleep," 21–22
"Frost at Midnight" (Coleridge), 235–36
"Further in Summer than the Birds" (#1068) (Dickinson), 125

"Garden, The" (Marvell), 108
Gascoigne, George (1535?–77)
   "Gascoigne's Good Night," 122
"Gascoigne's Good Night" (Gascoigne), 122
"Gate, The" (Muir), 104
Gay, John (1685–1732)
   "A New Song of Similes," 268
"Going, The" (Hardy), 384
Goldsmith, Oliver (1730–74)
   "Retaliation," 27
"Good-Night to the Season" (Praed), 391
"Graveyard" (Ferry), 170
Gray, Thomas (1716–71)
   "Elegy Written in a Country Church-Yard," 71
"Great Men have been among us" (Wordsworth), 29
"Great Merchant, The, Dives Pragmaticus, Cries His Wares" (Newbery), 227
Gunn, Thom (b. 1929)
   "His Rooms in College," 257
   "In Praise of Cities," 159, 160
   Misanthropos, 320–21, 321–22
   "Moly," 106–7
   "My Sad Captains," 319

"Half hour for coffee and at night, A" (Cunningham), 323–24
Hamlet (Shakespeare), 236
Hardy, Thomas (1840–1928)
   "At a Hasty Wedding," 431

"An August Midnight," 191
"Channel Firing," 121
"The Darkling Thrush," 85
"The Going," 384
"I Look into My Glass," 81
"Neutral Tones," 241
"The Oxen," 65
"The Self-Unseeing," 23
"Side by Side," 312–13
Heaney, Seamus (b. 1939)
   "Kinship," 428
"Heart asks Pleasure—first—, The" (#536) (Dickinson), 419
Henry IV, Part II (Shakespeare), 252
Henry V (Shakespeare), 254
Henry VI, Part II (Shakespeare), 372
Herbert, George (1593–1633)
   "Artillery," 190
   "The Flower," 158
Herbert of Cherbury, Edward, 1st Baron (1583–1648)
   "Ode upon the Question Moved, An, Whether Love Should Continue Forever?" 83
"Heron, The" (Roethke), 106
"Heron Totem" (Stephens), 256
Herrick, Robert (1591–1674)
   "A Conjuration, to Electra," 66
   "Delight in Disorder," 67
Hine, Daryl (b. 1936)
   "Bluebeard's Wife," 95
"His Rooms in College" (Gunn), 257
"Home Is So Sad" (Larkin), 90
Hood, Thomas (1799–1845)
   "Our Village," 272–73
Hope, A. D. (b. 1907)
   "Man Friday," 134–35, 286–88
Hopkins, Gerard Manley (1844–89)
   "Duns Scotus's Oxford," 301
   "Inversnaid," 308
   "The Lantern Out of Doors," 35
"Horatian Ode, An: Upon Cromwell's Return from Ireland" (Marvell), 270
"Hotel Normandie Pool, The" (Walcott), 232
"Hunting of the Snark, The" (Carroll), 390
"Hymns of the Marshes" (Lanier), 227

"I fynde no peace and all my warre is
    done" (Wyatt), 447
"If there's no ruling" (Daryush), 325
"I heard a Fly buzz—when I died—"
    (#465) (Dickinson), 125
"I Look into My Glass" (Hardy), 81
In Memoriam A. H. H. (Tennyson), 117,
    183–84
"Inniskeen Road: July Evening" (Kava-
    nagh), 122, 123
"In Praise of Cities" (Gunn), 159, 160
"In the Bleak Midwinter" (Rossetti), 479
"In the Egyptian Museum" (Lewis),
    129–30
"Inversnaid" (Hopkins), 308
"Inviting a Friend to Supper" (Jonson),
    464
"I Saw the Bird That Can the Sun En-
    dure" (Spenser), 102
"I Saw the Bird That Dares Behold the
    Sun" (Spenser), 101–2
"I sing of a maiden" (ballad), 309

Jarrell, Randall (1914–65)
    "A Soul," 171
Jerusalem (Blake), 338
"John Mouldy" (de la Mare), 452
Johnson, Samuel (1709–84)
    "On the Death of Dr. Robert Levet,"
    91
Jonson, Ben (1573–1637)
    "Inviting a Friend to Supper," 464
Julius Caesar (Shakespeare), 425–26
"Jumblies, The" (Lear), 305
Justice, Donald (b. 1925)
    "Anonymous Drawing," 417
    "A Man of 1794," 334–35
    "My South: On the Porch," 349–50
    "Ode to a Dressmaker's Dummy," 442
    "Sadness," 195

Kavanagh, Patrick (1905–67)
    "Inniskeen Road: July Evening," 122,
    123
Keats, John (1795–1821)
    "The Eve of St. Agnes," 93
    "Lines Supposed to Have Been Ad-
    dressed to Fanny Brawne," 82

King Lear (Shakespeare), 113
"Kinship" (Heaney), 428
Kinzie, Mary
    "After Frost at Midnight," 322–23
    "Midwinter," 173–74
    "Objet," 370
    "The orchard dying—," 415
    "Plague Summer," 432–33
    "Reading During Marriage," 318
Koethe, John (b. 1945)
    "The Realm of Ends," 118, 119

"Lady, Weeping at the Crossroads"
    (Auden), 166, 167
"Laily Worm and the Machrel of the Sea,
    The" (ballad), 420–21
Lamb, Charles (1775–1834)
    Satan in Search of a Wife, 391
    "She Is Going," 453–54
"Lament" (Abelard), 421
"Lament for the Makaris" (Dunbar), 419
Landor, Walter Savage (1775–1864)
    "Dull Is My Verse," 421
"Landscape with Self-Portrait"
    (Nemerov), 127–28
Lanier, Sidney (1842–81)
    "Hymns of the Marshes," 227
"Lantern Out of Doors, The" (Hopkins),
    35
Larkin, Philip (1922–85)
    "Home Is So Sad," 90
    "The Trees," 180
"Last Hill in a Vista" (Bogan), 177
Lear, Edward (1812–88)
    "The Jumblies," 305
Lewis, Janet (1899–1998)
    "In the Egyptian Museum," 129–30
"Lie, The" (Ralegh), 453
"Lines Supposed to Have Been Addressed
    to Fanny Brawne" (Keats), 82
"London" (Blake), 153
"longe love, that in my thought doeth
    harbar, The" (Wyatt), 245–46
Longfellow, Henry Wadsworth
    (1807–82)
    Song of Hiawatha, 474
"Long-legged Fly" (Yeats), 294
"Lotos-Eaters, The" (Tennyson), 417

"Lovers Infinitenesse" (Donne), 410
Lowell, Robert (1917–77)
  "Mr. Edwards and the Spider," 60–61
  "Lying in a Hammock at William Duffy's Farm in Pine Island, Minnesota" (Wright), 53

Macbeth (Shakespeare), 193, 373
"Mad Gardener's Song" (Carroll), 288–89
"Maid's Song" (Randall), 211
"Man Friday" (Hope), 134–35, 286–88
"Man of 1794, A" (Justice), 334–35
Marvell, Andrew (1575?–1634)
  "The Garden," 108
  "An Horatian Ode: Upon Cromwell's Return from Ireland," 270
"Mattie Groves" (ballad), 419
"Melodic Trains" (Ashbery), 54
"Memory" (Bogan), 91
Merrill, James (1926–95)
  "From the Cupola," 207
  "An Urban Convalescence," 258
"Midwinter" (Kinzie), 173–74
Millay, Edna St. Vincent (1892–1950)
  "Spring," 56
"Mill-Race, The" (Winters), 39–41
Milton, John (1608–74)
  Paradise Lost (Book I), 93–94, 99
  Paradise Lost (Book II), 112
  Paradise Lost (Book VI), 388
  Paradise Lost (Book VII), 388
  Paradise Lost (Book IX), 77, 97, 98, 99, 100, 101, 408
  Paradise Lost (Book X), 194, 409
Misanthropos (Gunn), 320–21, 321–22
"Moly" (Gunn), 106–7
"Months have ends—the Years—a knot, The" (#423) (Dickinson), 267
Moore, Marianne (1887–1972)
  "An Egyptian Pulled Glass Bottle in the Shape of a Fish," 318
Moore, Thomas (1779–1852)
  "Believe Me if All Those Endearing Young Charms," 277
Morris, John N. (1931–97)
  "The Unburied," 370–71
Morris, William (1834–96)
  "For the Bed at Kelmscott," 406

"Mr. Edwards and the Spider" (Lowell), 60–61
Muir, Edwin (1887–1959)
  "Ballad of Hector in Hades," 145–46, 146–47
  "Childhood," 252, 253
  "The Enchanted Knight," 69
  "The Gate," 104
"My Life had stood—a Loaded Gun" (#754) (Dickinson), 125
"My Lute and I" (Wyatt), 300–301
"My Papa's Waltz" (Roethke), 63
"My Sad Captains" (Gunn), 319
"My South: On the Porch" (Justice), 349–50

Nemerov, Howard (1920–91)
  "Again," 96
  "Landscape with Self-Portrait," 127–28
  "The Sanctuary," 105
  "Writing," 243
"Neutral Tones" (Hardy), 241
Newbery, Thomas (fl. 1563)
  "The Great Merchant, Dives Pragmaticus, Cries His Wares," 227
"New Song of Similes, A" (Gay), 268
"Nights are getting cold" (Shiki), 328

"Objet" (Kinzie), 370
"Ode to a Dressmaker's Dummy" (Justice), 442
"Ode to Evening" (Collins), 270
"Ode upon the Question Moved, An, Whether Love Should Continue Forever?" (Herbert of Cherbury), 83
"Old Man's Winter Night, An" (Frost), 192–93
"Old Mother Goose" (nursery rhyme), 299
Oliver, Raymond (b. 1936)
  "Cyclic," 178
  "Structures," 78
"On a Bird Singing in Its Sleep" (Frost), 21–22
"On the Death of Dr. Robert Levet" (Johnson), 91
"Operations: Desert Shield, Desert Storm" (Wilner), 35–38

"orchard dying—, The" (Kinzie), 415
Othello the Moor of Venice (Shakespeare), 464
"Our Village" (Hood), 272–73
Owen, Wilfred (1893–1918)
  "Strange Meeting," 271–72
"Oxen, The" (Hardy), 65

Paradise Lost (Milton)
  Book I, 93–94, 99
  Book II, 112
  Book VI, 388
  Book VII, 388
  Book IX, 77, 97, 98, 99, 100, 101, 408
  Book X, 194, 409
"Philip Sparrow" (Skelton), 267, 299–300
"Photographs from a Book: Six Poems" (Ferry), 169
Piers Plowman, 310–11
"Piled for burning" (Boncho), 328
"Pity of Love, The" (Yeats), 331
"Plague Summer" (Kinzie), 432–33
Plath, Sylvia (1932–63)
  "Edge," 56
Pope, Alexander (1688–1744)
  The Dunciad, 398
  "Epistle to Bathurst," 283–84
  An Essay on Criticism, 282
  An Essay on Man, 409
"Poplar Field, The" (Cowper), 228
"Postcard from the Volcano, A" (Stevens), 117–18
Pound, Ezra (1885–1972)
  "Ts'ai Chi'i," 329
"Poverty" (Traherne), 189–90
Praed, Winthrop Mackworth (1802–1839)
  "Good-Night to the Season," 391
"Prayer for My Daughter, A" (Yeats), 275
Prelude, The (Wordsworth), 409–10
"Prospero to Ariel" (Auden), 312

Ralegh, Sir Walter (ca. 1552–1618)
  "As You Came from the Holy Land of Walsinghame," 297–98
  "The Lie," 453
  "Three Thinges There Bee," 249
Randall, Julia (b. 1923)

"Adam's Dream," 270
  "Boundbrook," 278
  "Maid's Song," 211
"Reading During Marriage" (Kinzie), 318
"Realm of Ends, The" (Koethe), 118, 119
"Resolution and Independence" (Wordsworth), 120
Resurrection (Yeats), 153
"Retaliation" (Goldsmith), 27
Richard II (Shakespeare), 236
Rime of the Ancient Mariner, The (Coleridge), 195–96, 278, 470
"Rizpah" (Tennyson), 392
Robinson, Edwin Arlington (1869–1935)
  "Captain Craig," 253–54
Roethke, Theodore (1908–63)
  "The Coming of the Cold," 108
  "The Heron," 106
  "My Papa's Waltz," 63
Romance of the Rose, The (Chaucer), 263
Romeo and Juliet (Shakespeare), 449
"Rose-Cheekt Laura" (Campion), 475
Rossetti, Christina (1830–1894)
  "In the Bleak Midwinter," 479
Rossetti, Dante Gabriel (1828–82)
  "The Woodspurge," 148
"Rugby Chapel" (Arnold), 332

"Sadness" (Justice), 195
"Sanctuary, The" (Nemerov), 105
Satan in Search of a Wife (Lamb), 391
"Satire I" (Wyatt), 204, 233
Saul (Browning), 392
Schuyler, James (1923–90)
  "A Few Days," 55
"Seen Through a Window" (Ferry), 196–97
"Self-Unseeing, The" (Hardy), 23
Shakespeare, William (1564–1616)
  Antony and Cleopatra, 439
  Hamlet, 236
  Henry IV, Part II, 252
  Henry V, 254
  Henry VI, Part II, 372
  Julius Caesar, 425–26
  King Lear, 113
  Macbeth, 193, 373

Othello the Moor of Venice, 464
Richard II, 236
Romeo and Juliet, 449
Sonnet 5 ("Those howers that with gentle worke did frame"), 41
Sonnet 31 ("Thy bosome is indeared with all hearts"), 156
Sonnet 71 ("Noe Longer mourne for me when I am dead"), 116, 210, 422
Sonnet 73 ("That time of yeeare thou maist in me behold"), 316, 481
Sonnet 94 ("They that have the powre to hurt, and will doe none"), 248
Sonnet 110 ("Alas 'tis true, I have gone here and there"), 28
Sonnet 116 ("Let me not to the marriage of true mindes"), 474
The Tempest, 474
Troilus and Cressida, 59
"She Is Going" (Lamb), 453–54
"Shield of Achilles, The" (Auden), 165–66
Shiki (1867–1902)
"Nights are getting cold," 328
"White butterfly," 328
"Side by Side" (Hardy), 312–13
Sidney, Sir Philip (1554–86)
"When to My Deadly Pleasure," 280n. 19
"Single Sonnet" (Bogan), 73
"Sir Patrick Spens" (ballad), 295–96
Skelton, John (1460?–1529)
"Philip Sparrow," 267, 299–300
"Slow Pacific Swell, The" (Winters), 202–3
"Song for a Lyre" (Bogan), 89
Song of Hiawatha (Longfellow), 474
"Song: She Dwelt Among th' Untrodden Ways" (Wordsworth), 163
Sonnets (Shakespeare). *See* listing by number and first line under "Shakespeare, William."
"So set its Sun in Thee" (#880) (Dickinson), 79
"Soul, A" (Jarrell), 171
Spenser, Edmund (1552–99)
The Faerie Queene, 462

"I Saw the Bird That Can the Sun Endure," 102
"I Saw the Bird That Dares Behold the Sun," 101–2
"Spoiler's Return, The" (Walcott), 285–86
"Spring" (Millay), 56
"Spring" (Thomson), 423
"Stand Whoso List" (Wyatt), 86
Steele, Timothy (b. 1948)
"Toward Calgary," 138
Stephens, Alan (b. 1925)
"Heron Totem," 256
Stevens, Wallace (1879–1955)
"The American Sublime," 54
"Fabliau of Florida," 343
"A Postcard from the Volcano," 117–18
Strand, Mark (b. 1934)
Dark Harbor, 206
"Strange Meeting" (Owen), 271–72
"Structures" (Oliver), 78
"sudden chill—, A" (Buson), 328
"Summer Wish" (Bogan), 54
Swinburne, Algernon Charles (1837–1909)
"By the North Sea," 391

"Tam Samson's Elegy" (Burns), 397
Tempest, The (Shakespeare), 474
Tennyson, Alfred Lord (1809–92)
In Memoriam A. H. H., 117, 183–84
"The Lotos-Eaters," 417
"Rizpah," 392
"Ulysses," 224
Thomson, James (1700–1748)
"Spring," 423
"Three Thinges There Bee" (Ralegh), 249
"Tintern Abbey" (Wordsworth), 116, 137, 174
"'Tis good—the looking back on Grief—" (#660) (Dickinson), 24–25
"To a Friend Whose Work Has Come to Nothing" (Yeats), 109
"To Be Sung on the Water" (Bogan), 76
"Toward Calgary" (Steele), 138
Traherne, Thomas (1637–74)
"Poverty," 189–90

"Trees, The" (Larkin), 180
Troilus and Cressida (Shakespeare), 59
"Ts'ai Chi'i" (Pound), 329

"Ulysses" (Tennyson), 224
"Unburied, The" (Morris), 370–71
"Urban Convalescence, An" (Merrill),
    258

"Valediction, A: Forbidding Mourning"
    (Donne), 156
"Verses Supposed to Be Written by Alex-
    ander Selkirk, During His Solitary
    Abode in the Island of Juan Fernan-
    dez" (Cowper), 240

Walcott, Derek (b. 1930)
    "The Hotel Normandie Pool," 232
    "The Spoiler's Return," 285–86
Watts, Isaac (1674–1748)
    "Against Idleness and Mischief," 467
"When to My Deadly Pleasure" (Sidney),
    280n. 19
"White butterfly" (Shiki), 328
Whitman, Walt (1819–92)
    "Cavalry Crossing a Ford," 423
    "The World Below the Brine," 339
Wilbur, Richard (b. 1921)
    "Exeunt," 179
Wilner, Eleanor (b. 1937)
    "Operations: Desert Shield, Desert
        Storm," 35–38
Winters, Anne (b. 1939)
    "The Mill-Race," 39–41
Winters, Yvor (1900–1968)
    "The Slow Pacific Swell," 202–3
"Witch, The" (Yeats), 292
"With a Copy of Swift's Works"
    (Cunningham), 279
"With the Shell of a Hermit Crab"
    (Wright), 175
"Woodspurge, The" (Rossetti), 148
Wordsworth, William (1770–1850)
    "Composed upon Westminster
        Bridge," 143–44, 393

"Great Men have been among us," 29
    The Prelude, 409–10
    "Resolution and Independence," 120
    "Song: She Dwelt Among th' Untrod-
        den Ways," 163
    "Tintern Abbey," 116, 137, 174
    "World Below the Brine, The" (Whit-
        man), 339
Wright, James (1927–80)
    "Lying in a Hammock at William
        Duffy's Farm in Pine Island, Min-
        nesota," 53
    "With the Shell of a Hermit Crab," 175
"Writing" (Nemerov), 243
Wyatt, Sir Thomas (1503–42)
    "I fynde no peace and all my warre is
        done," 447
    "The longe love, that in my thought
        doeth harbar," 245–46
    "My Lute and I," 300–301
    "Satire I" ("Myne owne John Poynz"),
        204, 233
    "Stand Whoso List," 86

Yeats, William Butler (1865–1935)
    "Balloon of the Mind," 161
    "Byzantium," 276
    "A Drinking Song," 64
    "Easter 1916," 172, 293
    "The Fish," 304
    "Long-legged Fly," 294
    "The Pity of Love," 331
    "A Prayer for My Daughter," 275
    Resurrection ("Two Songs from a Play"),
        153
    "To a Friend Whose Work Has Come
        to Nothing," 109
    "The Witch," 292
"You have here no otherness"
    (Cunningham), 324–25
"Young Woman, A" (Ferry), 332–33

SUBJECT INDEX

Boldface page numbers indicate that the poem is quoted in the text at this point rather than simply referred to or discussed.

Abelard, Peter: "Lament," **429**

Abrams, Meyer H., 492

absolute construction: defined, 384; in graphic schema of syntax, 382; in hyperbaton, 421; in Johnson's "On the Death of Dr. Robert Levet," 91

abstraction: balancing particulars against, 368; defined, 384; in graphic schema of diction, 382; metaphor contrasted with, 436; and polysyllabism, 111, 137, 404; starting with the thing and moving to the thought, 381

accent, 217–21; defined, 384–85; in graphic schema of meter and prosody, 383; marking, 222, 463; and meter as pulling against one another, 213; stress contrasted with, 463. *See also* intervals

accentual-syllabic verse, 217–61; accent in, 385;

assumption of, 293, 296; defined, 385; in graphic schema of line, 383; in graphic schema of meter and prosody, 383; illustrative poems, 505–6; isochrony, 425; meter in, 437; in metrical history of English, 215; rhythm in, 212; threshold between accentual verse and, 290–94

accentual verse, 290–313; advantages of, 369; alliteration in, 386, 387; auditory setting of, 303; as cadential verse, 398; as counted form, 290; defined, 385–86; in graphic schema of line, 383; in graphic schema of meter and prosody, 383; in graphic schema of stanza and rhyme, 383; as harder to hear in period of free verse, 290; illustrative poems, 505; in metrical history of English, 215; pattern withheld in, 291; pithy

quality of, 308; podic verse contrasted with, 302, 303; as quintessentially spoken, 290; syllabic verse compared with, 313–14, 315, 316; threshold between accentual-syllabic verse and, 290–94; and the two-stress unit, 308–12; of Yeats, 291–94. *See also* expandable time; hemistich

"A Clock stopped—" (#287) (Dickinson): continuum of metaphor in, **154**

"Adam's Dream" (Muir): visionary dream in, 363

"Adam's Dream" (Randall): rhyme in, **270**

"Address to the Unco Guid, or the Rigidly Righteous" (Burns): mixed diction of, 132–**33**, 405

adjacent rhyme, 271, 455

adnomination: as bringing out shape and logic of word formation, 357; defined, 386; in graphic

adnomination (*continued*)
schema of diction, 382;
in graphic schema of
trope, 382; in Milton, 99
"Adonais" (Shelley): hex-
ameter in, 218; Spenser-
ean stanza in, 462
adversatives: in Byron and
Auden, 81; defined,
386; launching the sub-
junctive with, 366
adynaton: defined, 386; in
graphic schema of rheto-
ric and mode, 382; as
hyperbole, 421
"Ae fond kiss, and then we
sever" (Burns): trochaic
meter in, **475**
"After Frost at Midnight"
(Kinzie): as alcaic,
322–23
"After the Persian" (Bo-
gan): anaphora in, 393;
as imagist free verse,
341–42; nondeclarative
syntax in, 88
"Afterwards" (Hardy): ana-
pestic gallop avoided in,
392–93
"Again" (Nemerov): de-
scriptive syntax in,
96–97; diction of, 127;
literal symbol in, 144
"Against Idleness and Mis-
chief" (Watts): syntactic
inversion in, **467**
Age of Anxiety, The
(Auden): expandable
time in, **306**–7; "un-
earned significance" in,
308
"Album Leaves" (Randall):
quotation in, 174–75
alcaics: as syllabic form,
322–23
Alexander, Cecil: trochaic
meter used by, 226
Alexandrines: illustrative

poems, 507; as syllabic,
218, 314
*Alice's Adventures in Wonder-
land* (Carroll): syntac-
tic inversion in, **467;**
zeugma in, 481–**82**
allegory, 159–62; on con-
tinuum of comparison,
476; defined, 386–87;
in graphic schema of
trope, 382; metaphor
contrasted with, 436,
437; narrative line re-
quired in, 160; personi-
fication emerging from,
445
"Allegro, L'" (Milton): bi-
syllabic words in, 220;
and primacy of immedi-
ate scene, 158
Allen, Donald M., 483
Allen, John Alexander, 484
alliteration: in accentual
verse, 386, 387; acciden-
tal association in, 308;
Anglo-Saxon model of,
309; in biblical free
verse, 337; defined,
387–88; in graphic
schema of diction, 382;
in graphic schema of
stanza and rhyme, 383;
in graphic schema of
trope, 382; in Milton,
98–99; and overstress-
ing, 443; and rhyme,
262, 263; as thickening
verbal texture, 140–41.
See also assonance
allusion, 164–75; contin-
uum of, 390; on contin-
uum of comparison,
475, 476; defined,
388–90; in epigrams,
358; in graphic schema
of rhetoric and mode,
382; in graphic schema
of trope, 382; from lit-

eral symbol to classical,
155; modesty of scale re-
quired in, 168; overt
forms of, 173–75; re-
marks on using, 172; to
social and economic
conditions, 173
Alpers, Paul J., 493
Alter, Robert, 398
alternating rhyme: appear-
ance of, 264; in hymn
meter, 418; illustrative
quatrains with, 504–5;
rhyme scheme of, 271,
455
"Always" (Strand): tenor
and vehicle coinciding
in, 156; verisimilitude
of suggestion in, 155
"American Sublime, The"
(Stevens): lineation in,
54
Ammons, A. R.: free verse
of, 341, 342
Amours de Voyage (Clough):
conversational style in,
401; dactyls in, 402–3,
402, 403
amphibrach: as alternative
in anapestic poems,
228–29; in ballads, 227;
defined, 390–91; in
graphic schema of meter
and prosody, 383; in
"Green Gravel," 174; il-
lustrative poems, 505–6;
in limericks, 433; in lit-
erary poems, 228; in
nursery rhymes, 227,
390; as rare in English,
227; in triple meter,
472; Victorian use of,
392
analytical concepts, 380,
382
anapest: amphibrachs as al-
ternatives in anapestic
poems, 228–29; de-

fined, 391–93; in graphic schema of meter and prosody, 383; in Hardy's "Neutral Tones," 240–41; illustrative poems, 506; in limericks, 433; as rare in English, 227; as rising foot, 226, 391, 437; substituting for an iamb, 465; as taking over an iambic line, 458; in triple meter, 472; as varying iambs, 307, 393

anapestic gallop, 240–41, 391, 392

anaphora: in Bogan's "Baroque Comment," 58; defined, 393; in graphic schema of line, 382; in graphic schema of rhetoric and mode, 382; and isochrony, 425. *See also* isocolon; tag

"Anaphora" (Bishop): and anaphora, 393

anastrophe: defined, 393; as syntactic inversion, 467–68

anatomy: and Auden's "In Praise of Limestone," 360; defined, 394; in graphic schema of rhetoric and mode, 382

Anchor Anthology of Sixteenth-Century Verse, The (Sylvester), 490

"And Did Those Feet" (Blake): compound sentences in, 80

"Andrea del Sarto" (Browning): speaker of, 208–9

"Anecdote of the Jar" (Stevens): haiku feeling of, 329

Anniversaries (Donne): anatomy in, 394; as expository verse, 374

"Anonymous Drawing" (Justice): heterometric rhyme in, **417**

Answerable Style: Essays on "Paradise Lost" (Stein), 500–501

antimimetic meter, 251–59

antithesis: in biblical free verse, 337; in couplets, 401; defined, 394; in graphic schema of line, 382; in graphic schema of rhetoric and mode, 382; in Hebrew verse, 51, 53; in Hope's "Man Friday," 134–36, 288; and monosyllables making stress, 247, 248, 250; in Petrarchan mode, 446

Antony and Cleopatra (Shakespeare): mixed trope in, 438–**39**

aporia: defined, 394; in graphic schema of rhetoric and mode, 382; as meiosis (deflation), 421

apposition: absolute construction compared with, 384; defined, 394–95; in graphic schema of syntax, 382; in hyperbaton, 421; and juxtaposition, 65, 394, 395

archetype: on continuum of comparison, 477

argumentative subordinating sentences, 47, 468

Arnold, Matthew: "Rugby Chapel," 330, **332,** 448. *See also* "Dover Beach"

Articulate Energy: An Inquiry into the Syntax of English Poetry (Davie), 498

"Artillery" (Herbert): rhetoric of, 190

Ashbery, John: long-line works, 55; "Melodic Trains," **54**–55

"Ash-Wednesday" (Eliot): two-stress unit in, 311

"As I Walked Out One Evening" (Auden): adynaton in, 421

"Aspen and the Stream, The" (Wilbur): as dialogue poem, 360

assonance: defined, 395; in Milton, 99; Pope on, 366

Astrophel and Stella (Sidney): decasyllabic line in, 317; sonnets as complete poems, 462

asyndeton: in baroque poetry, 340; defined, 395

"As You Came from the Holy Land of Walsinghame" (ballad): desolate quality of, 355; irregularity of, 296–98, **297–98;** mixed metaphor in, 438; triple measures in, 266

"At a Hasty Wedding" (Hardy): contrary-to-fact argument in, 82; syntactic inversion in, 84; as triolet, **431**

"At a Low Bar" (Ferry): isochrony in, 304; juxtaposition in, 62–**63**

Attridge, Derek: on ballad meter, 268; on Burns stanza, 397; on common meter as normative in English, 420; *The Rhythms of English Poetry,* 496; on two-stress unit, 266; on unrealized fourth beat, 267, 293–94

Auden, W. H.: abstract diction turning into per-

Auden, W. H. (*continued*)
sonification in, 140; accentual verse of, 386; adversatives of, 81; "age of anxiety," 375; allusion to social and economic conditions in, 173; "As I Walked Out One Evening," 421; ballad as influencing, 278; in Bate and Perkins's *British and American Poets,* 486; "But in the Evening the Oppression Lifted," **139**–40; *The Dyer's Hand,* 496; *Elizabethan and Jacobean Poets, Marlowe to Marvell,* 485; "In Memory of Sigmund Freud," 140, 316; "In Praise of Limestone," 140, 360; "Lay your sleeping head my love," 226; line consciousness of, 68; literal symbol in, 434; "Lullaby," 474; *Medieval and Renaissance Poets, Langland to Spenser,* 485; on modernization, 86n; monosyllabism in, 114; pararhyme in, 271, 443; "Paysage Moralisé," 366; pithy darts of rhyme of, 358; *Poets of the English Language,* 485–86; *The Poet's Tongue,* 485; "The Quest," 362; *Restoration and Jacobean Poets, Milton to Goldsmith,* 485; rhyming on the phrase in, 67–68; *Romantic Poets, Blake to Poe,* 485; sestinas of, 459; "Sonnets from China" (from *In Time of War* sequence), 362, 462; starting a

poem with "But," 366, 386; "The Summer Holds," 173; syllable-count variation in, 318; tension in, 470–71; *Victorian and Edwardian Poets, Tennyson to Yeats,* 485; "A Walk After Dark," 73; writing on poetry, 483n. See also *Age of Anxiety, The;* "Fall of Rome, The"; "Lady, Weeping at the Crossroads"; *Letter to Lord Byron; Sea and the Mirror, The;* "Shield of Achilles, The"

"Auguries of Innocence" (Blake): the small implicating the great in, **153**

Augustan poetry: defined, 396; in graphic schema of rhetoric and mode, 382. *See also* Pope, Alexander

"August Midnight, An" (Hardy): rhetoric in, **191**–92

"Autumn—" (Basho): as haiku, **328**

"Autumn" (Clare): amphibrachs in, 228

bacchius: defined, 396; as not viable in English, 229, 396, 438

Baker, David, 493

Baker, Howard, 493

Baker, William E., 497

ballad, 266–70; amphibrachs in, 227; arguments of, 210–11; common meter in, 400; defined, 396; echo tradition of, 277; English ballads, 298, 400, 429; exercise in ballad of

metamorphosis, 354–55; in graphic schema of rhetoric and mode, 382; in graphic schema of stanza and rhyme, 383; holdovers from leonine verse, 265; illustrative poems, 503, 504; intensity of, 266; irregular ballads, 294–98; juxtaposition in, 265; leonine rhyme in, 429; metaphysical ballads, 278–79; metrical norm of, 266; movement toward literary stanza, 269; recession of technique in, 451; refrains in, 264, 452; rhyme in, 263–66; rule of two in, 266–67, 457; Scottish ballads, 48, 74, 298, 396, 400, 451; stanzas in, 264; triple meter in, 266, 472; unrealized beat in, 267–69, 420. *See also* ballad meter

ballad meter (ballad stanza): alternating rhyme in, 455; as basic stanza in English, 418; clausal mode of, 439; defined, 396; as hymn meter, 418–19; illustrative quatrains with alternating rhyme, 504; symmetry of, 268. *See also* common meter

"Ballad of Hector in Hades" (Muir): ballad meter in, 418; and law of simplified focus, 428; literal symbol in, **145–47,** 434, 477; metonymy in, 438; persona of, 445; personification in, 446; recession of technique in, 369n; self-dramatizing persona of, 210; six-line "quatrains" in, 421

ballad stanza. *See* ballad meter

"Balloon of the Mind" (Yeats): allegory in, **161**–62, 387; over-stressed line in, 443

"Barbara Allen" (ballad): incremental repetition in, 264

Barfield, Owen, 497

"Baroque Comment" (Bogan): anaphora in, 393; anastrophe in, 468; asyndeton in, 395; as biblical free verse, 340; epithet in, 411; isomorphism in, 57–**58;** juxtaposition in, 65; metaphor in, 436–37; periphrasis in, 444–45; word order in, 481

"Baroque Wall Fountain in the Villa Sciarra, A" (Wilbur): primacy of immediate scene in, 157–58

Basho: "Autumn—," **328**

Bate, Walter Jackson, 486

Baudelaire, Charles: "La Beauté," 314–15

Beardsley, Monroe, 213

"Beauté, La" (Baudelaire): syllabification and caesural division in, 314–15

"Believe Me if All Those Endearing Young Charms" (Moore): aura of song in, **277**

Belitt, Ben, 476

"Belle Dame Sans Merci, La" (Keats): reduced line in, 452

Belloc, Hilaire, 410

"Ben Jonson Entertains a Man from Stratford" (Robinson): as dramatic monologue, 357

Beowulf: Anglo-Saxon alliterative model in, **309–10;** auditory setting of, 303n. 11

"Beowulf" and the Appositive Style (Robinson), 500

Berryman, John: "Dream Songs," 449

Betjeman, John. *See* "Death in Leamington"

Beum, Robert, 337, 493

biblical free verse (syntactical free verse), 336–40; defined, 396; frame of expectation of, 369; in graphic schema of meter and prosody, 383; illustrative poems, 506; imagist free verse compared with, 340

"Birches" (Frost): mimetic meter in, 255; trochaic inversion in, 474

"Birds at Winter Nightfall" (Hardy): as triolet, 431–32

Bishop, Elizabeth: "Anaphora," 393; "The Fish," 201, 333; "In the Waiting Room," 421; "A Miracle for Breakfast," 459; poems growing in mind of, 34–35; "Sestina," 459; sestinas of, 459. *See also* "Cirque d'Hiver"; "Crusoe in England"; "Filling Station"

"Bishop Blougram's Apology" (Browning): subjunctive mood in, 464–**65**

bisyllabic words: stress in, 220, 458

Black Mountain school, 483

Blake, William: "And Did Those Feet," 80; "Auguries of Innocence," **153;** *Jerusalem,* **338;** "Milton," 443; the small implicating the great in, 152–53. *See also* "London"

blank sonnet: defined, 396

blank verse: cut-and-paste as danger with, 372; defined, 397; end-stopped, 101–6; enjambment in, 4, 5, 101, 397; evolution of, 49–50; exercises, 7–8, 352; as feeling less artificial than stanzaic forms, 368–69; flatness as risk of, 369; form follows theme in, 242–45; in graphic schema of line, 383; in graphic schema of meter and prosody, 383; hexameters in, 218; illustrative poems, 506; loosening into free blank verse, 471; Milton's use of, 50, 98, 397; and passage, 443–44; pattern of, 4; regularized line-endings required for, 216. *See also* free blank verse

blason: in graphic schema of rhetoric and mode, 382; in Petrarchan mode, 446

"Bluebeard's Wife" (Hine): descriptive syntax of, 94–**95;** Spenserean stanza in, 462

"Blueberries" (Frost): anapests in, 393

Bogan, Louise: "The Changed Woman," **419–20;** "'Come, Sleep, . . . ,'" 353; "Fifteenth Farewell," 447; "Medusa," 88; *A Poet's Alphabet: Reflections on the Literary Art and Vocation,* 497; "Rhyme," 467–68; "Roman Fountain," 88; "Song for the Last Act," 88; stylistic range of, 88; subphrasal cut in, 341; "Summer Wish," **54, ** 360. *See also* "After the Persian"; "Baroque Comment"; "Cassandra"; "Daemon, The"; "Last Hill in a Vista"; "Memory"; "Single Sonnet"; "Song for a Lyre"; "To Be Sung on the Water"

Bold, Alan, 265

Boncho: "Piled for burning," **328**

Borges, Jorge Luis, 164, 181

"Borough, The" (Crabbe): monosyllabism in, 440; plain style as low style in, **120**

Borroff, Marie, 306–8, 497

"Boundbrook" (Randall): as metaphysical ballad, **278**

"Break, Break, Break" (Tennyson): isochrony in, 305

Breslin, Paul, 205

breve: defined, 397; in Nabokov's three-symbol scansion, 222, 435

Bridges, Robert: light rhyme in, 430

"Bristowe Tragedie, The" (Chatterton): ornamented quatrains of, **269**

British and American Poets, Chaucer to the Present (Bate and Perkins), 486

Brogan, T. V. F., 492

Bronson, Bertrand, 298n. 6

Brooke-Rose, Christine, 143n, 434, 471, 476, 497

"Brothers, The" (Muir): visionary dream in, 363

Browning, Robert: "Andrea del Sarto," 208–9; "Bishop Blougram's Apology," 464–**65;** dramatic monologues of, 357–58; "The Englishman in Italy," **228;** *The Ring and the Book,* 468; *Saul,* **392;** speakers in monologues of, 188

Bruns, Gerald L., 497

Bunyan, John: *Pilgrim's Progress,* 455

Burckhardt, Sigurd, 498

Burke, Kenneth, 494

Burns, Robert: "Address to the Unco Guid, or the Rigidly Righteous," 132–**33,** 405; "Ae fond kiss, and then we sever," **475;** aura of song in, 277; diction-shifting in, 132–33; "A Red, Red Rose," 163, 460; "Tam Samson's Elegy," **397,** 452–53; "To a Mouse," 132, 153

Burns stanza: defined, 397; extrapolation beyond the quatrain in, 274; in graphic schema of stanza and rhyme, 383; reduced line in, 452

"Burnt Norton" (Eliot): visionary theme of, 363; Wilner's "Operations" compared with, 19

Burton, Richard: monosyllabism in, 439

Buson: "Deer in rain—," **328;** restraint in, 201; "A sudden chill—," **328**

"But in the Evening the Oppression Lifted" (Auden): extremes of syllable count in, **139–40**

Byron, George Gordon, Lord: adversaries of, 81; analogies as persuasive, 164; "Darkness," 92–93; "Epistle from Mr. Murray to Dr. Polidori," **285;** ottava rima of, 274–75; pararhyme in, 271; rhyme flaunted by, 289. See also *Don Juan*

"By the North Sea" (Swinburne): amphibrachs in, **391**

"Byzantium" (Yeats): alliteration in, 387; epithet in, 411; ottava rima in, 275–**76;** stanzas in, 276–77

cadential verse: defined, 398; imbalance required for, 293. *See also* accentual verse

caesura: in Baudelaire, 314; defined, 398; and foot, 225n. 10, 244, 398; in fourteeners heard as a line, 414; in graphic schema of meter and prosody, 383; in graphic schema of syntax, 382; in Oliver's "Structures," 77–79; in scansion, 223–25; and syntax, 68; and trochaic inversion, 472, 473

Calvary (Yeats): plain style in, 15

Campion, Thomas: "Rose-Cheekt Laura," **475;** "There Is a Garden," 163

"Candle Indoors, The" (Hopkins): personification in, 446

Canterbury Tales (Chaucer): like endings in, **430**

"Captain Craig" (Robinson): elision in, 449; too-regular meter in, **253–54**

caret, 236, 294n, 304

Carew, Thomas: "To Saxham," 359, 471

Carmina Burana (songs): leonine rhyme in, 262, **429**

Carroll, Lewis: *Alice's Adventures in Wonderland,* **467,** 481–**82;** "The Hunting of the Snark," **390**–91; "Mad Gardener's Song," **288–89;** rhyme flaunted by, 289

Carruth, Hayden, 487

Carryl, Charles: leonine rhymes in, 429

"Cassandra" (Bogan): persona of, **209**–10, 445; personification in, 446

catchphrase: and monosyllables making stress, 247; in rhyming on the phrase, 66, 67, 283, 455

"Cavalry Crossing a Ford" (Whitman): imagism in, **423**

"Changed Woman, The" (Bogan): long meter of, **419–20**

"Channel Firing" (Hardy):

burlesque diction of, **121**

Chapman, George, 402, 414–15

character, 187–200

Chatman, Seymour, 494

Chatterton, Thomas: "The Bristowe Tragedie," **269**

Chaucer, Geoffrey: *Canterbury Tales,* **430;** as closer to prose than Pope, 280; in metrical history of English, 215–16, 303; *The Romance of the Rose,* **263**–64, 280

chiasmus: defined, 398–99; in graphic schema of meter and prosody, 383; in graphic schema of rhetoric and mode, 382; in graphic schema of stanza and rhyme, 383; in Pope, 281–82; and rhyming on the phrase, 281–82

Chickering, Howell D., Jr., 302n. 9, 310n. 20, 332n. 3

Child, Francis James, 298n. 6

"Childhood" (Muir): antimimetic meter in, **252–53;** literal symbol in, 143; personification in, 445

choriamb: defined, 399

"Church Going" (Larkin): light rhyme in, 429–30; low and high diction in, 123; praise-of-setting theme of, 360

"Cirque d'Hiver" (Bishop), **42–43;** as approaching the ballad, 278, 505; beginning of, 16; heterometric rhyme in, 273, 274; juxtaposition in, 426; metonymy

in, 162, 438; the small made large in, 152; theme striking out from the expected, 32–33

Clare, John: "Autumn," 228

clausal mode, 439

clause: in absolute construction, 384; as coinciding or diverging from the line, 75, 399; on continuum of syntax, 47, 468; defined, 399; in graphic schema of syntax, 382. *See also* hypotaxis

"Clerk Colvill" (ballad): allusion in, **167–68**

cliche: defined, 399; of feeling, 376–78; in graphic schema of diction, 382; in graphic schema of rhetoric and mode, 382; literal symbol versus, 375–79; Pope in making of, 284

"Clock stopped—, A" (#287) (Dickinson): continuum of metaphor in, **154**

Clough, Arthur High. See *Amours de Voyage*

coincidence, 48; as analytical concept, 382; of clause and line, 75; defined, 399–400; of phrase and line, 75–76, 369; with respect to rhyme, 71–72; tension requiring, 72, 471; variety providing tension against, 351

Coleridge, Samuel Taylor: "Dejection: An Ode," 85–**86,** 274. *See also* "Frost at Midnight"; *Rime of the Ancient Mariner, The*

Collected Essays of J. V. Cunningham, The (Cunningham), 498

Collins, William: hymn meter in, 418; "Ode to Evening," 269–**70**

"Comedian as the Letter C, The" (Stevens): periphrasis in, 445

Come Hither: A Collection of Rhymes and Poems for the Young of All Ages (de la Mare), 487

"'Come, Sleep, . . .'" (Bogan): as mad song, 353

"Coming of the Cold, The" (Roethke): syntactic surprise in, **108**

common meter: as basic stanza in English, 418; defined, 400; and fourteeners, 218, 414; in graphic schema of stanza and rhyme, 383; as hymn meter, 418–19; illustrative quatrains with alternating rhyme, 504. *See also* ballad meter; unrealized beat

comparison. *See* trope

complex subordinating sentences, 47, 468

"Composed upon Westminster Bridge" (Wordsworth): anaphora in, **393;** literal symbol in, **143–44,** 400; personification in, 437, 445; syntactic inversion in, 467

compound sentence: on continuum of syntax, 47, 468; defined, 400; formation of, 80; in graphic schema of syntax, 382. *See also* parataxis

concrete diction: balancing particulars against abstractions, 368; concrete plain style, 178; defined, 400; in graphic schema of diction, 382; and monosyllabism, 111

conjunctions: adversatives, 386; in asyndeton, 395; in compound sentences, 80, 400; monosyllabic, 220; in parataxis, 443

"Conjuration, to Electra, A" (Herrick): muscularity of syntax of, 353–54; rhyming on the phrase in, **66**

consonantal clang, 308

consonants: elision, 406; pararhyme, 443; quantity, 451; rhyme, 454. *See also* alliteration

context: as environment in which poems grow, 9–10; relevant context, 14; required for scanning lines, 219, 221, 458; in writing your way through a poem, 5

context makes meter, 239–46; as analytical concept, 381, 383; as scansion rule, 221, 458

continuum, 46–47; of allegory, 386; of allusion, 390; as analytical concept, 380, 382; defined, 400–401; of diction, 47, 150, 368, 401, 404; of the stanza, 278–79; of syntax, 46–47, 149, 401, 468; three points required for, 47; of trope, 148–52, 400, 475–76

"Contrary Impulses: The Tension Between Po-

etry and Theory" (Koethe), 495

contrary-to-fact argument, 82, 440, 464

contre-rejet, 303n. 10

conventions, 26–34; experimenting with, 13; overturning, 27–29

conversational style: in alcaics, 323; defined, 401; in graphic schema of diction, 382; in graphic schema of rhetoric and mode, 382; and number of syllables, 111; playing off cliche, 399

"Coole and Ballylee, 1931" (Yeats): as accentual-syllabic, 292

copula: defined, 401; in graphic schema of syntax, 382; as non-verb, 93n, 367, 441; in trope, 476

counted forms, 290–329

counting songs, 330

couplet: defined, 401–2; as earliest and most obvious rhymed form, 262; exercise in couplet narrative, 350–51; in graphic schema of stanza and rhyme, 383; hypotactic sentences in, 80; illustrative poems, 504; in narratives, 284–89; rhyme in, 68; rhyming on the phrase in, 282–84. *See also* fourteeners; heroic couplet

Cowley, Abraham: "Ode upon Doctor Harvey," 274

Cowper, William: "The Poplar Field," **228**–29. *See also* "Verses Supposed to Be Written by

Alexander Selkirk, During His Solitary Abode in the Island of Juan Fernandez"

Crabbe, George: "The Borough," **120,** 440; plain style in, 447

"Cradle Song" (Dekker): refrain in, 452

cretic: defined, 402; false cretics, 241n; as not viable in English, 229, 438

"Crusoe in England" (Bishop): the knife in, 377–**78,** 461; simile in, 461

Cuddon, J. A., 490–91

Cunningham, J. V.: *The Collected Essays of J. V. Cunningham,* 498; and couplet of Pope, 283n; "For My Contemporaries," 79, **126**–27; "A half hour for coffee and at night," **323–24;** poetry compared to chess by, 378–79; rhyme wit of, 359; syllabics of, 323–25; on syllabic verse in English, 317; syllable count in, 318; "With a Copy of Swift's Works," **279;** writing on poetry, 483n; "You have here no otherness," **324–25**

"Cyclic" (Oliver): as concrete plain style, **178**–79; diction of, 404; literal symbol in, 149, 434; speaker and rhetoric in, 196, 198

dactyl: in classical epic, 418; defined, 402–4; as falling foot, 226, 402,

437; in graphic schema of meter and prosody, 383; illustrative poems, 506; as rare in English, 227; in triple meter, 472; Victorian use of, 392

"Daemon, The" (Bogan): deriving the meter of, 239, 240; end-stopping in, 407; juxtaposition in, **62**

Dalmon, Charles: amphibrachs in, 228

Daniel, Arnaut: sestinas of, 459

Dark Harbor (Strand): fourteeners in, 219; free blank verse of, 334, 415; meiosis in, **206,** 421; melody of vowel passage in, 366

"Darkling Thrush, The" (Hardy): literal symbol in, 143, 149, 400; Romantic diction of, 120–**21;** subjunctive and parataxis juxtaposed in, 84–**85;** symbol in, 466; trope in, 143

"Darkness" (Byron): descriptive syntax of, **92**–93; strong verbs disappearing in, 368

Darley, George: *Ethelstan; or the Battle of Brunaburgh,* **427,** 428

Daryush, Elizabeth: "If there's no ruling," **325**–26; "Still-Life," 316; syllabics of, 325–26; on syllabic verse in English, 317; syllable count in, 318. *See also* "Drought"

Davie, Donald, 46, 451, 498

Davies, R. T., 487

Dawn in Britain, The (Doughty): word order in, **481**

"Death in Leamington" (Betjeman): amphibrachs in, 391; continuum analysis of, 151; diction of, **126**

"Death of the Hired Man, The" (Frost): monosyllabism in, **115;** six weak monosyllables in, 214

declaration: defined, 404; in Ferry's "Seen Through a Window," 348; perspective provided by, 366; as simplest syntax, 79–80

declarative sentence: on continuum of syntax, 47, 468; defined, 404; in graphic schema of syntax, 382; indicative mood of, 424; joining, 80. *See also* parataxis

"Deer in rain—" (Buson): as haiku, **328**

"Dejection: An Ode" (Coleridge): extrapolation beyond the quatrain in, 274; splitting compounds creating tension in, 85–**86**

Dekker, Thomas: "Cradle Song," 452

de la Mare, Walter: *Come Hither: A Collection of Rhymes and Poems for the Young of All Ages,* 487; "John Mouldy," **452**

"Delight in Disorder" (Herrick): rhyming on the phrase in, **67**

derived meter: as analytical concept, 383; defined, 404; in graphic schema

derived meter (*continued*)
of meter and prosody,
383; in scansion, 221,
458; two categories of,
226
"Descriptive" (Ferry):
end-stopping in, **103**–4;
monosyllables making
stress in, 247; rhetoric
of, 196; simile in, 461
descriptive poetry, 202,
334, 462
descriptive subordinating
sentences, 47, 468
descriptive syntax, 92–97
"Deserted Village, The"
(Goldsmith): syntactic
inversion in, 466
"Design" (Frost): etymo-
logical style in, 412; and
Hardy's "An August
Midnight," 192n; wit
in, 157
Deutsch, Babette: "The
fallen flower," **327**–28;
*Poetry Handbook: A Dic-
tionary of Terms,* 491
dialect, 131–33; and over-
stressing, 443
dialogue: exercise in dia-
logue in nonce stanzas,
360–61
Dickinson, Emily: "A
Clock stopped—"
(#287), **154;** diction
styles of, 125–26; "Fur-
ther in Summer than
the Birds" (#1068),
125, 455; "The Heart
asks Pleasure—first—"
(#536), **419,** 479; hymn
meter in, 418; "I Felt a
funeral, in my Brain"
(#280), 353; "I heard a
Fly buzz—when I
died—" (#465), **125;**
"The Months have

ends—the Years—a
knot" (#423), 268; "To
One denied to drink"
(#490), 354, 479;
"Twas like a Maelstrom,
with a notch" (#414),
162. *See also* "My Life
had stood—a Loaded
Gun" (#754); "So
set its Sun in Thee"
(#808); "'Tis good—
the looking back on
Grief—" (#660)
diction, 111–41; contin-
uum of, 47, 150, 368,
401, 404; defined,
404–5; difficult diction,
126–31; as element of
poetry, 45; graphic
schema of, 382; mixed,
382, 405; and mode,
439; and rhetoric, 454;
and rhythm, 136–40,
457; in self-conscious
speakers, 188; and sylla-
ble, 111–13, 405; and
syntax, 399, 469; and
trope, 140–41. *See also*
abstraction; concrete
diction; conversational
style; etymological style;
monosyllabism; plain
style; polysyllabism
*Dictionary of Literary Terms
and Literary Theory, A*
(Cuddon), 490–91
dimeter: defined, 405; in
graphic schema of meter
and prosody, 383; iam-
bic, 217; illustrative cou-
plets, 504; illustrative
quatrains with alternat-
ing rhyme, 504; in lim-
ericks, 433; versus two-
stress, 312–13
dipodic verse: defined,
405–6; in graphic

schema of meter and
prosody, 383; in graphic
schema of stanza and
rhyme, 383; nursery
rhymes, 299, 405; as
podic verse, 299; pre-
valence in English, 444;
rule of two, 405,
457
"Discursive Mode, The:
Reflections on the Ecol-
ogy of Poetry" (Hope),
495
discursive poetry, 334, 374
*Discussions of Poetry: Form
and Structure* (Murphy),
495
distance, 187–200
"Divine Meditations"
(Donne): monosyllables
making stress in, 247;
syntax of, 80
Dodgson, Charles L. *See*
Carroll, Lewis
"Dolls' Wash, The" (Ew-
ing): heterometric
rhyme in, **272**
Don Juan (Byron): adversa-
tives in, 386; comic
rhymes of, 134; histori-
cal rhyming in, 449; ot-
tava rima in, **275;** rhym-
ing on the phrase in,
456; stanzas in, 276–77,
463
Donne, John: *Anniversa-
ries,* 374, 394; clausal
mode in, 439; decasyl-
labic line in, 317; "Di-
vine Meditations," 80,
247; "Elegy X," 317;
"Lovers Infinitenesse,"
410; monosyllabism in,
440; outlandish meta-
phor in, 175, 176; plain
style in, 114, 116, 447;
podic free verse of, 331;

"Twickenham Garden,"
157. *See also* "Loves Dei-
tie"; "Valediction, A:
Forbidding Mourning"
"Do Not Go Gentle"
(Thomas): as villanelle,
431
double meter: in graphic
schema of meter and
prosody, 383
Doughty, Charles M.: *The
Dawn in Britain,* **481**
"Dover Beach" (Arnold):
allegory in, 387; begin-
ning of, **15**, 16, **17**–19;
heterometric rhyme in,
273; surprising shifts in,
33
dramatic extremes,
200–211
dramatic monologue,
208–10; of Browning,
357–58; defined, 406; in
graphic schema of rheto-
ric and mode, 382; mad
songs, 353; and rheto-
ric, 454
dramatic poetry: as better
behaved than written
verse, 373–74; blank
verse in, 49–50; heroic
quatrain in, 417; illustra-
tive poems, 503; over-
stressed line in, 334. *See
also* dramatic mono-
logue
dramatic syntax, 194
Drayton, Michael: "The
Moone-Calfe," 255–56
"Dream Songs" (Berry-
man): elision in, 449
"Drinking Song, A"
(Yeats): isomorphism in,
426; juxtaposition in,
64, 426
"Drought" (Daryush): half-
meaning in, 416; intran-

sitive verbs in, 425; as
syllabic verse, **326**
Drummond de Andrade,
Carlos, 206
Dryden, John: "A Song for
St. Cecilia's Day," 274
du Bellay, Joachim, 101–2
"Dull Is My Verse" (Lan-
dor): meiosis in, **421**
Dunbar, William: "Lament
for the Makaris," **419,**
452
Dunciad, The (Pope): an-
tithesis in, 394; chias-
mus in, **398**
"Duns Scotus's Oxford"
(Hopkins): as podic
verse, **301**, 302; *rejet*
in and *contre-rejet* in,
302n. 9
Dyer, John: "Grongar
Hill," 471
Dyer's Hand, The (Auden),
496

"Earth with Thunder
Torn, The" (Greville):
unexpected compari-
son in, 175–76
"Easter 1916" (Yeats): as
accentual, **293;** allusion
in, **172;** personification
in, 445; as podic free
verse, 331–32; two-
stress unit in, 311
Ecclesiastes 12: antithesis
in, 394
echo: attraction of,
277–78; in ballads, 267
"Edge" (Plath): lineation
in, **56,** 58
"Egyptian Pulled Glass
Bottle in the Shape of a
Fish, An" (Moore): as
imagist free verse, 340;
syllabic norm veering
into accentual-syllabic,

471–72; syllable-count
variation in, **318**–19
elective stress, 234–36; as
analytical concept, 383;
defined, 406; for getting
to the heart of rhythm,
381; in graphic schema
of line, 383; in graphic
schema of meter and
prosody, 383; in Strand's
Dark Harbor, 219n
elegant variation, 445
"Elegy Written in a Coun-
try Church-Yard"
(Gray): syntactic inver-
sion in, **71**
"Elegy X" (Donne): deca-
syllabic line in, 317
Eliot, T. S.: "Ash-
Wednesday," 311; in
Bate and Perkins's *Brit-
ish and American Poets,*
486; blank verse loosen-
ing into free blank
verse, 471; "Burnt Nor-
ton," 19, 363; exagger-
ated diction in, 422;
"Little Gidding," 363,
415; monosyllabism in,
114; *Selected Essays,* 498;
on the three voices of
poetry, 187; unrhymed
blank verse of, 334.
*See also Waste Land,
The*
elision: defined, 406–7; in
graphic schema of meter
and prosody, 383; mark
for, 222n. 8; variability
of, 449
*Elizabethan and Jacobean Po-
ets, Marlowe to Marvell*
(Auden and Pearson),
485
*Elizabethan and Metaphysi-
cal Imagery: Renaissance
Poetic and Twentieth-*

Elizabethan and Metaphysical Imagery (continued)
   Century Critics (Tuve), 501
Elizabethan Poetry: Modern Essays in Criticism (Alpers), 493
emblem, 465–66, 477
"Enchanted Knight, The" (Muir): allusion in, 390; hypotaxis in, 81; metamorphosis in, 355; recession of technique in, 451–52; syntactic inversion in, **69**–70, 466; syntactic surprise in, 109
end-stopping: defined, 407; in graphic schema of line, 382, 383; in graphic schema of stanza and rhyme, 383; in Gray, 71; implications of, 101–7; in lineation, 434; and rhyme, 101–3, 454–55; in Shakespeare's *Henry VI, Part II*, 372–73; as suggesting persuasion and definiteness, 365. *See also* stichic
end words, 459
English ballads, 298, 400, 429
English language: common (ballad) meter as basic stanza of, 419; iamb and trochee in, 226; iamb as metrical norm for, 212; losing its endings, 216, 280; meter in, 437; metrical histories of, 215–16; pentameter in, 444; spontaneous bent for equalized time in, 294; stichic and melic in, 279–80; syllabic verse

in, 315–16, 317; syllabification in, 314, 315; triple feet as rare in, 227
"Englishman in Italy, The" (Browning): amphibrachs in, **228**
enjambment: in alcaics, 323; avoiding repetition with, 95–96; in blank verse, 4, 5, 101, 397; counterpoint to, 73; defined, 407; in descriptive syntax, 94–95; in free verse, 54, 369; in graphic schema of line, 382, 383; in graphic schema of stanza and rhyme, 383; half-meaning created by, 59, 416; in lineation, 434; minimal, 103–5; and rhyme, 68; in Shakespeare's later work, 50; stanza skewed by, 279; strength of, 76–77
envoi, 459
epic poetry: heroic couplets in, 417; hexameter in, 418; illustrative poems, 503; of Milton, 194, 397, 439. *See also* epic simile; mock epic
epic simile: defined, 407–10; as didactic, 461; in graphic schema of trope, 382; overt comparison in, 156
epigram: defined, 410–11; exercise in epigram of condemnation, 358–59; in graphic schema of rhetoric and mode, 382
"Epistle from Mr. Murray to Dr. Polidori" (Byron): couplets of, **285**
"Epistle to Bathurst" (Pope): cliche in, 376; rhyming on the phrase

in, 67, **283–84;** zeugma in, 482
"Epistle to Dr. Arbuthnot" (Pope): rhyming on the phrase in, 67
"Epitaph on Elizabeth, L. H." (Jonson): metonymy in, 152
"Epithalamium" (Spenser): stanza in, 463
epithet: in Bogan's "Baroque Comment," 340; defined, 411; in graphic schema of diction, 382; in graphic schema of syntax, 382; and kenning, 427
equalized time: defined, 412; English spontaneously seeking, 294; in isochrony, 304. *See also* isochrony
"Equanimity" (Murray): anatomy in, 394
Eras and Modes in English Poetry (Miles), 499
Essay on Criticism, An (Pope): rhyming on the phrase in, **282**–83; on vowel alliteration, 366; zeugma in, 281
Essay on Man, An (Pope): epic simile in, **409;** rhyming on the phrase in, 455–56
Essays on the Language of Literature (Chatman and Levin), 494
Ethelstan; or the Battle of Brunaburgh (Darley): kenning in, **427,** 428
etymological style, 129–30; as analytical concept, 382; as bringing out shape and logic of word formation, 357; defined, 412; in graphic schema of diction, 382;

in graphic schema of trope, 382

etymology: of cliches, 376; defined, 412; and pun, 151. *See also* etymological style

"Evangeline" (Longfellow): dactyls in, 227

"Eve of St. Agnes, The" (Keats): descriptive syntax in, **93;** hexameter in, 418; non-verbs in, 441; Spenserean stanza in, 462

Ewing, Juliana Horatia: "The Dolls' Wash," **272**

exercises, 347–79; advanced, 352–66; blank verse, 7–8; order of, 368–72; scansion, 238–39; starting out, 348–52

"Exeunt" (Wilbur): heterometric rhyme in, 273–74; length of vowel in, 450–51; plain style in, **179**

expandable time: in accentual verse, 303, 306–13; as analytical concept, 381, 383; defined, 412–13; in graphic schema of meter and prosody, 383

expository verse, 374

"Fabliau of Florida" (Stevens): as imagist free verse, **343**

Faerie Queene, The (Spenser): as allegory, 159, 386; non-verbs in, 441; Spenserean stanza in, **462**

"fallen flower, The" (Deutsch): as haiku, **327**

falling feet: dactyls, 226, 402, 437; trochees, 226, 437

falling meter: in accentual-syllabic verse, 437; and cadential verse, 398; defined, 413; as derived meter, 226; and feminine line ending, 413. *See also* falling feet

"Fall of Rome, The" (Auden): enjambment in, 77; exception to coincidence in, **72;** juxtaposition in, 426–**27;** neologism in, 441; rhyming on the phrase in, 68

false cretics, 241n

false pyrrhics, 229, 230, 450

false spondees, 229, 231, 462

"Far Field, The" (Roethke): diction of, 131

"February: Valentine's Day" (Hine): Alexandrines in, 218

feminine line ending: in alcaics, 322, 323; defined, 413; and rhyming stress, 271

Ferry, David: accent used to indicate pronunciation, 70n; allusion in, 169, 170; "At a Low Bar," 62–**63,** 304; "Graveyard," 169–**70,** 389. *See also* "Descriptive"; "Photographs from a Book: Six Poems"; "Seen Through a Window"; "Young Woman, A"

"Few Days, A" (Schuyler): allusion in, 389; lineation in, **55,** 58–59

fiduciary symbols, 451

Fields, Kenneth, 490

"Fifteenth Farewell" (Bogan): line and phrase diverging in, 447

"Figured Wheel, The" (Pinsky): "word-heaping" in, 340n. 13

figures of speech: defined, 413; in flamboyant speakers, 188; in graphic schema of rhetoric and mode, 382; and rhetoric, 454; trope contrasted with, 475. *See also* adnomination; anaphora; antithesis; asyndeton; pun; zeugma

figures of thought, 142–86; defined, 413; in graphic schema of trope, 382; trope as embracing, 142, 475. *See also* trope

"Filling Station" (Bishop): as podic verse, **301**–2; as sprung free verse, 333

"First Essay on Interest" (Murray): anatomy in, 394

"Fish, The" (Bishop): as self-dramatizing, 201; as sprung free verse, 333

"Fish, The" (Yeats): dramatic syntax in, 194–95; isochrony in, **304;** as moving against iambic tetrameter, 302; symbol in, 400

"Fish, the Man, and the Spirit, The" (Hunt): epithet in, 411; neologism in, 441

"Flower, The" (Herbert): as bordering on cliche, 399; extrapolation beyond the quatrain in, 274; heterometric rhyme in, 273, 442;

"Flower, The" (*continued*)
mixed trope in, 143;
and primacy of imme-
diate scene, **158**–59;
subjunctive mood in,
81

foot: and caesura, 225n.
10, 244, 398; defined,
413; dipodic verse draw-
ing attention away from,
405; in graphic schema
of meter and prosody,
383. *See also* amphi-
brach; anapest; bac-
chius; choriamb; cretic;
dactyl; iamb; metrical
inversion; pyrrhic foot;
spondee; substituted
feet; trochee

form: choices for express-
ing theme, 5; as inhib-
iting, 345; list of poems
by form, 503–7; reading
within and across, 10; as
suggestive, 345–46; va-
riety provided by, 346;
writing in form, 345–
501. *See also* form fol-
lows theme

"Formation of the Heroic
Medium, The" (Baker),
493

form follows theme,
107–10; as analytical
concept, 382; in blank
verse, 242–45; defined,
414; and formal com-
plexity, 87; form spark-
ing theme, 347; sound
imitating sound, 255

"For My Contemporaries"
(Cunningham): diction
of, **126**–27; syntax of,
79

"For the Bed at Kelm-
scott" (Morris): as di-
podic verse, **406**

*Founding of English Metre,
The* (Thompson), 501
"Four Master Tropes"
(Burke), 494

fourteeners: and common
meter, 218, 414; de-
fined, 414–15; in
graphic schema of meter
and prosody, 383; in
Strand's *Dark Harbor,*
219

fragment. *See* sentence
fragment

free blank verse, 333–36;
blank verse loosening
into, 471; defined, 415;
frame of expectation of,
369; in graphic schema
of meter and prosody,
383; illustrative poems,
506

free verse, 330–443; accen-
tual and syllabic verse
harder to hear in period
of, 290; apposition in,
65; and cadential verse,
398; central choice re-
garding line breaks, 369;
defined, 415; four free-
doms of, 330, 381; in
graphic schema of line,
383; in graphic schema
of meter and prosody,
383; illustrative poems,
506–7; isomorphism in,
426; lineation in,
53–56; lines connecting
in bursts of alternating
energy, 371; and pas-
sage, 443; prose overlap
of, 290. *See also* biblical
free verse; free blank
verse; imagist free verse;
podic free verse; verset

*Free Verse: An Essay on Pros-
ody* (Hartman), 499

French language: Alexan-

drines, 218, 314; syllabi-
fication in, 314, 315,
465

"From the Cupola" (Mer-
rill): drama in, **207**–8;
mimetic meter in,
258–59; personification
in, 354; rhyming on the
phrase in, 455

Frost, Robert: "Birches,"
255, 474; blank verse of,
334; "Blueberries," 393;
couplets in, 402; "The
Death of the Hired
Man," **115,** 214; "The
Gift Outright," 250,
251; "Mending Wall,"
115, 247; monosylla-
bism in, 115, 440; "The
Most of It," 22; "Nei-
ther Out Far Nor In
Deep," 107; plain style
in, 447; "Stopping by
Woods on a Snowy Eve-
ning," 307. *See also* "De-
sign"; "Old Man's Win-
ter Night, An"; "On a
Bird Singing in Its
Sleep"; "Strong Are
Saying Nothing, The"

"Frost at Midnight" (Cole-
ridge): as blank verse, 7;
delicacy and reserve of,
237–38; diction of, 404;
elective stress in,
235–36; false pyrrhics
and false spondees in,
230–31

Frye, Northrop, 160

Fuller, Roy: "The Green
Hills of Africa," 103n

"Further in Summer than
the Birds" (#1068)
(Dickinson): diction of,
125; rhyme in, 455

Fussell, Paul, 94, 327, 398,
491

"Garden, The" (Marvell): conception of the body in, 208; syntactic surprise in, **108**

Garrett, John, 485

Gascoigne, George: "Of Money," 466; on word order, 259–60. *See also* "Gascoigne's Good Night"

"Gascoigne's Good Night" (Gascoigne): alliteration in, 387; fourteeners sounding like common meter, 414; low diction in, 121–**22**

"Gate, The" (Muir): enjambment in, **104**–5; metaphor in, 436; reduced line in, 452

Gay, John: "A New Song of Similes," **268**

genitive link, 476

"Gift Outright, The" (Frost): monosyllables making stress in, 250, 251

Gilbert, W. S., 272

glosa: in graphic schema of stanza and rhyme, 383; as linked form, 432

"Going, The" (Hardy): absolute construction in, **384;** layered metaphor in, 176

Goldensohn, Lorrie, 32

Goldsmith, Oliver: "The Deserted Village," 466. *See also* "Retaliation"

Goliard poets, 262, 428–29

"Good-Night to the Season" (Praed): amphibrachs in, **391**

Googe, Barnaby: plain style in, 120, 447

grammar: becoming attentive to, 69; defined,

415. *See also* like endings; morphology; syntax

Grammar of Metaphor, A (Brooke-Rose), 497

"Graveyard" (Ferry): allusion in, 169–**70,** 389

Gray, Thomas: "Elegy Written in a Country Church-Yard," **71;** hymn meter in, 418; line consciousness of, 68

"Great Men have been among us" (Wordsworth): deriving the meter of, 239, 241–42; as deviating from sonnet form, **29;** sentence fragment in, 90–91

"Great Merchant, The, Dives Pragmaticus, Cries His Wares" (Newbery): amphibrachs in, **227**–28

"Green Gravel" (song), 174

"Green Hills of Africa, The" (Fuller), 103n

Greville, Fulke: "The Earth with Thunder Torn," 175–76

Groden, Michael, 491

"Grongar Hill" (Dyer): iambic tetrameter in, 471

Gross, Harvey, 308, 319

Gunn, Thom: "Hardy and the Ballads," 494; on "The Laily Worm," 265–66; "My Sad Captains," **319**–20; syllabics of, 319–22. *See also* "His Rooms in College"; "In Praise of Cities"; *Misanthropos;* "Moly"

haiku, 326–29; defined, 415–16; in graphic

schema of stanza and rhyme, 383; hinge moment in, 327, 416; illustrative poems, 507

"Half hour for coffee and at night, A" (Cunningham): as syllabic verse, **323–24**

half-meaning, 59–61; as analytical concept, 382; defined, 416; discordant meter compared with, 239; enjambment in creation of, 59, 416; in graphic schema of line, 382; in graphic schema of syntax, 382; and threshold, 49, 471; in Wilner's "Operations: Desert Shield, Desert Storm," 57

Hamlet (Shakespeare): coded flowers in, 147; infinitives in, 424; variable stress in, 236–**37**

Harbage, Alfred, 372–73

Hardison, O. B., Jr., 492

Hardy, Thomas: "Afterwards," 392–93; "An August Midnight," **191**–92; "Birds at Winter Nightfall," 431–32; "Channel Firing," **121;** "The Going," 176, **384;** high and low diction used by, 120–21; "In Tenebris II," 481; "In Time of 'The Breaking of Nations,'" 131; line consciousness of, 68; literal symbol in, 149; neologisms of, 121; plain style in, 447; "Side by Side," **312–13;** syntactic inversion in, 70–71; "The Voice," 402. *See also* "At a Hasty Wed-

Hardy, Thomas (*continued*)
ding"; "Darkling
Thrush, The"; "I Look
into My Glass"; "Neu-
tral Tones"; "Oxen,
The"; "Self-Unseeing,
The"; "Walk, The"
"Hardy and the Ballads"
(Gunn), 494
Harmonium (Stevens), 342
Harper Anthology of Poetry
(Nims), 488–89
Hartman, Charles O., 55n,
57n, 231n. 20, 341,
483n, 499
Heaney, Seamus: "Kin-
ship," 427; *North,* 386,
427
"Heart asks Pleasure—
first—, The" (#536)
(Dickinson): hymn me-
ter in, 479; short meter
in, **419**
Hebrew verse: antithesis
in, 394; defined, 416; in
graphic schema of meter
and prosody, 383; in
graphic schema of syn-
tax, 382; line in, 51–53
hemistich: in accentual
verse, 386; defined,
416–17; in graphic
schema of meter and
prosody, 383; major
stave, 417; in Old En-
glish poetry, 309, 332n
Henry IV, Part II (Shake-
speare): mimetic meter
in, 251–**52**
Henry V (Shakespeare): mi-
metic meter in, **254;**
subjunctive mood in,
440
Henry VI, Part II (Shake-
speare): drab blank verse
of, **372**–73
Herbert, George: "Artil-
lery," 190; "Prayer,"

476; reduced line in,
452. *See also* "Flower,
The"
Herbert, Zbigniew, 206
Herbert of Cherbury, Ed-
ward, 1st Baron: "Ode
upon the Question
Moved, An, Whether
Love Should Continue
Forever?" **83**
heroic couplet: defined,
417; exercise in couplets
in praise of place,
359–60; in graphic
schema of stanza and
rhyme, 383
heroic quatrain: defined,
417; exercise in table-
talk with, 356–58; illus-
trative poems, 505
"Heron, The" (Roethke):
end-stopping in, 105–**6;**
hypotaxis in, 422; literal
symbol in, 149; sen-
tence construction in,
80
"Heron Totem" (Ste-
phens): mimetic meter
in, **256**
*Hero's Way: Contemporary
Poems in the Mythic Tradi-
tion* (Allen), 484
Herrick, Robert: "A Con-
juration, to Electra," **66,**
353–54; "Delight in
Disorder," **67;** satiric
meiosis in, 205
"Her Vision in the Wood"
(Yeats): as accentual-
syllabic, 291–92
heterometric rhyme,
272–74; defined, 417; in
graphic schema of line,
383; in graphic schema
of stanza and rhyme,
383; in odes, 442; in Re-
naissance poetry, 361
hexameter: in blank verse,

219; defined, 418; in
graphic schema of meter
and prosody, 383; iam-
bic, 218; in Shelley's
"Adonais," 218; in
Spenserean stanza, 462
Hiawatha syndrome, 474
high style: on continuum
of diction, 404–5; in
graphic schema of dic-
tion, 382; in graphic
schema of rhetoric and
mode, 382; high diction
mixed with low, 120–
26
Hine, Daryl: on Alexan-
drines, 218; "Blue-
beard's Wife," 94–**95,**
462; "February: Valen-
tine's Day," 218; *In and
Out,* 393; pararhyme in,
443; pithy darts of
rhyme of, 358; "The
Trout," 134, 454–55;
"Vowel Movements,"
366
"His Rooms in College"
(Gunn): as blank verse,
7; mimetic meter in,
256–**57;** syntax of, 79;
trochaic inversion in,
474
Hobsbaum, Philip, 271–
72, 330n. 2, 333, 334,
371, 499
Hollander, John, 269,
302n. 10, 392, 492,
494–95
"Home Is So Sad" (Lar-
kin): sentence fragment
in, **90;** trope in, 92
Homer: epithet in, 411.
See also *Iliad*
homoeoteleuton. See like
endings
Hood, Thomas: "Our Vil-
lage," **272**–73
Hope, A. D.: "The Discur-

sive Mode: Reflections on the Ecology of Poetry," 495. *See also* "Man Friday"

hopeful constructions, 464

Hopkins, Gerard Manley: "The Candle Indoors," 446; "Inversnaid," **308;** monosyllabic line in, 112–13; podic free verse of, 330, 331; "That Nature is a Heraclitean Fire and of the comfort of the Resurrection," 112, 443. *See also* "Duns Scotus's Oxford"; "Lantern Out of Doors, The"

"Horatian Ode, An: Upon Cromwell's Return from Ireland" (Marvell): epigram in, 410–11; stanzas of, **270**

"Horses, The" (Muir): allusion in, 390; visionary dream in, 363

"Hotel Normandie Pool, The" (Walcott): pyrrhic-spondee combination in, 231–33, **232**

Housman, A. E.: allusion in, 168–69; diction-shifting in, 133–34; rhyming on the phrase in, 66

Howard, Richard: poems of cultural gossip, 358

Howell, W. S., 492

Hunt, Leigh: "The Fish, the Man, and the Spirit," 411, 441

"Hunting of the Snark, The" (Carroll): amphibrachs in, **390–91**

hymn meter: defined, 418–21; in graphic schema of stanza and rhyme, 383. *See also* ballad meter; common me-

ter; long meter; short meter

"Hymns of the Marshes" (Lanier): anapests in, **227**

"Hymn to Proserpine" (Swinburne): anapestic gallop avoided in, 392

hyperbaton: defined, 421; in graphic schema of syntax, 382; as syntactic inversion, 467–68

hyperbole: defined, 421–22; in graphic schema of rhetoric and mode, 382. *See also* adynaton

hypotaxis: defined, 422; in graphic schema of syntax, 382; suppleness obtained from, 362; as syntactic extreme, 80–83; in twist in advance of start of poem, 354

hypothetical mood. *See* subjunctive mood

iamb: in accentual-syllabic verse, 217–18; anapests as varying, 307, 393; defined, 422; in fourteeners, 414; illustrative poems, 506; marking accent for, 422, 435, 458; as metrical norm for English, 212; preparation for writing with, 347; as rising foot, 226, 437; substitution for, 465. *See also* trochaic inversion

iambic hexameter, 218

iambic pentameter: in blank verse, 4, 397; defined, 422; in free blank verse, 333–36, 415; in graphic schema of meter and prosody, 383; in he-

roic couplets, 417; in heroic quatrains, 417; illustrative poems, 506; in metrical history of English, 215–16; in Milton, 50, 97–101; in ottava rima, 443; overstressing and understressing in, 229–38; in Spenserean stanza, 462; in sprung verse, 330n. 2; syllabics compared with, 316; too-regular, 253–54; uncertain syllables in Wyatt's, 245–47

iambic tetrameter: in accentual-syllabic verse, 217, 471; illustrative poems, 506

"Idea of Order at Key West, The" (Stevens): end-stopping in, 101, 108; as stichic, 463

"I Felt a funeral, in my Brain" (#280) (Dickinson): as mad song, 353

"If there's no ruling" (Daryush): as syllabic verse, **325**–26

"I heard a Fly buzz— when I died—" (#465) (Dickinson): diction of, **125**

Iliad (Homer): Bogan's "Cassandra" compared with, 210; epic simile in, 407–8; fourteeners in Chapman's translation of, 414–15

"I Look into My Glass" (Hardy): short meter of, 419; subjunctive mood in, **81;** syntax of, 79

image: defined, 422–23; in Dickinson's "My Life had stood—a Loaded Gun" (#754), 154; in good metaphor, 176; in

image (*continued*)
   graphic schema of
   trope, 382
imagism: defined, 423; in
   graphic schema of rheto-
   ric and mode, 382; in
   graphic schema of
   trope, 382; and the
   haiku, 326, 327, 329.
   See also imagist free verse
imagist free verse, 340–43;
   brevity and breathtaking
   stasis as anchors of, 369;
   categories of, 53n. 4; de-
   fined, 423; in graphic
   schema of meter and
   prosody, 383; illustrative
   poems, 506–7; metrical
   borrowing in Kinzie's
   "Midwinter," 174
Imitations of Horace (Pope):
   zeugma in, 482
imperative: in Bogan, 88;
   defined, 423
imperative mood: defined,
   423–24; as mood, 440
implied offbeat: defined,
   424; in graphic schema
   of meter and prosody,
   383; and isochrony, 425;
   and unrealized fourth
   beat, 478–79; in Yeats's
   "Easter 1916," 294
In and Out (Hine): anapests
   in, 393
incremental repetition,
   264; in graphic schema
   of rhetoric and mode,
   382; in graphic schema
   of stanza and rhyme,
   383
indicative mood: defined,
   424; in graphic schema
   of syntax, 382; as mood,
   440; subjunctive con-
   trasted with, 81
infinitive: defined, 424; in

graphic schema of syn-
   tax, 382
In Memoriam A. H. H.
   (Tennyson): alliteration
   in, 387; personification
   in, 182–85, **183–84;**
   plain style in, **117;** voice
   in canto from, 189
In Memoriam stanza: illus-
   trative quatrains, 504
"In Memory of Sigmund
   Freud" (Auden): ab-
   stract diction turning
   into personification in,
   140; meter compared
   with iambic pentameter,
   316
"Inniskeen Road: July
   Evening" (Kavanagh):
   allusion in, 165; epithet
   in, 411; half-meaning
   in, 416; metonymy in,
   438; plain style in,
   122–23
"In Praise of Cities"
   (Gunn): allegory in,
   159–60, 437; neologism
   in, 441; personification
   in, 182, 387; under-
   stressed line in, 478
"In Praise of Limestone"
   (Auden): abstract dic-
   tion turning into per-
   sonification in, 140;
   praise-of-environment
   theme of, 360
"In Tenebris II" (Hardy):
   word order in, 481
intention, 34–35
interrogative sentence: in
   graphic schema of syn-
   tax, 382
interspersed rhyme, 271,
   455
intervals: in accentual-
   syllabic verse, 217–61;
   defined, 425; in graphic

schema of meter and
   prosody, 383. *See also*
   isochrony
"In the Bleak Midwinter"
   (Rossetti): unrealized
   beat in, **479**
"In the Egyptian Mu-
   seum" (Lewis): apposi-
   tion in, 395; etymologi-
   cal style of, **129–30,**
   412; exception to coin-
   cidence in, 72–73;
   speaker and rhetoric in,
   199–200
"In the Waiting Room"
   (Bishop): meiosis in,
   421
"Intimations Ode"
   (Wordsworth): hetero-
   metric rhyme in, 273
"In Time of 'The Break-
   ing of Nations'"
   (Hardy): diction of, 131
intransitive verb: defined,
   425; in graphic schema
   of syntax, 382; as weak-
   est verb, 367
inversion: in graphic
   schema of line, 382; in
   graphic schema of rheto-
   ric and mode, 382. *See
   also* metrical inversion;
   syntactic inversion
"Inversnaid" (Hopkins):
   promotion of stress ab-
   sent in, **308**
"Inviting a Friend to Sup-
   per" (Jonson): absolute
   construction in, 384;
   subjunctive mood in,
   464
ionic. *See* rising ionic
irregular alternating
   rhyme, 271, 455
irregular ballads, 294–98
irregular odes. *See* Pindaric
   odes

Isaiah 2: antithesis in, 394

Isaiah 49: tags in, **52;** as verset, 338

"I Saw the Bird That Can the Sun Endure" (Spenser): end-stopping and rhyme in, **102–3**

"I Saw the Bird That Dares Behold the Sun" (Spenser): end-stopping and absence of rhyme in, **101–2**

"I Sing of a Maiden" (ballad): two-stress unit in, 308–**9**

isochrony: the boundaries of, 303–5; defined, 425; expandable time contrasted with, 413; in graphic schema of meter and prosody, 383; metric distinguished from podic verse by, 330n. 1; in "Old Mother Goose," 299, 330n. 1; in Yeats's "The Witch," 292–93. *See also* equalized time

isocolon: defined, 425–26; in graphic schema of rhetoric and mode, 382; in graphic schema of syntax, 382; tag compared with, 52n

isometric rhyme. *See* heterometric rhyme

isomorphism: as analytical concept, 382; defined, 426; in graphic schema of line, 382; in metric verse, 62; as occurring in all verse, 57

James, Henry, 444, 445

Jarrell, Randall. *See* "Soul, A"

Jerusalem (Blake): as biblical free verse, **338**

Job 38: as Hebrew verse, **416**

"John Brown's body lies a' mouldering in the grave" (song), 218

"John Mouldy" (de la Mare): reduced line in, **452**

Johns Hopkins Guide to Literary Theory and Criticism, The (Groden and Kreiswirth), 491

Johnson, J. W., 279

Johnson, Samuel: "Short Song of Congratulation," 226. *See also* "On the Death of Dr. Robert Levet"

Jonson, Ben: "Epitaph on Elizabeth, L. H.," 152; "Inviting a Friend to Supper," 384, **464;** plain style in, 447; prose preliminaries used by, 348; "Still to Be Neat," 162; "To Penshurst," 359

Jubilate Agno (Smart): anaphora in, 393

Julius Caesar (Shakespeare): isocolon in, **425–26**

"Jumblies, The" (Lear): isochrony in, **305;** refrain in, 453

Justice, Donald: "Anonymous Drawing," **417;** "A Man of 1794," 334–36, **334–35;** "My South: On the Porch," **349–50,** 387; "Ode to a Dressmaker's Dummy," **442;** plain style in, 447; "Sadness," **195**

juxtaposition, 62–65; with absolute constructions, 384; apposition and, 65,

394, 395; in ballads, 265; on continuum of likeness, 400; in couplets, 401; defined, 426–27; in graphic schema of line, 382; in graphic schema of rhetoric and mode, 382; in graphic schema of syntax, 382; and isomorphism, 426

Kavanagh, Patrick. *See* "Inniskeen Road: July Evening"

Keats, John: "La Belle Dame Sans Merci," 452; descriptive syntax in, 93; "Lines Supposed to Have Been Addressed to Fanny Brawne," **82;** "Ode to a Nightingale," 466; "Ode to Psyche," 441; "To Autumn," 400. *See also* "Eve of St. Agnes, The"

kenning, 185–86; defined, 427–28; double epithet as resembling, 411; in graphic schema of diction, 382; in graphic schema of trope, 382

King James Version of the Bible, 337

King Lear (Shakespeare): diction of catalogue of weeds in, **113;** monosyllabic lines requiring interpretation in, 255; pun in, 450

"Kinship" (Heaney): kenning in, 427

Kinzie, Mary: "After Frost at Midnight," **322–23;** epigram of condemnation, **358–59;** "Midwinter," **173–74;** "Objet,"

Kinzie, Mary (*continued*)
370; "The orchard dy-
ing—," **415;** "Plague
Summer," **432–33;**
"Reading During Mar-
riage," 317–**18;** sonnet
of secondary character,
362
Kipling, Rudyard: "Seal
Lullaby," 228, 429;
"The Way Through the
Woods," 479
Kitsch, 377
Knights, L. C., 495
Koethe, John: "Contrary
Impulses: The Tension
Between Poetry and
Theory," 495; playing
off cliche, 399; "The
Realm of Ends," **118,
119**
Kreiswirth, Martin, 491
Kundera, Milan, 377

"Lady, Weeping at the
Crossroads" (Auden):
absolute construction
in, 384; allusion in,
166–68, **166, 167,** 388,
390; as ballad, 278; bal-
lad meter in, 419; deriv-
ing the meter of, 239,
240; enjambment in,
77; imperative mood in,
423–24; meiosis in,
204–5; syntactic inver-
sion in, 84
"Laily Worm and the
Machrel of the Sea,
The" (ballad): desolate
quality of, 355; Gunn
on, 265–66; repetition
and interpolation in,
168, 265; as wavering
between short and
common meter, **420–
21**

"Lake Isle of Innisfree,
The" (Yeats): triple feet
of, 331
Lamb, Charles: *Satan in
Search of a Wife,* 391–92;
"She Is Going," **453–54**
"Lament" (Abelard): leo-
nine rhymes in, **429**
"Lament for the Makaris"
(Dunbar): as long meter,
419; refrain in, 452
Landor, Walter Savage:
"Dull Is My Verse," **421**
"Landscape with Self-
Portrait" (Nemerov): as
blank verse, 7; diction
of, 127–29, **127–28,**
404, 405; half-meaning
in, 60; metaphor of a
top in, 176; personifica-
tion in, 387; scansion
of, 222, 223
*Language and the Poet: Ver-
bal Artistry in Frost, Ste-
vens, and Moore* (Bor-
roff), 306–8, 497
Lanier, Sidney: "Hymns of
the Marshes," **227**
"Lantern Out of Doors,
The" (Hopkins), **35;** be-
ginning of, 15, 16, 17;
literal symbol in, 145;
metonymy in, 145,
162n, 438; specialized
diction in, 130; surprise
in, 33
Lanz, Herbert, 230n. 19
Larkin, Philip: "Home Is
So Sad," **90,** 92; and law
of simplified focus, 428;
pararhyme in, 272; plain
style in, 447; speakers
of, 188; "The Whitsun
Weddings," 7, 123. *See
also* "Church Going";
"Trees, The"
"Last Hill in a Vista" (Bo-

gan): antithesis in, 394;
declarative sentences in,
404; meiosis in, 422;
nondeclarative syntaxes
in, 88; nuanced meta-
phor in, **177**
law of simplified focus: as
analytical concept, 382;
defined, 428; in graphic
schema of line, 382; in
graphic schema of
trope, 382; in Hopkins's
"The Lantern Out of
Doors," 33; and literal
symbol, 145, 428
"Lay your sleeping head
my love" (Auden): as
trochaic, 226, 474
Lear, Edward: hetero-
metric rhyme in, 272;
"The Jumblies," **305;**
limericks of, 433; "The
Owl and the Pussycat,"
429; unlikely rhymes in,
134
"Legem Tuam Dilexi"
(Patmore): hexameter
in, 418
leonine rhyme: in ballads,
265; in *Carmina Burana,*
262; defined, 428–29;
disappearance of, 264;
in graphic schema of
stanza and rhyme, 383;
in Lamb's *Satan in Search
of a Wife,* 392
Letter to Lord Byron
(Auden): light rhyme in,
429; rhyme royal in,
457; rhyming on the
phrase in, 456
Levin, Samuel R., 494
Lewalski, Barbara K., 488
Lewis, Janet. *See* "In the
Egyptian Museum"
"Lie, The" (Ralegh): re-
frain in, **453**

lifts, 386, 416

light rhyme: articulating endings in, 218n; in Bunyan' *Pilgrim's Progress,* 455; defined, 429–30; in graphic schema of stanza and rhyme, 383

like endings: defined, 430–31; in graphic schema of stanza and rhyme, 383; in graphic schema of syntax, 382; and rhyme, 263, 280

limerick: defined, 433; in graphic schema of stanza and rhyme, 383; unlikely rhymes in, 134

line, 51–74; all other features following from, 10–11; anaphora in organizing, 393; as carrier of sense, 380; as carrier of sound, 380; and clause, 75, 399; continuum analysis of, 149; defined, 433; as element of poetry, 45; ending, 51; graphic schema of, 380, 382, 383; illustrative poems, 505–7; logic of the, 51–56; and meter, 437; and mode, 439; as most obvious thing about a poem, 51; the passage, not the line, 372–75; and phrase, 75–76, 447; in place, 57–68; and sentence, 4–5, 49, 279; and stress, 373; and syntax, 75–79, 469, 470; in tension, 68–74; and theme, 5; and verse, 480; in writing your way through a poem, 6. *See also* caesura; end-stopping; enjamb-

ment; lineation; reduced line

lineation: defined, 434; in free verse, 53–56; in graphic schema of line, 382

"Lines Supposed to Have Been Addressed to Fanny Brawne" (Keats): hypothetical subjunctive in, **82**

linked form: defined, 431–33; exercise in linked form using lines by another, 355–56; in graphic schema of stanza and rhyme, 383

linking verb. *See* copula

litanies: anaphora in, 393

literal symbol, 143–48; to classical allusion from, 155; versus cliche, 375–79; on continuum of metaphor, 148–49, 400; on continuum of trope, 475, 476; defined, 434–35; as figure of thought, 413; in graphic schema of trope, 382; and law of simplified focus, 145, 428; metaphor contrasted with, 466; personification emerging from, 182, 445; as specific before they are general, 378; and threshold, 471

literary stanza, 269–70

"Little Gidding" (Eliot): free blank verse of, 415; visionary theme of, 363

Livy, 410

Logic and Rhetoric in England 1500–1700 (Howell), 492

"London" (Blake): allusion in, 173; metonymy in,

162n; the small implicating the great in, **153**

"Longe Love, that in My Thought Doeth Harbar, The" (Wyatt): as more syllabic than accentual, 331; trochaic inversion in, 473; uncertain iambic pentameter of, **245–46**

Longfellow, Henry Wadsworth: "Evangeline," 227; *Song of Hiawatha,* **474;** "To the Driving Cloud," 402

"Long-legged Fly" (Yeats): as at limit of accentual-syllabism, **294**

Longman Dictionary of Poetic Terms (Myers and Simms), 492

long meter: defined, 435; in graphic schema of stanza and rhyme, 383; as hymn meter, 419–20; illustrative quatrains with alternating rhyme, 504

"Lotos-Eaters, The" (Tennyson): descriptive subordinating sentence in, 468; heterometric rhyme in, **417**

"Lovers Infinitenesse" (Donne): epigram in, **410**

"Loves Deitie" (Donne): deriving the meter of, 239, 240; plain style in, 116

Lowell, Robert: blank sonnets of, 396; cutting-and-pasting in, 372; as rhyming in passing, 68. *See also* "Mr. Edwards and the Spider"

Lowry, Malcolm, 496

low style. *See* plain style
"Lying in a Hammock at William Duffy's Farm in Pine Island, Minnesota" (Wright): isomorphism in, 57; juxtaposition in, 64–65; lineation in, **53**
lyric poetry: all features of plain-style following from sentence and line, 10; illustrative poems, 503; Marvell's iambic tetrameter, 471; recession of technique in, 451; Smith on, 500; stichic and melic, 279; two ways of approaching, 1–2

Macbeth (Shakespeare): epithet in, 411; metrical irregularity in, 373; monosyllabic lines requiring interpretation in, 255; monosyllabism in, 440; muscular pentameter of, **373;** personification in, 446; verb metaphor in, 476; voice in, **193**–94
Macksey, Richard, 491
macron: defined, 435; in Nabokov's three-symbol scansion, 222, 397, 458, 463
"Mad Gardener's Song" (Carroll): rhyming on the phrase in, **288–89**
mad song, exercise in trimeter, 352–54
"Maid's Song" (Randall): as metaphysical ballad, 210–**11**
main line-stress, 223; defined, 435; in graphic schema of line, 383; in graphic schema of meter

and prosody, 383; and half-meaning, 416; marking, 458; and meaning making stress, 458
Major Poets of the Earlier Seventeenth Century (Lewalski and Sabol), 488
major stave, 417
Malcontent, The (Marston): mimetic meter in, 255
"Man Friday" (Hope): anastrophe and hyperbaton in, 468; antithesis in, 134–36, **134–35,** 288; couplets of, **286–88,** 351, 402; hypotactic sentences in, 80–81; imperative mood in, 423; metaphor in, 177–78
"Man of 1794, A" (Justice): free blank verse of, 334–36, **334–35**
Marston, John: *The Malcontent,* 255
Marvell, Andrew: chiasmus in, 281; "The Garden," 208; "An Horatian Ode: Upon Cromwell's Return from Ireland," **270,** 410–11; iambic tetrameter in, 471; "To His Coy Mistress," 281; "Upon Appleton House, To My Lord Fairfax," 359; "Upon the Hill and Grove at *Bill-borow,*" 359
masculine line ending: in alcaics, 322; defined, 435; and rhyme in English, 216; and rhyming stress, 271
"Matinees" (Merrill): comparison from different realms in, 176
"Mattie Groves" (ballad): unrealized beat in, **419**

Mayakovsky, Vladimir, 164
McAuley, James, 213, 222n. 9, 499
meaning makes stress, 247–53; as analytical concept, 381, 383; and main line-stress, 458; as scansion rule, 221, 458–59. *See also* elective stress
measure: defined, 435. *See also* dimeter; foot; hexameter; pentameter; tetrameter; trimeter
Medieval and Renaissance Poets, Langland to Spenser (Auden and Pearson), 485
Medieval English Lyrics (Davies), 487
"Meditations in a Time of Civil War" (Yeats): hexameter in, 418; praise-of-place theme of, 359
meditative poetry: all features of plain-style following from sentence and line, 10; couplets in, 402; exercise in blank verse meditation, 352; illustrative poems, 504; Milton extending blank verse to, 50; ottava rima in, 274, 443; rhyme royal in, 271, 457; Shakespearean drama contrasted with, 374; stanzas in, 277; two ways of approaching, 1–2; of Winters, 202
"Medusa" (Bogan): nondeclarative syntax in, 88
meiosis: defined, 435; in graphic schema of rhetoric and mode, 382; hy-

perbole contrasted with, 421; as opportunity to try on a mask, 381; in psychological surrealism, 205–6; in satire, 204–5. *See also* aporia

melic: and stichic in English, 279–80

"Melodic Trains" (Ashbery): lineation in, **54–55**

"Memory" (Bogan): metaphor in, 177; sentence fragment in, **91,** 459; trope in, 92

"Mending Wall" (Frost): argument as expressed in, 115; meaning making stress in, 247

"Merlin Enthralled" (Wilbur): metamorphosis in, 355

Merrill, James: "Matinees," 176; pithy darts of rhyme of, 358; rhyme wit of, 359; "An Urban Convalescence," 257–**58,** 450. *See also* "From the Cupola"

Metamorphoses (Ovid), 355

metaphor: continuum of, 148–52; on continuum of comparison, 476–77; on continuum of trope, 475, 476; defined, 435–37; from different realms, 175–76; double epithet as coded, 411; as figure of thought, 413; in flamboyant speakers, 188; great and small and inner and outer compared, 152–54; and image, 422–23; layered, 176–78; literal symbol contrasted with, 466; mixed metaphor, 438; as movement from phys-

ical to spiritual, 181; periphrastic, 444; poems creating natural metaphors, 142; simile compared with, 460; simple replacement, 476; the verb-metaphor, 367, 476. *See also* allegory

metaphysical ballads, 278–79

metaphysical poets: outlandish metaphor in, 175

meter: and accent as pulling against one another, 213; antimimetic meter, 251–59; in ballads, 266; defined, 437–38; expectation as constant, 221, 458; graphic schema of, 383; in graphic schema of meter and prosody, 383; juxtaposition in metrical verse, 61–62; as a limit, 213–14, 261; mimetic meter, 251–59; other than iambic, 226–29; playing against rhythm, 212–14, 219; reading aloud for mastering, 347–48; syntax coinciding with, 399; and word order, 259–61, 480. *See also* accent; context makes meter; falling meter; foot; responsion; rising meter; scansion

Meter in English: A Critical Engagement (Baker), 493

metonymy, 162–64; allusion making use of, 173; in free blank verse, 335; on continuum of comparison, 475, 476; on continuum of trope, 476; defined, 438; as figure of thought, 413;

in graphic schema of trope, 382; in Hopkins's "The Lantern Out of Doors," 145; in Jonson's "Epitaph on Elizabeth, L. H.," 152; personification emerging from, 182, 445. *See also* literal symbol

Metre, Rhythm and Verse Form (Hobsbaum), 499

metrical borrowing, 173–75

metrical inversion: defined, 438; in graphic schema of meter and prosody, 383. *See also* trochaic inversion

Middle English, 310

"Midwinter" (Kinzie): quotation and metrical borrowing in, **173–74**

Miles, Josephine, 338, 439, 499

Millay, Edna St. Vincent: "Spring," **56**

"Mill-Race, The" (Winters), **39–41;** beginning of, 15, 16; as biblical free verse, 339–40; kenning in, 185–86; neologism in, 441; range of trope in, 185; speaker in, 188–89; surprising shifts in, 33

"Milton" (Blake): parataxis in, 443

Milton, John: adnomination in, 386; "L'Allegro," 158, 220; blank verse in, 50, 98, 397; descriptive syntax in, 93–94; etymological diction in, 130; "Il Penseroso," 158; phrasal mode in, 439; prefix parallel in, 250–51; *Samson Agonistes,* 273; the

Milton, John (*continued*) sentence and the pentameter passage in, 97–101; syntactic inversion in, 70; tension in, 471. See also *Paradise Lost*

mimetic meter, 251–59

"Miracle for Breakfast, A" (Bishop): as sestina, 459

mirror words, 357

Mirrour for Magistrates, A (Sackville): rhyme royal in, 457

Misanthropos (Gunn): speakers of, 208; syllabics of, 208n, **320–22**; vehicle in, 480

Missing Measures: Modern Poetry and the Revolt Against Meter (Steele), 500

mixed diction: in graphic schema of diction, 382; possibilities of, 405

mixed metaphor, 438

mixed trope: defined, 438–39; in graphic schema of trope, 382; in Hardy's "The Darkling Thrush," 143; and kenning, 427; in Larkin's "The Trees," 199

mock epic: couplets in, 402; defined, 439; in graphic schema of rhetoric and mode, 382; Pope's *The Rape of the Lock* as, 152

mode: as analytical concept, 382; defined, 439; graphic schema of, 382; illustrative poems, 503–4. *See also* dramatic poetry; lyric poetry; narrative poetry

modernization, 86n

Modern Poetry and the Idea of Language (Bruns), 497

"Moly" (Gunn): asyndeton in, 395; end-stopping in, **106–7**; monosyllabic line in, 113; speaker of, 208

monosyllabic words: in making stress, 247–51, 458; stress in, 220, 458

monosyllabism, 111–13; defined, 439–40; in graphic schema of diction, 382; metaphoric range deriving from, 142; and overstressed line, 136–40; in the plain style, 114–26, 404, 447; and rhythm, 457; and spondees, 463; stress requiring interpretation with, 254–55

Monro, Harold, 461

"Months have ends—the Years—a knot, The" (#423) (Dickinson): unrealized beat in, **268**–69

mood: defined, 440. *See also* imperative mood; indicative mood; subjunctive mood

"Moone-Calfe, The" (Drayton): mimetic meter in, 255–56

Moore, Marianne: subphrasal cut in, 341; syllabic norm veering into accentual-syllabic, 471–72; syllable-count variation in, 318. *See also* "Egyptian Pulled Glass Bottle in the Shape of a Fish, An"

Moore, Thomas: "Believe Me if All Those Endearing Young Charms," **277**

Moral Epistles (Pope): catchphrases in, 283

morpheme: defined, 440; in rhyme, 280; root, 386; in syllabic verse, 314

morphology: abstraction affecting, 384; defined, 441; in graphic schema of syntax, 382

Morris, John N.: "The Unburied," 343, **370–71**

Morris, William: "For the Bed at Kelmscott," **406;** *The Story of Sigurd the Volsung,* 392

"Most of It, The" (Frost): natural world speaking in, 22

"Mr. Edwards and the Spider" (Lowell): extrapolation beyond the quatrain in, 274; half-meaning in, 60–61; heterometric rhyme in, 442

Muir, Edwin: "Adam's Dream," 363; allusion in, 389–90; "The Brothers," 363; coincidence and tension in, 399–400; line consciousness of, 68; literal symbol in, 471; plain style in, 447; rhyme as background technique in, 74; speakers of, 188; "The Horses," 363, 390; "The Return," 363; visionary dreams of, 363. *See also* "Ballad of Hector in Hades"; "Childhood"; "Enchanted Knight, The"; "Gate, The"

Murphy, Francis, 495

Murray, Les A.: anatomy in, 394

Murray, Nicholas, 18n. 5

Myers, Jack, 492

"My Life had stood—a Loaded Gun" (#754) (Dickinson): diction of, **125**–26; metaphor in, 154; Petrarchan exaggeration in, 246n. 29

"My Lute and I" (Wyatt): as podic verse, **300–301**

"Myne owne John Poynz" (Wyatt). *See* "Satire I"

"My Papa's Waltz" (Roethke): jauntiness of, 211; juxtaposition in, **63–64**

"My Sad Captains" (Gunn): syllabics of, **319**–20

"My South: On the Porch" (Justice): alliteration in, 387; detail in, **349–50**

Nabokov, Vladimir, 221–22, 230, 293, 377, 398, 499

narrative poetry: and allegory, 160; couplets in narratives, 284–89, 402; exercise in couplet narrative, 350–51; illustrative poems, 503; ottava rima in, 443; passage and line in, 374; rhyme royal in, 271, 457; Shakespearean drama contrasted with, 374; Spenserean stanza in, 462. *See also* ballad; epic poetry; meditative poetry

near rhymes: natural effect of, 289; pararhyme, 271

"Neither Out Far Nor In Deep" (Frost): endstopping in, 107

Nemerov, Howard: diction of, 127–29; literal symbol in, 149, 471; "never *ask* a poet what he means," 15; "Runes," 445. *See also* "Again"; "Landscape with Self-Portrait"; "Sanctuary, The"; "Writing"

neologism: defined, 441; in graphic schema of diction, 382; of Hardy, 121

"Neutral Tones" (Hardy): deriving the meter of, 239, **240**–41; monosyllables making stress in, 247; periphrasis in, 444

New American Poetry, The (Allen), 483–84

Newbery, Thomas: "The Great Merchant, Dives Pragmaticus, Cries His Wares," **227**–28

New Book of Forms, The: A Handbook of Poetics (Turco), 493

New Criticism, 14

"New Song of Similes, A" (Gay): unrealized beat in, **268**

"Nights are getting cold" (Shiki): as haiku, **328**

Nims, John Frederick, 366, 413n. 20, 483n, 488–89, 495, 496

"Noble Rider and the Sound of Words, The" (Stevens), 389n

nonce stanzas: exercise in dialogue in, 360–61

non-counted forms, 330–43

nonsense rhymes: triple meter in, 472

non-verb, 367–68; de-

fined, 441; in Milton, 93n; stress in, 220

North (Heaney): as accentual verse, 386; kenning in, 427

Norton Anthology of Poetry (third edition), 484–85

Norton Anthology of Poetry (fourth edition), 487–88

"No Second Troy" (Yeats): metonymy in, 335n

Notes on Prosody and Abram Gannibal (Nabokov), 499

nursery rhymes: amphibrachs in, 227, 390; as dipodic, 299, 405; echo tradition of, 277; implied offbeat in, 424; as podic, 330; rhyming on the phrase in, 456

"Objet" (Kinzie): pauses played against continuity in, **370**

octave: defined, 441; in graphic schema of stanza and rhyme, 383; in sonnets, 462

ode: and Auden's "In Praise of Limestone," 360; and biblical free verse, 337; defined, 441–42; in graphic schema of rhetoric and mode, 382; in graphic schema of stanza and rhyme, 383; heterometric rhyme in, 417; in passages, 444

"Ode to a Dressmaker's Dummy" (Justice): heterometric rhyme in, **442**

"Ode to a Nightingale"
(Keats): symbol in, 466
"Ode to Evening" (Collins): stanzas diffused in,
269–**70**
"Ode to Meaning" (Pinsky): rhetoric of direct
address in, 442
"Ode to Psyche" (Keats):
rhetoric of direct address in, 441
"Ode upon Doctor Harvey" (Cowley): extrapolation beyond the quatrain in, 274
"Ode upon the Question
Moved, An, Whether
Love Should Continue
Forever?" (Herbert of
Cherbury): contrary-to-fact stanzas in, **83**
"Of Culture" (Steele):
anatomy in, 394
offbeat: defined, 442; in
graphic schema of meter
and prosody, 383. *See
also* implied offbeat
"Of Friendship" (Steele):
anatomy in, 394
"Of Money" (Gascoigne):
syntactic inversion in,
466
Old English: hemistich
patterns in, 332n; poetic
lines as displayed in, 309
"Old Man's Winter Night,
An" (Frost): periphrasis
in, 444; the speaker in,
192–93; syntactic inversion in, 468; trochaic inversion in, 214, 473
"Old Mother Goose"
(nursery rhyme): as dipodic, **299;** isochrony
in, 299, 330n. 1
Oliver, Raymond. *See*
"Cyclic"; "Structures"
"On a Bird Singing in Its

Sleep" (Frost): beginning of, 16; change of
direction in, **21–22;** coincidence creating balance in, 86; literal symbol in, 143; subjunctive
mood in, 464; surprising shifts in, 33; symbol
in, 466; understressed
line in, 478
On Extended Wings: Wallace Stevens's Longer Poems (Vendler), 501
"On Musicality in Verse"
(Burke), 494
onomatopoeia: defined,
442; in graphic schema
of diction, 382; in
graphic schema of
trope, 382
"On the Death of Dr.
Robert Levet" (Johnson): absolute phrases in,
91; apposition in, 395;
hymn meter in, 418;
trope in, 92
"Operations: Desert
Shield, Desert Storm"
(Wilner), **35–38;** allusion in, 19, 388–89,
390; beginning of, 15,
16, 19–21; isomorphism
in, 57; low and high
diction in, 123–24; personification in, 182; surprising shifts in, 33; verisimilitude of suggestion
in, 155
Opie, Iona, 174, 489
Opie, Peter, 174, 489
optative constructions, 464
order: choices for expressing theme, 5
Osborn, Marijane,
310n. 19
Othello the Moor of Venice
(Shakespeare): subjunctive mood in, **464**

ottava rima, 274–76; defined, 443; exercise in
ottava rima vision, 363;
in graphic schema of
stanza and rhyme, 383;
illustrative poems, 505;
in passages, 444
"Our Many Meters:
Strength in Diversity"
(Nims), 495
"Our Village" (Hood):
heterometric rhyme in,
272–73
overstressed line: defined,
443; in Frost's blank
verse, 334; in graphic
schema of diction, 382;
in graphic schema of
line, 382, 383; in
graphic schema of meter
and prosody, 383; in
iambic pentameter,
229–38; and monosyllabism, 136–40; spondees
creating, 463
Ovid: *Metamorphoses,* 355
Owen, Wilfred, 443;
"Strange Meeting,"
271–72
"Owl and the Pussycat,
The" (Lear): leonine
rhymes in, 429
"Oxen, The" (Hardy): allusion in, 165, 168, 388,
390; rhyming on the
phrase in, **65–66**
*Oxford Book of Children's
Verse, The* (Opie and
Opie), 489
*Oxford Nursery Rhyme
Book, The* (Opie and
Opie), 489

pantoum: in graphic
schema of stanza and
rhyme, 383; as linked
form, 432
Paradise Lost (Milton): allit-

eration in, 387–**88;** caesura in, 298; descriptive syntax in, **93–94;** elision in, 449; enjambment in, **77;** epic simile in, 407, **408–9;** etymological style in, 412; form following theme in, 242, 244–45; imperative mood in, 423; meiosis in, 421; metonymy in, 163; monosyllabism in, **112, 440;** motives altering meaning in, **194;** overt comparison in, 156; the sentence and pentameter in, **97, 98, 99, 100, 101;** simile in, 461; Stein's *Answerable Style: Essays on "Paradise Lost,"* 500–501; syntactic inversion in, 70, 466; typography of, 94; unrhymed pentameter of, 333

parallelism: anaphora as highlighting, 58; in Hebrew verse, 51, 52, 337, 416; and monosyllables making stress, 247, 250–51

pararhyme, 271–72; defined, 443; in graphic schema of stanza and rhyme, 383

parataxis, 80; defined, 443; in graphic schema of syntax, 382; linear play with juxtaposition, 384; subjunctive mood juxtaposed with, 84–85

passage: as analytical concept, 382; defined, 443–44; in graphic schema of syntax, 382; the passage, not the line, 372–75; the sentence and the pentameter passage in Milton, 97–101. *See also* stanza

past participles, pronunciation of, 448

Patmore, Coventry: "Legem Tuam Dilexi," 418

"Paysage Moralisé" (Auden): as sestina, 366

Pearl poet, 307, 308

Pearson, Norman Holmes, 485–86

"Penseroso, Il" (Milton): and primacy of immediate scene, 158

pentameter: defined, 444; in graphic schema of meter and prosody, 383; illustrative couplets, 504; illustrative extended quatrains, 505; rhyme royal, 457. *See also* iambic pentameter

Perec, Georges, 366

Pericles (Shakespeare): iambic tetrameter in, 471

periphrasis: defined, 444–45; in graphic schema of rhetoric and mode, 382; in high style, 405; and kenning, 427; resisting, 198

Perkins, David, 486

Perloff, Marjorie, 499–500

persona: defined, 445; in graphic schema of rhetoric and mode, 382; in graphic schema of trope, 382; in mad song exercise, 353; the poem as record of exact physical state of the, 378; and rhetoric, 187, 454

personification, 182–84; defined, 445–46; in graphic schema of trope, 382; as growing out of literal symbol, 182, 445; in Merrill's

"From the Cupola," 354; metaphor contrasted with, 436, 437; in modern poetical use, 387

Petrarcha, Francesco, 446

Petrarchan: defined, 446–47; deviating from conventions of, 27–28; in graphic schema of rhetoric and mode, 382; rhyme pattern of, 462; speakers of, 188; of Wyatt, 246

"Philip Sparrow" (Skelton): as podic verse, **299–300;** suppressed fourth beat in, **267**

"Photographs from a Book: Six Poems" (Ferry): allusion in, **169;** apposition in, 395; from literal symbol to classical allusion in, 155

phrasal mode, 439

phrase: in absolute construction, 384; as coinciding or diverging from the line, 75–76, 447; on continuum of syntax, 47, 468; defined, 447; in graphic schema of syntax, 382

Piers Plowman: strong-stress rhythm of, **310–11**

"Piled for burning" (Boncho): as haiku, **328**

Pilgrim's Progress (Bunyan): light rhyme in, 455

Pindaric odes: heterometric rhyme in, 273; illustrative poems, 505

Pinsky, Robert: "The Figured Wheel," 340n. 13; "Ode to Meaning," 442; "Shirt," 340n. 13, 394; *The Situation of*

Pinsky, Robert (*continued*)
Poetry: Contemporary Poetry and Its Traditions, 500
"Pity of Love, The" (Yeats): triple feet of, **331**
plain style, 114–26; on continuum of diction, 404; defined, 447–48; in graphic schema of diction, 382; in graphic schema of rhetoric and mode, 382; high diction mixed with, 120–26; modern evolution, 178–82; monosyllabism in, 114–26, 404, 447; non-verbs in, 367; word order in, 480
Plath, Sylvia: "Edge," **56**, 58; "Elm," 353
podic free verse, 330–33; defined, 448; frame of expectation of, 369; in graphic schema of meter and prosody, 383; illustrative poems, 506; as podic verse, 299–303
podic verse, 299–303; isochrony distinguishing metric verse from, 330n. 1; isochrony in, 304; in nursery rhymes, 330. *See also* dipodic verse; podic free verse
"Poem" (Williams): haiku feeling of, 329
Poetic Closure: A Study of How Poems End (Smith), 500
Poetic Diction: A Study in Meaning (Barfield), 497
Poetic Meter and Poetic Form (Fussell), 491
Poetics of Indeterminacy, The (Perloff), 499–500
poetry: anthologies, 483–90; as an art, 1–2;

as the art of fending something off, 46, 197–98; beginnings, 13–21; critical volumes on, 496–501; dictionary of poetic terms, 380–482; the elements, controlled in time, 215–343; elements of relation and resemblance, 45–214; essays and essay collections, 493–96; handbooks, 490–93; as imbedded in progression and indebted to surprise, 33; and intention, 34–35; looking at a poem from within, 380; the poet's poem as dead, 15; pressure as outward in, 161; prose as differing from, 254n. 2; as provisional, 2, 13, 24; reading poems as if you were writing them, 13–14; rhyming moving into the popular realm, 263; sense and sounds as parallels in, 1–2; view of the artistic process, 13–43; wholeness of a poem, 22; writing exercises, 347–79
"Poetry, Theories of" (Abrams), 492
Poetry Handbook: A Dictionary of Terms (Deutsch), 491
Poet's Alphabet, A: Reflections on the Literary Art and Vocation (Bogan), 497
Poets of the English Language (Auden and Pearson), 485–86
Poet's Tongue, The (Auden and Garrett), 485

"Polar Expedition" (Spender): literal symbol in, 434–35
polysyllabic words: pronunciation of, 449; stress in, 220–21, 457–58; in syllabic verse, 290
polysyllabism, 111–13; abstraction and, 111, 137, 404; and rhythm, 457; and understressed line, 136–40, 477–78
Pope, Alexander: antithesis in, 394; balanced satiric couplets of, 374–75; Chaucer as closer to prose than, 280; chiasmus in, 281–82; cliche making of, 284; The Dunciad, 394, **398;** "Epistle to Dr. Arbuthnot," 67; An Essay on Man, **409,** 455–56; Imitations of Horace, 482; kenning in, 427–28; Moral Epistles, 283; pyrrhic foot in, 230n. 19; rhyme flaunted by, 289; rhyme wit of, 359; rhyming on the phrase in, 67, 281–84; strong verbs disappearing in couplets of, 368; tropes of uneven comparison in, 282; unrhymed pentameter of, 333–34; voice of, 187; "Windsor Forest," 426; zeugma in, 152, 280–81. *See also* "Epistle to Bathurst"; Essay on Criticism, An; Rape of the Lock, The
"Poplar Field, The" (Cowper): anapests and amphibrachs in, **228**–29

Porter, Peter: pararhyme
in, 272
"Postcard from the Vol-
cano, A" (Stevens):
plain style in, **117–18;**
simile in, 461
Pound, Ezra: free verse of,
341, 342; and the haiku,
326, 327; imagist free
verse of, 423; "Ts'ai
Chi'i," **329**
"Poverty" (Traherne): lit-
eral symbol in, 434;
rhetoric of, 189–91,
189–90
Praed, Winthrop Mack-
worth: "Good-Night to
the Season," **391**
"Prayer" (Herbert): simple
replacement in, 476
"Prayer for My Daughter,
A" (Yeats): editorial dic-
tion of, 404; ottava rima
in, **275;** rhyming on the
phrase in, 456–57; stan-
zas in, 276–77
predicative mode, 439
prefixes: meaning makes
stress on, 250–51, 458
Prelude, The (Words-
worth): blank verse in,
397; epic simile in,
409–10; phrasal mode
of, 439; plain style in,
117
Preminger, Alex, 492
prerhymes: in epigrams,
358; rhyme as stronger
than, 267; in rhyming
on the phrase, 67, 455
Prince, F. T., 483n
*Princeton Encyclopedia of
Poetry and Poetics,* 492–
93
Prior, Matthew: *Solomon,*
401–2
pronunciation: defined,

448–49; in elision,
406–7; in graphic
schema of diction, 382;
in graphic schema of
meter and prosody,
383; of past participles,
448
prose: Chaucer as closer to
than Pope, 280; free
verse overlapping with,
290; meter as distin-
guishing from verse,
437; poetry as differing
from, 254n. 2; prose
draft approach to writ-
ing poetry, 348; and syn-
tax, 469
prosody: critical volumes
on, 496–501; defined,
450; graphic schema of,
383
Prosody Handbook, A (Sha-
piro and Beum), 493
"Prospero to Ariel"
(Auden): abstract dic-
tion turning into per-
sonification in, 140;
two-stress unit in,
311–**12**
"Prothalamium"
(Spenser): elective stress
in, 235
Proverbs 26: tags in, **52**
psalms: anaphora in, 393
Psalms 70: tags in, **51–52**
Psalms 121: tags in, **53**
psychological surrealism,
205–6
pun: adnomination having
effect of punning, 386;
chiasmus and zeugma
involving, 282; compar-
ison in, 154; on contin-
uum of diction, 47; on
continuum of trope,
149, 151–52, 475, 476;
defined, 450; in graphic

schema of diction, 382;
in graphic schema of
trope, 382
punctuation: in compound
sentences, 400; omitting
in scansion, 222n. 9; and
pauses, 68
*Purity of Diction in English
Verse* (Davie), 498
pyrrhic foot: defined, 450;
in eighteenth-century
poetry, 230n. 19; false
pyrrhics, 229, 230, 450;
in graphic schema of
meter and prosody, 383;
as not viable in English,
229, 438; pyrrhic-
spondee combination,
231–33, 235; in rising
ionic, 457

quantity: in classical verse,
290n, 437; defined,
450–51; in graphic
schema of meter and
prosody, 383
quatrain: in ballads, 264,
396, 400; defined, 451;
exercise in descriptive,
348–49; in graphic
schema of stanza and
rhyme, 383; in hymns,
418; illustrative ex-
tended or varied, 505; il-
lustrative with alternat-
ing rhyme, 504–5; long
meter, 419, 435; in pas-
sages, 444; short meter,
419, 460; unrealized
beats in ballad, 267–69.
See also heroic quatrain
"Quest, The" (Auden):
portraits in, 362
*Quest for Reality: An Anthol-
ogy of Short Poems in En-
glish* (Winters and
Fields), 490

"Quintets for Robert Morley" (Murray): anatomy in, 394
quotation, 173–75

Ralegh, Sir Walter: "As You Came from the Holy Land of Walsinghame," **296–98;** "The Lie," **453.** *See also* "Three Things There Bee"
Randall, Julia: "Adam's Dream," **270;** "Album Leaves," 174–75; "Boundbrook," **278;** "Maid's Song," 210–**11;** metaphysical ballads of, 278
Rape of the Lock, The (Pope): couplets in, 402; historical pronunciation in, 448; kenning in, 426–27; as mock epic, 152; periphrasis in, 445; puns in, 151–52, 401, 450; rhyme in, 455; syntactic inversion in, 466; too-regular meter parodied in, 253; zeugma in, 281
"Reading During Marriage" (Kinzie): stress variation in, 317–**18**
"Reading Poetry Aloud" (Bate and Perkins), 486–87
realization, 14
"Realm of Ends, The" (Koethe): plain style in, **118, 119**
recession of technique, 48; as analytical concept, 380, 382; defined, 451–52; of half-meaning, 61; of meter, 253; in Muir's "Ballad

of Hector in Hades," 369n; of rhyme, 74
"Red, Red Rose, A" (Burns): simile in, 163, 460
reduced line: defined, 452; in graphic schema of meter and prosody, 383; in graphic schema of stanza and rhyme, 383; in Muir's "The Gate," 105; in Yeats's ottava rima, 275
refrain: in ballads, 264, 452; defined, 452–54; in graphic schema of stanza and rhyme, 383; unlike linked form, 431; reduced line compared with, 452
rejet, 302n. 10
Renaissance poetry: allegory in, 159, 386; Bogan compared with, 31; deliberate unnaturalness in, 156–57; and nature, 26; past participles as pronounced in, 448–49; plain style of, 116, 120, 447; quatrains losing popularity in, 418; subjunctive mood in, 82; Tuve on, 501
"Resolution and Independence" (Wordsworth): plain style in, **120;** rhyme royal in, 457
responsion: in confirming meter, 240; defined, 454; in Kinzie's "After Frost at Midnight," 323
Restoration and Jacobean Poets, Milton to Goldsmith (Auden and Pearson), 485
Resurrection (Yeats): displacements of size in

song from, **153;** metonymy in, 162n
"Retaliation" (Goldsmith): polarities and reversals of style in, **27;** satiric meiosis in, 205; surprising shifts in, 33–34
"Return, The" (Muir): visionary dream in, 363
rhetoric, 187–211; contemporary poetry excluding play of, 29; continuum analysis of, 149; in conversational style, 401; defined, 454; dramatic extremes, 200–211; as element of poetry, 45; graphic schema of, 382; and mode, 439; in odes, 441; and persona, 187, 454. *See also* figures of speech; hyperbole; meiosis
rhyme, 262–89; adjacent rhyme, 271, 455; as background technique, 74; in ballads, 263–66; coincidence with respect to, 71–72; defined, 454–55; and end-stopping, 101–3, 454–55; and enjambment, 68; full and near, 271; graphic schema of, 383; illustrative poems, 504–5; interspersed rhyme, 271, 455; last-line, 271; and like endings, 430; loss of endings affecting English, 216, 280; meaning in, 280; medieval function of, 262; minimum thresholds for, 271; modern rhyme and syntactic clash, 279–81; morphemes in, 280; in

podic free verse, 332; pronunciation affecting, 448–49; rhymed stanzas seeming bland, 369n; rules of, 270–76; symmetry versus alternation, 262–66; and word order, 480. *See also* alternating rhyme; heterometric rhyme; leonine verse; light rhyme; pararhyme; rhyming on the phrase

"Rhyme" (Bogan): hyperbaton in, 467–68

rhyme royal: alternating and adjacent rhyme in, 271; defined, 457; in graphic schema of stanza and rhyme, 383; illustrative poems, 505

Rhyme's Reason: A Guide to English Verse (Hollander), 492

rhyming on the phrase, 281–84; with alternating rhyme, 288–89; as analytical concept, 382; in Bishop's "Cirque d'Hiver," 273; in comic rhyme, 134; defined, 455–57; in epigrams, 358; in graphic schema of rhetoric and mode, 382; in graphic schema of stanza and rhyme, 383; in graphic schema of syntax, 382; thematic contrast expressed by, 65–68

rhythm: as accommodation of poet's own sound, 214; as combination, 212–14; continuum analysis of, 149; counted forms, 290–329; defined, 457; and

diction, 136–40; as element of poetry, 45; and mode, 439; playing against meter, 212–14, 219; pronunciation affecting, 448; standards as varying over time, 49; theme and style supported by, 251. *See also* accent

Rhythms of English Poetry, The (Attridge), 496

Richard II (Shakespeare): and elective stress, **236;** trochaic inversion in, 473

Rime of the Ancient Mariner, The (Coleridge): aura of song in, 277–**78;** rhetoric of, **195–96;** tension in, **470**

Ring and the Book, The (Browning): syntactic inversion in, 468

rising feet: anapests, 226, 391, 437; iambs, 226, 337

rising ionic: defined, 457; pyrrhic-spondee combination approximating, 231n. 20

rising meter: in accentual-syllabic verse, 437; defined, 457; as derived meter, 226. *See also* rising feet

"Rizpah" (Tennyson): anapests in, **392**

Robinson, Edwin Arlington: "Ben Jonson Entertains a Man from Stratford," 357; "Captain Craig," **253–54,** 449; character sketches of, 362

Robinson, Fred C., 303, 500

Roethke, Theodore: "The Coming of the Cold," **108;** "The Far Field," 131; on form, 345; garden lore in, 131; "My Papa's Waltz," **63**–64, 211. *See also* "Heron, The"

Rolle, Richard: leonine rhymes in, 429

Romance of the Rose, The (Chaucer): rhyme in, **263**–64, 280

"Roman Fountain" (Bogan): nondeclarative syntax in, 88

Romantic Poets, Blake to Poe (Auden and Pearson), 485

"Romantic Verse Form and the Metrical Contract" (Hollander), 494–95

Romeo and Juliet (Shakespeare): past participles as pronounced in, 448–**49;** zeugma in, 482

root, 386

"Rose-Cheekt Laura" (Campion): trochaic meter in, **475**

Rossetti, Christina: "In the Bleak Midwinter," **479**

Rossetti, Dante Gabriel: "The Woodspurge," 147–48, **148**

"Rugby Chapel" (Arnold): as podic free verse, 330, **332,** 448

rule of two: as analytical concept, 383; in ballads, 266–67, 457; defined, 457; in dipodic verse, 405, 457; in graphic schema of meter and prosody, 383; in short meter, 460

"Runes" (Nemerov): persona of, 445

Sabol, Andrew J., 488

Sackville, Thomas: *A Mirrour for Magistrates,* 457

"Sadness" (Justice): rhetoric of, **195**

"Sailing to Byzantium" (Yeats): literal symbol in, 149

Samson Agonistes (Milton): heterometric rhyme in, 273

2 Samuel 22: chiasmus in, 398-**99**

"Sanctuary, The" (Nemerov): enjambment in, **105;** literal symbol in, 143; tenor and vehicle coinciding in, 156; verisimilitude of suggestion in, 154-55

San Francisco poets, 483

"Sarah's Choice" (Wilner): biblical revision in, 351

Satan in Search of a Wife (Lamb): anapest in, **391**-92

satire: diction-extremes in satiric rhyme, 134-36; meiosis in, 204-5; in mock epic, 439; in psychological surrealism, 205-6; and retreat from an audience, 207

"Satire I" ("Myne owne John Poynz") (Wyatt): clause coinciding with line in, 399; meiosis in, **204;** trochaic substitutions in, **233**

Saul (Browning): anapests as too regular in, **392**

scansion, 221-25; defined, 457-58; derived meter, 221, 458; exercises for learning to scan, 238-39; in graphic schema of meter and

prosody, 383; metrical expectation mapped to actual words, 221, 458; steps in determining, 220-21, 457-58; and stress, 219-20, 457-58; and syntax, 223-25; three symbols required for, 221-22, 458. *See also* derived meter; scansion rules

scansion rules, 221; defined, 458-59. *See also* context makes meter; meaning makes stress

Schuyler, James: bridging his free-verse lines, 55; free verse of, 341. *See also* "Few Days, A"

Scott, Sir Walter: iambic tetrameter in, 471

Scottish ballads, 48, 74, 298, 396, 400, 451

Scragg, Donald, 302n. 9, 303n. 11

scudding, 229

Sea and the Mirror, The (Auden): anatomy in, 394; persona of, 445; "Prospero to Ariel," 140, 311-**12**

"Seal Lullaby" (Kipling): amphibrachs in, 228; leonine rhymes in, 429

secondary stresses, 220-21, 457

"Second Coming, The" (Yeats): etymological diction in, 130, 412

Second Shepherd's Play: rhyme in, 263

"Seen Through a Window" (Ferry): clause diverging from line in, 399; descriptive sentences in, 80; as model of description, 348-49;

rhetoric of, 196-98, **196-97,** 378

Selected Essays (Eliot), 498

"Self-Unseeing, The" (Hardy): rhetoric of, 195; settling on its ending, **23**-24; surprising shifts in, 33

sentence: all other features following from, 10-11; choice of sentence frames, 6; continuum of, 46-47, 468; defined, 459; in graphic schema of syntax, 382; and line, 4-5, 49, 279; and the pentameter passage in Milton, 97-101; and stanza, 279; in writing your way through a poem, 6. *See also* compound sentence; declarative sentence; imperative; sentence fragment; syntactic inversion; syntax

sentence fragment, 90-92; on continuum of sentences, 47, 468; defined, 459; in graphic schema of syntax, 382

sestet: defined, 459; in graphic schema of stanza and rhyme, 383; in sonnets, 462

sestina: defined, 459-60; exercise in sestina of early intuition, 363-66; in graphic schema of stanza and rhyme, 383

"Sestina" (Bishop), 459

"Sestina, The" (Nims), 496

"Sestina in Cantina" (Lowry), 496

"Shadows in the Water" (Traherne): editorial diction of, 404

Shakespeare, William:
Antony and Cleopatra,
438–**39;** blank verse
evolution in, 50, 397;
elective stress in, 234n;
Henry IV, Part II,
251–**52;** *Henry V,* **254,**
440; *Henry VI, Part II,*
372–73; *Julius Caesar,*
425–26; *Othello the
Moor of Venice,* **464;** past
participles as pro-
nounced in, 448; *Per-
icles,* 471; rhyme pattern
of sonnets, 462; *Richard
II,* **236,** 473; *Romeo and
Juliet,* 448–**49,** 482; Son-
net 31, **156;** Sonnet 65,
254; Sonnet 73, **316,**
470, **481;** Sonnet 76,
482; sonnets deviating
from convention, 28;
The Tempest, **474;** *Troi-
lus and Cressida,* **59,** 60;
unrhymed pentameter
of, 333; voice of, 187,
193. See also *Hamlet;
King Lear; Macbeth;* Son-
net 5; Sonnet 71; Son-
net 94; Sonnet 110;
Sonnet 116
Shakespearean Meanings
(Burckhardt), 498
"Shakespeare's Sonnets"
(Knights), 495
Shapiro, Karl, 337, 493
"She Is Going" (Lamb): re-
frain in, **453–54**
Shelley, Percy Bysshe: "Ad-
onais," 218, 462; pyrrhic
foot in, 230n. 19
"Shield of Achilles, The"
(Auden): allusion in,
165–66, 388, 390; epi-
thet in, 411; monosylla-
bism in, 440; visionary
theme of, 363
Shiki: "Nights are getting

cold," **328;** "White but-
terfly," **328**
"Shirt" (Pinsky): anatomy
in, 394; "word-
heaping" in, 340n. 13
short meter: common me-
ter compared with, 420;
defined, 460; in graphic
schema of stanza and
rhyme, 383; as hymn
meter, 419; illustrative
quatrains with alternat-
ing rhyme, 504; in
Lear's limericks, 433;
unrealized beat in, 479
"Short Song of Congratu-
lation" (Johnson): as
trochaic, 226
"Side by Side" (Hardy): as
accentual-syllabic,
312–13
Sidney, Sir Philip:
Astrophel and Stella, 317,
462; Bogan and, 30;
decasyllabic line in, 317;
"When to My Deadly
Pleasure," **280n. 19**
simile: on continuum of
comparison, 476; on
continuum of likeness,
400; on continuum of
trope, 475–76; defined,
460–61; as figure of
thought, 413; in graphic
schema of trope, 382;
tenor and vehicle in,
156. *See also* epic simile
Simms, Michael, 492
simple replacement, 476
Singing Game, The (Opie
and Opie), 174, 489
singleness of mind, 87–88
"Single Sonnet" (Bogan):
declarative sentences in,
404; elective stress in,
234; enjambment
masked in, 73; impera-
tives in, 88; metrical

variation in, 233–34;
theme as greater than
the form, **30**–32
*Sir Gawain and the Green
Knight* (romance): ex-
pandable time in,
412–13; *Pearl* poet as au-
thor of, 307, 308
"Sir Patrick Spens" (bal-
lad): end-stopping in,
107; irregularity of,
295–96; metonymy in,
162, 439, 477; triple
measures in, 266; why
Sir Patrick is sent to
Norway, 266, 266n. 8
*Situation of Poetry, The:
Contemporary Poetry and
Its Traditions* (Pinsky),
500
Skelton, John: "Philip
Sparrow," **267, 299–300**
slack syllables: defined,
462; in prose and non-
metrical poems, 220
slash, 222, 397, 435, 463
"Slow Pacific Swell, The"
(Winters): clause coin-
ciding with line in, 399;
couplets in, 402; literal
symbol in, 143; as self-
dramatizing, 201,
202–4, **202–3**
Smart, Christopher: *Jubi-
late Agno,* 393
Smith, Barbara Herrnstein,
267n. 11, 284, 500
"Snow Man, The" (Ste-
vens): diction of, 131
Solomon (Prior): couplets
in, 401–2
song: as chant, 269; echo
tradition of, 277. *See
also* ballad
"Song for a Lyre" (Bogan):
declaratives in, 88; lit-
eral symbol in, 434; nu-
anced metaphor in, 177;

"Song for a Lyre" (Bogan) (*continued*)
and primacy of immediate scene, 158, 159; syntactic inversion in, **89**

"Song for St. Cecilia's Day, A" (Dryden): extrapolation beyond the quatrain in, 274

"Song for the Last Act" (Bogan): nondeclarative syntax in, 88

Song of Hiawatha (Longfellow): trochaic meter in, **474**

"Song: She Dwelt Among th' Untrodden Ways" (Wordsworth): metonymy in, **163**–64

sonnet: blank sonnet, 396; defined, 462; exercise in dramatized description, 349–50; exercise in sonnet of secondary characters, 361–62; in graphic schema of stanza and rhyme, 383; haiku compared with, 327; illustrative poems, 505; rhyme patterns in, 462; tradition of, 9–10. *See also* octave; Petrarchan; sestet; volta

Sonnet 5 (Shakespeare), **41;** beginning of, 15, 16, 17; consonant thickening in, 451; neologism in, 121; personification in, 182; the start as instantly countered, 33

Sonnet 31 (Shakespeare): exaggerated posture of, **156**

Sonnet 65 (Shakespeare): mimetic meter in, 254

Sonnet 71 (Shakespeare): elective stress in, 235n; hypotaxis in, **422;** plain style in, **116;** as self-dramatizing, **210**

Sonnet 73 (Shakespeare): syllabic verse compared with, **316;** tenor and vehicle of, 470; word order in, **481**

Sonnet 76 (Shakespeare): zeugma in, 482

Sonnet 94 (Shakespeare): amphibrach as end-of-line substitution in, 390; "do" in, 368; monosyllables making stress in, **248**–49; rhyme in, 454; shift from abstract to concrete in, 327; trochaic inversion in, 473

Sonnet 110 (Shakespeare): as deviating from sonnet convention, **28,** 29; surprising shifts in, 33; trochaic inversion in, 473

Sonnet 116 (Shakespeare): antimimetic meter in, 252; argumentative subordinating sentence in, 468–69; contrary-to-fact argument in, 83; mimetic meter in, 254; trochaic inversion in, **474**

"Sonnets from China" (from Auden's *In Time of War* sequence): portraits in, 362; sonnets as complete poems, 462

"So set its Sun in Thee" (#808) (Dickinson): condensation and inversion in, 84; stylistic comparison with Jarrell, 79; subjunctive mood in, 353

"Soul, A" (Jarrell): allu-

sion in, **171**–72; compound sentences in, 80; declarative sentences in, 404; isochrony in, 304; stylistic comparison with Dickinson, 79

Sound and Form in Modern Poetry: A Study of Prosody from Thomas Hardy to Robert Lowell (Gross), 498

speech, 187–211

Spender, Stephen: "Polar Expedition," 434–35

Spenser, Edmund: "Epithalamium," 463; "I Saw the Bird That Can the Sun Endure," **102**–3; "I Saw the Bird That Dares Behold the Sun," **101**–2; phrasal mode in, 439; "Prothalamium," 235. *See also* *Faerie Queene, The*

Spenserean stanza: defined, 462; in graphic schema of stanza and rhyme, 383; illustrative poems, 505; in passages, 444; six-measure lines in, 218

"Spoiler's Return, The" (Walcott): couplets of, **285**–**86;** diction-shifting in, **131**–32

spondee: defined, 462–63; false spondees, 229, 231, 462; in graphic schema of meter and prosody, 383; as not viable in English, 229, 438; pyrrhic-spondee combination, 231–33, 235; in rising ionic, 457; substituting for an iamb, 465

"Spring" (Millay): lineation in, **56**

"Spring" (Thomson): imagism in, **423**

sprung verse: defined, 463. *See also* podic free verse

Stallworthy, Jon, 251n

standards, 48–49

"Stand Whoso List" (Wyatt): overstressing in, 443; tension in, **86–87**

stanza, 262–89; alcaics, 322–23; in ballads, 264; continuum of the, 278–79; defined, 463; extrapolation beyond the quatrain, 274; graphic schema of, 383; illustrative poems, 504–5; the literary stanza, 269–70; and passage, 443–44; and sentence, 279; in sestinas, 459; thinking in stanzas, 276–79. *See also* Burns stanza; ottava rima; rhyme royal; quatrain; Spenserean stanza

stanzaic poetry: blank verse as feeling less artificial than, 368–69; defined, 463; reduced line in, 452; refrains in, 452; stichic contrasted with, 463; as strophic, 463

"Star Gazers" (Wordsworth): fourteeners sounding like common meter, 414

Steele, Timothy: as attentive to word-length, 113n. 4; "Boundless Wealth from a Finite Store: Meter and Grammar," 496; *Missing Measures: Modern Poetry and the Revolt Against Meter,* 500; "Of Culture," 394; "Of Friendship," 394;

proverbial expressions in rhyme of, 136; writing on poetry, 483n. 1. *See also* "Toward Calgary"

Stein, Arnold, 500–501

Stephens, Alan: "Heron Totem," **256**

Stevens, Wallace: alliteration in, 140; "The American Sublime," **54;** "Anecdote of the Jar," 329; blank verse loosening into free blank verse, 471; "The Comedian as the Letter C," 445; exaggerated diction in, 422; "Fabliau of Florida," **343;** free blank verse of, 334; haiku as influence on, 327, 329; *Harmonium,* 342; imagist free verse of, 342–43; "The Noble Rider and the Sound of Words," 389n; "A Postcard from the Volcano," **117–18,** 461; seven-measure line used by, 218–19; "The Snow Man," 131; tension in, 470; voice of, 187. *See also* "Idea of Order at Key West, The"

stichic verse: defined, 463; Gascoigne on, 260; in graphic schema of line, 383; in graphic schema of meter and prosody, 383; in graphic schema of stanza and rhyme, 383; and melic in English, 279–80; and mode, 439; as mosaic-like, 94; softening in Hope's "Man Friday," 351; stanzaic contrasted with, 463

"Still-Life" (Daryush): syllabics of, 316

"Still to Be Neat" (Jonson): metonymy in, 162

"Stopping by Woods on a Snowy Evening" (Frost): expandable time in, 307

Story of Sigurd the Volsung, The (Morris): anapestic gallop avoided in, 392

Strand, Mark: "Always," 156; meiosis in, 205–6. See also *Dark Harbor*

"Strange Meeting" (Owen): pararhyme in, **271–72**

stress, 217–21; accent contrasted with, 463; in accentual-syllabic verse, 217–61; defined, 463; determining in scansion, 220–21, 457–58; in graphic schema of meter and prosody, 383; and light rhyme, 429; and line, 373; marking, 219, 463; and meter, 437; of monosyllabic verbs, 367; rhyming stress, 271; and rhythm, 457; in Romance languages, 315; secondary stresses, 220–21, 457; syllabic meter drawing attention away from, 290; variable stress, 236–38. *See also* elective stress; main line-stress; meaning makes stress; over-stressed line; slack syllables; understressed line

"Strong Are Saying Nothing, The" (Frost): anapests inserted among iambs of, 307, 393; compound sentences in, 80,

"Strong Are Saying Nothing, The" (Frost) (*continued*) 400; iambic pentameter in, 422; isochrony in, **304–5**

strong-stress meter. *See* accentual verse

strophic: defined, 463; in graphic schema of line, 383; in graphic schema of stanza and rhyme, 383. *See also* stanzaic poetry

"Structures" (Oliver): caesural pausing in, 77–79, **78**, 398; comparison as accurate in, 164; *contre-rejet* in, 303n. 10; periphrasis in, 445

Stryk, Lucien, 328

style: continuum analysis of, 149; critical volumes on, 496–501; rhythm supporting, 251. *See also* prosody

subjunctive mood: adversatives for launching, 366; defined, 463–65; in graphic schema of syntax, 382; as mood, 440; parataxis juxtaposed with, 84–85; suppleness obtained from, 362; types of, 81–83

subphrasal cut, 340–41

substituted feet: basic metrical expectation not changed by, 221, 458; defined, 465; in graphic schema of meter and prosody, 383; spondee, pyrrhic, cretic, and bacchius as, 229. *See also* metrical inversion

"sudden chill—, A" (Buson): as haiku, **328**

"Summer Holds, The"

(Auden): allusion in, 173

"Summer Wish" (Bogan): as dialogue poem, 360; lineation in, **54**

surrealism, psychological, 205–6

Surrey, Henry Howard, Earl of: versions of Wyatt's sonnets, 246

"Sweet and Low" (Tennyson): refrain in, 453

Swift, Jonathan: "Verses on the Death of Doctor Swift, D. S. P. D.," 134

Swinburne, Algernon Charles: "By the North Sea," **391;** dactyls in, 402; "Hymn to Proserpine," 392

syllabics, 313–29; accentual verse compared with, 313–14, 315, 316; advantages of, 369; alcaics, 322–23; as counted form, 290; of Cunningham, 323–25; of Daryush, 325–26; defined, 465; in English, 315–16, 317; in graphic schema of line, 383; in graphic schema of meter and prosody, 383; of Gunn, 319–22; as harder to hear in period of free verse, 290; illustrative poems, 507; pattern withheld in, 291; as quintessentially written, 290; and stress, 218; syllable count, 317–19; tanka, 326, 470. *See also* haiku

syllables: accent and stress, 217; accent describing average behavior of, 384; and diction, 111–

13, 405; elision, 406–7; and movement of verse in time, 215. *See also* monosyllabism; polysyllabism; syllabics

Sylvester, Richard, 490

symbol: on continuum of comparison, 476; on continuum of likeness, 400; defined, 465–66; in graphic schema of trope, 382. *See also* literal symbol

syntactical free verse. *See* biblical free verse

syntactic inversion, 83–84; in Bogan's "Song for a Lyre," 89; defined, 466–68; in graphic schema of syntax, 382; in Hardy's "An August Midnight," 192; lines in tension, 69–71; and meter, 261; suppleness obtained from, 362. *See also* anastrophe; hyperbaton

syntax, 75–110; continuum of, 46–47, 149, 401, 468; defined, 468–69; and diction, 399, 469; dramatic, 194–95; as element of poetry, 45; extremes of, 79–89; flexibility with, 108–10; form follows theme, 107–10; graphic schema of, 380–81, 382; ingenious perspectives provided by, 366; and line, 75–79, 469, 470; meter coinciding with, 399; and mode, 439; modern rhyme and syntactic clash, 279–81; pauses depending on, 68; and rhetoric, 454;

and scansion, 223–25; sentence fragment as minimal, 90–92; and trope, 469. *See also* clause; phrase; sentence; word order

Syntax in English Poetry 1870–1930 (Baker), 497

table-talk, exercise in, 356–58

tag: defined, 469; in graphic schema of rhetoric and mode, 382; in graphic schema of syntax, 382; in Hebrew verse, 51–52, 416; isocolon compared with, 52n

"Tam Samson's Elegy" (Burns): refrain in, **452–53**

tanka: defined, 470; as syllabic verse, 326

Taylor, Jane, 467

Tempest, The (Shakespeare): trochaic meter in, **474**

Tennyson, Alfred Lord: "Break, Break, Break," 305; "The Lotos-Eaters," **417,** 468; plain style of, 117; "Rizpah," **392;** "Sweet and Low," 453; "The Voyage of Maeldune," 402. See also *In Memoriam A. H. H.;* "Ulysses"

tenor: allegory and explicit, 159–62; closeness to vehicle, 162; defined, 470; in Dickinson's "My Life had stood—a Loaded Gun" (#754), 154; in epic simile, 409; in graphic schema of trope, 382; in literal symbol, 434, 466; in

metaphor, 436, 466; in mixed trope, 438; in simile, 156, 460–61; in symbol, 465–66

tension, 48; as analytical concept, 382; coincidence needed for, 72, 471; constant use of, 61; defined, 470–71; between line and sentence, 49; lines in, 68–74; in mixed diction, 405; variety providing, 351

tetrameter: in ballad meter, 396; in Burns stanza, 397; in common meter, 400, 418; defined, 471; in graphic schema of meter and prosody, 383; iambic, 217, 471; illustrative couplets, 504; illustrative extended quatrains, 505; in long meter, 419, 435; in short meter, 419, 460; trochaic, 471, 474, 475. *See also* rule of two

"That Nature is a Heraclitean Fire and of the comfort of the Resurrection" (Hopkins): monosyllabism of, 112, 443

theme: choices in treatment of, 5; conventions in determining, 26; and line, 5; and mode, 439; in onomatopoeia, 442; rhythm supporting, 251; trying to be true, 378–79. *See also* form follows theme

"There Is a Garden" (Campion): metaphor in, 163

Thomas, Dylan: "Do Not Go Gentle," 431

Thompson, John, 501

Thomson, James: "Spring," 423

"Three Thinges There Bee" (Ralegh): elective stress in, 406; monosyllables making stress in, **249–51;** plain style as low style in, 120; trochaic inversion in, 474

threshold: between accentual and accentual-syllabic verse, 290–94; as analytical concept, 382; defined, 471–72; of invention, 87; of the known, 49–50; and standards, 48–49; tension between line and sentence, 49

thresholds of choice, 48–50; in writing the poem you read, 21–26

"Tintern Abbey" (Wordsworth): as blank verse, 7; monosyllabism in, **116;** polysyllabism in, **137;** Randall quoting from, **174**–75; as self-dramatizing, 201

"'Tis good—the looking back on Grief—" (#660) (Dickinson): ambiguous second stanza of, 24–26, **24–25;** tension in, 470, 471

"To a Friend Whose Work Has Come to Nothing" (Yeats): hypotaxis in, 422; muscularity of syntax of, 354; subjunctive mood in, 353; syntactic surprise in, 108, **109**–10

"To a Mouse" (Burns): diction-shifting in, 132; the small implicating the great in, 153

"To Autumn" (Keats): literal symbol in, 400
"To Be Sung on the Water" (Bogan): apposition in, 395; enjambment in, **76**–77; line and phrase coinciding in, 447
"To His Coy Mistress" (Marvell): chiasmus in, 281
"To One denied to drink" (#490) (Dickinson): hymn meter in, 479; muscularity of syntax of, 354
"To Penshurst" (Jonson): praise-of-place theme of, 359
"To Saxham" (Carew): iambic tetrameter in, 471; praise-of-place theme of, 359
"To the Driving Cloud" (Longfellow): dactyls in, 402
"To the Small Celandine" (Wordsworth): as trochaic, 226
"Toward Calgary" (Steele): absolute construction in, 384; larger meaning in, 181–82; literal image in, 423; personification in, 182, 184; rhetoric of, 198; syntax of, 469; understressing and overstressing in, 137–39, **138**
"Tower, The" (Yeats): literal symbol in, 149
"Tower II, The" (Yeats): ottava rima in, 275
tradition: as broadening and limiting, 26; as environment in which poems grow, 9–10
Traherne, Thomas: "Poverty," 189–91, **189–90,**

434; "Shadows in the Water," 404
transitive verb: defined, 472; in graphic schema of syntax, 382; intransitive verb contrasted with, 425; as non-verb, 367
"Trees, The" (Larkin): half-meaning in, 416; plain style in, 179–**80;** rhetoric of, 198–99
trimeter: in ballad meter, 396; in common meter, 400, 418; defined, 472; exercise in trimeter mad song, 352–54; in graphic schema of meter and prosody, 383; iambic, 217; illustrative couplets, 504; illustrative extended quatrains, 505; illustrative quatrains with alternating rhyme, 504; in limericks, 433; rule of two for, 267; in short meter, 419, 460; unrealized beat in, 479
triolet: in graphic schema of stanza and rhyme, 383; as linked form, 431–32
triple meter: in ballads, 266, 472; defined, 472; as derived meter, 226; in graphic schema of meter and prosody, 383. See also amphibrach; anapest; dactyl
trochaic inversion (trochaic substitution): acceptable use of, 214; defined, 472–74; in graphic schema of meter and prosody, 383; as metrical inversion, 438; new unit of syntax beginning with, 244n;

"trochaic inversion" as superior term, 475
trochaic meter: dactyls substituting in, 402; defined, 474–75; illustrative poems, 506; in podic free verse, 331, 448; stress and accent in, 226
trochaic substitution. See trochaic inversion
trochaic tetrameter, 471, 474, 475
trochee: context as affecting, 221, 226; defined, 475; as falling foot, 226, 437; and light rhyme, 429–30. See also trochaic inversion; trochaic meter
Troilus and Cressida (Shakespeare): half-meaning in, **59,** 60
trope, 142–86; for baffling or inchoate experience, 354; comparison from different realms and metaphoric layers, 175–78; continuum of, 148–52, 400, 475–76; continuum of comparison, 476–77; defined, 475–77; and diction, 140–41; as element of poetry, 45; and fragment, 92; graphic schema of, 382; in Hope's "Man Friday," 136; overt comparison versus naturalistic suggestion, 154–59; poetry starting with the thing and moving to the thought, 381; and rhetoric, 454; in self-conscious speakers, 188; and syntax, 469. See also allusion; figures of

thought; metaphor; metonymy; mixed trope; personification; simile; symbol; tenor; vehicle
"Trout, The" (Hine): rhymes of, 134, 454–55
"Ts'ai Chi'i" (Pound): haiku feeling of, **329**
"Twas like a Maelstrom, with a notch" (#414) (Dickinson): metonymy in, 162
Turco, Lewis, 299, 304, 330n. 1, 493
Tuve, Rosalind, 157, 501
"Twa Corbies, The" (ballad): category phrases in, 265
"Twickenham Garden" (Donne): wit in, 157
two-stress unit: accentual verse and, 308–12; dimeter versus, 312–13; in dipodic verse, 299; rule of two, 457

"Ulysses" (Tennyson): infinitives in, 424; persona of, 445; plain style in, 117; scansion of, 222, 223, **224–25**
Unbearable Lightness of Being, The (Kundera), 377
"Unburied, The" (Morris): as imagist free verse, 343; varying tempos in, **370–71**
understressed line: defined, 477–78; in Frost's blank verse, 334; in graphic schema of diction, 382; in graphic schema of line, 382, 383; in graphic schema of meter and prosody, 383; in iambic pentameter, 229–38; and polysyllabism, 136–40, 477–78

unearned significance, 308
unfolding: in writing your way through a poem, 5
unrealized beat: in ballad quatrains, 267–69; in common (ballad) meter, 420; defined, 478–79; in graphic schema of meter and prosody, 383; and implied offbeat, 424; in Yeats's "Easter 1916," 293
"Upon Appleton House, To My Lord Fairfax" (Marvell): as "gracious home" poem, 359
"Upon the Hill and Grove at *Bill-borow*" (Marvell): as "gracious home" poem, 359
"Urban Convalescence, An" (Merrill): mimetic meter in, 257–**58;** pun in, 450

"Valediction, A: Forbidding Mourning" (Donne): as metaphysical-deliberative, 157–58; simile in, 156; verisimilitude of suggestion in, 154, 155–**56**
Valéry, Paul, 345
variable stress, 236–38
variation, elegant, 445
vehicle: in allegory, 159; closeness to tenor, 162; defined, 479–80; in Dickinson's "My Life had stood—a Loaded Gun" (#754), 154; in emblem, 465–66, 477; in epic simile, 409; in good metaphor, 176; in graphic schema of trope, 382; in metaphor, 436; in mixed trope, 438; in simile, 156,

460–61; in symbol, 465–66
Vendler, Helen, 501
Verbal Icon, The: Studies in the Meaning of Poetry (Wimsatt), 501
verbs: monosyllabic, 220; in normal word order, 459; in syntactic inversion, 467; the verb-metaphor, 367, 476. *See also* copula; infinitive; intransitive verb; mood; non-verb; transitive verb
verse: defined, 480; in graphic schema of line, 382; isomorphism in, 57; line as beginning and end of, 380; meter as distinguishing from prose, 437
verse paragraphs, 444
"Verses on the Death of Doctor Swift, D. S. P. D." (Swift): rhymes of, 134
"Verses Supposed to Be Written by Alexander Selkirk, During His Solitary Abode in the Island of Juan Fernandez" (Cowper): deriving the meter of, 239, **240;** elision in, 449
verset: biblical free verse based on, 337; defined, 480; in graphic schema of line, 383; in graphic schema of meter and prosody, 383. *See also* biblical free verse; Hebrew verse
Versification: A Short Introduction (McAuley), 499
Victorian and Edwardian Poets, Tennyson to Yeats (Auden and Pearson), 485

villanelle: in graphic schema of stanza and rhyme, 383; as linked form, 431

voice: choices for expressing theme, 5; Eliot on the three voices of poetry, 187

"Voice, The" (Hardy): dactyls in, 402

Voice That Is Great Within Us, The: American Poetry of the Twentieth Century (Carruth), 487

volta: in blank sonnet, 396; defined, 480; for description, 349; in graphic schema of rhetoric and mode, 382; in graphic schema of stanza and rhyme, 383; as shift, 327, 459, 462

"Vowel Movements" (Hine): shifting of main vowels in, 366

vowels: pararhyme, 443; rhyme, 449. *See also* assonance; quantity

"Voyage of Maeldune, The" (Tennyson): dactyls in, 402

Walcott, Derek: diction-shifting in, 131–32; "The Hotel Normandie Pool," 231–33, **232;** "The Spoiler's Return," **131–32, 285–86**

"Walk, The" (Hardy): literal symbol in, 149; self-presentation in, 200–201

"Walk After Dark, A" (Auden): resolution of line and sentence in, 73

Warnke, Frank J., 492

Waste Land, The (Eliot): anaphora in, 393; continuum analysis of, 150; Dantesque overtones in, 172, 173; elision in, 449

Watts, Isaac: "Against Idleness and Mischief," **467;** parodied by Carroll, 481

"Way Through the Woods, The" (Kipling): unrealized beat in, 479

Webster, John: Eliot influenced by, 334; *The White Devil,* 254–55

"When to My Deadly Pleasure" (Sidney): meter of, **280n. 19**

"White butterfly" (Shiki): as haiku, **328**

White Devil, The (Webster): monosyllabism of, 254–55

Whitman, Walt: biblical free verse of, 338–39; "Cavalry Crossing a Ford," **423;** "The World Below the Brine," **339**

"Whitsun Weddings, The" (Larkin): as meditation, 7; low and high diction in, 123

Wilbur, Richard: "The Aspen and the Stream," 360; "A Baroque Wall Fountain in the Villa Sciarra," 157–58; on dramatic poetry, 200; "Merlin Enthralled," 355. *See also* "Exeunt"

"Wilde Swans at Coole, The" (Yeats): metrical ambiguity of, 291; transitive verb making trope in, 425

Williams, William Carlos: free verse of, 342; haiku as influence on, 327,

329; "Poem," 329; subphrasal cut in, 341

Wilner, Eleanor: "Sarah's Choice," 351. *See also* "Operations: Desert Shield, Desert Storm"

Wimsatt, W. K., 144n, 213, 250n, 264n. 2, 280, 501

"Windsor Forest" (Pope): kenning in, 426

Winters, Anne. *See* "Mill-Race, The"

Winters, Yvor: on Eliot's blank verse, 334; *Quest for Reality: An Anthology of Short Poems in English,* 490. *See also* "Slow Pacific Swell, The"

"Witch, The" (Yeats): as accentual, **292**–93; accentual-syllabic dimeter contrasted with, 312; as podic free verse, 331–32

"With a Copy of Swift's Works" (Cunningham): as metaphysical, **279**

"With Ships the Sea Was Sprinkled Far and Nigh" (Wordsworth): law of simplified focus in, 145

"With the Shell of a Hermit Crab" (Wright): comparison from different realms in, **175,** 181; declarative sentences in, 404

"Woodspurge, The" (Rossetti): literal symbol in, 147–48, **148**

word order, 259–61; defined, 480–81; in graphic schema of diction, 382; in graphic

schema of line, 382, 383; in graphic schema of meter and prosody, 383; normal order, 459
words: automatic vocabulary, 378; choice of, 6–7; as "fiduciary symbols," 451; mirror words, 357; onomatopoeia, 442; in writing your way through a poem, 5–6. See also conjunctions; diction; etymology; neologism; verbs; word order
Wordsworth, William: allusion to social and economic conditions in, 173; blank verse in, 50, 334; "Intimations Ode," 273; plain style in, 120, 447; "Resolution and Independence," **120,** 457; "Song: She Dwelt Among th' Untrodden Ways," 163–64; "Star Gazers," 414; "To the Small Celandrine," 226; "With Ships the Sea Was Sprinkled Far and Nigh," 145. See also "Composed upon Westminster Bridge"; "Great Men have been among us"; Prelude, The; "Tintern Abbey"
"World Below the Brine, The" (Whitman): as biblical free verse, **339**
Wright, James. See "Lying in a Hammock at William Duffy's Farm in Pine Island, Minnesota"; "With the Shell of a Hermit Crab"
writing: as model for making sense of art, 3; two

central tasks of the writer, 378
"Writing" (Nemerov): alliteration in, 140–41, 388; form following theme in, 242–44, **243;** trochaic inversion in, 473; understressed line in, 478
Wyatt, Sir Thomas: aura of song in, 277; decasyllabic line in, 317; "I fynde no peace and all my warre is done," **447;** irregular verse of, 331; "My Lute and I," **300–301;** Petrarchan sonnets translated by, 446–**47;** plain style as low style in, 120, 447; podic verse of, 299, 300–301; reduced line in, 452; "Stand Whoso List," **86–**87, 443. See also "Longe Love, that in My Thought Doeth Harbar, The"; "Satire I"

Yeats, William Butler: accentual verse of, 291–94; analogies as persuasive, 164; Calvary, 15; "Coole and Ballylee, 1931," 292; Dante as influence on, 172–73; displacements of size in, 153; "A Drinking Song," **64,** 426; etymological diction in, 130; "Her Vision in the Wood," 291–92; "The Lake Isle of Innisfree," 331; literal symbol in, 149, 471; "Long-legged Fly," **294;** "Meditations in a Time of Civil War," 359, 418; "No Second

Troy," 335n; ottava rima of, 274–76, 363; "The Pity of Love," **331;** podic free verse of, 330, 331–32; prose preliminaries used by, 348; range of diction in, 124–25; Resurrection, **153,** 162n; "Sailing to Byzantium," 149; "The Second Coming," 130, 412; sentence forms used as an argumentative lexicon, 114–15, 140; "The Tower," 149; "The Tower II," 275; "The Wilde Swans at Coole," 291, 425. See also "Balloon of the Mind"; "Byzantium"; "Easter 1916"; "Fish, The"; "Prayer for My Daughter, A"; "To a Friend Whose Work Has Come to Nothing"; "Witch, The"
"You have here no otherness" (Cunningham): as syllabic verse, **324–25**
"Young Woman, A" (Ferry): beginning with a "that" clause, 366; podic free verse, **332–33;** as sentence fragment, 459; syntax of, 469

zeugma: defined, 481–82; in graphic schema of rhetoric and mode, 382; in graphic schema of trope, 382; in Pope, 152, 280–81; and rhyming on the phrase, 281–82

CREDITS

Author's Acknowledgment: As I look around the table at those who have helped me early and late, my editor Kathryn Kraynik takes a place near the head, for her ingenuity in helping me find the shape of this book. MK